COMMONLY USED SYMBOLS

Symbol	Term	Page Where Symbol Is Introduced
B	government bonds	40
BP	balance of payments	292
C	consumption spending	26
CU	currency	315
D	chequeable deposits	315
E	exchange rate	11
$\overline{E}$	fixed exchange rate	291
F	government transfer payments	40
G	government spending	26
I	investment spending	26
J	net investment income from foreigners	41
K	capital stock	126
K^*	desired capital stock	230
M	money supply	43
M_B	monetary base	318
N	employment	126
N^*	potential employment	125
P	price level	13
R	interest rate	95
R^K	rental price of capital	226
R_o	opportunity cost of money	329
RE	monetary reserves	316
S_g	government saving	41
S_p	private saving	41
S_r	rest-of-world saving	41
T	taxes	41
U	unemployment rate	65
U^*	natural rate of unemployment	65
W	wage rate	65
X	net exports	26
Y	GDP (or income)	26
Y_d	disposable income	74
Y^*	potential output (potential GDP)	26
Z	price shock	177
π	inflation rate	136
π^e	expected inflation	136

MACRO-ECONOMICS

The Canadian Economy

MACRO-ECONOMICS

The Canadian Economy

Robert E. Hall

John B. Taylor

STANFORD UNIVERSITY

Jeremy R. Rudin

UNIVERSITY OF BRITISH
COLUMBIA

W · W · NORTON & COMPANY · NEW YORK · LONDON

To Donna, Christopher, Anne, Jonathan, and Andrew
R.E.H.

To Allyn, Jennifer Lynn, and John Andrew
J.B.T.

To my family
J.R.R.

Cataloging in Publication Data

Hall, Robert Ernest, 1943–
    Macroeconomics: the Canadian economy / Robert E. Hall, John B. Taylor,
Jeremy R. Rudin. — 1st edition
        p.   cm.
    ISBN 0-393-95930-9
    1. Macroeconomics. 2. Canada—Economic conditions. 3. Canada—
Economic policy.   I. Taylor, John B. II. Rudin, Jeremy R. III. Title.
HB172.5.H347 1990
339.5'0971—dc20   89-77415
                                                                                    CIP

W. W. Norton & Company, Inc., 500 Fifth Avenue, New York, N.Y. 10110
W. W. Norton & Company, Ltd., 37 Great Russell Street, London WC1B 3NU

1 2 3 4 5 6 7 8 9 0

Contents

Part II   The Micro Foundations of Aggregate Demand

8   Consumption Demand   183

13   The Government's Budget Deficit and Aggregate Demand   356

Part III   The Micro Foundations of Aggregate Supply and Price Adjustment

14   Aggregate Supply and Economic Growth   379

Preface

NOWHERE IN economics does research develop as rapidly as in macroeconomics. Our goal has been to capture the spirit and content of this new research in a form that is manageable at the intermediate level and relevant to the modern Canadian economy. To this end we have based the book on an up-to-date yet simple approach that incorporates international trade and financial flows at every step of the analysis.

The late 1980s have seen the complete assimilation of the big idea of the 1970s: rational expectations. The results can be seen in every chapter of this book. Our discussion of consumption, investment, foreign trade, and money embraces rational expectations at many points. Even in areas—notably the sluggish adjustment of prices—where our model has properties disputed by leading rational expectations theorists such as Robert Lucas or Thomas Sargent, our analysis adopts rational expectations.

Recent years have seen an upsurge of interest in models where only real factors influence real variables. We devote some attention to the real business-cycle view in its several forms, although the main thrust of our analysis is toward a view in which both real and monetary factors shape the economy in the short run.

With all this attention to new developments, however, it remains our conviction that there is much that is worth retaining in traditional Keynesian and monetarist macroeconomics. In particular, two key ideas remain important in our thinking. First, output, not prices, responds strongly in the short run to shifts in demand; in the long run, prices adjust, returning the economy toward its potential level determined by the supply of labour and capital. Second, as a consequence of this, the level of employment and hence of disposable income is a given to households in the short run, so it is useful to look at the propagation of spending through the consumption function. In other words, we have not banished the expenditure process of elementary macroeconomics, though we move beyond it early in the book.

There is no need for open-economy considerations to form a complicated appendage to macroeconomic models. Using modern theories about the determinants of the exchange rate and its influence on real output we have incorporated trade and capital flows in our model in a rigorous way. At the same time, this has allowed us to dispense with the forest of shifting curves that often arises when foreign trade considerations are simply grafted onto a conventional closed-economy model.

Price adjustment, of course, is a basic fact of macroeconomics, and this book puts demand, supply, and price adjustment on an equal footing. There is more to the subject than IS-LM and aggregate demand, so we try not to spend so much time on the details of aggregate demand that aggregate supply and price adjustment become an addendum covered late in the course. Students get the basics of aggregate supply and price adjustment in the first few chapters of the book; later chapters uncover their origins in microeconomics and the stickiness of wages and prices that develops at the microeconomic level.

Chapters 4–7 constitute a complete macro model, capable of analysing all the major concerns of macroeconomics, including inflation. This minicourse develops the IS-LM model in two chapters, followed by analyses of price adjustment over time and macroeconomic policy. Foreign trade and financial flows are fully incorporated from the outset beginning with the realistic assumption that the exchange rate is flexible.

Throughout the book we have addressed topics of special interest to Canadians—for example: macroeconomic policy and regional disparity (Chapter 7), the effect of exchange rate changes on inflation (Chapter 10), the potential macroeconomic impact of the Canada-U.S. free trade agreement (Chapter 10), the pros and cons of exchange rate intervention (Chapters 11 and 18), innovations in Canadian financial markets (Chapter 12), proposals to deregulate key aspects of banking (Chapter 12), the independence of the Bank of Canada (Chapter 12), and Canada's participation at the annual economic summits (Chapter 18). While the book is about Canada, the United States is not ignored. Throughout the book, we discuss the substantial impact of the United States on the Canadian economy, and explicitly compare Canadian and American savings rates (Chapter 8), and unemployment rates and business cycles (both in Chapter 17).

Distinctive Features at a Glance

What, in our experience, makes this book work well as a class text? A short list includes the following features, most of which set this book apart from others in the field:

• Development early on of a *complete working macro model* with aggregate demand, aggregate supply, and price adjustment.

- Treating the *price level as a predetermined variable* consistently throughout the book for expositional simplicity.
- Discussion of the *open economy* from the outset and integration of this into the macro model throughout.
- Repeated use of *intertemporal budget constraints* that link savings to the accumulations of assets for consumers, firms, and government.
- A comprehensive treatment of the *microeconomic foundations of macroeconomic theory.*
- Careful exposition of the *empirical regularities* of the macroeconomy at the start of each chapter on micro foundations.
- Review of the *policy implications* of micro foundations for IS, LM, or price adjustment at the end of each chapter on micro foundations.

Pedagogical Features at a Glance

There are several strictly pedagogical features in the text that we have found enhance presentation of the material.

- *Summary boxes* draw together key ideas at appropriate places within each chapter. They serve a reinforcing function by allowing readers to check their understanding of one aspect of the analysis before tackling new material. And they also serve a review function, helping readers locate the building blocks of the analysis without rereading entire chapters.
- *Topic boxes* introduce special concepts related to the discussion in the text, including computing growth rates, quarterly GDP statistics, budget projections, indexing taxes, and the relationship between graphs and algebra. They also present discussion of historical examples, current policy issues, and other illustrations of points in the text.
- *Problems.* At the end of each chapter there are two types of problems: numerical and analytical. The numerical problems require the use of a hand calculator and usually take more time. We have found these useful for special projects. The analytical questions can be done with graphs or simple algebra. In addition, there are short questions for review.
- *References.* We have tried to keep footnotes to a minimum. Footnotes are used mainly to document a specific statement or reference in the text.
- *Parallel graphical and algebraic presentation.* In most cases arguments are presented in both graphical and algebraic form. We have found that some students learn better with graphs and some learn better with algebra, especially if the algebra is presented in a way that does not intimidate. Graphical arguments are not necessarily easier for all students and the algebra is provided to help those with a preference for algebra. Of course, graphical presentation usually helps with the intuition and we would expect even the less graphically inclined students to learn basics such as the Keynesian cross or IS-LM. A special effort has been made to demonstrate that graphs and algebra are just two ways to describe the same economic concepts. See especially the topic box on page 74.

- *Real-world examples.* Showing how economic theory works in practice is the best way to learn. Too often, however, these lessons of experience are placed at some distance from the analysis, with the result that students often sense that a barrier exists between macroeconomic models and the real world from which they are drawn. We have chosen to make the performance of the economy an integral aspect of the exposition, with new concepts constantly illuminated by examples.
- *Teaching supplements.* An *Instructor's Manual* that we have prepared is available from the publisher. This *Instructor's Manual* contains many teaching "tricks" to prompt students to become actively involved in the subject. These include macro-forecasting contests, policy projects on Bank of Canada monetary targeting, debate formats for lectures, and classroom skits to illustrate the forward-looking theory of consumption and other models. There are also references to more complicated material related to the text and answers to the questions posed in the text. An excellent *Study Guide* prepared with David H. Papell of the University of Houston to accompany the text is also available.
- *Computer software.* The MacroSolve package, written by Stephen R. King and Rick M. McConnell, embodies the IS-LM and price-adjustment equations developed in the text. The user can shift curves on the graphical display and see immediately how the economy reacts. The program also allows easy access to Canadian macroeconomic data.
- *Data sources.* In order to be as accurate and up-to-date as possible the data used in the preparation of the book were taken, whenever possible, from the CANSIM university base ('CANSIM' is an official mark of Statistics Canada), a computer data base maintained by Statistics Canada. As most readers do not have access to CANSIM, a printed source is cited for all of the data used in the tables and figures. Whenever possible the source given is *The Canadian Economic Observer*, Statistics Canada's new comprehensive economic publication. This makes it easy to look up additional related data, or to keep lectures up-to-date. If the data used are not included in that publication the *Bank of Canada Review* or the federal Department of Finance's *Quarterly Economic Review Annual Reference Tables* are cited, if possible. If it is necessary to cite any other Statistics Canada publications the catalogue number is used rather than the title, as it is easier to locate these publications by number. (Readers should note that because CANSIM is updated on its own schedule the data used in the tables and figures need not correspond precisely to the data available in any particular issue of the cited publications.)

A Guided Tour

The book starts with a mini-course in macroeconomic analysis in Part I that covers many important topics. We review the basic facts of macroeconomic fluctuations and develop a simple but complete model of the macroeconomy. Our approach to aggregate demand is standard, through the IS-LM apparatus. We include trade even in the first development of the IS curve. We have chosen to use the term 'aggregate supply' in its classical sense—a vertical line in the output-price diagram, showing the full-employment, or potential, level of output. The long-run equilibrium of the economy occurs at the intersection of aggregate demand and potential output.

The path to long-run potential is governed by the price-adjustment process. But the price level is unresponsive in the short run—output occurs where the aggregate demand curve intersects the predetermined price level. We do not drop the predetermined-price assumption when we bring the supply side into the picture. IS-LM remains our theory of output determination in each period of the dynamic analysis. Price adjustment comes into play the period after a policy or other change has affected output.

The expositional simplification we achieve in this way is enormous. We do not feel that the empirical evidence justifies the complexity of simultaneous determination of prices and output in each period. There is certainly no contradiction to the predetermined-price assumption if the period is a quarter of a year, and the assumption is valid as a close approximation if the period is a full year.

The adaptation of price adjustment to inflation ranks high among the ideas that have evolved in macroeconomics over the past two decades. We avoid characterising this adaptation solely as a matter of changing expectations. Even with rational expectations, price adjustment depends partly on recent inflation experience since contracts and other rigidities prevent quick adjustments. We discuss how the adaptation of expectations to inflation depends on how prices and wages are set.

After the short course in macroeconomic analysis, we go on to develop the micro foundations of aggregate demand in Part II. At the start of each chapter we present the key facts or puzzles that need to be explained. At the end of each chapter we look at the implications for IS-LM. The consumption chapter (8) develops a forward-looking theory of consumption based on the life cycle and permanent income formulations, emphasising the role of rational expectations. By establishing an intertemporal budget constraint, we avoid present discounted values and forbidding summations. Chapter 9, on investment, focusses on Dale Jorgensen's model. The first foreign trade chapter (10) focusses on flexible exchange rates, with a rational expectations model of the exchange rate as its centerpiece. The second chapter on foreign trade (Chapter 11) considers the fixed exchange rate case in theory and practice. Chapter 12, on the monetary system, considers the money supply process, including the role of the central bank in exchange rate intervention. That chapter also takes up money demand and recent changes in the Canadian monetary system. Chapter 13, on government, contains more material on the deficit and government debt than is customary alongside a standard treatment of automatic stabilisers and related subjects. When the intertemporal budget constraint for the government is presented, the idea is already familiar to the student from consumption and investment.

Part III contains much that we think is novel for an intermediate text. It is here that we develop the micro foundations of aggregate supply and price adjustment. Chapter 14 sets the stage with perfect price flexibility, long-term growth, and inflation. An appendix deals with the algebra of rational expectations models. Chapter 15 takes a careful look at the real business-cycle model and the imperfect information model of aggregate supply developed by Robert Lucas. Chapter 16 deals with micro foundations and macro implications of overlapping wage setting. It also discusses markup pricing and the optimal contract model of Costas Azariadis, Martin Baily, and others. Chapter 17 discusses the implications of price adjustment for the dynamic behaviour of the macroeconomy and compares these implications with actual experience.

Part IV pulls the analysis together into a comprehensive treatment of macroeconomic policy evaluation. Chapter 18 takes up general policy issues such as time inconsistency, multiplier uncertainty, targets and instruments, and the rational expectations critique of policy evaluation. The emphasis is on policy rules, rather than on one-time policy changes. The inflation-unemployment trade-off appears as a policy frontier between output stability and price stability. International policy coordination is discussed, as are suggestions for improving the policy frontier.

Acknowledgments

Early drafts of both the first and second U.S. editions were used in several intermediate macroeconomics courses at Stanford, and we thank the students and teaching assistants for their very helpful comments. We are deeply grateful to the many teachers and students at Stanford and elsewhere who wrote to us with their comments. This book is immeasurably better than it would have been without their feedback.

During the preparation of the Canadian edition we were fortunate to have had the sage advice of Keir Armstrong, Paul Boothe (University of Alberta), David Johnson (Wilfred Laurier University), E. H. Oksanen (McMaster University), Douglas Purvis (Queen's University), Peter Sephton (University of New Brunswick), and P. Sharma (Carleton University) and the sterling research assistance of Edgardo Sepulveda.

Finally, we would like to thank Drake McFeely, Donald Lamm, Nancy Palmquist, and Deborah Makay of W. W. Norton for outstanding editorial help and advice.

	R.E.H.
Stanford	J.B.T.
Vancouver	J.R.R.
December 1989	

PART I

Fundamentals of Macroeconomics

1

The Macroeconomy

THE ECONOMY is always in motion. Most of the movement is upward. Production of cars, steel, personal computers, and apartment buildings rises each year. Firms hire more and more workers to make these products. But in some years, production falls, workers are laid off, and unemployment rises.

As you read this book, the economy is at some stage of its ceaseless pattern of fluctuations. This year's upturn or downturn is temporary. And as it occurs, longer-run, more slowly evolving forces—such as population growth and technological progress—are leading to more lasting increases in output as the economy grows over time. The current fluctuation is a temporary diversion from the longer-run growth path.

Fluctuations in output and employment are among the most regular and persistent facts of economics. Although there are undoubtedly some new or special features of the current upturn or downturn in economic activity, such fluctuations themselves are not new. They have been recorded for hundreds of years. Economists have developed a branch of economic theory, called **macroeconomics,** to explain these fluctuations. This book is about macroeconomics. Macroeconomics seeks to explain why fluctuations happen and to investigate policies that can mitigate them.

The word **macro**economics was coined to distinguish the subject from **micro**economics. Microeconomics is the study of how individual consumers and firms behave, and how the market system allocates scarce resources. Microeconomics is not usually concerned with the temporary fluctuations in the economy. But it is a mistake to isolate macroeconomics from microeconomics. When macroeconomists try to explain the fluctuations in the economy they must look at the behaviour of consumers and firms, the organisation of labour markets and industry, the workings of financial markets, and even the machinations of governments. They rely on microeconomics when they do so. Macroeconomics is only as good as the microeconomics that underlies it.

During the past 15 years economic fluctuations in Canada and other countries have been larger and more erratic than at any time since the Great Depression of the 1930s. Most people sense this and are therefore more concerned than ever with the ups and downs of the economy. A recession has substantial effects on our economic welfare. Layoffs during recessions and the inability to find work during periods of high unemployment create severe hardships. Poverty rises during recessions. Even for those who don't lose their jobs, lower incomes reduce what can be consumed; lower incomes also reduce what can be invested to increase the productive capacity of the economy in the future.

Other important variables also fluctuate as the economy goes through its ups and downs. Fluctuations in inflation, interest rates, and the international value of the Canadian dollar all accompany the fluctuations in the economy. These key economic variables move together in reasonably predictable ways. We will have a lot to say about the relationships among output, employment, interest rates, prices, and exchange rates. Indeed, macroeconomics has been more successful in predicting relationships among variables than it has been in predicting the levels of the variables. For instance, macroeconomists are not much better than anyone else in forecasting interest rates. But they can tell you that a fall in the value of the dollar will probably accompany a fall in interest rates, and they can tell you why.

The media give high priority to economic fluctuations, and this is some indication of their importance. Newspaper headlines like 'UNEMPLOYMENT REACHES HIGHEST LEVEL IN FOUR YEARS,' 'INFLATION HITS FIVE-YEAR LOW,' and 'DOLLAR PLUNGES TO NEW DEPTHS' record the ups and downs in the economy. Economic fluctuations are also big items on the platform of any national political campaign. The incumbents usually try to claim credit for any good news, such as a drop in inflation, while the challengers blame them for the bad news, such as a high unemployment rate.

1.1 Recent Performance of the Macroeconomy

Figure 1–1 documents the fluctuations of the Canadian economy over the 20-year period from 1968 to 1987. The coloured line in the figure traces **real gross domestic product (GDP),** a concept we will examine in more detail in the next chapter. Real GDP is the actual, physical production of cars, trucks, rock concerts, films, haircuts, and every other good or service that people in Canada prepare for trade with one another or with the rest of the world. We get real GDP by summing up the dollar value of production, and then adjusting for any price changes that have occurred from year to year.

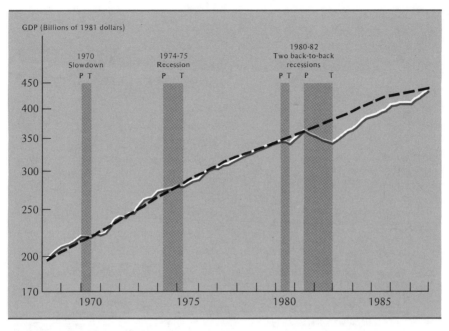

Figure 1–1.   REAL GDP IN CANADA, 1968–87.
The coloured line shows what has happened to real GDP. During the periods that are shaded, real GDP grew very slowly or declined. The black line shows what real GDP would have looked like if it had grown smoothly during the period instead of fluctuating as it did. Source: *Canadian Economic Observer,* Table 1.3.

The vertical axis in Figure 1–1 shows the values of real GDP in 1981 prices. The horizontal axis indicates the year. The figure also shows how Statistics Canada classifies periods of slow growth of the economy. A **recession** is a period of time during which GDP falls or grows very slowly. There are three recessions shown in Figure 1–1. A period of very slow growth that is both mild and brief is termed a **slowdown.** There is one period that is classified as a slowdown in Figure 1–1. The beginning of a recession is called the **peak,** and is marked with a P in the figure. The end of a recession is called a **trough,** and is marked with a T. Between the shaded areas the economy is growing fairly rapidly—these periods are called **recoveries,** or **expansions.**

Note that GDP tended to rise during the 20-year period. There is a growth trend because of a growing labour force and increased capital stock, and because of technological improvements. The black dashed line in the chart indicates the steady upward trend that underlies the behaviour of real GDP. This trend line is called **potential GDP.** Real GDP fluctuates around potential GDP as the economy goes through successive recessions and recoveries.

Fluctuations do not occur at regular intervals. They certainly cannot be anticipated with great accuracy, and this is what makes macroeconomic

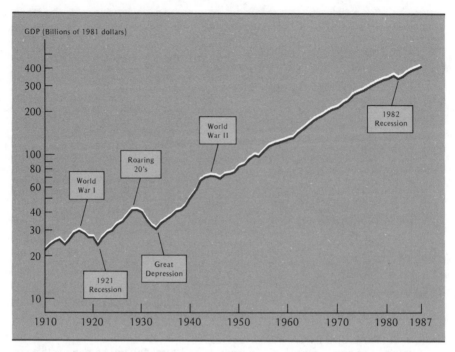

Figure 1–2. REAL GDP, 1910–87.
The largest decline in real GDP occurred from 1929 to 1933, the years of the Great Depression. Another important contraction occurred in the early 1920s. Both were more serious than any recession since 1950. Note: GNP rather than GDP for 1910–25. Sources: *Canadian Economic Observer*, Table 1.3, and M.C. Urqhuart, 'New Estimates of GNP, Canada, 1870–1926,' in S. Engerman and R. Gallman, eds., *Long Term Factors in American Economic Growth*, University of Chicago Press, 1986.

forecasting both difficult and interesting. For example, the recovery that began in 1975 was relatively long, whereas the recovery that began in 1980 was very short.

Figure 1–2 gives a longer perspective on the fluctuations in economic activity, showing the ups and downs in the economy over the last 77 years. The most noticeable single fluctuation during this period was the downturn during the Great Depression of the early 1930s. Note, however, that the recession in the early 1920s and the subsequent boom in the late 1920s were also comparatively large in magnitude. Although economic fluctuations in Canada have not ceased, they appear to have diminished in magnitude compared to this earlier period.

EMPLOYMENT

Fluctuations in employment follow closely the fluctuations in real GDP. Figure 1–3 shows the ratio of employed workers to the working-age popula-

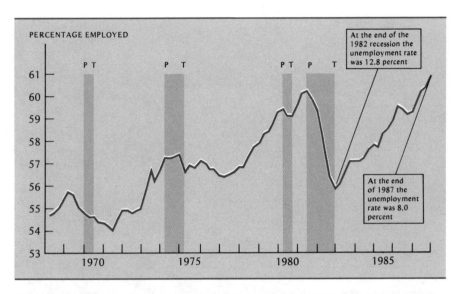

Figure 1–3.   EMPLOYMENT AS A PERCENTAGE OF WORKING-AGE POPULATION.
Recessions are periods of declining employment, measured as a fraction of the working-age population. Because of the fluctuations in employment, recessions influence a large fraction of the public. Source: *Canadian Economic Observer*, Table 2.1.

tion for the same 20-year period covered by Figure 1–1. Employment fell rapidly as the economy went through each of the recessions during this period. Firms laid off workers as the economy's production fell, and hired fewer new workers. As the economy began to recover after each downturn, employment again grew as firms called workers back to work and hired many new workers. This close association between production and employment as the economy fluctuates is one of the key facts of macroeconomics. Recurrent recessions are serious social problems, because they involve large-scale job losses.

Mirroring the drops in employment are the increases in the **unemployment rate,** which is the percentage of workers who are not working but who are looking for work. When employment falls the unemployment rate rises as workers are laid off. For example, during 1983 the unemployment rate rose to 12 percent. By the start of 1988 it had fallen to under 8 percent.

INFLATION

Another important fact of economic fluctuations is their correlation with the rate of **inflation**—the percentage change in the average price of all goods in the economy. In general, prices tend to rise faster when the economy is operating near its peak. Conversely, prices tend to rise less rapidly when the economy is near a trough. These rises and falls lag behind the fluctuations in real GDP.

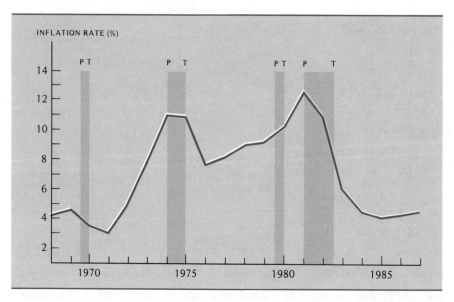

Figure 1–4.   THE RATE OF INFLATION.
Starting in the late 1960s, the rate of inflation rose. In the 1980s, it began to decline. Bursts of inflation have preceded or accompanied recessions. Typically, inflation subsides to some extent just after recessions. Source: *Canadian Economic Observer,* Table 3.2.

Figure 1–4 shows the rate of inflation. The chart demonstrates that almost all of the significant declines in the rate of inflation occurred just after recession periods. Are recessions a necessary part of the disinflation process? This is one of the central concerns of this book.

INTEREST RATES

Interest rates also tend to fluctuate over the business cycle. The interest rate is the amount charged for a loan by a bank or other lender per dollar per year, expressed as a percent. For instance, if your roommate lends you $100, for which she asks you to pay her $110 a year from now, the interest rate is 10 percent. Figure 1–5 shows one representative interest rate, the Treasury bill rate, during the same period that we previously considered. The Treasury bill rate measures how much the government pays to borrow. There was a general rise in interest rates starting in the 1960s as inflation rose. As we will see, interest rates usually rise with inflation to compensate lenders for the falling purchasing power of the dollar. The interest rate minus the expected rate of inflation is called the **real interest rate.**
However, the fluctuations of interest rates during the recessions are most dramatic. Interest rates are **procyclical;** they rise during recovery periods

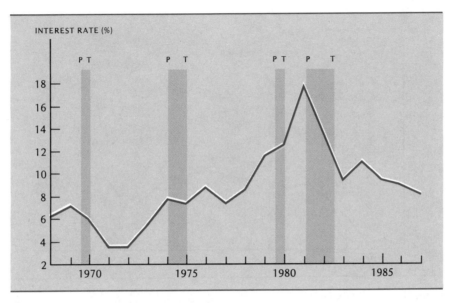

Figure 1–5. THE TREASURY BILL INTEREST RATE.
Like other interest rates, the rate on Treasury bills reaches a peak just before a recession and then usually falls sharply. Source: *Canadian Economic Observer,* Table 10.1.

and fall during recessions. They are also one of the most volatile of macroeconomic variables, and the most difficult to predict. Nevertheless, as Figure 1–5 makes clear, these interest rate fluctuations are intimately related to the fluctuations in production and employment. A thorough understanding of interest rate behaviour is crucial to any explanation of economic fluctuations.

A variable closely related to the interest rate is the **money supply.** The money supply consists of currency and the deposits that people have at banks and certain other financial institutions. The money supply is controlled by the Bank of Canada, which is an agency of the federal government.

The behaviour of the money supply is shown in Figure 1–6. The chart shows the money supply divided by the price level, or **real money.** There seems to be a relationship between money and the timing of recessions and booms. The relationship suggests that changes in the money supply may be causing the fluctuations in the economy. In the theory that we develop in this book the money supply is a primary force in economic fluctuations.

The ideas, theories, and models we study in this book endeavour to explain why GDP and employment fluctuate so much. They will also try to provide reasons for the cyclical movements of inflation, interest rates, and the money supply as well as a number of other macroeconomic variables.

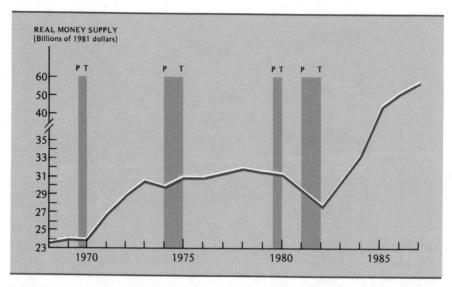

Figure 1–6.   THE MONEY SUPPLY.
The money supply divided by the price level—real money—seems to decline before re-
cessions. The general trend in real money is positive because the growth in the economy
creates a need for more money to assist in buying and selling goods. Sources: *Canadian
Economic Observer,* Table 1.1 (GDP deflator), and *Bank of Canada Review,* Table E1
(M1-A).

Macroeconomic Fluctuations

1. The economy undergoes recessions and recoveries at irregular intervals. Recessions are periods of contracting economic activity; recoveries are periods of above-average economic growth after a
   recession. Over the long haul the economy expands as population
   and technical progress increase output along the trend of potential
   GDP.

2. The physical volume of output—measured by real GDP—contracts
   in a recession and expands in a recovery.

3. Employment moves closely with output. Recessions are periods of
   job loss, that is, rising unemployment.

4. The period between World War I and World War II saw two very
   large contractions. Recessions have continued since World War II.
   In the early 1980s the overall contraction was the worst since the
   Great Depression.

5. Inflation generally subsides in the wake of a recession.

6. Interest rates usually reach a peak just before a recession starts and
   then fall considerably during the recession.

1.2 Exchange Rates

An **exchange rate** is the amount of a foreign currency that can be purchased with one Canadian dollar. For example, in May 1988, our exchange rate with the United States was .81. Thus one Canadian dollar purchased 81 U.S. cents. Another way to think of an exchange rate is the price that foreigners must pay to buy Canadian dollars using their currency. When foreigners purchase Canadian goods they pay for these goods with Canadian dollars. Thus in May 1988 a cup of coffee that cost one Canadian dollar in Halifax would have cost an American 81 U.S. cents. Similarly, Canadians purchase foreign goods using foreign currencies. A cup of coffee that cost one U.S. dollar in New York in May 1988 would have cost a Canadian visitor 1.23 Canadian dollars (1/.81 = 1.23). *in Cdn dollars*

There is an exchange rate between the Canadian dollar and every foreign currency. It is common to concentrate on the Canada-U.S. exchange rate because the United States is by far our largest trading partner, accounting for almost 70 percent of Canadian merchandise imports and over 75 percent of Canadian merchandise exports. However, Canada trades extensively with other countries as well. Rather than keep track of all of our exchange rates separately it is a useful simplification to consider an average of these exchange rates. A **trade-weighted exchange rate** is an average of the exchange rates between the Canadian dollar and several different currencies, with those countries that trade more with Canada given more weight.

Often when the value of the Canadian dollar is changing relative to the U.S. dollar it is also changing in the same direction relative to other currencies. When this happens the Canada-U.S. and trade-weighted exchange rates must move in the same direction. But the U.S. dollar and trade-weighted exchange rates can move in opposite directions at the same time. During much of 1983, for example, the Canadian dollar was falling against the U.S. dollar but rising against the British pound, French franc, and German mark. At that time the Canada-U.S. exchange rate fell while the trade-weighted exchange rate rose. The Canada-U.S. and trade-exchange weighted exchange rates are shown in Figure 1–7.

The exchange rate influences how expensive foreign goods are compared to Canadian goods. For example, suppose that the Canadian dollar prices of Canadian goods and the U.S. dollar prices of U.S. goods were constant while the Canada-U.S. exchange rate rose. U.S. goods would become less expensive relative to Canadian goods. As we will see in Chapters 5 and 10, this will cause Canadians to buy more U.S. goods while Americans buy fewer Canadian goods.

But this is not the only way that foreign goods can become more attractive. Suppose that the prices of Canadian goods rose while both the U.S. dollar price of U.S. goods and the exchange rate were unchanged. Canadian goods would become relatively more expensive compared to U.S. goods. Once again Canadians would want to buy more U.S. goods while Americans would want to buy fewer Canadian goods.

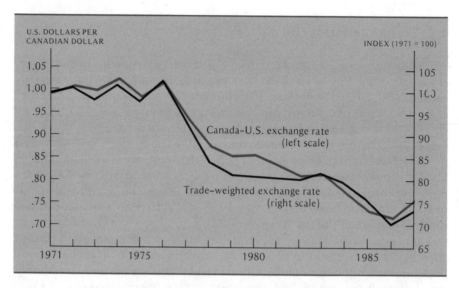

Figure 1–7.   THE CANADA-U.S. AND TRADE-WEIGHTED EXCHANGE RATES.
Canada's exchange rates with other countries have fluctuated widely since 1976. The Canada-U.S. and trade-weighted exchange rates have not always moved in the same direction. Source: *Canadian Economic Observer*, Table 10.1.

The **real exchange rate** is a measure that takes into account both of the influences on the relative attractiveness of foreign and domestic goods: the exchange rate and the prices of the goods. To compute the real exchange rate let E be the exchange rate, P be the level of prices in Canada, and P_u be the price level in the U.S. Then the real exchange rate is EP/P_u. Holding U.S. prices constant, an increase in the exchange rate or an increase in prices will increase the real exchange rate. Either way, an increase in the real exchange rate makes foreign goods more attractive.

1.3 Explaining Fluctuations: Flexible or Sticky Prices?

At the core of any theory of macroeconomic fluctuations is an explanation of how the economy responds to economic forces. How does GDP adjust when a new technology is introduced? What if there is a sudden increase in demand for new factories and machines because of a massive buildup of defence spending? What if the price of oil is quadrupled because a cartel of producers cuts back on production? In constructing an explanation of how the economy responds to these forces, the macroeconomist constructs a **model.** A model is simply a description of how consumers and firms behave and how they interact with each other in markets.

The earliest economic theories about the determination of GDP went as follows: At a given moment, there is a certain amount of productive capacity in the economy. The level of the capacity depends on the number of factories and machines and the number of workers. Full employment will prevail in the economy, because if unemployment developed it would quickly disappear as wages fell enough to stimulate the demand for labour. The basic theory of supply and demand assumes that prices or wages would adjust quickly so that supply would equal demand. Analogously, early theories of macroeconomics supposed that wages and prices for the whole economy would adjust quickly to keep labour and machines fully employed. Prices were assumed to be *flexible* enough to bring about a complete and quick adjustment.

According to such a theory, a change in overall demand in the economy would result in a change in the price level, but not in the level of production. The workings of a macro model with flexible prices are shown in the simple macroeconomic supply-demand diagram in Figure 1–8.

The productive capacity of the economy is shown as a vertical line. The productive capacity is determined by the volume of productive factors— capital and labour—and is unrelated to the price level. In later chapters, we will have much more to say about productive capacity, because it is a concept that retains an important role in modern macroeconomics. Productive capacity determines **potential output,** labelled Y^* in Figure 1–8. Potential output is the amount of output that can be produced from the existing capital stock and labour force.

Figure 1–8 also shows an **aggregate demand curve,** which slopes downward. Aggregate demand is the total amount of demand throughout the economy. Demand depends on the price level—the total amount demanded

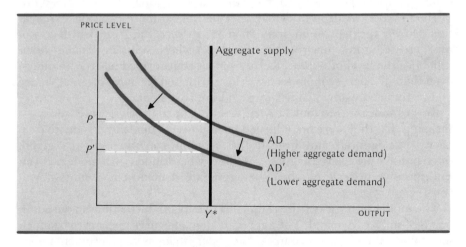

Figure 1–8. THE MODEL WITH PERFECTLY FLEXIBLE PRICES.
The level of output, measured by real GDP, is determined by the capital stock and the number of workers, neither of which responds to the price level. Consequently, aggregate supply is a vertical line. Aggregate demand is a downward-sloping schedule, but demand does not influence the level of output. If the aggregate demand schedule shifts downward, from AD to AD' only the price level changes; output remains the same.

is higher if the price is lower. The negative relationship is due to financial factors: A higher price level increases the demand for money and credit and raises interest rates. Higher interest rates then lower demand. We will have much more to say in later chapters about aggregate demand, which has a central role in all macroeconomic theories.

With perfectly flexible prices the economy always operates at the intersection of aggregate demand and aggregate supply. If the price level happened to be too high, so that demand fell short of supply, and unemployment threatened, then the price level would fall immediately by just enough to stimulate demand and restore equilibrium.

What is interesting and important about this model is that demand influences only the price level, not the level of output. If a change in economic policy shifts demand downward, prices fall immediately. Output remains unchanged. With perfectly flexible prices, *shifts in demand cannot explain recessions and booms.* Shifts in demand explain only variations in inflation.

To explain the continuing pattern of major fluctuations in output and employment, this type of model has to say that potential GDP is shifting. But potential GDP depends on the amount of capital and the number of people available for work, neither of which seems likely to fluctuate much from one year to the next. The model seems an unpromising way to explain recessions and booms.

This type of model with perfectly flexible prices was essentially what economists in the early twentieth century used for analysing the macroeconomy. The Great Depression in the 1930s saw a drop in real GDP that was so large—28 percent from 1929 to 1933—and similar changes in other countries, that an explanation based on a drop in potential GDP seemed out of the question. A drop in demand seemed like a more plausible explanation. During the depression, John Maynard Keynes, the great British economist, created a new macroeconomic model where shifts in demand *could* influence the level of output. Keynes's ideas transformed macroeconomics, even though macroeconomists have since criticised Keynes's original theory and introduced many qualifications and improvements.

Keynes's idea was to look at what would happen if prices were 'sticky'— meaning that they were not adjusted in response to demand. Productive capacity was ignored and instead the economy operated with a given, unresponsive price level. Figure 1–9 shows what happens in a model with an unresponsive price level when the aggregate demand curve shifts downward.

The model with sticky prices allows us to explain fluctuations in output in terms of shifts in demand. The aggregate demand curve appears to be much less stable than is potential output. Each year, changes in government policy shift demand. Investment demand fluctuates. Consumers change their moods and spend less or more. The demand for exports shifts as conditions in other countries change. The model with sticky prices opens up a way for each of these demand shifts to influence output, whereas the model with flexible prices says that output can change only when potential output changes.

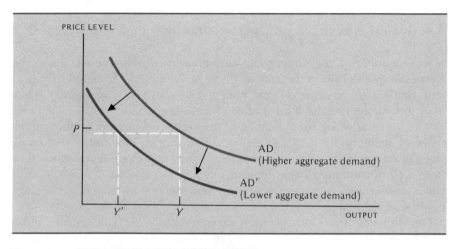

Figure 1–9.   THE MODEL WITH STICKY PRICES.
In the model with sticky prices, output is not necessarily equal to potential. The economy operates on its aggregate demand schedule, at a given price level. If aggregate demand falls, the price level remains unchanged. Output falls instead.

Models with Flexible Prices and Sticky Prices

THE MODEL WITH FLEXIBLE PRICES

1. The price level fluctuates immediately to keep the aggregate demand for output equal to potential output. Unemployment and other unused resources do not occur. $Y = AS$.

2. Potential GDP is determined by the capital stock and by the number of workers, neither of which is likely to shift very much from one year to the next.

3. Output is determined by the productive capacity of the economy. The demand schedule determines the price level.

THE MODEL WITH STICKY PRICES

1. Output does not necessarily equal potential GDP. The price level is fixed, and output is aggregate demand at the fixed price.

2. When demand shifts, output shifts.

3. Because aggregate demand seems to be less stable than is potential GDP, the model with sticky prices is more successful in explaining short-run fluctuations in output.

1.4 Recent Advances in Macroeconomics

Macroeconomics has undergone tremendous developments since the Keynesian revolution in the 1930s. These developments have led to important changes in actual economic policy. The changes in economic policy have in turn altered the nature of the fluctuations.

The acceptance of Keynesian ideas brought recognition of the importance of maintaining a steady growth of aggregate demand. After many years of research, the importance of controlling aggregate demand has now been well documented both theoretically and empirically, though there is still considerable controversy among macroeconomists about the best method of control.

One important school, the **monetarists,** usually identified with Milton Friedman, formerly of the University of Chicago, now of the Hoover Institution at Stanford University, holds that steady money growth will best stabilise the growth of aggregate demand.

Macroeconomists in the **Keynesian** school have argued that changes in taxes and government spending are also desirable. James Tobin of Yale University and Franco Modigliani of M.I.T. are macroeconomists usually identified with this school. They also favour the active use of monetary policy to offset other sources of instability, in place of the passive, steady growth policy of the monetarists.

In the 1960s, some Keynesians began to think that controlling aggregate demand could virtually eliminate economic fluctuations; for example, in 1969 Martin Bronfenbrenner entitled a book *Is the Business Cycle Obsolete?* and argued that it was. More recent research and the actual experience in the 1970s and 1980s have shown this to be a false hope. We now know that aggregate demand management will not eliminate economic fluctuations, or be able to bring unemployment permanently to very low levels.

In recent years, progress in macroeconomics has been substantial in two areas: price adjustment and expectations.

PRICE ADJUSTMENT

Price adjustment is the process through which firms adjust their prices in response to changing demand and supply conditions in their markets. The new theories of price adjustment attempt to fill in gaps in the simple model with sticky prices. First, the assumption of sticky prices might be reasonable for the short run but is clearly false in the long run. Second, in an inflationary environment many prices are continually increasing. Price-adjustment theories had to describe how price setting would incorporate the steadily rising trend in prices. Third, early theories of price adjustment were vague about the microeconomic reason for the slow adjustment. New theories of price adjustment have provided better explanations based on labour contracts and lack of information firms have about the nature of the changes in demand. All the newer theories about price adjustment show explicitly that potential GDP matters in the long run. In fact, in the long run, the economy returns to potential.

RATIONAL EXPECTATIONS

Expectations about the future are an important part of all macroeconomic theories. In *The General Theory of Employment, Interest and Money,* Keynes talked about expectations repeatedly. Keynes emphasised the erratic nature of expectations, that they could shift around randomly with no rational explanation. One of the most interesting recent theoretical developments is the hypothesis of **rational expectations.** The hypothesis has influenced macroeconomic thinking deeply, and many parts of this book show the influence. Consumption, investment, and price adjustment are areas where we have to deal forthrightly with the issues of how people form their expectations.

The principle of rational expectations holds that firms and consumers form expectations about the future 'rationally.' This simply means that they make the most of the information that is available to them. If they know from past experience that the Bank of Canada increases money growth in order to lower interest rates whenever there is an increase in unemployment, then they will expect the Bank of Canada to act the same in the future, unless information to the contrary is provided. Or, if they know that a 3-year tax cut has been passed, they will anticipate a reduction in their tax bill 3 years down the road and adjust their behaviour accordingly.

The rational expectations assumption is used so much in this book—in the analysis of consumption, investment, and wage and price determination —that you may find the idea somewhat routine. But it is important to keep in mind that rational expectations has been the subject of considerable controversy. Frequently, rational expectations is taken as a shorthand phrase to stand for propositions that economic policy is ineffective and that inflation can be reduced quickly without a recession. We will explain later in the book how these propositions can be derived from strong, unrealistic assumptions and why we think the propositions are wrong. But it is not rational expectations that makes the propositions wrong.

With these new developments in macroeconomics, new schools of thought are emerging that have only loose connections with the older schools such as Keynesians and monetarists. Virtually all macroeconomists today accept the idea of rational expectations in one form or another, even though the idea was rejected initially by traditional Keynesians.

Today two broad schools of thought have been categorised by researchers. The **new classical** school includes economists such as Robert Lucas of the University of Chicago and Thomas Sargent of Stanford University. The new classicals accept the idea of rational expectations but maintain that prices adjust very quickly, like the classical economists assumed. A branch of this school, called the **real business-cycle** school, including Edward Prescott of the University of Minnesota and Charles Plosser of the University of Rochester, maintains that monetary factors or aggregate demand are relatively unimportant in explaining economic fluctuations.

The **new Keynesian** school includes economists such as Olivier Blanchard of M.I.T. and Edmund Phelps of Columbia University. The new Keynesians also accept the idea of rational expectations, but maintain that wages and prices adjust slowly and that this slow adjustment is the key to explaining economic fluctuations. There is a sense in which the new Keynesians could just as accurately be called new monetarists, for this school emphasises the importance of money and also maintains that the economy eventually returns to some natural level of output.[1]

How Did Today's Macroeconomists Come to Study Economics?

Macroeconomists—whether traditional Keynesian, monetarist, new classical, or new Keynesian—began studying economics for many different reasons. Some got interested because the hardships of the Great Depression of the 1930s touched them personally. For others it was
pure chance. But whatever the reason, they all liked it and stuck with it. Here are some answers to the question 'How did you come to study economics?' from some macroeconomists whose work we will study in this book.[*]

Franco Modigliani

[Laughter] That's a good question. I'd say, by chance. I started my university years with the expectation that I would become a doctor, because my father was one. . . . At the last moment I realized that I wasn't cut out for that profession; I cannot stand the sight of blood. So I went into law, which is in Italy very general.

Then there was a national competition among university students to write an essay about the effect of price controls. I decided to participate. . . . I wrote my essay and won first prize. The judges said that I should pursue the study of economics and so I began.

James Tobin

I went into economics for two reasons. One was that as a child of the Depression I was terribly concerned about the world. It seemed then

[*] The answers come from separate interviews published in Arjo Klamer, *Conversations with Economists*, Rowman and Allanheld, 1984.

---

[1] Of course no categorisation can be complete for long because new research is always developing new ways of thinking. For example, a recent school of thought to emerge might be called the *market power school*, based on research by Oliver Hart of M.I.T., N. Gregory Mankiw of Harvard, and others. These researchers explain unemployment in recessions with models of oligopoly or monopoly in which firms or workers have some market power.

that many of the problems were economic in origin. If you thought that the world should be saved, and I did, then economics looked like the decisive thing to study. The second thing was that you could have your cake and eat it too, because it was an intellectually fascinating subject.

Robert E. Lucas, Jr.

I have always liked to think about social problems. It may have something to do with my family. We always argued about politics and social issues. I studied history. . . . But I came around to the view that economic forces are central forces in history, and started trying some economics. It was a big shock to me to find books in English that were incomprehensible to me. . . . [Like] Keynes's *General Theory.* I still can't read Keynes. [Laughter] I realized I couldn't pick it up as an amateur. So I got into economics in a professional way and got my Ph.D. at Chicago.

Thomas J. Sargent

[Long pause and hesitation] I liked it when we studied it in college. But also I was truly curious, ever since I was a kid, about what causes depressions. The Great Depression had a big effect on me: a lot of people in my family got wiped out. My grandfather ran a quarry in the construction business, and he got wiped out. My other grandfather was in the radio business, and he got wiped out. It was the common story.

1.5 The Macroeconomic Model Used in This Book

Although many alternative theories are discussed, a main model appears throughout this book. This model combines the new theories of price adjustment, the new theories of rational expectations, and the earlier Keynesian ideas about aggregate demand and output determination. It is introduced first in a rudimentary, or 'no-frills,' form in Chapters 4 through 7, and then in a more complete form later in the book.

The basic ideas in the rudimentary model can be explained as follows: In the short run prices and wages do not adjust. Workers' wages are set at a particular level for about a year, and firms usually set their price and wait to see what the market will buy at that price. But eventually prices begin to adjust and reach their market-clearing level; aggregate demand will eventually equal potential GDP.

How does the economy move from a situation where output is greater or less than potential GDP to the situation where aggregate output equals potential GDP? The process of price adjustment does the job. The simplest expression of the idea of price adjustment is: *When output is less than potential*

GDP, *there is pressure on prices to adjust downward. When output exceeds potential* GDP, *there is pressure on prices to adjust upward.*

The slow adjustment of wages and prices has important implications for macroeconomics. If a disturbance moves the economy away from its potential growth path, then the slow adjustment of prices will prevent the economy from returning to potential quickly. Prolonged departures of the economy from potential, such as we observed in Figure 1–1, will then occur. Moreover, if prices adjust slowly, then changes in prices or inflation will occur with a lag. As we will show in considerable detail, price rigidities are capable of explaining both the economic fluctuations and the price movements associated with these economic fluctuations.

The rest of the book is a systematic development of the interrelationships among these three factors: aggregate demand, aggregate supply, and price adjustment. In the short run, aggregate demand determines output because the price level is fixed. In the long run, the supply of productive factors determines output and aggregate demand determines the price level. The price-adjustment equation tells how the economy makes the transition from the short to long run.

Review and Practice

MAJOR POINTS

1. Output and employment expand and contract at irregular intervals.

2. Other measures of the state of the economy, like interest rates and inflation, also track fluctuations.

3. The exchange rate is the amount of foreign currency that can be purchased with one Canadian dollar. The real exchange rate is a measure that takes into account both of the influences on the relative attractiveness of foreign and domestic goods: the exchange rate and the prices of the goods.

4. With flexible prices, output is set by supply conditions alone; output is always at its potential level. The model with flexible prices has problems explaining large movements of output.

5. The model with sticky prices says that output need not be equal to potential output. Output is determined by aggregate demand given a fixed price level. The price level does not change to equate demand with supply.

6. In the model with sticky prices, fluctuations in output are caused by shifts in aggregate demand.

7. The price-adjustment process describes the transition from the short run to the long run. Prices fall when output is below potential GDP and rise when it is above. The price movements move the economy in the direction of potential GDP.

KEY TERMS AND CONCEPTS

Fluctuations	Recovery	Peak
Recession	Trough	Gross domestic product

Real GDP	Unemployment rate	Flexible prices
Exchange rate	Potential GDP	John Maynard Keynes
Trade-weighted exchange rate	Procyclical	Keynesians
	Model	Monetarists
Real exchange rate	Aggregate supply	Price adjustment
Rate of inflation	Aggregate demand	Rational expectations
Rate of interest	Sticky prices	

QUESTIONS FOR DISCUSSION AND REVIEW

1. Which of the following are procyclical?
   a. Interest rates   c. Inflation
   b. Employment   d. Money supply

2. Explain the difference between potential GDP and real GDP.

3. Describe a typical macroeconomic fluctuation, starting from a peak.

4. What are the determinants of potential GDP?

5. How have economic fluctuations changed during the last 75 years?

6. Explain the difference between the Canada-U.S. exchange rate, a trade-weighted exchange rate, and the real exchange rate.

7. How does GDP respond to aggregate demand when prices are perfectly flexible?

8. How does GDP respond to aggregate demand when prices do not adjust?

PROBLEMS

Numerical

1. Real output in the United States is given below for the years 1953 through 1987. All of the data are in billions of 1982 U.S. dollars.

1953	1,435	1971	2,485
1954	1,416	1972	2,609
1955	1,495	1973	2,744
1956	1,526	1974	2,729
1957	1,551	1975	2,695
1958	1,539	1976	2,826
1959	1,629	1977	2,959
1960	1,665	1978	3,115
1961	1,709	1979	3,192
1962	1,799	1980	3,187
1963	1,873	1981	3,249
1964	1,973	1982	3,166
1965	2,088	1983	3,279
1966	2,208	1984	3,501
1967	2,271	1985	3,608
1968	2,366	1986	3,713
1969	2,423	1987	3,820
1970	2,416		

    a. Plot U.S. real output over this period. Put real output on the vertical axis of the graph and the year on the horizontal axis.

    b. Estimate potential output by drawing a smooth trend line through the points on the graph. Identify any shifts in the trend of potential. By what percent did real output grow during this period?

    c. Identify the fluctuations of real output around potential output. How many complete (peak-to-peak) economic fluctuations occurred during this period? How closely do fluctuations in U.S. output correspond to fluctuations in Canadian output?

2. Suppose that the aggregate demand curve in a particular year is given by the algebraic expression $Y = 3,000 + 1,000/P$, where Y is output and P is the price level. Potential output is $Y^* = 4,000$.

    a. Draw the downward-sloping aggregate demand curve and the vertical aggregate supply curve to scale on a diagram with the price level P on the vertical axis and output Y on the horizontal axis.

    b. Suppose that prices are flexible. Find the price level and show it on the diagram.

    c. Now suppose that the following year the aggregate demand curve is given by $Y = 3,000 + 1,100/P$. In what direction has the curve shifted? If output remains at potential, what is the new price level? What was the rate of inflation between the two years?

    d. If prices are instead assumed to be sticky, what will the new level of output be? Will there be pressure on the price level to move upward or downward? Explain.

3. We have the following data on interest rates and the price level (in Canada) for the years 1977–87:

Year	Price Level	Interest Rates
1977	67.9	—
1978	73.9	—
1979	80.7	—
1980	88.9	12.8%
1981	100.0	17.7
1982	110.8	13.6
1983	117.2	9.3
1984	122.3	11.1
1985	127.2	9.4
1986	132.4	9.0
1987	138.2	8.2

    a. Calculate the rate of inflation for the years 1978–87. Note: The rate of inflation this year is given by 100 times the price level this year minus the price level last year, all divided by the price level last year.

    b. Calculate the expected rate of inflation for the years 1980–87 assuming (i) people expect the rate of inflation to be the average rate of inflation in the two previous years, and (ii) people have perfect foresight and expected inflation just equals actual inflation.

    c. For each of the assumptions in Part b, calculate the real interest rate for the years 1980–87.

    d. In light of this example, explain why economists have such a difficult time measuring the real interest rate.

Analytical

1. What explains the fluctuations in output in models where prices are flexible? In models where prices are sticky?

2. Comment on the following two explanations of the large drop in output in the early 1980s in Canada:
   a. 'There was a decline in aggregate supply. Potential output declined because the number of people available for work declined.'
   b. 'There was a decline in aggregate demand. With very high interest rates, consumers and firms purchased fewer goods so that production and employment declined.'
   Which statement seems more plausible? Which statement is consistent with the macro model with flexible prices and which with the model with sticky prices?

3. Explain how the debate between the current schools of macroeconomic thought resembles the macroeconomic debates of the 1930s. In what way is this debate different from those between the Keynesians and the monetarists?

4. Would Keynes have argued that prices in the 1930s were too low or too high? Explain.

5. Explain briefly the idea behind rational expectations. Why is the theory of expectations important when discussing the real interest rate?

2

Measuring Economic
Performance: Output and
Income

IN CHAPTER 1 we examined the behaviour of several key
macroeconomic variables—production, employment, inflation. In this
chapter and the next we show how these and other important variables are
defined and measured.

2.1 Gross Domestic Product

We begin with **gross domestic product (GDP).** GDP refers to production during a particular time period, which we will usually take to be a year, or a
quarter of a year. GDP is the *flow* of new products during the year or the
quarter.

There are three different ways to think about and measure GDP. First, we
can measure **spending** on goods and services by different groups—households, businesses, government, and foreigners. Second, we can measure
production in different industries—agriculture, mining, manufacturing,
and so on. Last, we can measure the total wage and profit **income** earned by
different groups producing GDP. Each of these measures has its own special
purpose, but they all add up to the same thing. We consider each in turn in
the next three sections.

How do we know that the total amount of spending is equal to the total value of production, which in turn is equal to the total amount of income? Think about an individual firm. Suppose the value of its production is $1 million. It is unlikely that its sales are exactly $1 million in that year—suppose its sales are $900,000. For accounting purposes, we treat the remaining $100,000 as spending. It is the firm's investment in inventories of its own goods and is included as part of total investment. Both at the level of the firm and at the level of the whole economy, the equality of production and spending is the result of considering inventory investment as part of spending.

The equality of the value of production and income also derives from accounting principles. Our firm takes in $900,000 in one year. In addition, we add in the $100,000 value of its inventory accumulation as sales, for a total of $1 million. The firm pays out $450,000 in wages. That amount is counted in the incomes of the workers. The firm pays $50,000 in interest, which is counted in the incomes of whoever holds the firm's bonds. It pays $400,000 for its raw materials, which is counted in the incomes of the sellers of materials or of their employees, bondholders, etc. The residual, $1,000,000 - $450,000 - $50,000 - $400,000 = $100,000$, is the profit earned by the owner of the firm, which counts as part of the owner's income. All of the receipts of the firm from its sales are paid out to somebody as income. The value of production and the total amount of income generated are the same.

As a result of the two accounting rules—including inventories in spending and computing profit as the residual between sales and expenses—it is always true that production, spending, and income are exactly the same. This kind of relation is called an **identity**—it is the inevitable outcome of the accounting system, not a statement about how the economy works.

The alternative measures of GDP are gathered together in the system of national accounts. Economists and statisticians at **Statistics Canada,** an agency of the federal government in Ottawa, are responsible for collecting the GDP data and publishing the national accounts. Many of the ideas behind GDP were developed by the late Simon Kuznets of Harvard University. He won the Nobel Prize in economics in 1971 for this work.

2.2 Measuring GDP through Spending

Total spending on goods and services produced in Canada during any period can be broken down as follows:

Gross domestic product = Consumption
+ Investment
+ Government purchases
+ Net exports (or exports minus imports).

Using symbols this key identity can be written on one line:

$$Y = C + I + G + X$$
where Y = Gross domestic product
C = Consumption
I = Investment
G = Government spending
X = Net exports (exports minus imports).

CONSUMPTION

Consumption is defined as spending by *households*. It includes purchases of (1) **durable goods,** such as washing machines, stereos, and cars, (2) **nondurable goods,** such as food, clothing, and gasoline, and (3) **services,** such as haircuts, medical care, and education. Spending on new houses is the only type of household spending that is not included in consumption. Instead it is included in fixed investment.

INVESTMENT

Investment consists of **fixed investment** and **inventory investment.** Fixed investment is the purchase of new factories, machines, and houses. Inventory investment is the change in inventories at business firms. We first discuss fixed investment.

Fixed Investment. Fixed investment is broken down into **nonresidential** fixed investment and **residential** fixed investment. Nonresidential fixed investment is spending on structures and equipment for use in business. Steel mills, office buildings, and power plants are examples of structures. Trucks, lathes, and typewriters are examples of equipment. Residential fixed investment is spending on construction of new houses and apartment buildings. The term 'fixed' connotes that these types of investment goods will be around for a long time, and distinguishes fixed from inventory investment, which is much more temporary, as we will see below. The term 'fixed' is conventionally dropped when the meaning is implicit from the context, and we will follow this convention.

Investment is a *flow* of new capital during the year that is added to the *stock* of capital. The capital stock is the total amount of productive capital in the economy—it includes all the buildings, equipment, and houses. The capital stock increases from one year to the next as a result of investment. However, because the capital stock is constantly wearing out, part of the investment reported in each year's GDP is actually devoted to replacing worn-out capital, not increasing the capital stock. What is reported in GDP is *gross* investment. This accounts for the term 'gross' in GDP. Statisticians have a number of ways of estimating the loss of the existing capital stock from one year to the next. This loss is called **depreciation**. **Net investment** is defined as follows:

$$\text{Net investment} = \text{Gross investment} - \text{Depreciation}.$$

We have the following relation:

$$\text{Capital stock at the end of this year} = \text{Capital stock at the end of last year} \\ - \text{Depreciation during this year} \\ + \text{Gross investment during this year}.$$

By rearranging this equation and putting in the definition of net investment, we have:

$$\text{Net investment} = \text{Capital stock at the end of this year} \\ - \text{Capital stock at the end of last year}.$$

These equations hold whether we are looking at total investment or separately at nonresidential and residential investment. An alternative to GDP is **net domestic product,** or NDP; it includes only net investment. GDP, on the other hand, includes this year's gross investment.

Inventory Investment. Now consider inventory investment, which is simply the change in the stock of inventories held at businesses.

$$\text{Inventory investment this year} = \text{Stock of inventories at the end of } this \text{ year} \\ - \text{Stock of inventories at the end of } last \text{ year}.$$

For example, when a publisher produces and stores 10,000 copies of a newly printed book in its warehouse, the books are counted in GDP as inventory investment. Even though no one has yet purchased the books, they must be counted in GDP because they have been produced. If subsequently you purchase a book directly from the publisher, consumption is up by one book and inventory investment is down by one book; GDP does not change, nor should it since there is no new production. When the publisher sells a book to a bookstore, the publisher's inventory investment is down by one book and the bookstore's inventory investment is up by one book. Total inventory investment does not change, and neither does GDP.

Inventory investment is positive when inventories are increasing, and negative when inventories are decreasing. In 1981 inventory investment was 1.4 billion dollars. In 1982, a recession year, it was −9.8 billion dollars. If inventory investment were not added to spending when computing GDP, we would underestimate production when inventory investment was positive, as in 1981, because spending would be less than production; similarly we would overestimate production when inventory investment was negative, as in 1982, because spending would be more than production.

As the data for 1981–82 show, inventory investment adds to the fluctuations of GDP. **Final sales** is a measure that excludes inventory investment.

Final sales is defined as GDP minus inventory investment. Final sales fluctuates less than GDP.

GOVERNMENT PURCHASES

Government purchases are the sum of federal, provincial, and local government purchases of goods and services. In 1987, provincial and local government purchases were 77 percent of total government purchases. Schools, road construction, and military hardware are examples of government purchases. Government purchases are only part of the total government *outlays* that are included in budgets. Government purchases exclude such items as welfare payments and interest payments on the public debt that are included in government outlays. In 1987 purchases of goods and services accounted for 45 percent of total government outlays.

The distinction between consumption, investment, and government is based primarily on the type of purchaser rather than on the type of product that is purchased. If a Chevrolet is purchased by a household it goes into consumption—as a consumer durable. If it is purchased for use by a business, it goes into investment—as business fixed investment in equipment. If it is purchased by government, it goes into government purchases. (Statistics Canada does provide a tabulation of investment in buildings and equipment by the government.) The only exception to this rule is residential investment, which includes all housing purchases whether by households, businesses, or government.

IMPORTS AND EXPORTS

Canada has an open economy. An open economy is one with substantial interaction with other countries. Canada has experienced a growing volume of transactions with the rest of the world, and GDP has to take these into account. **Exports** are deliveries of goods and services that were made in Canada to foreigners. Imports are deliveries of goods and services that were made outside Canada to Canada.

Part, but not all, of Canadian exports represent goods and services *produced* in Canada. The other part has been imported to Canada and then sold abroad, perhaps as part of manufactured products. For example, General Motors Canada might put a radio imported from Japan into a Chevrolet that is exported to the United States. We want to subtract the radio from the exported car, if we are measuring goods produced in Canada. More generally, if goods are imported from abroad and purchased by Canadian consumers, businesses, or governments, the goods should not be counted in a measure of Canadian production. For these reasons imports are subtracted from spending and exports are added to spending when computing GDP. In other words, only **net exports,** that is, *exports less imports,* are added to the total volume of spending when computing GDP. Note that this decomposition of GDP does not tell you what part of consumption was imported and what part was produced in Canada. Nor does it break down investment, government purchases, or exports between domestic and imported components. The total of net exports is sometimes referred to as the **trade balance.** When net exports are positive there is a **trade surplus.** When net exports are negative there is a **trade deficit.**

THE RECENT RECORD

Table 2–1 shows how Canadian GDP broke down in 1987. Consumption is the biggest component—almost 60 percent—of GDP. Services is the biggest component of consumption—about 50 percent. Services (restaurants, utilities, housing, transportation, and the like) have been growing as a share of consumption.

Fixed investment is about 18 percent of GDP. Nonresidential fixed investment is much larger than residential fixed investment. Government purchases are larger than investment, at about 20 percent of GDP. Exports and imports are each about 25 percent of GDP in recent years with export somewhat larger. The Canadian economy has always depended heavily on international trade and this dependence is growing. In the 1950s and early 1960s exports usually accounted for less than 20 percent of GDP.

These 1987 shares are fairly typical for consumption, investment, government purchases, exports, and imports in any recent year. Inventory investment fluctuates dramatically, and can be negative as well as positive; no year is typical. Final sales were slightly less than GDP in 1987 since inventory investment was positive.

Table 2–1. GROSS DOMESTIC PRODUCT IN 1987—THE SPENDING SIDE (billions of dollars)

Gross domestic product	549.7
Consumption	323.0
Durables	49.4
Nondurables	123.2
Services	150.4
Investment	103.6
Fixed investment	101.6
Nonresidential	62.7
Residential	38.9
Inventory investment	2.0
Government purchases	119.2
Net exports	3.9
Exports	144.2
Imports	140.3
Final sales	547.7

Note: Final sales is GDP less inventory investment.
Source: *Canadian Economic Observer,* Table 1.2.

Bringing Astronomical Numbers Down to Earth

Table 2–1 shows that GDP was $549.7 billion in 1987. With all the zeros this looks like $549,700,000,000. An astrophysicist would write it 5.497×10^{11}. How can we make intuitive sense of such large numbers?

The best way to bring numbers like this down to size is simply to divide by the population—that is, to calculate GDP per person. The population of Canada was 25.6 million in 1987. GDP per capita in Canada was thus $21,473 (549,700,000,000/25,600,000 = 21,472.66).

Canadian consumption in 1987 was $323 billion. This amounts to about $12,617 per capita for food, clothing, transportation, and other consumer items. On average, every man, woman, and child in Canada consumed $12,617 of goods and services in 1987.

Government purchases of goods and services were $119.2 billion in 1987. This amounted to $4,656 per capita for national defence, schools, highways, police, and so on. The sum of private consumption plus public consumption per capita in Canada in 1987 was $17,273.

Net exports were $3.9 billion in 1987, or about $152 per capita. In other words, on average, every person in Canada made $152 more goods that were sold abroad than they bought goods that were made abroad.

WHICH SPENDING ITEMS SHOULD BE INCLUDED?

In deciding which spending items to include in computing GDP, we must be careful to avoid double counting. For example, the purchase of a 10-year-old house should not be counted; that house was counted 10 years ago when it was constructed. Similarly, the purchase of the assets of Canadian Pacific Airlines by Pacific Western Airlines in 1986 should not be counted; Canadian Pacific's maintenance facilities, for example, were included in business fixed investment when they were built.

To avoid double counting, we also do not include the purchase of **intermediate goods.** These are goods that are converted into other goods in the production process (for example, steel is an intermediate good used in the production of cars). We only include purchases of the **final goods,** such as the cars themselves. The value of the steel is included in GDP as part of a car when someone buys the car. The purchases of steel by automobile manufacturers are not counted.

In computing GDP, we value different types of goods, such as apples and oranges, using the price of each good that is paid by the purchaser. The price includes sales and excise taxes. If apples cost twice as much as oranges, then each apple will contribute twice as much to GDP as will each orange.

REAL GDP

GDP is a dollar measure of production. In comparing one year to another, we run into the problem that the dollar is not a stable measure of purchasing power. In the 1970s especially, GDP rose a great deal not because the economy was actually growing rapidly but because the dollar was inflating. For comparisons across years, we need a measure of output that adjusts for inflation. We want GDP *in constant dollars,* or, as we will generally call it, **real GDP.** In contrast, the GDP that we have looked at so far is sometimes called **nominal GDP.** From 1972 to 1987 nominal GDP grew by about 406 percent from $108.6 billion to $549.7 billion. During the same period real GDP grew by about 73 percent. The conversion from nominal to real makes a big difference.

The concept of real GDP is straightforward. We want to measure consumption, investment, government purchases, and exports in physical rather than dollar units. Further, we want to subtract imports in the same physical units, so that real GDP is a measure of production in Canada.

To compute consumption in real terms, the national income statisticians gather data on the prices of consumption goods in great detail. They take the data on the corresponding detailed flows of goods to consumers and restate them in 1981 dollars. For example, suppose the retail price of a typical shirt rose from $10 in 1981 to $15 in 1988. The flow of shirts to consumers was $300 million in 1981 and $500 million in 1988. Consumption of shirts in real terms was $300 million in 1981 dollars in 1981 and $330 million in 1981 dollars in 1988. The $330 million is computed as

$$P_b/P_t$$

[500 million 1988 dollars] $\times$ [(10/15) 1981 dollars per 1988 dollar]
= 330 million 1981 dollars.

The same type of adjustment for price change is applied to each detailed category of consumption, investment, government purchases, exports, and imports. Then real GDP is real consumption plus real investment plus real government purchases plus real exports less real imports.

Table 2–2 shows the breakdown of real GDP for the four-year period that spans the deep 1981–82 recession in Canada. This recession was preceded by record high interest rates in the summer of 1981. As we will see later, the high interest rates were the result of events in the United States and policy actions by the Bank of Canada. There are many figures in Table 2–2, but with some study they give a good account of what happened to the Canadian economy. With a close look, at least five interesting facts can be gleaned.

1. Real GDP fell from 1981 to 1982, and then rose in 1983 and 1984. This decline and subsequent rise is the essential feature of an economic cycle. Each cycle begins with a contraction of real GDP, reaches a trough, begins an expansion, and then reaches a peak. The next cycle starts with the next contraction.

2. Real GDP fell by more than final sales in 1982, since inventory investment declined. In fact, inventory investment became negative—firms drew down their inventories because they anticipated lower sales during the recession. The decline in inventories made the recession worse than it otherwise would have been.

Table 2–2.   REAL GROSS DOMESTIC PRODUCT, 1981–84
(billions of 1981 dollars)

	1981	1982	1983	1984
Gross domestic product	356.0	344.5	355.4	377.9
Consumption	196.2	191.0	197.5	206.7
Durables	28.1	24.6	27.5	31.1
Nondurables	81.4	79.2	79.7	81.7
Services	86.7	89.2	90.3	93.9
Investment	78.1	57.6	64.2	63.7
Fixed investment	76.7	66.8	66.6	67.6
Nonresidential	56.1	49.6	46.5	47.4
Residential	20.6	17.2	20.1	20.2
Inventory investment	1.4	−4.2	−2.4	3.9
Government purchases	78.0	80.3	80.9	82.4
Net exports	3.9	15.9	14.8	18.0
Exports	96.9	94.8	100.8	118.7
Imports	93.0	78.9	86.0	100.7
Final sales	354.6	353.7	357.8	374.0

Source: *Canadian Economic Observer*, Table 1.3.

3. Consumption fell in 1982, as high interest rates made borrowing for automobiles, furniture, and appliances costly. Also, people postponed purchases of big-ticket items until better times.
4. Both residential investment and nonresidential investment fell sharply in 1982. The high interest rates made it difficult to borrow to finance both housing and factory construction. Both types of investment had not risen back to the 1981 figure by 1984.
5. Both exports and imports fell in 1982 and rose thereafter. Imports fell because Canadian demand for all types of goods and services, including imported ones, fell. Exports fell because a recession also occurred in the United States in 1982, and the United States is our largest trading partner. Net exports rose because imports fell more than exports. This occurred for two reasons. First, the recession in the United States was less severe than in Canada. As a result, the reduction in the demand for our goods by Americans was not as great as the reduction in our demand for foreign goods. Second, the value of the Canadian dollar declined relative to the U.S. dollar. This made Canadian goods relatively more attractive to Americans while making U.S. goods relatively less attractive to Canadians. (Both of these factors are discussed in more detail in Chapters 5 and 10.)

Quarterly GDP Statistics and Recessions

The spending data reported in Tables 2–1 and 2–2 are *annual*. They give the flow of spending for a year. *Quarterly* GDP data are also available for Canada. These give the spending flows for a quarter of a year. Quarterly data are useful for understanding shorter-run movements of business cycles. Private forecasting firms and government agencies all use quarterly models of the economy. Quarterly data on real GDP are reported in the newspapers as soon as they are available, usually a few weeks after the quarter is over. Although some economists consider that a downturn qualifies as a recession only if real GDP declines for two consecutive quarters, Statistics Canada uses a more flexible approach for dating recessions.* Some important conventions of the reporting of quarterly data are illustrated in the following comparison.

Year: Quarter	Real GDP	Year	Real GDP
1985:1	389.4	1985	395.2
1985:2	391.9		
1985:3	395.6		
1985:4	403.9		
1986:1	405.1	1986	407.7
1986:2	408.3		
1986:3	408.6		
1986:4	408.9		
1987:1	415.4	1987	424.1
1987:2	420.6		
1987:3	426.9		
1987:4	433.7		

The flow of GDP in each quarter is stated at an annual rate, which means that the actual flow each quarter is multiplied by 4. If you add up the four quarterly flows for each year, and divide by 4, you get the annual figure reported at the right.

* See Phillip Cross, 'Special Study: The Business Cycle in Canada 1950–1981', in *Current Economic Analysis*, March 1982, Statistics Canada catalogue number 13-004E.

2.3 Measuring GDP through Production: Value Added

GDP can also be computed by adding up production of goods and services in different industries. As we observed on the spending side, we must avoid counting the same items more than once. Many industries specialise in the

Computing Growth Rates

The growth rate of a variable between two periods, in percent, is defined as *the change in the variable divided by the value of the variable in the first period multiplied by 100.* Thus, the growth rate of real GDP from 1986 to 1987 is

$100 \times$ (real GDP in 1987 − real GDP in 1986)/(real GDP in 1986)
= $100 \times (424.1 - 407.7)/(407.7) = 100 \times (13.7)/(407.7)$
= 3.4 percent.

Growth rates are usually converted to 'annual rates' because everyone is used to annual rates. For a change from one year to the next the growth rate is already at an annual rate. For the growth rate from one quarter to the next the annual rate is approximated by multiplying the quarterly growth rate by 4.

production of intermediate goods that are used in the production of other goods. If we want each industry's production to include the contribution of those industries to total GDP, then we want to take the production of intermediate goods into account.

The concept of **value added** was developed to prevent double counting and to attribute to each industry a part of the GDP. The value added by a firm is the difference between the revenue the firm earns by selling its products and the amount it pays for the products of other firms it uses as intermediate goods. It is a measure of the value that is added to each product by firms at each stage of production.

For General Motors of Canada, for example, value added is the revenue from selling cars less the amount it pays for steel, glass, and the other inputs it buys.

For a car dealer, value added is the revenue from selling cars less the wholesale cost of the cars. The value added to a car by a car dealer takes the form of a convenient showroom, ample selection, advice (for what it's worth), and final preparation and testing. The car dealer produces these services by hiring salespeople and car mechanics, renting showroom and garage space, borrowing money to hold a big inventory of cars, and keeping the profits. Wages, rents, interest, and profits are thus what make up value added at each firm.

GDP is the sum of the value added by all the firms in Canada. If a firm sells a final product, the sale appears in that firm's value added but does not appear anywhere else. On the other hand, if a firm sells its output as an input for another firm, that sale appears negatively in the other firm's value added. Products sold by one firm to another are called **intermediate products.** When the two firms are added together in the process of computing

Table 2–3. VALUE ADDED BY INDUSTRY IN 1987
(billions of dollars)

Gross domestic product at factor cost	379.0
Agriculture	11.8
Fishing, trapping, logging, and forestry	3.5
Mining	21.8
Construction	27.0
Manufacturing	74.6
Transportation and storage	18.2
Communication	10.9
Wholesale and retail trade	45.8
Finance, insurance, and real estate	54.3
Community, business, and personal services	75.4
Utilities	11.8
Government	23.7

Source: *Canadian Economic Observer*, Tables 1.15 and 1.16.

GDP, sales of intermediate products wash out. When a firm imports a product, the transaction appears negatively in that firm's value added, but does not appear positively in the value added of any Canadian firm.

A breakdown of real GDP in terms of the value added by various industries is given in Table 2–3 for 1987. These figures tell some interesting stories about the modern Canadian economy. We tend to think of the economy as producing goods—lumber, wheat, cars—but the non-goods-producing sectors make up well over half of the economy. We also often think of Canada as having a resource-based economy. But the primary industries—agriculture, fishing, mining, and forestry—account for only 10 percent of the economy, and this is only half the contribution of manufacturing.

You may have noticed that the figure given for real GDP in 1987 in Table 2–3 is smaller than the one given on page 32. The figure on page 32 is real GDP measured using market prices. These prices, which are the prices faced by consumers such as yourself, include indirect taxes (and occasionally subsidies) like the provincial sales tax. When Statistics Canada computes real GDP by industry it excludes these taxes and subsidies, resulting in a smaller figure. This is called **real GDP at factor cost,** as noted in Table 2–3. The term 'at factor cost' signifies that this approach measures the contribution of a good to GDP according to the amount paid for the inputs (factors) used to produce it. The approach taken in computing the number reported for real GDP on page 32 measures the contribution of a good to GDP according to its market price, which reflects taxes and subsidies as well as factor costs.

2.4 Measuring GDP through Income

The Canadians who produce GDP receive income for their work. This income provides a third way to compute GDP. To see the relation between GDP and income, think again about the value added of a car dealer. Value added is the difference between the revenue from selling cars and the wholesale cost of cars. That difference must be somebody's income. Part of the difference is the wages the car dealer pays to salespeople and mechanics. Another part is the rent that the car dealer pays to a landlord for the use of the showroom and garage. Another part is the interest that the car dealer pays to a bank for loans to finance inventory. The rest of the difference is profit, which goes into the income of the owner of the car dealership. Thus, all of the value added shows up in income, in the form of either wages, rent, interest, or profit. Since we know that the sum of all firms' value added is GDP, the sum of all incomes must also equal GDP.

To compute national income we need to recognise that not all of the income generated by activity that takes place within Canada's borders is paid to Canadians. For example, many factories that operate in Canada are owned by Americans; the profits from these factories are therefore paid to foreigners. In addition, many Canadians earn income from investments that they have made in other countries.

The total payments to foreigners that arise from activity in Canada usually exceed the total payments that Canadians receive from their investments in other countries. Deducting the difference between these two totals from GDP yields **gross national product (GNP)**. Thus gross domestic product is the total income generated within Canada's borders while gross national product is the total income of Canadians, regardless of where it was generated.[1]

In computing national income, Statistics Canada also excludes the indirect taxes paid by Canadians. Indirect taxes are taxes such as the retail sales tax and gasoline tax that form part of the purchase price of a good or service. (By contrast, income taxes are paid directly to the government; they are not indirect taxes.) Statistics Canada further deducts the amount that our buildings and equipment have depreciated; these are called *capital consumption allowances*. Finally, accounting for a small amount of measurement error (the statistical discrepancy) yields **net national income** at factor cost, as shown in Table 2–4. The term 'net' signifies that depreciation has been deducted from the 'gross' figure, and the term 'at factor cost' signifies that indirect taxes have been excluded.

A large amount of national income is diverted by the government and by businesses before it reaches wage earners or shareholders. But government and businesses also augment the income of some people by paying social security and other benefits. The national accounts contain two concepts of income that take account of these diversions and augmentations. **Personal income** is total income received by the public before income taxes, contributions to government pension plans, and other direct payments to govern-

---

[1] It is now conventional to measure real output in Canada in terms of GDP rather than GNP. This accords with the practice of most other industrialised countries with the exception of the United States (reminiscent of that country's continued disregard for the metric system). Using GDP has some other advantages over the use of GNP as well: GDP is more closely related to employment within Canada, and it is easier to reconcile with measurements of output by province.

Table 2–4. THE RELATION BETWEEN GDP AND NET NATIONAL INCOME AT FACTOR COST IN 1987
(billions of dollars)

Gross domestic product at market prices		549.7
plus:	Investment income received from nonresidents	7.0
less:	Investment income paid to nonresidents	23.6
equals:	Gross national product at market prices	533.1
less:	Indirect taxes net of subsidies	58.0
less:	Capital consumption allowances	63.3
less:	Statistical discrepancy	.1
equals:	Net national income at factor cost	411.7

Source: *Canadian Economic Observer,* Table 1.4.

ments, and **disposable personal income** is total income after these payments.

While most of Canadians' personal income is earned through labour, about one-third comes from other sources. Of these, government is the most important, providing income directly through transfer payments such as unemployment insurance benefits, and indirectly through interest payments on the public debt. Canadians also receive income from farms and other unincorporated businesses, as shown in Table 2–5. Disposable personal income was $363.8 billion, or $14,211 per capita in 1987. Consumption per capita was $12,617, so all but $1,594 of income per capita was consumed.

How much of domestic income is earned by workers and how much is profit? Table 2–6 shows the breakdown for 1987. About 69 percent of national income was earned by labour; this includes payments to workers in wages and salaries as well as fringe benefits. The profit share includes not

Table 2–5. SOURCES AND DISPOSITION OF PERSONAL INCOME IN 1987
(billions of dollars)

Labour income	295.7
plus: Income from farms and unincorporated businesses	37.2
plus: Investment income (including interest on the public debt)	61.4
plus: Transfers from government	67.6
plus: Other transfers	1.3
equals: Personal income	463.2
less: Income taxes	70.0
less: Employer and employee contributions to social insurance and government pension funds	25.0
less: Other direct taxes	4.4
equals: Personal disposable income	363.8

Source: *Canadian Economic Observer,* Table 1.5.

Table 2–6.   LABOUR AND PROFIT SHARES OF NATIONAL INCOME IN 1987
(billions of dollars)

Labour income	295.7	Labour share 69 percent
Pre-tax corporate profits	57.2 ⎫	
Income from farms and unincorporated businesses	37.3 ⎪	
Interest and miscellaneous investment income	41.3 ⎬	Profit share 31 percent
Adjustment for change in the value of inventories	−3.1 ⎭	
Net domestic income at factor cost	428.4	

Source: *Canadian Economic Observer*, Table 1.1.

only corporate profits, but also rental income, proprietors' income, and net interest income. Since labour plus profits exhaust income, the profit share was 31 percent in 1987. These relative shares are fairly stable from year to year. In 1966 the labour share of domestic income was also 69 percent. Note that net domestic income at factor cost as reported in Table 2–6 differs from net national income at factor cost as reported in Table 2–4 by the amount of net investment income received from foreigners.

THE UNDERGROUND ECONOMY

Some productive activity that should be included in GDP in principle is difficult to measure because it is deliberately hidden. Activity is sometimes hidden to avoid paying taxes on the proceeds (for example, babysitters who do not file income tax returns) or because the necessary approval has not been obtained (for example, construction undertaken without a building permit). Statistics Canada estimates that the 'underground' economy is about as large as 3 percent of GDP, although other researchers have made higher estimates. One reason that these estimates differ is that Statistics Canada excludes illegal activities from GDP by definition while some other researchers include the production of all goods and services, whether legal or not, in their estimates of GDP.

The term **underground economy** refers to production which is sold but not reported. Lack of reporting is not the only reason for omitting production from GDP.

For example, suppose that your parents work during the day and you have a young brother who needs to be looked after between the time that school lets out and the time that your parents return from work. If your parents pay a day-care centre to supervise your brother then the supervision provided is counted as part of GDP. If you subsequently volunteer to look after your brother (and receive no explicit payment for this) then GDP would be reduced. Although your brother is still being supervised after school, this supervision has been changed from a market activity (your parents pay the day-care centre) to a non-market activity (simply part of family life).

Most non-market activity is excluded from GDP (one exception is farmers' consumption of their own produce). It is worth keeping in mind that GDP is meant to measure only market activity, by and large. It would be impossible to measure the value of all activity that could potentially be provided by a market because so many aspects of our private lives could be included. For example, Statistics Canada would have to try to keep track of how often people find blind dates for their friends because this is also done by dating services that charge a fee for this service.

The System of National Accounts

1. Gross domestic product (GDP) is the production of goods and services in Canada. The spending, value added, and factor income measures of GDP are all equivalent ways of thinking about GDP; differences arise only because some measurements are made at market prices and others are made at factor cost. In particular the national income identity says that spending on GDP is equal to the income earned from producing GDP.

2. Consumption, investment, government purchases, and net exports are the four basic components of spending. Consumption is the largest component and investment and net exports are the most volatile components.

3. The investment component of GDP includes the replacement of depreciating capital. It is thus gross investment. Net investment is gross investment less depreciation. Net domestic product is GDP less depreciation.

4. Real GDP is a measure of production that is adjusted for the effects of inflation. It measures the physical volume of production. Nominal GDP measures the dollar volume of production.

5. Final sales is GDP less inventory investment. It fluctuates less than GDP.

6. To avoid double counting we measure the contribution of each industry by its value added and do not include any goods that were produced in an earlier year.

7. Disposable personal income is the amount of national income that is available for households to spend. It is the sum of personal income from all sources including the government, minus direct tax payments and contributions to government pensions.

2.5 Saving and Investment

Saving is defined as disposable income minus consumption. An important, but sometimes confusing, fact is that *saving must equal investment.* To see this, consider first a closed economy with no government and therefore no taxes. Then,

$$\text{Spending on GDP} = \text{Consumption} + \text{Investment.}$$

Also, from the definition of saving,

$$\text{National income} = \text{Saving} + \text{Consumption.}$$

Since spending on GDP equals national income, we know that

$$\text{Consumption} + \text{Investment} = \text{Saving} + \text{Consumption}$$

or

$$\text{Investment} = \text{Saving.}$$

The equality of saving and investment follows from nothing but the definitions of GDP and income. As long as the statisticians adhere to these definitions, there is no possibility that investment can ever differ from saving. We don't have to say, 'If our theories hold, saving and investment will be equal.' No matter how investors and consumers behave, saving and investment will be equal.

The simple identity that saving equals investment becomes more complicated for an open economy interacting with other economies in the world. By borrowing, a country can invest more than it saves. By lending, a country can save more than it invests. The ability to borrow or lend permits investment to be undertaken at the most efficient place and time. Borrowing means accumulating financial liabilities. Lending means accumulating financial assets. These financial assets and liabilities have implications for macroeconomic behaviour. An important example is the borrowing of the federal government to finance its budget deficit. As the stock of government bonds (liabilities of the government) grows, the interest payments on the debt may require increasing future taxes or printing more money, either of which has macroeconomic implications.

SAVING AND INVESTMENT IN AN OPEN ECONOMY

We now look at saving and investment flows at the sector level. The economy is divided into three sectors: private (households and private businesses), government, and the rest of the world. Some more symbols will save space. Let

F = Government transfers to the private sector → *trb pymts*
N = Interest on the government debt

(int on bonds)

T = Taxes,
J = Net investment income received from foreigners
S_p = Private saving (saving of the private sector)
S_g = Government saving
S_r = Rest-of-world saving

and recall that we previously defined

Y = GDP
C = Consumption
I = Investment
G = Government spending, and
X = Net exports.

Private Saving. For simplicity we will ignore depreciation. From the definition of saving we know that private saving is disposable income minus consumption (C). Disposable income is GDP (Y) plus net investment income from foreigners (J) plus the impact of the government ($F + N - T$). Therefore:

$$S_p = (Y + J + F + N - T) - C. \qquad (2-1)$$

Government Saving. For simplicity we will treat all government expenditures as government consumption. That is, investment will be assumed to equal zero for the government sector. Hence, government saving equals income (tax receipts, net of transfer payments and interest payments) minus purchases of goods and services:

$$S_g = (T - F - N) - G. \qquad (2-2)$$

Government saving is also called the government **budget surplus** or **budget deficit**. The budget is in surplus when G is less than $(T - F - N)$ and in deficit when G is greater than $(T - F - N)$.

Rest-of-World Saving. Recall that we defined private saving as total payments received by the private sector minus total outlays of the private sector. **Rest-of-world saving** with respect to Canada is defined in the same way. The rest of the world receives payments from Canada for our imports from abroad. It also receives payments that arise from investments that foreigners have made in Canada (for instance, the dividends paid by Ford of Canada to the parent company in Detroit). We have to subtract from this the payments that foreigners make to Canadians for our exports and the payments that arise from investments that Canadians have made in other countries (for instance, the interest on a U.S. government bond owned by someone in Edmonton). The difference between our imports and exports is net exports, but with the sign reversed ($-X$). The difference between investment income payments made to foreigners and those received from foreigners is net investment income, but also with the sign reversed ($-J$). The sum of net exports and net investment income from foreigners ($X + J$) is called the **current account.** Thus rest-of-world saving with respect to Canada is the negative of the current account:

$$S_r = -(X + J). \tag{2-3}$$

If the current account is negative, then rest-of-world saving with respect to Canada is positive.[2] This is termed a **capital inflow** because it indicates that savings generated abroad are being used in the Canadian economy.

It is important to note that these equations do not imply that saving equals investment for any of the sectors individually. However, for the three sectors as a whole, saving must equal investment. The sum of the three sectors' saving is

$$S_p + S_g + S_r = (Y + J + F + N - T) - C + (T - F - N - G) - (X + J). \tag{2-4}$$

Everything cancels out on the right-hand side except $Y - C - G - X$, which from the income identity is equal to investment, I. Thus, private saving plus government saving plus saving from the rest of the world equals investment. This identity is of great importance in interpreting movements in investment and saving. Because of large shifts in the saving of these three sectors in recent years, the identity deserves particular emphasis, as is illustrated in Table 2–7.

Table 2–7.   GROSS SAVING AND INVESTMENT FOR 1985–87
(billions of dollars)

	1985	1986	1987
Gross private domestic saving	113.3	108.1	118.1
plus: Government saving	−33.5	−27.4	−25.1
plus: Capital inflow	3.3	12.1	10.6
plus: Statistical discrepancy	.6	−1.2	.0
equals: Gross private domestic investment	83.7	91.6	103.6

Note: Government businesses are included in private saving. Capital inflow is net of change in official reserves.
Source: Statistics Canada, 13-001.

Table 2–7 shows the movement in gross investment in Canada between 1985 and 1987. The 9 percent increase in investment between 1985 and 1986 occurred, despite the decline in private saving, because of increased government saving (a smaller deficit) and a large increase in capital from abroad. Investment in new factories and equipment in Canada continued to grow largely because of the willingness of foreigners to invest in Canada. For example, Honda of Japan was building an auto assembly plant in Alliston, Ontario, in 1986.

As a result, net foreign investment accounted for over 10 percent of Ca-

[2] There is one possible exception to this which is noted when we discuss changes in official foreign exchange reserves in Section 2.6.

nadian investment spending in 1986 and 1987. The United States has also experienced large government deficits and slow or negative growth in private savings in recent years, resulting in an even greater dependence on foreign investment. Foreign sources accounted for about 22 percent of U.S. investment spending in 1986 and 1987; some of these investments were made by Canadians.

SAVING AND CHANGES IN ASSETS

To illustrate how these saving and investment decisions relate to the accumulation of assets and liabilities, consider two types of financial assets: government bonds and government money (currency). Money and bonds are financial liabilities of the government and are financial assets of the private sector. We call bonds B and money M. Let the symbol Δ represent a change from one year to the next. Then ΔM means change in money and ΔB means change in bonds.

The excess of saving over physical investment can be used to increase assets or reduce liabilities. Suppose that the entire government saving can only be used either to reduce the national debt or to reduce money. The relation between government saving and asset accumulation is thus summarised as

$$S_g = -(\Delta M + \Delta B). \tag{2-5}$$

Since the government deficit is $-S_g$, Equation 2–5 equivalently says that the deficit must be financed by issuing money or by issuing bonds. Sometimes Equation 2–5 is called the **government budget identity.** If the private sector restricts itself to money and bonds, then the excess of private saving goes into either money or bonds. That is,

$$S_p = I + \Delta M + \Delta B_p. \tag{2-6}$$

The subscript p on B means that this is the private holding of bonds. Finally, if the rest of the world invests only in government bonds, then we have

$$S_r = \Delta B_r. \tag{2-7}$$

The subscript r on B means that this is foreign holdings of Canadian government bonds. By adding the assets for these three equations together we find again that $I = S_p + S_g + S_r$, the saving equals investment identity for the economy as a whole. As is clear from these equations, a government deficit generates an increase in either money or government bonds or both. A capital inflow from abroad results in an accumulation of Canadian debt abroad. In this sense the Canadian current account deficit is used to help finance the government budget deficit.

2.6 Transactions with the Rest of the World: The Balance of Payments Accounts

We have already discussed transactions with other countries: imports and exports of goods, factor payments from and to foreigners, and capital inflows and outflows with the rest of the world. Statistics Canada also tabulates many aspects of our transactions with foreigners in the balance of international payments. Although there are no concepts in the balance of payments accounts that we have not already discussed, you will frequently hear about various types of deficits using the terminology of these accounts. It is important to understand what these mean. The balance of payments accounts are divided into the **capital account** and the **current account.** The capital account keeps track of international borrowing, for example, when a Canadian company borrows from a foreign bank. It also keeps track of international trade in assets, for example, the purchase of foreign stocks by Canadians. Thus the capital account includes transactions that involve acquiring direct ownership of resources by purchasing land, buildings, and companies (this is termed **direct investment**), and transactions that involve acquiring financial assets by making bank loans or buying stocks and bonds (this is termed **indirect** or **portfolio investment**).

Purchasing a stock and making a loan are quite similar; in both cases one party acquires a claim on some future payments from the other (dividends in the case of the stock, installment payments in the case of the loan). When a foreigner acquires a claim on a Canadian the capital account is increased by the value of the claim. When a Canadian acquires a claim on a foreigner the capital account is reduced by the value of that claim. Thus the capital account is positive when Canadians have sold more claims to foreigners than they have acquired from foreigners. This is termed a **capital inflow.** A positive capital account balance indicates that, as a group, Canadians are becoming more indebted to foreigners. But it also indicates that foreign capital is being made available to Canadians in order to increase the Canadian stock of physical capital, or for other purposes.

Canada's capital account balance in 1987 is summarised in Table 2–8. Canadian direct investment abroad exceeded direct investments by foreigners in Canada, so the net direct investment balance is negative. This was more than offset by the large inflow in portfolio investment. In practice, it can be difficult to keep track of these international capital flows. As a result, there is a large 'statistical discrepancy' in the capital account.

Table 2–8. CANADIAN CAPITAL ACCOUNT IN 1987
(billions of dollars)

Net direct investment	−1.6
plus: Net portfolio investment	19.6
plus: Statistical discrepancy	−3.0
equals: Capital account balance	15.0

Source: *Bank of Canada Review,* Tables J1 and J3.

One type of international transaction in assets is omitted from the capital account. The Canadian government maintains a stock of foreign currency. This is called Canada's **official reserves** (or **foreign exchange reserves**). The reason for these reserves is discussed in Chapters 11 and 12. For now, you should note that changes in official reserves provide another way that Canadians can increase or reduce their claims on foreigners.

All other international transactions are entered on the current account. The current account is broken down into a number of smaller accounts. The *merchandise account* keeps track of trade in goods: items such as wheat and automobiles. In recent years Canada has almost always had a surplus in merchandise trade. The *service account* keeps track of trade in items such as travel, freight, and business services. In recent years Canada has usually had a deficit in services trade. However, the merchandise surplus has usually exceeded the services deficit so that Canada's net exports of goods and services taken together have been positive from 1978 to 1987.

The balance on investment income has long been negative. Canadians are net debtors relative to the rest of the world. In 1987, for example, Canadians as a whole owned $214 billion less in foreign assets than foreigners owned of Canadian assets. As a result, we receive less investment income from abroad than we pay to foreigners.

The Canadian current account balance in the recent past is shown in Figure 2–1. The current account balance has shifted between positive and neg-

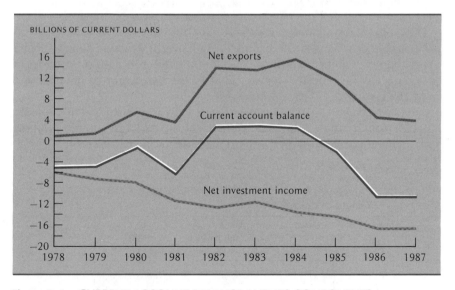

Figure 2–1. CURRENT ACCOUNT BALANCE AND ITS COMPONENTS.
In the 10-year period shown here, net exports have always been positive and net investment income has always been negative. The current account has been both positive and negative. The data are given in nominal terms; thus part of the reason for the widening of the gap between net exports and net investment income is simply the inflation that took place during these years. Source: *Canadian Economic Observer*, Table 1.17.

Table 2-9. CANADIAN CURRENT ACCOUNT IN 1987
           (billions of dollars)

Merchandise trade balance	11.0
plus: Services trade balance	−7.1
equals: Net exports	3.9
plus: Investment income balance	−16.6
plus: Transfer balance	2.1
equals: Current account balance	−10.6

Source: *Canadian Economic Observer*, Table 1.17.

ative, largely depending on whether the net export surplus has exceeded the net investment income deficit. (The current account also includes transfers between Canadians and foreigners, such as inheritances received by Canadians from abroad.)

In 1987 the current account was negative, as shown in Table 2–9. That is, Canadians acquired more in the way of goods, investment income, and transfers from foreigners than foreigners acquired from us. How is this possible?

It must be that foreigners acquired more claims on Canadians (that is, acquired more Canadian assets) than Canadians acquired of foreigners. Indeed, the difference between these two must equal the current account deficit. If official reserves are unchanged, then the capital account surplus must equal the current account deficit. The sum of the current account and the capital account is called the **balance of payments.** Thus if official reserves are unchanged the balance of payments must equal zero.

The current and capital accounts will not offset each other exactly if official reserves do change. For example, the current account deficit can be larger than the capital account surplus, but the difference must be made up by a reduction in official reserves. That is, the balance of payments must equal the change in official reserves.

Canada's balance of payments position in 1987 is summarised in Table 2–10. The capital inflow (capital account surplus) was large enough to allow both a current account deficit and an increase in official reserves.

Table 2-10. CANADIAN BALANCE OF PAYMENTS IN 1987
            (billions of dollars)

Current account balance	−10.6
plus: Capital account balance	15.0
equals: Change in official reserves	4.4

Source: *Bank of Canada Review*, Tables J1 and J3.

Review and Practice

MAJOR POINTS

1. There are three ways to measure and think about GDP: the spending side, the production side, and the income side. The components of spending are consumption, investment, government spending, and net exports. The components of production are the values added by each industry. The components of income are wages, profits, and interest.

2. Real GDP is the physical volume of production, after the effects of rising prices have been removed. Real GDP growth has averaged about 4 percent per year in the last 20 years, but there have been many fluctuations. Potential GDP is real GDP after the economic fluctuations have been removed. Nominal GDP is just GDP without adjustment for inflation or for economic fluctuations.

3. Value added is the difference between revenue and purchases of goods and services by a firm. It is the firm's contribution to GDP. GDP for the whole economy is the sum of value added across all producers.

4. Depreciation is the loss of capital from wear and tear. Net investment is gross investment less depreciation. Net domestic product is GDP less depreciation.

5. Conceptually, income and production are equal. All of value added is somebody's income. In the national accounts, there are various measures of income. Net national income at factor cost is GNP plus net investment income from abroad less depreciation and less sales and excise taxes. Personal income is labour and investment income plus transfers from the government. Disposable personal income is personal income less income taxes and social insurance contributions.

6. The balance of payments is the sum of the current account and the capital account. The current account consists principally of net exports and net investment income from abroad. The capital account keeps track of borrowing and lending between Canadians and foreigners. If we experience a current account deficit this must be financed by a capital account surplus or a reduction of the government's foreign exchange reserves, or both.

7. An important implication of the equality of income and product is the equality of saving and investment. It will always be the case that investment equals private saving plus the government surplus plus the capital inflow from abroad.

KEY TERMS AND CONCEPTS

Gross domestic product	Personal disposable income	Intermediate goods
Value added	Government purchases	Government saving
Consumption	Imports	Real GDP
Gross national product	Exports	Nominal GDP
Fixed investment	Depreciation	Balance of payments
National income	Net investment	Current account
Net national income	Net domestic product	Capital account
Net domestic income	Final sales	Official reserves
Inventory investment	Factor incomes	
Personal income	Private saving	

QUESTIONS FOR DISCUSSION AND REVIEW

1. Explain why spending on GDP is equal to income earned from producing GDP.

2. Identify which of the following are flows and which are stocks: consumption; government bonds outstanding at the end of last year; government purchases; inventories; inventory investment; depreciation; factories and equipment in Canada on December 31, 1985; the budget deficit.

3. Explain how real GDP is calculated.

4. Which components of spending fluctuate the most over the cycle?

5. Why must the sum of the current account and the capital account equal the change in official reserves?

PROBLEMS

Numerical

1. The following are data for the Canadian economy for 1986 in millions of dollars.

Gross investment expenditures	91,744
Pre-tax corporate profits	46,124
Exports of goods and services	137.459
Interest and other investment income	39,586
Indirect taxes less subsidies	53,825
Income from farms and non-farm unincorporated businesses	34,560
Inventory valuation adjustment	−1,789
Investment income received from foreigners	7,207
Statistical discrepancy in spending approach	−131
Investment income paid to foreigners	23,761
Imports of goods and services	132,879
Capital consumption allowances	59,438
Government purchases of goods and services	112,986
Statistical discrepancy in net national income	−132
Personal consumption expenditures	297,304
Labour income	274,607

   a. Compute GDP using the spending approach.
   b. Compute net national product.
   c. Compute net domestic income.
   d. Compute net national income two ways.

2. Fill in the blanks.
   a. If investment is $100 billion, private saving is $120 billion, and capital inflow from abroad is $10 billion, then the government budget deficit is _____ billion.
   b. If the stock of inventories in the economy was $90 billion at the end of 1985 and $110 billion at the end of 1986, then inventory investment for 1986 is _____ billion.
   c. If GDP is $500 billion, investment income received from foreigners is $5 billion, and investment income paid to foreigners is $20 billion, then GNP is _____.

3. (Warning: This problem is tough.) Data on an economy are given in the following tables (billions of dollars).

	Purchases of Intermediate Inputs from						
Industry	Agriculture	Mining	Manufacturing	Transportation and Utilities (T&U)	Trade	Finance, Insurance, and Real Estate (FIRE)	Services
Agriculture	—	1	19	14	7	7	18
Mining	8	—	21	4	18	18	8
Construction	21	21	22	23	18	15	5
Manufacturing	54	153	—	139	20	106	11
T&U	1	60	20	—	25	55	12
Trade	9	7	464	79	—	76	8
FIRE	0	13	24	36	14	—	7
Services	4	9	104	29	56	73	—

	Purchases of Capital from		
Industry	Construction	Manufacturing	Abroad
Agriculture	2	3	1
Mining	11	12	2
Construction	0	8	1
Manufacturing	21	132	14
T&U	8	17	3
Trade	27	25	0
FIRE	143	6	0
Services	19	15	1

Industry	Imports of Inputs	Sales to Government	Sales to Consumer	Exports	Wages
Agriculture	12	8	12	37	60
Mining	90	9	1	21	88
Construction	2	23	0	0	98
Manufacturing	181	188	21	206	315
T&U	5	5	101	13	132
Trade	2	6	935	15	287
FIRE	3	11	178	5	256
Services	6	4	583	21	195

Government wages: 337

Assume that consumer and government purchases from abroad are zero, and that there is no inventory investment.

a. Compute consumption, investment, government purchases, exports, and imports. Compute GDP from these.
b. Compute value added for each industry. Calculate GDP by summing all value added. Is it equal to GDP from Part a? (Hints: Government value added is its wage payment. In calculating value added, do not subtract capital inputs.)
c. Compute profit for each industry as sales less purchases of current inputs (do not subtract investment). Compute net domestic income as total profit plus total wages. Is it equal to GDP?
d. Compute net exports.

4. Consider a closed economy with expenditure totals for a year given by

Consumption	1,300
Investment	500
Government purchases	500
Government tax receipts	400
Depreciation	200

Suppose that the financial assets in the economy consist of money and bonds. Assume that money equals 500 at the start of the year, and that government bonds equal 700 at the start of the year.

a. Assuming that 90 percent of government deficits are financed by bonds, calculate the new levels of bond and money holdings for the private sector and for the government.

b. Show how the total change in government liabilities—money (M) + bonds (B) —can be computed in two ways.

Analytical

1. Identify which of the following purchases is counted as part of GDP. You purchase a used lawn mower at a garage sale. General Motors of Canada purchases tires from Goodyear of Canada to equip new Chevrolets. General Motors of Canada purchases tires from Goodyear of Canada to replace worn tires on executives' company cars. A neighbour hires you to babysit for an evening. You purchase a share of Air Canada. A neighbour breaks your window with a golf ball, and you purchase a new window. You pay your tuition for the semester.

2. As part of its drive to replace welfare with workfare, the government decides to redesignate $100 million in welfare benefits as government wages. The recipients become government employees.

a. For each of the methods used in calculating GDP, describe the effect of this policy change.

b. Suppose now that the workfare recipients are removed from the government payroll and are moved into the payroll of the newly incorporated Workfare, Inc. As part of its support for the workfare program, the government stands ready to subsidise Workfare, Inc., if its sales do not cover its costs. Since Workfare, Inc., has no products to sell, the subsidy ends up being the full $100 million. How does this arrangement affect your answers to Part a?

3. Suppose that automobile purchases were to be treated like housing purchases in the national accounts. How would that affect saving? Investment?

4. Determine whether the following statements are true or false, and explain why.

a. The current account deficit is equal to the government budget deficit plus investment less private domestic saving.

b. If GDP were measured at the prices firms receive for the products they sell, then sales and excise taxes would not be subtracted from GDP in computing national income.

c. The importance of different goods in GDP is determined by their relative price: For example, the production of one ounce of gold counts much more in GDP than the production of one ounce of steel.

5. In 1986, spending by Americans on personal consumption, private investment, and government operations totalled 104 percent of U.S. GNP. How is that possible?

6. Explain how the current account deficit in 1986 helped finance the large government budget deficit as well as the large increase in private gross investment in Canada. Should Canadians care whether foreigners or other Canadians hold the Canadian public debt?

7. Suppose initially that exports are zero and imports are $10 billion. Then assume that the government places a ban on imports. Assume that the spending habits of consumers, firms, and government remain the same (i.e., they spend the same amount but substitute domestic goods for imports).
   a. What happens to GDP?
   b. What happens to each category of savings (assume taxes remain unchanged)?
   c. Does total savings still equal investment?

8. Suppose that in a given year Canadian foreign trade consists of some consumer importing a single Honda Accord for $12,000 (1.8 million yen). Here are some possible financial transactions to accompany the purchase: (i) The consumer pays with $12,000, which Honda puts in its Canadian bank account. (ii) The consumer pays with 1.8 million yen that he happens to have in a Japanese bank account. (iii) The consumer pays with $12,000; Honda invests the proceeds in Canadian Treasury bills. (iv) The consumer purchases 1.8 million yen on the foreign exchange market from some anonymous Canadian foreign exchange trader, and then pays for the car.
   a. Is Canada running a current account surplus or deficit?
   b. For each of the financial transactions described above, explain the effect the transaction has on the Canadian capital account. What is the sum of the current account and capital account balances?

3

Monitoring the Economy: Inflation and Employment

THE SYSTEM OF NATIONAL accounts discussed in Chapter 2 does not cover all of the important measures of economic performance. In this chapter we take up two measures—inflation and employment—that are not only more visible to unsophisticated observers, but have formed the basis of most policy initiatives of the past 25 years. In the first case, the cost of living is measured by a price index that is not part of the accounts, though it is closely related. As for the second case, employment and unemployment, while these are possibly the most important dimensions of performance, they are not part of the national accounts at all.

3.1 Measuring Inflation

Almost everybody watches the rate of inflation. It is a major indicator of how the economy is doing, and changes in inflation are closely related to fluctuations in real GDP. The **rate of inflation** is defined as the percentage rate of change in the general price level from one period to the next. The general price level is a measure of the purchasing power of the dollar, or the amount of goods and services the dollar can buy. For example, one measure of the price level was 138 in 1987, which means that the same basket of goods that cost $100 in 1981 cost $138 in 1987. Much of the original economic research on measuring the general price level was done by Irving Fisher of Yale University in the 1920s. There are now two approaches to measuring the general price level: constructing **price indexes** directly from data on the prices of thousands of goods and services, and calculating **implicit price indexes,** or **deflators,** by dividing a component of nominal GDP by the same component of real GDP.

PRICE INDEXES

A price index is a ratio showing the price of a basket of goods and services in various years in relation to the price of the basket in a base year. The index is 100 in the base year and correspondingly higher in later years if the prices of the things in the basket have risen. The most conspicuous price index is the **consumer price index (CPI).** This index measures the cost of living for a typical urban family. Statistics Canada computes it in the following way: Once every 4 years or so, Statistics Canada makes a survey of the buying habits of Canadian families. The survey covers not only the products they buy in stores, but other expenditures like the purchases of houses. Then Statistics Canada makes a long list of goods and services whose prices they can determine once a month. From the survey of buying habits, they estimate the quantities of each item bought by the average family. The list includes whole milk, for example. The amount of whole milk in the CPI basket is greater than the fraction of income that the typical family spends on whole milk. The price of whole milk is considered representative of the prices of other dairy products that are not included in the index.

Every month, Statistics Canada sends surveyors into stores to write down the actual prices of goods and services. When discounts are available, they take them into account. Statistics Canada is particularly careful about new car prices because they have a large role in the price index and few people actually pay the sticker price for a new car.

Each month, Statistics Canada computes the new level of the price index by using the detailed prices to compute the cost of the CPI basket. The basket is chosen so that its price was 100 in 1981, which means that the index had the value 100 in 1981. Almost all the prices going into the index have risen since 1981. In 1987, the index was 138, so on average prices had risen 38 percent in 6 years. Some prices have risen more than others. The 1987 level of eggs was 103, while the level of cable television service was 166; both started at 100 in 1981.

Figure 3–1 shows the history of the Canadian price level as measured by the CPI since 1960. Inflation was moderate in the early 1960s, gained momentum in the late 1960s and early 1970s, and reached two peaks in 1974 and 1981. Inflation moderated in the 1980s.

The CPI is the most widely used measure of the purchasing power of the Canadian dollar. When people make an agreement that is set in dollars and want to protect themselves against inflation, they can write in a provision that payments rise in proportion to the increase in the CPI. This practice is called **cost-of-living adjustment (COLA)** and is used in some government

Figure 3–1. THE PRICE LEVEL.
The consumer price index measures the price of a bundle of goods and services representative of the purchases of a typical family. By construction, it has the value 100 in 1981. Because of inflation at varying rates since 1981, the index stood at 138 in 1986. Source: *Canadian Economic Observer,* Table 3.2.

programs such as pension payments and family allowances and in some collective bargaining agreements that spell out the terms of employment for unionised workers.

The government puts out another major price index in addition to the CPI called the **industrial products price index (IPPI).** Instead of measuring the prices actually paid by consumers, it measures the prices charged by producers at various stages in the production process. There is no clear basis for the choice of weights for the IPPI, comparable to the market basket that gives the weights for the CPI. As a result, there is much less interest in the monthly value of the IPPI itself. However, Statistics Canada reports all of the detailed prices going into the IPPI and these prices and the price indexes computed from them are the best source of information about prices of crude materials and intermediate goods. Some economists think that the raw materials price index, which is based on the prices of crude inputs such as wood, ore, and fuels, is one of the most sensitive early warning indicators of future inflation.

IMPLICIT PRICE INDEXES

The construction of data on nominal and real GDP results in another type of price index. The purpose of measuring real GDP is to get rid of the price effects in nominal GDP. Thus, the ratio of nominal GDP to real GDP is a measure of prices. It is called the **GDP implicit price index** or **GDP deflator.** For example, in the fourth quarter of 1987 nominal GDP was $570.5 billion. Real GDP was 433.7 billion 1981 dollars. The GDP deflator for the fourth quarter of 1987 was $100 \times 570.5/433.7 = 131.5$. That is, with a base of 100 in 1981, the price level according to the GDP implicit price index was 131.5.

Each component of GDP has an implicit price index. For example, the ratio of nominal consumption to real consumption is the **consumption implicit price index.** It is used as an alternative to the CPI as a measure of the cost of living.

Remember that GDP does not include imports. Correspondingly, the GDP deflator does not count the prices of imported goods. The **implicit price indexes** for consumption, investment, and government spending do include imported goods. As a result, if import prices fall the implicit price indexes for these components of GDP will not rise as quickly as the overall GDP index. For example, import prices fell 2.7 percent in 1987 according to the import implicit price index. This was due to the strength of the Canadian dollar (the effect of the exchange rate on import prices is discussed more fully in Chapter 10). The GDP implicit price index rose by 4.3 percent in 1987. The government implicit price index rose by the same amount but the consumption index rose only 3.7 percent and the investment index only 3.1 percent.

Over the long term however, the GDP implicit price index and the consumption implicit price index tell the same story about the Canadian price level. And the consumption implicit price index and the consumer price index behave similarly as well. These two price indexes do differ somewhat, in part because the CPI includes the cost of owning a home while this is not included in the consumption implicit price index (new home prices are included in the residential construction implicit price index, while the cost of acquiring an existing home is excluded because the construction took place in a previous period).

Inflation, Price Indexes, and Implicit Price Indexes

1. Inflation is the rate of increase in the price level. The price level is an average of all prices in the economy.

2. There are two types of measures of the price level: price indexes and implicit price indexes or deflators. The consumer price index (CPI) and the industrial products price index (IPPI) are the two major price indexes. The weights on the individual prices in the CPI are based on a survey of consumer buying habits. The GDP implicit price index is the ratio of nominal GDP to real GDP. It is a measure of the prices of all goods and services produced in Canada.

3. The CPI is used for cost-of-living adjustments in some union contracts and government programs.

3.2 Measuring Employment, Unemployment, and Wages

Employment falls along with production during recessions, and rises again during recoveries. Over the long haul, employment grows along with potential GDP, as firms hire more workers to produce the growing output. The principal source of information about labour market activity in Canada is the **Labour Force Survey.** About 48,000 households are interviewed each month by Statistics Canada to find out whether each member of the household was employed. Everyone who did any work for pay or profit, including unpaid work on a family farm, is counted as employed for that month. The results are blown up by multiplying by about 200 so that they are good estimates of the total number of workers employed that month in the whole economy (each household in the survey stands for a little over 200 households in the population). Some other people who did not work—notably those on vacation—are also counted as employed.

Total employment was 11.9 million in 1987, up by .3 million from its level of 11.6 million in 1986 and up by 1.3 million from its level of 10.6 million in the recession year of 1982. The long recovery and expansion of the mid-1980s involved substantial growth in employment, as expansions generally do. On the other hand, employment falls during recessions. Employment reached a peak of 11.0 million in June 1981 and then fell to a trough of 10.5 million in November 1982.

HOURS PER WEEK AND TOTAL HOURS

The number of hours worked each week varies among workers and over time. Some people normally work part time for only a few hours a week and others work 60 to 70 hours. Among people who get paid by the hour, the average factory worker now puts in about 39 hours per week, while the average health-care worker puts in about 28 hours. Also, the number of hours per week falls during recessions and rises during expansions. When demand is booming many workers are asked, or choose, to work overtime. For example, in the 1979–80 recession, average weekly hours in manufacturing fell from 39.1 hours in November 1979 to 37.6 hours in July 1980, and rose again to 38.9 hours in June 1981. For many decades there has also been a downward trend in hours of work in some industries. For example, the standard work week in manufacturing has declined steadily from 59 hours in 1901 to about 39 hours at present.

For all these reasons, employment by itself is not a complete measure of labour input to the economy. Total hours of work—the number of people working multiplied by the hours of work of the average worker—is a better measure. Statistics Canada publishes an index of total hours for the business sector. This index is shown in Figure 3–2 for the period from 1968 to 1987.

When the level of real output of the economy declines, total hours of

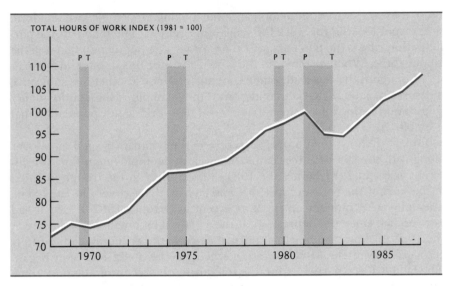

Figure 3-2. TOTAL HOURS OF ALL WORKERS.
The total amount of work performed in Canada, measured by the hours of all workers, fluctuates along with the business cycle. In the slowdown of 1969–70 and the recession of 1981–82 total hours worked declined. Growth in total hours was negligible in the 1974–75 recession although some growth did occur during the brief recession of 1980. Source: Statistics Canada, 15-204.

work decline. The work force feels the effects of a recession in the form of fewer hours of work per week, as well as in the possibility of being laid off. Their pay declines in either case even if the wage rate does not change.

UNEMPLOYMENT

One of the most important questions in macroeconomics is why the economy does not provide work for the entire labour force. Even in the best of times, people are unemployed. They are interested in working and are available for work, but have not found jobs. One of the principal purposes of the Labour Force Survey is to determine how many people are unemployed each month. High unemployment is the single most important signal of distress in the economy.

The Labour Force Survey counts you as unemployed if you did not work at all during the survey week and you were looking for work. In each survey, several million people are found to be unemployed. The **labour force** is defined as the number of persons 15 years of age or over who are either working or unemployed. The **unemployment rate** is the percentage of the labour force that is unemployed.

There are millions of people who are not working but who are not counted as unemployed. They are considered out of the labour force because they are retired, in school, at home looking after their own children, sick, or not looking for work for some other reason. The **labour force participation rate** is the percentage of the working-age population that is in the labour force. Whether one is in the labour force or not is sometimes a matter of opinion; this has lead some economists to look at other less subjective measures of labour market conditions. One example is the **employment/population ratio.** This is the percentage of the working-age population that is employed.

Table 3–1 shows the number of people in the population aged 15 or over along with the labour force, employment, and unemployment for four different years: in 1981 before the 1981–82 recession, at the trough in 1982, at the start of the recovery in 1983, and later in the recovery in 1987. The unemployment rate got up to 12.8 percent in October 1982, a level it had not reached since the depression of the 1930s. The unemployment rate at the 1981 peak was higher than normal because the economy had not fully recovered from the 1980 recession when the 1981–82 recession began. The labour force participation rate fell during the recession, because some workers became discouraged looking for work and left the labour force to retire early, go back to school, or do something else. Note that the employment/population ratio tells about the same story as the unemployment rate during this period.

Table 3–1. UNEMPLOYMENT, LABOUR FORCE, AND THE POPULATION

	1981	1982	1983	1987
Millions of people:				
(1) Aged 15 or over	18.38	18.66	18.92	19.83
(2) In labour force	11.90	11.96	12.18	13.12
(3) Employed	11.01	10.64	10.73	11.96
(4) Unemployed	.90	1.31	1.45	1.17
Percentage:				
Labour force participation rate, (2)/(1)	64.8	64.1	64.4	66.2
Unemployment rate, (4)/(2)	7.5	11.0	11.9	8.9
Employment/population ratio, (3)/(1)	59.9	57.0	56.7	60.3

Source: *Canadian Economic Observer,* Table 2.1.

Figure 3–3 shows how the average annual unemployment rate behaved during the period since 1950. Unemployment moves with the business cycle. When real GDP is high relative to the trend path of potential GDP, unemployment is low. When output is at low levels in the depths of recessions, unemployment is high.

Note that in normal times—when real GDP is equal to potential GDP—unemployment is not zero. Even in boom times there is some **frictional unemployment.** When workers enter the labour force for the first time or after a spell out of the labour force, they need some time to find a job. During this

Figure 3–3. THE UNEMPLOYMENT RATE.
The unemployment rate has fluctuated between 2 and 13 percent since 1950. Unemployment rises during recessions and falls during expansions. There has also been an upward drift in the unemployment rate. Sources: *Canadian Economic Observer,* Table 2.1, and *Historical Statistics of Canada,* Series D233.

period they are counted as unemployed. Similarly, when workers quit their jobs, there will frequently be a span of time before they find new jobs. Movements from one job to another are particularly common for young workers as they find out what type of job they are best suited for. This is one reason why young workers have higher unemployment rates than older workers. In addition, there are some low-skilled workers who are frequently unemployed. Additional training for such workers would reduce the unemployment rate. Finally, workers in seasonal occupations such as fishing are often unemployed for part of every year.

The term economists use for the unemployment rate that prevails in normal times is the **natural rate of unemployment.** The natural rate of unemployment now seems to be about 7 percent. It was apparently closer to 5 percent in the 1960s. The reasons for the increase in the natural unemployment rate in the past two decades are not well understood. One possible reason is that the proportion of the labour force that is made up of people who are not the sole support of their families has increased. This makes leaving and reentering the labour force more likely. Another possibility is the increased generosity of the unemployment insurance system. This makes prolonged job searching less costly.

When the national unemployment rate changes, the unemployment rates in all of the regions of Canada tend to change in the same direction. However, unemployment rates are persistently different across the regions. From 1973 to 1987 the Atlantic region (Newfoundland, Prince Edward Island, Nova Scotia, and New Brunswick) always had a higher unemployment rate than any other region, while the lowest rate was found either in Ontario or in the prairie region (Alberta, Saskatchewan, and Manitoba). For example, in 1987 the unemployment rate was 14.1 percent in the Atlantic region but only 6.1 percent in Ontario.

OKUN'S LAW

There is a useful shorthand formula that closely approximates the cyclical relationship between unemployment and real GDP. It is commonly called **Okun's law,** after its discoverer, Arthur Okun, who used it to illustrate the effects of macroeconomic policy when he was an advisor to the U.S. government in the 1960s. Okun's law says that for each percentage point by which the unemployment rate is *above* the natural rate, real GDP is about 2 percent *below* potential GDP. The percentage departure of GDP from potential is called the **GDP gap.** For example, if unemployment is 9 percent, 2 percentage points above the natural rate of 7 percent, then real GDP is about 4 percent below potential. The GDP gap is minus 4 percent.

The Labour Market in the 1960s and the 1980s

The 1960s and the 1980s both had economic expansions of unusual length. The 1968 and 1987 years show the labour market under more or less standard conditions—neither suffering from a recent recession nor enjoying super-heated conditions. In 1968 the unemployment rate was 4.5 percent. In 1987, the unemployment rate was 8.9 percent. By that measure, unemployment was considerably worse in the 1980s than in the 1960s. Jobs seemed to be harder to find.

Unemployment insurance (UI) data tell a mixed story. Unemployment insurance is a federal government program that temporarily supplements the incomes of workers who have lost their jobs. To be covered by UI, a person must have worked a specified number of weeks before they lost their job. In 1968 the UI system paid 3.2 weeks of benefits per person covered while in 1987 it paid 4.6 weeks per person covered. However, claims submitted were relatively lower in 1987 than in 1968; 27 per 100 workers covered instead of 37.

By another measure jobs seemed easier to find in 1987. The help-wanted index, which measures the volume of job vacancy advertising placed by employers, was at 47 in 1968 compared to 120 in 1987.

In interpreting these figures it is important to keep in mind the many changes that have taken place in Canadian labour markets in the last 20 years or so. An unemployment rate of 8.9 percent, while high, does not represent as much financial hardship in 1987 as it would have implied in 1968. This is because a larger proportion of the unemployed had other sources of income in 1987—a working spouse or parent, or UI benefits. The increased generosity of the UI system means that more UI benefits would have been paid in 1987 than in 1968 even under otherwise identical labour market conditions. Finally, much of the help-wanted advertising in 1987 may have been about highly skilled jobs that few of the unemployed could quality for. Thus it may be difficult for some people to find jobs even when there are many vacancies.

WAGES

Remember that the income side of the national accounts reports the total earnings of workers. Total labour compensation divided by total annual hours of work gives a measure of the average hourly wage paid to workers in Canada. Statistics Canada calls this **compensation per hour.** Compensation per hour includes the value of fringe benefits as well as cash wages. Wages are the most important component of the cost of production.

Wages and prices generally moved together throughout the swings in inflation in the 1970s. The **real wage** is the hourly average wage divided by the cost of living. From the point of view of workers, it measures the purchasing power of the wage—the amount of goods and services that can be bought with one hour of work. From the point of view of employers, it measures the real cost of labour input. The real wage since 1950 is shown in Figure 3–4.

The real wage grew steadily until 1978 when it fell sharply due to a combination of wage controls imposed by the federal government, depreciation of the Canadian dollar, and substantial growth in labour supply. The real wage fell again in 1982 and 1983 in the aftermath of a severe recession which reduced labour demand.

3.3 Productivity

Productivity is the amount of output produced per unit of input. Because labour is the most important input, the most popular measure of productivity is **labour productivity**, or output per hour of labour. When economists talk about productivity they usually mean labour productivity. A broader measure of productivity, called **total factor productivity**, is output per generalised unit of input (factor is a general term for an input like labour or capital). The generalised unit counts capital, energy, and materials as inputs in addition to labour. However, output per unit of labour and total factor productivity for Canada as a whole tell about the same story for recent years.

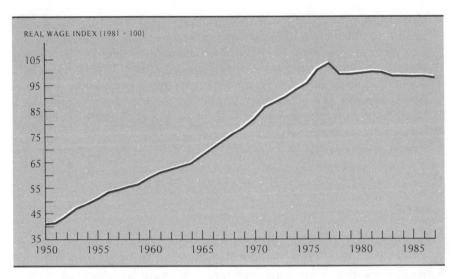

Figure 3–4. THE REAL WAGE.
The real wage is the ratio of the dollar wage (compensation per hour) to the cost of living (the consumer price index). In 1987 the real wage was 5 percent below its peak value according to this measure, but nearly as high as its peak value using the consumption implicit price index instead of the CPI. This figure shows the calculation made using the CPI. Sources: Statistics Canada, 15–204, and *Canadian Economic Observer,* Table 3.2.

Statistics Canada computes labour productivity for the economy as the ratio of real GDP originating in the business sector to the total hours of work in that sector. The recent history of labour productivity is shown in Figure 3–5. Productivity has generally been increasing as workers have become more efficient and have had more and better machines to work with. This increase in productivity underlies the growth in real wages that we saw in the previous section. But productivity is also procyclical. It rises more quickly in booms, and less quickly (or even falls) in recessions. Firms tend to keep skilled workers on the payroll and let them produce fewer items in slack times, rather than lay them off and run the risk that they will find jobs elsewhere. They make up for their low productivity in bad times with higher productivity in good times.

Although the CPI and the consumption implicit price index appear to move together quite closely, they are not identical. The seemingly small differences between them can make a substantial difference in the calculation of the real wage. Using the CPI as the measure of the cost of living, the real wage peaked in 1977 and was 5 percent below its peak value in 1987. Using the consumption implicit price index the real wage peaked in 1982 and was only .3 percent below its peak value in 1987.

Productivity growth has been disappointing since 1973 in all of the major industrialised countries. In Canada, productivity has declined slightly in each of three serious recessions, and the intervening expansions have not been strong enough to bring productivity growth back to its previous trend.

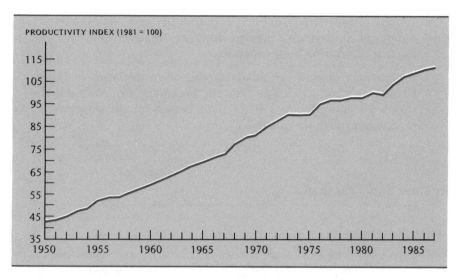

Figure 3–5. LABOUR PRODUCTIVITY IN NONAGRICULTURAL BUSINESS.
Productivity is the amount of output produced per hour of work. The general trend in
productivity has been upward. Productivity tends to drop in recessions. The drop in productivity was especially pronounced in the recessions of 1974–75 and 1981–82. Source:
Statistics Canada, 15–204.

Economists disagree about the reasons for the post-1973 productivity slowdown. Some stress the role of the increases in oil prices. Others point to the
level of expenditures on research and development and say that it is insuffi-
cient to support enough technical innovation. Still others say that we are not
investing enough in new machines and factories. Of all the puzzles about the
recent performance of the economy, the slowdown in productivity growth is
perhaps the most difficult one for economists to solve.

Employment and Productivity

1. Employment is closely related to output fluctuations.

2. The unemployment rate is the percentage of the labour force that
   is unemployed. The participation rate is the percentage of the
   working-age population that is in the labour force.

3. The unemployment rate is closely related to the deviations of real
   GDP from potential GDP. This relation is called Okun's law.

4. The wage rate is the amount paid to workers per hour, week, or
   month of work. The real wage measures the purchasing power of
   the wage payment. The real wage grew steadily in Canada until
   1978, but had not passed its previous peak by 1987.

5. Labour productivity is defined as output per unit of labour input. Labour productivity has been growing for a long time, though with fluctuations during business cycles.

6. Productivity growth in Canada slowed down in the early 1970s. Growth of productivity permits the real wage to grow, and the slowdown in productivity is the main reason for the slowdown in real wage growth in Canada.

Review and Practice

MAJOR POINTS

1. The consumer price index is the number of dollars required to purchase a market basket of goods and services typical of the consumption patterns of Canadians.

2. Implicit price indexes, or deflators, can be calculated by dividing a component of nominal GDP by the same component of real GDP. The consumption deflator is widely used by economists as an alternative to the CPI. The overall GDP deflator is a measure of the price of domestic production; it does not include the price of imports.

3. The best measure of total labour input to the economy is the total number of hours worked by all workers each year. That measure tends to move in proportion to real GDP.

4. A good measure of hourly wages is total labour earnings divided by total hours worked. The real wage is the ratio of the hourly wage to the price level. The real wage in Canada grew smoothly until 1978. In 1987 the real wage was still below its previous peak.

5. The unemployment rate is the percentage of the labour force that is actively looking for work but has not found work. Many people who are not working are not counted as unemployed because they are not looking for work. The unemployment rate has varied between 2 and 13 percent since 1950. Okun's law describes the relation between unemployment and real GDP: For every 2 percent by which real GDP departs from its trend path, the unemployment rate departs in the opposite direction from its normal level by 1 percentage point.

6. A simple measure of productivity is the ratio of real GDP to labour input. In Canada, productivity has grown smoothly except in recession years. Productivity growth slowed appreciably after 1973.

KEY TERMS AND CONCEPTS

Price indexes	Unemployment rate
Consumer price index	Participation rate
Producer price index	Rate of inflation
Implicit price indexes	Frictional unemployment
Labour force	Natural rate of unemployment

Okun's law   Real wage

GDP gap   Labour productivity

QUESTIONS FOR DISCUSSION AND REVIEW

1. What is the difference between high prices and inflation?

2. What is the difference between being unemployed and not working? Give some examples of people not at work who are not unemployed.

3. Explain why unemployment falls when output rises. In the process, mention what happens to employment.

4. Describe how the real wage, employment, and hours of work influence the purchasing power of earnings.

PROBLEMS

Numerical

1. Suppose that Okun's law between unemployment and GDP is given by

$$(Y - Y^*)/Y^* = -2(U - U^*),$$

where U is the unemployment rate, U^* is the natural rate of unemployment, Y is GDP, and Y^* is potential GDP. Unemployment is measured as a fraction. Suppose that the natural rate is 7 percent; that is, $U^* = .07$.
   a. Calculate the GDP gap for each of the years in 1983–87 using the following unemployment data: $U = 11.9, 11.3, 10.5, 9.6$, and 8.9 percent, respectively.
   b. Real GDP for these same years is as follows: $355, $379, $395, $408, and $424 billion. Using these data and your answers to Part a, calculate potential GDP for each of these years. What is the average growth rate of potential GDP?
   c. Suppose that from 1987 to 1991, potential GDP continues to rise at the average rate of growth for the previous 5 years. By how much must actual GDP increase in that time in order to reduce the unemployment rate to 7 percent in 1991?

2. The consumer price index for the 1978–82 period and the GDP implicit price index are listed below.

	CPI	GDP Implicit Price Index
1978	73.9	74.2
1979	80.7	81.6
1980	88.9	90.2
1981	100.0	100.0
1982	110.8	108.7

   a. Calculate the rate of inflation according to both measures from 1979 through 1982. What might explain the differences between the two?
   b. Suppose that the hourly wage rate for a group of workers that sign an employment contract for the 3-year period starting in 1979 is indexed to the CPI according to the formula

$$\Delta W/W = .03 + .5\Delta\text{CPI}/\text{CPI}.$$

   Calculate the actual increase in the wage during each year of the contract period. If the wage was $12.00 in 1979, what was it in 1980, 1981, and 1982? What happens to the real wage measured in terms of the CPI?
   c. Repeat your calculations with .03 reduced to 0 and .5 increased to 1. What indexing formula would the workers' employer have preferred? Is there any rea-

son for the employer to have been happy with the other formula before the actual inflation experience was known?

3. The CPI is calculated for a fixed market basket. It measures the change in the cost of the market basket from the base year until the current year. An index with the market basket fixed in the first year—like the CPI—is called a Laspeyres index. An alternative index—called the Paasche index—is based on a market basket in the end year. It measures the change in the cost of a market basket fixed in the end year. Suppose that the base year is 1973. Suppose that the market basket contains only two items, peanut butter and gasoline, and that the quantities consumed in 1973 and 1974 are:

	Peanut Butter	Gasoline
1973	100 jars	50 gallons
1974	150 jars	45 gallons

Suppose that the price of peanut butter increased from $1.00 per jar in 1973 to $1.20 per jar in 1974, and that the price of gasoline increased from $.50 per gallon to $2.00 per gallon.

a. Calculate the rate of inflation for the Laspeyres (CPI) index and the Paasche index.

b. Will inflation calculated using the Laspeyres index always exceed inflation calculated with the Paasche index? (Hint: Use standard indifference curve analysis.)

c. Workers often receive an adjustment in their wages equal to only a fraction of inflation as calculated using the CPI. In view of the preceding analysis explain why workers would likely be better off than they were before if they were fully compensated for inflation. Would this also be the case if inflation was calculated using the Paasche index?

Analytical

1. Okun's law suggests that over the course of the business cycle a change in the unemployment rate of 1 percentage point will be accompanied by a 2 percent change in output. Using the formula:

$$Y = (Y/H)(H/N)(1-U)L,$$

where Y/H is output per hour worked, H/N is hours per worker, N is the number of employed workers, U is the unemployment rate, and L is the labour force, explain in what direction and why some of the factors other than Y and U might change. (Note that if $W=XYZ$, then for small changes, the percentage change in W is given by the sum of the percentage changes in X, Y, and Z. Note also that $1-U = N/L$, and that a change in the unemployment rate of 1 percentage point corresponds to approximately a 1 percent change in N/L.)

2. An empirical regularity in the Canadian economy is that roughly 30 percent of output goes to capitalists in the form of earnings of capital, while 70 percent goes to workers in the form of wages.

a. Using the formula given in Question 1, show that the increase in the average hourly wage will be given by the growth in productivity per man hour, Y/NH.

b. From Figures 3–4 and 3–5 it appears that real wage growth slowed even more than productivity growth in the last 15 years. Does this imply that there has been a rise in the share of output going to the owners of capital?

3. Suppose that on January 1, 1992, the government creates 100,000 new jobs. Only those currently without jobs may apply. The new jobs attract 300,000 applicants, half of whom would not otherwise be looking for work in January.
   a. Is the labour force for January changed from what it would have been in the absence of these new jobs? By how much?
   b. Assuming that without the new jobs the labour force would have been 10 million and the unemployment rate 7 percent, what will the unemployment rate for January now be?

4

Spending Balance

MEASURES of income, spending, and employment, of the sort we have examined in Chapters 2 and 3, are the cornerstones of macroeconomics. But having established the evidence, how do we explain it? In the rest of this book we develop a system for analysing macroeconomic fluctuations. The theory, or model, presented is used by economists for forecasting business cycles, for determining the size and timing of government policy action to mitigate the effects of recessions or to combat inflation, and for asking what went wrong in particular episodes such as the Great Depression in the 1930s or the 'Great Inflation' of the 1970s. Such models are the 'bread and butter' of macroeconomic analysis.

We begin, in this chapter and the next, by presenting the basic methods used by economists to analyse aggregate demand. We will use the ideas about aggregate demand to explain short-run fluctuations of GDP around the potential GDP path; that is, the movements associated with recessions and booms in economic activity. According to Okun's law, which we discussed in Chapter 3, the overall level of unemployment can be closely tied to the fluctuations of actual GDP around potential GDP. Hence, understanding the fluctuations in actual GDP relative to potential GDP will also provide an explanation for observed periods of unemployment.

Our first step is to explain the concept of spending balance. In the process, we will develop a simple model that explains the determination of GDP.

4.1 An Overview

In Chapter 2 we noted that GDP could be defined and measured in three alternative ways: as **spending** on goods and services, as **production** of goods and services, and as **income** received by workers and firms. It is a simple matter of accounting identities that these three alternatives will give the same answer for total GDP, aside from measurement error and statistical discrepancies. When we move beyond accounting identities to a theory of what determines the fluctuations of GDP, however, it makes quite a difference which one of these concepts is used. In practice, it has turned out to be useful to focus first on the spending side.

Firms produce goods because people have decided to buy them. Aggregate demand theory starts by examining spending decisions. For example, consider how a macroeconomist goes about projecting the growth of GDP for the upcoming year. The macroeconomist begins with a projection of the spending demands of consumers, firms, and governments. If a personal tax cut is coming up, then the macroeconomist will naturally anticipate a larger amount of demand for consumption goods by households. If interest rates are projected to rise because of a change in monetary policy, then investment demand from firms is likely to be lower. If there is a public clamour for decreased government spending, then government demand is likely to fall. By adding up the spending demands of the various sectors of the economy the macroeconomist obtains an estimate of aggregate spending. This total then serves as the projection for GDP for the upcoming year. While it will be necessary to check whether these spending projections are consistent with incomes—in a way to be made clear below—the basic forecast is obtained from an analysis of the spending decisions in the economy. Because the total spending forecast is an aggregation of demand in all sectors of the economy, we refer to the total as **aggregate demand.** Implicitly the macroeconomist is making an assumption that aggregate demand determines the amount of goods produced in the economy. This assumption is central to our analysis of economic fluctuations.

A FIRM'S RESPONSE TO CHANGES IN DEMAND

To see why the macroeconomist's assumption that aggregate demand determines output is usually a reasonable assumption, we need to consider the typical behaviour of business firms at the microeconomic level. Under normal conditions most business firms operate with some excess capacity, and respond to increases in demand by producing more goods. In Canada the average level of capacity utilisation in manufacturing industries is roughly 80 percent. Some machines are left idle on standby; others are run for only two of three shifts. Hence firms have considerable leeway to produce more by increasing capacity utilization when demand increases. If additional labour is necessary to operate the equipment more intensively, it is usually possible to have some workers increase their hours per week, to recall some workers from layoff status, or even to hire additional workers. The natural rate of unemployment is about 7 percent, indicating that additional workers can be hired in the short run, even at full employment. Hence, for both capital and labour inputs to production, there is considerable short-run flexibility for firms to meet an increase in the demand for their products. And though we have been speaking entirely in terms of increases in demand, the same response occurs for declines in demand. A firm will produce less when the demand for its product declines. In sum, both increases and decreases in demand for a firm's product get translated into increases and decreases in production. In the economy as a whole, short-run fluctuations in aggregate demand result in similar fluctuations in GDP. In this sense, the assumption that 'demand determines output' is a reasonable one for analysing most short-run fluctuations of GDP from its long-run growth path.

Firms not only adjust their production in response to changes in demand, they also adjust their prices. When an increase in demand results in a firm producing at above-average operating levels, it usually increases its prices as well. Similarly, a decline in demand that brings the firm to below-normal operating levels will result in a price adjustment below what would have been appropriate otherwise. By adjusting its price in this way the firm can usually both increase its profits in the short run and encourage a shift in demand to a more desirable level from the firm's point of view.

There is a crucial difference, however, between the adjustment of production and the adjustment of prices in response to a change in demand: *Prices appear to be very 'sticky' compared to production; the adjustment of prices occurs gradually, whereas the adjustment of production and employment occurs almost instantaneously.* Economists have only recently begun researching the reasons for this slow price adjustment on the part of firms, and we will summarise this exciting and important research in Part III. The implication of this slow price adjustment is that changes in aggregate demand first result in changes in production, much as described above, and only later in changes in prices. In fact, in the very short run it is usually a good approximation to ignore price adjustment and focus on the changes in production.

We have left out one important aspect of firm behaviour in our discussion so far. Many firms maintain a stock or inventory of their finished products on their shelves, so that when there is an increase in demand the immediate response is usually to meet the demand out of the inventory. Conversely, a drop in demand can be matched by an accumulation of inventory. Clearly, changes in demand that are exactly matched by changes in inventory will not affect production or GDP. However, for the economy as a whole, increases in sales are met with increases in production. Thus, as an approximation it is possible to ignore inventory adjustments and assume that changes in demand are directly translated into changes in production. A full treatment of the process of inventory adjustment is given in Chapter 9.

AN EXAMPLE: THE FURNITURE INDUSTRY

Production in the furniture industry rises and falls by large magnitudes in response to changes in demand. Consider what happens in the furniture industry when there is a decrease in demand for furniture.

Such a decrease occurred in the recession that took place from August 1981 until December 1982. High mortgage interest rates and lower incomes reduced residential and nonresidential construction activity which in turn reduced the demand for new furniture.

As a result, furniture production fell almost 25 percent in real terms from 1981 to 1982 even though the recession had already begun in the latter half of 1981. The number of manufacturing workers in the furniture industry fell by 12 percent as workers were laid off or let go. The remaining workers were asked to work shorter hours so that total person-hours worked in the industry fell by slightly more than 12 percent. With fewer hours worked, total wage payments fell by 10 percent even though the average hourly wage rose somewhat due to the general price inflation that took place in 1982. The profits of furniture manufacturers also decreased, reducing dividend payments to owners and bonus payments to managers. Furniture industry workers, managers, and owners thus had less income to spend, and this further reduced the demand for goods and services in the economy.

With the recovery that began in 1983 all of these effects were reversed. By 1985 the industry had reached roughly the same levels of production, employees, and person-hours employed that had prevailed in 1981.

4.2 Consumption and Income

From this simple microeconomic description of firm behaviour, we now proceed to investigate **spending balance.** When the economy is in spending balance, spending decisions generate a level of GDP consistent with the income underlying the spending decisions.

THE INCOME IDENTITY

We presented the spending components of demand in Chapter 2 using the accounting identity

$$Y = C + I + G + X, \qquad \text{The Income Identity} \qquad (4\text{--}1)$$

where Y is GDP, C is consumption, I is investment, G is government spending, and X is net exports. GDP, consumption, investment, government spending, and net exports in this identity are all measured in real terms as discussed in Chapter 2.

We also saw in Chapter 2 that after subtracting depreciation, indirect taxes, and certain other items from GDP we get income. This relationship between GDP and income is important for the theory of aggregate demand because spending is heavily influenced by disposable income. In order to keep the analysis as simple as possible, we consider an economy in which income and GDP are the same; this implies that there is no depreciation or indirect taxation. Then the variable Y on the left-hand side of Equation 4–1 is income as well as GDP. The identity says that income equals the sum of consumption, investment, government spending, and net exports. For this reason it is called the **income identity.**

Although Equation 4–1 looks very simple, it is a key part of the theory. It represents two important ideas. First, total aggregate spending determines GDP—for reasons discussed in the previous section. Second, GDP is equal to income. Because GDP is equal to income we will frequently use the words interchangeably in our discussions. To avoid confusion, keep in mind that GDP, or simply *output,* and *income* always take on the same value and are always represented by the same symbol Y.

We now consider the components of aggregate demand. We start with consumption.

THE CONSUMPTION FUNCTION

How do consumers make their spending decisions? The **consumption function** is a description of the total consumption demand of all families in the economy. It states that consumption depends on **disposable income.** Disposable income, as we saw in Chapter 2, is income less taxes. The consumption function is based on the simple idea that the larger a family's disposable income, the larger that family's consumption will be. Thus, total consumption for all families in the economy will be larger if disposable income in the economy is larger.

The consumption function should be viewed as a simple approximation of actual consumption demand. Clearly consumption depends on other things besides current income: wealth, expected future income, and the price of goods today compared to tomorrow. We will discuss these and other factors that affect consumption in Chapter 8. The more elementary consumption function used in this chapter was first introduced to the study of macroeconomics by Keynes. Despite its simplicity, it has proved remarkably versatile as a macroeconomic tool.

The consumption function can be written algebraically as

$$C = a + bY_d. \qquad \text{The Consumption Function} \qquad (4-2)$$

Specifically, this algebraic formula says that consumption C is equal to some constant a plus another constant b times disposable income Y_d. Both constants $(a$ and $b)$ are positive. The constant a describes an element of consumption that is independent of disposable income. Less formally, Equation 4–2 simply says that consumption depends positively on disposable income.

When studying algebraic relationships like the consumption function in macroeconomics, it is very important to distinguish between the constants and the variables. Sometimes the constants are called **coefficients.** In this consumption function the variables are C and Y_d. The constants, or coefficients, are a and b. Variables move around; constants stay fixed. To highlight this important distinction we use lowercase letters for constants and uppercase letters for variables. This convention is used throughout this book.

Example. If the coefficient $a = 80$ and the coefficient $b = .9$, then the consumption function looks like this:

$$C = 80 + .9Y_d.$$

If disposable income is \$3,000 billion, then consumption will be $80 + .9 \times 3,000$, or \$2,780 billion. If disposable income rises to \$4,000 billion, then consumption will rise to $80 + .9 \times 4,000$, or \$3,680 billion. If disposable income increases by \$1,000 billion, consumption changes by \$900 billion. Note how the variables, consumption and disposable income, change in this calculation but the coefficients stay fixed.

The coefficient b is called the **marginal propensity to consume.** It measures how much of an *additional* dollar of disposable income is spent on consumption. For the numerical values stated in the last paragraph, 90 percent of each additional dollar of income is spent on consumption.

We can also represent the consumption function graphically, as in Figure 4–1. The vertical axis measures consumption. The horizontal axis measures disposable income. The consumption function is shown as a straight, upward-sloping line. It indicates that as disposable income increases so does consumption.

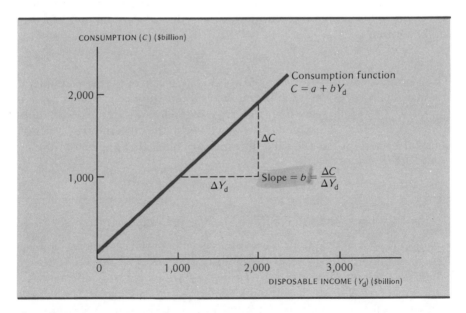

Figure 4–1.   THE CONSUMPTION FUNCTION.
Consumption depends on income. The upward-sloping line shows that higher levels of disposable income correspond to higher levels of consumption. The slope of the line tells us how much consumption changes when disposable income changes. The slope of the line equals the marginal propensity to consume.

The Consumption Function

1. Disposable income is the amount of income that people have available to spend after taxes.

2. The consumption function says that there is a predictable relationship between disposable income and consumption. The higher disposable income, the higher consumption.

3. The marginal propensity to consume is the fraction of an increase in disposable income that is consumed.

We can also write the consumption function in terms of income rather than disposable income. Disposable income is obtained by adding government transfer payments to income and then subtracting income taxes. For simplicity we will assume for now that there are no transfer payments. (If you prefer, you can include transfer payments by treating the term 'taxes' as short for: taxes paid less transfer payments received.) If the tax *rate* is given by the constant t, then total tax payments are tY. Disposable income Y_d equals income Y minus taxes tY. Thus, we can write disposable income as $Y_d = (1 - t)Y$. For example, if the tax rate t is .3 and income Y is $4,000 billion, then taxes are $1,200 billion and disposable income is $2,800 billion. By replacing disposable income Y_d with $(1 - t)Y$, the consumption function can be written

$$C = a + b(1 - t)Y. \tag{4-3}$$

This says that consumption depends positively on income. For example, if the marginal propensity to consume b is .9 and the tax rate t is .3, then $b(1 - t) = .63$. An increase in income of $100 billion will increase consumption by $63 billion. This alternative way to write the consumption function is useful because it has the same income variable Y that appears in the income identity.

Graphs, Slopes, and Intercepts versus Algebra and Coefficients

Figure 4–1 and Equation 4–2 express exactly the same idea—that consumption depends positively on disposable income—in two different ways: graphically and algebraically. A third way is *verbal* presentation and analysis, which, although sometimes less precise, is necessary if you want to explain your economic ideas to those without economic training.

In general a graph is a diagram with a line or lines showing the relationship between two variables. The lines can be straight, as with the consumption line, or they can be bending, as with the aggregate demand curve studied in the next chapter (Figure 5–10). Relationships that are shown by straight lines are called *linear* relationships to distinguish them from bending lines. Sometimes lines are called **schedules,** a term that derives from the presentation of the relationship numerically as two columns of numbers that look like a train schedule. Graphs provide a more intuitive understanding, and, because visual images are sometimes easier to recall, graphs are good memory aids.

Algebra frequently provides more accurate and direct answers, and is needed in more complex problems. Frequently only a rough sketch is needed for a graphical analysis, but it is important to know that there is a precise connection between a graphical and an algebraic representation of an economic relationship. The variable on the vertical axis of a graph is usually the one on the left-hand side of the equal sign in the algebraic expression. For the consumption function, the variable on the left-hand side is consumption. The variable on the horizontal axis is usually the one on the right-hand side of the equal sign in the algebraic expression. For the consumption function, the variable on the right-hand side is disposable income. The place where the vertical axis and horizontal axis cross sometimes represents the zero value for both variables, but this is not necessary. It is important to look carefully at the scale on a diagram. For diagrams that are simply rough illustrations, no numerical scale will appear.

The place where the consumption line crosses the vertical axis in Figure 4–1 is called the **intercept.** It equals the coefficient a in the algebraic expression. It gives the value of consumption when disposable income is zero. More generally, the intercept of any line is the place where the line crosses the vertical axis.

The steepness of the consumption line is measured by its **slope.** The slope tells us how much consumption increases when income increases by one unit. The slope of the line is the coefficient b in the algebraic expression. Thus, if disposable income increases by an amount ΔY_d, then consumption increases by an amount ΔC given by b times ΔY_d. On the graph we move to the right by ΔY_d and up by b times ΔY_d. In general, a perfectly flat horizontal line has a slope of zero, and a perfectly vertical line has a slope of infinity. If the slope is positive then we say that the line slopes *upward* as we move from left to right; if the slope is negative then the line slopes *downward* as we move from left to right. The slope of the consumption function is positive (b is greater than zero), and clearly the consumption line slopes upward.

4.3 The Point of Balance of Income and Spending

So far we have discussed the determinants of only one of the components of spending—consumption—but we already have the ingredients of an elementary theory of income or GDP determination. Before considering the determinants of the other components of spending, we illustrate how this theory works. To do this, we will make two simplifications. First, we will temporarily ignore net exports by assuming that imports and exports are always equal to zero. We will return imports and exports to the model in the next section of this chapter. Second, values for investment and government spending will be taken from *outside* the model. Variables determined outside a model are called **exogenous variables.** Of the five variables that we discussed so far (income Y, consumption C, investment I, government spending G, and net exports X), this leaves two, consumption C and income Y, to be determined *inside* the model. Variables that are determined inside a model are called **endogenous variables.**

This basic idea that the endogenous variables must simultaneously satisfy a number of relationships is central to macroeconomic analysis. In the chapters that follow we will elaborate on this simple theory by adding more endogenous variables and more relationships that they must satisfy.

The elementary model consists of two basic relationships: the income identity, summarised algebraically in Equation 4–1, and the consumption function, summarised algebraically in Equation 4–3. These two relationships can be used to determine values for the two endogenous variables of the model: consumption C and income Y. *The values for C and Y are determined by requiring that both the consumption function and the income identity are satisfied simultaneously.*

Once we determine income and consumption in this way, we will have also determined GDP, of course, because income equals GDP. We illustrate the determination of income and consumption first using graphs and then using algebra.

GRAPHICAL ANALYSIS OF SPENDING BALANCE

In Figure 4–2 spending is measured on the vertical axis and income on the horizontal axis. Two intersecting straight lines are shown, a **spending line** and a **45-degree line.**

The spending line (the flatter of the two) shows how total spending depends on income. Total spending is the sum of consumption, investment, and government spending. In this model only consumption depends on income, through the consumption function. Investment and government spending are exogenous. The spending line is obtained by adding the consumption function in Equation 4–3 to investment and government spending. The equation corresponding to the spending line is

$$\text{Spending} = \underbrace{a + b(1 - t)Y}_{\substack{\text{Consumption from} \\ \text{Equation 4–3}}} + \underbrace{I}_{\substack{\text{Exogenous} \\ \text{investment}}} + \underbrace{G.}_{\substack{\text{Exogenous} \\ \text{government spending}}}$$

The spending line thus incorporates the consumption function.

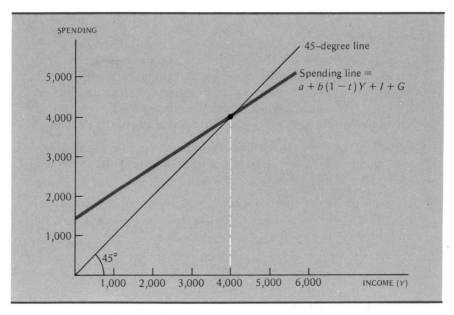

Figure 4–2. SPENDING BALANCE.
The intersection of the two lines shows where consumption and income satisfy both the consumption function and the income identity. The point of intersection is the solution to the model consisting of Equations 4–1 and 4–3.

The 45-degree line is drawn halfway between the vertical spending axis and the horizontal income axis. For any point on the 45-degree line, income equals spending. This line thus represents the income identity. The line makes a 45-degree angle with the horizontal axis; hence its name. Sometimes Figure 4–2 is called a 'Keynesian 45-degree' diagram, or a 'Keynesian cross' diagram, because of its early use to illustrate this simple model with a Keynesian consumption function.

The point of intersection of the spending line and the 45-degree line is the point where consumption and income satisfy both relationships of the model. On the 45-degree line, the income identity is satisfied. On the spending line, the consumption function is satisfied. The intersection of the two lines thus gives the value of income that we are looking for. At this point total spending in the economy equals total income, and consumption spending satisfies the consumption function. Income and spending are in balance.

The 45-degree line is steeper than the spending line. The 45-degree line has a slope of 1. The consumption function has a slope $b(1 - t)$, which is less than 1. For example, if $b = .9$ and $t = .3$, then $b(1 - t) = .63$. Because the lines have different slopes, they will always intersect.[1]

---

[1] See the box on pp. 74–75 for a review of the concept of slope.

Spending Balance

1. The simple model of income determination consists of two relationships, the consumption function and the income identity. The
   model determines two endogenous variables: consumption and
   income. Three exogenous variables—investment, government
   spending, and net exports—are determined outside the model.

2. Spending balance occurs when consumers are choosing their consumption levels, C, on the basis of a level of income that is the same
   as the level $Y = C + I + G$.

3. In terms of the equations, spending balance occurs at levels of consumption C and income Y that obey both the consumption function
   and the income identity.

ALGEBRAIC SOLUTION

The levels of consumption and income can also be found algebraically.
Substitute the consumption equation, 4–3, into Equation 4–1, eliminating X
by setting it equal to zero for now. The result is

$$Y = \underbrace{a + b(1 - t)Y}_{C} + I + G. \tag{4-4}$$

The bracket below Equation 4–4 shows where C in the income identity has
been replaced by the consumption function. Equation 4–4 has one endogenous variable: Y. Recall that I and G are exogenous variables. The variable Y
appears on both sides of Equation 4–4. To solve the equation for Y we
gather together both terms involving Y on the left-hand side of the equation. Doing so we see that the value of Y that solves Equation 4–4 is given by

$$Y = \frac{a + I + G}{1 - b(1 - t)}. \tag{4-5}$$

This is the solution of the model and corresponds exactly to the value of Y,
which is at the point of intersection in Figure 4–2. The solution value for
consumption can then be obtained by plugging this value into the consumption function (4–3). That is,

$$C = a + b(1 - t)Y, \tag{4-6}$$

where Y comes from Equation 4–5.

Example. Suppose that investment equals $650 billion, and government
spending equals $750 billion. Suppose, as in the previous examples, that the
marginal propensity to consume, b, equals .9, the constant a equals 80, and

the tax rate, t, equals .3. Then, according to the formula in Equation 4–5, income equals

$$\frac{80 + 650 + 750}{1 - .9(1 - .3)} = \frac{1,480}{.37},$$

or $4,000 billion. GDP is also equal to $4,000 billion. Using the consumption function (Equation 4–6) we get that consumption equals

$$80 + .9(1 - .3)(4,000),$$

or $2,600 billion.

Does a Tax Cut Pay for Itself?

When the government cuts the tax rate it stimulates the economy. At the same time, the stimulus increases the government's tax revenue because the amount of income being taxed increases. This led to the argument, commonly heard in the United States in the early 1980s (the beginning of the administration of Ronald Reagan), that a tax cut could pay for itself. As we will see, our model implies that this is only partly true.

The effect of a tax cut is to increase the fraction of GDP that flows to families as disposable income. In 1987 that fraction was 364/550 or 66.2 percent. Suppose instead that a tax cut in 1987 had increased this proportion to 69 percent. In other words, suppose that t was reduced by 2.8 percentage points.

Equation 4–5 is the easiest way to figure out how a cut in the tax rate raises GDP. The actual values of investment, I, and government purchases, G, for 1987 were 86 and 87 billion 1981 dollars. We will assume that the intercept in the consumption function, a, is 7, and the marginal propensity to consume, b, is .87. Then the base level for real GDP in 1987, according to Equation 4–5, should have been 424 billion 1981 dollars. Had the lower tax rate been in effect in 1987, real GDP would have been 450 billion, again according to Equation 4–5, with the lower tax rate. Real GDP would have increased by 26 billion on account of the tax cut, had the cut been in effect in 1987.

Government revenue without the tax cut would have been 33.8% × 424 = 143 billion 1981 dollars. Revenue with the lower tax rate but higher level of GDP would be 31.0% × 450 = 140 billion. The tax cut would lower revenue by 3 billion. That is, the higher level of GDP would not be enough to offset the lower tax rate.

The tax rate reduction does pay for a good deal of itself, however. Suppose someone had tried to compute the lost revenue without taking account of the stimulus of GDP. It might be calculated as the cut in the tax rate, 2.8 percent, times the level of GDP before the tax cut, 424 billion, or 12 billion. But counting the favorable effect of the resulting economic expansion means that revenue only fell by 3 billion. The difference of 9 billion is the amount of the possible revenue loss that was paid back by the expansion, according to these calculations.

In later chapters, we will give some reasons why expansion resulting from a tax cut might not be as vigorous as the one considered here. In particular, we will stress the importance of the response of monetary policy. Still, it will remain true that a tax cut pays for some part of itself.

HOW SPENDING BALANCE IS MAINTAINED

It is important to understand the logic of finding the values of consumption and income that satisfy both the consumption function and the income identity. When people consume more in stores, firms will produce more. As we discussed in the microeconomic example, the firms will then employ more workers, or have their existing workers spend more time on the job. Their added production increases the wage incomes of their existing and new workers and adds to the profits of the owners of the firms. This added income in turn stimulates more consumption. When spending is in balance, the income that consumers are receiving is the same as the income generated by their spending.

What happens if spending is not in balance? Suppose that consumers are spending too much relative to their incomes. The economy would then be in an untenable situation. Consumers would notice that they were spending too much and would contract their consumption. But then firms would produce less and workers' incomes would fall. The process of contraction would continue until consumption fell to a point of balance with income.

How do we know that contraction of income and consumption will ultimately reach a point of balance rather than continuing to a complete collapse of the economy? When families contract their consumption because their income falls, the contraction in consumption is less than the fall in income. Some of the fall in income results in reduced taxes, so that disposable income does not fall as much as national income. Moreover, the marginal propensity to consume is less than 1, so that the fall in disposable income results in a smaller reduction in consumption. The smaller reduction in consumption thus generates a smaller drop in income on the second round. So the process of consumption and income contraction converges to a new lower point of balance. A numerical example of this type of convergence is presented in Table 4–1, page 83.

We do not present a formal model of the detailed process by which the economy reaches spending balance. The reason is that the process seems to operate quickly—more quickly than the business cycle or price adjustment. Our model assumes that the economy has already reached spending balance over each period of observation. Balance is not achieved by magic. But it is a useful simplification to talk about the economy after it has gone through the process.[2]

THE MULTIPLIER

In order to show how the elementary model can be used to analyse the short-run fluctuations in the economy, we consider what happens to income when there is a change in one of the exogenous variables. Suppose, for example, that there is a *decrease* in investment *I*. The exact reasons for the decrease are not important at this time, but for concreteness you may think of a sudden decline in expected profitability which reduces firms' desire to invest. What are the implications of this decline in investment demand?

We first consider the situation graphically using the spending line and 45-degree line in Figure 4–2, reproduced in Figure 4–3. The new diagram shows the impact of a decline in exogenous investment. It *shifts* the spending line downward by the amount of the decline in investment. If investment falls by $1 billion then the spending line shifts down by $1 billion. To see this, note that the intercept of the spending line is $a + I + G$. Hence, the change in the intercept is the same as the change in investment; government spending is not changing and *a* is constant. Figure 4–3 shows that income is lower as a result of the downward shift in the spending line.

Note that the decline in income is larger than the shift in the spending line, because the slope of the spending line is greater than zero. The economy thus 'multiplies' the decline in investment into an even larger decline in income and GDP. This mechanism is called the **multiplier**. The steeper the spending line, the larger the decline in income.

The effect of the decline in investment on income can be calculated algebraically. Looking back to Equation 4–5, if we change investment by an amount ΔI then the change in income will be given by

$$\Delta Y = \underbrace{\frac{1}{1 - b(1 - t)}}_{\text{The Multiplier}} \Delta I. \qquad (4\text{–}7)$$

This is obtained by writing Equation 4–5 in terms of the changes in the variables, and noting that neither government spending nor the constant coefficient changes. All that is left is the change in investment.

The term $1/[1 - b(1 - t)]$, which multiplies the change in investment in Equation 4–7, is the multiplier. It is a general expression for the change in

---

[2] Some elementary texts describe the adjustment process by focussing on inventories: If output is greater than spending, inventories begin to rise and this leads firms to cut back on output. Output and spending are thus brought into equality. As we stated above, we prefer not to introduce inventories at this stage of the analysis. We feel that the description in the text is a close approximation to reality. Many types of businesses—medical services, education—do not hold inventories of finished products yet their production responds to changes in demand.

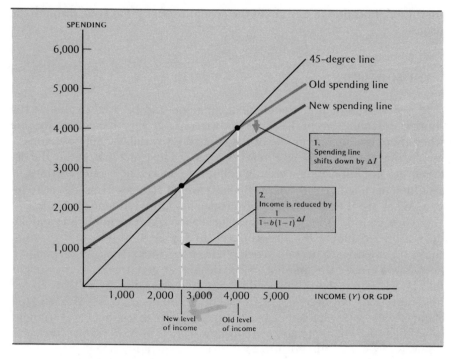

Figure 4–3.   THE MULTIPLIER.
A decrease in investment demand shifts the spending line down. The new point of intersection is at a lower level of GDP. The decline in GDP is larger than the decline in investment, illustrating the multiplier mechanism. (Note that the drop in investment shown in
the diagram is much larger than would be possible in the Canadian economy. The drop is
exaggerated here so that it can be easily seen in the diagram.)

income associated with a change in investment. Since $b(1-t)$ is less than 1,
the value of expression 4–7 is greater than 1. Hence, the change in GDP is
greater than the change in investment, just as we found using the graphical
analysis. Note that the larger the marginal propensity to consume, b, the
larger the multiplier.

   Example. If the marginal propensity to consume, b, is equal to .9 and the
tax rate, t, is .3, then the multiplier is equal to $1/.37$ or about 2.7. A $1 bil-
lion decrease in investment results in a $2.7 billion decrease in income or
GDP. Similarly, a $1 billion *increase* in investment results in a $2.7 billion increase in income or GDP.

   This example can be used to illustrate the explicit actions of consumers
and firms that result in the multiplier process. Suppose that a $1 billion de-
crease in investment occurs because home builders become pessimistic
about the housing market and build fewer new houses. Initially, the decreased purchases of new houses decrease income and GDP by $1 billion. But
the reduced construction activity means that the incomes of workers in
those companies will be reduced as they work fewer hours or are laid off.

The income of shareholders of construction companies will also be reduced, because of the decline in profits. In this example, the income of workers and shareholders falls by the full $1 billion. If the workers and shareholders have a marginal propensity to consume of .9 and pay taxes equal to 30 percent of their income, then they will reduce their consumption by $.63 billion. Hence, GDP is cut by another $.63 billion. The total reduction in GDP is now $1.63 billion.

But this is not the end. There is a third round. The workers and owners of the firms where the owners and employees of the construction companies cut their purchases by $.63 billion will have a reduction in their income of this same amount. With the same taxes and marginal propensity to consume, they will thus cut their consumption by .63 times $.63 billion, or by $.397 billion. The total reduction in GDP is now $2.027 billion. The process will continue for a fourth and fifth round and so on, but by this time the reduction in income will be diversified across many different firms in the economy. Some of the reduced consumption demand will certainly get back to the construction companies themselves.

If we keep summing the reduction in GDP at all these rounds we will eventually get a $2.7 billion reduction in GDP—the same as the direct computation using the multiplier. As we mentioned above, the total effect of these spending reductions on GDP would usually occur in a fairly short period, certainly less than a year. The different rounds of production are summarised in Table 4–1. Note how the eventual $2.7 billion reduction of GDP that we calculated directly through the multiplier is almost reached after just a few rounds. Note also how convenient it is to use the multiplier rather than go through all these tedious calculations.[3]

Table 4–1. EXAMPLE OF THE MULTIPLIER PROCESS (billions of dollars)

	Reduction in GDP		
	This Round	Sum to Date	Calculation
Round 1	1.000	1.000	Exogenous drop in investment
Round 2	.630	1.630	$b(1-t)(1) = (.630)(1)$
Round 3	.397	2.027	$[b(1-t)]^2(1) = (.397)(1)$
Round 4	.250	2.277	$[b(1-t)]^3(1) = (.250)(1)$
Round 5	.158	2.434	$[b(1-t)]^4(1) = (.158)(1)$
Round 6	.099	2.534	$[b(1-t)]^5(1) = (.099)(1)$

[3] The formulas for the calculations in the far right column of Table 4–1 add up to the formula for the multiplier: that is,

$$\frac{1}{1 - b(1-t)} = 1 + b(1-t) + [b(1-t)]^2 + [b(1-t)]^3 + \ldots$$

This result can be shown using the formula for a geometric series. A formal algebraic model of the adjustment process could come from putting *past* income rather than current income in the consumption function. This leads to a dynamic model—called the dynamic multiplier—that describes how consumption adjusts over time after a sudden change in investment.

Fluctuations in investment have always been associated with cyclical fluctuations in GDP. Such fluctuations in investment were emphasised by Keynes as an essential source of business-cycle fluctuations. One of Keynes's main contributions was to show that relatively small fluctuations in investment could lead to large fluctuations in GDP. The mechanism underlying Keynes's theory was the multiplier; our example of a decline in investment leading to a large decline in GDP provides a simple illustration of Keynes's theory.

Changes in the other exogenous variable—government spending—also result in changes in income. The analysis is exactly the same as investment. An increase in government spending will raise income and GDP by a greater amount. The same multiplier process is at work. In fact, the formula for the government spending multiplier—the amount that income increases when government spending increases—is exactly the same as the investment multiplier.

The government spending multiplier can be derived in the same way that the investment multiplier was derived. To show this we have again reproduced the 45-degree line and spending line from Figure 4–2 in Figure 4–4. An increase in government spending will *raise* the spending line in Figure

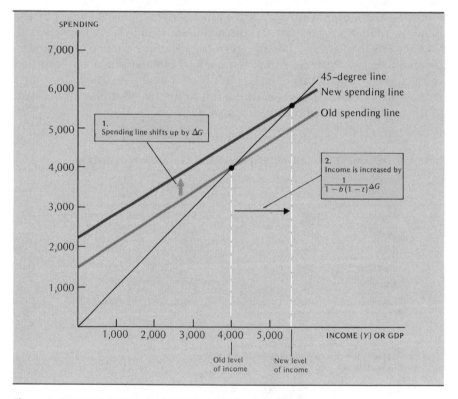

Figure 4–4.   THE GOVERNMENT SPENDING MULTIPLIER.
An increase in government spending shifts the spending line up. Income or GDP expands by the multiplier times the increase in government spending.

4–4. This has an even larger effect on income, because of the multiplier process. Knowing the size of the government spending multiplier is important for assessing the impact of a change in government policy on the economy.

The Multiplier

1. When investment rises, GDP rises; investment is part of total GDP.

2. As GDP rises, disposable income also rises, so consumption rises.

3. The increase in GDP is larger than the increase in investment, because of the increase in consumption. The multiplier measures the amount of GDP stimulated by an increase in investment.

4. The formula for the multiplier is $\dfrac{1}{1 - b(1 - t)}$.

5. The government spending multiplier is exactly the same as the investment multiplier. When government spending increases, GDP increases by a larger amount.

4.4   Spending Balance with Foreign Trade

Now that we have examined the role of consumption in determining spending balance we are ready to consider the key role played by foreign trade in this process. We will no longer assume that net exports are zero; instead we will consider how net exports and output are interrelated.

EXPORTS AND IMPORTS

As we saw in Chapter 2, foreign trade is divided into exports, sales of goods and services to the rest of the world, and imports, purchases of goods and services from the rest of the world. **Net exports** are simply exports less imports. When exports are greater than imports, there is a **trade surplus;** conversely, when exports are less than imports, there is a **trade deficit.**

Consider the income identity (Equation 4–1) once again. Recall that this income identity tells us two things: (1) Income and GDP are the same thing, and (2) aggregate demand—as measured by total spending—determines GDP. In thinking about how imports and exports affect aggregate demand for goods produced in Canada, keep in mind that consumption C, investment I, and government spending G by Canadians all include some purchases of goods and services abroad. In order to get a measure of how much of Canadian demand is for goods produced in Canada, we need to subtract imports. For example, if Canadians buy 100,000 more cars, then consumption rises by 100,000 cars. But if all these cars are imported from abroad then imports increase by 100,000 cars and aggregate demand for Canadian goods (Y) does not change. The reason we add exports to the identity is straightforward: When foreigners increase their purchases of goods produced in Canada, aggregate demand increases.

We will develop a relation between net exports and the level of Canadian income. The relation is negative. There is no reason to think that Canadian exports are much affected by Canadian income; they are affected instead by incomes in the countries purchasing the imports. But imports are affected by Canadian income. When Canadian income rises, consumers increase their spending on imported as well as domestic goods. Part of investment is also imported; when the total rises, the imported part rises.

We can summarise the relation between income and net exports in a **net export function:**

$$X = g - mY. \tag{4-8}$$

Here g and m are constants. For each dollar that GDP rises, imports rise by m dollars. Exports remain unchanged, so net exports fall by the same m dollars.

Compare the net export function with the consumption function, which we discussed earlier in this chapter. Net exports, like consumption, depend on income. But net exports *decline* by m dollars for each dollar increase in income, whereas consumption *rises* by b dollars for each dollar increase in income (b is the marginal propensity to consume). The reason that net exports decline with income is that imports rise by m dollars for each dollar increase in income. For this reason the coefficient m is sometimes called the **marginal propensity to import.** The dependence of net exports on income means that we need to take account of the response of net exports to income when we calculate the effects of monetary and fiscal policy, much as we took account of the response of consumption earlier in this chapter.

Now we can proceed exactly as we did before, developing an equation for spending balance by putting the net export function and the consumption function into the income identity. We did that before to get Equation 4–4, except that net exports were set to zero in that equation. The corresponding equation is

$$Y = a + b(1 - t)Y + I + G + g - mY. \tag{4-9}$$

Again, we can solve for the value of Y at the point of spending balance. Previously, we got Equation 4–5. Now we get

$$Y = \frac{a + I + G + g}{1 - b(1 - t) + m}. \tag{4-10}$$

Note how the impact of a change in government spending on output is

$$\frac{1}{1 - b(1 - t) + m}.$$

This is the **open-economy multiplier.** Note that the multiplier is smaller when the marginal propensity to import is larger. By setting m equal to zero the multiplier is the same as the multiplier for a closed economy. For example, if the marginal propensity to consume b is .9, the tax rate t is .3, and the marginal propensity to import m is .1, then the multiplier is $1/.47 = 2.1$, compared with a multiplier of $1/.37 = 2.7$ for the closed economy.

$$\rightarrow \frac{1}{1-b} = \frac{1}{1-0.9} = \frac{1}{0.1} = 10$$

The Decline of the Multiplier

At your first exposure to the multiplier, you may be very impressed. If the marginal propensity to spend, b, is .9 and there are no taxes, then the multiplier is 10! But then when you consider the role of taxes in draining off income, you get the multiplier in Equation 4–7, which we said might be about 2.7. Then when we considered the fact that some of the purchasing power stimulated by growth in demand would go into imports rather than domestic spending, the multiplier dropped some more, to 2.1 or even less.

Other factors, which we will study in later chapters, will further reduce the multiplier. In the next chapter, we will consider the fact that higher demand raises interest rates, and these in turn discourage investment and net exports. Then the multiplier in our standard example will be only 1.1.

The analysis of the multiplier we present in this book is close to the New Keynesian school. Some of the other schools of thought we mentioned in Chapter 1 are skeptical about the multiplier. Some monetarists think that the multiplier is virtually zero. The new classical and real business-cycle schools assert that the multiplier is low; moreover, to the extent that they believe that government spending stimulates output, it is through a different mechanism than the one we developed in this chapter. Briefly, in the real business-cycle model, higher government spending raises the interest rate, and a higher interest rate stimulates more work effort.

At this point, we can begin to analyse how policy or other economic forces affect the trade surplus. Recall from Chapter 2 that the trade surplus, as measured in the national accounts, is just net exports. Anything that lowers net exports will reduce the trade surplus. Looking at the net export function, Equation 4–8, we can see that net exports, in turn, respond negatively to the level of GDP. Combining the two, we can say that forces that raise GDP will also reduce the trade surplus. In particular, an increase in government spending, G, will raise GDP according to the multiplier derived in Equation 4–10. Thus, increases in G reduce the trade surplus. Since increases in G also raise the fiscal deficit, we can see that the trade balance and government budget balance are related—when the government takes an action that raises its own deficit, it causes the trade surplus to fall as well.

sell securities

In Chapter 2, we noted that a reduction in the trade surplus would cause the current account (the sum of the trade surplus and net investment income from foreigners) to decline. Without a change in the government's foreign exchange reserves a current account deficit will result in an equal increase in the amount that Canadians have borrowed abroad.

Thus suppose that the government wants to increase spending without raising taxes or reducing its foreign exchange reserves. In this scenario, the government will be forced to borrow to pay for the increased spending. We know that part of this borrowing will be done abroad through the capital inflow that must accompany a decline in the current account in this circumstance. So instead of obtaining all of the resources to be devoted to government spending from the domestic economy, some of them will come from foreign economies.

In the rest of the book, the models we develop will all take account of trade and the open economy.

Spending Balance in an Open Economy

1. Net exports appear in the income identity for an open economy.

2. The net export function describes the negative relation between income and net exports. It arises because higher Canadian income causes higher Canadian imports from other countries.

3. The multiplier in an open economy is smaller than in a closed economy.

4. Events that raise GDP, such as higher government spending, cause net exports to fall and the trade surplus to fall. Part of an increase in the fiscal deficit is financed overseas through a higher current account deficit.

Review and Practice

MAJOR POINTS

1. It is reasonable to set up a model for the short run in which firms respond to an increase in demand by producing more output rather than by raising prices.

2. Spending balance occurs when the public is making its spending plans on the basis of a level of income that is consistent with the GDP that is the sum of their spending.

3. The consumption function expresses the positive relation between income and consumption.

4. Spending balance occurs when consumption plus investment plus government purchases add up to the level of GDP upon which the consumers made their consumption plan.

5. The investment multiplier expresses the relation between investment and GDP. When investment rises by $1 billion, GDP rises by more than $1 billion because consumption rises as GDP rises.

6. Spending balance for an open economy occurs when the sum of all spending, including net exports, equals GDP.

7. The multiplier for an open economy is less than the multiplier for a closed economy.

8. An increase in government spending increases both the fiscal deficit and the current account deficit.

KEY TERMS AND CONCEPTS

Spending balance   Multiplier

Aggregate demand   Investment multiplier

Income identity   Government spending multiplier

Consumption function   Marginal propensity to import

Disposable income   Net exports

Marginal propensity to consume   Net export function

Exogenous variable   Trade surplus

Endogenous variable   Current account deficit

QUESTIONS FOR DISCUSSION AND REVIEW

1. How do firms typically respond to an increase in demand in the short run?

2. What happens to consumption if income rises? If taxes are cut?

3. What is true at the point of spending balance? What happens if the economy is not at a point of spending balance?

4. What happens to GDP if consumers change their behaviour and the coefficient a in the consumption function increases?

5. Why does an increase in investment or government purchases bring about a large increase in GDP?

6. Explain why the open-economy multiplier is smaller than the closed-economy multiplier.

7. How does an increase in government spending affect the trade deficit?

PROBLEMS

Numerical
1. Suppose that the model of the economy is given by

$$Y = C + I + G + X$$
$$C = a + bY_d$$
$$Y_d = (1 - t)Y$$
$$X = g - mY$$

where $I = \$650$ billion, $G = \$750$ billion, and the constants take the following values: $a = 80$, $b = .9$, $t = .3$, $g = 400$, $m = .1$.

a. Show that the value of GDP at the point of spending balance is $4,000 billion.

Note that this is the same value found for the closed economy in the example on pages 78–79. Compared to that model, is spending higher or lower? Is the multiplier higher or lower?

b. What proportion of investment is private saving? Government saving? Saving by the rest of the world?

c. Now suppose that I increases by $100 billion. By what proportion of the increase in investment do each of the three categories of saving increase?

Analytical

1. Imagine that you operate an economic forecasting firm. Your stock in trade is that you know the true model of the Canadian economy. It is given by

$$Y = C + I + G + X$$
$$C = a + bY_d$$
$$Y_d = (1 - t)Y$$
$$X = g - mY$$

where I and G are exogenous, and it is assumed that you have numerical values for all of the constants in the model.

a. Of the four spending components, which must you forecast before arriving at a forecast for the Canadian GDP? Explain.

b. Now suppose that you are trying to forecast GDP for a centrally planned economy in which the production schedules for all goods are determined a year in advance. Would forecasting C, I, G, and X be a very good way of forecasting GDP?

2. For the model given in Problem 1, explain why private saving, government saving, and saving by the rest of the world are all endogenous variables.

3. Suppose the economy is described by the following simple model:

$$Y = C + G$$
$$C = a + bY_d$$
$$Y_d = (1 - t)Y$$

a. Give an expression that relates private saving, S_p, to disposable income. This is called the saving function.

b. What must the relationship be between private saving and the government budget deficit? (Hint: Refer back to the discussion in Chapter 2 concerning the relationship between saving and investment.)

c. Solve for the values of S_p and the budget deficit; that is, derive an expression for each that is a function only of the exogenous variable G, and the constants in the model. Are your expressions consistent with your answer to Part b?

4. Balanced budget multiplier: Consider the following simple model with investment and government spending exogeneous.

$$Y = C + I + G$$
$$C = a + bY_d$$

Disposable income Y_d is given by $Y - T$, where T is total taxes. Suppose that taxes are not directly related to income so that T can be increased or decreased independently of income.

a. Derive the change in Y associated with an increase in taxes T. Show the results graphically and algebraically. What is the tax multiplier? That is, what is $\Delta Y / \Delta T$?

b. Compare the tax multiplier with the government spending multiplier derived in the text. Aside from the difference in signs, which is larger? Why?

c. Now increase government spending G and taxes T by the same amount. For this change the government budget deficit $G - T$ does not change. If the budget was balanced before it will still be balanced. What happens to income Y in this case? Perhaps surprisingly it increases. Calculate by how much. That is, using algebra calculate $\Delta Y/\Delta G$, setting $\Delta G = \Delta T$. The result is called the balanced budget multiplier.

5. For the model given in Problem 1, which of the following statements are true?
   a. An exogenous increase in net exports (i.e., an increase in g) raises the trade surplus and lowers the government budget deficit.
   b. An increase in investment lowers the government budget deficit and lowers the trade surplus.
   c. An increase in government spending and taxes of the same amount leaves both the government budget deficit and the trade surplus unchanged.

6. Imagine an economy in which the government spent all of its tax revenues, but was prevented (by a balanced budget requirement) from spending any more; thus $G=tY$, where t is the tax rate.
   a. Explain why government spending is endogenous in the model.
   b. Is the multiplier larger or smaller than the case in which government spending is exogenous?
   c. When t increases, does Y increase, decrease, or stay the same?

5

Financial Markets and Aggregate Demand

IN THIS CHAPTER we move from spending balance to demand analysis by considering the roles of financial markets, interest rates, and investment. We develop three crucial pieces of macroeconomic analysis —the IS curve, which summarises ideas about spending balance, the LM curve, which describes equilibrium in the money market, and the aggregate demand curve.

5.1 Investment and the Interest Rate

In the aggregate demand system we developed in Chapter 4, there were two exogenous forces that potentially can affect aggregate demand—investment and government spending. In this section we present an extension of that aggregate demand model. The extension has two important features: First, **financial variables**—interest rates and the supply of money—are shown to play an important role in the determination of aggregate demand, and, second, investment depends on these financial variables. Investment is no longer determined outside the model. Investment now becomes an endogenous variable.

The addition of financial variables to the model means that we will be concerned with the effects of changes in the money supply and interest rates, as well as with government spending. In Canada the money supply is controlled by the **Bank of Canada**—the country's central bank, created by an act of Parliament in 1934. Changes in the money supply are referred to as **monetary policy.** The money supply can have powerful effects on the economy and everyone who is concerned about the performance of the macroeconomy pays close attention to the opinions expressed by the governor of the Bank of Canada. **Fiscal policy,** on the other hand, involves changes in government spending, taxes, and transfers. Fiscal policy is determined by the federal and provincial governments. Hence, the extended model will permit us to examine important public policy questions concerning the prime minister, the provincial premiers, and the Bank of Canada. Such questions involve the relative importance of monetary versus fiscal policy and the appropriate mix of these policies.

In the basic model, you may have noticed that aggregate demand was independent of the price level. We talked about the possibility of firms adjusting their individual prices, but the general or average level of prices had no direct effect on demand. As soon as we add financial variables, we will find that aggregate demand depends on the price level: As the price level increases, aggregate demand decreases. Aggregate demand, and hence real GDP, will also change if there is a shock to the price level—such as when the price of oil jumped upward in 1974. Such shocks can affect the overall price level significantly. Unless monetary or fiscal policy offsets the shock, there will be a recession or a boom. The issue of how policy should respond to price shocks is one of the most important macroeconomic problems facing policy makers today.

THE INVESTMENT DEMAND FUNCTION

When we change investment from an exogenous variable to an endogenous variable, we need to specify a behavioural relationship to explain how investment is determined within the model. The relationship we use to describe investment is a simple but fundamental one. It states that investment depends negatively on the interest rate. This means that the demand for investment goods—the new factories, offices, and equipment used by business firms, as well as the new houses built for residential use—is low when interest rates are high, and vice versa.

The major reason for this negative relationship is that business firms and consumers finance much of their investment purchases by borrowing. When borrowing costs are high because of high interest rates, firms and consumers will tend to make fewer investment purchases. High borrowing costs effectively make investment goods more costly. Note that even if borrowings are not the source of funds for investment—such as when the funds come from selling financial securities—the interest rate should matter. If interest rates are high, then not holding those securities will represent a larger loss of income on those securities than if interest rates were low. Hence, people will be reluctant to sell those securities in order to purchase physical investment goods.

In algebraic terms the relationship for investment demand, called the **investment function,** can be represented as

$$I = e - dR. \tag{5-1}$$

As before, I is investment. Investment is now assumed to depend on R, the interest rate. Investment is measured in billions of dollars, and the interest rate is measured in percentage points. Equation 5–1 says that investment demand is equal to a constant e minus another constant d times the interest rate. The coefficient d measures how much investment falls when the interest rate increases by 1 percentage point. Note that we have kept the convention that lowercase letters represent constant coefficients, while uppercase letters represent variables. The investment function is shown graphically in Figure 5–1. It is a downward-sloping line.

Example. Suppose e equals 750 and d equals 2,000; then Equation 5–1 looks like

$$I = 750 - 2,000R.$$

When the interest rate is 5 percent, investment I is $750 - 2,000(.05)$, or $650 billion. An increase in the interest rate of 1 percent reduces investment by $20 billion. Note that we speak about the interest rate R as a percent, but use decimals in algebraic formulas: 'The interest rate is 5 percent' means $R = .05$. This convention is used throughout the book.

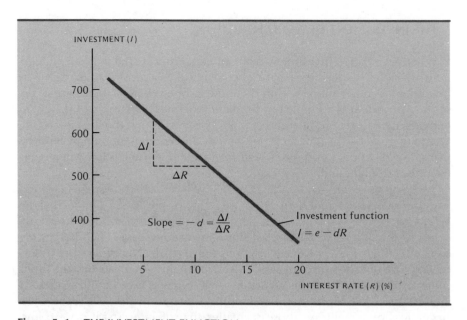

Figure 5–1.   THE INVESTMENT FUNCTION.
When the interest rate rises, the demand for investment falls. A higher interest rate means that the cost of funds required for investment is higher; only those investment projects that are particularly profitable will be undertaken.

THE MEANING AND INTERPRETATION OF *R*

Note that, in changing investment from an exogenous variable to an endogenous variable, we have introduced a new endogenous variable into the model: the interest rate *R*. There are, of course, many different interest rates in a modern economy: rates on *long*-term securities, rates on *short*-term securities, rates on *risky* securities, and rates on *safe* securities. When we use the term '*the* interest rate,' we are therefore simplifying the financial structure of the economy. In thinking about this simplification—that is, in trying to relate *R* to something you can read about or look up in a newspaper—it is useful to imagine an average or representative interest rate that represents the behaviour of all the different types of rates. For many purposes this abstraction is not too bad; interest rates on different types of securities—while not equal—tend to move in the same direction. That is, when interest rates on risk-free Treasury bills are abnormally high, so are interest rates on more risky corporate bonds. Of course, there are sometimes differences between short- and long-term interest rate behaviour—known as term structure variations—which can be relevant for investment. However, we will focus on the average representative interest rate *R*.

It is also important to distinguish between the **real interest rate** and the **nominal interest rate.** The nominal interest rate is simply the rate that you read about in the newspaper or that banks place in their windows to indicate what they will pay for different types of deposits. The real interest rate corrects the nominal rate for expected changes in the price level. Specifically, the real interest rate is the nominal interest rate minus the expected rate of inflation. For example, if your bank is paying 10 percent on deposits for a year, and you expect inflation to be 6 percent for the year, then the real rate of interest for you is 4 percent. The real rate of interest measures how much you will earn on your deposit after taking account of the fact that inflation will have increased the price of goods that you might purchase in a year. We usually mean the real interest rate when we use the symbol *R* in this book, but we do not generally add the adjective 'real,' unless the meaning is ambiguous, or we want to point out a particular reason to distinguish between the real and the nominal rates. Of course, for low rates of inflation the real rate and the nominal rate are very close.

The Investment Function

1. Investment demand is negatively related to the interest rate. When funds are more expensive, less investment takes place. The investment function describes this negative relationship.

2. The interest rate *R* that is in the investment function is an average of the many interest rates that we observe at banks and in the financial markets.

Portfolio Investment and Macro Investment

The difference between the macroeconomist's use of the term 'investment' and its use in casual conversation may be a stumbling block. Macroeconomic investment, I, is limited to purchases of newly built houses, plant, equipment, and inventories. When a business or a family buys stocks, bonds, existing real estate, or other portfolio items, they also think of them as investments because these assets (should) provide a financial return. Such investments are not counted as macroeconomic investment, however, because they are just movements of existing assets from one person to another. They do not create any new productive facilities. When one person buys stock, somebody else sells that stock; one person's investment is another's disinvestment.

But portfolio opportunities still matter, because they always loom as an alternative to macroeconomic investment. A business can invest in plant, equipment, and inventories, and presumably it will enjoy a high return, or else why would it stay in that industry? But if its corporate treasurer recommended investing in a new plant predicted to provide a 5 percent return at a time when government securities were paying 6 percent, he would soon enjoy the status of ex-corporate treasurer.

What kind of competition is macroeconomic investment up against? In 1987, portfolio investments scored the following returns:

Toronto Stock Exchange dividend rate	2.6%
Nonchequeable savings accounts	4.8
6-month Treasury bills	8.1
5-year trust company guaranteed investment certificates (GICs)	9.6
Medium-term corporate bonds	10.3

The returns to bonds generally grow higher as they get riskier. Interestingly, the best investment historically has been the stock market, where capital gains have more than made up for the lower dividend rates.

If a business concludes that the likely return to a new plant is better than any of these other returns, taking into consideration taxes, capital gains, future inflation, and so on, then it will decide to build the plant. Hence the returns on alternatives, such as bonds, are an important determinant of the level of investment.

5.2 Net Exports and the Interest Rate When the Exchange Rate Is Flexible

Now that we have included the interest rate in our model we need to modify the net export equation to take this into account. The relationship between net exports and the interest rate is somewhat indirect but it is important.

Recall from Chapter 1 that the real exchange rate determines how expensive foreign goods are compared to Canadian goods. A higher real exchange rate makes Canadian exports more costly to foreigners while making imports less costly to Canadians. An increase in the real exchange rate will therefore reduce the demand for net exports by reducing export demand and increasing import demand.

How do we incorporate this negative relationship between net exports and the real exchange rate into our complete model of aggregate demand? We must add another term to the net export function (Equation 4–8) to incorporate the negative effect of the real exchange rate on net exports:

$$X = g - mY - n\frac{EP}{P_u}. \tag{5-2}$$

Once again, X is net exports and Y is income or GDP. The expression EP/P_u is the real exchange rate, which depends on the nominal exchange rate E, the Canadian price level P, and the U.S. price level P_u. The constants in Equation 5–2 are g, m, and n.

Net exports are related to the interest rate because the real exchange rate is related to the interest rate. This comes about as follows. Usually the government allows the financial markets to determine the level of the exchange rate (E in Equation 5–2). This is called a **flexible** or **floating exchange rate.** When the exchange rate is flexible the principal influence on the exchange rate is the interest rate. When the Canadian interest rate rises relative to the U.S. interest rate, for example, it becomes more attractive for U.S. investors to lend to Canadian businesses and governments. To do this, U.S. investors must first trade their U.S. dollars for Canadian dollars; therefore the demand for Canadian dollars rises. At the same time, the increase in the Canadian interest rate relative to the U.S. rate makes it less attractive for Canadian investors to lend to Americans. As a result, Canadians are less willing to exchange Canadian dollars in return for U.S. dollars. Thus Canadian dollars become more attractive relative to U.S. dollars and so the price of Canadian dollars—the exchange rate—rises. As long as prices are slow to react, an increase in the exchange rate (E) will increase the real exchange rate (EP/P_u).

We summarise this relationship in the following equation for the real exchange rate:

$$\frac{EP}{P_u} = q + vR. \tag{5-3}$$

As before, EP/P_u is the real exchange rate and R is the interest rate. Equation 5–3 also contains coefficients q and v. Holding everything else constant, an increase in the Canadian interest rate will increase the real exchange rate. Combining Equations 5–2 and 5–3 shows how net exports are influenced by the interest rate. This yields:

$$X = g - mY - n(q + vR). \tag{5-4}$$

An increase in the Canadian interest rate will make lending to Canadians more attractive; this raises the real exchange rate which in turn reduces the demand for net exports.

Example. Suppose g is 500, m is .1, n is 100, q is .75, and v is 5. Then Equation 5–4 is

$$X = 425 - .1Y - 500R.$$

Net Exports

1. In addition to being negatively related to income, net exports are negatively related to the interest rate.

2. The negative relation to the interest rate occurs because higher Canadian interest rates raise the real exchange rate. The higher real exchange rate decreases exports and increases imports, thereby decreasing net exports.

5.3 The Money Market and the Interest Rate

Our next step is to explain how the interest rate is determined. The explanation relies on the theory of the demand for money.

THE DEMAND FOR MONEY

When we speak of **money** we have a rather special meaning in mind. Money is the currency issued by the Bank of Canada—for example, coins and bills—together with the chequing account balances held by the public in banks.[1]

Money is used to facilitate the purchase and sale of goods. When we buy goods we usually pay with currency, or with a cheque. Money does not include the much larger amounts of wealth held in mutual funds, bonds, corporate stock, and other forms, even though these forms of wealth are measured in dollars, because they are not usually used to pay for goods.

Three basic propositions about the demand for money are important for macroeconomics.

---

[1] By 'banks' we mean banks that accept deposits from the public, such as the Bank of Nova Scotia. These banks are often referred to as chartered banks, because such banks require a form of government approval called a charter in order to operate. As we will see, the Bank of Canada is very different from the chartered banks. We do not include deposits at the Bank of Canada in the definition of money.

1. *People will want to hold less money when the interest rate is high and, conversely, will want to hold more money when the interest rate is low.*

This means that there is a negative relation between the demand for money and the interest rate R. People hold money for transactions purposes, to pay daily expenses and monthly bills. But they could obtain higher earnings by keeping their wealth in other forms, such as savings accounts or bonds. Currency pays no interest. And even though many chequeable deposits now pay interest, the rate is less than on other forms of wealth. Because of this, people tend to economise on the use of money for transactions purposes. A common way to do this is to go to the bank more often to withdraw money from a high-interest savings account to obtain currency, or simply to transfer funds to a lower-interest chequing account. With more frequent trips to the bank, a smaller amount can be withdrawn each time from savings accounts. This means that, on average, a smaller amount of currency or chequing balances will be held by the individual. For example, you could go to the bank every week, rather than every month, to obtain currency and thereby hold a smaller amount of currency on average.

How much economising will occur will depend on the interest rate. The interest rate R represents how much a consumer or firm could earn by holding more in forms that pay full interest instead of in currency, which pays no interest, or chequing deposits, which pay less than full interest. Clearly the more that can be earned by holding those other forms—the higher is R—the less money an individual will want to hold.

2. *People want to hold more money when income is higher and, conversely, less money when income is lower.*

The more a family receives as income, the more the family will normally be spending, and the more money the family will need for transactions purposes. When income increases, the transactions demand for money increases. More money will be needed to buy and sell goods.

This means that there is a positive relationship between income Y and the demand for money. As income in the economy increases, on average each family's income increases and the demand for money in the entire economy increases.

3. *People want to hold more money when the price level is higher and, conversely, less money when the price level is lower.*

If the price level rises people will need more dollars to carry out their transactions, even if their real income does not increase. At a higher price level, goods and services will be more expensive; more currency will be needed to pay for them and cheques will be written for larger amounts.

This means that the demand for money is an increasing function of the price level. The positive relation between money demand and the price level is critical for macroeconomics. This is how the price level affects aggregate demand, as we indicate below.

To summarise these three basic ideas, the demand for money depends negatively on the interest rate R, positively on income Y, and positively on the price level P. An algebraic relationship that summarises the effect of these three variables on the demand for money is presented in the following equation:

$$M = (kY - hR)P. \tag{5-5}$$

Here M represents the amount of money demanded by firms and consumers. The other variables in Equation 5–5 have been defined already: P is the price level, R is the interest rate, and Y is income or GDP.[2] The lowercase symbols k and h are constant positive coefficients. The coefficient k measures how much money demand increases when income increases. The coefficient h measures how much money demand declines when the interest rate increases. Equation 5–5 is called the **money demand function.** It is a more complicated algebraic expression than the equation we used previously for consumption and investment demand. The money demand function shows that money demand depends on three variables (the interest rate R, income Y, and the price level P), whereas consumption demand and investment demand each depend on only one variable.

Example. If k equals .1625 and h equals 1,000, then Equation 5–5 looks like

$$M = (.1625Y - 1,000R)P.$$

If income Y is \$4,000 billion, the interest rate is 5 percent ($R = .05$), and the price level P is 1, then the demand for money is equal to \$600 billion. An increase in income of \$10 billion will increase the demand for money by \$1.625 billion. An increase in the interest rate of 1 percentage point will decrease the demand for money by \$10 billion.

THE MONEY SUPPLY

The Bank of Canada determines the level of the **money supply.** In Chapter 7 we will study the interesting question of how the Bank of Canada goes about setting the money supply. For now, we will assume that the Bank of Canada has picked a certain level for the money supply.

We will also assume that the demand for money and the supply of money are equal. For this reason we do not introduce a new symbol to represent the money supply. The variable M means both money supply and money demand. Since these are always equal, this should cause little confusion. (Recall that the symbol Y also refers to two variables: income and GDP.)

How does the demand for money become equal to the supply of money? Suppose that the demand is greater than the supply. Since the supply of

---

[2] Note that the appropriate interest rate for the money demand function is the nominal rate. Most alternatives to holding currency such as bonds pay a nominal interest rate. In order to keep our analysis simple we place the real interest rate, R, in the money demand function. If inflation is low this is a very good approximation.

money is fixed by the Bank of Canada, the demand for money must fall if the two are to be equal. The demand for money can adjust down by an increase in the interest rate, a decline in the level of income, or a decline in the price level. For example, an increase in the interest rate will cause people to demand less money. In principle, all three variables could move, but in practice income and especially interest rates adjust more quickly, and do most of the job of bringing demand into equality with supply.

Money and the Interest Rate

1. Money is currency plus the balances in chequing accounts.

2. The demand for money falls if the interest rate rises, if income falls, or if the price level falls.

3. The Bank of Canada determines the money supply.

4. The demand for money equals the supply of money. The interest rate and income move as necessary in any year so that money demand equals money supply.

5.4 The IS-LM Model

Our objective is to use the economic relationships introduced in the previous sections to determine GDP, investment, consumption, net exports, the interest rate, and the price level. These relationships represent the theory of how people behave. There are five economic relationships: the income identity, the consumption function, the investment demand function, the net export function, and the money demand function. The theory implies that all five relationships must hold at the same time.

The method of analysis proceeds as follows. We take as given the values for the variables determined outside our model in any year, for example, 1991. These are the exogenous variables: the money supply M and government spending G. They are determined by the Bank of Canada and the various levels of government. For simplicity, we will at first assume that the federal government is the only source of government spending. We want to find values for income, consumption, investment, net exports, the interest rate, and the price level that are implied by the model and by the values of the money supply and government spending for that year. We also want to find out what happens if the money supply or government spending changes. Will interest rates and output rise or fall, and by how much? We proceed in two stages.

First, we put the price level on the back burner, and focus our efforts on finding GDP, the interest rate, consumption, investment, and net exports for the year. We can put the price level aside because it doesn't move very much in any one year. Recall that prices are sticky and adjust only gradually. It is very convenient for us to be able to look away from the price level and focus on the other variables; fortunately this is in tune with how the economy actually works.

Second, we find how much the price level is adjusted by firms, based on the demand for their products that we have calculated for the year.

Note that this method treats the price level a little differently from the other economic variables determined by the theory. Because the price level adjusts only after a period of time, its value this year is essentially predetermined by conditions in previous years. Since the price level is predetermined, we call it a **predetermined variable,** to distinguish it from the endogenous variables that are determined within the model during the year. The endogenous variables are GDP, consumption, investment, net exports, and the interest rate. The economic relationships and the key macroeconomic variables are summarised in the box below.

Key Macro Relationships (the Theory) and the Major Variables

Macro Variables

The *Endogenous* Variables:		The *Exogenous* Variables:	
Name	Symbol	Name	Symbol
Income	Y	Government purchases	G
Consumption	C	Money supply	M
Investment	I		
Net exports	X		
Interest rate	R		

The *Predetermined* Variable:

Name	Symbol
Price level	P

Five Relationships (How the Variables Interact with Each Other)

Algebra		Name	Numerical Example
$Y = C + I + G + X$	(4–1)	Income identity	
$C = a + b(1 - t)Y$	(4–3)	Consumption function	$C = 80 + .63Y$
$I = e - dR$	(5–1)	Investment function	$I = 750 - 2{,}000R$
$X = g - mY - n(q + vR)$	(5–4)	Net exports	$X = 425 - .1Y - 500R$
$M = (kY - hR)P$	(5–5)	Money demand	$M = (.1625Y - 1{,}000R)P$

Suppose that the price level is given. For example, suppose that $P = 1$. Then the five macro relationships will determine values for the five remaining endogenous variables. The situation is analogous to that in Chapter 4 where we had to find values for two variables to satisfy two relationships. We first use graphs and then algebra.

Because graphs only allow for two variables, we need to reduce the five relationships to two relationships. A way to do this was originally proposed in 1937 by J. R. Hicks, the British economist who won the Nobel Prize in 1972. Hicks's graphical approach, called the IS-LM approach, is still used widely today because of its great intuitive appeal.[3]

goods mrkt in equil

THE IS CURVE

The **IS curve** is shown in Figure 5–2. *The IS curve shows all the combinations of the interest rate R and income Y that satisfy the income identity, the consumption function, the investment function, and the net export function.* In other

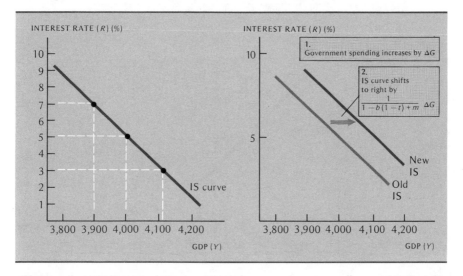

Figure 5–2. THE IS CURVE.
The IS curve shows all the combinations of the interest rate *R* and income *Y* that satisfy the consumption, investment, and net exports functions, and the income identity. As shown in the left-hand panel, it is downward sloping; an increase in the interest rate reduces investment and net exports. Through the multiplier, GDP falls. The right-hand panel illustrates how the IS curve shifts to the right when government spending increases.

[3] See J. R. Hicks, 'Mr. Keynes and the Classics: A Suggested Interpretation,' *Econometrica*, Vol. 6, pp. 147–159, 1937. The IS–LM model acquired its name this way. At all points on the IS curve, investment demand, 'I,' is equal to the demand for saving, 'S,' where saving is defined in the broad sense used in Chapter 2. At all points on the LM curve, the money supply, 'M,' is equal to money demand. The 'L' stands for money demand; it comes from the term *liquidity preference*, which is a synonym for money demand. (Money is more liquid—easier to exchange for goods and other items—than bonds or corporate stock.)

words, it is the set of points for which spending balance occurs. The left-hand panel of Figure 5–2 shows how higher levels of the interest rate are associated with lower levels of GDP along the IS curve.

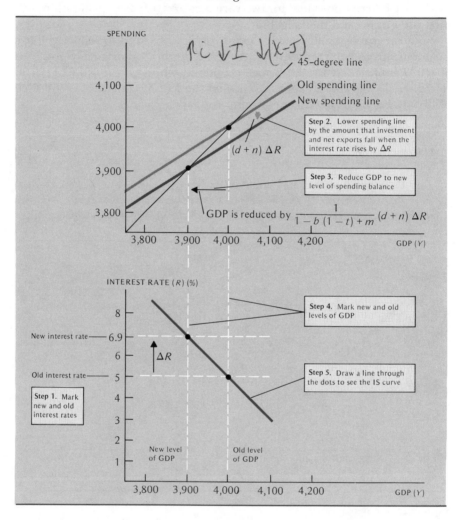

Figure 5–3. GRAPHICAL DERIVATION OF THE IS CURVE.
The upper part of the diagram shows the 45-degree line and spending line. The lower part of the diagram is the graph where the IS curve is to be drawn. The lower diagram has the interest rate on the vertical axis, and GDP on the horizontal axis. Points on the graph are obtained as described in the instructions placed in boxes on the diagram. Start with an interest rate and find the position of the spending line for that interest rate. (Higher interest rates will lower the spending line because they reduce investment and net exports.) Then find the resulting level of GDP that satisfies the requirements of spending balance. Note how the slope of the IS curve will depend on the marginal propensity to consume b, the tax rate t, and the marginal propensity to import m, because these affect the multiplier. Note also that the slope depends on the sensitivity of investment and net exports to changes in the interest rates, controlled by the coefficients d and n.

Slope. The first thing to remember about the IS curve is that it is downward sloping. Understanding the intuitive economic reason for this downward slope is very important. *The IS curve is downward sloping because a higher interest rate reduces investment and net exports, and thereby reduces GDP through the multiplier process.* To find a specific point on the IS curve, choose an interest rate and calculate how much investment will result using the investment function. Subtract nR from the export function. The higher the rate of interest, the lower the level of investment and net exports. Pass this level of spending through the multiplier process to find out how much GDP will result. The more of both, the more GDP. The interest rate and this level of GDP are a point on the IS curve. A self-contained explicit graphical derivation of the IS curve is shown in Figure 5–3.

Shifts. The second thing to remember about the IS curve is that *an increase in government spending shifts the IS curve to the right.* An increase in government spending increases GDP through the multiplier; as GDP increases we move the IS curve to the right. Note that, conversely, a decrease in government spending pushes the IS curve to the left.

To find how much the IS curve shifts, pick an interest rate R and calculate a corresponding level of investment and net exports. Now increase government spending. Through the multiplier process, output will increase by the multiplier times the increase in government spending. Holding the interest rate constant, the IS curve shifts to the right along the horizontal GDP axis by the amount of the multiplier times the increase in government spending. This is shown in the right-hand panel of Figure 5–2.

THE LM CURVE

The **LM curve** is shown in Figure 5–4. *The LM curve shows all combinations of the interest rate R and income Y that satisfy the money demand relationship for a fixed level of the money supply and for a predetermined value of the price level.* The left-hand panel of Figure 5–4 shows that higher levels of the interest rate are associated with higher levels of GDP along the LM curve.

Slope. The first thing to remember about the LM curve is that it slopes upward. The reason for this is somewhat involved, but important to keep in mind: Imagine that the interest rate increases. What must happen to income if money demand is to remain equal to money supply? An increase in the interest rate R reduces the demand for money. But the money supply is fixed. Hence, income must adjust to bring money demand back up. A rise in income is what is required. A rise in income will increase the demand for money, and offset the decline in money demand brought about by the rise in the interest rate. In sum, the increase in the interest rate is associated with an increase in income. Thus the LM curve is upward sloping.

To understand better the derivation of the LM curve, it is helpful to introduce the concept of **real money.** Real money is defined as money M di-

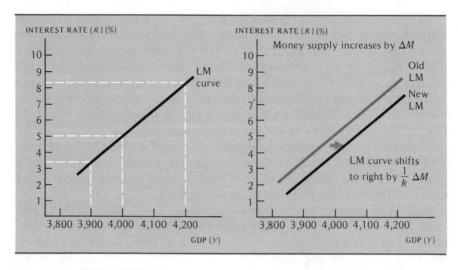

Figure 5–4.   THE LM CURVE.
The LM curve shows the values for the interest rate and income such that the supply of money is equal to the demand for money. As shown in the left-hand panel the LM curve is upward sloping. The right-hand panel shows how an increase in the money supply shifts the LM curve to the right.

vided by the price level P. Because the term 'real money' is used so much in macroeconomics we sometimes use the term **nominal money** when we mean just plain money M. Real money M/P is a convenient measure of money that corrects for changes in the price level. For example, if money increases by 10 percent and the price level increases by 10 percent, then real money does not change. The money demand function back in Equation 5–5 can be written in terms of real money if we simply divide both sides by the price level. That is,

$$M/P = kY - hR. \tag{5–6}$$

This says that the demand for *real* money depends positively on real GDP and negatively on the interest rate. The real money demand equation is an attractive way to think about money demand because it depends on two rather than three variables. Looking at Equation 5–6 we see that real money demand consists of two parts: One part, kY, increases with income, while the other part, $-hR$, decreases with the interest rate. Of course the same economic principles apply whether we write the money demand function in terms of real money or nominal money.

Looking carefully at Equation 5–6 it seems pretty clear why the LM curve slopes up. If the Bank of Canada is holding nominal money constant, and the price level isn't moving, then real money is also constant. If real money is constant, then an increase in the interest rate R, which reduces money demand by hR, must be offset by an increase in Y, which increases money demand by kY. Hence, when the interest rate R increases, income Y increases.

A self-contained graphical derivation of the LM curve, based on this line of reasoning, is shown in Figure 5–5. The left-hand panel of Figure 5–5 is a graph of the demand for real money as a function of the interest rate. Real money demand decreases with the interest rate. But note that an increase in GDP increases money demand and this shifts the money demand line to the right. If money demand is to stay equal to money supply, then the interest rate must increase, as shown in the diagram.

Shifts. The second thing to remember about the LM curve is that *an increase in the money supply shifts the LM curve to the right.* Conversely, a decrease in the money supply shifts the LM curve to the left. Looking again at Equation 5–6, we can get an economic understanding for this. An increase in the money supply increases the variable on the left-hand side, M/P. If money demand is to remain equal to money supply, then either output Y must rise or the interest rate R must fall. If we hold the interest on the LM diagram at a particular value, then output Y must increase, and the LM curve shifts to the right.

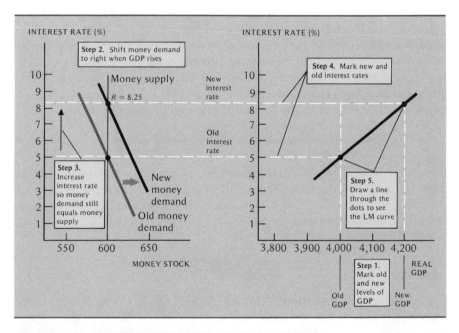

Figure 5–5. GRAPHICAL DERIVATION OF THE LM CURVE.
The left-hand panel shows the demand for real money as a function of the interest rate. The demand schedule slopes downward because higher interest rates make the public conserve on money holdings. Money demand shifts to the right if real GDP rises. Higher GDP causes the public to hold more real money at a given interest rate. The LM curve is constructed in the right-hand panel. The instructions show how to get points on the curve. Start with a level of GDP and find the money demand suitable for that level. Then find the interest rate that equates money demand and money supply. The LM curve traces out the market-clearing interest rate for different levels of GDP.

Changes in the price level also shift the LM curve. Again, look at the symbols in Equation 5–6 to keep track of what is going on. An increase in the price level reduces real balances. Hence, an increase in the price level does exactly the same thing to the LM curve as a decrease in the money supply. *An increase in the price level shifts the LM curve to the left.* The rationale: An increase in the price level means that less real money is available for transactions purposes. This means that either the interest rate must rise or real income must fall to reduce money demand. Either way the LM curve shifts to the left. Conversely, a decrease in the price level shifts the LM curve to the right, just like an increase in the money supply.

ALGEBRAIC DERIVATION OF THE IS AND LM CURVES

The algebraic statement that defines the IS curve is the expression of spending balance; that is, the GDP, Y, generated as total spending is equal to the level of income, Y, that consumers and importers assumed in making their spending decisions:

$$Y = a + e + g - nq + [b(1 - t) - m]Y - (d + nv)R + G. \qquad (5\text{–}7)$$

Note that the right-hand side is just the consumption function plus the investment function plus the net export function plus government spending. We want to express the IS curve as an equation giving the value of R that gives spending balance at a specified level of Y. We solve Equation 5–7 for R by moving the R term to the left-hand side and dividing by $d+nv$:

$$R = \frac{a + e + g - nq}{d + nv} - \frac{1 - b(1 - t) + m}{d + nv}Y + \frac{1}{d + nv}G. \qquad \text{IS Curve} \quad (5\text{–}8)$$

Government spending, G, increases the interest rate for a given level of income. Graphically, this looks like a shift of the IS curve to the right, a result that we saw in Figure 5–2. A higher value of G raises the IS curve or, equivalently, shifts the IS curve to the right.

The coefficient

$$\frac{1 - b(1 - t) + m}{d + nv}$$

that multiplies Y in Equation 5–8 is the slope of the IS curve. Note that the slope of the IS curve depends on the sensitivity of investment to the interest rate, represented by the coefficient d. The algebraic formula shows that the slope of the IS curve is small—which means that the IS curve is fairly flat—if investment is very responsive to the interest rate. Then, small changes in the interest rate result in large changes in investment, and hence large fluctuations in GDP. Similarly, the IS curve will be flat if net exports are highly sensitive to the real exchange rate, that is, if the coefficient n is large, and if the real exchange rate is highly sensitive to the interest rate, that is, if the coefficient q is large. What matters is the sum of the investment and net export effects, $d+nv$. Note also that the IS curve will be flat if the marginal propensity to consume b is large, if the tax rate t is small, or if the marginal propensity to import, m, is small. In these cases, the multiplier is large and changes in the interest rate have large effects on GDP.

An Example of an IS Curve. With the numerical values summarised in the box on page 102, the IS curve is

$$R = \frac{1,255}{2,500} - \frac{1 - .53}{2,500}Y + \frac{1}{2,500}G$$

or

$$R = .502 - .000188Y + .0004G. \qquad \text{Numerical Example} \atop \text{of IS Curve} \qquad (5\text{--}9)$$

The slope of the IS curve is $-.000188$: Along the IS curve, when GDP rises by \$100 billion the interest rate falls by 1.88 percentage points. The IS curve that appears in Figure 5–2 is drawn accurately to scale for this numerical example. The IS curve on the left is drawn for government spending G equal to \$750 billion. The shift in the IS curve to the right in Figure 5–2 is due to an increase in government spending of \$40 billion.

The algebraic expression for the LM curve is obtained simply by moving R to the left-hand side of the money demand equation (5–6) and dividing by the coefficient h. That is,

$$R = \frac{k}{h}Y - \frac{1}{h}\frac{M}{P}. \qquad \text{LM Curve} \qquad (5\text{--}10)$$

Equation 5–10 says that an increase in real money balances M/P lowers the interest rate for a given level of income. This means that the LM curve shifts to the right, a result that corresponds to the graph in Figure 5–4. The slope of the LM curve is k/h. Note that the slope of the LM curve k/h is small—meaning that the LM curve is fairly flat—if the sensitivity of money *elastic* demand to the interest rate is large, that is, if the coefficient h is large. Then, a small decline in the interest rate raises the demand for money by a large amount and requires a large offsetting decrease in income. The small change in the interest rate combined with the large change in income trace out a flat LM curve. Note also that the LM curve is flat if the sensitivity of money demand to income, k, is small.

An Example of an LM Curve. With the numerical values summarised in the box on page 102, the LM curve is

$$R = \frac{.1625}{1,000}Y - \frac{1}{1,000}\frac{M}{P}$$

or

$$R = .0001625Y - .001\frac{M}{P}. \qquad \text{Numerical Example} \atop \text{of LM Curve} \qquad (5\text{--}11)$$

This LM curve is drawn to scale in Figure 5–4. The shift of the LM curve in the right-hand side of Figure 5–4 corresponds to an increase in the money supply of $40 billion.

FINDING INCOME *Y* AND THE INTEREST RATE *R*

Finally we are ready to find the values of the interest rate and income that are predicted by the theory. We first proceed graphically. To satisfy all five relationships of the model, the values of *R* and *Y* must be on both the LM curve and the IS curve—that is, at the intersection of the LM curve and the IS curve. The IS curve takes care that the theory of consumption, investment, and net exports and the income identity are satisfied, while the LM curve takes care that the theory of money demand and money supply is satisfied. The values of the interest rate and income that we are looking for are thus at the intersection of the LM curve and the IS curve. The intersection is shown graphically in Figure 5–6.

Once we have determined the levels of income *Y* and the interest rate *R* we can determine consumption *C*, investment *I*, and net exports *X*. Consumption is obtained by putting the value of income into the consumption

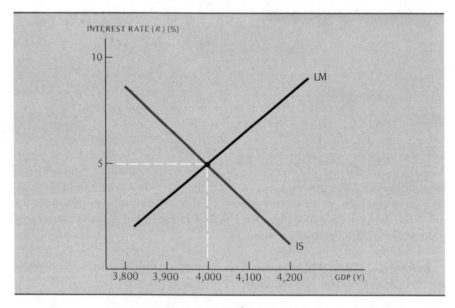

Figure 5–6. THE INTERSECTION OF THE IS CURVE AND THE LM CURVE.
The values of the interest rate and income predicted by the macro model occur at the intersection of the IS curve and the LM curve. For these values, all five relationships of the model are satisfied. Along the IS curve consumption demand, investment demand, net export demand, and the income identity are satisfied. Along the LM curve money demand equals money supply.

function, investment is obtained by putting the value of the interest rate into the investment function, and net exports are obtained by putting income and the interest rate into the net export function.

Recall that all these predictions of the model are made with the price level fixed, on the 'back burner.' This is fine for the short run—for about a year or so—but for no longer. We look at what happens to the price level in the next chapter.

5.5 Policy in the IS-LM Model

MONETARY POLICY

We are now ready to make the IS-LM approach go to work. Consider monetary policy. What happens if the Bank of Canada increases the money supply? We now know that an increase in the money supply shifts the LM curve to the right. The effect of such a change on the interest rate and income is shown in Figure 5–7. As the left-hand panel indicates, the theory predicts that *when the money supply increases the interest rate falls and GDP rises.* This increase in GDP will probably put upward pressure on prices, but we are saving the details for the next chapter.

What is actually happening in the economy when the Bank of Canada increases the money supply? Immediately after the increase there is more money in the economy than people demand. This tends to make the interest rate fall, so the demand for money increases. The lower interest rate then stimulates investment and net exports, which raises GDP through the multiplier process. In sum, GDP rises and the interest rate falls.

FISCAL POLICY

Suppose that the federal government increases defence spending. We now know that an increase in government spending pushes the IS curve to the right. Figure 5–7 shows what happens to interest rates and GDP. In the right-hand panel *an increase in government spending increases the interest rate and increases income.*

What is going on in the economy when the government purchases more goods? First, the increase in government demand increases GDP through the multiplier. But the increase in GDP will increase the demand for money: More money is needed for transactions purposes. Since the Bank of Canada does not change the money supply, we know that interest rates must rise to offset the increase in money demand that came from the increase in GDP. This increase in the interest rate will reduce investment demand and net exports and thus offset some of the stimulus to GDP caused by government spending. The offsetting negative effect is called **crowding out.**

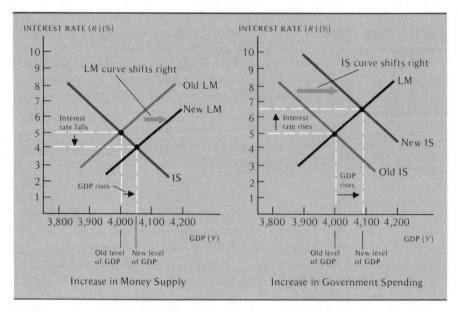

Figure 5–7.   EFFECTS OF MONETARY AND FISCAL POLICY.
In the left-hand panel, an increase in the money supply shifts the LM curve to the right, thus raising GDP and lowering the interest rate. In the right-hand panel, an increase in government spending shifts the IS curve to the right, thus raising GDP and raising the interest rate. A comparison of the two panels illustrates a fundamental difference between monetary policy and fiscal policy: An expansionary monetary policy lowers interest rates and an expansionary fiscal policy raises interest rates.

Numerical Example. Explicit numerical values for the effect of changes in the money supply and government spending can be obtained from the numerical IS and LM curves given in Equations 5–9 and 5–11. First set R in the IS curve equal to R in the LM curve. This is the algebraic equivalent of the graphical intersection of the LM and IS curves. Setting Equation 5–9 equal to Equation 5–11 means

$$\underbrace{.502 - .000188Y + .0004G}_{\text{IS curve}} = \underbrace{.0001625Y - .001\frac{M}{P}}_{\text{LM curve}}.$$

Isolating Y on the left-hand side of this equation gives the simpler form

$$Y = 1{,}432 + 1.14G + 2.855\frac{M}{P}. \tag{5-12}$$

Suppose that the money supply M is \$600 billion, that government spending G is \$750 billion, and that the price level is 1. Then Equation 5–12 says that GDP is equal to \$4,000 billion. Plugging this value for Y into either the equation for the IS curve or the equation for the LM curve, we find that the interest rate is 5 percent. Figure 5–6 is drawn accurately to scale for these values. Equation 5–12 says that an increase in government spending of $1 billion increases real GDP by $1.14 billion, for a ratio of 1.14. Compare this effect with the government spending multiplier of 2.1 that we found in the model where investment is exogenous and net exports depend only on income. The effect is smaller when we take account of the financial system, because interest rates rise and crowd out investment spending. As for monetary policy, if the price level is 1, then an increase in the money supply of $1 billion increases GDP by $2.855 billion.

IS-LM in the Business Pages

Not many reporters are versed in the IS-LM model. It's not surprising to find statements like this one in the financial pages:

A new recession is feared because higher government spending is raising interest rates. Those higher rates are discouraging housing purchases and plant and equipment investment.

More government spending shifts the IS curve outward. The economy moves up and to the right along the LM curve. It is true that interest rates are higher, but this is a symptom of higher GDP, not something that will cause a decline in GDP.

And

The only way to head off the impending recession is to bring the government's deficit under control. Otherwise, high interest rates will choke off economic activity.

It is true that an anti-deficit move (lower spending or higher taxes) will lower interest rates by moving the IS curve inward, but the result will be to worsen, not head off, an incipient recession.

THE RELATIVE EFFECTIVENESS OF MONETARY AND FISCAL POLICY

Monetary and fiscal policy differ in how effective they are in shifting aggregate demand. Two important issues must be faced in determining the relative effectiveness of monetary and fiscal policy:

1. The sensitivity of **investment demand** and **net exports** to interest rates
2. The sensitivity of **money demand** to interest rates

The issues can be given graphical interpretations in terms of the *slopes* of the IS curve and the LM curve. First, think about it intuitively.

→ not much change in Y

When Is Fiscal Policy Relatively Weak? An expansionary fiscal policy will have a relatively *weak* effect on aggregate demand if interest rates rise a lot and have a large negative effect on investment and net exports. The fall in investment and net exports will offset the positive effect that government spending has on aggregate demand. The fall in investment and net exports will be large under two circumstances, corresponding to the two issues listed above.

→ elastic

1. If the sensitivity of investment demand and net exports to the interest rate is *very large.* Then a rise in interest rates will reduce investment and net exports by a considerable amount.   *inelastic*
2. If the sensitivity of money demand to the interest rate is *very small.* Then the increase in money demand that arises as a result of the increased government expenditures will cause a big rise in the interest rate. (The small interest rate sensitivity means that the interest rate has to move a lot.)

Another property of the economy that affects the strength of fiscal policy is the spending multiplier (see p. 81). A high spending multiplier means more effective fiscal policy. However, if the economy has high interest sensitivity of investment and net exports and low interest sensitivity of money demand, even a very large multiplier will not result in strong effects of fiscal policy.

When Is Fiscal Policy Relatively Strong? An expansionary fiscal policy will have a relatively *strong* effect on aggregate demand if interest rates don't rise by much or have a small effect on investment and net exports. This occurs under circumstances opposite to those listed under weak fiscal policy.

When Is Monetary Policy Relatively Weak? An expansionary monetary policy will have a relatively *weak* effect on aggregate demand if the drop in interest rates that occurs when the money supply is increased is small or has little influence on investment and net exports. This occurs under two circumstances.

→ inelastic

1. If the sensitivity of investment demand and net exports to interest rates is *very small.* Then investment is not stimulated much by the decline in interest rates.   *elastic*
2. If the sensitivity of money demand to interest rates is *very large.* Then the increase in the money supply doesn't cause much of a drop in interest rates. (A small drop in interest rates is sufficient to bring money demand up to the higher money supply.)

When Is Monetary Policy Relatively Strong? An expansionary monetary policy will have a big effect if interest rates fall by a large amount and stimulate investment and net exports in a big way. This occurs under circumstances opposite to those listed under weak monetary policy.

THE IS-LM INTERPRETATION

The IS curve is relatively flat if investment demand and net exports are very sensitive to interest rates, because small changes in interest rates are associated with big changes in demand. Conversely, the IS curve is relatively steep if investment and net exports are very insensitive to interest rates.

The LM curve is relatively flat if money demand is very sensitive to interest rates, because small changes in interest rates are sufficient to reduce money demand when it increases with a change in income. Conversely, the LM curve is relatively steep if money demand is very insensitive to interest rates.

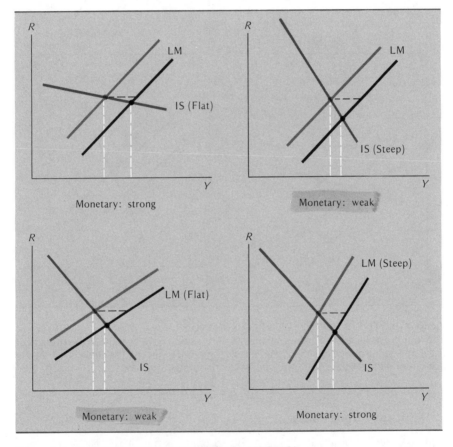

Figure 5-8.   MONETARY POLICY, WEAK OR STRONG?
The four IS-LM diagrams illustrate all the possibilities that have bearing on the strength of monetary policy. In some cases the IS curve is flat; in other cases the LM curve is flat. In every case the LM curve is shifted outward by the same amount. At the bottom of each diagram the answer to 'Weak or strong?' is given.

With these IS slope and LM slope interpretations of the interest rate sensitivities, we now can review the previous discussion using the IS-LM diagrams. Eight cases exhaust the possibilities, and are shown in Figures 5–8 and 5–9.

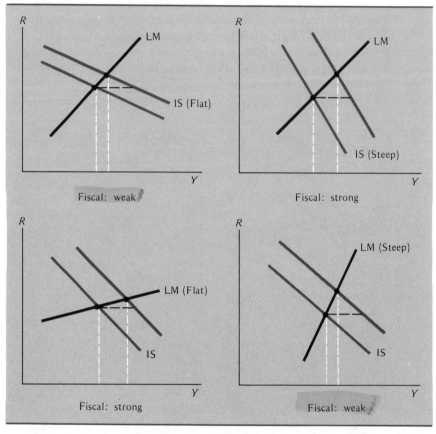

Figure 5–9. FISCAL POLICY: WEAK OR STRONG?
The four IS-LM diagrams illustrate all the possibilities that have bearing on the strength of fiscal policy. In some cases the IS curve is flat; in other cases the LM curve is flat. At the bottom of each diagram the answer to 'Weak or strong?' is given.

Weak and Strong Policy

1. Monetary policy is strong if the IS curve is flat or the LM curve is steep. Monetary policy is weak if the IS curve is steep or the LM curve is flat.

2. Fiscal policy is strong if the IS curve is steep or the LM curve is flat. Fiscal policy is weak if the IS curve is flat or the LM curve is steep.

3. For given slopes of the IS and LM curves, fiscal policy is more effective if the spending multiplier is large.

5.6 The Aggregate Demand Curve

In preparation for our analysis of price change and inflation in the next chapter, we now derive the **aggregate demand curve.** The aggregate demand curve is shown in Figure 5–10. The aggregate demand curve tells how much people will demand at a given level of prices. The higher the price level, the less aggregate demand. Hence, as with most demand curves in microeconomics, the aggregate demand curve is downward sloping.

Except as a mnemonic device to remember which way the aggregate demand curve is sloped, the analogy between the standard microeconomic demand curve and the aggregate demand curve of macroeconomics is a weak one, and should not be emphasised. The ideas behind the aggregate demand curve are much different from those that underlie the typical demand curve of microeconomics. In particular, it is important to keep in mind that the financial system—the demand and supply for money—lies behind the aggregate demand curve.

Figure 5–11 is a graphical derivation of the aggregate demand curve. In the top part of Figure 5–11 is an IS-LM diagram. Recall that changes in the price level shift the LM curve. Higher prices shift the LM curve to the left, and lower prices shift the LM curve to the right.

Now suppose that the price level rises. The LM curve shifts to the left, raising the interest rate, lowering investment and net exports, and ultimately lowering GDP. Thus, a higher price level reduces GDP because it increases the demand for money. The increase in demand causes interest rates to rise and causes GDP to fall. The different values for the price level and GDP constitute the aggregate demand curve.

Figure 5–10.   THE AGGREGATE DEMAND CURVE.
On the left is the aggregate demand curve (AD). It shows that aggregate demand is a declining function of the price level. On the right, the aggregate demand curve shifts to the right if either monetary or fiscal policy is expansionary.

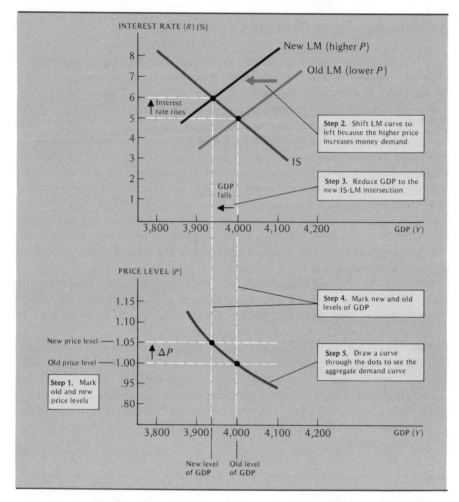

Figure 5–11.   DERIVATION OF THE AGGREGATE DEMAND CURVE.
An increase in the price level shifts the LM curve to the left. This raises interest rates and reduces output. The resulting negative relationship between the price level and GDP is summarised in the aggregate demand curve.

The IS, LM, and Aggregate Demand Curves

1. The aggregate demand curve shows what level of GDP will be demanded given a particular price level.

2. The two economic principles governing the aggregate demand curve are spending balance and the equality of the demand for and supply of money.

3. Spending balance is summarised by the IS curve. The IS curve is downward sloping because higher interest rates reduce investment and net exports and therefore reduce GDP. An increase in government spending pushes the IS curve to the right.

4. The condition that the supply of and the demand for money are equal is summarised by the LM curve. The LM curve is upward sloping. An increase in the money supply pushes the LM curve to the right.

5. The aggregate demand curve slopes downward. A higher price level means that real money balances are lower and therefore that the interest rate is higher. This means that investment, net exports, and GDP are lower.

6. An increase in government spending or an increase in the money supply shifts the aggregate demand curve to the right.

MONETARY AND FISCAL POLICY

Changes in the money supply and in government spending both shift the aggregate demand curve. This is shown in the right-hand panel of Figure 5–10. Suppose that the money supply increases. At a given price level, aggregate demand rises. More money means that a lower interest rate equates money demand with money supply. A lower interest rate stimulates more investment and net exports, which in turn requires a higher level of GDP for spending balance. In sum, the aggregate demand curve shifts to the right when the money supply increases.

Fiscal policy also shifts the aggregate demand curve. An increase in government spending shifts the aggregate demand curve to the right. At a given price level more government spending means more aggregate demand. Conversely, a decrease in government spending shifts the aggregate demand curve to the left.

Numerical Example. How do we get the aggregate demand curve using algebra? We have already got it. On page 112 Equation 5–12 represents the intersection of the IS and LM curves. It shows how GDP falls when the price level rises: The price level appears in the denominator on the right-hand side of Equation 5–12. Equation 5–12 is the aggregate demand curve. For the numerical example that we have been considering throughout this chapter, it shows how much GDP falls when the price level rises.

Note that the aggregate demand equation 5–12 also depends on the money supply M and government spending G. Changing M and G in this equation corresponds to the shifts in the aggregate demand diagram shown in Figure 5–10.

Review and Practice

MAJOR POINTS

1. Investment depends on the interest rate. A higher interest rate discourages some investment projects and lowers total investment.

2. Net exports also depend negatively on the interest rate. A higher interest rate attracts capital from other countries; this drives up the exchange rate and lowers net exports.

3. The demand for money also depends negatively on the interest rate.

4. When the Bank of Canada is holding the money stock constant, the interest rate has to move as necessary to equate the demand for money with the given money supply.

5. At a higher price level and the same money stock, a higher interest rate is needed to equate money demand with supply.

6. At a higher price level and the same money stock, a lower income level is needed to equate money demand with supply.

7. The IS curve shows the level of GDP that brings spending balance for each interest rate. It slopes downward.

8. The LM curve shows the interest rate that brings equality of supply and demand in the money market for each level of GDP. It slopes upward.

9. The IS-LM model answers questions about the effect of policy over the period when it is reasonable to consider prices fixed. Monetary expansion raises output and lowers the interest rate. Fiscal expansion raises output and raises the interest rate.

10. The intersection of the IS and LM curves tells the levels of GDP and the interest rate for a given price level and fiscal-monetary policy. It corresponds to a point on the aggregate demand schedule.

KEY TERMS AND CONCEPTS

Interest rate	Money demand function
Real interest rate	Money supply
Nominal interest rate	Bank of Canada
Investment function	Monetary policy
Net export function	Fiscal policy
Crowding out	IS curve
Flexible exchange rate	LM curve
Money	Aggregate demand curve

QUESTIONS FOR DISCUSSION AND REVIEW

1. What are the important determinants of aggregate demand? For each one, trace out what happens if it changes.

2. Why does a higher price level raise the interest rate? What could the Bank of Canada do to prevent the increase in the interest rate?

3. Explain why the IS curve slopes downward.

4. Explain why the LM curve slopes upward.

5. Explain why the aggregate demand curve slopes downward.

6. Why does a decrease in government spending reduce interest rates?

7. Why does an increase in the money supply reduce interest rates?

PROBLEMS

Numerical

1. This problem pertains to the numerical example listed in the box on page 102. Set the price level equal to 1.
   a. Use the algebraic form of the aggregate demand curve to find the level of GDP that occurs when the money supply is $600 billion and government spending is $750 billion.
   b. Use the IS curve and the LM curve to find the interest rate that occurs in this same situation. Explain why you get the same answer in each case.
   c. Use the consumption function to find the level of consumption, the investment function to find the level of investment, and the net export function to find the level of net exports for this same situation.
   d. Show that the sum of your answers for consumption, investment, government spending, and net exports equals GDP.
   e. Repeat all the previous calculations if government spending increased to $850 billion. How much investment is 'crowded out' as a result of the increase in government spending? How much are net exports crowded out?

2. Savings and budget deficits: This problem pertains to the numerical example in the text and makes use of the answers to Problem 1.
   a. Set government spending at $750 billion and the money supply at $600 billion. Calculate government saving (the budget surplus). Calculate the level of private saving, and show that private saving plus government saving equal investment.
   b. Now repeat your calculations for a level of government spending equal to $850 billion. Does private saving plus government saving still equal investment? Why not?
   c. Explain why private saving increases as a result of government spending. In light of your calculations evaluate the statement: 'Government budget deficits absorb private saving that would otherwise be used for investment purposes.'

3. Compare the IS curve in the numerical example on page 109 with the IS curve that you get by increasing the coefficient d to 4,000.
   a. What is the slope of each IS curve? Explain in words why the second IS curve is flatter.
   b. For which value of d does an increase in the money supply have a larger effect on output? Why?

   c. Derive the aggregate demand curve in each case. Which has a larger coefficient for M/P? Is this consistent with your answer to Part b?

4. Compare the LM curve in the numerical example on page 109 with the LM curve that you get by increasing the coefficient h to 2,000.
   a. What is the slope of each LM curve? Explain why the slopes are different.
   b. For which value of h is monetary policy more powerful? Explain.
   c. Derive the aggregate demand curve in each case. Which has a larger coefficient for M/P? Is this consistent with your answer to Part b?

5. Using the numerical example of the chapter, calculate values for the money supply and government spending that will increase GDP from $4,000 billion to $4,100 billion *without changing the interest rate at all*.

6. The following relationships describe the imaginary economy of Nineland:

$$\begin{aligned}
Y &= C + I & &\text{(Income identity)} \\
C &= 90 + .9Y & &\text{(Consumption)} \\
I &= 900 - 900R & &\text{(Investment)} \\
M &= (.9Y - 900R)P & &\text{(Money demand)}
\end{aligned}$$

Y is output, C is consumption, I is investment, R is the interest rate, M is the money supply, and P is the price level. There are no taxes, government spending, or foreign trade in Nineland.
   The year is 1999 in Nineland. The price level is 1. The money supply is 900 in 1999.
   a. Sketch the IS curve and the LM curve for the year 1999 on a diagram and show the point where the interest rate and output are determined. Show what happens in the diagram if the money supply is *increased* above 900 in 1999.
   b. Sketch the aggregate demand curve. Show what happens in the diagram if the money supply is *decreased* below 900 in 1999.
   c. Derive an algebraic expression for the aggregate demand curve in which P is on the left-hand side and Y is on the right-hand side.
   d. What is the value of output and the interest rate in 1999 when the money supply is 900?

Analytical
1. Higher interest rates reduce investment and increase foreign saving. What then must happen to the combination of private and government saving after a rise in interest rates? If neither private nor government saving depends directly on the interest rate, how can this change come about?

2. Graphically derive the LM curve, as in Figure 5–5, using instead a graph that relates money demand to income. (Hint: Put the stock of money on the vertical axis and income on the horizontal axis, and set this diagram above the LM diagram.)

3. Consider the following statements: (i) The IS curve is steep when investment is insensitive to the interest rate. (ii) The LM curve is flat when money demand is insensitive to income. (iii) The LM curve is flat when money demand is sensitive to the interest rate. (iv) The IS curve is flat when the marginal propensity to consume is high.
   a. Explain in words why each of these statements is true.
   b. Confirm algebraically that each statement is true. (Hint: Begin by deciding which coefficient in the model changes. Then show how a change in that coefficient affects the expression for the slope of the IS or LM curve.)

4. Suppose that money demand depended only on income and not on interest rates.
   a. What does the LM curve look like in this case?
   b. Show graphically that G has no effect on the level of output, Y. What does G affect?
   c. Show the same thing algebraically. Explain why the LM equation becomes the aggregate demand equation.

5. Show how the IS curve and the LM curve can be shifted to get a decline in output without a change in interest rates. What kind of mix of monetary and fiscal policy is needed to do this?

6. Suppose that two administrations, one Liberal and the other Conservative, both use fiscal and monetary policy to keep output at its potential level, but that the Liberal administration raises more in taxes and maintains a larger money supply than the Conservative administration.
   a. On a single graph, show how the IS and LM curves of these two administrations differ.
   b. Indicate whether the following variables will be higher under the Liberal or Conservative administration, or whether they'll be unchanged: consumption; investment; net exports; government saving; private saving.
   c. Under which administration will foreign holdings of Canadian financial assets grow more slowly?

6

Aggregate Supply and Price Adjustment

As WE saw in Chapter 5, aggregate demand determines output in the short run. A reduction in aggregate demand, for example, reduces GDP and throws the economy into a recession. But this is just the first stage. As prices begin to adjust, the economy will be able to recover and return to its potential output. In the long run, the aggregate supply of basic resources in the economy will determine output.

In this chapter, we will look first at the determinants of **aggregate supply** —the labour force, the stock of productive capital, and technology. Aggregate supply defines the economy's potential GDP. We then study the price-adjustment process, and the movement of the economy from situations where aggregate demand is above or below potential to situations where aggregate demand equals potential.

6.1 Aggregate Supply

The supply side of the macroeconomic model describes the economy's capabilities for producing output. The important determinants of aggregate supply are:

1. The number of people available for work and their productivity
2. The amount of equipment, structures, land, and other types of capital
3. The technology

LABOUR

Not everybody in the population is in the labour force. It is against the law for children to work; many adults are in school, working at home, or in retirement; quite a few others are unable to work because they are disabled or sick. Some people are committed to working full time no matter what the incentives; others will choose the level of their work effort depending on the incentives provided by the labor market.

We define **potential employment** (N^*) as the volume of employment that the entire population would choose given existing incentives. It is the total amount of work that would be done if everybody could find a job and earn as much as people like themselves are already earning. Notice that potential employment is not the absolute maximum amount of work that the population is capable of doing. It is the amount they would want to do given the existing real wage, which, as we saw in Chapter 3, measures the purchasing power of wages. The real wage is the actual wage paid, W, divided by the price level, P. Potential employment might rise if the real wage increased.

In our analysis potential employment does not depend on any of the major macro variables: output, consumption, investment, the interest rate, or the price level. It is exogenous. Though potential employment depends on the real wage W/P, it does not depend on the price level P. The reason is that actual wages are assumed to vary in proportion to the price level, so that a change in the price level does not affect the real wage. This is a fairly realistic assumption for short-run macroeconomic fluctuations. Potential employment is not fixed, however. It grows steadily as the population grows.

The unemployment rate is not zero when employment is equal to potential employment. It is equal to about 7 percent. As we saw in Chapter 3, this level of unemployment is called the natural rate of unemployment, and is greater than zero partially because of transitional periods of unemployment when workers change jobs or are looking for new jobs. The unemployment rate is above the natural rate when employment is below potential employment; conversely, the unemployment rate is below the natural rate when employment is above potential employment.

CAPITAL

In any given year, the volume of physical capital—factories and equipment—is determined by investment in previous years. The capital stock increases from one year to the next as long as gross investment is greater than the depreciation of the capital stock. As long as net investment is positive, the capital stock is growing. However, any investment project undertaken this year to increase the capital stock won't add to the stock until the project is complete, which usually takes at least a year. In any case, the capital stock is so large that the flow of new investment can have little effect on it in a short span of time.[1] Chapter 14 will provide more detail on this point. For now all that matters is that capital, like potential employment, is independent of the other macro variables in any one year. Hence, we will treat the capital stock as if it were exogenous. We use the symbol K for the existing capital stock.

TECHNOLOGY

The technology tells us how much output can be produced from the amount of labour and capital used in production. A simple way to describe the technology is in terms of a **production function,** which shows how much output can be made from given amounts of labour and capital. The production function can be represented using symbols as follows:

$$Y = F(N,K). \tag{6-1}$$

This is simply shorthand notation for saying that the output Y that is produced in the economy depends on employment N and capital K. (Reading out loud we say: 'Y is a function F of N and K.') The notation F with parentheses after it means a general function of the variables listed in parentheses. With such a notation we are not specific about what the function actually looks like, whether it is linear or the square root of N, or whatever.

The production function relates output to employment and capital whatever their levels, even if employment is below potential. It would tell us how much real GDP would be produced, for example, if there were a very severe depression and only half the normal number of people were at work.

POTENTIAL GDP

To determine the aggregate supply capabilities of the economy, we ask: How much output could be produced if employment were at its potential level and all the existing capital were in use? The answer is

$$Y^* = F(N^*,K). \tag{6-2}$$

The level of output, Y^*, is called **potential GDP.** It is the amount of output that would be produced if everybody who wanted to work could find a job. For this reason, Y^* is also frequently called the **full-employment level of output.** Recall that in Chapter 1 we compared actual GDP with estimates of potential GDP. Relative to actual GDP, potential GDP appears to grow steadily.

---

[1] Technically, the capital stock is a predetermined variable, like the price level in our analysis. Its current value is determined by events in the past. But the capital stock is even 'stickier' than the price level, and for this reason we ignore the fact that it depends on investment in our analysis of macroeconomic fluctuations. It could not be ignored in a study of long-term growth.

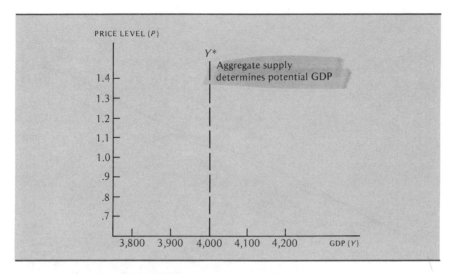

Figure 6–1.   AGGREGATE SUPPLY AND POTENTIAL GDP.
Potential GDP does not depend on the price level. It is marked on the price-GDP diagram as a vertical line. Potential GDP would be affected by changes in the incentives to work, the volume of capital, and technology.

Potential GDP is not influenced by the price level or the other macro variables because potential employment is not influenced by these variables. In the price-GDP diagram that we used in Chapter 5 to draw the aggregate demand curve (Figure 5–10), potential output would be marked as a vertical line.[2] This is shown in Figure 6–1. Actual GDP fluctuates around potential GDP. In any year actual GDP can be either above or below potential GDP.

Do not be confused because potential GDP does not move in Figure 6–1, even though we have seen that potential GDP is steadily growing. Figure 6–1 shows the situation in a single year. If we wanted to show how potential GDP grows, we could move the potential GDP line to the right. In Figure 6–2, we show the upward-sloping trend line of potential GDP and look at the fluctuations of actual GDP around potential GDP.

Aggregate Supply

1. Aggregate supply describes the amount of output that the basic resources of the economy are capable of producing.

2. Potential employment is the volume of employment that would

[2] Some economists talk about the vertical aggregate supply schedule as the *long-run* aggregate supply schedule. They then use the term 'short-run aggregate supply' for what we call the price-adjustment process. We believe that these are two very different concepts, so we reserve aggregate supply for issues genuinely concerned with the supply side of the economy. Price adjustment has to do with the interaction of demand and supply, so it is confusing to call it aggregate supply.

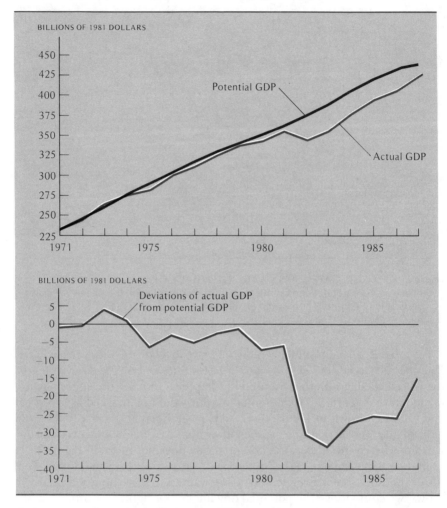

Figure 6–2. ACTUAL GDP RELATIVE TO POTENTIAL GDP, 1971–87.
The top chart shows how potential GDP grew and how actual GDP fluctuated around it. The deviations of actual GDP from potential GDP are shown in the lower panel. Source: *Canadian Economic Observer*, Table 1.3.

occur if everybody was working who wanted to at prevailing incentives.

3. Potential output is the amount of output that can be produced, as shown by the production function, from potential employment and the existing capital stock.

4. Aggregate supply is the same as potential GDP. On a price-GDP diagram, it is marked by a vertical line at a level of output equal to potential output. Aggregate supply, or potential GDP, does not depend on the price level.

6.2 Price Stickiness and the Determination of Output and Unemployment in the Short Run

Recall that prices are sticky in the sense that they are not adjusted quickly by firms in response to demand conditions. Firms wait a while before adjusting their prices. For some period of time, therefore, the price level is stuck at a predetermined level. It is during this time that sellers are waiting to see how demand conditions change before they adjust their prices again. Prices eventually adjust, of course, but not until the next time period—a year or quarter later, for example. For the time being the price level is predetermined.

DETERMINATION OF OUTPUT

Figure 6–3 shows how aggregate demand determines output at some predetermined price. The aggregate demand curve is the same one derived in the previous chapter. The predetermined price is shown by the horizontal line drawn at P_0. GDP is determined by the point of intersection of the aggregate demand curve and the flat predetermined-price line.

Shifts in the aggregate demand curve—caused perhaps by changes in the money supply or government spending—will result in increases or decreases in output. A rightward shift in the aggregate demand curve results in an expansion of output; a leftward shift in the aggregate demand curve results in a contraction of output.

Figure 6–3. DETERMINATION OF OUTPUT WITH PREDETERMINED PRICE.
The horizontal line shows the price level predetermined for this year at level P_0. This year's output is at the intersection of the aggregate demand schedule and the horizontal line. In the left-hand panel the intersection occurs at the level of output marked Y_0. In the right-hand panel the aggregate demand curve shifts right, and output expands from Y_0 to Y_1.

The price level inherited from last year, when combined with the aggregate demand curve, determines the level of output. Output can be below potential output. Then we will observe unemployment and other unused resources. Or output can exceed potential output. These two possibilities are shown in Figure 6–4, where we have superimposed the vertical potential GDP line to indicate potential. In the left-hand panel of Figure 6–4, output is below potential. In the right-hand panel output is above potential.

Although the price level doesn't change immediately when firms find themselves producing above or below their potential, there is pressure for a price adjustment. When demand is below potential output there is pressure toward a downward move in prices; conversely, when demand is above potential there is pressure for an increase in prices.

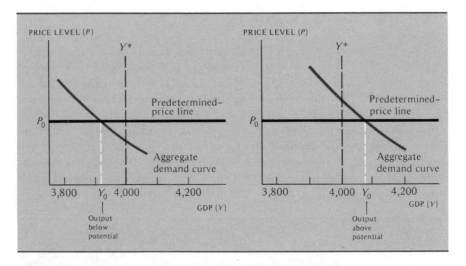

Figure 6–4.   GDP CAN BE ABOVE OR BELOW POTENTIAL GDP.
On the left, the level of output is below potential. On the right, the level of output is above potential. Both of these positions will exert pressure on firms to change prices. On the left there is pressure to lower prices. On the right there is pressure to raise prices.

How the Real Business-Cycle School Views Economic Fluctuations

The real business-cycle school, led by Edward Prescott of the University of Minnesota, Charles Plosser of the University of Rochester, and others, believes that monetary forces have little or no effect on employment and output. Only non-monetary or 'real' factors such as technical change affect output.

Members of the school disagree strongly with the ideas of Figure 6–4. They argue that the economy is always at the intersection of aggregate supply and aggregate demand (see, for example, Edward Prescott, 'Theory Ahead of Business Cycle Measurement,' *Federal Reserve Bank of Minneapolis Quarterly Review*, Fall 1986, pp. 9–23). They see no reason to develop a monetary or aggregate demand theory to explain fluctuations in total output because they feel that these fluctuations are due to technological factors.

Because it is an observed fact that output and employment go through recessions and booms, real business-cycle theorists have to interpret those fluctuations as movements along an elastic supply curve or as shifts of the supply curve. They posit random shifts up and down in the production function. In years of high productivity, people work harder and output and employment are both high. Recessions are times when technology has regressed and people want to work less. The properties of the aggregate supply curve that we have described in this chapter are inconsistent with the real business-cycle view. The aggregate supply curve in Figure 6–1 doesn't shift left or right from year to year the way GDP does.

Real business-cycle theory, which is discussed in more detail in Chapter 15, Section 1, is highly controversial and is accepted by only a minority of macroeconomists. But it is a stimulating and important development which may influence the way many macroeconomists think.

This adjustment leads to a changed price level for the *next year,* or period —not this year. For example, if aggregate demand is above potential in the year 2001, then the price level will be higher in 2002. When the aggregate demand curve is drawn to determine output for the year 2002, the predetermined price will be drawn at a higher level. If the intersection of the aggregate demand curve for the year 2002 and this new price line is still not at an output level equal to potential, then there will be a further adjustment in prices, but this will not occur until the year 2003. The process continues this way until aggregate demand equals potential output, at which point the desire for firms to adjust their prices will no longer be present. Whether or not the process converges depends on the explicit price-adjustment process, which we consider in the next section.

The process by which the price level changes from one year to the next is *dynamic* in the sense that the variables are changing from one period to the next. The impact of a change in the money supply, for example, has effects on the price level that take place over a number of years. The model that we use to describe this dynamic process is an example of a **dynamic model.** The dynamic model is illustrated in Figure 6–5.

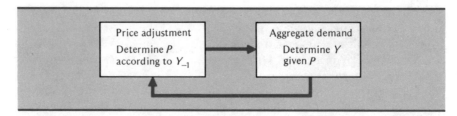

Figure 6–5. DYNAMIC ANALYSIS AND PREDETERMINED VARIABLES.
The price-adjustment process is shown on the left. It determines the current price level based on the recent past level of output. Then the aggregate demand schedule, shown on the right, determines the level of output given the price level.

Determination of Output in the Short Run

1. In the short run, the price level is predetermined. It can change over time but, in a given year, the events of that year have almost no impact on the price level.

2. The level of output is determined by the point on the aggregate demand schedule corresponding to the price level.

3. In the short run, output can be below or above its potential level.

DETERMINATION OF UNEMPLOYMENT

We noted in Chapter 3 that Okun's law establishes a close relation between real GDP and unemployment. When an adverse shock shifts the aggregate demand curve inward, real GDP falls, as shown in Figure 6–3. Figure 6–6 starts with that shift and shows how it generates an increase in unemployment as well. From the decline in real GDP, the lower left-hand diagram converts it into a change in the percentage deviation of GDP from potential, $(Y - Y^*)/Y^*$. Then the right-hand part of the diagram computes the resulting increase in unemployment by applying Okun's law.

A number of important mechanisms are at work in the process described in Figure 6–6. If GDP declines, employers need a smaller amount of labour input. They cut the length of the work week, they reduce the intensity of work, and they cut the size of the work force. Most of the workers who are laid off become unemployed. In addition, people who are looking for work find it harder to locate jobs. Because of the importance of hours reductions and the common pattern of retaining workers during temporary declines in demand (called labour hoarding), a 2 percent decline in GDP is associated with only a 1 percentage point increase in unemployment. This close negative relation is one of the most reliable generalisations that macroecono-

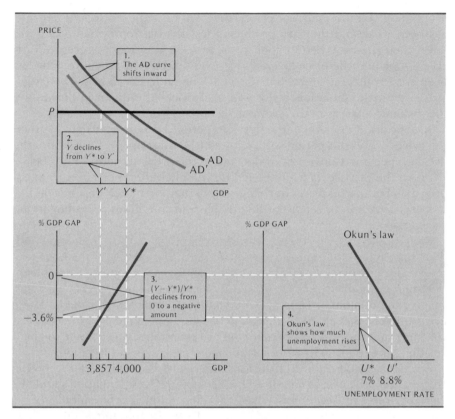

Figure 6–6.   DETERMINATION OF UNEMPLOYMENT.
The upper left-hand diagram shows the aggregate demand curve in its original position
and after it shifts inward. Output declines from Y* to Y'. The lower left-hand diagram
translates the GDP decline into percentage terms. The right-hand diagram uses Okun's
law to show the amount of increase in unemployment that occurs as a result of the decline in GDP.

mists have found. Whenever some force causes GDP to decline, you can be
confident that unemployment will rise.

6.3 Price Adjustment

Decisions about prices are made by individual firms. But, moving from the
level of the firm to the macro level is tricky. Finding a good way to model
aggregate price adjustment has occupied much of the research time of macroeconomics during the last 20 years. Mistakes in understanding price adjustment have generated some of the most glaring errors in the field of
macroeconomics.

   Firms adjust their prices in response to conditions in their markets. If demand has been strong and they are producing more than they think is ap-

propriate given their current prices, they will raise their prices. If demand has been weak and they are producing less than is appropriate, they will lower their prices. When we look at the process in terms of aggregate variables—GDP and the price level—prices will tend to rise whenever GDP has been above potential and will tend to fall when it has been below potential. We have already mentioned this aspect of price adjustment in illustrating the dynamic analysis in the previous section.

Specifically, if demand in the previous period Y_{-1} is greater than Y^*, then the price level P this period will be raised (the subscript "-1" indicates the previous period). Conversely, if demand in the previous period Y_{-1} is below Y^*, then the price level P will be bid down. The difference $Y_{-1} - Y^*$ measures the pressure on prices to change. Note that, because P depends on Y_{-1}, it is *predetermined,* or set, according to demand conditions prevailing in the recent past.

Firms make their price decisions with the prices of their inputs in mind. The most important input is labour. Hence, the behaviour of the wage rate is a major determinant of price adjustment. Wages tend to rise when conditions in the labour market are strong. Remember that, when real GDP is high relative to potential, unemployment is low and employment is high. These are conditions that are likely to lead to rising wages. Wage pressure comes at the same time as the direct pressure on prices and the two combine to give a relation between the deviation of GDP from potential and inflation.

Economic intuition and historical experience both support the notion that market pressure, as measured by $(Y_{-1} - Y^*)/Y^*$, and inflation should be related. Recently, economists have developed microeconomically based theories of price adjustment, and Chapter 16 will go into the details of some of these theories. What follows is a first look at the way price decisions by firms become magnified into an aggregate price-adjustment equation.

RELATIVE PRICE SETTING AND IMPERFECT INFORMATION

The price adjustment made by one firm will be *relative* to what that firm feels is the prevailing level of prices for its product. The reason for making a price adjustment is to change the price relative to other prices in the economy. When General Motors sets the suggested retail price for Chevrolets for the upcoming year, it is important that the company take account of what price Ford is likely to set. If GM comes out with a Chevrolet price that is way above the Ford price it will suffer a loss of sales, which it might have avoided had it known what Ford was up to. The prevailing level of prices— that is, the level of prices for closely related products during the price-setting period—is an integral part of the information a firm requires to make a good pricing decision.

Firms do not know with certainty the relevant prevailing level of prices. Moreover, because the firm is likely to keep its price at the new level for some time into the future, knowing the appropriate prevailing price will require estimating the future pricing decisions of other firms that will be setting their prices in the upcoming months. The firm must therefore form an estimate or expectation of the prevailing price level in the economy. If GM expects the price of Fords to hold steady, then it is more likely to hold its Chevrolet price steady. If GM expects Ford to increase its prices by 10 percent, then it will be more willing to raise its Chevrolet price by that amount, give or take the desired relative price adjustment it desires.

Suppose that firms try to raise their own prices above the prevailing price when demand conditions are strong and real GDP is above potential. Specifically, suppose that the typical firm raises its own price f percentage points above its forecast of the prevailing price for every percent by which GDP exceeds potential. In other words,

$$\frac{\text{Firm's price}}{\text{Forecasted prevailing price}} = 1 + f \frac{Y_{-1} - Y^*}{Y^*}.$$

For example, if the coefficient f equals .3 and the proportional deviation of GDP from potential, $(Y_{-1} - Y^*)/Y^*$, is .1, then the firm's price divided by its forecasted prevailing price will be 1.03. In other words, the firm's price will be 3 percent higher than the forecasted prevailing price.

Now suppose that the typical firm forecasts the prevailing price to be the same as last year's price; that is, the forecasted prevailing price equals P_{-1}. Then we can write the resulting price-adjustment equation as

$$\frac{P}{P_{-1}} = 1 + f \frac{Y_{-1} - Y^*}{Y^*}. \tag{6-3}$$

Now, if we replace the 1 in Equation 6–3 by P_{-1}/P_{-1} and move it to the left-hand side, we get

$$\pi = f \frac{Y_{-1} - Y^*}{Y^*}, \tag{6-4}$$

where the Greek letter π stands for the **rate of inflation** $(P - P_{-1})/P_{-1}$. It says that the rate of inflation is positively related to the deviation of real GDP from potential. Such a relationship is called a **Phillips curve** after A. W. Phillips who first studied it.[3]

Forecasting this year's prevailing price to be the same as last year's price would not be a good assumption for price adjustment if prices were expected to rise in the future. Suppose that firms expect inflation. They must forecast the growth of the prevailing price and, if a relative price increase is called for, increase their own prices faster than the prevailing price is in-

---

[3] A. W. Phillips fit this type of relationship to data for the United Kingdom from 1861 to 1957. The fit was very good. Phillips actually related percentage changes in wages to the unemployment rate. See 'The Relationship between the Unemployment Rate and the Rate of Change in Money Wage Rates in the United Kingdom, 1861–1957,' *Economica*, November 1957, pp. 283–299.

creasing. If GM, for example, forecast the price of Fords to increase by 10 percent, and desired a 2 percent cut in the relative price of Chevrolets to stimulate sales, it would increase its Chevrolet price by 8 percent. The implication of this type of behaviour is to add a term π^e to the Phillips curve:

$$\pi = \pi^e + f \frac{Y_{-1} - Y^*}{Y^*}. \qquad (6\text{--}5)$$

Note that this equation is the same as Equation 6–4 with expected inflation π^e added to the right-hand side. The curve is illustrated in Figure 6–7. When inflation becomes expected at the rate π^e, it shifts the Phillips curve upward.

The Phillips curve with the expectation term has an important property: If real GDP is above potential GDP on a permanent basis, then the rate of inflation will never stop increasing. As actual inflation rises, expected inflation, π^e, will also begin to rise: As firms see actual inflation increasing they will begin to expect higher inflation. But then actual inflation will have to be even higher, because GDP can exceed potential only if actual inflation exceeds expected inflation. This property of the price-adjustment equation has been called the **accelerationist** or, equivalently, the **natural rate property.** The terminology comes from the property that if real GDP is brought above its potential level, Y^*, then the inflation rate will rise and the price level will accelerate. There is no way for real GDP to be held constantly

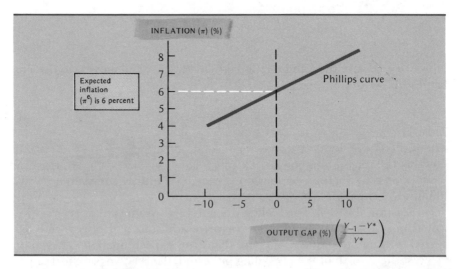

Figure 6–7. THE PHILLIPS CURVE.
The higher GDP is relative to potential, the higher will be the rate of inflation. When GDP is below potential, the Phillips curve predicts that inflation will be below the expected rate of inflation. In booms, when GDP is above potential, actual inflation will exceed expected inflation. The higher the expected rate of inflation, the higher is actual inflation. The expectational shift is important in explaining persistent inflationary periods, like the 1970s, in Canada.

above its natural level without inflation constantly rising limitlessly. In an economy with reasonably stable prices, the level of real GDP will tend to be near potential, on the average.

This relationship between expectations and price adjustment was developed in the late 1960s by Edmund Phelps of Columbia University, and independently by Milton Friedman. At the time that they developed the relationship most economists had not considered the role of expectations in the Phillips curve. Friedman presented his controversial theory at a large convention of economists in his presidential address to the American Economic Association in 1967.[4] At that time inflation was still pretty low and many economists were skeptical of the Friedman-Phelps theory. As it turned out, data that became available in the 1970s showed that Friedman and Phelps were right.

Figure 6–8 shows that there has been a stable Phillips curve price-adjustment relationship of the type proposed by Phelps and Friedman for the pe-

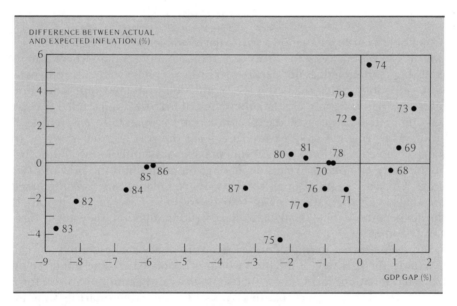

Figure 6–8.   PRICE ADJUSTMENT IN CANADA SINCE 1968.
The horizontal axis shows the percentage departure of GDP from potential. The vertical axis shows the amount of inflation relative to the expected amount. Years in the upper right are ones when output was above potential and inflation exceeded expectations. Years in the lower left are recession years when output was low and inflation subsided. Most years fit into the general pattern predicted by the price-adjustment relationship. In this diagram, the expected inflation rate is measured as the inflation rate in the year before. Source: *Canadian Economic Observer,* Tables 1.3, 1.13.

[4] Friedman's presidential address is found in Milton Friedman, 'The Role of Monetary Policy,' *American Economic Review,* March 1968, pp. 1–17. Phelps first published his results in Edmund S. Phelps, 'Money Wage Dynamics and Labor Market Equilibrium,' *Journal of Political Economy,* July–August 1967, pp. 678–711.

riod since 1968. The vertical axis measures the amount by which inflation exceeds expectations and the horizontal axis measures the gap between actual and potential GDP. According to the theory, this relationship should be stable over time and upward sloping. This is by and large the case except for an apparent leftward shift in the mid-1980s.

WHAT DETERMINES EXPECTED INFLATION?

So far we have said nothing about what determines the expected inflation term π^e in the price-adjustment equation. The simplest idea is that π^e depends on past inflation. Suppose, for example, that GM thinks that the price of Fords will increase at 60 percent of last year's inflation rate. Suppose that all firms forecast inflation in the same way. Then the expectation π^e would be set to $.6\,\pi_{-1}$. Equation 6–5 would then become

$$\pi = .6\,\pi_{-1} + f\,\frac{Y_{-1} - Y^*}{Y^*}. \tag{6-6}$$

This Phillips curve is based on a particularly simple model of expected inflation. It is a rational way for firms to forecast in an economy where abnormally high inflation does not persist year after year but eventually returns to lower inflation, so that the best guess of inflation would be simply a fraction (like .6) of past inflation. On the other hand, if high inflation tended to last a long time, then people would expect inflation to come down only a little, if at all. They might simply extrapolate from the past and set $\pi^e = \pi_{-1}$. In more complex inflationary environments, expected inflation would probably be more complex, perhaps depending on inflation in the previous two years. Or firms might attempt to guess where inflation was heading based on what they expect the Bank of Canada to do with the money supply: If they expect the Bank of Canada to start fighting inflation, they might forecast less inflation.

But even if firms attempted to bring future policy changes into their calculations, the past rate of inflation would probably have some influence on expected inflation. Firms know that some prices will continue to rise for a while, even if they suspect that the Bank of Canada would start fighting inflation right away. Some price increases would already have been announced by other firms, and these will take place in any case. Wage setting is also a factor in price decisions, and wage increases negotiated in earlier years would continue. The relative price-setting idea in the price-adjustment theory described above is also important for wage setting. For unionized workers, such as the Canadian Auto Workers, the contractual nature of wage setting is conspicuous. Contracts frequently set wages for as much as 3 years in advance. The contracts of different unions are set at different times. When wage contracts are renegotiated, they are influenced by the wages currently being paid to workers under contracts settled in previous years, and by what other workers are likely to get in upcoming years. The expected rate of increase in prevailing wages is thus influenced by past wage decisions, as well as by upcoming wage decisions. Overlapping contracts mean that expected inflation will be related to past inflation even if forecasters are perfectly rational and forward-looking.

We will come back to alternative ideas about expected inflation in Chapter 16. For now we will use Equation 6–6 as our Phillips curve.

Note that the larger the difference between real GDP and potential GDP, the faster will be the reduction in inflation. Suppose, for example, that the coefficient f in the price-adjustment equation is equal to .2. This value implies that a 5 percent fall of real GDP below potential GDP, which lasts for one year, will reduce the rate of inflation by 1 percent. When output is 10 percent below normal for one period the rate of inflation will be reduced by 2 percent. Of course, the price-adjustment equation works the other way around as well. If real GDP rises above potential GDP, then there will be an increase in inflation.

Price Adjustment

1. The process of price adjustment moves the economy toward potential GDP. When the price level is too high, GDP is less than potential, prices fall, demand rises, and eventually full employment is restored.

2. If no inflation is expected, the price-adjustment equation relates the rate of inflation to the deviation of GDP from potential.

3. Under conditions of expected inflation, the price-adjustment relation is shifted upward by the amount of the expected inflation.

4. A simple model of expected inflation is that expected inflation is given by a fraction of last year's inflation.

6.4 Combining Aggregate Demand and Price Adjustment

The aggregate demand curve, in combination with price adjustment, governs the dynamic response of the economy to a change in economic conditions. As an example, we will look at what happens to the economy when the money supply is increased. We assume the economy starts out with zero inflation and GDP equals potential GDP. The increase in money initially pushes the aggregate demand curve to the right and increases output. Gradually prices rise to bring the economy back into equilibrium at potential GDP. We now trace out the path of GDP as it returns to potential.

On the left in Figure 6–9 we show the aggregate demand curve intersecting the predetermined-price line. The intersection occurs where output is

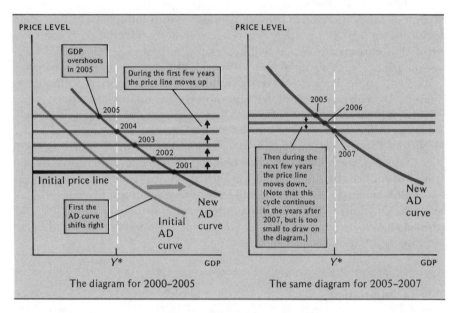

Figure 6-9. AGGREGATE DEMAND AND PRICE ADJUSTMENT.
The diagram on the left shows the aggregate demand curve intersecting the predetermined-price line at potential GDP (Y*). After an increase in the money supply the aggregate demand curve shifts to the right. Then the price line begins to shift up and output declines. GDP falls below potential GDP, but then there is downward pressure on prices and the price line begins to fall. This is shown in the diagram on the right, where we see the same aggregate demand curve during the years after 2005.

equal to potential GDP. Suppose that this is the situation in the year 2000 but that starting in 2001 the Bank of Canada increases the money supply. The aggregate demand curve shifts to the right, and GDP expands. The economy goes into a boom during 2001, and GDP is above potential GDP. Since the stimulus to aggregate demand comes from monetary policy we know from the IS-LM method of the last chapter that the interest rate falls, stimulating investment spending. Then the multiplier expands GDP. All this occurs during the year that the money supply increased.

With firms now operating above potential, they will adjust their prices upward. The price line will shift up. We can easily calculate the exact size of the price adjustment in 2002 using the price-adjustment equation (6–6): Calculate the inflation rate $(P - P_{-1})/P_{-1}$ associated with the level of GDP for 2001. Multiply this inflation rate by the previous price level P_{-1} to get the absolute change in the price level, $P - P_{-1}$, and hence the price level P for 2002. We shift the price line in Figure 6–9 upward by the amount of this price increase. Assuming that the Bank of Canada does not increase the money supply again, the same aggregate demand curve continues to apply in 2002. Thus, the new point of intersection of aggregate demand and the price line occurs at a lower level of output compared with 2001. The economy moves up and to the left along the aggregate demand curve.

What is happening in the economy? At a higher price level more money is demanded by people for transactions purposes. But since the Bank of Canada doesn't increase the money supply again, this puts upward pressure on the interest rate. The higher interest rate reduces investment below what it was in 2001, and this reduction has multiplier effects throughout the economy. GDP falls.

According to Figure 6–9, GDP is still above potential in 2002. Thus there will be another upward adjustment in the price level. This time the price adjustment will be the sum of two effects. The two effects correspond to the two terms on the right-hand side of the price-adjustment equation (6–6). Because there was inflation the year before, there will be expectations of continuing inflation in 2002. This factor will add to inflation. On the other hand, output is no longer so far above potential. The contribution from that term in the Phillips curve will be smaller. In the scenario in Figure 6–9, the price rises even more in 2003 than it did in 2002. Again the aggregate demand curve doesn't move, so output falls again in 2003. As before, the interest rate rises because of the increased demand for money, and this reduces investment.

If output is still above potential or if inflation is still above where it started in 2000, there will be another price adjustment. Hence, GDP will continue to fall. Note that GDP will fall below—overshoot—potential because expected inflation keeps the price line moving up.

This overshooting is shown in Figure 6–9 where GDP falls below potential GDP in the year 2005. But this overshooting creates forces that reverse the decline in GDP and bring it back to potential GDP. When actual GDP is below potential GDP, the depressed economic conditions place downward pressure on prices. As firms bid down their prices the price line begins to shift down as shown in the right-hand panel of Figure 6–9. As the price line reverses its previous movement and begins to shift down, GDP will start to rise. The process continues period after period until GDP eventually returns to potential. In Figure 6–9 we show GDP getting very close to potential in the year 2007, though there are tiny movements (too small to see on the diagram) after that. By 2007 inflation has returned to zero, where it began in 2000, though the price level has permanently increased. The price level has increased by the same amount that the money supply increased.

Note how the graphical analysis in Figure 6–9 is divided into different phases. In the first phase (on the left), the price line is moving up. In the second phase (on the right), the price line is moving down. The graphs are divided into phases because it is confusing to draw in the new price lines in 2006–2007 on top of the previous ones for 2000–2005. Rather, the new diagram on the right has simply omitted the previous price lines. The important thing to imagine visually is that the price line moves up and then reverses direction, moving down. Getting out a pencil and paper and shifting the price lines yourself will convince you of the dynamic nature of this adjustment process. Alternatively this movement can be shown very nicely with computer graphics in which you can see the price line moving gradually over time (see the box on p. 143).

The fact that the economy returns to potential GDP, as shown in Figure 6–9, is a key result of macroeconomic theory. In the long run, an increase in money does not increase GDP. The increase in money eventually leads to an increase in the price level of the same magnitude. This raises interest rates back to where they were before the monetary expansion, and eventually reduces investment back to its original level. Note that all other variables—except the price level—are also back to where they were before the increase in the money supply. In the long run the increase in money had no effect on real variables. For this reason we say that money is *neutral* in the long run. But money is not neutral in the short run. It has a powerful effect on output in the short run before prices have had a chance to adjust. The same analysis holds in reverse for a decline in the money supply.

Figure 6–10 summarises how GDP and the price level move over time according to the above calculations. The upper panel shows GDP and the lower

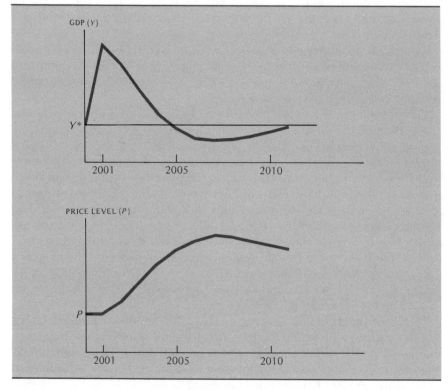

Figure 6–10. GDP AND THE PRICE LEVEL AFTER AN INCREASE IN MONEY.
The top panel shows GDP and the bottom panel shows the price level. Time (years) is measured on the horizontal axis of both diagrams. The money supply is increased in the year 2001, which is marked on both graphs. At first, GDP increases and the price level does not move. In 2002 the level of GDP begins to fall, and the price level begins to rise. The movements continue in 2003 and so on until GDP returns to potential GDP, and the price level rises by the full amount that the money supply increases.

High-Tech Macro Graphics

As is clear from the discussion in this chapter the adjustment of the economy to a change in the money supply or government spending is a dynamic process that takes place over a number of years. To illustrate this process with graphs it is necessary to keep the curves in the diagrams shifting year after year. These shifting curves trace out the movement of the economy as in Figure 6–9.

But just as one or two snapshots in the sports pages or even a chalk talk after the game cannot capture all the action of a football game,

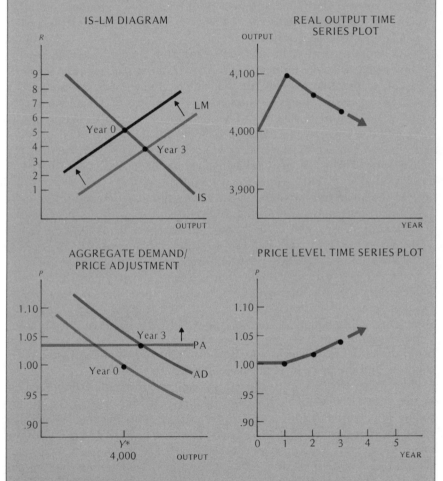

A MACROSOLVE COMPUTER SCREEN.
This is what the computer screen looks like after 3 periods. The arrows indicate the direction of movement. Note that the upper left-hand panel is the standard IS-LM diagram discussed in Chapter 5, the lower left-hand panel is Figure 6–9, and the right-hand panels are those shown in Figure 6–10.

neither can the printed page or a blackboard completely capture the action of the economy as it responds to changes in government policy. Fortunately, recent advances in computer technology now permit a more comprehensive picture of the action in macroeconomics.

MACROSOLVE, a computer program written by Stephen King and Rick McConnell to go along with this text, provides state-of-the-art computer graphics that show how the curves of macroeconomics shift over time. On an IBM-PC or compatible computer or an Apple Macintosh the program simultaneously shows not only the AD curve and price-adjustment diagram in Figure 6–9, but also the IS-LM diagram, and even the time series charts for output and prices in Figure 6–10. Just as video replay helps both players and coaches (not to mention the fans) in football, MACROSOLVE is a great boon to students and teachers in macroeconomics.

As an illustration of how MACROSOLVE works, the sketch above shows what the computer screen looks like three periods after an increase in the money supply (the same case considered in the text).

There are four charts on the screen. In the upper left-hand area is the standard IS-LM diagram. The increase in the money supply has shifted the LM curve to the right from its initial position in period 0. By period 3, however, the LM curve is shifting back to the left as prices are rising. The arrows in the sketch illustrate the movement of the LM curve that you would see on the computer screen.

In the lower left-hand area is the same aggregate demand price-adjustment diagram shown in Figure 6–9, but only with the price line that applies in period 3. Note how the aggregate demand curve has shifted to the right, and that the price line is shifting up.

Finally, on the right are the two time series charts that appear in Figure 6–10, now with only the first three periods shown and with arrows indicating how the lines would be extending themselves on the computer screen.

panel shows the price level. Note how GDP returns to potential after overshooting and the price level permanently rises to a new level.

Fiscal policy works a little differently from monetary policy. Suppose that in the same circumstances government spending, rather than the money supply, is increased in 2001. Again the aggregate demand curve shifts to the right just as in Figure 6–9, and GDP rises. But now, from IS-LM results of the previous chapter, we know that interest rates rise during the first year, crowding out investment and net exports and partly offsetting the stimulus to demand from government spending. As the price level begins to rise, interest rates rise further, and more investment and exports are crowded out.

In the long run GDP returns to potential GDP even though government spending has been increased. As a result we know that in the long run investment spending and net exports must have been reduced by exactly the same amount that government spending was raised. Otherwise, the income identity would be violated. In the long run fiscal policy completely crowds out investment spending and net exports. The rise in the price level increases the demand for money, leading to higher interest rates and less investment spending and net exports.

ALGEBRAIC DERIVATION

The response of the economy to a change in the money supply can also be analysed with algebra. Suppose the aggregate demand curve is the one considered in the examples in Chapter 5. Setting G equal to 750 in Equation 5–12 yields

$$Y = 2{,}287 + 2.855\frac{M}{P}. \tag{6–7}$$

Combining this aggregate demand curve with one of the price-adjustment equations, 6–6, describes the evolution of the economy. We then use Equation 6–6 along with Equation 6–7. The algebraic calculations proceed in flip-flop fashion, just like the graphical analysis: Take the price level as given, use Equation 6–7 to find output Y, and plug the value of output into Equation 6–6. Calculate the inflation rate π and the price level P for the next year. Then go back to Equation 6–7 with the new price level, determine a new output level, and so on. The answers you get at each stage are the same as the ones that can be read off the numerical scales in Figure 6–9.

We have now completed our first description of the complete macroeconomic model. In the short run, the price level inherited from the previous year together with the current aggregate demand schedule determine the level of output. In the medium run, the process of price adjustment moves the economy closer to potential GDP. Eventually, the economy will reach potential GDP. Our next step is to use this complete model to examine the important issues of monetary and fiscal policy.

The Movement to Potential GDP

1. The aggregate demand curve and the price-adjustment line govern the movement to potential GDP. After being pushed away from potential GDP by monetary policy or fiscal policy—whether toward slack or overfull employment—the economy will eventually reach potential GDP.

2. Because expected inflation responds to past inflation, the economy overshoots potential GDP. However, it will still eventually reach potential GDP.

3. An increase in the money supply increases GDP in the short run, but eventually this effect wears off as the price level rises. In the long run an increase in the money supply has no effect on GDP.

4. An increase in government spending also increases GDP in the short run, though there is some reduction in investment and net exports. In the long run, the stimulus to GDP is completely offset by a decline in investment and net exports as interest rates rise. In the long run fiscal policy completely crowds out investment spending and net exports.

Review and Practice

MAJOR POINTS

1. Potential GDP is the level of real GDP that would be produced if everybody was working who wanted a job given existing incentives.

2. The aggregate supply schedule is a vertical line; supply equals potential GDP no matter what the price level.

3. In the long run, the economy moves to potential GDP.

4. In the short run, the price level is predetermined. GDP is determined by aggregate demand at the predetermined price level.

5. The process of price adjustment takes the economy to potential GDP over time. When output exceeds potential, prices rise; when output is below potential, prices fall.

6. If inflation becomes expected by the public, the price-adjustment schedule is shifted upward by the amount of the expected inflation.

7. The economy reaches potential GDP through the repetition of price adjustment year after year. Each year, conditions in the previous year determine the price level coming into the year. Then the aggregate demand curve determines GDP.

8. Because expected inflation fluctuates according to recent actual inflation, the economy overshoots its potential on the way to its final resting point at potential.

KEY TERMS AND CONCEPTS

Aggregate supply	Predetermined price level
Potential employment	Dynamic model
Production function	Price adjustment
Potential output	Phillips curve
Full-employment level of output	Expected inflation
Aggregate supply schedule	Accelerationist property

QUESTIONS FOR DISCUSSION AND REVIEW

1. What determines potential employment? Why doesn't potential employment depend on the price level?

2. What is the justification for taking the capital stock as given?

3. Explain how the Phillips curve is derived from a model of relative price setting. What happens to the Phillips curve if firms expect inflation?

4. Explain why money is neutral in the long run but not in the short run.

5. Does government spending completely crowd out private investment and net exports in the long run? What about the short run? Why?

6. Why does the economy overshoot potential GDP when expectations of inflation depend on last year's inflation?

7. What is the accelerationist hypothesis? What would happen to inflation if policy makers attempted to hold unemployment below the natural rate year after year?

8. If firms expect the Bank of Canada to start fighting inflation with an aim to bringing it to zero, will their expectations of inflation suddenly drop to zero? Why?

PROBLEMS

Numerical
1. Suppose the economy has the aggregate demand curve derived in the examples of Chapter 5. That is,

$$Y = 2{,}287 + 2.855\frac{M}{P}$$

and the price-adjustment schedule

$$\pi = 1.2\left(\frac{Y_{-1} - 4{,}000}{4{,}000}\right).$$

The money supply is $600 billion.

a. Plot the aggregate demand curve and the potential GDP line. Explain why the *aggregate demand curve is not a straight line*.
b. If $P_0 = .5$ what will Y_0 be? Will this place upward or downward pressure on prices?
c. Compute the path of the economy—that is, calculate GDP, the price level, and inflation—for each year until GDP is within 1 percent of potential.
d. Diagram the economy's path on the demand curve plotted in Part a. Then, draw your own version of Figures 6–9 and 6–10. (You may assume that inflation was initially zero.) From these graphs, does the economy overshoot or converge directly to equilibrium?
e. Assume now that inflation is given by $\pi = .6\pi_{-1} + 1.2\,[(Y_{-1}-4{,}000)/4{,}000]$. Compute the path of the economy for the first five years, and diagram the economy's path as in Part d. Now is there overshooting?
f. In Part e, what does the $.6\pi_{-1}$ term in the price-adjustment equation represent? Explain the relationship between this term and overshooting.

2. Again, suppose that the model of the economy is given by
$$Y = 2{,}287 + 2.855(M/P)$$
$$\pi = .6\pi_{-1} + 1.2[(Y_{-1}-4{,}000)/4{,}000].$$

where $P_0 = 1$ and $\pi_0 = 0$.

a. For what value of M will GDP equal potential? Assuming that $M = \$550$ billion, calculate output, inflation, and the price level for Years 0 through 5.
b. Using the numerical IS-LM equations given in Chapter 5, find out what happens to the interest rate, consumption, investment, and net exports in each of these years. What is the long-run equilibrium value for each of these variables?

c. Note that income, consumption, and investment tend to overshoot and undershoot at the same time. Using the IS-LM diagram, explain why this is necessarily so. Why isn't the same true of net exports?

Analytical

1. In view of Okun's law, is it possible for both output and the unemployment rate to increase from one year to the next? Explain.

2. According to the price-adjustment equation 6–6, is inflation a predetermined variable? Explain.

3. Using the expectations-augmented Phillips curve, explain what happens when the unemployment rate decreases for one year and then returns to the natural rate. Then describe what happens when the unemployment rate stays below the natural rate year after year.

4. From a position of potential GDP and zero inflation the government increases defence spending. Describe qualitatively, using words and graphs but no algebra, what happens to GDP, the price level, interest rates, consumption, investment, and net exports. Assume at first that expectations of inflation remain at zero. Then describe how your answers change if expectations of inflation depend on last year's inflation.

5. Suppose that there is a sudden and permanent decline in potential GDP. Describe the behaviour of prices, output, interest rates, consumption, investment, and net exports.

6. Suppose that output is below potential output in Year 0. Prices that year are given by P_0. In Year 1 (with the level of potential output unchanged) the Bank of Canada stimulates the economy by shifting the aggregate demand curve until it intersects the point (P_0, Y^*).
   a. Sketch the aggregate demand curve for Years 0 and 1. Describe the action taken by the Bank of Canada.
   b. Assume that the price-adjustment process is given by Equation 6–6. If inflation in Year 0 was zero, how will prices behave in Year 1? Sketch the price-adjustment curve for Year 1.
   c. Explain why output in Year 1 will be above potential.
   d. In which direction should the Bank of Canada have shifted the aggregate demand curve in order to set $Y_1 = Y^*$? Is it possible to say?
   e. Given the Bank of Canada's action, is it possible to say whether prices will increase or decrease in Year 2? Why or why not?

7. The Phillips curve originally described a relationship between inflation and unemployment. In this problem we look at some of the properties of the Phillips curve.
   a. Use Okun's law and the price-adjustment equation given in 6–5 to derive a relationship between inflation and unemployment. Is inflation related to current or past values of unemployment? Sketch a graph of this relationship, with inflation on the vertical axis and unemployment on the horizontal axis.
   b. How would a change in Y^* shift the curve? How about a change in U^*?
   c. How would a change in π^e shift the curve?
   d. In view of your answers to Parts b and c, how might the Phillips curve have actually shifted in the 1970s? Explain.

8. When thinking about the adjustment process, remember that underlying the aggregate demand curve are the IS and LM curves.
   a. During the adjustment process, is it the IS or LM curve that moves? Why does it move?

b. Assume that the economy is initially in equilibrium and then the IS curve is shifted out. Using the IS and LM graphs, show the adjustment process (i) for the case when the economy returns directly to equilibrium, and (ii) for the overshooting case.

c. Repeat Part b for the case where the LM curve is initially shifted out.

9. Suppose that at the end of 1988 Y is equal to potential, $P=1.2$, and $M=\$720$ billion. Assume that prices in 1988 have risen by 5 percent. The aggregate demand and price-adjustment equations for the economy are given by:

$$Y = Y_0 + 2.855 \, (M/P)$$
$$\pi = \pi^e + f[(Y_{-1}-Y^*)/Y^*].$$

a. What is the real money supply? What is the nominal money supply?

b. Suppose the Bank of Canada wishes to maintain output at potential for each of the years 1989 through 1992. If $\pi^e=\pi_{-1}$, what are the required increases in the real and nominal money stocks for each of the four years? Repeat your calculations for $\pi^e = .6\pi_{-1}$.

c. Qualitatively, how would your answers to Part b differ if the Bank of Canada expected government spending to increase in each of these years?

7

Macroeconomic Policy: A First Look

MONETARY AND fiscal policy have powerful effects on the economy. Changes in the money supply or in government spending have an immediate impact on real GDP and a delayed impact on the price level. An increase in the money supply, for example, will stimulate output and employment in the short run, with inflation rising later, and real GDP eventually returning to normal.

Because monetary and fiscal policies have such powerful effects on the economy they are constantly being discussed and debated. In early 1988, for example, members of Parliament, private-sector economists, academics, and journalists were all evaluating the anti-inflationary stance being taken by John Crow, the governor of the Bank of Canada. The governor's decisions have an impact on all of us, as for instance on those of us buying or selling a home and concerned about what happens to mortgage interest rates.

Discussions about fiscal policy have recently focussed on the federal government deficit. Concerns about interest rates and investment were part of the reason. An increase in government spending will obviously increase the deficit if not matched by an increase in taxes. Our analysis shows that an increase in the deficit will increase interest rates, and crowd out some investment even as it stimulates the economy in the short run.

In this chapter we take a systematic look at the formulation and evaluation of macroeconomic policy, that is, monetary and fiscal policy. The fact that monetary and fiscal policy have the potential to affect the economy

150

suggests that these policies might be used to improve macroeconomic performance. We will want to investigate whether this is the case.

Sometimes there are economic **shocks** or **disturbances** to the economy that might call for policy intervention. We distinguish between two types of disturbances in this chapter: **aggregate demand disturbances** and **price disturbances.** An aggregate demand disturbance is some event other than a change in policy that shifts the aggregate demand curve. A price disturbance is some event that shifts the price-adjustment relationship. The immediate effect of a price disturbance is to change the price level, unless policy acts to offset the disturbance. Another important policy problem is disinflation—getting the inflation rate down after it has been built into the economy. This chapter considers the appropriate policy responses.

We will also consider the issue of how to choose between monetary and fiscal policy. Both types of policies can shift aggregate demand, but they have different effects on investment and net exports.

7.1 Shocks and Disturbances to the Economy

Unforeseen or unpredictable events are commonplace in the economy. At the most basic level, many of the relationships we use to describe the economy depend on human behaviour, which is frequently erratic. Keynes used the term 'animal spirits' to characterise the moods of business people. Other economic relationships depend on technology—the money demand relationship, for example, depends on how technically advanced the financial system is. It seems that, no matter how successful we are in describing the systematic parts of economic behaviour, there will always be some room for uncertainty, and thus for shocks and disturbances to our economic relationships. The model we developed in Chapters 4 through 6 would certainly be affected by such shocks.

SHOCKS TO AGGREGATE DEMAND

Consider some examples of shocks to the behavioural relationships of the extended model of aggregate demand:

1. A recession in the United States reduces American demand for Canadian goods. Net export demand falls.
2. A new type of credit card makes it easier to get by with less cash. The money demand schedule shifts inward.

These two examples are illustrated graphically in Figure 7–1. Recall that net export demand depends on both income and the interest rate. Given a particular level of income, say, $Y = Y_0$, we can draw the relationship between net exports and the real interest rate as the downward-sloping line shown in Figure 7–1. If U.S. income falls, net export demand will be lower at each

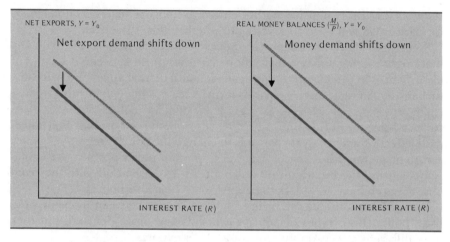

Figure 7–1.   SHOCKS: DOWNWARD SHIFTS IN NET EXPORTS AND MONEY DEMAND.
On the left, a reduction in U.S. demand for Canadian goods shifts the net export schedule downward. On the right, changes in financial markets reduce money demand. The money demand function shifts inward.

possible interest rate, given that $Y = Y_0$. The decline in money demand would shift the demand for money inward for each interest rate, once again taking the level of income as unchanged.

Disturbances can be distinguished according to whether they are temporary or permanent. This distinction is important for policy makers: A temporary disturbance might be ignored because its effects will disappear soon anyway. In practice it is difficult to distinguish between temporary and permanent shocks when they occur.

ANALYSING THE EFFECTS OF AGGREGATE DEMAND SHOCKS

Disturbances both to spending and to money demand, the two major components of our model of aggregate demand, shift the aggregate demand curve: The downward shift in net export demand pushes the aggregate demand curve to the left. The downward shift in money demand has the same effect as an increase in the money supply, which we know shifts the aggregate demand curve to the right.

These shifts in the aggregate demand curve have immediate impacts on real GDP, as shown in Figure 7–2.

From the analysis used in Chapter 6 we can trace out the full dynamic movement of the economy in response to the aggregate demand shocks:

1. With real GDP below potential GDP after the drop in net exports, the price level will begin to fall. Firms have found that the demand for

Figure 7-2.   DISTURBANCES SHIFT THE AGGREGATE DEMAND SCHEDULE.
On the left, aggregate demand has shifted inward because of the decline in the net export schedule. On the right, aggregate demand has shifted outward because of the decline in money demand. On the left, GDP falls at first. Then the economy moves down and to the right along the AD schedule until it finally reaches equilibrium again at a lower price. On the right, GDP rises at first. Then the economy moves up and to the left along the AD schedule until it reaches equilibrium again at a higher price.

their products has fallen off and they will start to cut their prices. This drop in the price level is shown in Figure 7-2 as a movement down and to the right along the aggregate demand (AD) schedule. The lower price level causes the interest rate to fall. With a lower interest rate, investment spending and net exports will increase. The increase in investment and net exports will tend to offset the original decline in net exports. This process of gradual price adjustment will continue as long as real GDP is below potential GDP. By the time that real GDP has again recovered and returned to potential GDP, investment and net exports will have increased by just the amount that net exports fell in the first place. The interest rate will be lower by enough to stimulate this much investment and net exports. In the long run, real GDP will be back to normal, but during the period of gradual price adjustment the economy will have gone through a recession with an increase in unemployment.

2. When the demand for money drops, the aggregate demand curve will shift outward. The interest rate drops; investment, net exports, and consumption rise. But higher GDP will cause prices to rise, tending to raise the interest rate. Through this process of gradual price adjustment the economy will eventually return to normal. In the meantime, however, the economy has experienced a period of inflation and a boom in economic activity.

To summarise the examples, in both cases there is a shock to aggregate demand that temporarily moves the economy away from potential GDP and sends the economy into either a boom or a recession. Through gradual adjustment of the price level the economy eventually returns to normal.

SHOCKS TO THE PRICE LEVEL

The shocks considered so far had the effect of shifting the aggregate demand curve. Another type of shock occurs when the price level shifts. There are several reasons why this might occur:

1. The price of an input to the economy might suddenly rise; the best example is an increase in the price of oil, such as occurred in the 1970s. Suppose that the members of the Organization of Petroleum Exporting Countries (OPEC) increase the price of crude oil; the aim is to increase the relative price of crude. But other price setters in petroleum-related industries—gasoline, heating oil, plastics, etc.—will at first increase their own price not knowing whether a change in profit margins is necessary. This will tend to increase the price of all petroleum-related products. Moreover, prices in other energy industries will also tend to increase. Unless there is a fall in the price of other goods, when the producing countries increase the price of crude oil there will be an increase in the overall price level.

2. A large group of workers—perhaps during a union negotiation—may get a wage increase that is abnormally high. When firms pass on the wage increase in the form of higher prices, there will be an upward shift in the price—a price shock.

3. Firms might simply make a mistake and increase their prices, perhaps because they mistakenly expected an increase in inflation.

4. The Canada-U.S. exchange rate may fall dramatically. The Canadian dollar prices of some of the goods that are imported from the United States would rise. The prices of many internationally traded goods are set in U.S. dollars. As a result, the Canadian dollar prices of these goods would increase when the Canada-U.S. exchange rate falls, even if these goods are not purchased from Americans.

A price shock is shown in Figure 7–3. If monetary and fiscal policies do not change, then real GDP will fall below potential GDP. After the initial price shock the economy will be operating below its full-employment level at Y_1. With no increase in the money supply, this will in turn cause prices to fall as firms try to cut prices to increase sales. The fall in prices corresponds to a downward movement in the price-adjustment curve, which will continue until real GDP is equal to potential GDP. Eventually, therefore, the economy returns to normal operating levels. In the meantime the price shock has caused a recession. The period of recession puts downward pressure on prices and offsets the original price shock.

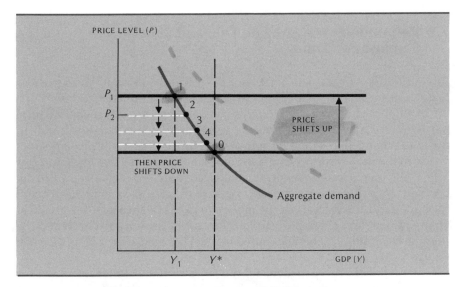

Figure 7–3.   AN UPWARD SHOCK IN THE PRICE LEVEL.
Real GDP is reduced when the price level jumps up—the economy moves to point 1, up
and to the left along the aggregate demand curve. Then the process of price adjustment
causes the economy to return gradually to its original equilibrium as the price level falls.

Economic Shocks

1. There can be unexpected shifts in spending—for example, the
   amount of investment undertaken by businesses at any given interest rate might rise or fall.

2. There can be unexpected shifts in the money market—for example, the amount of money demanded by the public at any given interest rate might rise or fall.

3. Spending or money market shifts will in turn shift the aggregate
   demand curve. At first, real GDP will rise or fall. Later, as price adjustment occurs, real GDP will return to equilibrium and the price
   level will move to a permanently different level.

4. Prices may shift unexpectedly as well. When that occurs, real GDP
   will change at first. Then price adjustment will return the economy
   to its original equilibrium. Neither the price level nor GDP will
   change in the long run.

7.2 Responding to Aggregate Demand Shocks: Stabilisation Policy

In considering appropriate responses to aggregate demand shocks, let us first consider the case of a fall in the demand for our exports. This occurs, for example, whenever the United States experiences a recession. Unless the Bank of Canada takes action the aggregate demand curve will shift to the left. What action would be appropriate for the Bank of Canada? An increase in the money supply would lower the interest rate. The lower interest rate would increase investment. It would also cause the exchange rate to depreciate, restoring some of the lost export demand and curbing the demand for imports. If the increase in the money stock is just the right size, its effect on investment and net exports will exactly offset the leftward movement in the aggregate supply schedule caused by the U.S. recession. This is shown in Figure 7–4.

Other types of aggregate demand shocks raise many of the same issues for aggregate demand policy. Suppose, for example, that there is an investment boom caused by business optimism that pushes the aggregate demand schedule to the right. Without any policy response we know from the discussion above that this will result in a temporary increase in GDP followed by a period of increase in the rate of inflation. Policy makers could avoid this instability by taking some action to reduce aggregate demand: The money supply or government spending could be reduced or, alternatively, taxes could be raised. Any of these actions would have the effect of bringing the aggregate demand schedule back to the left.

The type of aggregate demand policy outlined in these two examples is called **countercyclical stabilisation policy,** because it attempts to counter

Figure 7–4. FALL IN EXPORT DEMAND.
A fall in export demand shifts the aggregate demand schedule to the left, reducing real GDP. Timely action by the Bank of Canada to increase the money supply could prevent it.

those disturbances to the economy that otherwise would cause cyclical fluctuations in real GDP and the price level. Such a policy is also sometimes called *activist,* because the policy makers are actively manipulating the instruments of monetary and fiscal policy.

WHEN DO MACROECONOMISTS DISAGREE ABOUT STABILISATION POLICY?

The underlying objective of policy in the above examples is to maintain a steady or stable level of aggregate demand. The importance of a stable aggregate demand is one that has been recognised by most economists since the 1930s. Even economists who normally differ on other issues agree on the principle that it is desirable to maintain a stable growth of aggregate demand. Keynesians such as the late Walter Heller of the University of Minnesota and James Tobin of Yale University agree with monetarists such as Milton Friedman on this point. As we showed in Chapter 2, the Canadian economy has been much more stable in the period following World War II —even if one includes the turbulent 1970s and early 1980s. Many economists feel that this improvement in macroeconomic performance is related to the recognition of the importance of stable aggregate demand growth.

If macroeconomists agree on such a basic issue as the goal of stable aggregate demand growth, then what is all the highly publicised controversy and disagreement about? Primarily, it is about the means of achieving this goal. Monetarists—including Milton Friedman, Allan Meltzer of Carnegie-Mellon University, and Karl Brunner of the University of Rochester—argue that the most effective way to maintain a steady growth of aggregate demand is to keep the rate of money growth constant. But how does such a view make sense in light of our previous arguments that timely changes in the money supply can be used to offset disturbances to the economy?

Monetarists have no disagreement about the powerful effects that changes in the money supply can have on real GDP in the short run—for example, Milton Friedman has said, 'Because prices are sticky, faster or slower monetary growth initially affects output. . . . But these effects wear off. After about two years the main effect is on inflation.'[1] However, for a number of reasons, monetarists feel that it is not possible to use monetary policy in the way that we illustrated. Their criticism of activist policy is that the impact of monetary policy occurs with a lag and the length of this lag is uncertain. Because of the lag, monetary stimulus or restraint may come too late. In an attempt to offset a decline in investment, the policy response may come after the recession is over, when the economy is recovering back to potential GDP. This might add to the expansion in economic activity and exacerbate the economic fluctuation. Figure 7–5 illustrates this possibility. Because of the practical difficulties of conducting monetary policy in an

---

[1] See *Newsweek,* July 12, 1982, p. 64.

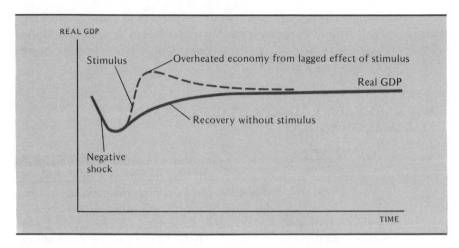

Figure 7–5. LAGS IN POLICY.
A change in the policy instrument that arrives too late might exacerbate the fluctuations in the economy.

uncertain world, monetarists argue that attempts to manipulate monetary policy to offset disturbances to the economy could result in more rather than fewer fluctuations in economic activity.

A second argument of the monetarists against activist countercyclical policy is that the instruments of policy might be used to overstimulate the economy and bring about higher and higher rates of inflation. In our examples of countercyclical policy we never considered the possibility that policy makers might try to push the economy beyond its potential output, Y^*. But clearly this is feasible. With prices temporarily sticky, real GDP can be raised above potential output Y^*. The long-run consequence of such a policy will be a higher price level, but, in the short run, real GDP growth could appear quite attractive. The danger of such an inflationary policy becomes quite serious when policy decisions are made in a political environment. The long-run disadvantages of such a policy may be overlooked in favour of short-run advantages when election day nears. This is one of the arguments in favour of placing restrictions on the ability of the federal government to affect the policy decisions of the Bank of Canada. The relationship between the Bank of Canada and the federal government is discussed on pages 321–22.

Other arguments against the use of countercyclical policy have come from the new classical macroeconomists, such as Thomas Sargent of Stanford University and Neil Wallace of the University of Minnesota. The argument here is quite different from that of the monetarists; it questions whether systematic changes in the instruments of aggregate demand policy can have any effect at all on real GDP and employment. The new classical school focusses directly on the issue of price stickiness, which we have taken for granted in most of our discussion. If prices are not sticky—that is, if they are adjusted instantaneously without a lag—then any systematic attempt to use policy to affect real GDP will be offset by changes in the price level. In such a world aggregate demand policy has no role at all except to control prices.

A second related point of the new classical view is that the need for policy intervention is not adequately justified. For example, in the case where an increase in investment brings about a boom in the economy, the appropriate aggregate demand policy is to offset this boom by a contractionary monetary policy. The justification for such a policy is that it reduces the fluctuations in real GDP and the price level. However, the behaviour of investment is altered as a result of the policy. The objection raised by the new classical school is that it might be more harmful to cut the investment demand than it would be to have the fluctuations in real GDP and the price level.

Policy Response to Demand Shocks

1. When an aggregate demand shock occurs, monetary or fiscal policy can offset the shock. Whatever inward or outward shift of the aggregate demand curve has taken place can be reversed through a policy move in the opposite direction.

2. Though almost all economists agree on the desirability of stable aggregate demand, many believe that active policy might add to the instability rather than offset it. Monetarists generally oppose enacting policy that attempts to act against aggregate demand shifts.

3. Another argument against active policy comes from the new classical school. They argue that a systematic policy of offsetting demand disturbances won't have any effect on GDP.

7.3 Responding to Price Shocks

The response to a price shock raises some more difficult issues than does the response to a demand shock. Even under the best of circumstances—no lags or uncertainty in the conduct of policy—such a shock will inevitably affect either the price level or real GDP.

Suppose, for example, that there is a price shock of the type illustrated in Figure 7–6. As we discussed above, with no policy response, such a price shock tends to reduce real GDP and raise the price level. This is shown in the left-hand panel of Figure 7–6.

Now, suppose that the monetary authorities increase the money supply in response to the price shock. As shown in Figure 7–6, this shifts the aggregate demand curve outward and tends to mitigate the downward fluctua-

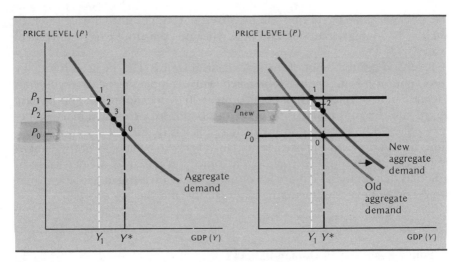

Figure 7–6. MONETARY RESPONSE TO A PRICE SHOCK.
On the left, monetary policy does not respond to the price shock. The shock raises the price level from P_0 to P_1. Output falls from $Y*$ to Y_1. Then the price-adjustment process starts. In the next year the price level drops to P_2. Eventually prices fall back to normal and output returns to potential output. On the right, monetary policy responds to the price shock. The money supply is increased and the aggregate demand curve moves outward. At the new intersection of the price line (point 1), there is less downward pressure on the price level because output at Y_1 is closer to potential than in the panel on the left. Assuming that the new aggregate demand curve is maintained, eventually the price level falls to the level marked P_{new}.

tion in real GDP. However, the increase in the money supply will exacerbate the fluctuation in the price level. If output does not fall much below potential there will be little downward pressure on the price level. The price level will stay high for a longer time and never return to normal if the money supply is not reduced again. As shown in the right-hand panel of Figure 7–6, the price line will remain at a higher level if the aggregate demand curve remains at its new higher position. In the sense that there is less downward pressure on the price level so that it never returns to normal, there is thus less price stability with the policy that tries to offset the fluctuation in real GDP. In other words, with a supply shock there is a trade-off between the stability of real GDP and the stability of the price level.

Policies that increase the money supply in response to positive price shocks are called **accommodative policies.** A policy that holds the money supply constant is called **nonaccommodative.** Figure 7–7 summarises, for the two policies, the behaviour of GDP and the price level after a price shock. The plots show the results of the calculations of GDP and the price level from Figure 7–6. Clearly the accommodative policy is better in terms of the performance of GDP, but is worse in terms of the performance of the price level.

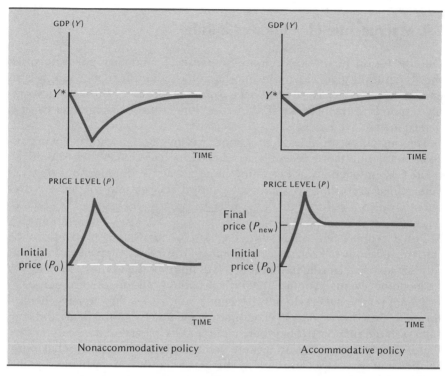

Figure 7–7. THE RESPONSE OF THE PRICE LEVEL AND GDP TO PRICE SHOCKS FOR ACCOMMODATIVE AND NONACCOMMODATIVE POLICIES.
These charts summarise the calculations from Figure 7–6. The nonaccommodative policy is shown on the left and the accommodative policy is shown on the right. Output is more stable with the accommodative policy, but the price level is less stable.

Policy Response to Price Shocks

1. In the absence of a policy response (that is, with a nonaccommodative monetary policy), a positive price shock causes a rise in the price level and a sustained period of economic slack.

2. Price shocks create a serious problem for policy. If policy tries to limit the decline in GDP from a positive price shock, it will make the price level less stable. If it tries to head off the inflation, it will deepen the recession.

7.4 Macroeconomic Policy as a Rule

Our discussion of the appropriate response of monetary policy to price shocks naturally gives rise to the question of whether the money supply is an exogenous variable, as we have been assuming all along. If the money supply responds to the price level, then it no longer can be exogenous for it is determined in the model.

Treating policy variables as exogenous has long been a tradition in macroeconomics. But more recently an alternative view, that they should be treated as endogenous, is becoming more attractive. Endogenous policy is determined according to some behavioural relationship, or what is frequently called a **policy rule.** The most frequently discussed policy rule in macroeconomics is the fixed growth rate rule for the money supply that Milton Friedman and other monetarists have advocated. A fixed growth rate rule is simply to keep the growth rate of the money supply constant. But this is a very special rule in that it involves no response of the money supply to economic events. A more general rule would call for some response.

Even if policy makers do not determine policy according to a mechanical formula, they do respond to economic events much like the firms and consumers in the economy. Their behaviour and its impact on the economy are therefore probably more accurately described by a systematic behavioural relationship. If so, we can think of the behavioural relationship as a policy rule.

We saw in Section 7.3 that an accommodative monetary policy was one that reacted to a positive price shock with an increase in the money supply. We showed the effect of this type of policy on the fluctuations of real GDP and the price level, by treating the money supply as exogenous. If the Bank of Canada regularly, or systematically, reacted to price disturbances in this way, then we would say that the Bank was following an accommodative policy rule. The money supply would not be an exogenous variable. It would join the list of endogenous variables to be determined in the basic macroeconomic model. As with the other endogenous variables, a behavioural relationship would describe how the monetary authorities determined the money supply. In fact, the policy rule *is* that behavioural relationship.

The derivation of the policy rule and its effects on the economy can be shown graphically. In Figure 7–8 we show how the monetary authorities react to price shocks. There are several different price lines drawn. Each line represents a price shock of different magnitude. For each price shock, we show how the Bank of Canada reacts by shifting the aggregate demand schedule outward. This accommodative reaction leads to intersections of the aggregate demand curve and the price line at higher levels of real GDP than would otherwise occur, shown by the dark line. This line represents the combined effect of the accommodative policy and the price shocks. Note that it is downward sloping—like an aggregate demand curve—but it is steeper than the aggregate demand curve without the influence of policy.

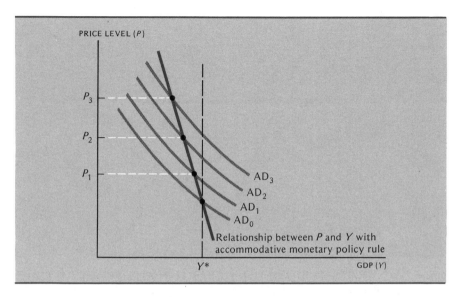

Figure 7–8. EFFECT OF AN ACCOMMODATIVE POLICY RULE.
If the price shock is small, so that the price level is P_1, the Bank of Canada sets the money supply so that the AD schedule is AD_1. For larger shocks that raise the price level to P_2 or P_3, the Bank raises the money stock more, so that the corresponding AD schedule is AD_2 or AD_3. The set of intersections traces out the policy rule schedule. This schedule includes the monetary response.

The policy of responding *as a rule* to price shocks causes the economy to behave as if it had a steeper aggregate demand curve. The more accommodative the policy, the steeper the policy rule curve.

In Figure 7–9 we have drawn the two curves that correspond to alternative policy rules. The first policy rule is quite simple: Leave the money stock fixed. Thus GDP is determined by the price level and the usual aggregate demand curve. The second policy rule is accommodative. In this case GDP is found using the price level and the policy rule schedule, which is derived as in Figure 7–8.

Note that when there is a price shock the accommodative rule results in a smaller decline in GDP than does the fixed money stock rule. However, the smaller negative gap leads to less subsequent downward pressure on prices, and therefore less price stability over a longer period of time. A more accommodative policy rule would produce a steeper policy rule schedule. If such a rule was in place the price shock would cause an even smaller change in output, and this would result in even less downward pressure on prices in the future. Thus more accommodative policies result in greater stability of real GDP but less stability of prices. Less accommodative policies tend to increase price stability but at the cost of less real GDP stability.

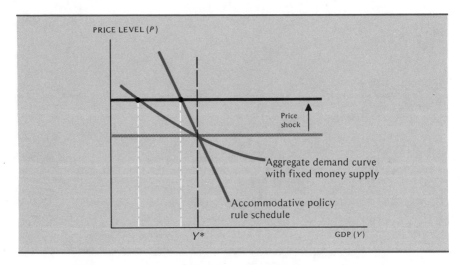

Figure 7–9. AGGREGATE DEMAND UNDER ALTERNATIVE MONETARY POLICY RULES.
More accommodative policy makes the policy rule schedule steeper. As a result, the downward shift in output after a price shock is smaller the more accommodative the policy.

WHY FOCUS ON POLICY RULES?

Aside from the desire to model the economy and the effect of policy as accurately as possible, there are two important reasons why policy analysis in recent years has concentrated on rules rather than on exogenous changes in the policy instruments. These reasons will come up naturally in our later discussions of policy rules, but are worth mentioning briefly now. One reason is the recognition that expectations of policy can influence how policy affects the economy. If people anticipate a certain policy, then they will act differently than if that policy were unanticipated. By stipulating policy as a rule, policy makers are implicitly stating how policy will react to future contingencies. That the money supply will increase if there is a positive price shock is an example of such a rule.

A second reason for the emphasis on rules is the problem of time inconsistency. Unless there is a systematic way for policy makers to commit themselves to operating in a particular way in the future, there will be a temptation to change their plans from what they announce. That is, policy makers will be tempted—in order to stimulate the economy—to do things differently from what they had promised. The advantage of policy rules in such situations is that rules commit policy makers to behaving in a certain predictable way—as long as they do not break the rule! We will come back to the problem of time inconsistency in Chapter 18.[2]

---

[2] The importance of time inconsistency for macroeconomics was first pointed out in Guillermo Calvo, 'On the Time Inconsistency of Optimal Policy in a Monetary Economy,' *Econometrica*, Vol. 46, pp. 1141–1428, 1978, and in Finn Kydland and Edward Prescott, 'Rules Rather

---

Policy Rules

1. When macro policy is conducted according to a rule, it means that the policy instruments become endogenous variables—they respond in a known way to changes that occur in the economy.

2. One important example of a rule is the way the Bank of Canada responds to a price shock. The Bank can emphasise price stability by not adjusting money growth after a shock, which will worsen unemployment. Or, it can limit unemployment by adding to inflation through monetary expansion.

3. Many economists favour policy rules because their use may have favourable effects on the economy through expectations and because a binding rule may prevent shortsighted attempts to overstimulate the economy.

7.5 Disinflation

The problem of maintaining price stability in the face of price shocks is closely related to another type of price stabilisation problem: that of bringing down the rate of inflation when it has become too high and has become incorporated into people's expectations and price-setting behaviour. This latter problem is called the problem of **disinflation:** that is, reducing the rate of inflation. This problem requires us to pay close attention to the role of expectations in the Phillips curve.

The Phillips relationship, as we saw in Chapter 6, can be written

$$\pi = \pi^e + f \frac{Y_{-1} - Y*}{Y*}. \tag{7-1}$$

The most challenging problem of disinflation occurs when the expected rate of inflation equals last period's inflation rate; $\pi^e = \pi_{-1}$. With this expectation of inflation the only way that inflation can be reduced is by letting actual output Y drop below potential output $Y*$. Equation 7-1 states that the *change* in the rate of inflation over its previous level π_{-1} depends on the percentage deviation of GDP from potential GDP.

The Phillips curve tells us that if the inflation rate is viewed by the policy makers as being too high and in need of reduction, then some type of a recession is inevitable. The essential policy questions related to disinflation are how long and how deep the recession should be. In other words, how sharply should the policy makers reduce the policy instruments to bring

---

about a path for real GDP that is consistent with the desired reduction in inflation?

SETTING POLICY TO HIT A TARGET LEVEL OF GDP

To answer this question, we first need to show how the policy instruments, such as the money supply or government spending, can be manipulated to get a desired path for real GDP. Recall that, with the price-adjustment equation, the price level is predetermined during the course of any particular year. Recall also that monetary and fiscal policies shift the aggregate demand curve to the right or left. The intersection of the aggregate demand curve with the price line gives the current value of real GDP. Hence, by changing monetary policy the Bank of Canada can achieve just about any value of real GDP that it wants. Note that this ability of the monetary authorities to pinpoint real GDP perfectly needs to be qualified by the inherent uncertainty and lags in the effect of monetary policy that we discussed above. In addition, we know that aiming for a value of real GDP above potential GDP will soon result in an inflationary spiral. But in the policy problem considered here, this latter possibility is not an issue because the aim of policy is to set real GDP below potential GDP in order to put downward pressure on prices and reduce the rate of inflation.

So far we have used the aggregate demand method to find a level of GDP for a given level of the money supply or government spending. Now we must work the method in *reverse*. We want to find a level for the money supply for a given target level of GDP. The idea is illustrated in Figure 7–10. The economy is shown to be operating at potential output, Y^*. Suppose that the Bank of Canada wants to set the money supply to push the economy to a lower target level, Y_1. What level of the money supply should it choose? The answer, as shown in the right-hand panel of Figure 7–10, is to reduce the money supply to the level that sets the aggregate demand curve at a point of intersection with the predetermined-price line at the target level of output Y_1.

Numerical Example. Suppose that the aggregate demand curve is the one that we studied in Chapter 5, Equation 5–12, namely,

$$Y = 1,432 + 1.14G + 2.855\frac{M}{P}. \tag{7-2}$$

Suppose that government spending G has been set at \$750 billion and that the predetermined price level P equals 1. Potential GDP is \$4,000 billion. The Bank of Canada now wants to choose a money supply M to bring actual GDP below potential to \$3,900. For $G = 750$ and $P = 1$, the aggregate demand curve looks like

$$Y = 2,287 + 2.855M. \tag{7-3}$$

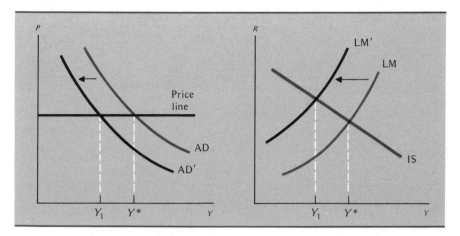

Figure 7–10.   AGGREGATE DEMAND IN REVERSE: THE MONEY SUPPLY IS SET TO HIT A GDP TARGET.
The left-hand panel shows the situation in the economy. Output is equal to potential output, Y^*. The Bank of Canada wants to set the money supply so that the output is reduced to the level Y_1. To do this it must shift the aggregate demand curve inward from AD to AD'. As shown in the right-hand panel, the Bank thus reduces the money supply by an amount that makes the LM curve shift in and intersect the IS curve at a level of output equal to Y_1.

The level of the money supply is found by setting output Y in Equation 7–3 equal to 3,900 and finding M. The answer is

$$M = \frac{3,900 - 2,287}{2.855} = \frac{1,613}{2.855}, \tag{7–4}$$

or 566. Note how this calculation is just the reverse of setting M to a value and finding Y, as we did in the numerical example in Chapter 5.

ALTERNATIVE DISINFLATION PATHS

Suppose that the rate of inflation has risen to 10 percent, and that the Bank of Canada wants to disinflate. Table 7–1 shows three alternative paths for the deviation of GDP from potential GDP, $(Y - Y^*)/Y^*$, and corresponding paths for the inflation rate. Year zero shows the starting point, with inflation at 10 percent and GDP equal to potential GDP. The Bank of Canada begins to take actions to reduce inflation in Year 1. The values in Table 7–1 are obtained directly from the Phillips curve in Equation 7–1. For these calculations, we assume that the coefficient f in Equation 7–1 is .2. Recall also that we assume that the public believes that inflation will persist unless the Bank contracts the economy. The simple model of expected inflation with this property that we use is $\pi^e = \pi_{-1}$. Inflation expected this year is last year's actual inflation.

Table 7–1.   THREE PATHS FOR INFLATION AND THE GDP GAP

Year	Path 1 GDP Gap	Path 1 Inflation	Path 2 GDP Gap	Path 2 Inflation	Path 3 GDP Gap	Path 3 Inflation
0	0	10	0	10	0	10
1	0	10	−5	10	−10	10
2	0	10	−5	9	−10	8
3	0	10	−5	8	−10	6
4	0	10	−5	7	−10	4
5	0	10	−5	6	0	2
6	0	10	−5	5	0	2
7	0	10	−5	4	0	2
8	0	10	−5	3	0	2
9	0	10	0	2	0	2
10	0	10	0	2	0	2

Note: The GDP gap is the deviation of GDP from potential measured in percent; that is, gap = $(Y - Y^*)/Y^*$ times 100. Inflation is the percentage change in the price level. Each path shows the GDP gap and inflation over a 10-year period. The calculations are made with the Phillips curve of Equation 7–1 with f equal to .2. In the first path, policy holds real GDP at its potential level. Inflation stays at 10 percent. In the second path, real GDP is depressed below potential. Inflation drops steadily to 2 percent. When it reaches 2 percent, policy eases and GDP pulls back up to potential. In the third path, policy is even more contractionary at first; GDP is 10 percent below normal. Inflation drops to 2 percent sooner than in the second path.

The three alternatives given in Table 7–1 are all feasible for the Bank of Canada to undertake. Clearly, if the Bank can pick any value of output Y it wants in the short run, it can also pick any value for the deviation of output from potential output, $(Y - Y^*)/Y^*$, since potential GDP (Y^*) is exogenous. By setting the money supply so that the aggregate demand curve is in the appropriate place, the Bank can set output and hence the deviations of output from potential output to the desired level.

The three alternatives were selected to indicate the kind of choice that the monetary authorities have to make when faced with excess inflation. Perhaps the most important thing to note about the choices is that none of them is a good one. The latter two involve a recession, as the inflation rate is decreased. The first avoids a recession, but gets no reduction in inflation.

The second two paths are both successful in getting the inflation rate down from 10 to 2 percent. But there are important differences between the two paths. Path 2 involves a longer, but shallower recession. GDP is just 5 percent below potential for the entire period of the disinflation. However, it takes 8 years to get the inflation rate down to 2 percent. Path 3 involves a shorter recession, but it is quite deep. GDP is 10 percent below potential. In this case the inflation rate is reduced more quickly, reaching 2 percent in 4 years. Clearly, more extreme possibilities are open to policy makers. Or a compromise between Path 2 and Path 3 is another possibility. The paths we have presented in Table 7–1 are meant to be representative of the choices facing policy makers. We illustrate in Figure 7–11A how Paths 2 and 3 differ.

In comparing these paths it is important to note their implications for unemployment. Suppose that the natural rate of unemployment that corresponds to potential GDP is 7 percent. Recall from Chapter 3 that Okun's law translates a GDP gap of 1 percent into .5 percentage point of unemployment. Thus, for Path 2 the unemployment rate rises to 8.5 percent for 8 years, and for Path 3 the unemployment rate rises to 12 percent for 4 years. Of course the unemployment rate stays at 7 percent, the natural rate, for all years in Path 1.

Assuming that some reduction in inflation is desired, we must rule out Path 1. The choice is between Path 2 and Path 3. If very high unemployment is to be avoided, then a more gradual approach is appropriate. Moreover, the more gradual approach is better because it gives people more time to adjust their plans.

An illuminating way to compare the two disinflation paths is shown in Figure 7–11B. The rate of inflation is on the vertical axis and the GDP gap is on the horizontal axis. At the start of the disinflation, the inflation rate of 10 percent and the GDP gap of zero are shown by the point labeled '0' in the diagram. The alternative possibilities for inflation and the GDP gap are then shown as two big Cs emanating from this initial point and ending up at the final point. The C for Path 3 is much more elongated than the C for Path 2. This illustrates how Path 3 pushes the economy into a deeper recession than does Path 2.

The alternative possibilities in Figure 7–11B are very similar to the choices faced by policy makers in the early 1980s. The Bank of Canada had become increasingly concerned about inflation and began a new, more restrictive, policy in 1981. In a speech made after the new policy was implemented, Gerald Bouey, then the governor of the Bank of Canada, reiterated the Bank's resolve to 'reduce the rate of inflation by restraining the rate of monetary expansion' even though he recognised that 'the process of reducing inflation is painful and costly.'[3]

Figure 7–12 shows the actual rates of inflation and the GDP gap that occurred, starting from 1981. The combination of restrictive Canadian monetary policy and a recession in the United States brought about by a similar policy reduced aggregate demand in Canada in 1982. The substantial decline in the rate of inflation did not occur until the next year. By the mid-1980s the rate of inflation as measured by the GDP implicit price index had stabilised at about 3 percent. The economy emerged from the recession with a steady growth rate, but growth was not fast enough to return the economy all the way to potential by 1987.

[3] Speech by Gerald K. Bouey given in Ottawa on April 6, 1982, reprinted in the *Bank of Canada Review,* April 1982.

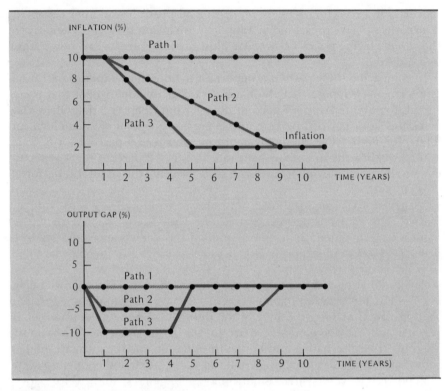

Figure 7–11A.   A COMPARISON OF TWO DISINFLATIONS.
Path 2 shows a long, shallow recession (lower panel) and a slow decline in inflation (upper panel). Path 3 shows a short, deep recession and a speedy decline in inflation. Path 1 has no recession and no disinflation.

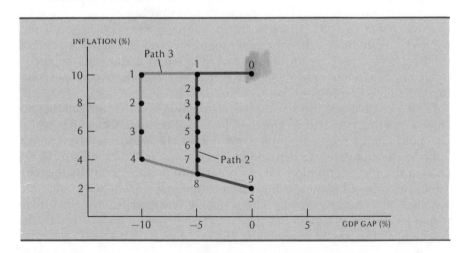

Figure 7–11B.   INFLATION AND GDP DURING TWO DISINFLATIONS.
The inflation rate is on the vertical axis; the GDP gap is on the horizontal axis. Both disinflation paths start at '0' and end at the same point. Path 3 shows a much deeper recession than does Path 2.

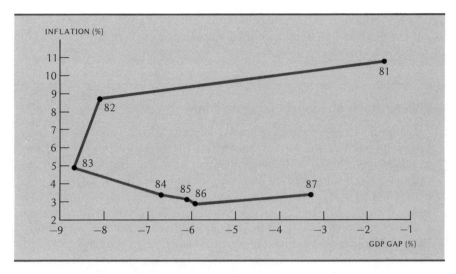

Figure 7–12.   THE 1981–87 DISINFLATION.
As money growth was reduced, GDP fell far below potential. The tight monetary policy was continued and eventually inflation came down. Compared to our Paths 2 and 3 in Figures 7–11A and 7–11B, the actual path looks more like the deeper recession path.

Comparing the actual 1981–87 experience with the two alternative paths, Paths 2 and 3, it looks as if the Bank attempted to bring about something closer to Path 3. The fall in GDP was sufficient to bring inflation down much more quickly than in the gradual path. As a result, the rate of increase in the GDP implicit price index fell from 11 percent in 1981 to 5 percent two years later and about 3 percent in the year after that.

However, the recession may have been more severe than the Bank intended. Peter Howitt of the University of Western Ontario has argued that the Bank of Canada misinterpreted developments in the money and foreign exchange markets, resulting in greater monetary restraint than was necessary for the Bank's anti-inflation goals.[4] This episode is discussed more fully in Chapter 18.

In 1988 the new governor of the Bank of Canada, John Crow, faced a similar decision. The rate of inflation as measured by the CPI had been roughly 4 percent per year since 1986. In a speech made at the University of Alberta, Crow stated that he was not satisfied with this level of inflation, even though it had been roughly stable. He said that his goal was to achieve price stability, that is, to bring the inflation rate down to zero. Nonetheless, at that time he was not willing to use a very restrictive monetary policy in order to reduce the rate of inflation. Although the recession of 1982 had produced a

[4] See Peter Howitt, *Monetary Policy in Transition: A Study of Bank of Canada Policy, 1982–85*, C.D. Howe Institute/Prentice-Hall, 1986.

significant reduction in the rate of inflation, the new governor was reluctant to put the economy through a similar experience once again.[5]

Other Schools of Thought on Disinflation

Figure 7–12 seems to give strong support to the general view we have expressed in this book: It takes time for prices to adjust, and during that time, there can be large departures of GDP from potential. A negative shock to aggregate demand, such as one chosen by the Bank of Canada to bring inflation to an end, sends the economy into recession.

Other schools of thought do not agree that recession is inevitably the result of a policy to bring down inflation. One of the most influential critics of the view expressed in this book is Thomas Sargent of Stanford University. Sargent has written,

... Inflation only *seems* to have a momentum of its own; it is actually the long-term government policy of persistently running large deficits and creating money at high rates which imparts the momentum to the inflation rate. An implication of this view is that inflation can be stopped much more quickly than advocates of the "momentum" view have indicated and that their estimates of the length of time and the costs of stopping inflation in terms of foregone output ... are erroneous. This is not to say that it would be easy to eradicate inflation. On the contrary, it would require far more than a few temporary restrictive fiscal and monetary actions. It would require a change in the policy regime; there must be an abrupt change in the continuing government policy, or strategy, for setting deficits now and in the future that is sufficiently binding as to be widely believed [emphasis added].*

Sargent examines the experiences of four countries—Austria, Hungary, Germany, and Poland—in the aftermath of World War I to test his theory. In his view, the magnitude of the recession that accompanied huge decreases in the inflation rate in these countries was small in those instances where there was a complete change in government policy and the public believed that highly expansionary fiscal and monetary policy had ended.

* 'The Ends of Four Big Inflations,' in Robert E. Hall, ed., *Inflation: Causes and Effects,* a National Bureau of Economic Research Project Report, University of Chicago Press, 1982, pp. 41–97.

---

[5] The text of the University of Alberta speech can be found in John Crow, 'The Work of Canadian Monetary Policy,' reprinted in *Bank of Canada Review,* February 1988. In a speech at the University of British Columbia some months later Crow stated explicitly what recent events had revealed; he was not prepared to engineer a recession in order to reduce the inflation rate.

Disinflation

1. The price-adjustment equation is the key to understanding the problem of disinflation. Unemployment must rise above its natural rate to reduce inflation.

2. Monetary policy can be set to aim for a target for GDP. Policy makers have a choice of disinflationary paths—the more unemployment they choose, the faster disinflation will occur.

3. From 1981 through 1984, rapid disinflation occurred in Canada, with GDP well below potential and high rates of unemployment.

7.6 Monetary Policy and Regional Disparity

A recession raises the unemployment rate in all regions of the country, but the strength of the effect varies by region. For example, in the 1982 recession employment fell more than 5 percent in Quebec and British Columbia, while the decline was only 2.4 percent in Ontario and 1.3 percent in the prairie provinces. The recovery in employment has also been uneven. From 1982 to 1987 employment grew 3 percent per year on average in Ontario, 1.6 percent per year in British Columbia, and .9 percent on the prairies.

It is not possible to have different monetary policies for each region. Monetary policy affects the economy through its impact on financial markets. Canadian financial markets are highly integrated across the country. For example, an increase in the demand for bank loans in any single region will increase the interest rate on these loans in every region as funds are drawn from across the country into the region with the increase in demand. This is as it should be. The financial markets efficiently transfer funds from savers seeking high returns to the borrowers who are best able to generate these returns, wherever the savers and borrowers are located.

Even if it were possible to force banks to charge different interest rates in each region this would have no effect on regional disparities. If someone in Nova Scotia was able to borrow from a bank at 9 percent while someone in Ontario could only borrow at 12 percent then it would be in both their interests for the Nova Scotian to lend to the Ontarian at some intermediate rate. With enough borrowers active in each province, regional interest rates would again be equalised.

As the Bank cannot have different policies for each region it cannot base its policy solely on events in the region with the highest unemployment rate. For whatever reasons, the natural rate of unemployment appears to be higher in the Atlantic provinces than the (roughly) 7 percent natural rate that prevails, on average, in the rest of the country. The only way that Bank of Canada policy can lower the Atlantic unemployment rate to 7 percent is to use a policy that is so stimulative that output in Atlantic Canada exceeds potential output (so that unemployment will be lower than the natural rate). Such a stimulative policy would lift output above potential in the rest of the country at the same time. The positive output gap would cause a substantial increase in inflation. Meanwhile, the reduction in unemployment would only be short-lived because output cannot remain above potential indefinitely.

Some of the regional impacts of monetary policy are offset by other government policies. For example, while the national monetary policy led to a particularly high unemployment rate in the Atlantic provinces in 1982, the unemployment insurance program transferred purchasing power into the Atlantic provinces at the expense of the relatively more prosperous regions. The federal government also maintains an array of programs designed specifically to combat regional disparities (although these have had only limited success so far).

7.7 Monetary versus Fiscal Policy

In our discussion of policy in this chapter we did not emphasise the different qualities of monetary and fiscal policy. Either policy can shift the aggregate demand curve and thus affect output and prices. Here we discuss some of the issues that arise in the choice between monetary and fiscal policy.

Recall that *fiscal* policy is a change in government purchases of goods and services (G), a change in transfer payments (F), or a change in taxes (T). Each of these changes affects aggregate demand. Purchases directly add to demand, and transfers and taxes change income, which changes demand indirectly through the consumption function. A more **expansionary** (or a **looser) fiscal policy** is an increase in government purchases, an increase in transfers, or a decrease in taxes. A **contractionary** (or **tighter) fiscal policy** is the reverse.

Recall also that *monetary* policy is a change in the money supply (M). A more **expansionary,** or looser, **monetary policy** is an increase in the money supply. A **contractionary,** or tighter, **monetary policy** is a decrease in the money supply.

Note that we frequently measure changes in monetary and fiscal policy relative to growing trends in the variables. Thus, a contractionary fiscal policy frequently means a reduction in the growth *rate* of government expenditures (rather than an absolute decline) or an increase in the growth *rate* of taxes (rather than an absolute increase). Similarly, a contractionary monetary policy frequently means a reduction in the growth rate of money.

Recall from our discussion in Chapter 5 that both fiscal and monetary policy are capable of shifting the aggregate demand schedule. A fiscal expansion stimulates spending directly. It causes the interest rate to rise. If the fiscal expansion raises government purchases or stimulates consumption by raising disposable income, then the higher interest rates tend to depress investment and net exports. By contrast, a monetary expansion lowers the interest rate. Investment and net exports grow and consumption responds to that growth through the multiplier.

Even though both policies affect the basic variables of our analysis—output and the price level—in the same way by shifting the aggregate demand schedule, there are important differences in their other effects. These differences are mediated by the interest rate. Monetary expansion favours investment and net exports, whereas fiscal expansion through higher government purchases or tax cuts discourages investment and net exports.

Review and Practice

MAJOR POINTS

1. One important type of macroeconomic shock shifts the aggregate demand curve. Such a shock can originate anywhere in the spending and financial parts of the economy.

2. The other important type of shock shifts the price level.

3. In principle, monetary and fiscal policy can be used to offset shifts in aggregate demand, so that the shifts have little effect on GDP or the price level. But some economists question the feasibility or the wisdom of trying to counteract every demand shift.

4. Price shocks create a much more serious problem for policy. Without a policy response, shocks bring lower GDP and higher inflation. Policy can limit the GDP decline only by adding to the inflation.

5. It is advantageous to adopt a policy rule and to follow the rule each time a macro shock occurs. Some rules limit variations in unemployment at the cost of high variability in inflation. Other rules stabilise prices at the cost of variable unemployment. No rule achieves the ideal of low variation in both unemployment and inflation.

6. Another policy issue is how to phase out inflation once it is established. Policy can choose between ending inflation rapidly, with high unemployment, or disinflating gradually, with unemployment closer to the natural rate.

7. The government can put its aggregate demand policy into effect with either monetary or fiscal policy.

KEY TERMS AND CONCEPTS

Aggregate demand disturbance	New classical view on policy
Price disturbance	Accommodation of price shock
Accommodative policy	Policy rule
Countercyclical stabilisation policy	Disinflation
Activist policy	

QUESTIONS FOR DISCUSSION AND REVIEW

1. What are some of the possible reactions of the economy in the short run to an event that causes an aggregate demand shift? A price shock? What about in the long run? What if both types of shocks occur at the same time?

2. Explain how the economy would respond to a negative price shock if there were no policy response.

3. What are the dangers of a vigorous response to a demand shock? What are the benefits?

4. Explain how the Bank of Canada can choose the slope of the aggregate demand curve.

5. Explain why an extended period of excess unemployment is needed to bring about disinflation. Do you find your explanation completely convincing?

6. What factors should policy makers consider in deciding whether to use fiscal or monetary policy to shift the aggregate demand curve?

7. Why can fiscal policy be used to try to address regional disparities while monetary policy cannot?

PROBLEMS

Numerical

1. Suppose the economy is initially described by the following equations:

$$Y = C + I + G$$
$$C = 80 + .63Y$$
$$I = 750 - 2,000R$$
$$M = .1625Y - 1,000R$$
$$\pi = 1.2\ [(Y_{-1} - 4,000)/4,000]$$

The money supply is equal to $600 billion, government spending is $750 billion, and output is at its potential level of $4,000 billion with a price level of 1. Then there is a money demand shock. The new money demand equation is given by

$$M = .1625Y - 2,000R.$$

a. In the year of the shock, compute the value of GDP, the price level, interest rates, and the real money supply.
b. Using aggregate demand curves, illustrate the economy's path in the year of the shock, and in subsequent years.
c. Calculate the new long-run equilibrium values for income, prices, interest rates, and the real money supply.
d. Could the Bank of Canada have done something to avert the adjustment process? If no, why not? If yes, describe exactly what they could have done.

2. Repeat Exercise 1, assuming now that the shock is to investment. The new investment equation is given by

$$I = 800 - 2,000R.$$

What change in fiscal policy, if any, would have offset the shock?

3. Suppose the economy has the aggregate demand schedule

$$Y = 2,287 + 2.855\ \frac{M}{P}$$

and a price-adjustment schedule

$$\pi = .6\pi_{-1} + 1.2[(Y_{-1} - Y^*)/Y^*] + Z,$$

where Z is an exogenous price shock; potential GDP is $Y^* = 4,000$.

a. Graph the aggregate demand schedule for $M = 600$. Graph the price-adjustment schedule. Find the price level for $Z = 0$.
b. Suppose the economy starts with a price level of 1.0 and zero expected inflation. A price shock of 5 percent occurs in the first year ($Z = .05$). No further price shocks occur ($Z = 0$ in all future years). Trace the path of the economy back to potential by computing the values of the price level, GDP, unemployment, and expected inflation in each year for 5 years.
c. Repeat the calculations for the following monetary accommodation: The money supply is 5 percent higher starting in the second year. Compare this new path for inflation and unemployment to the original path.
d. Suppose, instead, that monetary policy tries to limit inflation by contracting the money stock by 5 percent starting in the second year. Repeat the calculations and compare to the original path.
e. Now suppose that there is no price shock ($Z = 0$ in all years), but that the economy starts with expected inflation of 3 percent. Compute the path to potential. How much excess unemployment (over the natural rate of 7 percent) occurs in the process of returning to potential? Use Okun's law.

4. Consider the following model of aggregate demand:

$$C = 835 + .56Y_d \qquad \text{(Consumption)}$$
$$I = 640 - 2,000R \qquad \text{(Investment)}$$
$$M = 139.5P/ (R + .66) \quad \text{(Money demand)}$$

Government taxes (T) equal tY where the tax rate t is .29. Government purchases G are constant at 690. Each time period represents one year. In addition, prices adjust according to

$$\pi = \pi_{-1} + .3[(Y_{-1} - Y^*)/Y^*] \quad \text{(Price adjustment)}$$

Suppose that it is January 1991 and that you have just been hired as an advisor to the governor of the Bank of Canada. Because the Bank is trying to put on a low-budget image, the governor asks you to bring a hand calculator to your new job. History has repeated itself and the rate of inflation in 1990 was 10 percent. That is, the price level increased from .909 in 1989 to 1.0 in 1990. The Bank of Canada set the money supply for 1990 at 186, and the real output in the economy in 1990 was equal to potential. What was potential output in 1990?

Assume that potential output remains constant at its 1990 value for the rest of the 1990s. What follows pertains to your new job at the Bank.

a. The governor asks you what actual output will have to be in 1991, 1992, and 1993 in order for inflation to be reduced to 7 percent in 1992, to 4 percent in 1993, and then held constant at 4 percent for 1994. What is your answer based on the above model?
b. The governor decides to disinflate the economy according to the path that you calculated in Part a, and asks you to give a recommendation about where to aim the money supply in 1991, 1992, and 1993 to achieve this path. What do you say?
c. Suppose the governor ignores your recommendation and increases the money

supply by 20 percent to 223 in 1991. What will happen to output in 1991 and inflation in 1992?

Analytical

1. Suppose that the economy is initially in equilibrium and that there is a permanent increase in money demand. The following year the money supply is increased so that at the old equilibrium level of prices, income, and interest rates, money supply equals money demand.
   a. Illustrate the shock and the Bank of Canada's reaction to it with an aggregate demand graph. Using arrows, like in Figure 7–2, sketch the economy's path.
   b. What happens to prices, income, and interest rates in the year of the shock, the year immediately following the shock, and all subsequent years?
   c. Whose views of countercyclical stabilisation policy does this example illustrate?

2. Evaluate the following statement: It is price changes, not higher prices, that bother people so much. Therefore, the best response to a price shock is full accommodation. This will prevent output from falling below potential, as well as avoiding any additional price changes.

3. Explain the following statement: The reason that price shocks pose a dilemma for policy makers is that they cannot directly control the price level. Contrast this situation to the case of aggregate demand shocks.

4. Suppose that the Bank of Canada fully accommodates a price shock, shifting out the aggregate demand curve until aggregate demand equals Y^* at the higher price level. The behaviour of both income and the price level are given by the following graphs:

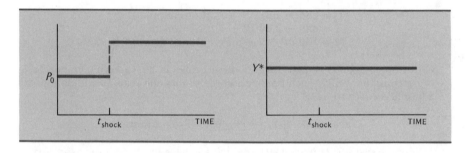

   a. Assuming that aggregate demand is given by the usual relationship, which of the following equations must describe the adjustment of prices?

   $$\pi = f[(Y_{-1}-Y^*)/Y^*] \qquad\qquad \pi = .6\pi_{-1} + f[(Y_{-1}-Y^*)/Y^*]$$

   b. Assume now the same policy response, but that prices are governed by the other equation. Describe the path followed by output and prices.

5. Suppose the Bank of Canada used monetary policy to keep the interest rate at 7 percent no matter what else happened in the economy.
   a. When would such a policy be inflationary? How would the nominal money stock and output behave in this instance?
   b. When would such a policy be deflationary? How would the nominal money stock and output behave in this instance?
   c. What other policy is available for targeting the interest rate? What are its advantages?

6. 'Stagflation' was a term coined in the 1970s to describe a sustained period of high

inflation and unemployment. Using graphs, describe how stagflation may come about in the wake of a price shock.

7. The 'political business cycle' is said to occur because the party in power expands policy in the election year in order to get reelected. How could this be prevented?

8. One example of a monetary policy rule is $Y=Y^*$.
   a. What does the aggregate demand curve look like for such a policy rule?
   b. Explain why the money stock is an endogenous variable under such a rule. How is the money stock affected by price shocks? By aggregate demand shocks?
   c. Explain why $P=P_0$ is not a feasible policy rule.

9. Suppose that a new federal government is elected after making the following campaign promises: lower inflation, lower taxes, and higher government spending.
   a. Explain why the achievement of all three goals would require an extremely restrictive monetary policy.
   b. Could the same rate of disinflation be achieved with a less restrictive monetary policy and a more restrictive fiscal policy? If not, why not? If so, explain how the following variables would be affected: output, inflation, interest rates, consumption, investment, the trade balance, and the government budget deficit.

PART II

The Micro
Foundations of
Aggregate
Demand

8

Consumption Demand

THE STUDY of consumer behaviour—what, how much, and when individuals consume—has been a lifetime occupation of thousands of economists. This is not surprising for the consumer occupies center stage in economics. A first principle of microeconomics is that consumers choose their consumption plans in order to maximise their satisfaction or utility. And ever since Adam Smith the performance of an economic system has been judged by how efficiently it allocates scarce resources to satisfy the wants of consumers. It is natural, therefore, to start with consumers in our examination of the micro foundations of macroeconomics.

Traditionally, macroeconomists have been concerned with consumption because consumption is such a large and important component of aggregate demand. In Part I we saw that consumption is over one-half of all spending and that the response of consumption to changes in income—the consumption function—is a crucial ingredient in macroeconomic analysis. In the first section of this chapter we look at the empirical evidence on consumption. We show that this evidence raises questions about the simple consumption function and then we show how consumption theory has been reconstructed in light of this empirical evidence. We also examine the response of consumption to interest rates.

8.1 Fluctuations in GDP, Consumption, and Income

As the overall economy grows and fluctuates, so does consumption. Figure 8–1 shows how real GDP and personal consumption expenditures have grown and passed through cycles together during the last four decades.

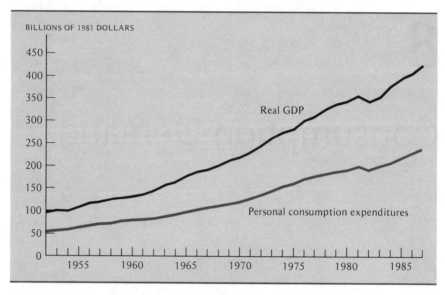

Figure 8–1. CONSUMPTION EXPENDITURES AND GDP.
Real GDP and real personal consumption expenditures grow at about the same rate over long periods of time so that, on average, consumption expenditures maintain roughly a 55 percent share of GDP. However, over the business cycle, consumption expenditures fluctuate much less than GDP. Consumption expenditure is less volatile than the other components of GDP. Source: *Canadian Economic Observer,* Table 1.3.

Note that, *over the long run, consumption expenditures and GDP grow at about the same rate, but, over short-run business cycles, consumption expenditures fluctuate less than GDP.*[1] For example, in the deep recession of 1982 real GDP fell 3.2 percent, but real consumption spending dropped only 2.6 percent. In the recovery of 1984 real output rose by 6.3 percent but the increase in consumption was not as sharp, only 4.6 percent. This relatively smooth behaviour of consumption expenditures compared to GDP is one of the most important facts of the business cycle.

The smoothness of consumption differs greatly by type of consumption. Figure 8–2 shows the breakdown of personal consumption expenditures into its three components: durables, nondurables, and services. Note that the relatively smooth behaviour of consumption expenditures is most striking for services, which grow steadily regardless of the fluctuations in the economy. Nondurables fluctuate more, but much of the business cycle fluctuation in consumption expenditures is due to durables. When recessions occur people reduce their purchases of durable items such as furniture and automobiles much more than nondurable items such as food or services

[1] Note that the increasing gap between real GDP and real consumption in Figure 8–1 is not inconsistent with the fact that the *ratio* of real consumption to real GDP remains constant. The gap gets larger as the level of the two series increases.

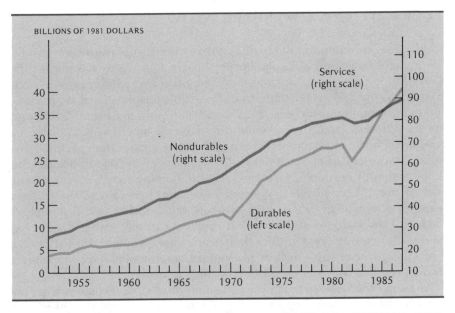

BILLIONS OF 1981 DOLLARS

**Figure 8–2. FLUCTUATIONS IN THE COMPONENTS OF REAL PERSONAL CON-
SUMPTION EXPENDITURES.**
Expenditures on services grow smoothly with little cyclical fluctuation. Expenditures on
durables are the most volatile component of consumption. Source: *Canadian Economic
Observer*, Table 1.6.

such as entertainment. Note, too, that services now represent the largest
and fastest-growing component of consumption. As services become more
important we might expect overall consumption expenditures to become
less volatile.

Overall consumption behaviour would show even smaller fluctuations if
we looked at the true economic measure of **consumption** rather than at
consumption expenditures. The distinction between consumption and
consumption expenditures is a subtle one, but takes on special importance
in the case of durables. Consider a car, for example. Expenditure on a car
occurs at the time that we buy the car and bring it home from the car dealer,
even if we finance it by borrowing. Consumption of the car is then spread
out over several years as we drive the car and it gradually deteriorates
through normal wear and tear. Expenditure occurs when the car is acquired; consumption occurs as the car is used up. Consumption of durables
is spread out more over time and is smoother than expenditure on them.
For services and nondurable items there is no meaningful distinction between consumption and expenditure: When we purchase a haircut we consume it at the same time. Because consumption of durables fluctuates less
than expenditures on durables, it is clear that total consumption has smaller
fluctuations than total consumption expenditures.

GDP AND PERSONAL DISPOSABLE INCOME

Why does consumption fluctuate less than GDP? Part of the answer can be found in the behaviour of disposable personal income. As we saw in Chapter 4, according to the simplest theory, consumption depends on personal disposable income: When fluctuations in disposable income are small, fluctuations in consumption will be small as well. We stressed in Chapter 2 that GDP is very different from the personal disposable income that is available to consumers for spending. GDP is about 50 percent greater than personal disposable income. Part of GDP is not really income at all because it includes the depreciation of machines, factories, and the housing stock. An important part of GDP is unavailable to consumers because it is paid to the various levels of government in the form of taxes. Still another part is ploughed back into corporations in the form of retained earnings rather than being paid out to consumers. On the other hand, some people receive transfers from the government—such as unemployment compensation or pension payments—that are not related to current production.

Although the difference between GDP and disposable income is large on average, what is more important for our purposes is that the difference shrinks during recessions and expands during booms. Taxes fall during recessions, and transfers increase because more people collect unemployment insurance and welfare. Therefore disposable income does not fall as much as GDP. These changes in taxes and transfers are sometimes called **automatic stabilisers** because of their stabilising effect on disposable income; we will be studying them in more detail in Chapter 13. Retained earnings also fall during recessions, because corporations don't cut their dividends very much, further mitigating the effect on disposable income. The sum of these effects is shown in Figure 8–3, where real GDP and real disposable income are plotted for the years 1952–87.

Figure 8–3 shows that personal disposable income fluctuates less than GDP. On average, when GDP falls during a recession disposable income does not fall as much. There are exceptions to this general rule, but, again, on average, over this period a fall in real GDP of $10 billion reduced real disposable income by only $4.5 billion.[2]

THE RELATION BETWEEN REAL DISPOSABLE INCOME AND CONSUMPTION

As we have just seen, part of the reason that consumption fluctuates less than real GDP is that disposable income fluctuates less than GDP. But can all

---

[2] This relationship was estimated by comparing real disposable income and real GDP in Canada each year during the 1952–87 period. The least-squares relation between the *change* in real disposable income and the *change* in real GDP has a slope coefficient of .45. The least-squares line is the straight line that minimises the sum of squared vertical distances between the dots and the line.

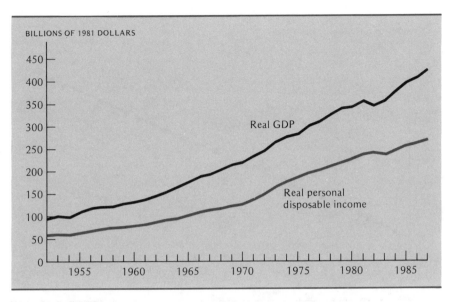

BILLIONS OF 1981 DOLLARS

Figure 8–3. REAL GDP AND REAL PERSONAL DISPOSABLE INCOME.
Disposable income fluctuates much less than real GDP. The automatic stabilisers—taxes and transfers—as well as the dividend policies of corporations prevent disposable income from falling as far as GDP during recessions. Source: *Canadian Economic Observer*, Tables 1.3, 1.5, and 1.12.

of consumption behaviour be explained by current personal disposable income as the simplest consumption function would suggest? In Figure 8–4 we examine the relationship between personal consumption expenditures and personal disposable income for the period from 1952 through 1987. Each dot in Figure 8–4 represents real consumption and real disposable income in Canada for one year. We can summarise the relationship by drawing a straight line through the dots.[3] The straight line gives the relationship

$$C = 11.1 + .81Y_d, \tag{8–1}$$

where C and Y_d are measured in billions of 1981 dollars. Equation 8–1 is in the form of the simple consumption function; the **marginal propensity to consume** (MPC) is .81. Figure 8–4 indicates that consumption is sometimes less and sometimes greater than predicted by the simple consumption function. The errors are measured by the vertical distances between the line and the dots in Figure 8–4. The errors appear to be small. The simple consumption function seems to give a surprisingly good description of consumption.

[3] We estimated this relationship by finding the straight line that minimises the sum of the squared vertical distances between the dots and the line (that is, the least-squares line) for the years from 1952 through 1987.

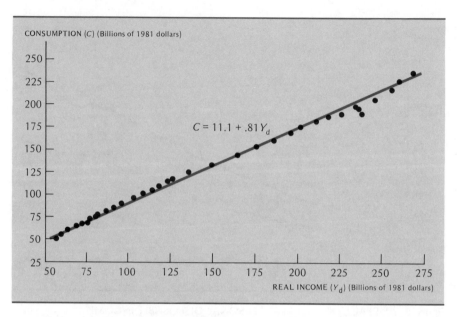

Figure 8–4. THE RELATION BETWEEN REAL DISPOSABLE INCOME AND REAL CON-SUMPTION EXPENDITURES.
The horizontal position of each dot shows real disposable income in that year and the vertical position shows real consumption in that year. The straight line is a simple consumption function that is fit through the scatter of dots. The vertical distances between the line and the dots measure the error in the consumption function. Source: *Canadian Economic Observer*, Table 1.3.

8.2 Defects in the Simple Keynesian Consumption Function

Unfortunately, Figure 8–4 paints too rosy a picture about the reliability of the simple consumption function. Although the errors in Figure 8–4 appear small to the naked eye, for some purposes—such as forecasting or policy analysis—they are actually quite large. A more revealing picture of the errors is found in Figure 8–5, where the error in the simple consumption function is plotted for each year. The vertical scale in Figure 8–5 is much larger than the vertical scale in Figure 8–4. This magnifies the errors much as does an enlargement of a photograph and makes them easier to analyse.

A very large negative error occurred in 1982. People consumed much less than normal given their disposable incomes; they acted as if they distrusted their income figures in that year. Why? Perhaps they were becoming pessimistic about their incomes in the future: The unemployment rate in Canada reached levels not seen since the Great Depression of the 1930s, interest rates were at heights that had never been seen before, and the stock market fell sharply. These uncertainties about the future could have led to caution and increased saving.

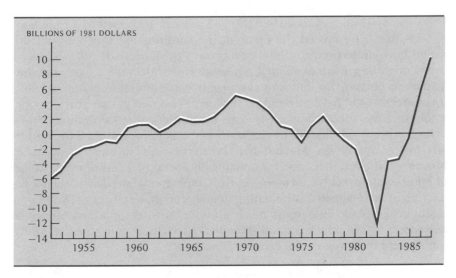

Figure 8–5. ERROR ANALYSIS IN THE SIMPLE CONSUMPTION FUNCTION.
This diagram gives a microscopic view of the errors in the simple consumption function that are barely visible in Figure 8–4. It blows up the distance between the actual consumption-income dots and the simple consumption-income line in Figure 8–4. The distances are then plotted each year from 1952 through 1987. A big negative error is evident in 1982, and a big positive error is evident in 1987. Source: The errors are computed from the consumption and income data used for Figure 8–4.

At the other extreme an enormously large positive error occurred in 1987. People consumed much more than normal of their disposable income. Perhaps they were then more optimistic about the future: The stock market was booming for most of the year, inflation remained low, and unemployment was falling back towards a more normal level. Perhaps as a result consumers felt that the economy would resume the robust and sustained growth that had been experienced earlier.

Note that these informal but plausible explanations of the errors in the simple theory imply a much more sophisticated consumer than the one that simply looks at current income, as the Keynesian model postulates. Expected future income enters the decision. The main contribution of the newer theories of consumption described in the next section is to bring these expectations of the future explicitly into account.

THE EFFECT OF CONSUMPTION ERRORS ON FORECASTING AND POLICY

Some perspective on the practical importance of these errors in the consumption function can be gained by looking at their effect on economic forecasting and policy. These errors can have significant effects on economic forecasts. For example, the error in the consumption function in

1987 was $10 billion. From 1986 to 1987 real GDP increased by $16 billion. A forecaster who missed the error in the consumption function in 1987 would have underpredicted real GDP growth by more than 100 percent—predicting GDP growth of about 1.5 percent rather than the 4.0 percent that actually occurred. By ignoring the negative consumption error in 1982, forecasters would have missed the decline in real GDP in that year.

These large forecasting errors can obviously lead to economic policy errors. More fiscal stimulus might have been called for in 1982 if the unusually low consumption demand had been correctly forecast in advance. Moreover, if consumers don't automatically spend 81 cents of every dollar of additional disposable income—as the simple model predicts—then a reduction in taxes aimed at stimulating demand might not work as planned; it might generate too little or too much stimulus. More complicated consumer behaviour makes policy-making difficult, especially if policy makers don't understand the more complicated behaviour.

SHORT-RUN VERSUS LONG-RUN MARGINAL PROPENSITY TO CONSUME

There is one systematic feature of the errors in the simple consumption function that is difficult to see in the charts with a naked eye, but which nonetheless has provided a crucial insight and stimulus to advanced research on consumption: *On average, consumption is smoothed out compared to disposable income; consumption fluctuates less than disposable income.* This phenomenon can be detected and illustrated by using the concept of the long-run and short-run marginal propensity to consume. Figure 8–6 shows how the long-run and the short-run marginal propensities to consume differ for total consumption. The **long-run marginal propensity to consume** tells us how much consumption will increase over the long haul when personal disposable income rises. For total consumption the long-run marginal propensity to consume is .81, as we have already seen in Equation 8–1.

The **short-run marginal propensity to consume** tells us how much consumption will rise over the short run—during one year or during one business cycle—when disposable income rises. As Figure 8–6 illustrates, the short-run marginal propensity to consume is less than the long-run marginal propensity to consume.

Table 8–1 shows the actual difference between the short-run and the

Table 8–1. SHORT-RUN AND LONG-RUN MARGINAL PROPENSITY TO CONSUME, 1953–87

	Total Consumption	Nondurables Plus Services	Durables
Long-run MPC	.81	.66	.15
Short-run MPC	.55	.37	.18

Note: The long-run MPCs are based on the least-squares fit of the annual *levels* of real consumption and real disposable income. The short-run MPCs are based on the fit of the year-to-year *changes* in the same two variables.

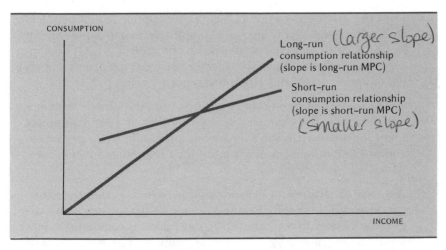

Figure 8–6.   THE MARGINAL PROPENSITY TO CONSUME IN THE SHORT RUN AND IN THE LONG RUN.
The steeper line shows how consumption rises with income in the long run. Its slope is the long-run marginal propensity to consume (MPC). The flatter line shows how consumption rises with income in the short run. Its slope is the short-run MPC.

long-run marginal propensity to consume in Canada from 1953 to 1987 for total consumption and two of its components. The short-run marginal propensity to consume can be calculated statistically by noting how much consumption changes from one year to the next when disposable income changes. For total consumption the short-run MPC is .55, compared with .81 for the long-run MPC. The difference is even more pronounced for consumption of nondurables plus services: Nondurable and services consumption falls by 37 cents in the short run for each dollar decrease in disposable income, but the fall is 66 cents over the long run if that dollar shortfall in income persists. Note that the difference between the long-run and the short-run MPC is reversed for durable expenditures; unlike the other components of consumption, durables are more sensitive to income in the short run than in the long run. A complete theory of consumption has to come to grips with these empirical observations.

GDP, Consumption, and Income

1. Consumption fluctuates much less than GDP. The least stable component of consumption expenditures is durable consumption. Services and nondurable consumption grow more smoothly.

2. The main reason that consumption fluctuates less than GDP is that disposable income fluctuates less than GDP. Consumption is financed out of disposable income.

3. Over the past few decades in Canada consumption has more or less tracked income according to a simple Keynesian consumption function with a marginal propensity to consume of .81. Of each incremental dollar of disposable income, 81 cents has been spent on consumption goods and 19 cents has been saved.

4. There have been significant deviations from the simple consumption function. For example, in the recession of 1982 consumers spent much less than the simple consumption function predicted, and in 1987 they spent much more than the simple function predicted.

5. A systematic feature of consumption behaviour is that the short-run marginal propensity to consume is less than the long-run marginal propensity to consume. Over short periods consumption falls less than the amount by which income falls; over longer periods of time, a decrease in consumption begins to catch up to a decrease in income.

8.3 The Forward-Looking Theory of Consumption

A number of different theories of consumption have been developed in response to the deficiencies in the simple consumption function. The most durable and widely accepted today are the **permanent-income theory** developed in the 1950s by Milton Friedman and the **life-cycle theory** developed independently at about the same time by Franco Modigliani of the Massachusetts Institute of Technology.[4] The two theories are closely related, and together they have served as a foundation for most of the rational expectations research on consumption in macroeconomics in the 1970s and 1980s. We will refer to them jointly as the **forward-looking theory of consumption.** The theory embodies the basic idea that individual consumers are forward-looking decision makers. The life-cycle theory gets its name from its emphasis on a family looking ahead over its entire lifetime. The permanent-income theory is named for its distinction between permanent income, which a family expects to be long-lasting, and transitory income, which a family expects to disappear shortly. In practice the theories differ primarily in the types of equations used to express the basic idea of forward-looking consumers and to implement this idea empirically.

[4] Friedman published his findings in 1957 in a famous book *A Theory of the Consumption Function* (Princeton University Press); the findings on the life-cycle theory were published in a series of papers, the most important of which are F. Modigliani and R. E. Brumberg, 'Utility Analysis and the Consumption Function: An Interpretation of Cross-Section Data,' in K. K. Kurihara (ed.), *Post-Keynesian Economics,* Rutgers University Press, pp. 388–436, and A. Ando and F. Modigliani, 'The "Life-Cycle" Hypothesis of Saving: Aggregate Implication and Tests,' *American Economic Review,* Vol. 53 (March 1963), pp. 55–84.

Like the simple consumption function, the forward-looking theory of consumption assumes that families or individuals base their consumption decisions on their disposable incomes. To simplify matters we will begin by ignoring factors other than disposable income that might also influence consumption, such as interest rates. The forward-looking theories break ranks with the simple consumption function by saying that consumers do not concentrate exclusively on this year's disposable income. Instead, they also look ahead to their likely future disposable income, which will depend on their future earnings from working, on their future income from wealth they have accumulated, and on how high taxes will be in the future. Based on their current income and expected future disposable income they decide how much to consume this year after taking account of their likely consumption in future years as well.

The consumption decision is thus much like a plan; this year's consumption is the first year of a plan that covers perhaps the next 50 years. Next year, the plan will have to be adjusted to take account of all the new information that has become available, but if everything works out as expected the plan will be followed. Although few consumers actually sit down and work out formal forward-looking plans in great detail, it is likely that a significant fraction do some informal planning when they borrow to buy now, planning to pay off the loan later with future anticipated earnings, or when they save for retirement. We will talk about a very self-conscious plan, of the sort that an economist might make, but we recognise that most families are much more informal in their planning.

THE INTERTEMPORAL BUDGET CONSTRAINT

To describe how such a planning process results in a consumption decision, we will focus on a single family. The family could consist of a single individual, but would more typically be a family with parents and children. The first aspect we will look at is the budget constraint the family faces. The budget constraint applies not to one single year, but to many future years taken together. The constraint is more flexible in any one year than it is over time; in any one year a family can consume more than its disposable income by borrowing or by drawing down some of its financial assets. But a family can't go on forever consuming more than its disposable income— eventually it will run out of assets or places to borrow. The family faces an **intertemporal budget constraint** that limits its consumption over the years. In some years, a family will consume less than its income; the excess of income over consumption—saving—is then added to the family's financial assets and can be used for consumption in later years. Consumption this year is thus reduced so that consumption in later years can be increased. The budget constraint incorporates the accumulation of assets that results from savings.

The intertemporal budget constraint can be described in words as follows:

Assets at the beginning of next year
= Assets at the beginning of this year
+ Income on assets this year ⎱
+ Income from work this year ⎰ Disposable income ⎱ Saving
− Taxes paid this year ⎰
− Consumption this year

Assets include items such as bank deposits, bonds, corporate stock, and pension funds. There are two types of income: (1) income on assets, such as interest payments from the bank where the family holds its deposits, and (2) income from work. If a family adds to its assets then it also adds to its future income on those assets. Hence it is important to distinguish between the two types of income.

Disposable income is, of course, income on assets plus income from work minus taxes. Note that the budget constraint simply states that each year's savings—disposable income less consumption—is added to assets.

To give a clearer picture of the intertemporal budget we introduce the following symbols:

A_t = Assets at the beginning of year t
R = Interest rate on assets
E_t = Income from work during year t
T_t = Taxes during year t
C_t = Consumption during year t

The small subscript indicates the year. The interest rate (R) tells us how much income a given amount of assets will earn. For example, if the interest rate is 5 percent and assets A_t equal \$1,000 in year t then income on assets is \$50 in year t. (The interest rate R is the *real* interest rate, that is, the nominal interest rate less the expected rate of inflation.)

Using these symbols the intertemporal budget constraint can be written as

$$A_{t+1} = A_t + RA_t + E_t - T_t - C_t. \tag{8-2}$$

The six algebraic terms in Equation 8–2 correspond one-for-one with the six items listed in the budget constraint that we wrote in words above. The subscript $t + 1$ indicates assets at the beginning of year $t + 1$. (For example, if year t is 1988 then year $t + 1$ is 1989.) The budget constraint, Equation 8–2, applies to all years of the family's future—working years and retirement years. By applying this equation year after year, the family can figure out what its asset position will be many years in the future, given expectations about the interest rate, income from work, and taxes. By reducing consumption this year the family can increase its assets in future years. The increased assets—plus the interest earned on these assets—could be used for consumption on timely items such as the children's education, for retirement, or as a bequest. (The interest rate R is measured in fractions in this formula: If the interest rate is 5 percent then set R equal to .05 in Equation 8–2. Then R times A, for example, equals $50 if A equals $1,000.)

A consumption plan is feasible if it does not involve an impractical asset position at any time in the future. Any positive amount of assets is practical, since it means the family is lending to others, rather than borrowing. For most people, it is impractical to have their assets drop significantly below zero. Our concept of assets is *net* across all borrowing and ownership of the family—if a family buys a house with a 20 percent down payment and takes on a mortgage for the remaining 80 percent, its net asset position is positive. The value of the house as an asset exceeds the liability of the mortgage. Borrowing from a positive net asset position is perfectly practical—almost everybody does it. But it is difficult to borrow when there is a negative net asset position. An exception might be medical school students who can borrow because their expected future incomes are so favourable.

PREFERENCES: STEADY RATHER THAN ERRATIC CONSUMPTION

Many different consumption plans are feasible. As long as the family is careful not to consume too much, it has a wide choice about when to schedule its consumption. It could consume very little in the early years and build up significant assets by middle age. Or it could consume as much as possible and keep its assets only barely positive. Which of the feasible plans will the family choose? The forward-looking theory of consumption assumes that *most people prefer to keep their consumption fairly steady from year to year*. Given the choice between consuming $10,000 this year and $10,000 next year, as against $5,000 this year and $15,000 next year, people generally choose the even split. There are exceptions but it seems reasonable that most people prefer not to have ups and downs in their standard of living.

Figure 8–7 shows a typical path for income for a family with a steady consumption plan. Income from employment is low in the early years and gradually rises until retirement as job experience and seniority increase. During retirement income from work is zero. Note how consumption is relatively large compared to income in the early years of work; young families tend to borrow when they can in anticipation of greater future income in later years. During the years immediately before retirement, consumption is relatively low as the family saves more in anticipation of retirement. Finally, during retirement consumption is much greater than income as the family draws down its assets.

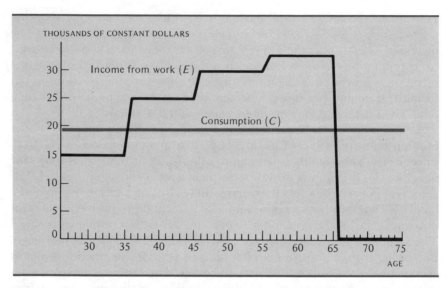

Figure 8–7. ILLUSTRATION OF STEADY CONSUMPTION COMPARED TO INCOME GROWTH AND DECLINE.
Income from work is assumed to grow as experience and seniority increase and then drop to zero during retirement. Thoughtful forward-looking consumers who prefer a smooth consumption path will tend to borrow during their early years, save in their middle-age years, and draw down their assets during retirement.

PREFERENCES: HOW LARGE AN INHERITANCE FOR THE NEXT GENERATION?

Figure 8–7 illustrates the important features of the typical smooth consumption path. But the assumption that families prefer a smooth consumption path is still not sufficient to pin down one consumption path among those that are feasible. The family can choose a high smooth consumption plan or a low smooth consumption plan. Different smooth paths of consumption will leave the family with different levels of assets at the end of the parents' lifetimes. Figure 8–8 shows the path of assets for the smooth consumption path already shown in Figure 8–7 (Path 2) along with asset paths for higher (Path 1) and lower (Path 3) consumption paths.

A higher consumption path leaves fewer assets at the end of the lifetime. To pin down the consumption path completely we need to make an assumption about what the parents' preferences are for assets at the end of their lifetimes. How much will they want to leave to the next generation as inheritance? If parents are convinced that their children can make it on their own, they may prefer to consume most of their assets during retirement. Or they might want to reward their children for doing well by giving a large bequest. There is little agreement among economists on what motivates be-

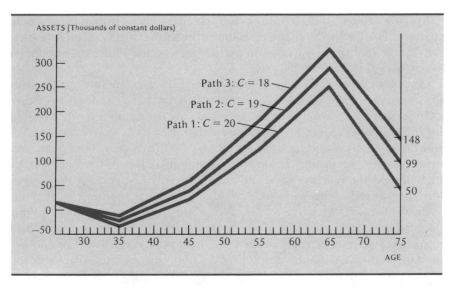

Figure 8–8. ASSETS AND BEQUESTS UNDER SMOOTH CONSUMPTION PATHS, STARTING WITH $15,000.
If consumption follows Path 1 over the family's lifetime, assets will follow the path marked 1, with little left for the next generation. If consumption follows Path 2, sufficiently more assets are accumulated to leave more for the next generation. Along Path 3, consumption is even lower and assets left for inheritance are even higher.

quests.[5] Fortunately, however, many of the important empirical predictions of the life-cycle and the permanent-income hypotheses hold regardless of what assumption we make about inheritance. We will discuss the effect of alternative assumptions below, where the assumption about inheritance does matter.

THE MARGINAL PROPENSITY TO CONSUME OUT OF TEMPORARY VERSUS PERMANENT CHANGES IN INCOME

It should already be apparent from Figure 8–7 that there is a relation between the family's current assets plus its expectations about future earnings from work and its consumption decision. If news comes along that the family is better off, either because it has higher assets today or because it expects higher earnings in the future, the family will adjust its consumption upward. Moreover, it will adjust its future consumption plans upward by about the same amount. If the family reacted to good news by changing only current consumption and not future planned consumption, it would be planning a consumption path that was not smooth.

[5] Douglas Bernheim, Andrei Shleifer, and Lawrence Summers argue that parents use bequests to influence their childrens' actions in 'The Strategic Bequest Motive,' *Journal of Political Economy*, Vol. 93 (December 1985), pp. 1045–1076.

By how much does consumption change when disposable income changes? For forward-looking consumers the answer depends on how long the change in income will last—in particular, whether the change is viewed as *temporary* or *permanent*.

Consider first the case where income increases permanently. An interesting and important example is a permanent cut in taxes, though any other change such as the winning of a lottery that pays the family a yearly payment for life would serve just as well. Suppose that the family learns that its taxes will be lower by a certain amount, say $1,000, this year, next year, and every year in the future. Disposable income increases in the first year by $1,000, and the increase is viewed as permanent. Assume that the tax cut was unexpected so that the family could not have planned for it in advance. If the family didn't change its consumption plans, future assets would pile up quickly. Next year, assets would be higher by $1,000. In later years, this would grow as interest compounded. But next year, there would be another increment to assets in the amount of $1,000, and in later years this too would earn compound interest. Moreover, if the family raised its consumption, assets would still pile up unless the increase in consumption were equal to the decrease in taxes, $1,000. The family's exact plan would depend on how much of the income improvement it wanted to pass on to the next generation. Assuming that the amount of the improvement passed on is zero we get a simple conclusion: *The marginal propensity to consume from the increase in disposable income is 1. Consumption rises by the full amount of the increase in income when the increase is viewed as permanent.* If the family wanted to pass on some of the increased income as a bequest then the marginal propensity to consume would be smaller.

Now consider a temporary tax cut of $1,000 that will last only one year; taxes are then expected to return to their normal level in the remaining years. Again assume that the tax cut was unexpected so that the family could not have adjusted its plans in advance. If the family raises its consumption by $1,000 in the year of the tax cut then it will finish the year with nothing extra saved. At the end of the year it will have to reduce its consumption to the level previously planned, which would go against the rule that consumption should be smooth. The family can achieve a better consumption plan by raising consumption less than the tax cut and accumulating some assets. Hence, the marginal propensity to consume will be less than 1. But how much less?

We can determine the amount by using the forward-looking model. If the family didn't change its consumption plans at all, the $1,000 would be added to the family's assets and start earning interest at rate R. Suppose that the interest rate is 5 percent. As the years passed, the increment to assets, including compound interest, would become quite large. After 50 years, $1,000 left to compound at 5 percent interest becomes $12,000. But rather than leave this much more for the next generation, the typical family will probably raise its planned consumption. If it raises planned consumption by the amount of the interest, $50 per year, then after 50 years the family will have just the additional $1,000, not the extra $11,000 in compound interest. Thus, one option for the family is to plan to consume an extra $50 per year and leave an extra $1,000 to the next generation. Or, the family could consume just a bit more and leave nothing extra to the next generation. The intertemporal budget constraint, Equation 8–2, can be used to figure out how much more than $50 the increase in consumption would have to be to exhaust the $1,000 windfall after 50 years.

The forward-looking theory predicts the following consumption rule from this planning process: *If a family receives an unexpected temporary increment to its disposable income, it will raise its consumption by the interest earned by the increment, plus a bit more if it does not want to pass the full amount on to the next generation.* If the tax cut is $1,000 then the rise in consumption is $50, or a little more if not all of the $1,000 is passed on. The marginal propensity to consume from the one-year temporary tax cut, or any other temporary increase in income, is a little greater than the interest rate, or about .05 in this example. It is far, far less than the marginal propensity to consume arising from a permanent increase in income, which is closer to 1. It is also much less than that suggested by the simple consumption function we looked at earlier in the chapter. The difference between the marginal propensity to consume out of a temporary change in income and the marginal propensity to consume out of a permanent change in income is the single most important feature of the newer theories of consumption based on a forward-looking consumer.

MPC from temporary ↑ income < MPC from permanent ↑ income.

ANTICIPATED VERSUS UNANTICIPATED CHANGES IN INCOME

In each of the above examples we assumed that the change in income was unanticipated. If the change was anticipated then the family would adjust its plans in advance. How? Suppose, for example, that the family learns about the temporary tax cut of $1,000 one year in advance. Then it would increase its consumption before the tax cut actually took place. Postponing the increase in consumption to the year of the tax cut would mean that the planned consumption path would not be smooth and this would violate the steady consumption rule. The increase in the consumption path would be slightly less than in the case where the tax cut was unanticipated simply because there is one more year of consumption to spread the improved income over. If the family wanted to leave the full $1,000 to the next generation then the increase in consumption would be slightly less than the interest rate times the tax cut. If the tax cut occurred with 50 years on the planning horizon then consumption would be spread over 51 years. The increase in consumption would thus be about $48.

Note that the marginal propensity to consume in the year that the tax cut is anticipated is astronomical. The change in income is zero in that year and consumption increases by about $48. The marginal propensity to consume is literally infinite! But the important point is that with forward-looking consumers the marginal propensity to consume depends not only on whether the change in income is temporary or permanent, but also on whether it is anticipated or unanticipated.

8.4 How Well Does the Forward-Looking Theory Work?

The key point of the forward-looking theory of consumption is that the marginal propensity to consume from new funds depends on whether the new funds are a one-time increment or will recur in future years. The marginal propensity to consume from temporary increases is low—only a little above the interest rate. The marginal propensity to consume from permanent increases in earnings is high—close to 1.

Consumption in the economy as a whole is the aggregation of the consumption decisions of millions of families. Most tests of the forward-looking model focus on aggregate consumption. Many of the events that matter a great deal for an individual family—births and deaths, promotions, winning big at the racetrack—don't matter at all in the aggregate. The 'law of large numbers' guarantees that purely random individual experiences do not influence the total. But some of the influences affecting individual families are common across all families, as, for example, when the economy goes into recession.

THE SHORT-RUN AND LONG-RUN MPC: A ROUGH CHECK OF THE THEORY

Before looking at the particular methods that Friedman, Modigliani, and other economic researchers have used to test this theory formally, let's see how well it explains the facts of aggregate consumption that we presented in the previous section. The most important statistical regularity that the simple consumption function misses is that the short-run marginal propensity to consume is less than the long-run marginal propensity to consume; that is, consumption does not increase as much with income over short-run business cycle periods as it does over long-run growth periods. If consumers usually expect short-run business cycle fluctuations in their income to be temporary, then forward-looking consumption theory provides an explanation for this finding. If they expect the drop in income that they experience during a recession to be temporary, then they will not cut their consumption as much as if they thought the drop was more lasting. Similarly, they will not increase their consumption so much during the boom stage of a cycle. Is it plausible that many consumers tend to view recessions and booms as temporary? The experience of much of the last 30 years is that business cycle recessions and booms have in fact been temporary. If consumers can remember this experience then an expectation that recessions are temporary seems reasonable. Moreover, economic forecasters usually predict a return to a steady growth path following a recession—they at least remember what happened in the last cycle—and their forecasts are covered on television, in newspapers, and in magazines. Thus the forward-looking theory of consumption seems to pass this rough check pretty well.

Why Is the Saving Rate Higher in Canada than in the United States?

Personal saving is the amount left over from personal disposable income after consumption expenditures and transfers to outside the personal sector are made. The **personal saving rate** is personal saving as a percentage of personal disposable income. For example, in 1987 personal disposable income in Canada was $364 billion, of which $35 billion was saved. Thus the savings rate was 9.6 percent (the calculation is $(35/364 \times 100 = 9.6)$. The 9.6 percent savings rate was the lowest in Canada since 1972. This low saving rate is just another way to think about the large error in the consumption function in 1987 shown in Figure 8–5 and discussed in the text (consuming an abnormally high fraction of disposable income is the same thing as saving an abnormally low fraction of disposable income).

A 9.6 percent savings rate is low by Canadian standards but it is quite high relative to recent U.S. experience. While Canadian and U.S. savings rates were similar up until 1976 the savings rate in Canada has been much higher than the U.S. rate since then. A study by Chris Carroll of M.I.T. and Lawrence Summers of Harvard showed that Canadian savings rates have been higher than U.S. rates even after accounting for differences in the way that saving is measured in each country.

Why is the saving rate higher in Canada? The forward-looking theory of consumption may provide part of the answer. Carroll and Summers state that perhaps 'the sharp increase in Canadian savings, which coincided with an increase in Canada's . . . unemployment rate [relative to the United States], was the result of a perception by Canadians that their economy had become a significantly more risky working environment, necessitating a higher rate of precautionary savings. This hypothesis is loosely supported by polls which indicate a large drop in the confidence of Canadians in their economy in the late 1970s.' *

Other factors have also been involved. In the mid-1970s the Canadian government introduced new tax incentives to encourage retirement saving that were not matched in the United States. And relative to the size of each economy, Canadian government budget deficits have been higher than in the United States. The potential significance of government budget deficits for saving behaviour is considered in Chapter 13.

* Chris Carroll and Lawrence H. Summers 'Why Have Private Savings Rates in the United States and Canada Diverged?' *Journal of Monetary Economics,* Vol. 20, 1987, pp. 249–279.

ANDO AND MODIGLIANI: DO ASSETS MATTER FOR CONSUMPTION?

One of the earliest formal statistical tests of the forward-looking theory was done by Albert Ando of the University of Pennsylvania in collaboration with Modigliani. Ando and Modigliani formulated consumption as depending on two factors: (1) current income from work and (2) total assets. In their formulation a change in income, given the value of assets, is assumed to be indicative of a permanent change in income (the current level of income would be representative of all future income). Hence, the marginal propensity to consume from a change in income from work—holding constant the level of assets—would be close to 1. The equation would have to be made more complicated if current income is known to be different from likely future income. On the other hand, their formulation assumes that a change in the value of total assets, given the level of income, would tend to be a temporary change—an example would be a one-time increase in the value of corporate stock. Hence, the marginal propensity to consume from a change in the value of total assets would be close to the interest rate. Algebraically, the Ando-Modigliani consumption function thus takes the form

$$C = b_1 Y_d + b_2 A, \tag{8-3}$$

where Y_d is disposable income, A is assets, and b_1 and b_2 are coefficients. Note that Equation 8–3 is a modification of the simple Keynesian consumption function: Assets have been added as a second factor to income. When Ando and Modigliani fit this simple equation to data in the United States during the period after World War II they found that b_1 was close to .7 and that b_2 was close to .06, thereby providing striking confirmation for their ideas about consumption. Moreover, the addition of total assets to the equation could eliminate some of the errors in the simple Keynesian consumption function that we noted earlier. For example, the high level of consumption relative to income in 1987 may have been due in part to the high value of the stock market during most of that year.

Events that began late in 1987 indicate that the relationship between stock prices and consumption is not so simple. After a number of small declines in stock prices the value of the shares traded on the Toronto Stock Exchange fell 15 percent in one week in October 1987. Stock prices rose somewhat in later months, but remained well below the levels reached between March and September of 1987. Nonetheless, there was no appreciable decline in real consumption spending following the stock market crash.

The lack of reaction of consumption to the stock market crash poses a challenge to the forward-looking theory of consumption, although perhaps not an insurmountable one. For example, consumers may have believed that the fall in stock prices would be only temporary. If so, then the forward-looking theory implies that they would not make any major changes in their consumption plans because they had not made any major changes in their expectations about their lifetime wealth. In addition, house prices continued to rise throughout this period. This could have increased homeowners' views of their own wealth and thereby offset the effect of lower stock values. Last, some consumers may have decided to leave smaller bequests to their children when stock prices fell, rather than to reduce their consumption.[6]

FRIEDMAN: DOES PAST INCOME MATTER FOR CONSUMPTION?

Friedman expressed the ideas about forward-looking consumers in a slightly different way. He simply defined permanent income as a fixed long-run level of income that has a present value equivalent to the family's assets and expected future income. All other changes in income are then viewed as transitory. Friedman then argued that the marginal propensity to consume from permanent income should be close to 1, and the marginal propensity to consume from transitory income should be closer to zero. Algebraically, he formulated the consumption function as

$$C = b_p Y_p, \tag{8-4}$$

where Y_p is permanent disposable income and b_p is a coefficient. According to Friedman's formulation b_p should be close to 1.

An important part of Friedman's formulation was his assumption that permanent income is an average of income over the last several years. Thus, if current income suddenly increased there would be only a small increase in permanent income; income would have to increase for several years in a row before people would expect that permanent income had increased. To test the theory he thus substituted an average of current income and previous income over the past several years for permanent income in Equation 8–4. Effectively, therefore, consumption should depend on past income as well as on current income. Past income should matter for consumption because it helps people to forecast future income. Although it is an admittedly simple model of people's expectations, Friedman found that his formulation of the consumption function fit the facts better than the simple Keynesian function with current income.

WHERE DO WE STAND NOW?

The empirical work of Ando, Modigliani, and Friedman is now more than 30 years old. Economic research in the 1970s and 1980s has led to more revealing tests of the forward-looking theory and has raised puzzling

---

[6] See the discussion in 'Economic Developments in Canada in the Second Half of 1987,' *Bank of Canada Review*, March 1988.

new questions. Three strands of the new research are particularly important: the use of rational expectations to measure future income prospects,
the analysis of data on the histories of thousands of individual families, and
case studies of particular economic policy 'experiments.'

Rational Expectations. The hypothesis of consumers as forward-looking
decision makers already postulates a considerable degree of rationality to
consumers. The hypothesis of rational expectations postulates more, but
not necessarily less plausible, rationality. Recall that Ando, Modigliani, and
Friedman postulated rather naive assumptions about what people expected
about their future income: It would tend to stay where it was recently. The
rational expectations approach attempts to look at the actual historical behaviour of income and use this to describe statistically how people expect income to behave in the future.

The approach is a statistical formalisation and a much finer version of the
rough check on the theory that we described at the start of this section.
Rather than just saying that people expect business cycles to be temporary,
the approach assumes that people act as if they have a little algebraic model
of the behaviour of income over the business cycle in their heads, and that
they use this model when guessing their future income. Of course, nobody
except perhaps an economist would actually use such a model in their personal family planning: The idea is that by watching television, reading the
newspaper, or just talking with friends people get a view of future economic
developments that is not much different from that of the average professional economist who actually uses such a model.

The rational expectations approach is used by many economists engaged
in macroeconomic research.[7] The most straightforward version of this approach is to substitute the forecasts of income from such a model into the
permanent-income equation, 8–4, for consumption. More technical versions substitute forecasts of future income into the intertemporal budget
constraint, Equation 8–2, and calculate the optimal plan for consumption
directly without the intermediate step of Friedman's permanent-income
equation. Using rational expectations this way clearly requires advanced
mathematical skills and understandably the approach has attracted economists who specialise in such skills.

---

[7] The research referred to is found in a series of papers published in the *Journal of Political
Economy:* Robert Hall, 'Stochastic Implications of the Life Cycle–Permanent Income Hypothesis: Theory and Evidence,' *Journal of Political Economy,* Vol. 86 (December 1978), pp. 971–
988, and Marjorie Flavin, 'The Adjustment of Consumption to Changing Expectations about
Future Income,' *Journal of Political Economy,* Vol. 5 (October 1981), pp. 974–1009. Lars Peter
Hansen and Kenneth Singleton have incorporated rational expectations into the budget constraint in a formal intertemporal planning process in their 'Stochastic Consumption, Risk Aversion, and the Temporal Behavior of Asset Returns,' *Journal of Political Economy,* Vol. 91 (April
1983), pp. 249–265. John Cuddington implements Hall's approach using Canadian data in
'Canadian Evidence on the Permanent-Income Rational Expectations Hypothesis,' *Canadian
Journal of Economics,* Vol. 15 (May 1982), pp. 331–335. All these papers are technically de-
manding. They are listed here as sources; we suggest them as reading only for the more mathe-
matically inclined students.

Does Consumption Take a Random Walk?

One of the more fascinating findings of rational expectations research on the forward-looking consumption theory is that consumption should follow a *random walk*. A random walk is a technical term that connotes the image of a drunken sailor walking around changing directions every few seconds in a completely unpredictable manner. The best forecast of which direction that sailor will be walking in the next few minutes is the direction he is now walking, regardless of where that direction is taking him. Similarly, in economics a variable follows a random walk if the best guess of the variable next period is the same as the variable this period. Many economists feel that common stock prices follow a random walk.

A family's consumption takes a random walk if the best forecast of that family's consumption next year is the family's consumption this year. Why should the consumption of a forward-looking family who has rational expectations follow a random walk? The only reason a forward-looking family would change its level of consumption would be if its income changed in a way that could not be predicted. Recall that consumption smoothing implies that the family will try to consume the same amount every year: Consumption next year should be the same as consumption this year, so should consumption the year after that, and so on. Hence, the best predictor of what a family will consume next year is what the family is consuming this year! This year's consumption reflects all the available information on the family's future income expectations.

Because the future is not certain, consumption next year will of course be different than the family planned. If there is a surprise increase in income because the family won the lottery, then consumption next year will be greater than planned. But with rational expectations any such changes that have not already been incorporated into the consumption plans are unpredictable. Hence, the best guess of consumption next period is consumption this period.

Many economists have tested the random walk theory of consumption. Although the theory is approximately correct there are some discrepancies. In particular, changes in consumption seem to be positively related to past income. This indicates that consumption is more sensitive to income than would be predicted by the simple forward-looking model with rational expectations. Some of the reasons for this excess sensitivity are described in the text.

Although much of this research is new, it is already clear that the forward-looking consumption theory does not fare as well when people are assumed to forecast rationally. One problem is that consumption is a bit too responsive to temporary changes in income, although clearly not as responsive as in the simple Keynesian consumption theory. In other words, the forward-looking theory with rational expectations suggests that the short-run marginal propensity to consume should be even smaller than is observed in the data summarised in Table 8–1.

Individual Family Histories. One of the most important improvements in our knowledge of the economy in recent years is the availability of data on the economic histories of individuals and families over a span of several years. At the University of Michigan, for example, a survey called the Panel Study on Income Dynamics has kept tabs on the major economic and personal events of thousands of U.S. families since 1969. Such surveys that collect information on individuals over a number of years are typically called **panel** or **longitudinal surveys.** They are useful to macroeconomists because they tell how families experience recessions and booms individually. Aggregate data tell us only about all families in the economy added together. One study has looked at how well the forward-looking consumption model performs in describing the consumption behaviour of about 2,000 families in the Michigan panel data set.[8] The results show an excess sensitivity of consumption to temporary changes in disposable income. The marginal propensity to consume from temporary income was about 30 percent of the marginal propensity to consume from permanent income. This seems a bit higher than the 10 percent ratio that the pure forward-looking model suggests. The results seem to say that about 80 percent of the families behaved according to the forward-looking model, while about 20 percent behaved according to a simple model in which consumption is proportional to disposable income.

Policy Experiments. Governments have sometimes used changes in income tax rates to try to stabilise the economy. According to Douglas Purvis of Queen's University and Constance Smith of the University of Alberta, the reasoning behind the income tax rate increase of 1966 was to reduce output growth and so moderate inflationary pressure.[9] Similarly, the income tax cuts that took place in 1974 and 1977 were designed to stimulate the economy, which was perceived to be growing too slowly.

In the United States, income taxes were raised temporarily in 1968 as an anti-inflation measure and reduced temporarily in 1975 in order to stimulate demand. According to the forward-looking theory of consumption, families who realised that these tax changes were temporary would adjust their consumer expenditures by only a small amount; if so, the policy changes would not have their desired effect of restricting demand in 1968 or stimulating demand in 1975. On the other hand, according to the simple

---

[8] Robert Hall and Fredric Mishkin, 'The Sensitivity of Consumption to Transitory Income: Estimates from Panel Data on Households,' *Econometrica,* Vol. 50 (March 1982), pp. 461–481.

[9] Douglas D. Purvis and Constance Smith, 'Fiscal Policy in Canada: 1963–84,' in John Sargent (ed.), *Fiscal and Monetary Policy,* University of Toronto Press for the Royal Commission on the Economic Union and Development Prospects for Canada, 1986.

consumption function, these tax changes would be translated into large changes in consumption and thereby in aggregate demand.

Although clearly not conceived as experiments, such changes in tax policy give economists a rare opportunity to test the predictions of the forward-looking theory of consumption. This is probably as close as macro-economists will ever get to a laboratory experiment. As it turned out, the response of consumption to the change in disposable income seemed to be small. After the increase in taxes in the United States in 1968 consumers simply saved less of their reduced income and thereby reduced their spending only slightly. In the second quarter of 1975 the rate of saving as a fraction of disposable income in the United States rose to almost 10 percent from about 6 percent in the first quarter. Almost all of the increase in disposable income was saved, evidently because people knew the temporary nature of the income changes.

Alan Blinder of Princeton University has systematically studied the response of consumer spending to temporary changes in consumer income using a rational expectations approach similar to that described above.[10] His overall finding was that the marginal propensity to consume from a temporary tax change is about half of the marginal propensity to consume from a permanent tax change. This ratio is a bit above that found in the Michigan panel data (.3). Blinder's data suggest that the world is split about 50–50 between forward-looking consumers and those who consume a constant proportion of their current disposable income. But Blinder emphasises that these estimates are not precise. Perhaps the most important lesson from these experiments is that the response of the economy to a temporary income tax change is not the sure, predictable stimulus predicted by the simple consumption function.

DEFECTS IN THE FORWARD-LOOKING MODEL

Overall the empirical research discussed above indicates that the forward-looking model works fairly well: The marginal propensity to consume from temporary income is always less than the marginal propensity to consume from permanent income, as the theory predicts. But why doesn't it work better? Why does consumption respond as much as it does to temporary income? One reason is that the tests might be incorrectly estimating expectations of future income. In the case of temporary tax changes, for example, families may not be so aware of the machinations of the government. Perhaps they pay no attention to the news about tax changes. If they, like most people, see the benefits of a tax cut in the form of reduced withholding deductions from their paychecks, they may mistakenly assume that

---

[10] Alan Blinder, 'Temporary Income Taxes and Consumer Spending,' *Journal of Political Economy*, Vol. 89 (February 1981), pp. 26–53. The figures on tax rebates and saving mentioned in the previous paragraph are tabulated in Blinder's paper.

this cut in deductions is permanent. Then they will apply their regular marginal propensity to consume from income, which will be, say, .8. Moreover, when they find their deductions back up to the old level, they will reduce consumption accordingly.

Or suppose the family pays close attention to the economic news and believes that a temporary tax cut will accomplish its purpose of stimulating the economy. The family will benefit in the next year or two from the more favourable performance of the economy. According to the life-cycle and permanent-income hypotheses, the family should immediately increase its consumption because of its expected increase in economic well-being. Even though such a family would spend only a little of its tax rebate, it might raise its total consumption level because of the improved national economy.

Another possibility is that consumers cannot borrow as easily as the forward-looking model suggests and that especially during recessions they cannot obtain the funds to maintain their consumption. Economists call such consumers **liquidity constrained.**[11] Such consumers might be described very well by the simple Keynesian model; they would increase their expenditures as they receive more income regardless of whether it is permanent or temporary.

In concluding our discussion of the forward-looking model of consumption, it is important not to lose sight of the central ideas by focussing too much on the particular equations or tests that express the ideas. The basic point is that families are thoughtful about consumption decisions. The way they react to a change in economic circumstances depends on the context of the change. If the change is transitory—if it involves a windfall gain or loss—consumption is likely to respond relatively little. If the change in income will sustain itself for the foreseeable future, consumption will change almost by the full amount of the change in income.

The Forward-Looking Model of Consumption

1. The forward-looking model of consumption tries to improve the simple consumption function by relating consumption to expected future income rather than just to current income. It pictures families as making a consumption plan well into the future.

2. The theory says that the marginal propensity to consume from one-time, transitory income is low, perhaps as low as .05. The marginal propensity to consume from permanent increases in income is close to 1.

---

[11] Walter Dolde has studied the problem of liquidity-constrained consumers in 'Capital Markets and the Short Run and Behavior of Life Cycle Savers,' *Journal of Finance,* Vol. 33 (May 1978), pp. 413–428.

3. When the government tries to influence consumption spending through tax policy, the effects are sensitive to the permanence of the policy change. A one-time tax cut probably has little effect on consumption spending. A permanent tax cut probably has a much larger influence.

8.5 Real Interest Rates, Consumption, and Saving

Thus far we have assumed that consumers want a steady consumption path. They would like to consume about the same amount this year as next year and every year thereafter. This is a reasonable assumption if the price of future consumption goods is not too low or too high relative to present consumption goods. But suppose that the price of future consumption goods is suddenly expected to change. For example, in April 1978 a joint federal-provincial initiative temporarily reduced provincial sales taxes in order to stimulate demand. A sales tax reduction affects consumers in a different way than an income tax reduction because it makes the price of consumption goods change over time. As the sales tax reduction was known to be temporary, forward-looking consumers chose to 'speed up' their purchases, especially of large items such as cars and appliances. Consider those consumers who, in March 1978, were planning to buy new cars in 1979. After the government announced that the sales tax on new cars would be reduced in 1978, but return to its original level in 1979, many of these consumers changed their plans and purchased their cars earlier in order to take advantage of the temporarily lower price.

The interest rate also becomes a factor in consumption because it too affects the price of future consumption relative to current consumption. In fact, the *real* interest rate is the relative price between present consumption and future consumption. It thus directly affects the choice of whether to consume more today or more tomorrow. Recall that the interest rate quoted in the newspaper, the *nominal* interest rate, does not correct for changes in purchasing power. The real interest rate R equals the nominal interest rate minus the expected rate of inflation π^e. For example, if the nominal interest rate is 11 percent, but prices are expected to rise at 4 percent per year, then the real interest rate is 7 percent. If you postpone one unit of consumption this year, you can consume 1.07 units next year by investing at an 11 percent nominal rate and losing 4 percent to inflation.

If the real interest rate is positive, as it generally is, people face an incentive to defer spending. A dollar saved today will buy more than a dollar of goods tomorrow. Hence people will tend to defer consumption unless they are too impatient. Economists have a measure of impatience called the **rate of time preference.** If the real interest rate is higher than the rate of time preference, then people will tend to shift their consumption a bit toward the next year. If the real rate of interest is high, today's consumption will tend to be low. This factor makes consumption negatively related to the real rate of interest. Saving, which is simply the difference between disposable income and consumption, is therefore positively related to the real rate of interest.

Changes in the interest rate do something else in addition to changing the price of tomorrow's goods relative to today's. They change income. If interest rates rise, for example, a family can earn a higher real return from its accumulated assets. This makes the family better off. On this account, planned consumption is higher. This increase in consumption might offset the reduced consumption that comes from the incentive to defer consumption from today to tomorrow. Hence, we can't say unambiguously whether consumption in the first year falls or rises—the *income* effect makes it rise while the incentive to make a *substitution* of future consumption for present consumption makes it fall. Similarly, the effect of change in the real interest rate on saving is also ambiguous.[12] Of course, this offsetting tendency of the income effect and the substitution effect is common to many relative price changes in economics—not only the interest rate.

It is a controversial matter whether or not consumption is negatively related to the interest rate.[13] The most difficult problem in interpreting the data is that consumption depends on disposable income as well as on the interest rate, and during the business cycle income and the interest rate tend to move together. It is difficult to separate out the effect of one variable on the other.

Another complication in examining the relation between real interest and consumption is that the real interest rate is not observed directly. What we observe is the nominal interest rate. To convert it to a real rate, we must subtract the expected rate of inflation. Measuring the expected rate of inflation is difficult.

EFFECT OF REAL INTEREST RATES ON WORK

There is one last complication in our analysis of consumption. For this whole chapter we have assumed that individuals do not or cannot change how much they work. Income from work was taken as exogenous. But some people are free to vary how much they work. In particular, if real interest rates rise the value of income from working today relative to tomorrow

---

[12] The income and substitution effects are shown graphically in the appendix to this chapter.

[13] Michael J. Boskin, 'Taxation, Saving, and the Rate of Interest,' *Journal of Political Economy*, Vol. 86 (April 1978, pt. 2), pp. 53–527, and E. P. Howrey and S. H. Hymans, 'The Measurement and Determination of Loanable-Funds Saving,' *Brookings Papers on Economic Activity*, Vol. 3, 1978, pp. 655–705, are two widely cited recent empirical studies of the effect of interest rates on consumption and saving in the United States.

will work harder

rises. People could gain from working harder and longer hours now and taking time off to spend the earnings later. Hence, in principle, income from work is a positive function of the real interest rate. Because saving is the difference between disposable income and consumption, this positive effect of real interest rates on income from working reinforces the negative effect of real interest rates on consumption to make saving positively related to income.

Detecting empirically the effect of real interest rates on work effort has proved even more elusive than detecting the effect of real interest rates on consumption. It appears that most people cannot or do not adjust their work effort very much in response to interest rate changes. This corresponds with casual observation.

Consumption, Saving, and the Interest Rate

1. The consumption planning process should take the interest rate into account. The real interest rate—the nominal interest rate less the expected rate of inflation—is the trade-off facing the consumer between current and future consumption. When real interest rates are high, future consumption becomes cheaper relative to consumption this year.

2. It is difficult to isolate the effect of interest rates on consumption in actual data. There is no strong empirical confirmation of the theoretical possibility that saving responds positively to real interest rates, at least for the variation in real interest rates that has been observed.

8.6 Consumption and the IS Curve

In Chapter 5 we introduced the IS curve. It shows all the combinations of real GDP and interest rates where spending balance occurs. To find a point on the IS curve, we consider a particular interest rate. Then we find the level of GDP that gives spending balance at the interest rate. The IS curve is downward sloping in the IS-LM diagram with the interest rate R on the vertical axis and output Y on the horizontal axis. The slope of the IS curve and how much it is shifted by fiscal policy are crucial for evaluating the effects of monetary and fiscal policy.

Recall that the simple Keynesian consumption function was used in the derivation of the IS curve in Chapter 5. How is the IS curve affected by the factors considered in this chapter?

R less sensitive on output

THE SLOPE OF THE IS CURVE

Consider first the slope of the IS curve. The smaller the marginal propensity to consume (MPC), the steeper the slope of the IS curve. A small MPC means that the multiplier is small and changes in interest rates thereby have a small effect on output. The results considered in this chapter make us scale down the MPC. We saw that consumers have a lower MPC out of disposable income because the cyclical fluctuations in disposable income are viewed as temporary. On this account the IS curve is steeper than it seemed in Chapter 5, because output is less sensitive to the interest rate.

However, the interest rate effects on consumption considered towards the end of this chapter have an opposite effect on the IS curve. If consumption depends negatively on the interest rate, then a higher interest rate will shift the consumption function down, in which case the level of GDP corresponding to spending balance will be lower. On that account the IS curve is flatter than it seemed in Chapter 5, because output is more sensitive to the interest rate.

On balance it is an empirical question whether the true IS curve that incorporates the issues raised in this chapter is flatter or steeper than the IS curve derived in Chapter 5.

SHIFTS IN THE CURVE DUE TO TAX CHANGES

The IS curve in Chapter 5 did not distinguish between temporary and permanent changes in taxes. A cut in tax payments of any kind would shift the IS curve to the right by the same amount and thereby stimulate output by the same amount. The forward-looking theory of consumption says that the shift in the IS curve should be much larger if the tax cut is permanent rather than temporary. A purely temporary tax cut would have a very small effect on the IS curve.

Because it is sometimes difficult to tell whether people think a tax cut is permanent or temporary, the forward-looking theory points to an element of uncertainty in our ability to determine how much the IS curve will shift in response to tax changes.

Finally, the forward-looking theory says that the IS curve will shift to the right in response to an *expectation* of future tax cuts. Future tax cuts will stimulate consumption today because lifetime disposable income has increased.

Review and Practice

MAJOR POINTS

1. Consumers finance their consumption from their incomes, and consumption has tracked income reasonably closely in Canadian history.

2. However, there have been significant deviations from a simple consumption function.

3. The forward-looking consumption theory relates consumption to current and expected future income rather than to just current income.

4. In this view, the marginal propensity to consume from transitory income is much lower than that from permanent changes in income.

5. Tax policy does not operate in a mechanical way through disposable income. Families raise their consumption only if a tax cut makes them feel better off, which may not happen with some types of cuts.

6. Though higher real interest rates ought to stimulate saving by making consumers defer consumption, this hypothesis has not been firmly established by the data.

7. The marginal propensity to consume is one of the determinants of the slope of the IS curve. Because of automatic stabilisers and the low short-run marginal propensity to consume of forward-looking consumers, the IS curve may be steep.

KEY TERMS AND CONCEPTS

Consumption

Disposable income

Keynesian consumption function

Marginal propensity to consume (MPC)

Long-run marginal propensity to consume

Short-run marginal propensity to consume

Forward-looking theory of consumption

Intertemporal budget constraint

Smooth consumption path

Friedman permanent-income model

Ando-Modigliani life-cycle model

Marginal propensity to consume out of temporary income

Marginal propensity to consume out of permanent income

Rational expectations tests

Panel data tests

Real interest rate

Rate of time preference

Income effect

Substitution effect

Automatic stabilisers

QUESTIONS FOR DISCUSSION AND REVIEW

1. List some of the reasons that disposable income is less than GDP. What factors tend to raise disposable income even though they are not part of GDP?

2. How can you tell if a simple consumption function governs the relation of consumption and income?

3. What is an estimate of the marginal propensity to consume from the historical relation of consumption to income? Why is this estimate probably an overstatement of the reaction of consumption to a temporary tax cut? What is an estimate of the short-run marginal propensity to consume?

4. Outline the way that a family might plan its consumption. How would it react to learning that tax rates are going to rise in the future?

5. Why is the marginal propensity to consume out of temporary income a bit above the real interest rate?

6. List some of the reasons that a tax cut has an uncertain effect on consumption.

7. Review all the steps involved in constructing the IS curve, including the possibility that consumption responds to the interest rate.

PROBLEMS

Numerical

1. Use the intertemporal budget constraint for this problem. To make calculations easy assume that a family lives for 5 years with 4 years of work and 1 year of retirement. (A more realistic assumption would be a 50-year horizon with 40 years of work and 10 years of retirement.) Consider a family that wishes to consume the same amount each year. Assume earnings of $25,000 per year and an interest rate of 5 percent. Assume initial assets of zero.

   a. Find the level of consumption such that the assets at the end of 5 years are roughly zero, say within $100. What is the level of assets at the beginning of retirement?

   b. Repeat the calculation of consumption, but with initial assets of $1,000. By how much does consumption rise? Compare this to the interest earnings on $1,000 at 5 percent, namely, $50 per year. Would the increase be closer to $50 if the family lived for 50 years?

   c. Repeat the calculation of consumption, with initial assets of zero, but with earnings of $26,000 per year. By how much does consumption rise? Explain why the increase in consumption is larger than in Part b.

2. Suppose that we have a consumption function of the form

$$C = 80 + .9Y_\mathrm{p},$$

where Y_p is permanent disposable income. Suppose that consumers estimate their permanent disposable income by a simple average of disposable income in the present and previous years:

$$Y_\mathrm{p} = .5(Y_\mathrm{d} + Y_\mathrm{d-1}),$$

where Y_d is actual disposable income.

   a. Suppose that disposable income Y_d is equal to $3,000 in Year 1 and is also equal to $3,000 in Year 2. What is consumption in Year 2?

   b. Suppose that disposable income increases to $4,000 in Year 3 and then remains at $4,000 in all future years. What is consumption in Years 3 and 4 and all remaining years? Explain why consumption responds the way it does to an increase in income.

   c. What is the short-run marginal propensity to consume? What is the long-run marginal propensity to consume?

   d. Explain why this formulation of consumption may provide a more accurate description of consumption than the simple consumption function that depends only on current income.

3. Suppose that consumption is given by the same equation as in Problem 2, but that consumers set their permanent income Y_p equal to the average of their expected income in all future years.

   a. Suppose that, as in the previous problem, disposable income was $3,000 in Years 1 and 2, but suppose also that in Year 2 consumers expect that disposable income will be $3,000 in all future years. What is consumption in Year 2?

   b. Suppose that in Year 3 disposable income rises to $4,000, and that consumers expect the $4,000 level to remain in all future years. What is consumption in Year 3?

c. Explain why consumption in Year 3 is different from that in Problem 2 even though the disposable income is the same.

4. Suppose again that consumption is given by the same equation as in Problem 2 and that permanent income is estimated in the same way as in Problem 2. Place this consumption function into a simple macro model like the one in Chapter 4. That is, disposable income Y_d is equal to income Y less taxes T, where taxes equal $.3Y$, and the income identity is $Y = C + I + G$.
   a. Suppose that in Year 2 investment I is $650 and government spending G is $750. Suppose that disposable income Y_d in Year 1 was $2,800. What are consumption, income, and disposable income in Year 2?
   b. Suppose that in Year 3 government spending increases to $800 and then remains at $800 for all future years. What are consumption, income, and disposable income in Year 3? (Make sure to use your calculation from Part a of disposable income in Year 2 when you calculate consumption in Year 3.)
   c. Calculate income and consumption for Years 4, 5, and 6. Do you see a pattern developing?
   d. Where do you think income will end up after it stops changing? Compare your answer to the simple case where consumption depends on current disposable income only, so that the multiplier formulas of Chapter 5 apply.

5. Suppose that the consumption function is given by

$$C = 130 + .63Y - 1,000R$$

rather than by the consumption function in Chapter 5. Add this consumption function to the other four equations of the macro model:

$$Y = C + I + G + X$$
$$M = (.1625Y - 1,000R)P$$
$$I = 750 - 2,000R$$
$$X = 425 - .1Y - 500R$$

Treat the price level as predetermined at 1.0, and let government spending be $750 and the money supply be $600.
   a. Derive an algebraic expression for the IS curve for this model and plot it to scale. Compare it with the IS curve in the examples of Chapter 5. Which is steeper? Why?
   b. Derive the aggregate demand curve and plot it to scale. How does it compare with the aggregate demand curve in the example of Chapter 5?
   c. Calculate the effect of an increase in government spending on GDP. Is the effect larger or smaller than in the case where consumption does not depend on the interest rate? Describe the process of crowding out in this case.
   d. Calculate the effect of an increase in the money supply on GDP. Is the impact larger or smaller than in the case where consumption does not depend on the interest rate? Explain.

6. The problem of the family choosing a consumption plan can be analysed using utility functions from intermediate microeconomics. In fact, this is how the forward-looking theory has been tested in recent research. Consider a very simple 2-year horizon for a family planning consumption. The family wants to determine how much to consume in Year 1 and in Year 2. Let consumption in Year 1 be C_1, and let consumption in Year 2 be C_2. Suppose that the family's satisfaction, or utility, from consuming C_1 and C_2 is given by the function

$$\text{Utility} = \sqrt{C_1} + \frac{1}{(1 + RT)} \sqrt{C_2},$$

where RT is the rate of time preference. Start with the rate of time preference equal to zero.

a. Show that this utility function means that the family prefers smooth consumption to erratic consumption. Which plan for consumption gives the family the greater utility: $3,600 in the first year and $4,900 in the next, or $4,250 in both years?

b. Show that when the rate of time preference is high the family will prefer to consume more in the first period. Do the following comparison: First set RT equal to zero and evaluate the utility of $3,600 in the first year and $3,000 in the second year versus $3,300 in both years; then raise RT to .25 and make the comparison again.

Analytical

1. Which of the following stylised facts are consistent with forward-looking theories of consumption? Which are not? Justify your answer in each case. Where the facts are not consistent with the theory, can you suggest some alternative explanations?
   a. The *marginal* propensity to consume out of current income is less for old people than for middle-aged people.
   b. The *marginal* propensity to consume out of current income is less for farmers than for most other occupations.
   c. Most European countries have both more extensive social welfare systems for older people and higher saving rates than does the United States.
   d. The saving rate in Canada fell from 1985 to 1987.
   e. The marginal propensity to consume out of temporary tax cuts is around .3 to .5.
   f. Across the population as a whole, people with lower incomes have lower saving rates than people with higher incomes.
   g. The amount of wealth in the economy is far greater than what current wage earners will consume in their retirement.

2. Suppose that actual GDP is below potential GDP, that inflation is low, and that the federal government wants to cut taxes in order to increase aggregate demand and bring the economy back to potential.
   a. Describe the situation using an IS-LM diagram. Show where you want the IS curve to move in order to reach potential.
   b. In light of the forward-looking theory of consumption, describe some of problems that might arise with the tax cut plan.

3. Draw a sketch of an IS-LM diagram. Compare two cases, one where the consumption function depends on the interest rate, the other where the consumption function does not depend on the interest rate. Compare the relative effectiveness of monetary and fiscal policy in the two different situations.

4. Explain the following puzzle: Saving depends positively on the interest rate, investment depends negatively on the interest rate, and saving equals investment. How does an increase in the money supply that lowers the interest rate and thereby increases investment also increase saving? It would seem that with the lower interest rate saving would be lower. What's going on?

5. An important implication of the permanent-income hypothesis is that fiscal policy operates with a lag.
   a. Explain why a permanent increase in government spending may cause the IS curve to shift out slowly over time, rather than shift out all at once.
   b. If permanent income is a weighted average of last period's and this period's income, what determines the speed at which the IS curve shifts out over time?

Appendix: A Graphical Approach to Consumption Planning

In this appendix we show how a two-period consumption planning problem can be represented graphically. Suppose that the representative family must choose how much to consume this year and next year. Figure 8–9 shows how the family's preferences for consumption in the two periods might look; the vertical axis is consumption next year (Year 2) and the horizontal axis is consumption this year (Year 1). The curved lines are **indifference curves**; they give the alternative values for consumption in the two years between which the family is indifferent. The slope of the line measures how many dollars of consumption next year must be given up when consumption this year rises by one dollar for the family to maintain the same level of satisfaction, or utility. This is sometimes called the **marginal rate of substitution** between consumption this year and consumption next year. The family is better off when the indifference curves are farther out and up.

The straight line in Figure 8–9 is simply the intertemporal budget constraint for the two periods. The slope of the line is $-(1 + R)$ because the family will have an additional $(1 + R)$ dollars of consumption next year for each dollar of consumption that is reduced (and thus saved) this year. (The equation for the budget line comes directly from Equation 8–2 with no taxes, no initial assets, and no bequest and is applied for two periods. Then Equation 8–2 is $A_2 = E_1 - C_1$ in Year 1, and $0 = (1 + R) A_2 + E_2 - C_2$ in Year 2. Putting A_2 into the equation for Year 1 gives the equation for the budget line.) The point on the line marked * represents the amount of income from work this year and next year. Moving up the line from * means that the family

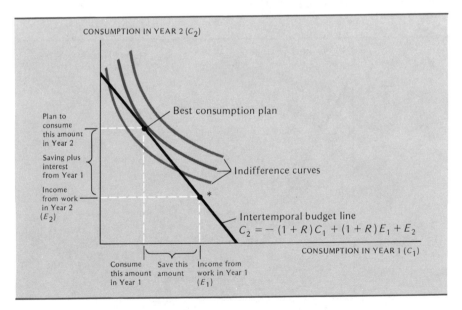

Figure 8–9. INDIFFERENCE CURVE AND INTERTEMPORAL BUDGET LINE FOR CONSUMPTION PLANNING.
The indifference curve is the combination of consumption in the two years that gives the same level of satisfaction to the family. The straight line is the budget constraint. The family tries to get to the highest indifference curve. This occurs where the indifference curve and the budget line just meet at a point of tangency.

is saving this year, because income is greater than consumption. Moving down on the line means that the family borrows this year.

The family tries to maximise utility or, in terms of the graph, to get to the highest indifference curve. This occurs at a point of tangency between the budget line and the indifference curve, as shown in the diagram. At this point the slopes are equal so we know that the marginal rate of substitution between consumption next year and consumption this year is equal to 1 plus the interest rate.

Now, suppose that the interest rate increases. This is shown in Figure 8–10. The budget line will then tilt in a steeper direction, pivoting around the point ∗. A higher level of utility is thereby achieved. As the graph is drawn, less is consumed this year. But note that this depends very much on how the indifference curves are drawn. (Try to draw another for which the reverse occurs.) The tilting of the curve represents the substitution effect, which certainly causes consumption this year to fall. But the budget line has also moved out to the right from where it was before on the indifference curve. This is the income effect. It certainly leads to more consumption today. The overall impact depends on which is stronger, the substitution effect or the income effect. In Figure 8–10 the substitution effect is stronger.

Now consider the effects of changes in income from work, assuming that the interest rate does not change. It is easy to see that a permanent change in income from work leads to a greater change in consumption than does a temporary change. Suppose that earnings in Year 1 increase but earnings in Year 2 do not. The budget line shifts out, raising consumption in both periods. The new budget line has the same slope as the original budget line (because, by assumption, the interest rate has not changed) and it passes through the point given by the now higher level of E_1 and the original level of E_2. Now suppose that the increase in income was permanent, so that

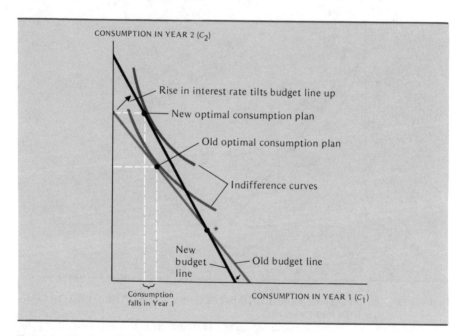

Figure 8–10.   INCREASE IN THE INTEREST RATE.
As the interest rate increases, the budget line gets steeper. This leads to a higher level of utility. As drawn, the family consumes less this period. But it is uncertain whether the family will consume less if other indifference curves are drawn.

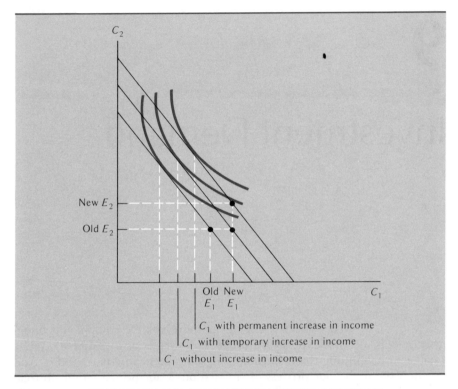

Figure 8–11.   TEMPORARY AND PERMANENT INCREASES IN INCOME.
With the interest rate unchanged an increase in earnings in either period shifts the budget line outward. This increases consumption in both periods. Thus a permanent change
in income has a larger effect than a temporary change.

E_2 also rose by the same amount as the increase in E_1. The budget line would shift
out again (now passing through the new values of E_1 and E_2), further increasing consumption in both periods. Thus the effect on consumption in Period 1 is greater
when the change in income in Period 1 is permanent rather than temporary. This is
shown in Figure 8–11.

9

Investment Demand

INVESTMENT IS one of the more volatile components of aggregate demand (net exports are roughly as volatile as investment). While smaller in magnitude than consumption, investment fluctuates more. And through the multiplier process its fluctuations lead to fluctuations in total output and income. Keynes argued that investment was the primary driving force in the economy, fluctuating erratically because of capricious shifts in business expectations, with consumption responding passively according to the simple consumption function.

In looking at the microeconomic underpinnings of investment we will see that Keynes's distinction between investment and consumption is not so pronounced. For one thing, investment, much as consumption, responds to income and output in a systematic way. When investment rises, it may be the result, not the cause, of an increase in spending elsewhere in the economy. Moreover, while investment decisions do depend on business expectations, these expectations are based on calculated estimates of future changes in demand and prices that businesses are likely to face. In making their investment decisions, business firms are at least as forward-looking as the consumers that we described in Chapter 8.

9.1 Fluctuations in Investment Spending

We saw in Chapter 2 that investment spending is divided into three categories:

1. Nonresidential fixed investment—business purchases of new plants and equipment

220

2. Residential fixed investment—construction of new houses and apart-
   ments
3. Inventory investment—increases in stocks of goods produced but not
   yet sold

Nonresidential fixed investment was 11.4 percent of GDP in 1987. Residential investment was 7.1 percent of GDP in the same year. But the shares
of the different types of investment in GDP are not a good measure of their
importance in economic fluctuations. Although plant and equipment investment is the dominant component of total investment, it is the most
stable over time. Since inventory investment is negative as stocks of unsold
goods fall and positive when stocks of goods rise, its share of GDP is not a
very meaningful statistic. Yet, inventory investment is particularly volatile
and has a major role in recessions. Finally, residential investment is important because housing construction drops when mortgage interest rates go
up.

Figure 9–1 shows how fixed investment is linked to overall economic activity. Weak investment spending was experienced during the recessions of
1953–54, 1957, 1960–61, and 1981–82. The fluctuations of investment
are larger in percentage terms than the fluctuations in real GDP. Unlike consumption, investment contributes more than its share to the fluctuations in
real GDP. Sometimes fluctuations in investment occur without fluctuations
in GDP, as long as consumption, government spending, or net exports move
in the opposite direction.

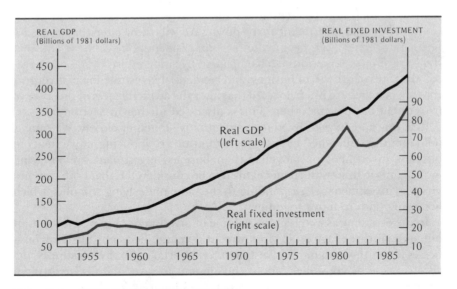

Figure 9–1.   FIXED INVESTMENT AND GDP.
Real fixed investment and real GDP tend to fluctuate together. However, the fluctuations
in fixed investment are larger than the fluctuations in total GDP. Source: *Canadian Economic Observer,* Table 1.3.

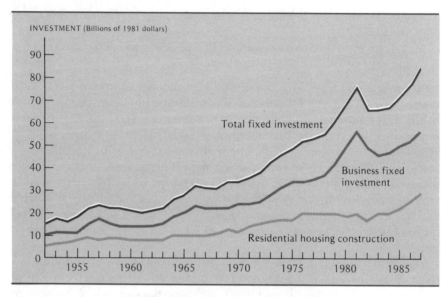

Figure 9-2. HOUSING VERSUS FACTORIES AND EQUIPMENT.
Separating housing investment from business investment reveals some important timing differences. Both business investment and housing investment fluctuate widely during recessions and booms. But housing investment appears to peak before business investment. Source: *Canadian Economic Observer*, Table 1.3.

The behaviour of the two components of fixed investment—business (nonresidential) and residential—is shown in Figure 9-2. In most recessions, residential investment turns down. We will show later that rising interest rates have large negative effects on residential investment and that the start of most recessions is accompanied by rising interest rates. One reason the rates of growth of business and residential investment may diverge is that tax changes are often enacted that alter the attractiveness of one type of investment but not the other. This is discussed further in Section 9.4.

Real GDP and *business* fixed investment move together closely. We cannot tell from the data whether movements in GDP are inducing movements in business investment or movements in business investment are inducing movements in GDP. A third mechanism to be considered is that both GDP and business investment are responding to the same underlying stimulus, which is causing both to move together.

In the economy as a whole, the volume of investment observed is the joint outcome of three factors: (1) **investment demand,** decisions made by businesses about the amount of investment to undertake; (2) **saving supply,** decisions made by consumers about the amount to save; and (3) **investment supply,** decisions made by producers of investment goods about how much to supply.

This chapter focusses on investment demand. A complete model of the economy that combines saving behaviour as described in Chapter 8 and the supply side of the economy is necessary to give a complete picture of investment. But we have already had a preview of the demand and supply process in Chapters 4 through 6. The economy reconciles the decisions of the various groups with the interest rate and the price of capital goods. If businesses want to invest more than consumers are willing to lend, the interest rate rises enough to depress investment and stimulate savings to the point of equality. If businesses want to invest more than the producers of investment goods want to produce, the price of capital goods rises. Then investment demand falls and the supply of capital goods rises, again to the point of equality.

Investment Analysis

1. Investment is the flow of newly produced capital goods. It consists of plant and equipment investment, residential investment, and inventory investment.

2. Investment is much more volatile than consumption. Declines in business fixed investment often coincide with declines in the overall economy. Declines in housing investment often lead the declines in the overall economy.

3. The overall level of investment depends on three elements: the investment demand of firms and households, the funds available for investment, and the amount of investment goods produced. Interest rates and the prices of investment goods move to equate the three elements. In this chapter we focus on the demand side.

9.2 How a Business Looks at the Investment Decision

In examining the micro foundations of investment demand we will start with business fixed investment and look at the decision process of a typical business firm. From a firm's perspective there are really two decisions that can be distinguished. The first thing for the managers to decide is how many factories and machines they want. That is, what is the firm's desired **capital stock**? The second question is how fast to build the factories and when to order the machines that they want. That is, what is the **flow of investment**? The simple investment function that we introduced in Chapter 5 focuses on the flow of investment while ignoring the desired capital stock. Here we start with the question of the desired capital stock, and derive the flow demand subsequently.

It is helpful to pose the typical firm's problem in the following rather abstract way: Suppose a firm has already figured out how much output it plans to produce during the upcoming period, say a year. Further, suppose that, whatever capital it will use, it will *rent* from another firm in the equipment rental business. For example, a firm in the business of offering typing services to its customers would rent word-processing equipment from a computer-leasing firm. (Many firms own most of their capital, but we will look at that case a little later.) The idea of thinking about a firm's investment decision as a choice about how much capital to rent was developed by Dale Jorgenson of Harvard University. He developed such models of investment starting in the early 1960s.[1] It is a useful abstraction because it makes the capital decision much like the decision to employ other factors used in production, such as labour and raw materials.

How much capital will the firm choose to rent? Microeconomics tells us the answer: the amount that equates the marginal benefit to the marginal cost. The **marginal benefit** is the amount of dollars saved by using fewer of the other factors of production when more capital is employed. A firm with more capital will need fewer workers, less energy, or fewer materials to produce the same amount of output. For example, with a word processor, a firm offering typing services might require fewer hours from proofreaders and typists, and perhaps fewer correction materials (like Liquid Paper). Note that the firm must look ahead to determine the marginal benefit of employing more capital during the period that it will rent the capital. Firms are thus assumed to be *forward-looking* in this theory of investment.

The **marginal cost** of capital is just the rental cost charged by the renting firm. For example, it is the amount that the computer-leasing firm charges each year for word-processing equipment.

The firm's decision can be illustrated graphically. The most important input to production is labour, so consider the case where the input displaced by capital is labour. The production function relating labour input to output produced is shown in Figure 9–3. When there is more labour input, there is more output. For example, for the typing services firm, when typists and proofreaders work more hours, more typed pages are produced. When there is more capital in the firm, the production function relating labour input to output produced is shifted upward, as shown in Figure 9–3. In this case fewer hours given by typists and proofreaders result in the same number of typed pages. In Figure 9–3, N is the level of employment needed to produce planned output with the existing capital stock, and N' is the reduced level of employment needed to produce planned output if extra capital is rented. If the wage per worker is W, the marginal benefit of the extra capital is $(N - N')W$.

We assume that capital has a **diminishing marginal product,** which means that the amount of the upward shift in the production function and corresponding decrease in labour requirements decline as the amount of capital grows. For example, if the typing services firm began with one full-time typist and one half-time proofreader, the first word processor would

<hr />

[1] The basic framework described here is due to the work of Dale Jorgenson, in particular, his 'Capital Theory and Investment Behavior,' *American Economic Review,* Vol. 53 (May 1963), pp. 247–259.

Figure 9–3. THE PRODUCTION FUNCTION AND THE MARGINAL BENEFIT OF CAPITAL.
The production function shows the amount of output produced from different amounts of labour. The lower production function describes the situation with the existing capital of the firm. In order to produce the planned output, the firm will have to employ N workers. The upper production function applies if the firm decides to rent some extra capital. In that case, to produce the planned output, only N' workers need to be employed. The marginal benefit of capital is the reduced wage payments, $(N - N')W$.

result in more labour saved than a second word processor. The third and fourth word processors would displace essentially no labour. We can describe the relationship between capital and the marginal benefit of additional capital in a **marginal benefit of capital** schedule, as shown in Figure 9–4.

The marginal benefit of capital schedule is the firm's **demand curve for rented capital** as well. To choose its level of capital, the firm simply finds the

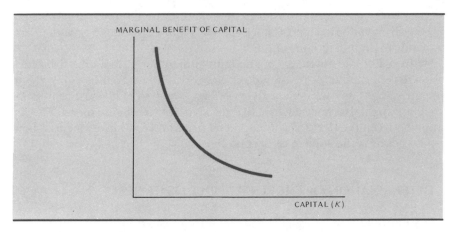

Figure 9–4.   THE MARGINAL BENEFIT OF CAPITAL SCHEDULE.
The marginal benefit of capital is a declining function of the amount of capital, because of the diminishing marginal product of capital. The position of the schedule depends on the level of planned output and on the wage rate.

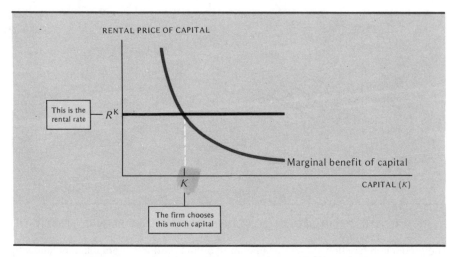

Figure 9–5. CHOOSING THE CAPITAL STOCK.
The marginal benefit of capital schedule is the firm's demand function for rented capital.
The firm chooses its capital stock by equating the marginal benefit of capital to its rental
price. With planned output and the wage rate held constant, the firm will choose to rent
more capital and employ less labour if the rental price falls.

amount of capital that equates the marginal benefit of capital to the marginal cost, which is the rental price. We call the rental price of capital R^K. The superscript K is a mnemonic for capital. Figure 9–5 illustrates the process.

What happens if the firm decides to produce more output? Looking back at Figure 9–3, you can see that producing more output with the same capital stock will require more labour. That, in turn, raises the marginal benefit of capital. To equate the marginal benefit to an unchanged rental price of capital, the firm will have to rent more capital. Figure 9–6 shows how the firm responds to an increase in output.

We have not said anything yet about investment, only about the firm's decision to rent capital. A firm could rent more capital without bringing about any investment in the economy as a whole. The firm might just rent some existing capital that another firm had decided not to rent anymore. The relation between the decisions of individual firms and total investment in new capital goods is the subject of Section 9.3.

DETERMINATION OF THE RENTAL PRICE OF CAPITAL

How would the market set the rental price of capital? We can answer this by looking at the costs faced by a rental firm—like a computer-leasing firm —that is in the business of owning machines and renting them out. We will make use of the following terms and assumptions:

Figure 9–6. EFFECT OF HIGHER OUTPUT.
When planned output rises and the rental price of capital and the wage remain the same, the firm's demand for capital rises. Higher planned output shifts the marginal benefit for capital schedule to the right. The firm's demand for rented capital rises from K to K'.

P^K is the price for purchasing a new machine from a producer of machines. The price is assumed to be unchanging for now. The price is measured in 'real' terms, that is, relative to the price of other noncapital goods, like haircuts or typing services.

R is the real interest rate.

d is the rate of depreciation. At the end of each year, the rental firm has to spend an amount d times the original amount spent on the machine P^K in order to make up for wear and tear on the machine.

R^K is the rental price of the equipment. This is the amount received by the rental firm for renting out the machine for one year.

First, consider the cost side of the rental operation. Suppose the rental firm decides to sell the machine after one year in the rental market. At the beginning of the year it borrows P^K to buy the machine at an interest rate of R and incurs an interest cost of RP^K. It has to pay dP^K to make up for depreciation. Total rental costs are therefore

$$(R + d)P^K. = R^K \qquad (9-1)$$

In words, Equation 9–1 states:

> The cost of renting out one machine for one year =
> (The rate of interest + The rate of depreciation)
> × The price of a new machine.

For example, if the price of a word processor is $10,000, the interest rate $R = .05$, and the depreciation rate $d = .15$, then the rental price is $2,000 per year.

What will be the market rental price? If the renter does not have a monopoly in the rental market, the market rental price will exactly equal the cost of renting. If it were any higher, new firms would enter the rental business and bid down the rent. If the rent were below cost, some rental firms would go out of business and rents would rise. Thus, the rental price of a machine for a year is just as spelled out above—the interest rate plus the rate of depreciation times the price of a new machine. Algebraically, we have

$$R^K = (R + d)P^K. \tag{9-2}$$

Now we can go back to Figure 9–5 and relate the demand for capital by the firm that uses capital to the underlying determinants of the rental price of capital. Remember that the firm's demand for capital is a declining function of the rental price, so that the demand for capital is a declining function of the price of new equipment and a declining function of the real interest rate.

Demand for Capital and Rental Price

1. The demand for capital declines if the rental price of capital rises. The rental price will rise if the price of new equipment rises or if the interest rate rises. *θ: ↓ demand for capital*

2. The demand for capital rises if planned output rises.

3. The demand for capital rises if the wage rises.

THE RENTAL PRICE AND THE DECISION TO BUY NEW CAPITAL GOODS

A good deal of the capital equipment in Canadian industry is in fact rented, so the analysis we have just presented is more than an abstraction. But the bulk of capital is owned by the firm that uses it in production. Moreover, the one-year perspective we used to solve for the rental price of capital is not representative. Most firms purchase capital for the long run. Their concern is not just with the payoff in the first year, but with the financial success of the project over a decade or more. They must look ahead and estimate the benefits of a new capital project under the assumption that it will operate for quite a number of years.

The attraction of Jorgenson's rental price approach is that it gives the same answer to the question of what should be the desired capital stock as the more realistic approach in which the firm buys the capital and uses it for

a number of years. Firms are constantly formulating and evaluating investment projects. An investment project that consistently earns more than the
rental price of capital is worth undertaking. The project is a winner because
the firm earns more than it would have to pay to borrow money to finance
the project plus pay to cover the depreciation of the capital required for the
project. Similarly, an investment project that consistently earns less than the
rental price of capital is not worth undertaking. It is a loser.

Because of the diminishing marginal product of capital, as the winning
projects are put into effect they will depress the earnings of future projects.
Eventually, the last winning project will earn just the borderline revenue,
namely, the rental price of the capital. On the margin, the firm taking a
long-term view and purchasing its own capital will reach just the same point
it would if it chose to rent capital and made a year-by-year decision about
the amount of capital to use. Both the capital budgeting approach and the
rental approach arrive at the same conclusion: *The firm makes use of capital
up to the point where the marginal benefit of capital equals the rental price of capital.*

Not all investment decisions fit neatly into this analysis. If the firm's technology requires that investment take place in large lumps—like building
blast furnaces or power plants—it may not be able to find a combination of
projects with the property that the marginal benefit of investment in each
year is just equal to the rental price of capital. It may have to settle for a situation where the marginal benefit is higher in some years and lower in
others. The basic criterion for selecting winning investment projects remains the same for these lumpy investments. On the average, the marginal
benefit of capital will be equated to the rental price even in those cases. An
investment theory based on the equality of marginal benefit and rental price
seems a reasonable approximation of dealing with the aggregate economy,
even when some of the thousands of firms in the aggregate are making decisions about lumpy investments.

EXPECTED CHANGES IN THE FUTURE PRICE OF CAPITAL

So far we have assumed that the relative price of capital, P^K, does not
change, and is therefore not expected to change. What happens if the relative price of capital goods is expected to change? The forward-looking
aspects of the firm's investment decision now become important. Consider
first the rental firm. Suppose that the price of capital is *expected* to *decrease*
during the period that the capital equipment is rented out. On this account
the rental firm stands to take a loss. It purchased the capital for P^K, and the
capital will be worth less than that, say P_1^K, next year when the equipment is
returned. The rental firm expects to lose $P^K - P_1^K$. In order to cover this expected loss, the rental firm will increase the rental price that it charges by
the exact amount of the expected loss. For example, if the price is expected
to fall from $P^K = \$1,000$ to $P_1^K = \$950$ next year, then it would increase the

rental price by $50. Conversely, if the rental firm expected an increase in the price of capital, it would stand to gain. It could cover its costs by charging a lower rental price. In general the rental price is decreased by the amount of the *expected* increase in price of capital, ΔP^K.

With capital goods prices expected to change, the formula for the rental price becomes the old formula in Equation 9—1 less the expected change in the price of capital equipment:

$$R^K = (R + d)P^K - \Delta P^K.$$

The same thing can be written a bit more compactly as

$$R^K = (R - \pi^K + d)P^K,$$

where the π^K is the expected percentage change in the relative price of capital equipment. Thus: $\Delta P^K / P^K$.

This modification of the earlier rental price formula becomes very important when the price of capital is expected to change by a large amount relative to the price of other goods. As we will see below, for example, changes in taxes can alter the effective price of capital. If these changes in taxes are *anticipated* by firms, then the rental price of capital will change. Since firms increase their desired capital stock when the rental rate falls, a decline in the rental rate due to an expected change in taxes will increase capital spending.

9.3 The Investment Function

To keep things simple in our derivation of the investment function, we will assume that firms purchase all of their capital. As we have just seen, the rental price of capital is the central economic variable for investment decisions.

The firm's **investment demand function** tells how much capital equipment the firm will purchase given its planned level of output and the rental price of capital. If the firm has been in business for a while, it will have an existing stock of capital at the beginning of the year. After examining the planned level of output and the rental price of capital, it will decide upon a level of capital to use during the year. Finally, it will purchase enough new capital to make up the difference. In a nutshell, this is the theory of investment.

Earlier, we showed that the firm chooses the amount of capital it uses by equating the marginal benefit of capital to the rental price of capital. When the amount of capital is high, the marginal benefit of further capital is low. By adjusting the amount of capital, the marginal benefit can be brought into equality with the rental price. The result of this process is the firm's **desired capital stock,** which we call K^*.

Where marginal benefit = marginal cost

An example of an algebraic formula describing the desired capital is

$$K^* = .5(W/R^K)Y. \tag{9-3}$$

In this formula, W is the wage rate, Y is the firm's level of output, and R^K is the rental price of capital. The formula says that the desired capital stock equals .5 times the ratio of the wage to the rental price of capital, times the level of output. Hence, the firm will want to increase its use of capital whenever the wage to rental price ratio rises. When labour becomes more expensive relative to capital, the firm substitutes toward capital. Whenever planned output Y rises the firm will also want to use more capital.

Now consider how the **actual capital stock** changes. Suppose that the firm finishes the last year with a capital stock of K_{-1} (the subscript '−1' means last year) that is not equal to the desired capital stock for this year, K^*. If there is no depreciation then the level of investment will increase the capital stock by the amount of the investment. That is, investment equals the change in the capital stock:

$$I = K - K_{-1}. \tag{9-4}$$

If the firm wants its capital stock K to equal the desired capital stock K^*, then its investment demand I during the year is obtained by substituting $K = K^*$ into Equation 9–4. That is,

$$I = K^* - K_{-1}. \tag{9-5}$$

This much investment added to its existing capital will give the firm its desired level of capital for this year. This formula is the firm's **investment function.** The investment function for the example formula for the desired capital stock K^* in Equation 9–3 can be written out as

$$I = .5(W/R^K)Y - K_{-1}. \tag{9-6}$$

Then it is apparent that *investment depends positively on the wage rate, negatively on the rental price of capital, and positively on output.*

The effect of output on investment is called the **accelerator.** To simplify the notation, set $.5(W/R^K)$ equal to the simple expression v. Then, Equation 9–3 states that $K^* = vY$. If the firm always adjusts its capital stock each year so that it is equal to the desired stock, then

$$K = vY \quad \text{and} \quad K_{-1} = vY_{-1} . \tag{9-7}$$

This year   Last year

Investment, which is the change in the capital stock, must therefore be given by the difference between the two expressions in Equation 9–7. That is,

$$I = vY - vY_{-1} = v\Delta Y. \tag{9–8}$$

In words, the *level* of investment I depends on the *change* of output ΔY. When output accelerates, that is, when its change gets bigger, investment is stimulated. A rise in output from one level to another causes a burst of investment, but if output remains at its higher level, investment subsides. This accelerator process seems to explain a large fraction of the movements in investment.[2] It certainly is part of the reason for the close association between investment and GDP that we noted at the beginning of the chapter.

DEPRECIATION AND GROSS INVESTMENT

If the capital stock depreciates, as of course it does in reality, then the investment equations we have derived so far are only for net investment; recall that net investment is the change in the capital stock. A gross investment equation can be easily derived by adding a term to Equation 9–6 that measures the part of investment that goes for replacing worn-out capital. One assumption is that a constant fraction d of the existing capital stock wears out each period.[3] Then d times K_{-1} is added to Equation 9–6 and to all the related forms of the investment demand function in this chapter. Depreciation accounts for a very large part of gross investment. In 1987, for example, gross private domestic investment was \$102 billion, while depreciation was \$63 billion. Net investment was therefore \$39 billion.

$$I = 0.5(W/R^K)Y - K_{-1} + dK_{-1}$$

Properties of the Investment Function

1. When the growth of output Y is high, investment is high.

2. When the rental price of capital (R^K) is high, investment is low. In particular:
   a. When the real interest rate is high, investment is low.
   b. When the price of new capital goods is high, investment is low.
3. When wages are high, investment is high.

---

[2] See Peter K. Clark, 'Investment in the 1970s: Theory, Performance and Prediction,' *Brookings Papers on Economic Activity*, Vol. 1, pp. 73–113, 1979.

[3] There has been relatively little research on replacement investment. A good but somewhat mathematical discussion is in Martin S. Feldstein and Michael Rothschild, 'Towards an Economic Theory of Replacement Investment,' *Econometrica*, Vol. 42, pp. 393–423.

LAGS IN THE INVESTMENT PROCESS

A somewhat unrealistic element in the investment function we just derived is that the capital stock is adjusted to its desired level immediately. The investment function in Equation 9–6 assumes that the firm puts new capital in place as soon as it becomes aware that the level of output, the rental price of capital, and the wage warrant the new capital. For some kinds of equipment, this assumption is reasonable. But for many projects, there is a **lag** of several years between the firm's realisation that new capital is needed and the completion of the capital installation. To put it another way, much of the investment occurring this year is the result of decisions made last year, the year before, and even the year before that. The decisions were governed by the expectations prevailing in those years about economic conditions this year. New information about this year's conditions that became available after the launching of the projects cannot affect this year's investment in those projects. Much of this year's investment was predetermined by earlier decisions.

To set down an algebraic expression of lags in the investment process, we will assume that firms invest so that their capital stock is adjusted *slowly* towards the desired capital stock. Suppose that firms change their capital stock by a fraction s of the difference between the desired capital stock and the capital stock at the end of the last year. That is,

$$I = s(K^* - K_{-1}). \qquad (9-9)$$

Comparing this equation with Equation 9–5 we see how the investment function is modified to take account of lags in the investment process. The investment demand function in Equation 9–9 has all the properties of the original investment demand function plus one more: The more slowly that the capital stock is adjusted (the smaller is s), the weaker will be the reaction of investment demand to any of its determinants—planned output, the rental price of capital, or the wage rate.

Economic researchers have reached the conclusion that the responsiveness of investment to its determinants is very much attenuated by lags.[4] No more than a third of investment can take place in the year that economic changes make it apparent to firms that more capital is needed. Investment in this category includes tools, trucks, office equipment, and other portable items that are not produced to order. Major investments like whole plants or new custom-made equipment take one or more years to put in place.

[4] See Peter K. Clark, 'Investment in the 1970s: Theory, Performance and Prediction,' *Brookings Papers on Economic Activity,* Vol. 1, pp. 73–113, 1979.

THE AGGREGATE INVESTMENT DEMAND FUNCTION

Our discussion has looked at investment in the firm. We need to go from the firm to the economy as a whole. We will assume that total investment in plants and equipment is governed by Equation 9–9, with the wage to rental ratio taken as an economy-wide average and output taken as total real GDP. Of course, going from the firm to the total economy involves an element of approximation, because the firms we are adding together do not all have the same investment functions. Still, an aggregate investment demand function is a reasonable approximation. Even if firms are diverse, the basic properties of the investment process still hold: Investment responds positively to planned output and negatively to the rental price of capital. The strength of the response depends on how quickly investment plans can be carried out.

The Investment Function

1. The firm's investment demand function tells how much investment it needs to make this year in order to raise its capital stock to the desired level. Investment demand depends negatively on the rental price of capital and positively on the planned level of output and on the wage.

2. Lags in putting new investment in place limit the response of investment to changes in its determinants. Between one-tenth and one-third of the ultimate amount of investment occurs in the first year.

9.4 Taxes and Investment

Taxation of capital tends to discourage investment by reducing the earnings the firm receives from its investment. This effect of taxation can readily be incorporated into the rental price formula.[5] We first consider the effect of permanent tax changes.

PERMANENT TAX CHANGES

Consider again our derivation of the rental price of capital. Suppose the rental firm has to pay a tax rate of u on rental income. In addition, suppose the rental firm receives a payment of z dollars as an investment incentive from the government for each dollar of capital purchased. We derived the

---

[5] This method of incorporating taxes into the rental price of capital is based on the work of Robert E. Hall and Dale W. Jorgenson, 'Tax Policy and Investment Behavior,' *American Economic Review*, Vol. 57 (June 1967), pp. 391–414.

formula for the rental price by equating the rental income of the rental firm to the costs of renting. We can modify that analysis to take account of taxes by equating the after-tax rental income to the after-tax costs of renting. After-tax rental income is $(1 - u)R^K$. The effect of the investment incentives is to make the cost of purchasing a machine equal to $(1 - z)P^K$. Equating after-tax rental income to after-tax costs gives

$$(1 - u)R^K = (R + d)(1 - z)P^K. \tag{9-10}$$

Dividing by $1 - u$ gives

$$R^K = \frac{(R + d)(1 - z)P^K}{1 - u}. \tag{9-11}$$

The net effect of taxation and investment incentives is to multiply the rental cost by $(1 - z)/(1 - u)$.

For example, suppose the marginal tax rate applied to the revenue from capital is 50 percent. That is, $u = .5$. This by itself would double the rental price of capital—if rental firms lose half their revenue to taxation, they have to double their earnings to cover the costs of holding capital.

Suppose further that there is an investment incentive of 10 percent, and that tax deductions for depreciation on investment are worth 30 cents of current benefits for each dollar of investment. The combined effect of the two make z equal .4. In this example, the tax multiplier in the rental price of capital, $(1 - z)/(1 - u)$, is .6/.5, or 1.2. The tax system adds 20 percent to the rental price of capital.

For investments that are financed by issuing debt or taking on mortgages, the tax system gives further incentives to invest because firms can deduct their interest costs as well. Suppose that borrowing adds another 20 cents in current tax benefits for each dollar of investment. In that case, z would be .6 and the tax multiplier would be .4/.5, or .8. Tax incentives then outweigh the direct effect of taxes, and the net effect of the tax system is to subsidise investment.

Changes in taxes and tax incentives for investment are powerful tools for changing investment spending. As shown in the box below, the tax changes announced in 1987 raised the rental price of capital by as much as 15 percent. A reduction in the corporate tax rate from 45 to 38 percent tended to lower the rental price, but an elimination of the investment tax credit, a lower depreciation allowance, and a reduction in the value of deductions for interest payments (due to the lower tax) tended to raise it by a larger amount.

Suppose the desired capital stock falls by .75 percent for each percentage point that the rental price of capital is increased (that is, the elasticity is −.75). Then the desired capital stock would fall by about 11 percent as a result of this legislation. If the capital stock of plants and equipment in Canada is about $1,000 billion, then this reduction would amount to a fall in investment of $110 billion. Even if it were spread over 10 years, the effect on aggregate demand in each year could be substantial.

The Effect of the 1987 Tax Reform on the Rental Price of Capital

Tax changes that were announced by the federal government in 1987, to take effect in 1988 and later, will have a large effect on the rental price of capital once they are in place. Among the many changes announced were a reduction in the combined federal-provincial tax rate on corporations from 45 percent to 38 percent, elimination of the 7 percent investment tax credit, and a reduction in the amount of depreciation of capital allowed for tax purposes. The effects of these changes on the tax parameters are approximately as follows:

Source of Change in Tax Parameters (u, z)	Values of Tax Parameters	
	Old Tax Law	New Tax Law
Effects on tax rate (u) Corporate tax rate cut from .45 to .38	$u = .45$	$u = .38$
Effects on investment incentives (z)		
1. Investment tax credit repealed	.07	.00
2. Less accelerated depreciation	.31	.27
3. Smaller deduction of interest costs because of lower tax rate	$\underline{.16}$	$\underline{.13}$
Total: (1) plus (2) plus (3)	$z=.54$	$z=.40$
Tax multiplier: $(1 - z)/(1 - u)$	$.46/.55=.84$	$.60/.62=.97$

Thus, tax reform will raise the rental price of capital by as much as 15 percent. This could cause a substantial drop in investment demand.

These tax changes have another more positive effect on business investment, however. They 'levelled the playing field' in the jargon of tax reformers. Investment incentives such as investment tax credits and accelerated depreciation tend to favour certain industries at the expense of others. By eliminating these incentives, tax rates will be more equal across industries. Investment will thereby be allocated more efficiently.

ANTICIPATED TAX CHANGES

The above calculations assume that the tax rates are always in effect and that tax changes are not anticipated by firms. If firms are forward-looking, as we have argued they are, then anticipations of future tax changes can also affect investment. The effects are tricky to calculate, and can go in a direction opposite from unanticipated changes.

Suppose, for example, that Canadian firms anticipated in 1987 that the 7 percent investment tax credit would be repealed in the near future. In fact, this is a very realistic example, because such a repeal was proposed in the 1986 federal budget.

Firms that anticipated such a change would realise that they would have to pay 7 percent more for capital goods after the repeal. Accordingly they would want to buy capital in 1987 before the effective price rise. If possible they would shift their purchases of equipment from later years to 1987.

Rental firms would also cut their rental price in 1987 in anticipation of the repeal of the investment tax credit. With the effective price of capital goods expected to increase, rental firms could charge less for rent because of the expected capital gain on the capital that they owned. With a decrease in the rental price there would be more investment in 1987. Hence, an *anticipated* elimination of the investment tax credit would increase investment in the year that the elimination was anticipated.

Anticipation of the repeal of the investment tax credit is probably one of the reasons why real business fixed investment grew 8.8 percent in 1987 after growing only 3.2 percent in 1986.

These same anticipatory effects can work in the opposite direction. If firms anticipated a reenactment of the investment tax credit, perhaps because of a prolonged economic slump, then the rental price of capital would increase at the time of anticipation, and investment would actually fall.[6]

TAXATION OF SAVINGS

It is sometimes suggested that investment spending (I) can be increased by changing the way that income is taxed in order to encourage private saving. The argument is simple: If people save more the interest rate will fall and investment will rise. But the argument is too simple. Even if we can ensure that Canadian private saving will increase this does not guarantee that Canadian investment spending will rise.

Recall from Chapter 2 that investment spending must equal the sum of private saving, government saving, and saving by the rest of the world with respect to Canada. Suppose that taxes on saving are reduced. While private saving will rise, government saving will fall due to reduced tax collections. The reduction in government saving may offset the increase in private saving. Even if we could increase private and government saving at the same time investment spending need not rise. The additional savings may be invested abroad, resulting in a capital outflow.

---

[6] For rational expectations approaches to consequences of anticipated changes in investment incentives, see Lawrence H. Summers, 'Taxation and Corporate Investment: A *q*-theory Approach,' *Brookings Papers on Economic Activity*, Vol. 1, pp. 67–140, 1981, and John B. Taylor, 'The Swedish Investment System as a Stabilization Policy Rule,' *Brookings Papers on Economic Activity*, Vol. 1, pp. 57–97, 1982.

Tax Incentives

1. The government can influence the level of investment through tax policy. Heavier taxation raises the rental price of capital and discourages investment.

2. Tax incentives such as investment tax credits and depreciation deductions lower the rental price of capital and stimulate investment.

3. Anticipated increases in tax incentives can reduce investment today, because firms will postpone their capital purchases until they can take advantage of the credit.

4. Tax changes that encourage private saving need not increase domestic investment spending.

9.5 Residential Investment

The economic theory of residential investment can be approached in much the same way as the theory of business investment. We can start again with the concept of the *rental price*. Because a significant amount of housing of all kinds is rented in the open market, there is nothing unfamiliar about the idea of a rental price of housing. Even though many Canadian families own their houses rather than rent them, we can examine their decision about how large a house to own by looking at the rental price they pay implicitly when they own. Let R^H represent the rental price for houses. As before, the rental price is the interest rate plus a rate of depreciation times the price of houses (P^H):

$$R^H = (R + d)P^H. \tag{9-12}$$

An important quantitative difference is in the rate of depreciation, d. The equipment that makes up the bulk of business investment depreciates at around 10 percent per year, so d is .10 in the formula for R^K. Houses hardly depreciate at all. A reasonable value for d in the formula for R^H is .02. Consequently, the real interest rate is a much larger fraction of the rental cost of housing than it is of the rental cost of business investment. As we will see, residential investment is much more sensitive to interest rates than is business investment.

The public has a demand function for housing just as it has a demand function for any good. When the rental price of housing is high, the public demands less rental housing. We can find the public's **desired stock of housing** by finding where the rental price of housing intersects the demand curve, as in Figure 9–7.

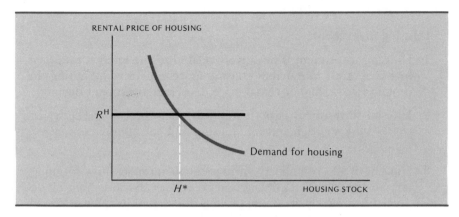

Figure 9–7.   DETERMINATION OF THE DESIRED HOUSING STOCK.
The desired stock of housing, $H*$, is found at the point on the demand curve for housing where the rental price of housing, R^H, has the value determined by the real interest rate and the price of houses.

Lags in housing construction are not nearly as long as in business investment. It is reasonable to suppose that the bulk of housing can be put in place within a year after a change in demand. The investment demand function for housing is just

$$I = H* - H_{-1}, \tag{9–13}$$

where H is the stock of houses and $H*$ is the desired stock of houses.

The accelerator principle operates for housing investment as well as for business investment. The stock of housing is related to the level of real income. Thus investment, which is the change in the stock, is related to the change in real income.

HOUSING INVESTMENT AND MONETARY POLICY

Of all the components of aggregate demand, housing investment is the most sensitive to real interest rates. We have already noted one reason for the sensitivity: Because housing depreciates at a low rate, the real interest rate is the dominant element in the rental price of housing. Most of what you pay your landlord is compensation for the capital tied up in your apartment. If you own a house, most of your annual cost is mortgage interest. Therefore, when monetary contraction or other influences raise interest rates, housing investment declines the most. The substantial drop in housing construction in 1982 seems clearly attributable to the high interest rates prevailing during that year and the previous one. Mortgage interest rates in 1982 were about 18 percent. On the other hand, housing construction increased in 1983 as mortgage interest rates dropped to 13 percent, even though nonresidential investment fell.

Housing Investment

1. Housing investment is negatively related to the interest rate R. A higher interest rate makes housing more expensive by raising the rental price. A higher rental price depresses investment demand.

2. Housing investment is positively related to real GDP. Higher incomes raise the demand for housing and so raise investment demand.

3. Housing is the component of investment most sensitive to monetary and fiscal policies through interest rates. Because housing depreciates so slowly, its rental price is dominated by interest cost.

9.6 Inventory Investment

Inventories are stocks of goods in the process of production and also finished goods waiting to be sold. On average, the value of the inventories held in the Canadian economy is about one-quarter the value of annual GDP. To put it another way, inventories were about equal to 3 months' GDP. The importance of inventories varies across the sectors of the economy. In manufacturing, for example, the value of inventories is close to 50 percent of annual manufacturing GDP. A significant amount of capital is tied up in inventories in the Canadian economy.

Inventories fit into the general framework for analysing investment set up at the beginning of this chapter. Inventories have a rental price, equal to the real interest rate times the price of goods held in inventory.

Firms choose a desired level of inventories by equating the marginal benefit of inventories to the rental price. What benefits do inventories provide the firm? We can distinguish two basic functions. First, and quantitatively most important, inventories are an intrinsic part of the physical production process. We will call this the **pipeline function** of inventories. In the oil industry, large amounts of oil are unavoidably in transit in pipelines at any moment. The pipeline function also includes goods in process. Inside an auto plant, you will always find stocks of parts ready to be made into cars together with a large number of cars partway through the assembly process. It would be costly to the auto manufacturer to coordinate the flow of parts and speed up the assembly process in order to cut down on the volume of inventories. The manufacturer has made a basic decision about the design of the production process that balances the advantages of inventories against their holding cost. About two-thirds of all inventories seem to be held because of the pipeline function.

The other third of inventories are finished goods. Auto plants have cars sitting in parking lots ready for shipment to dealers. The dealers themselves also keep quite a number of cars in their lots and showrooms. As a general matter, substantial inventories of finished goods ready for sale are held at the wholesale and retail level. One of the reasons for holding these inventories is to maintain a **buffer stock** to accommodate unexpected changes in demand. The buffer stock is the second major function of inventories. The grocery store keeps dozens of bottles of ketchup on the shelves because there is always a chance that an unusual number of people will buy ketchup on any given day.

Buffer-stock inventories are held at a certain average level that equates the marginal benefit to the rental cost. When sales surge, the inventories decline to below the desired stock. The firm then adjusts its purchases to replenish the stock. When sales fall short of expectations, inventories build up. The firm then decreases its purchases to run inventories down to their desired level.

Occasionally, unintended disinvestment and investment in buffer-stock inventories show up in the aggregate amount of inventory investment throughout the economy. For example, in the first quarter of 1986, aggregate final sales of goods in the Canadian economy declined in real terms. The production of goods continued to rise despite the drop in sales. As a result, inventory investment bulged. At annual rates inventory investment was $7 billion 1981 dollars in the first quarter of 1986. By the fall, production was brought down below the level of sales, and inventory investment was negative in the fourth quarter of 1986.

We can get an idea of the relative importance of the pipeline and buffer-stock influences on inventory investment by looking at the relationship between the *change* in real GDP and the *level* of inventory investment in the Canadian economy. Figure 9–8 shows this relationship for the years 1953–87.

We can draw two important conclusions about inventory investment from Figure 9–8. First, inventory investment tends to be closely related to changes in production. When higher levels of output are being produced, there are more goods in the pipeline. Filling up the pipeline to the higher level requires more inventory investment. Consequently, years of rapid GDP growth tend to be years of high inventory investment. This is the third important place where the accelerator principle is in operation. The accelerator effect is particularly strong for inventory investment, because lags are less important for inventories than for any other component of investment.

Second, there are occasional episodes when businesses are caught by surprise and inventories pile up or are depleted unintentionally. In these episodes, inventory investment departs from its usual relation to the change in real GDP. In Figure 9–8, the small number of dots away from the prevailing upward-sloping line are years when unintended depletion of inventories occurred. There is no systematic tendency for buffer stocks to absorb every

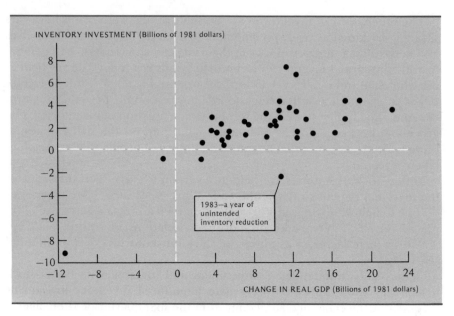

Figure 9–8.   INVENTORY INVESTMENT AND THE CHANGE IN GDP.
The amount of inventory investment tends to be closely related to the change in real
GDP. Each dot corresponds to a year in the period from 1953 through 1987. The horizontal axis shows the change in real GDP and the vertical axis shows the real amount of inventory investment. As a rule, inventory investment is high when real GDP is growing and low
when it is contracting. The major exception is 1983, when real GDP grew but inventory investment was negative. In 1983, there was probably unintended reduction of buffer
stocks because sales were unexpectedly high. As a general matter, intended changes in
inventory stocks dominate unintended changes. Years of high GDP growth are years of
high inventory investment and vice versa.

change in real GDP. Instead, big movements of buffer stocks are a rare surprise. Research on inventory behaviour has confirmed the general proposition that relatively few important movements of inventories can be traced to
surprises in sales.[7]

Inventory Investment

1. Inventories provide two benefits to firms. The production process
   involves a pipeline of partly produced goods. When the level of
   output is high the stock of goods in the pipeline is high. Inventories
   of finished goods also function as a buffer stock against unexpected
   changes in sales.

---

[7] See Albert A. Hirsch and Michael Lovell, *Sales Anticipations and Inventory Behavior*, John
Wiley & Sons, New York, 1969.

2. The pipeline function of inventories dominates inventory investment in most years, but occasionally economy-wide surprises in
   sales are large enough for changes in buffer stocks to contribute an
   important component to inventory investment.

3. The increase in pipeline inventories when output rises is a major
   part of the accelerator in the short run.

9.7 The Investment Function and the IS Curve

Total investment is the sum of investment in plants and equipment, residential housing, and inventory. We can summarise the ideas of this chapter in an
overall investment function. Investment depends positively on real GDP Y
and negatively on the interest rate R.

The accelerator principle is important in investment. Higher output requires firms to invest in new plants and equipment, it causes families to want
to increase their stock of housing, and it calls for higher pipeline stocks of
inventories. For all three reasons, an increase in GDP stimulates added investment. However, the stimulus is stronger in the short run than in the
long run. If the economy moves once and for all to a higher level of GDP,
there will be a bulge of investment as the economy moves to the new, higher
stock of plants, equipment, housing, and inventories desired at the new level
of GDP. Once the new stock is reached, investment will subside to normal
levels.

Investment depends negatively on the real interest rate. When the real
rental cost of plants and equipment rises, firms substitute toward other
inputs, especially labour. When the real rental price of housing rises, families substitute toward other forms of consumption. When the real cost of
holding inventories rises, firms reduce their stocks of inventories, though
this effect appears to be small. But the influence of higher real interest rates
in depressing total investment is unmistakable.

Investment is central to the IS curve—in fact, as we mentioned in
Chapter 5, the 'I' in IS stands for investment. The IS curve can be defined
as the set of combinations of real GDP and the interest rate where investment
and saving are equal.

As a general matter, the IS curve slopes downward because it takes a
lower interest rate to stimulate spending enough to achieve spending balance at a higher level of GDP. The investment function is a key part of that
process. Lower interest rates stimulate investment—the effect is most important for housing and least important for inventories. The interest sensitivity of investment is an important determinant of the slope of the IS curve.
If investment is highly responsive to the interest rate, the IS curve is flat—
small changes in the interest rate cause large changes in investment and thus
large changes in the level of GDP. If investment is not very responsive to in-

terest rates, and other components are also unresponsive, the IS curve will be steep. Because investment and other categories of spending are unable to respond in the very short run (say one month) to changes in interest rates, the IS curve is close to vertical in the short run.

Example. An investment equation with an accelerator effect might be

$$I = 350 + .1Y - 2,000R.$$

When combined with the consumption function and net export equation of Chapter 5, the IS curve is

$$R = .342 - .000148Y + .0004G.$$

Review and Practice

MAJOR POINTS

1. There are three types of investment: business purchases of new plants and equipment, construction of new housing, and addition to inventories.

2. A business determines its desired capital stock by equating the marginal benefit of capital to the rental price of capital. A household determines its desired stock of housing in the same way.

3. The desired capital stock falls if the rental price of capital rises. It rises if output or income rises. A business's desired capital stock rises if the wage rises, because it will substitute away from labour and towards capital.

4. The rental price depends on the real interest rate and the price of capital goods.

5. The investment function tells how much investment will occur in a given year depending on conditions in that year. Although firms would like to invest up to the point where actual capital equals desired capital, they generally cannot do so. Only a fraction of the move to the new level can occur in the first year.

6. Because of the lag in investment, a large fraction of the investment that occurs in one year is actually the result of investment projects initiated in earlier years. This part of investment is predetermined in the current year and does not respond to current economic conditions.

7. For plants and equipment, it is a good approximation to say that suppliers will supply whatever amount of new investment goods that businesses demand.

8. Tax incentives, including the depreciation deductions and interest deductions, have an important influence on investment. A higher investment credit lowers the rental price of capital and stimulates investment.

9. Inventory investment contributes an important part of the fluctuations in total investment. The stock of inventories tends to be proportional to real GDP, so an increase in GDP is accompanied by a period of inventory investment.

10. Overall, investment responds positively to real GDP; this response is called the accelerator. Investment responds negatively to the real interest rate.

11. The interest sensitivity of investment is a major determinant of the slope of the IS curve. If investment responds strongly negatively to interest rates, the IS curve is flat.

KEY TERMS AND CONCEPTS

Investment

Nonresidential fixed investment

Plant and equipment investment

Residential investment

Inventory investment

Investment demand

Marginal benefit of capital

Rental price of capital

Demand for capital

Rate of depreciation

Desired capital stock

Investment demand function

Accelerator

Tax incentives

Depreciation deductions

Desired stock of housing

Final goods inventories

Buffer stock function of inventories

Pipeline function of inventories

QUESTIONS FOR DISCUSSION AND REVIEW

1. What variables adjust so that the level of investment chosen by firms and households is equal to the amount of funds available for investment?

2. Why do investment and GDP move so closely together?

3. Suppose that a firm can reduce its energy bill by adding some capital. How does this enter the marginal benefit of capital schedule?

4. Why does the marginal benefit of capital schedule shift upward when output rises?

5. Explain the various predetermined elements in the investment function.

6. What are the effects of tax policy on investment in the long run?

7. Why is housing especially important in the economy's response to a high interest rate policy?

8. Explain exactly what happens to the three categories of investment as you move down the IS curve.

PROBLEMS

Numerical

1. Suppose that the demand for investment is given by the model

$$I = s(K^* - K_{-1}),$$

where K^* is the desired stock of capital given by

$$K^* = .1Y/R,$$

where Y is output and R is the interest rate. Assume that there is no depreciation and that $R = .05$. Let $s = .25$ to start.

a. Calculate the desired capital stock in Year 1 if output is 200. Calculate the level of investment in the first year if the capital stock was 400 at the beginning of the first year.

b. Suppose now that output rises from 200 to 250 in Year 2, and then remains at this new level forever. Calculate the level of investment and the capital stock in Years 2, 3, and 4. What are the new long-run levels of investment and capital? Explain why investment reacts with a lag to the increase in output.

c. Repeat the calculations in Parts a and b for $s = 1$ and comment on the difference between your answers.

2. Repeat Problem 1 for the case where investment is given by

$$I = s(K^* - K_{-1}) + .1K_{-1}.$$

The last term on the right is replacement investment. Explain the reason for the differences between the answers to Questions 1 and 2.

3. Suppose that the investment function is given by

$$I = 350 - 2{,}000R + .1Y$$

rather than by the investment function given in Chapter 5. Add this investment function to the other four equations of the IS-LM model:

$$Y = C + I + G + X$$
$$C = 80 + .63Y$$
$$X = 425 - .1Y - 500R$$
$$M = (.1625Y - 1{,}000R)P$$

Treat the price level as predetermined at 1.0, and let government spending be 750 and the money supply be 600.

a. Derive an algebraic expression for the IS curve for this model and plot it to scale. Compare it with the IS curve in the examples of Chapter 5. Which is steeper? Why?

b. Derive the aggregate demand curve and plot it to scale. How does it compare with the aggregate demand curve in the example of Chapter 5?

c. Calculate the effect of an increase in government spending on GDP. Is the effect larger or smaller than in the case where investment does not depend on output Y? Describe what is going on.

d. Calculate the effect of an increase in the money supply on GDP. How does the impact compare with the situation where investment does not depend on output?

4. Multiplier-accelerator interaction: Consider a macro model that has both a consumption function that depends on lagged income (like Friedman's permanent-income equation) and an investment equation that depends, with a lag, on changes in income. Ignore interest rate effects. In particular assume that the following equations describe the economy:

$$Y = C + I + G$$
$$C = 80 + .63Y_p, \text{ with } Y_p = .5(Y + Y_{-1})$$
$$I = 650 + .2(Y_{-1} - Y_{-2})$$
$$G = 750$$

a. By algebraic substitution of C and I into the income identity, obtain a single expression for output Y in terms of output in the previous years (Y_{-1} and Y_{-2}).

b. Calculate the constant level of output Y that satisfies all the relationships in the model. (Hint: Set $Y_{-1} = Y$ and $Y_{-2} = Y$ in the equation from Part a and solve for Y using algebra.)

c. Suppose that Y has been equal to the value that you calculated in Part b for the past 2 years (Years 1 and 2). But now suppose that government spending increases by $50 billion (in Year 3). Calculate the effect on output in Year 3. Calculate the effect on output in Years 4 through 10. Be sure to use the relationship that you derived in Part a, substituting the values for Y_{-1} and Y_{-2} that you calculated in the previous two steps.

d. Plot the values of Y on a diagram with the years on the horizontal axis. Do you notice any 'cyclical' behaviour in Y? Explain what is going on. (This algebraic model was originally developed by Paul Samuelson of M.I.T. while he was a student at Harvard in the 1930s.)

5. (This problem refers to the material in Appendix A.) Consider the case where the price of capital goods, P^K, and the revenues from investment, J, are the same each year. Work with the equation for the financial position V:

$$V_t = (1 + R)V_{t-1} - dP^K + J.$$

Always start with $V_0 = -P^K$. In the last period of the project the firm sells the capital good for P^K.

a. Show that, regardless of the length of the project, V is zero if the revenues from investment $J = (R + d)P^K$.

b. Calculate the financial position for each year of a 10-year project that costs $100,000 and earns a revenue of $16,000 per year. Use an interest rate of 5 percent and a depreciation rate of 10 percent. Is the project a winner or a loser?

c. Repeat the above calculation for an interest rate of 10 percent. Is the project a winner or a loser? Explain the difference between this answer and the answer to Part b.

Analytical

1. What theory of inventory investment predicts that inventory investment is negative when GDP suddenly rises? What theory predicts the opposite? For both theories explain what happens at firms during a sudden *decline* in GDP.

2. Consider a firm whose capital stock is initially equal to its desired capital stock, where $R = .05$, $d = .1$, $P^K = 100$, and P^K is initially not expected to change in the future.

a. Suppose P^K suddenly rises to 110. Ignoring taxes, what must the firm expect P^K to be next year in order for its desired capital stock to remain unchanged?

b. Suppose now that P^K is expected to return to 100 the following year and to remain at 100 in all future years. Assume that this is in fact what happens. Describe the behaviour of investment in the year of the price increase and in all future years. Consider both the case where the capital stock adjusts immediately to its desired level, and the case where it adjusts with a lag.

3. In this problem we consider an economy in which the price of *new* capital goods never changes. It is always equal to 100.

a. Assuming $R = .05$, $d = .1$, and a corporate income tax of 50 percent, what is the rental cost of capital?

b. The government is considering an investment tax credit (ITC) where 10 percent of the purchase price of a new capital good can be subtracted from a firm's taxes. Under such a proposal, what will the rental cost of capital be? Assuming that the ITC is unanticipated, describe the behaviour of I and K^* in the year that it is implemented.

c. Assuming that the old capital goods are perfect substitutes in production for new capital goods, what will the price of old capital goods be under the ITC? If the value of a firm's capital stock changes in the year the ITC is implemented, will this change directly affect the firm's investment decision?

   d. Assume now that such a proposal is announced a year ahead of time. What will the rental cost of capital be in the year in which firms learn about the ITC? Compare your answer to the rental cost calculated in Parts a and b. Explain any differences.

   e. Compare the level of investment in the year in which the ITC is announced to what it would be without the ITC. Compare the level of investment in the following year when the ITC is implemented to what it would be if the ITC was implemented *unannounced* that year.

4. How sensitive would you expect automobile production to be to the interest rate? In answering this question, consider (i) the sensitivity of the desired stock of automobiles to the interest rate, (ii) the lags in the adjustment of the automobile stock to its desired level, and (iii) the impact of changes in final automobile sales on inventory investment in automobile manufacturing.

5. Paradox of thrift: Suppose that investment demand depends on the level of income but not on the interest rate, according to the formula

$$I = e + dY$$

and that consumption also depends on income according to the consumption function

$$C = a + b(1 - t)Y.$$

   a. Sketch the spending line for the economy that shows how total spending increases with income Y. (Put spending on the vertical axis and income on the horizontal axis, like Figure 4–3 of Chapter 4.) Draw a 45-degree line and indicate where spending balance is.

   b. Suppose that consumers decide to be more 'thrifty,' to save more. They do this by reducing 'a' once and for all. Show the new point of balance in the diagram.

   c. What happens to investment as a result of consumers' attempts to save more? Explain.

   d. Explain the 'paradox of thrift' that the attempt to save more may result in a reduction in private saving. What happens to total saving?

   e. Explain why the paradox of thrift is a short-run phenomenon. Introduce interest rates into the investment function, and add a money demand function and price-adjustment equation to the model. If the economy is operating at potential GDP before the reduction in a, will it eventually return to potential after the reduction in a? What happens to saving and investment when prices have fully adjusted?

6. Suppose the desired capital stock is given by the expression

$$K^* = vY/R^K$$

where v is a constant and R^K is the rental cost of capital.

   a. Assuming that output in the economy is fixed at Y^*, will a permanent increase in the interest rate have a permanent or temporary effect on the level of investment?

   b. Is your answer to Part a consistent with the investment function incorporated in the IS curve?

   c. Suppose now that output in the economy is growing each period so that $\Delta Y = g$ where g is a constant increase in output (greater than zero). Assuming that the actual capital stock adjusts immediately to its desired level, answer Part a.

7. Sketch an IS-LM diagram. Compare two cases: one in which the investment demand function depends on income, the other where it is independent of income. In which case are both monetary and fiscal policy more effective? Explain.

8. Suppose that GDP is below potential GDP, and that inflation is low. The federal government is talking about reducing taxes on investment in order to get the economy back to potential.
   a. Sketch the situation on an IS-LM diagram. Show where you want to move the IS curve to get back to potential.
   b. In light of lags in the investment process and the forward-looking nature of firms' investment decisions, describe some of the problems that the policy makers need to worry about in enacting the tax legislation.

9. Consider a proposal to increase taxes on businesses and decrease taxes on consumers, keeping total revenue about the same. Describe the effects of this proposal on *investment demand*. Be explicit: Are these effects likely to occur immediately, or will they occur with a lag? Distinguish between the effects that work through the rental rate on capital and effects that work through the accelerator. Which of these two effects is likely to be larger in the long run?

Appendix A: Capital Budgeting and the Rental Price of Capital

In this appendix we show that Jorgenson's rental price approach gives the correct answer to the question of what should be the desired capital stock for a firm that *buys* capital. As discussed in the text the key result is that investment projects that earn more than the rental price will be undertaken, and those that earn less than the rental price will not be undertaken. We use a capital budgeting formulation of the firm's investment decision.

Suppose that a firm is considering buying some capital equipment that will contribute an amount J_t to revenue in each future year t. The year of the decision is $t = 0$. The equipment costs P^K.

The firm keeps track of its financial position—benefits less costs—for this capital project using an intertemporal budgeting process in the following way. Let V_t be the financial position in year t. The firm starts in the hole by the cost of the capital equipment, P^K. That is, the financial position in Year 0,

$$V_0 = -\text{The price of the capital equipment} = -P^K. \qquad (9\text{–}14)$$

For example, if the capital equipment cost \$1,000, then $V_0 = -\$1,000$. In the next year, the firm may be even deeper in the hole because it pays interest at rate R on the funds it used to pay for the project last year plus the additional spending it made at the end of last year to make up for wear and tear, or depreciation. For example, for the \$1,000 equipment, if the interest rate is 5 percent ($R = .05$), and 10 percent of the equipment needed to be replaced because of wear and tear ($d = .10$), then the financial position would be reduced by another \$50 + \$100 = \$150. On the other hand, the project contributed an amount J_0 to revenue in its first year. For example, if the revenue is \$200, the position in the project at the beginning of the second year is

$$V_1 = -\$1,000 - \$50 - \$100 + \$200 = -\$950. \qquad (9\text{–}15)$$

The same process repeats each year. In words:

> Position at the beginning of next year
> = Position at the beginning of this year
> + Interest at that position this year
> − Depreciation this year
> + Revenue from the project this year.

The general algebraic form is

$$V_t = V_{t-1} + RV_{t-1} - dP^K + J_{t-1}. \tag{9-16}$$

Note that this equation is like the intertemporal budget constraint from the forward-looking consumers in Chapter 8. It is essentially the firm's intertemporal budget for the project in question. At the end of the project, the firm will be able to sell the capital equipment. If the firm has been paying for all the wear and tear each year, so that the equipment is 'like new,' then the firm will be able to sell the equipment for what it paid for it. The firm will sell the equipment for P^K and the firm's financial position will be increased by P^K at the end of the project. (Recall that we assume that the price of new equipment is unchanging.)

With the repeated application of Equation 9–16, the firm can figure out its financial position in the project as long as the project is still in existence. The firm's projects will fall into two categories: **winners,** for which the position becomes positive (the initial investment pays itself back) and then becomes more and more positive, and **losers,** for which the position is always negative and the project never pays for itself. A reasonable theory of investment is that the firm goes with the winners and rejects the losers. This is equivalent to the capital budgeting recommendation, which says that projects that have a positive present discounted value should be undertaken, and those with a negative present discounted value should be rejected. The present discounted value of a project is simply the financial position V_t as we have defined it divided by $(1 + R)^t$. When the financial position is positive, so is the present discounted value. When the financial position is negative, so is the present discounted value.

Now, to prove that the rental approach gives the same answer as the capital budgeting approach we need to show that *an investment project that consistently earns more than the rental price is a winner; a project that consistently earns less than the rental price is a loser.*

Suppose a project earns exactly the rental price each year, that is,

$$J_t = (R + d)P^K. \tag{9-17}$$

As we noted, the financial position at the start is

$$V_0 = -P^K. \tag{9-18}$$

In the next period the financial position is

$$V_1 = -(1 + R)P^K - dP^K + J_0, \tag{9-19}$$

where we have used the budget equation, 9–16. Substituting $J_0 = (R + d)P^K$ into Equation 9–19, we get

$$V_1 = -(1 + R)P^K - dP^K + (R + d)P^K, \qquad (9\text{-}20)$$

which, after cancelling out terms on the right-hand side, simply equals $-P^K$. If you repeat this procedure to obtain the financial position after two years, V_2, three years, V_3, and so forth, you will find that the firm's financial position is always equal to minus *the current price of a machine*. At the end of the project the firm sells the machine. Because the firm receives the current price of the machine, P^K, the financial position at the end of the project is exactly zero. That is, the investment is just on the borderline between being a loser and being a winner.

If the investment earned a little more than the rental price each year, the firm's financial position would end up positive. The investment would be a clear winner. If the investment earned a little less than the rental price each year, the financial position would turn out negative. The firm would reject it. Hence, the rental price is the key factor in the investment decision, even though the firm is buying the capital.

Appendix B: Tobin's q and the Rental Price of Capital

We saw in Section 9.3 that investment takes place with a lag. This lag has implications for the observed relationship between investment, the rental price of capital, and a related variable called Tobin's q. To understand this relationship, suppose that the rental price R^K suddenly falls below the marginal benefit J of capital. The situation is illustrated in Figure 9–9, which is a replica of Figure 9–5. The firm will want to raise its capital stock until the marginal benefit of new capital is reduced to the new rental price. But if the firm must adjust its capital slowly, the marginal benefit of capital will remain above the rental price during the adjustment period when the firm is investing in new capital. Only when the adjustment is complete and the actual

Figure 9–9. DESIRED CAPITAL GREATER THAN ACTUAL CAPITAL.
When the rental rate on capital falls, firms do not immediately adjust their capital to the new desired level. The adjustment takes place with a lag. Until the capital stock is adjusted the rental price of capital R^K is below the marginal benefit of capital J.

capital stock equals the new desired level will the marginal benefit of capital equal the rental price. In the meantime, the greater is the difference between desired capital stock and the actual capital stock, the greater is the difference between the rental price and the marginal revenue of capital. Investment is positively related to this difference between J and R^K.

Alternatively stated, investment will be a positive function of the ratio of the marginal benefit of new capital J to the rental price of capital R^K. When this ratio (J/R^K) is greater than 1, the rental price is below marginal benefit of capital and the firm is investing in new capital. When the ratio is less than 1, the firm wants to reduce its capital stock and is thus not investing at all.

The ratio J/R^K of the marginal benefit of capital to the rental price of capital has an interesting interpretation. Suppose that the firm issues shares that can be bought or sold on a stock market, such as the Toronto Stock Exchange. If the interest rate on bonds is R, then the market value *(MV)* of the firm's shares should be such that the return on the shares, J/MV—the ratio of the marginal benefit of capital (J) to the value of the shares *(MV)* that represent ownership of that capital—is equal to the interest rate R. Then the return on holding the firm's shares is the same as the return on bonds. In other words, the market value MV of the firm's shares is directly related to the marginal benefit J of capital by the formula $MV \times R = J$. For example, if $J = \$10$ per share, and $R = .05$, then the market value MV of shares should equal $\$200$.

There is a similar relation between the price of capital at the firm, P^K, and the rental rate, R^K. Ignoring depreciation, the formula for the rental price of capital says that $P^K \times R = R^K$. Combining these two formulas we get

$$\frac{J}{R^K} = \frac{MV \times R}{P^K \times R} = \frac{MV}{P^K} = q.$$

The ratio on the far right (MV/P^K), the market value of the firm divided by the price of the firm's capital, is called Tobin's 'q,' after James Tobin of Yale University who emphasised the importance of the ratio for investment.[8] It is clear from our discussion thus far that investment should be positively related to q.

Tobin's q provides a very useful way to formulate investment functions because it is relatively easy to measure. Data on a firm's share price can usually be obtained from a stock exchange, and the price indexes for capital are tabulated as part of the system of national accounts. For this reason, Tobin's q is a useful gauge of the climate for investment. For example, in 1983 when investment was booming in the United States, Tobin's q in the United States was quite large, even though the measured real interest rate and the rental price of capital suggested an unfavourable climate for investment. The microeconomics of investment that underlie Tobin's q approach to investment are really no different from the rental price approach that we focus on in this chapter.

[8] See James Tobin and William Brainard, 'Asset Markets and the Cost of Capital,' in Bela Balassa and Richard Nelson (eds.), *Economic Progress, Private Values and Public Policy: Essays in Honor of William Fellner,* North-Holland, 1977, for more details about q.

10

Foreign Trade under a Flexible Exchange Rate

FOREIGN TRADE exerts a powerful influence on aggregate demand. For example, if consumers decide to purchase Swedish furniture instead of furniture produced in Canada, aggregate demand for Canadian goods will decline. The immediate short-run impact is a decline in GDP and employment in Canada.

By the standards of the seven largest industrial economies (the **G7**—Canada, France, West Germany, Italy, Japan, the United Kingdom, and the United States), the Canadian economy is heavily dependent on trade. In 1986, for example, 24 percent of Canadian production was exported, a proportion second only to Germany's and more than double that of Japan, a country which is often considered to be very export oriented. Imports accounted for 22 percent of Canadian spending in that year, a proportion second only to that of the United Kingdom.

The United States is by far our largest trading partner. In recent years roughly 70 percent of Canadian imports of goods came from the United States, and over 75 percent of the goods exported by Canadians were sent to the United States. A large part of Canada's exports arise from our natural resources: food, energy, metals, and forest products in particular. However, manufactured goods comprise up to 40 percent of our exports. Indeed, the largest single component of Canadian exports is motor vehicles and their parts, and virtually all of these are sent to the United States. Canada's imports are largely manufactured goods. Chief among these are motor vehicles and parts imported from the United States, and to a lesser extent, Japan and Europe. You may have noticed that motor vehicles form a large part of our exports to the United States and a large part of our imports from the United States. This occurs because Canadian consumers buy all of the models made by GM, Ford, and Chrysler while the Canadian plants operated by these companies produce only a few models in order to operate efficiently. For example, Canada produces more passenger vans than Canadian consumers want to buy and exports the rest to the United States.

Total Canadian exports almost always exceed total imports so that net exports are generally positive. However, the level of net exports varies widely from year to year. Along with investment, net exports is the most volatile component of GDP.

The international value of the Canadian dollar influences net exports and hence affects aggregate demand, GDP, and employment. Because so much of what Canadians purchase is imported, the value of the dollar can also affect the average level of prices in Canada. Fluctuations in the rate of exchange between the Canadian dollar and other currencies can be large and rapid, overwhelming the longer-run competitive factors that determine trade between countries, at least temporarily. For example, in 1987 the value of the Canadian dollar relative to the U.S. dollar rose steadily from 73 U.S. cents per Canadian dollar in January to 77 U.S. cents per Canadian dollar in December. Before the end of the year business people and labour unions involved in export-oriented industries were protesting that the rise in the Canadian dollar was eroding their competitive position in international markets.

In this chapter we examine the behaviour of the economy when the exchange rate is flexible, that is, when the government allows the financial markets to determine the exchange rate. This is the same situation that we considered in Part I. In the next chapter we will consider how the economy would be affected if the government chooses the exchange rate.

10.1 Foreign Trade and Aggregate Demand

Figure 10–1 shows what happened to the flows of goods and services into and out of Canada over more than 30 years. In almost every year exports have exceeded imports. The size of the trade surplus has varied substantially, however.

Recall from Chapter 2 that a trade surplus is not sufficient to ensure that the current account is also in surplus. Net investment income paid to foreigners by Canadians may exceed the trade surplus, producing a current account deficit.

As we discussed in Chapter 2, our accounts with the rest of the world must balance. If there is a current account deficit there must be a capital account surplus (capital inflow) or a reduction in official reserves, or both. Although it is tempting to think that a capital inflow occurs because of a

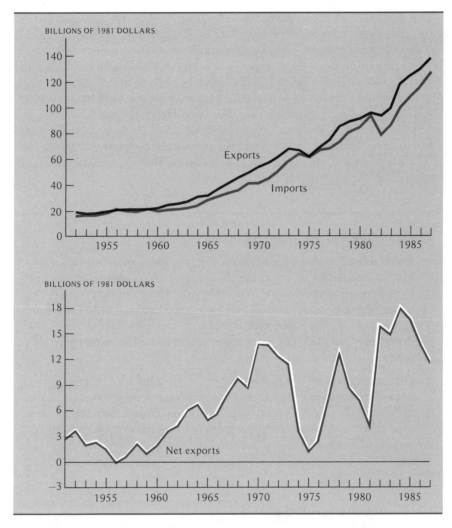

Figure 10–1.   EXPORTS, IMPORTS, AND NET EXPORTS IN 1981 DOLLARS.
The top panel shows the quantities of goods exported out of and imported into Canada
in constant 1981 dollars. The difference between the two is net exports, shown separately in the bottom panel. In almost every year exports have exceeded imports. The size
of the trade surplus has varied substantially, however. Source: *Canadian Economic Observer,* Table 1.3.

current account deficit, this would be somewhat misleading. As we will see,
decisions about international transactions in assets (the capital account) and
international transactions in all other items (the current account) are related
to each other by the fact that our international transactions must balance.
As shown in Table 2–10 (p. 46), in 1987 the current account deficit was
$10.6 billion and the capital account surplus was $15.0 billion. The difference between the two, $4.4 billion, was the increase in official reserves.

The real value of net exports (X) is the difference in the values of our exports and our imports once the effect of any changes in the prices of imports and exports have been eliminated. Although we will focus our attention on the determination of real net exports, it is worth keeping in mind that the prices of exports and imports can also have important effects. If, for example, the price of imports rises while the price of exports is unchanged the effect is that we have to give up more of the goods that we produce to get the same amount of the goods we import. The **terms of trade** is the name given to the ratio of the price of exports to the price of imports. If the price of imports rises relative to the price of exports, we say that there has been an adverse shift in the terms of trade.

Foreign Trade and Aggregate Demand

1. Foreign trade influences Canadian aggregate demand in two ways. First, Canadians can purchase their goods from abroad instead of from Canadian producers. When they do, their imports contribute to aggregate demand in the rest of the world instead of to Canadian aggregate demand. Second, foreigners can purchase goods produced in Canada. These exports enter Canadian aggregate demand.

2. Our accounts with the rest of the world must balance. If the sum of net exports and net investment income from foreigners is negative (that is, if there is a current account deficit), then there must be a capital account surplus (capital inflow) or a reduction in official reserves, or both.

10.2 The Exchange Rate

An **exchange rate** is the amount of a foreign currency that can be bought with one Canadian dollar. For example, on Friday, July 22, 1988, the exchange rate between the Canadian dollar and the U.S. dollar was .8327, or 83.27 U.S. cents per Canadian dollar. If you had gone to a bank with 10,000 Canadian dollars that day you could have purchased 8,327 U.S. dollars. Like other prices, exchange rates can change. The next business day (Monday, July 25) the value of the Canadian dollar had fallen to 82.32 U.S. cents. Your 10,000 Canadian dollars would have purchased 95 fewer U.S. dollars if you had waited over the weekend to make the transaction. The exchange rates between the Canadian dollar and foreign currencies are listed in the financial pages of most newspapers.

Note that we have defined an exchange rate as the number of units of foreign currency that can be purchased with one Canadian dollar. There is another way to report the rate at which Canadian currency can be traded for a foreign currency: how many Canadian dollars it takes to purchase one unit of the foreign currency. The number reported using one method is simply the inverse of the other. Thus on July 22, 1988, one Canadian dollar would buy .8327 U.S. dollar while it took $1/.8327 = 1.2009$ Canadian dollars to purchase one U.S. dollar.[1] As both ways of quoting the exchange rate convey the same information the choice between them is a matter of custom. In Canada, it is most common to quote the Canada–U.S. exchange rate as the number of U.S. dollars that can be purchased with one Canadian dollar, and that is the method we will use in this book. A convenient feature of that method is that when the value of the Canadian dollar increases relative to the U.S. dollar the exchange rate also increases. However, this is not the way that most other prices are quoted in the economy. In most other cases we state the number of Canadian dollars needed to purchase a unit of a good (for instance, salmon is $10 per kilogram), not the reverse (one dollar buys 100 grams of salmon).

Exchange rates are determined in the **foreign exchange market** where Canadian dollars and other currencies are traded freely. The foreign exchange market is not in one location; it is a global market. Banks all over the world actively buy and sell Canadian dollars and other foreign currencies for their customers. The banks are linked by a network of telecommunications that allows instantaneous contact around the globe. Because of different time zones, the foreign exchange market is open 24 hours a day.

In today's monetary system exchange rates are allowed to **float** against the currencies of other large countries. For this reason the system is called a floating or **flexible exchange rate system.** Canada and other major Western countries permit a free market in foreign exchange. The Canadian government does not attempt to fix the exchange rate with the U.S. dollar in a very narrow band as it did during much of the 1960s, nor do the other major industrial countries. This does not mean that the government is powerless to affect exchange rates or must ignore them when it sets macro policy. As we will see, changes in monetary and fiscal policy have strong influences on exchange rates, and these influences must be considered when setting macro policy.

As the United States is by far the most important country in Canada's international trade and financial relations, it is common to focus on the Canada–U.S. exchange rate. This is the approach that we will usually take in this book, and so we will refer to the Canada–U.S. exchange rate as 'the' exchange rate and denote it using the symbol E. There are some instances

[1] If you want to exchange Canadian and U.S. dollars at your bank you will find that the exchange rate is quoted in both of the ways described above. Moreover, one of the figures will be quite close to, but not exactly equal to, the inverse of the other. As a result, if you exchange 100 Canadian dollars for U.S. dollars and immediately exchange the U.S. dollars you received back into Canadian dollars, you will end up with a little less than 100 Canadian dollars. This is one way in which the bank makes a profit by exchanging currencies. Foreign exchange quotations in the newspaper reflect this practice as well.

Figure 10–2.   THE CANADA–U.S. AND TRADE-WEIGHTED EXCHANGE RATES.
The trade-weighted exchange rate is an average of exchange rates with many different currencies including the U.S. dollar, the French franc, the West German mark, the Japanese yen, and the British pound. As the United States is our major trading partner the Canada–U.S. exchange rate plays a large role in determining the trade-weighted exchange rate. Nonetheless, the U.S. and trade-weighted exchange rates sometimes behave differently. Source: *Canadian Economic Observer,* Table 10.1.

where this may be inappropriate, however. At those times we will also need to consider Canada's exchange rates with other countries. A convenient way to summarise this information is to form a **trade-weighted exchange rate.** This is an average of several different exchange rates, with the weight given to each country depending on the importance of that country in Canada's international trade. Various trade-weighted exchange rates can be constructed depending on the countries included and the weight assigned to each of them. Figure 10–2 shows one such trade-weighted exchange rate, along with the Canada–U.S. exchange rate, for the years 1971 to 1987.

The Canadian dollar fluctuated widely during this period. **Depreciation** of the dollar occurs when the exchange rate E falls. **Appreciation** of the dollar occurs when the exchange rate E rises. The annual averages used in Figure 10–2 somewhat understate the extent of exchange rate fluctuations. The Canadian dollar depreciated 34 percent from a high of 1.04 U.S. dollars in May 1974 to a low of .69 U.S. dollar in February 1986. Two years later the exchange rate had appreciated over 20 percent.

THE EXCHANGE RATE AND RELATIVE PRICES

In our discussion of the role of the exchange rate in foreign trade, we will usually assume that the United States is our only trading partner. While this convenient simplification is fairly realistic, it may sometimes be inappropriate. Under those circumstances we will want to consider events in other countries as well.

The **real exchange rate** is a measure of the exchange rate that is adjusted for changes in purchasing power between Canada and the United States. It is a measure of the relative price of goods produced in the United States compared with goods produced in Canada. The real exchange rate can be written in symbols as

$$\text{Real exchange rate} = \frac{\text{U.S. price of Canadian goods}}{\text{U.S. price of U.S. goods}} = \frac{E \times P}{P_u}.$$

Movements in the real exchange rate may differ from movements in the nominal rate. For example, if the nominal exchange rate is unchanging the real exchange rate will change if the rates of inflation in Canada and the United States are different. Figure 10–3 shows the nominal and real exchange rates between Canada and the United States for the years 1952–87.

The **nominal exchange rate** is the rate at which Canadian currency can be exchanged for U.S. currency. As we have defined it, this can be expressed in U.S. dollars. The real exchange rate is the rate at which Canadian goods can be exchanged for U.S. goods. It is most convenient to express this

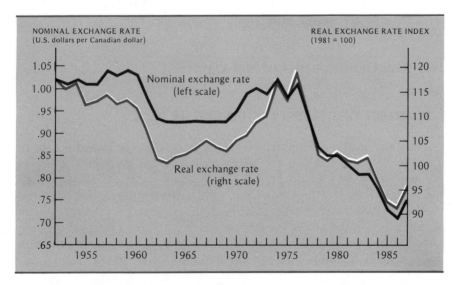

Figure 10–3. THE REAL AND NOMINAL EXCHANGE RATES WITH THE UNITED STATES. The real exchange rate between Canada and the United States is the nominal exchange rate adjusted for changes in the domestic purchasing power of the Canadian dollar and the U.S. dollar. When the real exchange rate falls, it means that Canadians find U.S. goods more expensive. The price of Canadian goods relative to U.S. goods fell from 119 in 1976 to 89 in 1986. Sources: *Canadian Economic Observer*, Tables 1.13 and 10.1, and *Economic Report of the President*, 1988, Table B-3.

as an index. Suppose, for example, that the only good produced in Canada was lumber and the only good produced in the United States was computers. Also suppose that the real exchange rate index rose from 100 in 1990 to 105 in 1991. This would indicate that a given amount of lumber could be exchanged for 5 percent more computers in 1991 than it could in 1990.

One way for the real exchange rate to rise is if the nominal exchange rate rises while prices in each country are unchanged. This would mean that Americans would have to pay more for Canadian goods compared to the price of goods produced in the United States. At the same time, Canadians would find that U.S. goods have become cheaper relative to Canadian goods. For example, if the nominal exchange rate rose from .70 to .80 the Canadian dollar price of a U.S.-made computer that cost 1,000 U.S. dollars would fall from 1,429 Canadian dollars to 1,250 Canadian dollars.

Recall our basic assumption that prices set by Canadian producers are fixed in the short run. Aggregate demand in this period, domestic or foreign, will not influence the dollar price level P in this period. We make the same assumption about the United States. The price level P_u set by U.S. producers is fixed in the short run.

The exchange rate E, on the other hand, varies minute by minute. Thus the real exchange rate (EP/P_u) varies minute by minute. The price of Canadian products in the United States is flexible in the short run because the exchange rate is flexible. By the same token, the Canadian dollar price of U.S. products is flexible in the short run.

10.3 The Determinants of Net Exports

THE EFFECT OF THE REAL EXCHANGE RATE

As we have just seen, fluctuations in the real exchange rate affect the demand for imports and exports. Imports depend positively on the real exchange rate. If the Canadian dollar is strong, it buys a lot of U.S. currency, and the goods sold by the United States are correspondingly cheaper. Overall, the effect of a higher real exchange rate is to divert some aggregate demand to the United States. Exports, too, are sensitive to the real exchange rate. A strong Canadian dollar—and therefore a high real exchange rate— makes Canadian goods more expensive in the United States.

THE EFFECT OF INCOME

In Chapter 4, we noted that net exports depend on Canadian GDP. Higher incomes make consumers spend more on imported products; this relation is particularly sensitive because many types of products that consumers spend extra income on, such as electronics and cars, are frequently imported. In addition, many investment goods are imported, such as machine tools. When GDP rises and investment strengthens, part of the increased investment goods come from abroad. Thus, in general, imports respond positively to GDP. On the other hand, there is little connection between Canadian exports and GDP. Hence net exports depend negatively on GDP.

THE EFFECT OF FOREIGN INCOME

Similarly, the income of foreigners, particularly Americans, affects the demand for Canadian exports. For example, every year in which Canadian exports declined (these are shown in Figure 10–1) was a recession year in the United States. Lower income in the United States reduced the demand for goods exported from Canada.

While the level of activity in the U.S. economy affects the demand for Canadian output, the level of Canadian output has a negligible effect on aggregate demand in the United States. This is a consequence of the fact that the U.S. economy is about 10 times the size of the Canadian economy. As a result, even though Canada–U.S. trade is roughly balanced, it accounts for as much as 20 percent of total Canadian output but only about 2 percent of total U.S. output. Therefore the level of output in the United States, which we will denote Y_u, is exogenous from the point of view of modelling the Canadian economy.

THE NET EXPORT FUNCTION

As we have seen, we can combine imports and exports into a single measure, net exports X, defined as exports less imports. Our conclusions about the determinants of net exports are:

1. Net exports depend negatively on the real exchange rate. When the Canadian dollar is strong, exports are lower and imports are higher. Net exports are lower on both counts.
2. Net exports depend negatively on real income in Canada. This dependence comes from subtracting imports, which depend positively on real income.

We can summarise these ideas in a simple algebraic formula:

$$X = g - mY - n\frac{EP}{P_u}. \qquad \text{Net Export Function} \qquad (10\text{--}1)$$

Equation 10–1 is the net export function. It says that net exports equal a constant g minus a coefficient m times income Y, minus a coefficient n times the real exchange rate. The net export function summarises how net

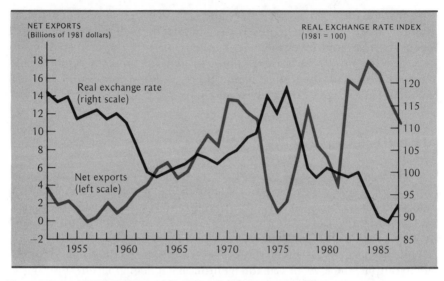

Figure 10–4. NET EXPORTS AND THE REAL EXCHANGE RATE.
The real exchange rate and net exports move at the same time, but in opposite directions. When the real exchange rate rises, net exports fall; conversely, when the real exchange rate falls, net exports rise. Sources: *Canadian Economic Observer*, Tables 1.3, 1.13,
and 10.1, and *Economic Report of the President*, 1988, Table B-3.

exports depend negatively on both income Y and the real exchange rate
(EP/P_u).

What about the effect of U.S. income? We have included this effect in the
coefficient g for simplicity. You may wish to think of g as depending directly
on U.S. income, for example,

$$g = g_0 + g_1 Y_u,$$

where g_0 and g_1 are positive constants.

How well does the net export function work? Figure 10–4 shows how
closely net exports and the real exchange rate were related during the
1970s and the early 1980s when the Canadian dollar was floating. The negative relation is quite evident; note that net exports tend to be high when
the real exchange rate is low and vice versa. We would not expect net exports always to increase whenever the real exchange rate falls because Figure 10–4 ignores the role of other key determinants of exports, notably
Canadian and U.S. income.

Example. A numerical example of the net export function can be written

$$X = 500 - .1Y - 100\frac{EP}{P_u}. \qquad \text{Numerical Example of} \atop \text{Net Export Function} \qquad (10\text{–}2)$$

Suppose that the price level in Canada and the price level in the United States are both predetermined at the value of 1.0. If output Y is 4,000 and the exchange rate E is 1.0 then net exports X equal zero. If output Y rises by 100, then net exports fall by 10 billion because imports rise by this amount. If the exchange rate falls from 1.0 to .7, then net exports would rise by 30.

Net exports is an endogenous variable that depends on the exchange rate. To complete our theory we therefore need to explain what determines the exchange rate.

Net Exports, Income, and the Exchange Rate

1. The exchange rate is the amount of foreign currency that can be exchanged for one dollar.

2. The real exchange rate is the exchange rate corrected for changes in the price level in Canada and abroad.

3. Net exports are negatively related to the real exchange rate and to real income.

10.4 Determination of the Exchange Rate

PURCHASING POWER PARITY

When the Canadian dollar appreciates, U.S. products become cheaper to Canadians. At the same time, Canadian products become more expensive in the United States. If Canada and the United States produced identical, readily transportable products, the exchange rate would not fluctuate in the short run. We would always buy from the cheapest producer. The exchange rate would always have the single value that equated the Canadian dollar prices of Canadian and U.S. products. The real exchange rate would never change. If Canada and the United States produced all the same products, the exchange rate could not fluctuate in the short run and would change in the longer run only by as much as prices in the United States rose by more than prices in Canada. This theory of exchange rate fluctuations is called **purchasing power parity.**

There are two reasons why the real exchange rate may changed nonetheless. First, not all of the goods and services that are produced in Canada and the United States can be transported to the other country. Such goods and services are called **non-tradeables.** For example, the price indexes P and P_u include the price of haircuts. An American may find that the price he pays for a haircut in New Orleans is more than the price he would pay to get his hair cut in Edmonton after converting the Canadian dollar price of the hair-cut to U.S. dollars. We would not expect this to influence the price of hair-cuts in either country, even in the long run. New Orleans barbers do not have to fear that their customers will fly to Edmonton to get their hair cut.

The other reason that the real exchange rate can change is that different countries produce different tradeable products. The private jet aircraft that are produced in Canada by the Canadair Corporation are not the same as the private jets produced in the United States by Gulfstream. If the Cana-dian dollar appreciates then the U.S.–built airplanes will become cheaper for Canadian purchasers, but Canadians will not stop buying Canadair jets entirely. Instead, Canadair's sales in Canada will be reduced somewhat and the Canadian sales of Gulfstream will increase somewhat.

The same thing happens in many other markets, but not all of them. Sim-ple goods, such as raw materials, are identical regardless of where they are made. In the absence of transportation costs and legal barriers to trade, the U.S. dollar price of these goods would always be the same regardless of where they are made. But a large proportion of the goods that Canada pro-duces do not fall into this category. Appreciation of the Canadian dollar makes it more difficult for Canadian producers of these goods to sell their output, but it does not wipe them out.

We will say that purchasing power parity holds between Canada and the United States when the U.S. dollar price of each tradeable good is the same whether the good was produced in Canada or the United States.[2] We can easily see that purchasing power parity does not always hold. If it always held then the real exchange rate would only change due to changes in the relative price of non-tradeable goods. As a result, the real exchange rate would change slowly, and in small steps. But the real exchange rate does not behave this way, as shown in Figure 10–3. The Organisation for Econo-mic Co-operation and Development (OECD) estimates that the nominal Canada–U.S. exchange rate (E) would have had to be .82 U.S. dollar per Canadian dollar in 1986 for purchasing power parity of the real exchange rate to hold. In fact, the nominal exchange rate was .72 in 1986.[3]

Why do we consider purchasing power parity if it is not a good explana-tion of the short-run behaviour of the exchange rate? The answer is that we would expect purchasing power parity to hold, on average, in the long run. In the long run purchasing power parity implies that the difference between Canada's inflation rate and the inflation rate of any other country will be roughly equal to the rate of depreciation of the Canadian dollar relative to

---

[2] The term *purchasing power parity* is sometimes used by different authors to mean slightly different things, as discussed in Mark Rush and Steven Husted, 'Purchasing Power Par-ity in the Long Run,' *Canadian Journal of Economics*, Vol. 18, (February 1985), pp. 137–145.

[3] Note that the purchasing power parity value of the nominal Canada–U.S. exchange rate need not be 1.00. Some people are misled into thinking this by the fact that the names of the currency units are the same in both countries. In fact, there is no more reason for 1 Cana-dian dollar to trade for 1 U.S. dollar than there is for 1 Canadian dollar to trade for 1 British pound or 1 Japanese yen or 1 Australian dollar.

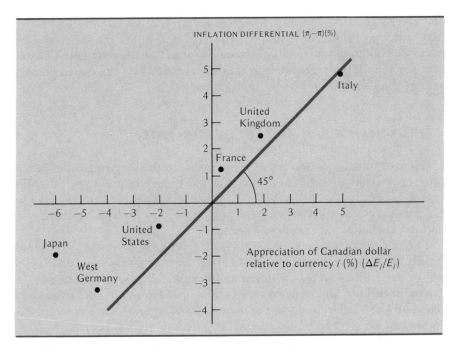

Figure 10–5.   INFLATION DIFFERENTIALS AND APPRECIATION OF THE CANADIAN DOLLAR RELATIVE TO SIX COUNTRIES, 1972–86.
The inflation rates are measured by the consumer price index in each country. The rates of inflation and appreciation are annual averages for the 15-year period. When the inflation differential is high, appreciation of the Canadian dollar against that country's currency is high. Source: *Economic Report of the President,* 1988, Tables B–108 and B–109.

that country's currency. That is,

$$\pi - \pi_i = \Delta E_i / E_i, \tag{10–3}$$

where π_i is the inflation rate in a given foreign country and E_i is the exchange rate between Canada and that country.

How accurate is this equation as a description of the long-run behaviour? In Figure 10–5 the inflation differentials and exchange rate appreciations between Canada and six economies are shown for the 15-year period from 1972 to 1986. The difference between inflation in each country (π_i) and inflation in Canada (π) is shown on the vertical axis. The rate of appreciation ($\Delta E_i / E_i$) of the Canadian dollar against each of the corresponding currencies is on the horizontal axis. The 45-degree line is then the relation between inflation differentials and exchange rate depreciation implied by Equation 10–3. The actual inflation rates and exchange rate behaviour come very close to the theoretical prediction. For example, of the six countries considered in the figure, Italy has had the weakest currency and the highest inflation rate compared to Canada. This relation between inflation and exchange rate behaviour is even more striking for countries with very high inflation rates. For example, from 1976 to 1986, the difference between the inflation rate in Argentina and that in Canada was about 250 percent per year. The Argentine currency depreciated by 240 percent per year against the Canadian dollar during that period.

THE EXCHANGE RATE AND THE INTEREST RATE

While purchasing power parity is important in the long run, other factors must be important in the short run. The most important of these other factors is interest rates. As we will see, policies in Canada that raise interest rates tend to cause the Canadian dollar to appreciate. Why are interest rates and the exchange rate positively related?

The financial markets of the major developed countries are closely linked. Investors are constantly comparing the returns they make by investing in the United States (in stocks and bonds that pay in U.S. dollars), in Japan, in Britain, and in many other countries. There are billions of Canadian and U.S. dollars and trillions of yen of 'hot money' that will migrate almost instantly to the place where it will earn the highest return.

Investors recognise that purchasing power parity will hold in the long run. As a result they have a belief or expectation about the future level of the exchange rate. Now suppose that the Canadian interest rate rises relative to the U.S. rate. U.S. investors will want to hold more Canadian bonds and fewer U.S. bonds. Thus they will want to sell their U.S. bonds, exchange the U.S. dollars they receive for Canadian dollars, and use these Canadian dollars to buy Canadian bonds. The increased demand for Canadian dollars will drive up the exchange rate.

How long can the Canadian dollar continue to rise? Recall that investors have some (unchanged) belief about the future level of the exchange rate. Thus as the exchange rate rises now it gets farther above its expected future level. The higher it is above its expected future level the farther it is expected to fall to reach that expected future level. Once the exchange rate rises enough, it will be expected to fall so far in the future that U.S. investors will no longer believe that it is to their advantage to hold Canadian bonds. They will reason as follows: The return that I can earn in Canadian dollars exceeds the return that I can earn in U.S. dollars. But I expect that by the time that I receive the Canadian payments the Canadian dollar will have depreciated. Thus when I exchange my Canadian earnings for U.S. dollars these Canadian dollars will purchase relatively few U.S. dollars. So I expect that my eventual return will be just as good if I invest in U.S. bonds instead of in Canadian bonds.

Another way of understanding this relationship is to think about it this way: If the Canadian interest rate rises relative to the U.S. interest rate, there would appear to be an incentive for a staggering capital inflow as vast amounts of U.S. capital sought the higher return available in Canada. But we do not ever observe such enormous capital flows. If we did, it would not be possible for the sum of the current and capital accounts to equal the change in official reserves, as we stressed in Chapter 2. It must be that something else happens at the same time that the interest rate changes so that investors do not want to make this enormous shift in their portfolios. That 'something else' is an increase in the exchange rate. As investors' beliefs about the future value of the exchange rate are unchanged, the current increase in the exchange rate means that the rate is above its expected future value. That is, the exchange rate is now expected to fall in the future. Once this expected depreciation is large enough, it eliminates the expectation that holding Canadian bonds will yield a higher return to U.S. investors than holding U.S. bonds.

Thus, given any U.S. interest rate, an increase in the Canadian interest rate will increase the exchange rate. This relationship is shown graphically in Figure 10–6.

In algebra, we can express the positive relation between the real exchange rate and the Canadian interest rate as

$$\frac{EP}{P_u} = q_0 + v(R - R_u), \tag{10-4}$$

where R is the Canadian interest rate, R_u is the U.S. interest rate, and q_0 and v are constants. This equation states that the real exchange rate will rise to the extent that the Canadian interest rate exceeds the U.S. rate, and will fall

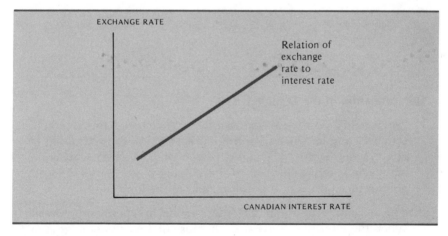

Figure 10–6. RELATION BETWEEN THE CANADIAN INTEREST RATE AND THE EXCHANGE RATE.
An increase in the Canadian interest rate relative to the U.S. interest rate will drive the exchange rate up as U.S. investors seek to buy Canadian bonds. Once the exchange rate has risen far enough, U.S. investors stop wanting to buy more Canadian bonds because at that point they believe that the Canadian dollar will subsequently depreciate enough to eliminate the advantage of holding Canadian bonds.

to the extent that the Canadian rate is below the U.S. rate. Just as we did for U.S. income, we can assume that the U.S. interest rate, while it may change, is unaffected by events in Canada. Thus R_u is exogenous in our model of the Canadian economy. We can then simplify Equation 10–4 as follows:

$$\frac{EP}{P_u} = q_0 + vR - vR_u$$

$$= (q_0 - vR_u) + vR$$

$$= q + vR, \tag{10-5}$$

where $q = q_0 - vR_u$. Thus an increase in the U.S. interest rate would reduce the value of q, and would thus reduce the real exchange rate. More details on the relation between the exchange rate and the Canadian interest rate appear in Appendix A to this chapter.

Example. The relation between the Canadian interest rate and the real exchange rate might be

$$\frac{EP}{P_u} = .75 + 5R. \quad \text{\small Numerical Example of Exchange Rate—Interest Rate Relation} \tag{10-6}$$

When the net export function, Equation 10–2, is combined with this relation, we get the numerical example of the net export relation we used in Chapter 5:

$$X = 425 - .1Y - 500R.$$

Determination of the Exchange Rate

1. Purchasing power parity says that the real exchange rate should be roughly constant. Increases in the price level in Canada would be offset by declines in the Canadian dollar exchange rate, leaving the real exchange rate unchanged. Purchasing power parity does not hold in the short run, but it does hold in the long run.

2. The exchange rate and the interest rate are positively related. When the interest rate rises, say because of an increase in government spending, the exchange rate also rises.

3. The relationship between the interest rate and the exchange rate comes about as investors shift their funds between different countries to obtain the best return. When the interest rate rises in Canada, investors buy Canadian dollar-denominated bonds and this drives up the exchange rate.

4. A high exchange rate implies that the Canadian dollar is expected to depreciate and this makes investors indifferent between high-interest Canadian dollar assets and lower-interest foreign assets.

10.5 The IS Curve and Economic Policy in an Open Economy

Recall that the IS curve describes the combinations of interest rates R and incomes Y that satisfy the income identity and the equations for spending: consumption, investment, and net exports. *Without* net exports in the income identity, the IS curve is downward sloping because higher interest rates reduce investment and, through the multiplier, reduce GDP. *With* net exports, more things happen to spending when the interest rate rises. An increase in the interest rate raises the exchange rate and thereby reduces net exports; this tends to augment the effect of the interest rate on investment and makes the IS curve flatter than it would be in a closed economy. Not only do high interest rates cause firms to invest less, they also cause Canadians to meet their needs with imported goods and foreigners to divert their demand away from Canadian products.

But the presence of net exports also reduces the size of the multiplier, and this tends to make the IS curve steeper. Net exports depend negatively on GDP. As GDP rises, part of the increase in spending goes abroad and does not enter domestic aggregate demand. This spillover abroad is sometimes called **leakage** and it reduces the size of the multiplier.

In Chapter 5, we derived the open-economy IS curve graphically. The next section adds some more details in the process of deriving it algebraically.

ALGEBRAIC DERIVATION OF THE OPEN-ECONOMY IS CURVE

The IS curve is derived algebraically by substituting the functions for consumption C, investment I, and net exports X into the income identity. That is,

$$Y = \underbrace{a + b(1 - t)Y}_{C} + \underbrace{e - dR}_{I} + G + \underbrace{g - mY - n(EP/P_u)}_{X}. \tag{10-7}$$

Putting the interest rate on the left-hand side gives

$$R = \frac{a + e + g}{d} - \frac{1 - b(1 - t) + m}{d} Y - \frac{n}{d} \frac{EP}{P_u} + \frac{1}{d} G. \tag{10-8}$$

This equation relates the interest rate R to output Y, the real exchange rate EP/P_u, and government spending G. To get the IS curve, substitute Equation 10–5 into Equation 10–8 in order to eliminate the real exchange rate:

$$R = \frac{a + e + g - nq}{d + nv} - \frac{1 - b(1 - t) + m}{d + nv} Y + \frac{1}{d + nv} G. \qquad (10\text{–}9)$$

The coefficient on Y shows that the IS curve slopes downward for two reasons: the negative response of investment to the interest rate, described by d, and the negative response of net exports, described by nv.

The IS curve of Equation 10–9 is exactly the same as the one we discussed in Chapter 5.

EFFECTS OF MONETARY AND FISCAL POLICY

Monetary and fiscal policy have important effects on trade and the exchange rate. Suppose that the Bank of Canada increases the money supply. This shifts the LM curve to the right, lowering interest rates and stimulating investment. The decline in interest rates depreciates the exchange rate; net exports rise. Because of the rise in investment and net exports, GDP rises. However, the increase in GDP tends to decrease net exports because imports rise. There are thus two offsetting effects of an increase in the money supply on net exports. Exports definitely rise, but imports might rise by a greater amount. In any case, interest rates fall, the Canadian dollar depreciates, and GDP rises. Conversely, when the money supply is decreased, interest rates rise, the Canadian dollar appreciates, and GDP falls.

Now suppose that government spending is increased. The IS curve is pushed to the right, and interest rates rise. The rise in interest rates reduces investment spending, but also causes the exchange rate to appreciate. The higher exchange rate reduces exports as Canadian goods become relatively expensive compared with foreign goods. Hence, the increase in government spending crowds out export industries as well as investment. Imports also rise because of the increase in the dollar and because GDP has increased. Thus an increase in government reduces the trade surplus (or increases the trade deficit), as it stimulates the economy.

The Budget Deficit and the Current Account Deficit

What happens to the current account deficit when the government runs a fiscal budget deficit? Suppose the budget deficit comes from a large tax cut that puts much more disposable income in the hands of consumers. There is no corresponding reduction in government spending, and consumers choose to spend most of the increase in disposable income. Then the IS curve shifts outward. This raises income and the interest rate. The increase in income reduces net exports, and the increase in the interest rate causes the exchange rate to appreciate, further reducing net exports. As discussed in Chapter 4, the tax cut will not 'pay for itself.' That is, even though income increases, the reduction in the tax rate on income will cause total tax revenues to fall. As government spending has not been cut, the government budget deficit will increase. Thus the government deficit increases at the same time that the trade surplus is reduced (or perhaps becomes a trade deficit).

If the government chooses not to change official reserves and if private investment and savings decisions are largely unaffected, then an increase in the budget deficit will cause a capital inflow. U.S. experience in the 1980s demonstrated this principle on a grand scale. The following chart shows how the tax cut of 1981, with large spending cuts, brought about a gigantic budget deficit. From current account surpluses at the beginning of the decade, very large current account deficits emerged in 1984, 1985, and 1986.

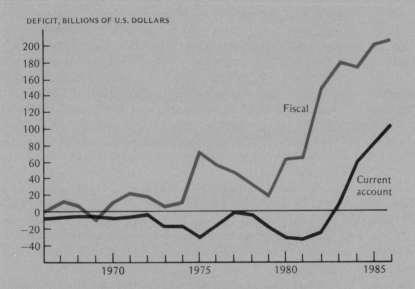

The budget deficit caused an accumulation of government debt. In a closed economy, the nation owes the debt to itself. But when the budget deficit is financed through a capital inflow, the borrowing is from the rest of the world. In effect, the United States owes the part of the national debt accumulated since 1981 to Japan and the other countries that have financed the U.S. current account deficit by running current account surpluses.

Current account deficits are not the inevitable result of budget deficits. The Canadian government deficit jumped from about $1 billion in 1981 to over $17 billion in 1982. Nonetheless the current account moved from a deficit in 1981 to a surplus in 1982. This was possible because of a dramatic increase in private saving in Canada, along with a fall in investment expenditures. The large government deficit persisted into 1986 but private saving fell and investment spending increased. These three things could happen simultaneously only if the current account went back into deficit, as indeed it did.

PRICE ADJUSTMENT

What happens in these alternative policy scenarios after the short run, that is, when firms begin to adjust their prices? Consider the monetary expansion first. Suppose that before the change in M output was equal to potential and both inflation and expected inflation were equal to zero. As discussed above, the increase in M would shift the LM curve outward, increasing output. As output would be above potential, the price level would begin to rise, starting in the next period. If M is held constant at its new level then the increase in the price level would reduce the level of real money balances. This would cause the interest rate to rise. The higher interest rate would cause output to fall for two reasons: Investment would be reduced, and the appreciation of the exchange rate caused by the higher interest rate would reduce net exports. Graphically, the LM curve would shift back towards its original position, as shown in the left-hand part of Figure 10–7. Note that the interest rate and real exchange rate will return to their original levels when output returns to potential.

Now consider the increase in government spending, again supposing that before the change in G output was equal to potential and both inflation and expected inflation were equal to zero. As discussed above, the IS curve would shift out, increasing output. Once again, this would set off an increase in prices that reduces real money balances, raises the interest rate and exchange rate, and thereby reduces both investment and net exports. Graphically, the LM curve shifts back toward the position that will set output equal to potential given the new IS curve. This is shown in the right-hand part of Figure 10–7.

Note that in this case the interest rate and real exchange rate are permanently higher after the price-adjustment process is complete. Why is this necessary? Output must return to potential, but the level of government spending has been permanently increased. Therefore the level of investment and net exports must be permanently reduced so that the sum of C, I, G, and X will once again equal Y^*.

This discussion of the price-adjustment process has considered the changes that will take place in the price level beginning in the period following a policy intervention. But this discussion is at least potentially incomplete. What if the changes in the exchange rate that are brought about by the policy change have an effect on prices that begins in the same period as the policy change? That is the topic of the next section.

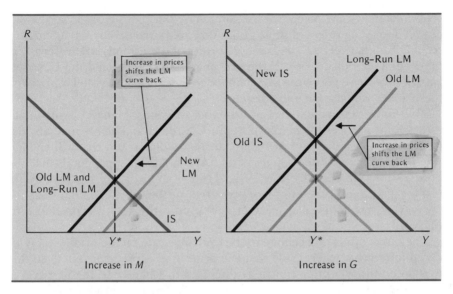

Figure 10–7. ADJUSTMENT OF THE OPEN ECONOMY TO POLICY CHANGES.
Starting with output equal to potential, an increase in M or G will raise output above potential and initiate inflation. The increase in the price level will reduce real money balances causing the interest rate to rise. This will reduce investment, and by raising the real exchange rate it will also reduce net exports. In the long run the LM curve will intersect the IS curve so that output is equal to potential.

Open-Economy IS Curve and Policy

1. The downward slope of the IS curve in an open economy comes in part from the positive relation between the interest rate and the exchange rate. Net exports decline when the interest rate rises.

2. The offset to fiscal expansion through crowding out is stronger in an open economy. Fiscal expansion raises the interest rate and depresses net exports as well as investment.

3. Monetary policy has an enhanced effect through the interest rate in an open economy. A monetary expansion lowers the interest rate and stimulates net exports as well as investment.

10.6 The Exchange Rate and the Price Level

One of the macroeconomic principles we have stressed in this book is that the price level is very unresponsive to most economic events in the short run. For example, a sudden contraction in monetary policy does not seem to have any measurable impact on the price level within the first year, even though its eventual effect is to lower prices considerably. One potential exception is that some prices will respond very quickly to changes in the exchange rate. The prices of some goods that are purchased by Canadians are set in U.S. dollars. The Canadian dollar price of these goods is therefore $1/E$ times the U.S. dollar price. If the exchange rate changes and the U.S. dollar prices of these goods are not changed then the Canadian dollar prices of these goods will change immediately.

This holds to some extent for a number of goods. Many U.S. manufacturers fix the prices of their exports in U.S. dollars. Their Canadian customers must pay the equivalent in Canadian dollars, and this will change when the exchange rate changes. And it also holds for some goods that are produced in Canada. The price of gold, for example, is set on a worldwide market in U.S. dollars. Thus a depreciation of the Canadian dollar will increase the Canadian dollar price of gold even if the gold was produced in Canada.

The direct effect of a change in the exchange rate on the price level is an exception to the general rule that the price level is predetermined, so this would constitute a price shock, as discussed in Chapter 6. If this effect is large, then the discussion of the effects of policy changes in a open economy must be amended to account for it.

Consider the example of an increase in the nominal money supply with output originally at potential. With the price level predetermined, the increase in the nominal money supply would increase the real money supply (M/P), shifting the LM curve to the right, increasing output and lowering the interest rate. The reduction in the interest rate would in turn reduce the exchange rate. If the depreciation increases the price level immediately, then part of the stimulative effect of the policy will be offset. This offsetting comes about because the price level would increase at the same time as the money stock so that the real money supply (M/P) would not increase as much as it would have if P had been unchanged. That is, we would need to analyse a simultaneous increase in the nominal money supply and a positive price shock.

The effect of the price change in future periods is the same as that of any price shock. If expected inflation depends on recent inflationary experience, then the price shock, by increasing current inflation, will also increase inflation in subsequent periods. For example, inflation in the year of the policy change will be increased. This will increase expected inflation in the year after the policy change, and the increase in expected inflation will lead to higher actual inflation, other things being equal.

This complication to the model can be safely ignored for policies that lead to small changes in the exchange rate. But what about a policy change that could lead to a substantial change in the exchange rate? There is a great deal of controversy among economists over the strength of the direct effect of a major change in E on the price level.[4] A quick glance at the data reveals why

---

[4] See, for example, Brian O'Reilly, Graydon Paulin, and Philip Smith, 'Responses of Various Econometric Models to Selected Policy Shocks,' Bank of Canada Technical Report No. 38, 1982.

the importance of this effect is uncertain. Those who believe that the direct effect of E on P is strong can point to 1977, a year in which the Canadian trade-weighted exchange rate depreciated by 10 percent and average import prices rose by 10 percent. Those who believe that the effect is weak can point to 1986, during which the trade-weighted exchange rate depreciated by 8 percent while average import prices hardly rose at all. By treating a substantial change in E as a price shock we can examine the consequences in our model under both assumptions.

10.7 The Effects of Trade Laws

The volume of Canada's imports and exports can be affected by changes in laws governing international trade enacted by Canada and by our trading partners. There are many legal measures that may affect trade. The most important ones are:

1. **Tariffs,** which are taxes on imported goods that do not apply to the same good if it is produced domestically
2. **Quotas,** which are limits on the quantity of particular goods that can be imported
3. **Subsidies,** which are direct or indirect payments to firms that make it easier for them to sell their goods in foreign markets

Such measures are called **protectionist,** because they seek to protect domestic producers from foreign competition. If Canada places a quota on shoe imports then the volume of shoe imports will fall. If the United States places a tariff on Canadian lumber then Canadian lumber exports to the United States will decline.

It might apear that more protectionism would make Canadians better off because it would help our producers, but this is usually not the case. First, consumers could suffer as prices would rise because of reduced competition from foreign suppliers. Second, microeconomics teaches us that trade barriers usually cause us to allocate our resources less efficiently. Third, if Canada made it more difficult for foreigners to sell their goods to Canadians then foreign governments might retaliate by enacting laws that discourage Canadian exports to their country. Even if our new trade law made us better off, the resulting retaliation could make us worse off overall.

Since the end of the Second World War Canadian governments have participated in a series of multi-country agreements to reduce tariff barriers. The first agreement was signed in 1947. There have been seven rounds of these negotiations since then, including the round that was ongoing while this book was in preparation. These agreements, called the **General Agreement on Tariffs and Trade (GATT),** have resulted in substantial reductions in Canadian and foreign tariff levels and an increase in the volume of our trade with other countries. In addition, Canada and the United States agreed to virtually unrestricted trade in motor vehicles and their parts. This agreement, often referred to as the Auto Pact, was signed in 1964. Accompanying these reductions in trade barriers, the percentage of Canadian GDP accounted for by exports and imports has risen.

The remaining barriers to trade that Canada maintains are concentrated in a few industries such as agriculture, footware, and textiles. These barriers consist mainly of quotas and subsidies. There is usually very little sentiment in favour of widespread protectionism in Canada, partly because we would be vulnerable to very damaging retaliation if we increased our trade barriers markedly.

This is not the case for our major trading partner, the United States. Although U.S. trade barriers are generally low, the U.S. government is inclined to enact protectionist measures whenever a recession occurs. This is largely due to the fact that the United States has little fear of retaliation by other countries because economically it is very powerful and relies relatively little on exports.

MACROECONOMIC EFFECTS OF U.S. PROTECTIONISM

A U.S. tariff or quota has the effect of shifting the Canadian net exports schedule in the direction of lower net exports given the exchange rate. That shift enters the spending process just as does any other shift in a spending schedule or a decrease in government purchases. The IS curve shifts to the left. The interest rate and GDP decrease along the LM curve, which remains unchanged. All the usual accompaniments to a spending contraction occur. In particular, the lower interest rate makes the Canadian dollar depreciate.

Because U.S. protectionism makes the Canadian dollar depreciate, the actual effect on trade is smaller than it might appear at first. Although a U.S. tariff makes Canadian exports more expensive for American purchasers, the weaker Canadian dollar offsets this to some extent. In other words, the exporting country pays part of the tariff, rather than the U.S. consumer. At the same time, the macroeconomic contraction in Canada becomes smaller, because if U.S. consumers see little price change, they will not cut their imports very much. Note that this effect cannot apply to quotas. If a quota on a particular good forces the quantity of imports to decline, a change in the exchange rate cannot offset this. However, if the decline in Canadian exports to the United States is large enough to reduce Canadian output and interest rates, then the fall in the exchange rate will stimulate the export of other goods to the United States somewhat.

Protectionism

1. Protectionist policies lessen foreign competition facing domestic producers. They generally help domestic producers and hurt do-

mestic consumers. They include tariffs on imports, quotas on the quantities of imports, and subsidies to domestic producers.

2. If one country introduces protectionist measures other countries may retaliate by erecting barriers to the first country's exports.

3. U.S. protectionist measures reduce Canada's net exports. They shift the IS curve inward, lower the interest rate, and reduce GDP.

The Canada-U.S. Free Trade Agreement

In 1988 the Canadian and U.S. governments began to implement a wide-ranging agreement on changes in trade policies called the **Canada-U.S. Free Trade Agreement (FTA).** This agreement may have a number of effects on the Canadian economy; here we consider its possible impact on macroeconomic stability.

The agreement provides for the eventual removal of all tariffs on Canada-U.S. trade, and restrictions on the imposition of non-tariff barriers. Although the balance of trade between Canada and the United States may be unchanged by the agreement, the volume of trade in each direction will increase somewhat. Further, some import and export activity that Canada now undertakes with other countries will be 'diverted' to the United States because tariffs on exports to, and imports from, countries other than the United States are not lowered under the FTA.

As a result, the proportion of Canadian production that is exported to the United States will be increased by the FTA, as will the proportion of Canadian spending that is devoted to U.S.-produced goods. How big this effect will be is uncertain, however, as most tarriffs between Canada and the United States were rather low before the FTA.

Greater concentration of Canadian trade with the United States will increase Canada's vulnerability to most shocks emanating from the United States. For example, a recession in the United States will have a greater effect on Canadian aggregate demand because more of Canadian production will be geared towards the U.S. market. A change in the Canada-U.S. exchange rate will have a greater effect on Canadian prices as more of our imports will have prices that are set in U.S. dollars.

However, the FTA could prevent a particular type of shock emanating from the United States—an increase in protectionism. Even without the FTA a great deal of Canadian output is purchased by Americans. It may be that the FTA, through its provisions and also through the cooperative atmosphere that its sponsors believe it will foster, will prevent the United States from enacting protectionist measures that would disrupt the Canadian economy.

Review and Practice

MAJOR POINTS

1. The long-run value of the exchange rate is determined by purchasing power parity. In the short run, expectations and conditions in financial markets create large deviations from purchasing power parity.

2. The interest rate differential between two countries is equal to the expected rate of depreciation.

3. When the real exchange rate is above purchasing power parity it is expected to decline to parity slowly.

4. There is a close relationship between the exchange rate and the interest rate. When interest rates are high the exchange rate also tends to be high.

5. The net export function depends negatively on income and on the real exchange rate.

6. The multiplier is smaller in an open economy than in a closed economy. This makes the IS curve steeper.

7. In an open economy an increase in the interest rate has a larger first-round effect on spending because it reduces net exports as well as investment. This makes the IS curve flatter.

8. An expansionary monetary policy lowers the interest rate and the exchange rate. Investment and exports are stimulated.

9. An expansionary fiscal policy raises the interest rate and the exchange rate. The policy crowds out the investment industries and the export industries.

10. A change in the exchange rate can have an immediate effect on the domestic price level by changing the domestic price of imported goods.

11. Protectionist policies undertaken by Canada's trading partners would reduce Canadian GDP in the short run. The resulting depreciation of the exchange rate would partially undo the effect of the protectionist measures.

KEY TERMS AND CONCEPTS

Purchasing power parity	Flexible exchange rate
Interest rate parity	Tariffs
Interest rate differential	Quotas
Exchange rate	Subsidies
Real exchange rate	Protectionism
Net export function	

QUESTIONS FOR DISCUSSION AND REVIEW

1. Explain how you would compare the return on a Canadian bond with the return on a U.S. bond.

2. What happens to the exchange rate between the Canadian dollar and the Italian lira when chronic inflation in Italy is well above inflation in Canada?

3. Why is it rational for investors to expect that the exchange rate will depreciate when it is above normal? Under what circumstances would it not be rational to expect this?

4. Summarise the steps and assumptions that link the exchange rate and the interest rate. What would happen to the relationship if the United States decided to use a more expansionary policy?

5. Describe what happens to consumption, investment, and net exports when you move down the IS curve.

6. What happens to net exports, investment, and consumption when government spending is decreased? Distinguish the long run from the short run.

7. What happens to net exports, investment, and consumption when the money supply is decreased? Why is monetary policy neutral in the long run, but not in the short run?

8. Describe the changes to the Canadian price of Japanese cars when the yen appreciates, in the short and medium runs.

9. What would happen to the interest rate, GDP, exchange rate, and trade balance if the United States placed a uniform 10 percent tariff on all imports?

PROBLEMS

Numerical
1. Consider a macro model consisting of the following relationships:

$$Y = C + I + G + X$$
$$C = 80 + .63Y$$
$$I = 350 - 2,000R + .1Y$$
$$M = (.1625Y - 1,000R)P$$
$$X = 500 - .1Y - 100(EP/P_u)$$
$$EP/P_u = .75 + 5R$$

where government spending G equals 750 and the money supply M equals 600. Suppose that the U.S. price level P_u is always equal to 1.0, and that the Canadian price level is predetermined at 1.0.
   a. Which are the endogenous variables and which are the exogenous variables in this relationship?
   b. Find the values of Y, R, C, I, X, and E that are predicted by the model.
   c. Derive an algebraic expression for the aggregate demand curve in which the money supply M, government spending G, and the price level P explicitly appear. For $M = 600$ and $G = 750$ draw the aggregate demand curve accurately to scale.
   d. Keeping the price level P at 1.0, calculate the effect a decrease in government spending of $10 billion will have on output, the interest rate, consumption, investment, net exports, and the exchange rate. Do the same thing for an increase in the money supply of $20 billion.

2. Using the same numerical example in Problem 1, calculate private saving, the government budget surplus, and the capital inflow from abroad for the case where $G = 750$ and $M = 600$. Show that the sum of these three equals investment. Repeat your calculation for $G = 740$ and for $M = 620$. Comment on what happens to the three components of saving.

3. For the same numerical example as in Problem 1 calculate a change in the mix of monetary and fiscal policy that will leave output equal to the level it is when $M = 600$ and $G = 750$, but in which the interest rate is 3 percent rather than 5 percent. Describe what happens to the value of the dollar, net exports, the government budget deficit, and investment for this change in policy.

4. Now assume that prices adjust according to the price-adjustment equation

$$\pi = 1.2(Y_{-1} - Y^*)/Y^*,$$

where π is the rate of inflation and Y^*, potential output, is equal to $4,000 billion. Continuing where you left off in Problem 1d, calculate the effect on the endogenous variables in the second, third, and fourth years after the increase in the money supply of $20 billion. Do the same for the decline in government spending of $10 billion. Describe the economy after prices have fully adjusted.

5. Consider a small economy that is much more open than the one in the previous examples. Its net export function is

$$X = 800 - .1Y - 400(EP/P_u)$$

and the relationship between the interest rate and the exchange rate is

$$EP/P_u = 10R + .5.$$

The other equations are the same.
a. Explain why this economy is more open.
b. Calculate what happens in the first year and in the long run when the money supply increases by $10 billion. Calculate what happens when government spending increases by $10 billion.

Analytical
1. Some members of the U.S. government are concerned that the United States bears too much of the cost of defending the Pacific Ocean. They would prefer that Japan shoulder more of this responsibility. Suppose it was agreed that the United States would spend less on defence and that Japan would spend more.
a. How would a reduction in defence spending affect the U.S. trade balance?
b. How would an increase in Japan's defence spending affect the U.S. trade balance?
c. To the extent that the United States and Japan purchase defence goods from each other, how will this affect your answer?

2. Purchasing power parity (PPP) is a theory of exchange rate behaviour as described in Section 10.4.
a. Explain why the real exchange rate changes very little under the theory of purchasing power parity.
b. What governs the behaviour of nominal exchange rates under PPP? Under what conditions are nominal exchange rates sticky?
c. Suppose that inflation in Canada is 4 percent while in the United States it is 7 percent. Under PPP, how does E change over time?
d. PPP clearly doesn't hold up in the short run; see Figure 10–3, where the real exchange rate is calculated using the GDP implicit price indexes for Canada and the United States. If the real exchange rate were instead calculated using price indices for manufactured goods, would you expect it to vary by more or less than it does in Figure 10–3?

3. On any given day, interest rates will differ from country to country. For example, Canadian government securities may pay 10 percent interest while comparable Japanese securities are paying 5 percent interest.
   a. Assume Japanese investors have access to Canadian securities. Why would any of them invest in Japanese securities when they could earn a higher interest rate on Canadian securities? Be specific.
   b. Is it likely that any Canadian investors would want to hold the Japanese securities?
   c. Suppose that PPP (see Question 2) holds exactly, that interest rates in Canada and Japan are 10 percent and 5 percent respectively, and that the Canadian inflation rate is 5 percent. If international investors are to be indifferent between holding Canadian and Japanese securities, what must the Japanese inflation rate be?

4. Given the net export function developed in this chapter, explain why the effect of fiscal policy on the trade balance is unambiguous, whereas the effect of monetary policy is ambiguous.

5. The topic box in Section 10.5 summarises the relationship between current account deficits and budget deficits.
   a. Are *increases* in the current account deficit an inevitable result of *increases* in the budget deficit?
   b. Consider the cases where investment is very sensitive to the interest rate and where it is very insensitive. Compare the effect that an increase in the budget deficit will have on the interest rate, the exchange rate, investment, and the current account deficit for each case.

6. In Chapter 5 we developed a model in which net exports were a function of the interest rate. In this chapter we have described in more detail why net exports depend on the interest rate.
   a. What factors determine the sensitivity of net exports to the interest rate?
   b. Consider the cases where net exports are very sensitive to the interest rate and where they are very insensitive. Compare the effect that an increase in the money supply will have on output, the interest rate, investment, and the trade balance for each case.
   c. Suppose foreign manufacturers maintain a fixed Canadian dollar price for their goods regardless of the exchange rate. Will this result in net exports being more or less sensitive to the interest rate?
   d. Given this behaviour, explain why the only way the monetary authorities could act to reduce the trade deficit is by inducing a recession.

7. Suppose that the economy is at potential, but that a trade deficit exists and is thought to be too large and the Canadian dollar is overvalued. Describe a change in monetary and fiscal policy that will keep the economy at potential, but will lower both the dollar and the trade deficit. Explain intuitively how the change in policy will bring about the desired results. Illustrate your answer using an IS-LM diagram.

8. Suppose that the economy is operating at potential but that inflation is thought to be too high. Macro policy will therefore have to turn contractionary, in order to reduce inflation. Describe the pros and cons of using monetary policy or fiscal policy to bring about the contraction, paying attention to the international factors.

Appendix A: The Interest Rate and the Exchange Rate under Rational Expectations

The purpose of this appendix is to derive the relationship between the real exchange rate and the real interest rate—Equation 10–4 and the example in Equation 10–6. The derivation requires that we consider expectations of exchange rate movements, and for this purpose we use the rational expectations assumption.

INTEREST RATE PARITY

The bond markets of Canada and other countries are closely linked. Investors are constantly comparing the returns they can make from holding their funds in assets denominated in Canadian dollars to the returns they can make in U.S. dollars, German marks, Japanese yen, British pounds, etc.

Suppose that an investor is comparing the return from holding a Canadian dollar-denominated bond to the return from holding a U.S. dollar-denominated bond. An investor comparing a Canadian bond with an American bond has to do more than compare the interest rates paid on the two bonds. The Canadian dollar earnings of the U.S. bond could be different from the interest rate because the Canadian dollar might appreciate or depreciate. Suppose that the U.S. bond pays 10 percent interest, and that the exchange rate is .8 U.S. dollar per Canadian dollar. Then a Canadian investor with 100 Canadian dollars could obtain 80 U.S. dollars, buy a U.S. dollar bond, and get back 88 U.S. dollars at the end of the year (interest plus principal). But suppose that the Canadian dollar depreciated by 2 percent over the year so that the exchange rate is .784 U.S. dollar per Canadian dollar at the end of the year. Then the 88 U.S. dollars could be exchanged back into about 112 Canadian dollars ($88/.784 = 112.2$). The net return on the U.S. bond, measured in Canadian dollars, is 12 percent, more than the stated interest of 10 percent on the bond in the United States. The depreciation of the Canadian dollar makes the difference.

Investors will compare the Canadian dollar interest rate to the U.S. dollar interest rate plus the expected rate of depreciation of the Canadian dollar. Suppose the Canadian dollar interest rate is 10 percent, the U.S. dollar interest rate is 5 percent, and the expected rate of depreciation of the Canadian dollar is zero. Then the comparison made by investors will strongly favour Canadian bonds. No investor would want to hold the U.S. dollar-denominated bonds in this situation.

What conditions would make investors willing to hold the U.S. dollar-denominated bonds? One answer, obviously, would be for the Canadian interest rate to fall to 5 percent, or the U.S. interest rate to rise to 10 percent. But even if interest rates remain different, the expected appreciation or depreciation of the Canadian dollar can bring the expected return on the two bonds into equality. When we observe that the Canadian dollar interest rate is 10 percent and the U.S. interest rate is 5 percent, we can reasonably guess that markets are expecting around a 5 percent annual depreciation of the Canadian dollar.

Of course the same relationship holds for bonds denominated in any foreign monetary unit. In general, *the interest rate differential between Canadian dollar bonds and bonds denominated in the foreign monetary unit is equal to the expected rate of depreciation of the dollar in terms of the foreign monetary unit.* More formally,

$$R - R_i = \text{Expected rate of depreciation of the Canadian dollar} \atop \text{with respect to the currency of Country } i, \qquad (10\text{--}10)$$

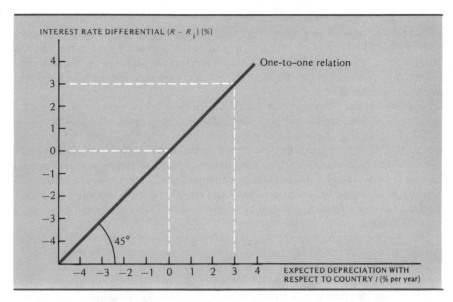

Figure 10–8. EXPECTED DEPRECIATION AND THE INTEREST RATE DIFFERENTIAL.
There is a one-to-one relationship between the interest rate differential and the expected depreciation of the Canadian dollar. If Canadian dollar bonds are yielding a higher interest rate compared to the bonds of Country i, investors must be expecting that the Canadian dollar will depreciate relative to the currency of Country i in the future. As the Canadian dollar depreciates, it will reward the holders of foreign bonds by enough to make up for the lower interest rate paid on the bonds.

where R is the Canadian dollar interest rate and R_i is the interest rate in the foreign country. For example, if $R = .05$ and $R_i = .10$, the expected rate of depreciation of the dollar is $-.05$. In other words, the Canadian dollar is expected to appreciate by 5 percent. This relationship between the interest rate differential and the expected depreciation is called **interest rate parity.** The relationship is shown graphically in Figure 10–8. The expected depreciation of the Canadian dollar is shown on the horizontal axis and the interest rate differential is shown on the vertical axis. The slope of the line is equal to 1. When the interest rate differential increases by 1 percentage point, the expected depreciation of the dollar increases by 1 percentage point.[5]

TESTING INTEREST RATE PARITY USING FUTURES MARKETS

We saw that purchasing power parity does not work in the short run. How well does interest rate parity work? To test the relationship we need a measure of investors' *expected* rate of depreciation of the currency. An easy way to find out what people expect about future exchange rate movements is to look at the **forward** or **futures markets** for foreign exchange. In a futures market for German marks, for

[5] If the interest rates in the interest rate parity condition are *real* rates, then the exchange rate should be the real exchange rate. If the interest rates are nominal then the exchange rate should be the nominal exchange rate. In this book we generally interpret the interest rates as real interest rates, and we do so here.

example, one can buy marks for delivery in the future, say a year from now. Futures markets reveal at what prices investors are willing to buy and sell foreign exchange in the future. The prices on forward or futures markets are found in the financial pages of most newspapers. Prices on forward markets are found along with other exchange rate quotes. Futures markets for foreign exchange are usually listed with wheat or soybean futures.

Suppose that the exchange rate for marks for delivery one year from now is 2.1 marks per Canadian dollar. Suppose that today's exchange rate is 2.0 marks per dollar. Then, according to the futures market, investors expect the dollar to appreciate against the mark by 5 percent. If interest rate parity holds then the dollar interest rate should be 5 percent below the German interest rate. In practice, the percentage difference between the futures exchange rate and the current exchange rate—the measure of expected depreciation—is almost exactly equal to the interest rate differential for any currency that can be freely traded. Interest rate parity seems to work fairly well.

This is not a complete test of interest rate parity, however. By using the futures market an investor covers the risk associated with changes in the exchange rate. A futures market locks in the yield by guaranteeing the exchange rate in the future. For this reason equality of the percentage difference between the current and future exchange rate, and the interest rate differential, is called **covered interest rate parity.** Without using the futures market the investor takes a chance that the exchange rate will be different from what was expected. The investor is exposed to the risk of a currency change.

An alternative test of (uncovered) interest rate parity that takes risk into account is based on the rational expectations method of estimating the expected future exchange rate. This approach supposes that investors predict the exchange rate based on how it has behaved in the past. Essentially investors are assumed to have a model of the exchange rate. By guessing what this model is, and by using it to project the size of appreciations and depreciations, the economists can see if interest rate parity holds. Such tests indicate that interest rate parity is a good approximation. Research undertaken by Allan Gregory of Queen's University indicates that interest rate parity is a useful theory of the Canada-U.S. exchange rate.[6]

THE EXCHANGE RATE AND ITS EXPECTED DEPRECIATION

Thus far we have related the interest rate differential to the expected rate of depreciation of the dollar. Our next step is to discuss how markets form expectations of the rate of depreciation of the dollar. We base our analysis on the idea of rational expectations.

Although not accurate in the short run, purchasing power parity is a reasonable guide for the tendency of the exchange rate in the long run. It appears that the ex-

[6] Allan W. Gregory, 'Testing Interest Rate Parity and Rational Expectations for Canada and the United States,' *Canadian Journal of Economics,* Vol. 20 (May 1987), pp. 289–305. Some aspects of the behaviour of exchange rates are not explained by interest rate parity. This is noted in Gregory's paper, and also in Lars P. Hansen and Robert Hodrick, 'Forward Exchange Rates as Optimal Predictors of Future Spot Prices: An Econometric Analysis,' *Journal of Political Economy,* Vol. 88 (Oct. 1980), pp. 829–853.

change rate has generally fluctuated around purchasing power parity, sometimes above and sometimes below. For example, when the exchange rate rose high above purchasing power parity in the early 1970s, it eventually fell back toward purchasing power parity in the early 1980s. When the dollar was very low in the mid-1980s, it eventually rose again.

Investors are likely to be aware of these general movements of the dollar. They therefore expect that when the dollar is high, the exchange rate will ultimately depreciate down to its normal level as set by purchasing power parity. Similarly, when the dollar plunges below the level of parity, investors expect the dollar to appreciate over the future, to restore parity in the long run. In general, there is a relationship between the expected rate of depreciation and the level of the exchange rate: *The higher the exchange rate, the larger the expected depreciation of the exchange rate; conversely, the lower the exchange rate, the larger the expected appreciation of the exchange rate.*

If the exchange rate returns to normal at a speed of w percent per year (if the speed is 10 percent per year then w would equal .10), then the relationship says

$$\text{Expected depreciation of the dollar} = w \, (\text{Exchange rate} - \text{Parity}), \quad (10\text{--}11)$$

where 'parity' stands for the level of purchasing power parity. For example, if the exchange rate is 1.3, purchasing power parity is 1.0 and w is .10 then expected depreciation is .03, or 3 percent per year. A graphical representation of the relation between the expected rate of depreciation and the level of the exchange rate is shown in Figure 10–9.

It is important to distinguish between the rational, expected future behaviour of

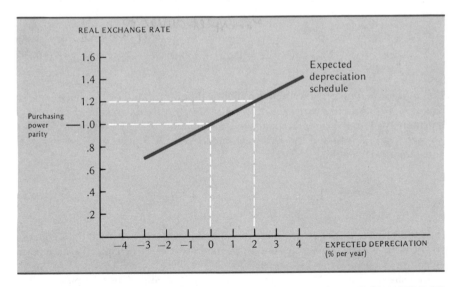

Figure 10–9. EXPECTED DEPRECIATION AND THE LEVEL OF THE EXCHANGE RATE. Based on past experience, investors expect the exchange rate to return to the level of purchasing power parity at a fairly slow rate. If the exchange rate is above the parity level, investors expect depreciation. If it is below, investors expect appreciation. There is an upward-sloping relation between the level of the exchange rate and the expected depreciation of the dollar.

the exchange rate as given by Equation 10–11 or Figure 10–9, on the one hand, and the actual behaviour of the exchange rate, on the other. The expected behaviour is smooth and slow, moving back to parity at a rate of perhaps 10 percent per year.[7] The actual behaviour is jerky, with possible movements of 10 percent in a single week. The foreign exchange market is like the stock market. It undergoes large, completely unexpected movements in response to surprising economic news. According to the rational expectations view, participants in the market have expectations of small movements in the exchange rate—sometimes up, sometimes down—even though large movements are the rule. The small movements give the best forecast on the average, given the information available to investors. Even the most informed expert cannot guess in advance all the movements that will occur.

Recall that we are deriving a relation between the dollar interest rate and the exchange rate. So far, we have two separate relations, summarised in Equations 10–10 and 10–11. One is between the interest rate differential and expected depreciation (Equation 10–10). The other is between the level of the exchange rate and expected depreciation (Equation 10–11). We can combine the two to get a relation between the interest rate differential and the level of the exchange rate:

$$R - R_u = w \text{ (Exchange rate } - \text{ Parity).} \qquad (10\text{–}12)$$

Equals expected
depreciation
from Equation 10–10

Equals expected
depreciation
from Equation 10–11

That is, when the Canadian dollar interest rate is high relative to the foreign interest rate, the exchange rate is high relative to parity.   We can rearrange Equation 10–12 as follows:

$$\text{Exchange rate} = \text{Parity} + (1/w)(R - R_u). \qquad (10\text{–}13)$$

This is just Equation 10–4 written in a slightly different way. The 'Exchange rate' in Equation 10–13 is the real exchange rate (EP/P_u), 'Parity' corresponds to q_0 in Equation 10–4, and $1/w$ corresponds to v in Equation 10–4. For example, if w is .2 (so that $v = 1/w = 5$) and the U.S. real interest rate is 5 percent $(R_u = .05)$, then Equation 10–13 yields:

$$\text{Exchange rate} = \text{Parity} + 5R - .25. \qquad (10\text{–}14)$$

If the purchasing power parity value of the real exchange rate is 1.0 then Equation 10–14 is identical to Equation 10–6 in the main text of this chapter because parity − .25 would be 1 − .25 which equals .75.

You may find the story behind the interest rate–exchange rate relationship a little indirect. It says that the Canadian dollar appreciates when Canadian interest rates rise because higher interest rates fit into the world economy only if the dollar is expected to depreciate, and, in order to depreciate, the dollar must appreciate first.

[7] This is a very rough estimate and is meant to suggest the slow expected movement.

What is going on in the economy to bring about these changes in the exchange rate? Suppose that the Canadian interest rate rises, both absolutely and relative to the U.S. interest rate. Canadian and U.S. investors will now find Canadian dollar securities more attractive. They will try to sell their U.S. dollar-denominated bonds and buy Canadian dollar-denominated bonds. At some point in this process, they will be trying to buy Canadian dollars and sell U.S. dollars. Consequently, the price of Canadian dollars relative to U.S. dollars—the exchange rate—must rise to clear the market. Thus the higher interest rate brings about an increase in the exchange rate. As the process proceeds, the higher exchange rate brings expectations of greater depreciation, until investors no longer find Canadian dollar bonds more attractive, even though Canadian dollar interest rates are still higher.

Appendix B: 'Overshooting' of Exchange Rates with Sticky Prices and Rational Expectations

We have based our theory of real exchange rate determination on rational expectations. We argued that the real exchange rate eventually returns to purchasing power parity, and that people rationally expect this return. This expectation theory enabled us to relate the *level* of the real exchange rate to the rate of appreciation or depreciation of the real exchange rate. Since the rate of depreciation is equal to real interest rate differentials, this led to an explicit relation between the real interest rate and the real exchange rate.

In recent years there has been considerable discussion among open-economy macroeconomists about **exchange rate overshooting.** Overshooting usually refers to a situation where the nominal exchange rate E overshoots its long-run value after an unanticipated but permanent increase in the money supply.[8] This occurs essentially because the exchange rate can move freely while prices cannot because they are sticky. In this appendix we show why overshooting may occur.

We consider a small country that takes as given the world interest rate and the world price level and within which a permanent unanticipated increase in the money supply occurs. According to our analysis, the permanent increase in the money supply will eventually raise the domestic price level and *depreciate* the currency by the same amount. In addition, in the long run, output will return to potential and all other real variables will return to normal.

In the short run, an increase in the money supply should reduce the domestic interest rate. For this to occur, however, there must be an expected appreciation of the currency. How do we get an expected appreciation when we know that in the long run the exchange rate will depreciate? As illustrated in Figure 10–10, this can occur if the exchange rate first **overshoots** its long-run value and then appreciates up towards that value. The initial sharp fall in the exchange rate will be unexpected, because the money supply increase was unanticipated. After that jump down, the exchange rate is then expected to move up again smoothly.

Now that we have calculated how the exchange rate behaves, we can complete our investigation of the effect of the money supply increase. As is illustrated in Figure 10–11, the aggregate demand curve shifts to the right. Since output is greater than potential, the price level begins to rise. Since the price level rises more slowly than

---

[8] The paper by Rudiger Dornbusch, 'Expectations and Exchange Rate Dynamics,' *Journal of Political Economy*, Vol. 84, pp. 1161–1176, 1976, led to much of the discussion of overshooting.

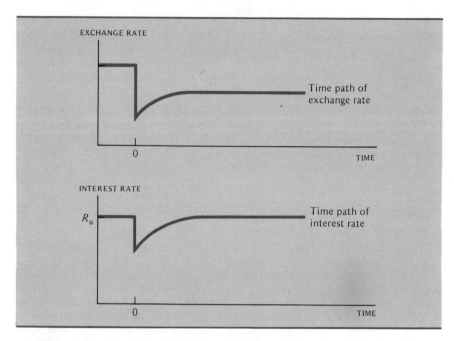

Figure 10–10. OVERSHOOTING: THE EXCHANGE RATE DEPRECIATES SHARPLY AND THEN GRADUALLY APPRECIATES.
When the money supply increases at Time 0, the exchange rate unexpectedly falls below its new long-run value. The subsequent appreciation is expected and permits the domestic interest to remain below the U.S. interest rate. The rate of change of the exchange rate declines as it gets closer to its long-run value.

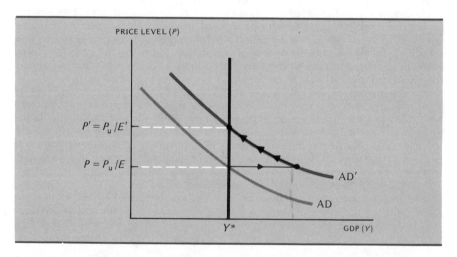

Figure 10–11. MONETARY POLICY WITH EXCHANGE RATE OVERSHOOTING.
Monetary expansion shifts aggregate demand from AD to AD'. Through the process of price adjustment, the economy reaches a new equilibrium at a higher price level, P', and a correspondingly lower exchange rate, E'.

the exchange rate falls at the point of impact, the real exchange rate (PE/P_u) falls and home goods are in greater demand than foreign goods. This stimulates exports from the home country. The price level will continue to rise until output returns to potential.

11

Foreign Trade under a
Fixed Exchange Rate

In the previous chapter we considered the determination of net exports when the government allows the financial market to determine the exchange rate. This is called a flexible, or floating, exchange rate. We saw that government policies such as a monetary expansion could affect the exchange rate, and we considered how changes in the exchange rate would affect the rest of the economy. In this chapter we consider the determination of net exports when the government chooses the exchange rate, rather than letting the financial market set the rate. This is called a **fixed exchange rate.**

At present the Canadian government does not fix the exchange rate. But analysis of this case will repay careful study for a number of reasons. First, Canada has used a fixed exchange rate in the past, so this analysis is needed to understand some of the past events in the Canadian economy. Second, some (but by no means all) economists advocate returning to a fixed exchange rate system. Our analysis of fixed exchange rates will allow us to assess the pros and cons of this proposal. Third, Canadian policy often combines some aspects of both fixed and flexible exchange rates. Thus we need to consider the fixed exchange rate case in order to understand and evaluate current policy.

11.1 Fixing the Exchange Rate

In order for the government to fix the Canada-U.S. exchange rate in today's economy, the government must ensure that the Canadian interest rate is equal to the U.S. interest rate. As a result, monetary policy must be dedicated to bringing about and maintaining this equality. To see this, consider this scenario:

Suppose that the government attempted to fix the exchange rate at some level $\overline{E}$ in the following way. A special agency of the government would be set up with instructions to trade Canadian and U.S. currencies with anyone who wanted such trades, but only at rate $\overline{E}$. Thus anyone who wanted to acquire U.S. dollars could purchase them from the agency for $1/\overline{E}$ Canadian dollars per U.S. dollar. The agency would collect Canadian dollars from buyers and give them U.S. dollars from the government's official reserves. Anyone who wanted to buy Canadian dollars could purchase them from the agency for $\overline{E}$ U.S. dollars each. The agency would pay out Canadian dollars and add the U.S. dollars it received in exchange to the stock of official reserves.

Such a scheme looks foolproof, but in the modern economy it would only work if the Canadian interest rate was equal to the U.S. rate. To understand why this is true we must return to the analysis of Section 10.4.

In the modern economy international financial markets are highly integrated. For example, it is very easy for Canadians to invest in the United States and for Americans to invest in Canada. Suppose the exchange rate is fixed at $\overline{E}$. If Canadian investors see that the Canadian interest rate is lower than the U.S. interest rate they will want to invest all of their financial capital in the United States. Thus they will swamp the government's foreign exchange agency with requests to trade Canadian dollars for U.S. dollars, and all of the government's official reserves will soon be exhausted in meeting this demand. With a flexible exchange rate the increase in the demand to trade Canadian dollars for U.S. dollars would cause the exchange rate to depreciate until investors no longer wanted to invest solely in the United States.[1] But under a fixed exchange rate, $\overline{E}$ cannot change now or in the future. Thus if the Canadian interest rate was less than the U.S. rate the government would soon exhaust its official reserves. Once this occurred there would be no way to keep the exchange rate fixed at $\overline{E}$.

Now suppose that the Canadian interest rate exceeded the U.S. interest rate while the exchange rate was fixed. In this case U.S. investors would want to buy Canadian bonds. The government's foreign exchange agency would be flooded with requests to give out Canadian dollars in return for U.S. dollars. The government's official reserves would build up enormously

---

[1] Recall that under a flexible exchange rate it is possible for the Canadian interest rate to differ from the U.S. interest rate without causing massive capital flows. For example, if the Canadian interest rate is less than the U.S. interest rate, Canadian investors will still be willing to invest in Canadian bonds if they expect that the Canadian dollar will appreciate enough in the future. They will reason as follows: To buy U.S. bonds I must buy U.S. dollars now. As I expect that the Canadian dollar will appreciate I believe that when the U.S. bond pays off I will be forced to trade the U.S. dollars for Canadian dollars at a time when U.S. dollars buy fewer Canadian dollars than they buy today. Thus, even though the rate of return that I would earn in U.S. dollars exceeds the rate of return I can earn in Canadian dollars, once I convert my U.S. earnings back to Canadian dollars I will be no better off than if I had bought the Canadian bond.

in a short period of time. Although it would be possible to continue this process indefinitely, the government would be tying up a vast amount of capital in foreign currency for which it had no use.

Thus if the government wants to commit itself to maintaining a fixed exchange rate over any significant length of time, it must be prepared to see that its policies result in the Canadian interest rate taking the same level as the U.S. interest rate. While, in principle, monetary or fiscal policy could be used to do this, in practice only monetary policy can be adjusted quickly enough to implement a fixed exchange rate policy successfully. As a result, if the government decides to fix the exchange rate the Bank of Canada must commit itself to the following rule for the money supply: Choose *M* so that the Canadian interest rate is equal to the U.S. interest rate.

We can analyse this graphically by drawing a horizontal line at the level of the U.S. interest rate, as shown in Figure 11–1. We call this horizontal line the **BP = 0 curve.** The name of the curve comes from the following observation. The exchange rate can be kept fixed without changing the level of official reserves if the Canadian interest rate is kept at the same level as the U.S. rate. As the balance of payments must equal the change in official reserves, this level is called the *BP* = 0 level.[2] The LM curve has not really disappeared in the model of Figure 11–1. We often do not bother to draw it when the exchange rate is fixed because we know that monetary policy will be conducted in such a way that the LM curve will intersect the IS curve at the interest rate indicated by the height of the *BP* = 0 curve.

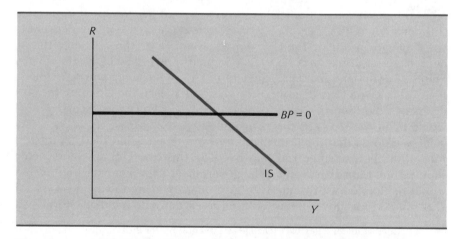

Figure 11–1.   OUTPUT DETERMINATION UNDER A FIXED EXCHANGE RATE.
The level of output is determined by the intersection of the IS curve and the BP = 0 curve. The height of the BP = 0 curve is given by the U.S. interest rate. The LM curve is not shown because we know that the money supply will be chosen so that the LM curve intersects the IS curve at the point that the IS curve crosses the BP = 0 curve.

[2] As we will see in Chapter 12, it is also possible to use changes in official reserves as part of a fixed exchange rate policy; even then the Canadian interest rate must be kept equal to the U.S. rate.

11.2 The Aggregate Demand Model under a Fixed Exchange Rate

In this section we consider how the algebraic and graphical model that we developed in earlier chapters must be modified if the exchange rate is fixed instead of flexible.

THE IS CURVE UNDER A FIXED EXCHANGE RATE

Recall that we derive the IS curve by substituting the equations for consumption (C), investment (I), and net exports (X) into the national income accounting identity $(Y = C + I + G + X)$. Thus suppose that the nominal exchange rate with the United States is fixed at some value $\overline{E}$ that is chosen by the government. Then

$$Y = \underbrace{a + b(1 - t)Y}_{C} + \underbrace{e - dR}_{I} + G + \underbrace{g - mY - n(\overline{E}P/P_u)}_{X}. \qquad (11\text{--}1)$$

Under a fixed nominal exchange rate the real exchange rate $\overline{E}P/P_u$ is a predetermined variable. We know this because the nominal exchange rate $(\overline{E})$ and the foreign price level (P_u) are given exogenously while the domestic price level (P) is predetermined. Thus, rearranging Equation 11–1 so that R is on the left-hand side yields

$$R = \frac{a + e + g}{d} - \frac{1 - b(1 - t) + m}{d}Y - \frac{n}{d}\frac{\overline{E}P}{P_u} + \frac{1}{d}G. \qquad (11\text{--}2)$$

Equation 11–2 reveals that under a fixed exchange rate the position of the IS curve depends directly on the real exchange rate.[3]

For example, if the level at which the exchange rate is fixed $(\overline{E})$ is reduced, then the IS curve will shift out. This will increase output in the short run because the reduction in the real exchange rate would increase the demand for net exports. This is shown in Figure 11–2. Note that in the left-hand panel of the figure a $BP = 0$ curve is shown but no LM curves appear. We know that the money supply will be set in such a way that the LM curve intersects the IS curve at the $BP = 0$ curve. In the right-hand panel these LM curves have been drawn in. You can see that they do not add any additional information to the analysis, but they do clutter the diagram.

---

[3] Under a flexible exchange rate the nominal exchange rate E is endogenous. Therefore the real exchange rate is also endogenous. In Chapter 10 we used the equation for the real exchange rate under a flexible rate (Equation 10–5) to eliminate EP/P_u from the net export equation. This yielded the flexible exchange rate IS equation (Equation 10–9). When the exchange rate is fixed we do not eliminate the real exchange rate from the IS equation because the real exchange rate becomes predetermined, rather than endogenous.

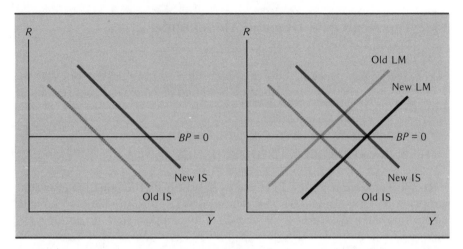

Figure 11–2.   EFFECT OF A REDUCTION IN $\overline{E}$.
The left-hand panel shows why output would increase. A reduction in the level at which
the exchange rate is fixed ($\overline{E}$) will reduce the real exchange rate, shifting the IS curve out
by stimulating net exports. Other shocks to spending such as an increase in government
spending or unexpectedly high investment would have a similar effect. The right-hand
panel shows where the LM curve would be before and after the reduction in $\overline{E}$.

MACROECONOMIC ADJUSTMENT WITH A FIXED EXCHANGE RATE

Suppose that output is equal to potential and then $\overline{E}$ is reduced. As shown
in Figure 11–2 this would reduce the real exchange rate, stimulating net
exports and shifting the IS curve out and raising output above potential.
How is long-run equilibrium restored when the exchange rate is fixed? As
output is raised above potential, inflation would occur in the future. This
would increase the price level (P), raising the real exchange rate ($\overline{E}P/P_u$).
Thus, over time, the IS curve would shift back to its original position as the
demand for net exports was reduced.

Now suppose that output was equal to potential and government spending was increased. Once again the IS curve would shift out raising output
above potential. In the long run inflation would raise the price level,
thereby raising the real exchange rate and reducing net exports. When output returns to potential the reduction in net exports caused by the change in
the real exchange rate would exactly offset the increase in government
spending.

The Macroeconomic Model under a Fixed Exchange Rate

1. In order to fix the Canada-U.S. exchange rate the Bank of Canada
   must commit itself to making sure that the Canadian interest rate is
   equal to the U.S. interest rate.

2. This commitment can be shown graphically by drawing a horizontal line at the level of the U.S. interest rate. This is called the $BP = 0$ curve. The money supply will be chosen so that the LM curve intersects the IS curve at the point where the IS curve crosses the $BP = 0$ curve.

3. Under a fixed nominal exchange rate the real exchange rate is a predetermined variable. The position of the IS curve depends on the predetermined value of the real exchange rate.

4. If output rises above potential the subsequent increase in the price level will raise the real exchange rate, discouraging net exports and shifting the IS curve back. If output is below potential the price level will fall, reducing the real exchange rate and shifting the IS curve out.

11.3 Pros and Cons of Fixed Exchange Rates

Economists who favour fixed exchange rates offer a number of arguments. Here are two of the most common. First, suppose that a depreciation of the exchange rate causes many prices in Canada to rise immediately. If so, then a depreciation will cause a substantial price shock. This will increase inflation now, and it will also increase inflation in the future due to its effect on expectations of future inflation. Thus fixing the exchange rate may improve price stability. Second, suppose that international trade is discouraged by fluctuations in nominal exchange rates. Then fixing the exchange rate would increase international trade. Because increased international trade can make an economy more efficient, this could increase the level of potential output.

Both of these suggested benefits are controversial. As discussed in Chapter 10, it may well be that depreciations cause only small, if any, price shocks. And it is far from clear that fixed exchange rates would encourage international trade. Given the uncertain nature of the benefits of fixed exchange rates, we should pay careful attention to the costs. Chief among these costs is that in order to increase exchange rate stability, other goals, such as output stability, might have to be sacrificed.

Suppose, for example, that Canadian output was equal to potential and the United States embarked on a restrictive monetary policy. In the short run this would raise the U.S. interest rate and reduce U.S. output. What would happen to Canadian GDP? This would depend on whether the exchange rate was flexible or fixed. The IS curve would shift in because the fall in U.S. income would reduce demand for Canada's exports. If the exchange rate was flexible, the increase in R_u would cause the Canada-U.S. exchange rate to fall as financial investments in the United States would become relatively more appealing than financial investments in Canada.

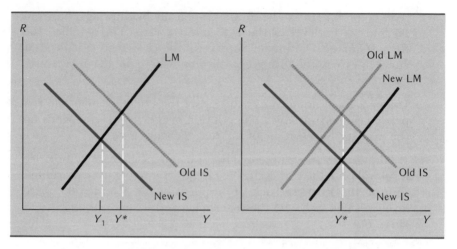

Figure 11–3. EFFECT OF A CONTRACTIONARY U.S. MONETARY POLICY UNDER A FLEXIBLE EXCHANGE RATE.
The left-hand panel shows what would happen if the money supply was not changed. The reduction in U.S. income would shift the IS curve back, although this would be partly offset by the depreciation of the Canadian dollar caused by the rise in the U.S. interest rate. Output would fall. The right-hand panel shows how monetary policy could be used to counteract the fall in output.

The fall in the exchange rate would stimulate net exports. Thus the inward shift of the IS curve due to the reduction in U.S. income would be partially offset by the depreciation of the exchange rate. Output would fall from Y^* to Y_1, as shown in the left-hand panel of Figure 11–3. In addition, monetary policy could be used to further counteract the fall in income. For example, an expansionary monetary policy could restore output to potential, as shown in the right-hand panel of Figure 11–3.

Under a fixed exchange rate the result would be quite different. The inward shift in the IS curve would tend to reduce output. There would be no exchange rate depreciation to mitigate this inward shift. Moreover, in order to maintain the fixed exchange rate, monetary policy would have to be directed to raising the Canadian interest rate to the new level of the U.S. interest rate. This is shown in Figure 11–4. The IS curve shifts in because of the fall in U.S. income and the $BP = 0$ curve shifts up because of the increase in the U.S. interest rate. The decrease in output is much greater than in the left-hand panel of Figure 11–3 where the exchange rate was flexible but the money stock was not changed. Moreover, the Bank of Canada cannot take any action to offset this fall in income when the exchange rate is fixed. Any increase in the money supply would cause the Canadian interest rate to fall below the U.S. interest rate, making it impossible to maintain the fixed value of the exchange rate.[4]

expansionary MP cannot be used

---

[4] It might be possible to use fiscal policy to stabilise output in this case. In Chapter 13 we discuss why this may not be practical, however.

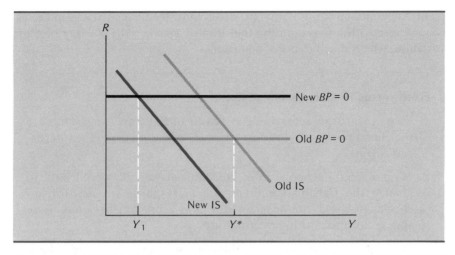

Figure 11–4.   EFFECT OF A CONTRACTIONARY U.S. MONETARY POLICY UNDER A
FIXED EXCHANGE RATE.
The reduction in U.S. income would shift the IS curve back. The increase in the U.S. interest rate would shift the $BP = 0$ curve up. The fall in output is greater than if the exchange rate was flexible. Moreover, monetary policy cannot be used to counteract this.

Now consider what would happen if the U.S. economy was unchanging
but a shock occurred in the Canadian economy. As long as the U.S. interest
rate is not changed Canada must hold its own interest rate constant in order
to keep the exchange rate constant. A shock in spending, such as unexpectedly strong investment, would shift the IS curve to the right, much as in Figure 11–2. GDP would rise by the full amount of the spending shift, together
with the resulting multiplier effects. The mitigating effects of higher interest rates that we would see under a flexible exchange rate would not occur
under a fixed rate. Thus GDP would be highly vulnerable to spending disturbances under a policy that kept the exchange rate constant.

Note that the flat $BP = 0$ curve also indicates that fiscal policy is more
powerful when the central bank stabilises the exchange rate. An increase in
government spending pushes the IS curve to the right. With floating exchange rates, we saw that the increase in government spending partially
crowds out private investment *and* net exports because interest rates rise
and the exchange rate appreciates. With the exchange rate fixed there is no
appreciation of the currency and the interest rate does not rise. Hence,
there is no crowding out. Production increases by the full amount of the
shift in the IS curve.

Of course, the Bank of Canada can pay attention to the exchange rate
without going as far as fixing it completely. For example, the Bank can pursue a policy of reducing or slowing changes in the exchange rate without
completely eliminating such changes. The important point is that making
monetary policy responsible for stabilising the exchange rate can prevent
monetary policy from achieving other goals, such as stability of employ-

ment. We cannot ask the Bank of Canada to prevent fluctuations in the exchange rate without recognising that it must sacrifice the stability of other variables, which may be more important.

Fixed versus Flexible Exchange Rates

1. Two of the arguments made in favour of fixed exchange rates are that fixed rates would reduce price shocks and encourage international trade.

2. With a fixed exchange rate, the Bank of Canada would have to change the Canadian interest rate in response to each foreign shock. It could not insulate GDP and employment from those shocks, as it can with a floating rate.

3. With a fixed exchange rate, a domestic spending shock would have a large effect on GDP. The normal cushioning through interest rate fluctuations would not occur, because it would cause exchange rate fluctuations.

11.4 International Experience with Fixed and Flexible Exchange Rates

From the end of World War II until the early 1970s most of the world economy operated under a system of fixed exchange rates. This system evolved out of an agreement between major trading nations at an international conference at Bretton Woods, New Hampshire, in 1944. The key economists participating in this conference were John Maynard Keynes, representing the United Kingdom, and Harry Dexter White of the U.S. Treasury. A leading member of the Canadian delegation was Louis Rasminsky, who eventually went on to become governor of the Bank of Canada from 1961 to 1972. Keynes and White favoured fixed rather than freely floating exchange rates based on the feeling that floating exchange rates were partly responsible for the poor performance of the world economy during the 1920s and the 1930s, compared with the better performance during a previous period of fixed exchange rates before World War I. However, they also recognised the need to change exchange rates under certain circumstances, and they therefore created a system that allowed for limited flexibility.

THE BRETTON WOODS SYSTEM

According to the Bretton Woods System, each country agreed to fix, or **peg**, the exchange rate for its currency in terms of the U.S. dollar. The nu-

Figure 11–5.   INTERVENTION BAND OF A FIXED EXCHANGE RATE SYSTEM.
Under the Bretton Woods System the monetary authorities of all participating countries
(except the United States) were committed to intervening whenever their exchange rate
with the United States threatened to leave the intervention band. A depreciation was
counteracted by a contractionary monetary policy, and an appreciation was counteracted by an expansionary policy.

merical value of this fixed exchange rate—for example, 2.80 U.S. dollars
per British pound sterling—was called the **par value**. Each country agreed
to intervene in currency markets to keep the exchange rate within 1 percent
above and 1 percent below its par value. The range between the **upper
intervention point** of plus 1 percent and the **lower intervention point**
of minus 1 percent was called the **intervention band** (see Figure 11-5).

Responsibility for maintaining these parities rested with the central banks
of each country, with the exception of the United States. The mechanics of
exchange rate intervention are discussed in Chapter 12, where central bank
activities are considered in some detail. The basic principle of exchange rate
intervention has already been set out. If the exchange rate with the United
States began to depreciate the central bank implemented a contractionary
policy. This raised the domestic interest rate and thereby raised the value of
the domestic currency relative to the U.S. dollar. If the exchange rate began
to appreciate the central bank turned expansionary. This lowered the domestic interest rate and depreciated the domestic currency relative to the
U.S. dollar.

Note that the United States had no active role to play in maintaining the
fixed parities. The U.S. dollar was termed the intervention currency for all
countries because all fixed parities were defined in terms of the rate of exchange for other countries' currencies with the U.S. dollar.

For those countries pegging their exchange rates to the U.S. dollar, the
exchange rate between any two other countries in the system was also fixed.
To see this, suppose that the Bank of England maintained a par value for the
British pound of exactly $4.00, and that the Bank of France maintained a
par value for the French franc of $.25. Then the exchange rate between
pounds and francs could not deviate from 16 francs per pound or, equivalently, .0625 pound per franc. If it did, then private international currency
traders could make enormous profits by selling in one market and buying in
another. A fixed exchange rate system in N countries requires that only $N -$
1 independent exchange rates need to be maintained by the monetary au-

thorities. All other exchange rates are maintained by private currency traders.

As part of the Bretton Woods agreement, two international monetary institutions were created. The **International Monetary Fund (IMF)** was set up to provide relatively short-term loans to countries in order to help them support their currencies during temporary periods of balance of payments difficulty. In the 1960s the IMF was authorised to create its own deposit money called Special Drawing Rights, which can be used for international payments between countries in place of the U.S. dollar. The other institution is known as the International Bank for Reconstruction and Development (or the **World Bank**). It was set up to make longer-term loans to developing countries. Today, the IMF and the World Bank are deeply involved in advising developing countries that are in debt to banks in the United States and other Western countries and policing their macroeconomic policies.

The original par values of the Bretton Woods agreement were based on the concept of purchasing power parity, which we discussed in Chapter 10. Under purchasing power parity, the price of similar goods in two different countries should be about the same. Hence, if an 8-ounce jar of jam costs $1.50 in New York City and £.5 in London, then purchasing power parity would imply that the exchange rate should be $3.00 U.S. per British pound. Of course, the actual purchasing power parity calculations at Bretton Woods were based on the average price of many commodities and services, not just jam.

INFLATION DIFFERENTIALS AND PARITY ADJUSTMENTS

If inflation is higher in one country than in another, then the exchange rate implied by purchasing power parity will change. Recalling the jam example, if the United States had an inflation rate of 10 percent while the British had an inflation rate of 20 percent, then after one year jam would cost $1.65 in New York City and £.60 in London; according to purchasing power parity the U.S. dollar would appreciate from $3.00 to $2.75— roughly a 10 percent appreciation. More generally, purchasing power parity indicates that *the exchange rate should appreciate by the difference between the foreign inflation rate and the domestic inflation rate.*

The economists and diplomats who drew up the Bretton Woods agreement knew that international differences in inflation and productivity growth could cause the original par values to get out of line, with undesirable consequences. Suppose that the rate of inflation in Britain exceeded that in the United States while the exchange rate between the countries was fixed. This would cause a trade deficit for Britain because British goods would become relatively expensive. This would tend to reduce output in Britain. Moreover, the Bank of England could not offset this through an expansionary policy. The only way to reduce the trade deficit would be through contractionary policies that reduced import demand. A fall in output would also slow the rate of inflation in Britain, making British goods more competitive with U.S. goods. Thus if British inflation exceeded U.S. inflation a painful period of disinflation would have to occur in order to maintain the fixed exchange rate.

To prevent this type of situation, the designers of the Bretton Woods System permitted adjustments in the par values in cases where a 'fundamental' imbalance would persist. These relatively infrequent parity adjustments were called **devaluations** when the exchange rate was lowered and **revaluations** when the exchange rate was raised. These terms are usually used instead of appreciation and depreciation for changes in par values in a fixed exchange rate system. *Markets* cause a currency to depreciate; the *government* devalues the currency. During the Bretton Woods period there were two instances where the British pound was devalued: first, from $4.00 U.S. to $2.80 U.S. in September 1949, and, second, from $2.80 U.S. to $2.40 U.S. in November 1967.

In practice, devaluations and revaluations did not occur as often as they needed to, given the differences in inflation rates. Devaluations were frequently postponed because they seemed to represent defeat for the government in power. The credibility of the government's commitment to maintaining parity was an important part of the system. To convince the markets that the country was committed to its pledge to maintain parity, the finance ministers would often put their own word and that of the government on the line. Once their commitment was widely publicised, it became difficult to devalue for this would seem like a broken promise.

Revaluations were also difficult. When a currency increases in value domestic producers are made less competitive relative to foreign producers. This reduces profits and employment in the export industries and in the industries that compete with foreign imports. Since a revaluation requires deliberate action on the part of the government, it is easy to blame the government for the loss of jobs and profits.

The most serious problem with the Bretton Woods System was that it was even more difficult to devalue the U.S. dollar. This problem led to the breakdown of the system starting in 1971. Under the Bretton Woods System the only way that the U.S. dollar could be devalued was for all countries to revalue their currencies against the dollar. The United States's part in the Bretton Woods agreement was a commitment to exchange the U.S. dollar for gold at a price of $35 U.S. per ounce. As inflation in the United States began to increase in the 1960s it became more and more difficult for the United States to maintain this commitment. For one thing, the general inflation made gold a bargain at $35 U.S. per ounce. But, more important, as prices rose in the United States relative to many of its trading partners, the demand for U.S. products fell compared with foreign products. United States expenditures abroad rose and foreign expenditures in the United States declined, leading to lower net exports, which was worsened by heavy U.S. military expenditures abroad. As in the early 1980s, much of the U.S. government's debt ended up being held by foreigners. By 1971 U.S. dollar securities held by foreign monetary authorities were over three times the amount of gold held by the U.S. government at Fort Knox. It had by that time become clear that the United States could not maintain its commitment.

WORLD INFLATION UNDER FIXED EXCHANGE RATES

If Country 1 fixes its exchange rate with Country 2, then Country 1 will find that its rate of money growth is similar to that of Country 2. To see this, suppose that Country 2 embarks on an expansionary monetary policy. The interest rate in Country 2 will fall. To maintain a fixed exchange rate Country 1 must reduce its interest rate to the new level experienced in Country 2. This calls for a monetary expansion in Country 1. This rough equality of money growth rates will tend to bring about a rough equality of inflation rates as well. This process is sometimes called 'importing inflation.' If Country 2 embarks on an expansionary monetary policy that causes inflation in Country 2, Country 1 must also embark on an expansionary policy that will also cause inflation in Country 1.

Canada under Bretton Woods

Although the Bretton Woods System operated from the end of World War II until the mid-1970s, Canada did not maintain a fixed exchange rate from 1950 to 1962 or from 1970 on. The decisions to let the exchange rate float despite the Bretton Woods agreement were made unilaterally. Although the IMF was displeased, there was no sanction that they could use to force Canada to comply with the agreement.

The major reason that the fixed parity was abandoned each time was to avoid the problem of 'importing inflation' described above. By and large, this was successful. For example, from mid-1970 to mid-1971 Canada was the only major country to have a floating exchange rate. At the same time, the Canadian inflation rate was lower than the rates of all of the countries adhering to fixed parities.

The exchange rate was fixed at 92.5 U.S. cents from 1962 to 1970. This was undertaken not only to honour Canada's commitment to the Bretton Woods System. Canada's unemployment rate had jumped substantially in the late 1950s and remained high by the standards of the day. Canadian policy makers felt that at a nominal exchange rate of 92.5 U.S. cents the real exchange rate would be relatively low. This would make Canada's exports more attractive to other countries, shifting the IS curve out (at least temporarily), and thereby stimulating the economy.

THE COLLAPSE OF BRETTON WOODS

On August 15, 1971, U.S. president Richard Nixon ended the United States commitment to sell gold at $35 U.S. per ounce. This in itself would not cause a devaluation of the U.S. dollar, unless all other countries agreed to shift their par values with the U.S. dollar. Such action would require difficult multilateral negotiations. Rather than going in empty-handed to such a multilateral negotiation with all other countries, the U.S. administration unilaterally enacted a special 10 percent tariff on imports, which would be eliminated only when its major trading partners agreed to revalue their currencies relative to the U.S. dollar. (Canada was maintaining a floating rate at the time.) The multilateral negotiations took place at the Smithsonian Institution in Washington, D.C. in December 1971, at which most countries agreed to revalue by various amounts. So the American strategy worked. Of course, it will never be known whether the United States needed to take such strong unilateral action to get what it wanted.

After the realignment of parities further efforts were made to reform the Bretton Woods System to prevent such problems in the future. The main goal of the United States during this period was to get more freedom to conduct its own domestic macroeconomic policy. Floating exchange rates seemed to offer this possibility, but there was no agreement on this point either within or outside the U.S. government.

World events had more to do with how the system evolved from the Smithsonian agreement than any formal reform effort. In 1973–74 the world price of oil increased fourfold. This increase affected some countries more strongly than others. Moreover, some countries chose policies designed to accommodate the price shock (as discussed in Chapter 7) while other countries chose nonaccommodative policies. Those countries with accommodative policies tended to have higher inflation but milder disruptions to output than those with nonaccommodative policies. As a result the increase in inflation was worse for some countries than for others, as shown in Figure 11–6. With widely different inflation rates in different countries, the Smithsonian parities were soon abandoned as countries found it increasingly difficult to maintain them.[5] The 1974–75 recession, which hit all countries (see Figure 11–7), put additional pressure on existing parities.

---

[5] Canada had already abandoned fixed parity before the oil shock. Canada's policy was more accommodative than Japan's, for example, as evidenced by the deeper recession and more rapid reduction of inflation experienced by Japan shown in Figures 11–6 and 11–7. The Canadian experience differed from Japan's in other ways as well because Canada was the only industrialised country that both imported and exported significant amounts of oil at the time of the oil shock (western Canadian oil was exported to the United States while eastern Canada imported oil from the Middle East). The existence of domestic oil supplies allowed Canada to temporarily control the price of oil by regulation without choking off the supply. Moreover, the Canadian economy partly benefited from the higher price for its oil exports. The United States was also a major oil producer (and also controlled oil prices temporarily) but it was not an oil exporter.

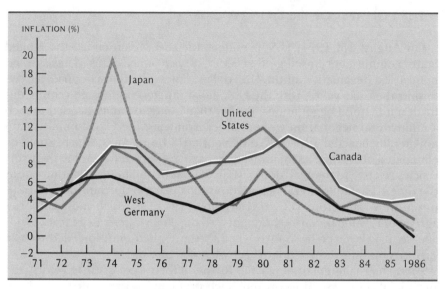

Figure 11–6.   INFLATION RATES IN FOUR COUNTRIES, 1971–86.
The inflation rate increased in most countries in 1973–74. The increase was larger in Japan than in Canada, the United States, and West Germany. The timing of the increase was also different in different countries. These discrepancies put additional pressures on existing exchange rate parities. Source: *Economic Report of the President,* 1988, Table B–109.

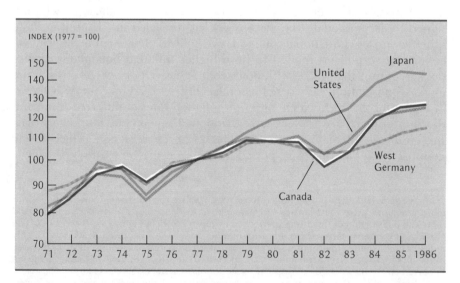

Figure 11–7.   INDUSTRIAL PRODUCTION IN FOUR COUNTRIES, 1971–86.
The 1974–75 recession hit all countries, but some countries chose different monetary and fiscal policies in response to it. This put additional pressure on exchange rate parities. Source: *Economic Report of the President,* 1988, Table B–109.

The desire of different countries to choose their own macroeconomic policies in response to the 1974–75 recession meant that exchange rates would have to shift further. Eventually most currencies began to float with no set parities, although there were considerable interventions aimed at preventing large movements. The world had emerged from the 1973–74 inflation and the 1974–75 recession with an essentially floating exchange rate system. It was not until January 1976 at an international conference in Jamaica that the IMF agreements were changed to reflect the reality of the floating exchange rate system. At that time the countries also agreed to abandon gold as a part of the international monetary system.

THE CURRENT SYSTEM

An international monetary system is a set of rules for each country's monetary authority that stipulates how exchange rates are to be determined. Like the rules of a domestic monetary system, international monetary rules can be either explicit or implicit. In the current system, some of the rules are stipulated explicitly in international agreements, but many have been adopted less formally by individual countries. The rules can stipulate that exchange rates be **fixed**, or that they be **floating**, or that they be **managed**, with policy makers attempting to 'lean against the wind' in order to smooth out exchange rate fluctuations.

The international monetary system continues to evolve. We will see that a number of European countries maintain fixed exchange rates among themselves, even though they all have floating exchange rates with the United States. Japan has a floating exchange rate, but the Bank of Japan has an active role in setting the value of the yen. Many Latin American and Caribbean countries fix their exchange rates to the U.S. dollar, and many African countries fix their currencies to the French franc.

Some economists think of the current international monetary system as a 'non-system.' There is certainly a lot of variety, as a glance at Table 11–1, which gives some of the different types of exchange rate arrangements used as of October 1986, will show. Five countries not listed in the table peg their currency to some other single currency.

The degree of central bank intervention in foreign currency markets has varied between countries and over time. The Bank of Canada renounced any intention to intervene in 1975. The Bank's stated policy was to gradually reduce the growth rate of a particular measure of the money supply (called M1) in order to reduce inflation, regardless of what happened to the interest rate or exchange rate. In fact, the Bank made some efforts to prevent depreciation of the Canadian dollar during the late 1970s. In 1981 the Bank officially concluded the policy of gradualism just described and concentrated on resisting depreciation of the exchange rate. Similar policy changes have occurred in the United States. In 1978 the United States intervened heavily to stop a depreciation of the U.S. dollar that was accelerat-

Table 11–1.   EXCHANGE RATE POLICIES IN SELECTED COUNTRIES

Independently Floating	European Monetary System	Crawling Peg	Pegged to U.S. Dollar	Pegged to French Franc
Australia	Belgium	Brazil	Barbados	Cameroon
Bolivia	Denmark	Chile	Egypt	C. African Rep.
Canada	France	Colombia	Ethiopia	Chad
Japan	W. Germany	Madagascar	Iraq	Congo
Lebanon	Ireland	Portugal	Nicaragua	Gabon
New Zealand	Italy	Somalia	Panama	Mali
Philippines	Luxembourg		Paraguay	Niger
Nigeria	Netherlands		Peru	Senegal
S. Africa			Syria	Togo
United Kingdom			Venezuela	
United States				
Uruguay				

Managed Floating	Pegged to Special Drawing Right	Pegged to Other Composites of Currencies	Limited Flexibility Against U.S. Dollar
Argentina	Burma	Algeria	Afghanistan
China, P.R.	Iran	Austria	Qatar
Ecuador	Jordan	Finland	Saudi Arabia
Greece	Kenya	Hungary	
Iceland	Libya	Kuwait	
India	Rwanda	Malaysia	
Indonesia	Seychelles	Norway	
Israel	Vietnam	Poland	
Korea		Romania	
Mexico		Singapore	
Pakistan		Sweden	
Spain		Thailand	
Turkey		Tunisia	
Yugoslavia		Zimbabwe	

Source: *International Financial Statistics,* International Monetary Fund, December 1986, p. 20 (selected countries).

ing as U.S. inflation got worse. This intervention was soon reduced after a temporary halt to the U.S. dollar's fall, but the U.S. dollar continued to depreciate. When the administration of Ronald Reagan came into office in 1981, it declared formally that the United States would not intervene in foreign exchange markets at all. By that time the U.S. dollar had begun to appreciate. After some pressure from European governments in 1983, the United States agreed to intervene to 'prevent disorderly markets'; this simply meant that the U.S. central bank (the Federal Reserve) would attempt to smooth out day-by-day exchange rate fluctuations.

In September 1985, at a famous meeting at the Plaza Hotel in New York, the United States, West Germany, Japan, Britain, and France made a joint commitment to lower the value of the U.S. dollar and to intervene to stabilise the four currencies against the U.S. dollar. Since then intervention has occurred. But none of the countries was willing to make exchange rate stabilisation the exclusive goal of monetary policy. The 1985 agreement was followed by a much larger appreciation of some of the currencies than was anticipated at the Plaza. In early 1987 the United States, Japan, and other countries intervened very heavily in foreign U.S. exchange markets in order to prevent the U.S. dollar from appreciating.

As Table 11–1 indicates, some countries—usually those with relatively high inflation rates—have a **crawling peg** system under which the currency is indexed to a domestic price index or some other indicator; the currency then appreciates or depreciates relative to the U.S. dollar according to how much that indicator moves. Brazil has one of the oldest crawling peg systems.

Eight European countries belong to a subsystem called the **European Monetary System (EMS)**, and maintain a fixed exchange rate among themselves. The EMS was created in 1979, when the countries each agreed to keep their currency within a fixed band around a par value set in terms of a composite unit (called the European Currency Unit) consisting of the currencies in the subsystem. The currencies are fixed within these limits among themselves, but as a group they jointly fluctuate against the U.S dollar and against the currencies of other countries. Figure 11–8 shows how the

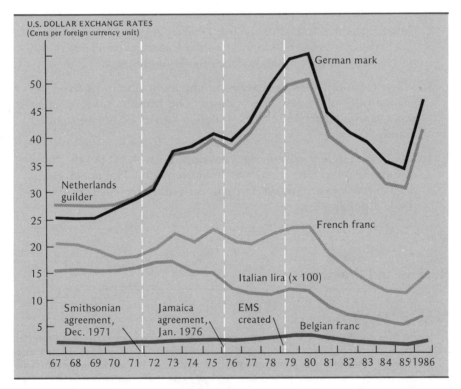

Figure 11–8. FIVE CURRENCIES IN THE EUROPEAN MONETARY SYSTEM.
Since 1979 the currencies in the system have been fixed to each other (with occasional adjustments), but collectively they float against the U.S. dollar. The chart shows how five of the currencies move together in synchrony against the U.S. dollar. The other countries show the same pattern. Source: *Economic Report of the President*, 1987, Table B–105.

exchange rates of five of these countries move against the U.S dollar. The Italian lira has been the weakest of the currencies, and now has a wider intervention band than the others.

Most of the countries in the world—about 90—operate with their exchange rates fixed to a single currency or to a composite of currencies. About 30 countries peg their exchange rate to the U.S. dollar. Of course, the currencies of these countries fluctuate against other countries' currencies in the world just as the U.S. dollar does. Another 40 countries peg their exchange rate to a composite including the IMF's Special Drawing Right.

The International Monetary System

1. From the late 1940s to the early 1970s, most of the major economies operated under the Bretton Woods System, with fixed exchange rates. Each central bank aimed to keep the value of its currency within a narrow band around its U.S. dollar exchange rate.

2. Canada declined to maintain a fixed exchange rate during much of this period. A major reason was that the Canadian government did not want to 'import inflation' from the United States.

3. When inflation rates vary across countries, a system of fixed exchange rates ultimately breaks down. The Bretton Woods System was abandoned in 1971 after inflation worsened in the United States.

4. Under the current system, the Canadian dollar floats but the Bank of Canada often tries to control its movements. The major European currencies are fixed relative to each other but float relative to the U.S dollar.

Review and Practice

MAJOR POINTS

1. When financial flows are important (as they are between Canada and the United States) a policy that fixes the exchange rate between two countries implies that the interest rates in the two countries will be equal. To fix its exchange rate with the United States, Canada would have to ensure that the Canadian interest rate was equal to the U.S. rate.

2. Under a fixed nominal exchange rate the real exchange rate is predetermined. As a result the position of the IS curve depends on the value of the real exchange rate. If output is not equal to potential, changes in prices will change the real exchange rate, shifting the IS curve so that long-run equilibrium is restored.

3. Economists who favour fixed exchange rates say that such rates will eliminate price shocks that arise from depreciations and encourage international trade. Other economists are skeptical about these benefits and point to the disadvantages of fixed exchange rates. Chief among these is that monetary policy can no longer be used to respond to shocks arising from the domestic or foreign economies.

4. If Country 1 fixes its exchange rate with Country 2, then Country 1 will have roughly the same inflation experience as Country 2.

5. The Bretton Woods System of fixed exchange rates began at the end of World War II. This system broke down when the participating countries wanted to respond to the oil shock in ways that led to widely different rates of inflation across countries.

KEY TERMS AND CONCEPTS

Floating or flexible exchange rate

Fixed exchange rate

Bretton Woods System

Devaluation and revaluation

Exchange rate intervention

European Monetary System

QUESTIONS FOR DISCUSSION AND REVIEW

1. Explain why a fixed exchange rate policy implies a particular monetary policy.

2. Explain why it is convenient not to draw the LM curve when graphically analysing an economy that has a fixed exchange rate policy.

3. Why is the response of GDP to government spending greater under a policy of fixed exchange rates than it is under a floating exchange rate?

4. What is the problem of 'importing inflation'?

5. Compare the Bretton Woods System with the European Monetary System.

6. How has Japanese monetary policy changed since the collapse of the Bretton Woods System?

7. Do you think that it would be possible to revive the Bretton Woods System? Do you think that it would be a good idea to do so?

PROBLEMS

Numerical
1. Consider a macro model of an economy consisting of the following equations:

$$Y = C + I + G + X$$
$$C = 80 + .63Y$$
$$I = 750 - 2,000R$$
$$M = (.1625Y - 1,000R)P$$
$$X = 500 - .1Y - 100(EP/P_u),$$

where government spending G equals 750. Suppose that the exchange rate is *fixed* at $E = 1$, that the foreign interest rate $R_u = .05$, and that both price levels P and P_u are predetermined at 1.0. (Note that the domestic interest rate R must equal .05.)

a. Explain why M rather than R is an endogenous variable in this model in contrast to the macro model with a flexible exchange rate.
b. Find the values of Y, C, I, X, and M that are predicted by the model.
c. Suppose that government spending G increases by $50 billion. Calculate what happens to the endogenous variables Y, C, I, X, and M. What mechanism brings about the change in the money supply? Is there any crowding out of investment or net exports by the fiscal policy expansion? Why or why not?

2. Suppose that prices in the economy in Problem 1 are determined by

$$\pi = 2 \left(\frac{Y_{-1} - Y^*}{Y^*} \right),$$

where $Y^* = \$4,000$ billion is potential GDP and $\pi = (P - P_{-1})/P_{-1}$ is the rate of inflation. Suppose that $G = 750$, $E = 1$, $R = R_u = .05$, $P_u = 1.0$. As in Problem 1, start out with a price level $P = 1.0$, but now let prices adjust after the first period.

a. Calculate the responses of Y, C, I, X, M, and P to a permanent increase in G of $10 billion. Give the numerical values in the first 4 years. Plot accurately the values for each variable against time for the first 4 years and then sketch what happens after the fourth year.
b. Is there any crowding out of investment or net exports after the first year? Why or why not?

3. Consider a model of a world economy consisting of only two countries.

$$
\begin{aligned}
Y &= C + I + G + X & Y_u &= C_u + I_u + G_u + X_u \\
C &= 80 + .63Y & C_u &= 80 + .63Y_u \\
I &= 750 - 2,000R & I_u &= 750 - 2,000R_u \\
M &= (.1625Y - 1,000R)P & M_u &= (.1625Y_u - 1,000R_u)P_u \\
R &= R_u \\
X &= -X_u = 100 - .1(Y - Y_u) - 100(EP/P_u)
\end{aligned}
$$

Variables without a subscript refer to one of the countries (say, Canada) and variables with the subscript u refer to the other country (say, the United States). Note that net exports from one country must equal the negative of net exports of the other country. Suppose that the price levels P and P_u are both predetermined at 1.0 and that the exchange rate E is fixed at 1.0.

a. Calculate the values of output, investment, consumption, government spending, net exports, and the money supply M_u if $G = 750$, $G_u = 750$, and $M = 600$.
b. Calculate what happens to these same variables if M increases by $50 billion, to $650 billion. Explain why the money supply M_u in the other country changes.
c. Calculate what happens to these same variables if G increases by $50 billion but M and G_u do not change.
d. Find a policy for the home country to follow to keep Y unchanged when G_u increases by $10 billion.

Analytical
1. Consider an economy with sticky prices under a fixed exchange rate. Explain why an increase in government spending will increase output by the same amount as in the simple spending balance model of Chapter 4.

2. In an economy with a fixed exchange rate, suppose that actual GDP is below potential GDP. Inflation is low and the objective is to bring the economy back to potential.

   a. Illustrate this situation with an IS-LM diagram.
   b. Describe a policy that can bring about the desired objectives. Would the policy
      be any different if investment was very sensitive to the interest rate?

3. Suppose that output is above potential and that government spending is unchanging. What causes the economy to return to potential under a flexible exchange
   rate if there is no change in government policy? What causes the economy to return to potential under a fixed exchange rate if there is no change in government
   policy? Explain the differences between the two cases.

4. Suppose the United states was committed to achieving and maintaining zero inflation. Would this make fixing the Canadian exchange rate with the United
   States more attractive to Canadian policy makers?

5. (This question uses material in Appendix A to Chapter 10, page 282.) Use Equation 10–10 to explain why, if Canada fixes its exchange rate with the United
   States, the Canadian interest rate must equal the U.S. interest rate. Make direct
   reference to the behaviour of investors and their expectations.

12

The Monetary System

A MONETARY system is an arrangement through which people express economic values and carry out transactions with each other. A well-developed monetary system is essential to a smoothly operating economy. History has shown that poorly developed monetary systems have been responsible for severe recessions and inflations. But even normal, everyday economic life is greatly facilitated by an efficient monetary system.

The monetary system is just one of many social arrangements that exist in any civilisation. Language is another. Weights and measures are a third. Some of these arrangements have evolved without formal or conscious social agreements; others have been the result of organised planning and formal agreement. Although monetary systems originally evolved informally in primitive cultures, in modern times most countries have enacted laws and institutions that define their monetary systems. One of the concerns of macroeconomics is whether certain revisions to these laws and institutions might improve macroeconomic performance.

The monetary system takes on a central role in aggregate demand because prices and wages do not move quickly enough to offset shifts in money supply or money demand. As we saw in Chapter 5, shifts in the LM curve—the curve for which money supply equals money demand—first result in changes in GDP, and later in changes in inflation. In this chapter we look at the microeconomic foundations of *money supply* and *money demand*. In doing so we will see that the monetary system is an intrinsically interesting part of the economy, and would be a subject worthy of study even without its role in macroeconomics.

12.1 The Elements of a Monetary System

A monetary system must specify two things: first, the way that payments are to be made; second, the meaning of the numbers that merchants put on goods and the numbers that appear in contracts. The first is called the **means of payment,** and the second the **unit of account.**

In most monetary systems one item is designated as a universally acceptable means of payment. Traditionally, it was a precious metal, gold or silver. With gold or silver serving as the means of payment, it was natural for merchants to price their goods with numbers that corresponded to units of these precious metals; horse traders would find it natural to charge a certain number of gold pieces for a horse. Hence, designated amounts of precious metals became units of account as well as a means of payment. For example, in England at the time of William the Conqueror, silver was the universally accepted means of payment and the pound of silver became the unit of account. Ever since, the English unit of account has been called the pound, though its purchasing power has become much less than the value of a pound of silver.

As financial systems developed, means of payment came into use that were different from the underlying unit of account. For example, until 1914 the unit of account in Canada was .4838 of an ounce of gold. That amount of gold was referred to as a dollar. But from 1820 on a common means of payment was paper money issued by private banks. A dollar bill from a bank carried a promise that it could be redeemed for gold at any time.

In the twentieth century, governments became more involved in the monetary system. In Canada, private banks are not allowed to issue dollar bills; only the Bank of Canada has that power. Moreover, the unit of account no longer has anything to do with gold. Instead, it is the government's dollar bill. Though dollar bills are widely used as means of payment, other means of payment are even more important, such as cheques and credit cards.

Although there is no law in Canada that requires prices to be quoted in dollars, nobody would choose to quote prices in another unit, such as French francs. The public is familiar with dollar prices and reluctant to think in any other terms. Even if you are good at doing arithmetic in your head, it is a lot more convenient to do all of your financial thinking in one set of units.

Together, the government's paper money and coins are called **currency.** Until the nineteenth century, currency was virtually the only means of payment. As monetary systems evolved during the nineteenth and twentieth centuries, currency began to be replaced by other means of payment in the great majority of transactions. Nevertheless, all transactions continued to be denominated in the units of the government's currency. By law, if you owe somebody a dollar debt, that person can require you to pay in currency. For larger debts, this right is rarely exercised. Instead, the person's right to receive currency sets up a situation where the two of you agree on some alternative, more convenient way to settle the debt. The other person may agree to accept a personal cheque from you. A cheque is an instruction to the banking system to make accounting entries to transfer wealth from you to the other person.

A great many customs exist about what means of payment are acceptable besides currency. In prisoner-of-war camps during the Second World War, prisoners used cigarettes as a means of payment. In modern times, credit cards are frequently an acceptable means of payment. Stores that accept credit cards let you know with a little sign in the window. Credit cards are another way to issue instructions to the banking system to transfer funds from one person to another. Like accepting cheques, the acceptance of a credit card in place of currency is voluntary. When you buy a house, neither a personal cheque nor a credit card is likely to be accepted. You will be expected to present a certified cheque, which is a promise by the bank itself to pay from its own funds and a guarantee that the funds actually exist. Customs differ by country as well. In Greece today, for example, currency rather than a personal cheque is a much more common means of payment than it is in Canada.

Monetary economists have attempted to pin down exactly what things should be counted as the means of payment.[1] Unfortunately, this is a very difficult task. Many techniques are available for conveying purchasing power. Currency and chequing accounts certainly should be counted as a means of payment. But what about the funds in savings accounts that can be electronically transferred in an instant to chequing whenever a payment is desired? Some means of payment, like credit cards, do not involve an asset at all. Despite these problems, the fact that there are means of payment other than currency is crucially important for monetary economics.

As there are a number of types of financial assets that are widely accepted as means of payment, and many more types of assets that are easy to transform into means of payment, the Bank of Canada uses a number of ways to keep track of the amount of wealth that is held in the form of 'money.' In Chapter 5, we used the term *money* to mean currency plus chequeable deposits. One measure that the Bank of Canada compiles that is similar in definition is **M1-A.** This includes currency held by the public, all chequeable deposits at chartered banks, and some other deposits that are held at chartered banks by firms rather than consumers. In 1987, M1-A averaged $79 billion.

M1-A does not include all chequeable deposits in the economy because it includes only those deposits held at chartered banks. These are the financial institutions with the word 'bank' in their names, for example, the Bank of

---

[1] The research discussed in D. Patinkin, *Money, Interest, and Prices,* covers much of the work on the various definitions of money.

Montreal. A large amount of chequeable deposits are also held at financial institutions that are not banks as such. These include trust companies, credit unions and, caisses populaires. Although these near-bank financial institutions function very much like chartered banks from their depositors' point of view, deposits at near-banks are not included in M1-A.

A broader measure of 'money' that does include deposits in near-banks is M2+. This measure, or aggregate, includes currency and all Canadian dollar chequeable deposits. It also includes many nonchequeable deposits that are easy to convert into chequeable deposits, such as nonchequeable personal savings accounts. M2+ is much larger than M1-A. In 1987, M2+ averaged $312 billion. Still other aggregates that include a different mix of financial assets are also measured by the Bank of Canada.[2]

The difficulty in determining exactly what should be counted as the means of payment indicates the difficulty in deciding which of the definitions of money one should look at. The choice of definition to use would not be a serious problem if the different monetary aggregates always moved together, but such movement is not the case. In 1985, for example, M1-A grew 36.4 percent while M2+ grew much more slowly, only 9.6 percent. The types of assets that can be used as means of payment change over time as the financial system evolves. As a result, a careful examination of changes in financial markets is a necessary part of interpreting the behaviour of monetary aggregates such as M1-A and M2+.

12.2 Money Supply: How the Bank of Canada Controls It

We now consider how the Bank of Canada controls the money supply. Assume that the money supply consists of currency (CU) and chequeable deposits (D) that individuals and firms hold at chartered banks. The money supply M is thus defined as

$$M = CU + D. \qquad (12-1)$$

Because chequeable deposits at chartered banks are part of the money supply, we must consider how the Bank of Canada's actions affect these deposits. Table 12–1 shows a set of balance sheets for four sectors of the economy: the private nonfinancial sector (consumers and businesses), the chartered banks, the Bank of Canada, and the government. This balance sheet shows how the sectors are related financially.

In the balance sheet assets are shown on the left and liabilities on the right. Assets are the things owned by the individual or organisation and liabilities are the amounts owed to others. For example, loans are assets for banks and liabilities for borrowers. Note that (with one exception) all of the

---

[2] The monetary aggregates are discussed in some detail in 'Monetary Aggregates in Canada: Some Recent Developments,' *Bank of Canada Review,* February 1988, and in other *Bank of Canada Review* articles referenced there.

Table 12–1.   FINANCIAL RELATIONSHIPS (BALANCE SHEETS) BETWEEN THE CHARTERED BANKS, THE BANK OF CANADA, THE GOVERNMENT, AND THE PRIVATE SECTOR

Private Nonfinancial		Chartered Banks		Bank of Canada		Government	
Assets	Liabilities	Assets	Liabilities	Assets	Liabilities	Assets	Liabilities
Currency (CU)					Currency (CU)		
Deposits (D)			Deposits (D)				
Bonds (B)		Bonds (B)		Bonds (B)			Bonds (B)
		Reserves (RE)			Reserves (RE)		
	Loans	Loans					
				Foreign Exchange Reserves (FX)			

things listed in these accounts appear at least twice—once in somebody's assets and again in somebody else's liabilities.

Currency (CU) *and Deposits* (D). The private sector holds currency that is issued by the Bank of Canada. The private sector also holds deposits at the chartered banks. These are assets of the account holders and liabilities of the banks.

Government Bonds (B). Government bonds are shown as a liability of the government. The private sector, the chartered banks, and the Bank of Canada hold bonds as assets.

Reserves (RE) must be held by law at a fixed fraction of the deposits that the chartered banks have as liabilities. These reserves can be held in two forms: as deposits at the Bank of Canada, or as paper money and coin in the vaults of the bank. To avoid double-counting this vault cash, the term currency (*CU*) will always refer to paper money and coin held outside the chartered banks.

Loans (L). One of the main reasons that banks are in business is to issue loans to their customers. They take deposits from some individuals and make loans to others. This is the **intermediation role** of the banks. They intermediate between individuals. But banks are important in macroeconomics because their liabilities (deposits) are part of the money supply.

Foreign Exchange Reserves (FX). The last line in the balance sheet shows the government's foreign exchange reserves or official reserves. As these are administered by the Bank of Canada they are included as an asset of the Bank. These are liabilities of the foreign governments that issued them. If foreign governments' balance sheets were shown in Table 12–1 there would be corresponding liability entries there.

The principal way in which the Bank of Canada controls the money supply is by selling bonds to, or by purchasing bonds from, the private sector. These purchases or sales of government bonds by the Bank of Canada are called **open-market operations.** To see how these open-market operations affect the money supply, we first define the **monetary base** (M_B). The monetary base is defined as currency plus reserves.[3] That is,

$$M_B = CU + RE. \tag{12–2}$$

The Bank of Canada does not try to exercise separate control of reserves and currency. Instead the Bank controls only the total of the two. The Bank lets the chartered banks and the private sector decide how much of the monetary base is currency and how much is reserves. Any bank can withdraw currency from its reserve account whenever it wants, and any bank can put currency into its reserve account and receive credit dollar for dollar. During the Christmas shopping season, for example, the public likes to hold more cash than usual. The banks therefore withdraw currency from their reserve accounts and make it available to their customers.

Using open-market operations the Bank of Canada can add to or subtract from the total amount of bank reserves plus currency whenever it chooses. An open-market operation to expand the monetary base involves a purchase by the Bank of government bonds. Look again at the balance sheet in Table 12–1. Suppose that a chartered bank sells a bond to the Bank of Canada. The chartered bank receives a credit in its reserve account that adds to the total amount of reserves. The simple fact that assets must equal liabilities in the Bank of Canada's balance sheet indicates that any purchase of bonds must lead to an increase in the sum of currency and reserves—that is, in the monetary base. Whenever a bank transfers funds to another bank, nothing happens to total reserves—one bank's reserves rise by the exact amount that the other bank's fall. But a purchase of bonds by the Bank of Canada must raise the monetary base. Similarly, a sale of bonds by the Bank must reduce the monetary base.

The effects of the Bank's open-market operations on the monetary base are shown in Table 12–2. The monetary base increased more than fourfold in 19 years. Note that the amount of currency is much larger than the amount of reserves. About three-quarters of the monetary base is currency.

There is a direct relationship between the monetary base and the money supply, and this is how the Bank of Canada achieves its control of the money supply. The relationship between the monetary base and the money supply is due to two factors:

[3] Phillip Cagan of Columbia University has done much of the research on the determination of the monetary base and its relation to the money supply, focusing on the United States. See his *The Determinants and Effects of Changes in the Stock of Money, 1875–1960,* Columbia University Press, 1965. Cagan refers to the monetary base as high-powered money.

Table 12–2.   CURRENCY, RESERVES, AND THE MONETARY BASE (billions of dollars)

	Jan. 1969	Jan. 1979	Jan. 1988
Currency	2.9	8.5	15.8
Reserves	1.7	5.9	5.5
Monetary base	4.6	14.4	21.3

Source: *Bank of Canada Review,* Tables C10 and E1.

1. Reserve requirements: Chartered banks are required to hold a certain ratio of their chequing deposits on reserve at the Bank of Canada. This ratio is called the **reserve ratio** (r). This ratio varies depending on the type of deposit. For non–interest-bearing chequing accounts the required reserve ratio was .1 (10 percent) in 1988. For personal, interest-bearing, chequeable deposits the required reserve ratio was .02 (2 percent). Assume (for simplicity) that there is only one type of chequing account. Then reserves (RE) are given by the formula

$$RE = rD. \tag{12–3}$$

2. Currency demand: Most people want to hold some of their money in the form of currency. We will discuss the determinants of currency demand in Section 12.3. For now we can describe this demand in terms of a simple ratio. The **currency deposit ratio** (c) measures how much currency people want to hold as a ratio of their deposits. For example, the currency deposit ratio c might equal .2. Currency demand is thus given by

$$CU = cD. \tag{12–4}$$

Now we can derive the relationship between the monetary base and the money supply. From the definition of the money supply,

$$M = CU + D = cD + D = (1 + c)D,$$
$$M_B = CU + RE = cD + rD = (c + r)D.$$

Dividing M by M_B, we get

$$M = \frac{1 + c}{r + c} M_B. \tag{12–5}$$

The coefficient that multiplies M_B is called the **monetary base multiplier,** which we will call m. If $r = .1$ and $c = .2$, then the monetary base multiplier is 4. Open-market operations that increase the monetary base by $1 billion would then increase M by $4 billion. Because of this multiplier, the monetary base is sometimes called **high-powered money.** Here the reserve ratio and the currency ratio are assumed to be fixed, so the Bank of Canada can control the money supply as accurately as it wants by controlling the monetary base. In reality, as we show in Section 12.3, the currency ratio can vary, so control of the money supply is not so simple.

REQUIRED RESERVES AND EXCESS RESERVES

In Canada, chartered banks are penalised if they allow their reserves to fall below their requirements. For this reason they always keep some **excess reserves** over and above their **required reserves.** This is illustrated in Table 12–3, which is a more detailed version of Table 12–1, focussing only on the chartered banks and the Bank of Canada. The amount of excess reserves is small because banks do not receive any interest on their reserve balances at the Bank of Canada. They prefer to keep reserves close to the minimum required amount and invest the rest of their funds in loans or bonds. In 1987, for example, excess reserves were usually less than ¹⁄₁₀th of 1 percent of the volume of deposits. Thus it is a good approximation to say that all bank reserves are required reserves.

Table 12–3.   RESERVES: REQUIRED, BORROWED, AND EXCESS

Chartered Banks		Bank of Canada	
Assets	Liabilities	Assets	Liabilities
			Currency
	Deposits		
Bonds		Bonds	
Loans			
Required reserves			Required reserves
Excess reserves			Excess reserves
	Borrowed reserves	Borrowed reserves	
		Foreign exchange reserves	

Would banks hold reserves if they were not required to hold them? Reserve requirements were initially enacted into law in order to make sure that banks would have enough funds on hand if their depositors wanted to cash in their deposits. Even without reserve requirements, banks would hold some reserves for this purpose, but probably much less than the required levels. Holding assets in interest-bearing short-term government securities is almost as safe as holding assets in reserves. Government securities can be readily sold if there is a need for cash. But reserves are also used to carry out the instructions of a bank's depositors to transfer reserves from one account to another and from one bank to another. A large bank executes several million transfer instructions from cheques, credit cards, and electronic requests every day. In the process, it will be holding positive amounts of reserves as a normal part of its business. Someone in the melon business always owns a certain amount of melons at any one time even though they turn over constantly. Similarly, someone in the reserve business is likely to own reserves. Again, however, the amount of reserves necessary to carry out the business of a bank is probably much less than present requirements.

THE BANK RATE

The Bank of Canada stands ready to lend funds to the chartered banks if they are in need of reserves. As shown in Table 12–3, chartered bank reserve borrowings are a liability of the banks and an asset of the Bank of Canada. However, the Bank of Canada does not want a chartered bank to look to it for a loan until the chartered bank has exhausted all other possible sources of borrowing. That is, the Bank of Canada is willing to lend to the chartered banks, but only as the lender of last resort. In order to ensure that the chartered banks do not look to the Bank of Canada first, the Bank sets the rate at which it is willing to lend to the chartered banks above the rate prevailing in the market. This rate is called the **bank rate.**

Specifically, each Thursday new issues of 91-day Government of Canada Treasury bills (T-bills) are auctioned. Chartered banks, investment dealers, and the Bank of Canada are allowed to submit bids for these bills; the higher the amount paid for the bills, the lower is their yield. The bank rate is then set for the week at $\frac{1}{4}$ of 1 percentage point above the average yield of Treasury bills sold at that day's auction. As a result, a chartered bank that is in need of funds would in general do better to liquidate some of its holdings of T-bills than to borrow from the Bank of Canada. Accordingly, the amount of borrowing by the chartered banks from the Bank of Canada is usually quite small.

Even though the bank rate is set automatically following the T-bill auction, many Canadian journalists persist in referring to it as 'the trend-setting Bank rate' as if the Bank of Canada explicitly chooses a different rate each week. While this is somewhat misleading, it is not too far wrong. The amount that the investment dealers and chartered banks are willing to bid for T-bills, and hence the yield established at the auction, is heavily influenced by the Bank of Canada's activities even if the Bank does not bid at the auction that week. If, for example, the Bank of Canada has been expanding the monetary base, then prevailing interest rates will be reduced and the bids submitted to the T-bill auction will result in lower yields.

THE BANK OF CANADA AND THE NEAR-BANKS

Trust companies and credit unions are often called **near-banks** because they function very much like the chartered banks. Near-banks are not required to maintain a specific fraction of their deposits as non–interest-bearing reserves. Near-banks do keep some currency in their vaults in order to meet their obligations; thus they do have some non–interest-bearing reserves. But the near-banks are free to choose the proportion of their deposits to hold in this form without regard for any government-mandated minimum.

The near-banks are too large to ignore in an analysis of money supply. For example, the monetary aggregate M2+, which includes deposits at near-banks, is more than 60 percent larger than the corresponding aggregate that excludes near-bank deposits. The base multiplier analysis can be extended to apply to a broader monetary aggregate that includes deposits at near-banks. This is carried out in the appendix to this chapter.

We can see that the existence of near-banks poses some additional problems for monetary control by the Bank of Canada. Recall that our earlier analysis showed that the Bank of Canada's control of our narrow definition of money would be undermined to the extent that the public's choice of the ratio of their currency holdings to their deposits at chartered banks varied. The extended multiplier analysis shows that the Bank of Canada's control over a broader monetary aggregate that includes near-bank deposits depends on other choices that are beyond the direct control of the Bank: the public's choice of the ratio of their bank deposits to near-bank deposits, and the near-banks' choice of the proportion of their deposits to hold in reserve.

SETTING MONETARY POLICY IN CANADA

Control of the Canadian money supply, with all of its implications for the exchange rate, interest rates, and output, is entrusted to the governor of the Bank of Canada. While the Bank of Canada is an agency of the federal government, the governor is not a subordinate of any member of the Cabinet. He (all of the governors to date have been male) is insulated from the pressures of day-to-day politics in a way that the minister and deputy minister of finance, the people responsible for fiscal policy, are not.

At first glance the governor's independence may seem limited. The governor is chosen by the federal government and is appointed for a seven-year term which may be renewed. There is nothing to stop a determined federal government from rewriting the legislation to remove a governor if it chooses; this in fact occurred in 1961. While the governor is in office he may implement monetary policy as he sees fit. However, if the government desires a change in policy it can issue a directive that instructs the governor in what policy to pursue. Under the current Bank of Canada Act this directive must be made public shortly after it is issued.

If we look only at the legislation governing the Bank of Canada we would underestimate the governor's independence, however. If the federal government wants to force the existing governor to change his policies it must mount a very public campaign against the governor. At the very least, the elected officials must publicly acknowledge that they have taken responsibility for the conduct of monetary policy, explicitly detail that policy, and overturn a long (although not unbroken) tradition of central bank independence in Canada.

In addition, the governor can add to the consequences that the government will face if it issues a directive. For example, when rumors surfaced that a directive would be issued to then-governor Gerald Bouey in 1982, Bouey let it be known that in that event he would resign and that financial markets should take this to mean that Canadian monetary policy was in disarray. It was widely believed that this would lead to a rapid fall in the exchange rate and a severe embarrassment for the federal government.

Of course, no governor wants to be forced to resign, and some may want to ensure that they are reappointed to a second term. And every governor has recognised that coordinated monetary and fiscal policies will be more effective than policies that are at odds with each other. As a result, it is always the practice of governors of the Bank to consult extensively with the federal government and to accommodate the government's desires within the broad limits of the existing monetary policy.[4]

DISTINGUISHING BETWEEN MONETARY AND FISCAL POLICY

Our analysis of the money supply and the monetary base raises some definitional questions about monetary and fiscal policy. The government budget identity implies a relationship between the monetary base, government bonds, and government expenditures that must be kept in mind when distinguishing between monetary and fiscal policy. The monetary base, government bonds, and the deficit are related to each other by the following government budget identity:

$$G + F + RD - T = \Delta M_B + \Delta B, \tag{12-6}$$

where G, F, R, and T are as defined earlier, D is the total government debt, ΔM_B is the change in monetary base, and ΔB is the change in government bonds. It says that the government budget deficit is financed by increasing either the monetary base or government bonds. Note that the base as well as government expenditure and taxes appear in this expression, so that there is a link between monetary policy and fiscal policy.

To separate monetary policy changes from fiscal policy changes, we therefore need to specify what is happening to budget financing.

---

[4] York University historian J. L. Granatstein provides a colourful short history of the political aspects of Canadian monetary policy in 'The Untouchables,' *Saturday Night*, April 1983. Reviews of Canadian monetary policy are published periodically by the C. D. Howe Institute. The two most recent monographs in this series are Peter Howitt, *Monetary Policy in Transition: A Study of Bank of Canada Policy, 1982–85*, Toronto, Prentice-Hall Canada, 1986, and Thomas J. Courchene, *No Place to Stand? Abandoning Monetary Targets: An Evaluation*, Montreal, C. D. Howe Institute, 1983.

Fiscal policy is defined as **bond-financed changes** in government expenditures and taxes. That is, the monetary base and the money supply remain unchanged, and bonds are issued if government spending increases or taxes are reduced.   *→ sell bonds*

Monetary policy is defined as an increase in the monetary base matched by a reduction in government bonds. This exchange of money for bonds is an open-market operation. Note that open-market operations do not affect government purchases (G), transfers (F), or taxes (T). Thus open-market operations do not affect fiscal policy.

The Monetary System and the Bank of Canada

1. The monetary system in Canada is based on the dollar, which is the unit of account and a means of payment.

2. The institutions most prominent in providing the means of payment are the Bank of Canada, the chartered banks, and the near-banks. The liabilities of the Bank of Canada—currency and reserves—make up the monetary base.

3. The money supply consists of currency and deposits at banks and near-banks. The supply of money is directly related to the monetary base.

4. The Bank of Canada controls the monetary base by buying and selling bonds. In doing so it controls the supply of money.

Financing Government through the 'Printing Press'

How much does Canada resort to the printing press to raise revenues to pay for government expenditures? The monetary base gives a good measure of this. Suppose, for example, that Parliament passes a bill authorising the armed forces to build new ships for an amount of $2 billion. But the government does not raise taxes to pay for the ships. In order to pay for the ship construction, the government issues bonds. But rather than selling the bonds to the public, it sells the bonds to the Bank of Canada in exchange for currency which it then pays out to the workers and firms that build the ships. In effect, the increase in government expenditures was financed by the printing of more currency. Note that the monetary base increased by $2 billion.

Just as in this example, the increase in the monetary base is a measure of the amount of government revenue that is raised each year through the printing press rather than through taxes or borrowing. In 1987 the monetary base increased by about $1.5 billion dollars. Compared to the $123 billion of federal government expenditures during 1987 this is a trivial amount: Only 1 percent of government expenditures were financed by the printing press in 1987. This small percentage is typical in recent Canadian history.

Many countries have resorted to the printing press to finance government expenditure at one time or another. About 80 percent of American Revolutionary War expenditures were financed by printing paper money called 'continentals.' So much money was printed that a serious inflation occurred: Prices rose by over 300 percent from 1776 to 1778, and by 1,000 percent from 1778 to 1780. Hence the phrase, 'not worth a continental.' The printing press set off even worse inflations in Germany and several other European countries in the 1920s, and in Argentina, Brazil, and other South American countries in the 1970s and 1980s.

12.3 Central Bank Activity under Exchange Rate Intervention

In this section we consider how the Bank of Canada will act if it wants to intervene in the foreign exchange market. The Bank may want to fix the exchange rate at a particular level or it may simply want to make exchange rate fluctuations smaller without completely eliminating them.

From Table 12–1 we see that the Bank's assets consist of bonds issued by the Canadian government and foreign exchange reserves. Recall that the monetary base is defined as currency plus bank reserves. Because assets must equal liabilities, we know that domestic credit plus foreign reserves equals the monetary base. That is,

$$\text{Monetary base} = \text{Domestic credit} + \text{Foreign reserves.} \qquad (12\text{--}7)$$

Suppose that the U.S. interest rate rises and as a result the Canadian dollar begins to depreciate. Also suppose that the Bank of Canada wants to counteract this change in the exchange rate. How does the Bank prevent depreciation? As U.S.-denominated bonds begin to look more attractive relative to Canadian bonds, the Bank of Canada must provide the increased demand for foreign exchange by selling foreign reserves in order to prevent the exchange rate from depreciating. It does this by entering the foreign exchange market and selling its foreign reserves for domestic currency. In other words, foreign reserves decrease. The decrease in foreign reserves lowers the monetary base, reducing the money stock. This reduces the amount of real money balances that are available, raising the Canadian interest rate. This in turn makes Canadian bonds relatively more attractive to investors.

If the Bank of Canada wants to fix the exchange rate it must continue to sell its foreign reserves until the money stock has been reduced enough that the Canadian interest rate equals the U.S. interest rate. At that point the relative attractiveness of U.S. bonds will be eliminated and it will no longer be necessary for the Bank of Canada to give up its foreign reserves to prevent the exchange rate from falling. Similarly, if the U.S. interest rate falls, the Canadian dollar will begin to appreciate. To prevent this, the Bank of Canada must sell Canadian dollars in return for foreign securities, which it adds to its stock of foreign exchange reserves. This increases the monetary base and hence increases the money supply. To fix the exchange rate the Bank continues to trade Canadian dollars for foreign reserves until the money supply has expanded enough to lower the Canadian interest rate back to match the U.S. rate.

Thus one way for the Bank of Canada to implement the commitment to fix the exchange rate is simply to buy Canadian dollars when the exchange rate starts to fall and to sell Canadian dollars when the exchange rate starts to rise. This will automatically reduce or expand the money stock so that the Canadian interest rate is made equal to the U.S. rate, as discussed in Chapter 11.

The Bank may want to reduce the size of fluctuations in the exchange rate without going so far as to eliminate them. In that case it can follow the procedure described above, except that it will stop short of preventing all changes in the exchange rate. For example, if the Bank wants to reduce the size of a depreciation it will buy Canadian dollars with its foreign reserves, but it will not buy enough to eliminate the depreciation entirely.

INTERNATIONAL EFFECTS OF CENTRAL BANK ACTIVITY UNDER FIXED RATES

As discussed in Section 11.4, if two countries have a fixed exchange rate then the rate of money growth in each country will tend to be similar. A good example of this is found in the experience of West Germany in the late 1960s and early 1970s before the end of Bretton Woods. During this time the United States was pursuing an expansionary monetary policy. In order to keep the mark from rising against the U.S. dollar the German central bank (the Bundesbank) had to sell marks and acquire U.S. dollars which it added to its foreign reserves. As shown in Figure 12–1, at the end of the 1960s the Bundesbank's holdings of foreign reserves increased sharply. This led to a similar sharp increase in the monetary base. Almost all of the increase in the monetary base during this period was due to the Bundesbank's foreign exchange operations.[5]

---

[5] This discussion is based on Ronald I. McKinnon, *Money in International Exchange: The Convertible Currency System,* New York, Oxford University Press, 1979.

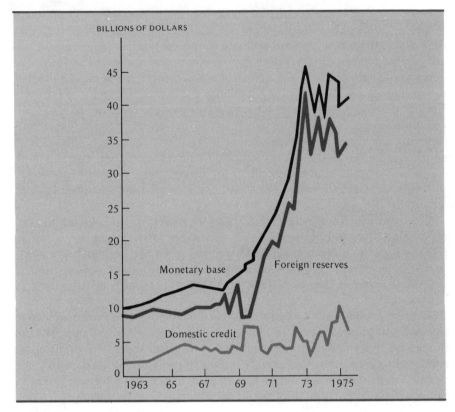

Figure 12–1.   THE EFFECT OF FOREIGN RESERVES ON THE MONETARY BASE: GERMANY, 1962–75.
As the Bundesbank prevented the mark from appreciating, it increased its holdings of foreign reserves and the monetary base expanded by about the same amount. Source: H.Cleveland and B. Brittain, *The Great Inflation: A Monetarist View,* National Planning Association (U.S.), 1976, p. 36.

OTHER OPTIONS FOR MAINTAINING A FIXED EXCHANGE RATE

We have learned that if the central bank wants to fix the exchange rate it must be willing to give up its prerogative to change the money supply as it sees fit, because the exchange rate will remain fixed only if the domestic and foreign interest rates are equal. Thus domestic monetary policy must be devoted to setting the domestic interest rate equal to the foreign rate. Here we ask if there are any circumstances that would allow for an independent monetary policy and a fixed exchange rate simultaneously.

A central bank normally responds to a potential depreciation of its currency by selling foreign reserves. Then the money supply contracts, the interest rate rises, and the potential depreciation is offset. However, it is possible for the central bank to sell foreign reserves and buy domestic credit at the same time in the same amount. Such a move is called a **sterilised intervention.** From Table 12–1, it is apparent that a sterilised intervention has no effect on the assets of the central bank. Thus it has no effect on the monetary base and no effect on the domestic economy.

Under modern conditions with highly integrated capital markets, it is unlikely that a sterilised intervention has much effect. A central bank would have to sell a huge volume of foreign reserves to defend its currency against a threatened depreciation. Its ability to make such a move is limited by its stock of foreign reserves. After the stock is exhausted, the bank would have to revert to normal monetary contraction.

Capital controls, such as restrictions on the amount of foreign currency that domestic residents can purchase, would permit the domestic interest rate to be different from the world rate. In fact, capital controls are still being used in many small countries for exactly this reason. Although they would enable monetary policy to be more effective, capital controls have the disadvantage that they reduce the efficiency of international capital markets. Economic efficiency requires that different types of capital be allocated according to their after-tax rate of return. Although there are already many taxes in the world that distort the allocation of capital, adding additional taxes would probably distort the allocation even further.

One of the consequences of fixed exchange rates is the likely need for capital controls. The Canadian government used capital controls during the first years of Canada's participation in the Bretton Woods System of fixed exchange rates. James Tobin, of Yale University, has argued that taxes or controls should be enacted so that capital does not move so quickly or by as much. Tobin argues that we should 'throw some sand' into the excessively efficient international financial system so that monetary policy can regain some control.[6]

12.4 The Demand for Money: Currency and Chequing Deposits

The alternative operating procedures for the Bank of Canada, outlined in Section 12.2, have significant macroeconomic implications. But before we can discuss them, we must examine the determinants of the demand for money.

Families and businesses constantly face decisions about how to conduct their financial affairs. They face big issues, such as how to finance the purchase of a house or a major capital investment, or how to hold wealth for retirement. They also face much smaller issues, such as whether to buy things with currency, cheques, or credit cards or by special credit arrangements or electronic transfers of funds. Their choices depend on their incomes, wealth, volume of transactions, and the relative prices of all the different financial services available in the market. There is no clean separation between specifically monetary decisions and more general economic decisions.

---

[6] James Tobin, 'A Proposal for International Monetary Reform.' *The Eastern Economic Journal,* Vol. 4, pp. 153–159, 1978.

At the most general level, we could look at the demands for currency and chequing deposits—or what we call money—as just parts of a large set of demand functions for financial instruments and services. Modern finance theory has tackled the question of how to set up these demand functions, taking into account the central role of economic uncertainty. Our approach is less general. Among the many demand functions, the demand for currency and chequing deposits is particularly important for macro issues.

James Tobin, who was awarded the Nobel Prize in economics for developing modern portfolio theory, first applied his portfolio ideas to the same money demand functions that we consider here.[7] Tobin was interested in developing a microeconomic foundation for the demand for money that Keynes had originally introduced in *The General Theory*. Keynes referred to the demand for money as **liquidity preference,** a term which is still used quite frequently, and which has permanently left the 'L' in the LM curve (the 'M' refers to the money stock). The term **liquid,** when applied to a financial instrument, means that it can be sold readily; money is the most liquid of all assets. The originator of many ideas about money demand, Keynes was responsible for stressing the importance of money demand in macroeconomic fluctuations.

Keynes distinguished among three motives in people's demands for money: a **transactions** motive, a **precautionary** motive, and a **speculative** motive. More recent research—such as Tobin's—has refined these categories, and Keynes's classification scheme has been revised somewhat. However, our discussion of money demand will touch on all three of these elements.

WHAT ARE THE OPPORTUNITY COSTS OF HOLDING FUNDS AS MONEY?

When you put funds in a chequing account, you are giving the bank the use of the funds. The bank earns the interest you would have earned if you had invested it. In exchange, the bank may pay you some interest, but less than what the bank is earning. In addition, if you have a sufficiently high balance, the bank may excuse you from service charges you would otherwise have to pay. Your opportunity cost per dollar in your chequing account is the interest you forego (the rate you might have received elsewhere less the amount you receive from the bank) less the avoided service charges. As usual in microeconomics, what matters precisely is the *marginal* opportunity cost—the interest foregone on the last amount added to your balance less the reduction in service charges if you took it out. For example, suppose you would earn 9 percent elsewhere and your bank pays 5 percent interest on chequing accounts. Suppose that, over the year, it will excuse you from $2

---

[7] See James Tobin, 'Liquidity Preference as Behavior Toward Risk,' *Review of Economic Studies,* Vol. 25 (February 1958), pp. 65–86.

in service charges if you raise your average balance by $100, so you earn 2 percent on the $100. Then your opportunity cost for the $100 of funds placed in your chequing account is

$$9\% - 5\% - 2\% = 2\%.$$

We call the opportunity cost of holding money R_o, the subscript 'o' standing for 'opportunity.' When you think about the added convenience of having another $100 in your account on the average over the year, you will keep in mind that you are sacrificing 2 percentage points of annual return on the funds.

Whatever complicated system the bank has for paying you interest on the one hand and charging you for services on the other, you can boil it down to an annual net opportunity cost of the account. This is the price we have in mind for chequing deposits as one of the many financial services available to you.

For currency, the computation of the opportunity cost is easy. There are no service charges at all. Currency pays no interest. Therefore, the cost of holding currency is just the foregone interest. If you are contemplating meeting your needs by holding an average amount of currency of $500, and you could earn 9 percent on the funds elsewhere, then the cost is just 9 percent of $500, or $45 per year.

Another hypothetical way of handling your finances might avoid money altogether. You could open a special savings account and obtain a credit card. Suppose that the savings account would allow you to write three cheques a month, one of which could pay for your credit card charges. You would pay for everything with the credit card. Suppose the special savings account pays you 8 percent interest (1 percent less than the 9 percent that you could get outside the bank) and the credit card has no finance charges if you pay the bill on time. If you keep an average balance of $2,500 in the account, your only cost would be the opportunity cost of 1 percent of $2,500, or $25 per year.

By now it should be clear that each type of financial service has its own opportunity cost. But consumers do not simply pick the cheapest service on the market. Different services have different characteristics. Choosing among them is like choosing laundry detergent at the grocery store.

THE TRANSACTIONS DEMAND FOR MONEY: AN INVENTORY THEORY

One of the reasons that families and businesses hold currency and keep funds in their chequing accounts is the same as the reason stores keep inventories of goods for sale. Because income is received periodically (say once every month) and expenditures occur every day, it is necessary to hold a

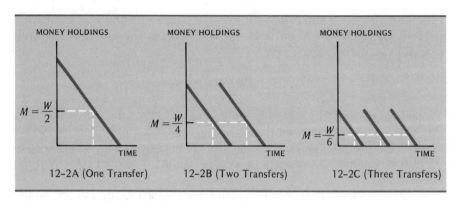

Figures 12–2A, B, and C.   THREE ALTERNATIVE MONEY MANAGEMENT STRATEGIES. In A, the family puts all its money in chequing at the start of the month. Average money holdings are large. In B, the family leaves half its income in a savings account at the start of the month and withdraws the rest at the middle of the month. Average money holdings are less than in A. In C, the family makes three withdrawals and money holdings are even lower. Hence, when there are more withdrawals, the money balance is lower.

stock of currency and chequing deposits. This inventory theory of the demand for money falls into Keynes's category of **transactions motive.**[8]

We first illustrate the inventory theory of money demand with a simple case. Suppose a family earns an amount W every month. The family consumes W over the month, in equal amounts each day. If the family draws down its money to zero just before being paid, then its money balance starts at W and declines smoothly to zero over the month. Figure 12–2A illustrates how the family's money holdings decline smoothly each day during the month. Its average level of money balances M is $W/2$. This family has a demand for money ($W/2$) that is proportional to its income W and does not respond to the prices of financial services. For one reason or another, the family has rejected ways other than money to hold its funds.

Next, take the same family with one additional financial option. It can have its paycheques deposited for free in a savings account. It can transfer any amount of funds to its chequing account. The cost of each transfer is k. The cost k includes the value of the time of the family members who make the transfer—it might involve a trip to the bank. The chequing account has an opportunity cost R_o. The family chooses an average balance to hold in its chequing account. The higher the average balance, the fewer transfers have to be made from the savings account. But the higher the average balance, the larger is the opportunity cost. The family wants to balance one cost against the other. For example, if the family makes one transfer at the be-

[8] The inventory theory of the demand for money was first worked out by William Baumol, 'The Transactions Demand for Cash: An Inventory Theoretic Approach,' *Quarterly Journal of Economics*, Vol. 56 (November 1952), pp. 545–556, and James Tobin, 'The Interest Rate Elasticity of the Transactions Demand for Cash,' *Review of Economics and Statistics*, Vol. 38 (September 1956), pp. 241–247.

ginning of the month its money balance is the same as in Figure 12–2A. If the family makes two transfers to chequing, one at the start of the month and one halfway through the month, as in Figure 12–2B, the average money balance is half as much as when the family makes one transfer. If three transfers are made, as in Figure 12–2C, the average money holdings are lower still.

In general, the average money balance, M, is half the amount transferred from savings to chequing on each transfer. The total number of transfers is the size of each transfer, 2 times M, divided into the total amount of consumption planned over the month, W. That is, the family will make $W/2M$ transfers during the month. The total cost of the transfers is k times $W/2M$ (remember that k is the cost of one transfer). The opportunity cost over the month is just R_o times the average balance, that is, R_oM. The family wants to choose its average balance to minimise the sum of the two costs. Algebraically it wants to find M to minimise total cost:

$$\frac{kW}{2M} + R_oM. \qquad (R\,CA)_{chg\,acct)} \qquad (12\text{–}8)$$

A famous theorem from management theory is the **square-root rule** for inventories.[9] The square-root rule says that stores should hold inventories proportional to the square root of sales. The same square-root rule applies to the demand for money. Specifically, the theorem says that the value of the average chequing balance M that minimises total cost is given by

$$M = \sqrt{\frac{kW}{2R_o}}. \qquad (12\text{–}9)$$

The square-root rule gives the family's transactions demand for cash. Note that the formula would be the same if they chose to keep their transactions balance in the form of currency instead of in a chequing account. In that case, because currency earns no interest, the opportunity cost of currency would be the interest rate paid on their savings account.

---

[9] Calculus is not necessary to derive the square-root rule. Rather one can use a 'complete the square' approach as follows. The total cost is

$$kW/2M + R_oM = \sqrt{(kW/2M + R_oM)^2}$$
$$= \sqrt{(kW/2M)^2 + kWR_o + (R_oM)^2}$$
$$= \sqrt{(kW/2M)^2 - kWR_o + (R_oM)^2 + 2kWR_o}$$
$$= \sqrt{(kW/2M - R_oM)^2 + 2kWR_o}.$$

The second term under the last square-root sign does not depend on M. Thus costs are minimised when the first term under the square-root sign is at its smallest value, which is zero. This term is equal to zero when

$$M = \sqrt{kW/2R_o},$$

which is the square-root rule. Alternatively, if you have had calculus you can differentiate Equation 12–8 with respect to M.

According to the square-root rule, the family holds less money if the opportunity cost R_o of holding money increases. The services of money are just like anything else the family consumes; they make do with less when the price rises. The square-root rule also says something about the relation between total spending and income W and the family's demand for money: Demand depends on the square root of total income. In comparing two families, one with double the income of the other, we should find that the second family has a transactions balance only 41 percent higher (the square root of 2 is 1.41).

MONEY AS A STORE OF WEALTH

Some families hold their wealth in the form of money—if they completely distrust all financial institutions they might accumulate dollar bills under a mattress. Criminal activities generate wealth that is held as currency to avoid detection. People who are not thinking very hard about their affairs sometimes leave large amounts idle in their chequing accounts at zero or low interest rates.

Hoards of inactive large-denomination paper money are apparently a large fraction of the total demand for currency. Over one-third of the total value of currency outstanding is in the form of $100 and $1,000 bills. The sheer volume of currency is surprising: There are about 9 million households in Canada; if the $19 billion in currency were distributed evenly among them, each would have $2,000 in currency at any one time. Very few families hold anything like this much. It is unlikely that businesses, which try to get their currency into the bank as quickly as possible, can account for much of the extra currency outstanding. Therefore, a few people must have extremely large hoards. Much of this cash is probably used in illegal activities such as drug dealing. Using cash instead of bank deposits makes it easier to hide illegal activity from the government because cash leaves no records.

Keynes's notions of precautionary and speculative demand for money fit into this store-of-wealth category. Under the precautionary motive individuals save some wealth in the form of money in case of an emergency need for funds. Since currency and chequing deposits are the easiest funds to obtain, it might seem natural to hold money for this purpose. However, in Canada, other interest-bearing assets serve the precautionary demand perfectly well. In politically unstable countries or in countries without a well-developed financial system, this motive for holding money would be more important.

Keynes's speculative motive captures the idea that changes in market interest rates will change the value of bonds. For individuals, bonds paying fixed interest rates are one of the main alternatives to holding the money in financial institutions. But, when interest rates rise, the price of these bonds falls.[10] Keynes argued that when interest rates were high more people would expect them to fall or, equivalently, would expect bond prices to rise, and would therefore want to hold bonds and less money. Thus, the demand for money declines as interest rates rise. Changes in bond prices also add risk to holding bonds. It was this risk that James Tobin formalised in his portfolio theory. People are assumed to be averse to risk; hence, they do not put all their wealth in a risky asset. Some of their wealth will be held as relatively riskless money. Unless they are unwilling to take on any risk, they will balance their wealth between money and bonds. This balancing gives rise to a demand for money as an aversion to risk.

THE DEMAND FOR CHEQUING DEPOSITS TO PAY FOR BANKING SERVICES

An important motive for holding chequing account balances is to pay the bank for the services it provides. With most chequing accounts, you can eliminate service charges by keeping a high enough balance. Instead of paying you interest and then charging you for the services you use, the bank offsets one against the other. In effect, you are earning a reasonable return on your wealth, but the return is paid in banking services rather than in cash.

One advantage of this system for consumers is that if interest is paid explicitly, it is taxable; if it is paid as banking services, it is not taxed. The 1987 federal income tax reform plan ended the deduction for the first $1,000 in interest earned from Canadian sources. This will make free services even more attractive to consumers.

For business customers, banks have traditionally linked loans and deposits. A business is more likely to get a loan if it has kept large deposits with a bank. Some loans require explicitly that part of the proceeds be kept as 'compensating balances,' which are inactive, non–interest-bearing balances in chequing accounts. Again, the bank is charging for its services by paying its depositors less than market interest rates on their deposits.

DEMAND FUNCTIONS FOR MONEY

We do not have any firm basis for dividing up the total demand for chequing account balances or currency into the categories just listed—transactions demand, store of wealth, and payment for banking services. We can offer a few rough guesses. First, the transactions demand for both forms of money appears to be a fairly small fraction of total demand. An upper-

---

[10] Interest rates and prices of existing bonds have an inverse relation. When the interest rate falls, the market price of a bond issued earlier rises. The bond continues to pay its interest payments, but new bonds have smaller payments. Hence, the old bond has a higher market price.

bound estimate of the amount of money the typical household should hold, on the average, for transactions purposes is $1,000. Then total transactions demand should not exceed $1,000 times 9 million, or $9 billion. In 1987, currency alone was $19 billion and chequing accounts far exceeded that amount.

Nobody holds currency to compensate a bank for services. Hence, the rest of the demand for currency presumably comes from people who want the anonymity it provides. For chequing accounts, probably much of the demand comes from the motive of compensating banks for services.

Because the transactions demand is a small fraction of total demand, the square-root rule cannot be sufficient to explain the total demand for money. Empirical studies of the demand for money indicate that money holdings have not grown quite as fast as income, but they have grown much more than the square root of income.[11]

The response of the demand for money to the price of holding money—the opportunity cost—is much more uncertain. For chequing accounts, it is hard to measure the price in the first place, because it involves both foregone interest and foregone service charges. We do not have any systematic information about the reduction in service charges that the typical bank customer can obtain by holding a larger chequing balance, but we can look at the relation between interest rates and cash holdings.

Currency holdings have declined gradually relative to GDP since 1960. This is shown in Figure 12–3. The relatively steep decline from 1972 to 1982 coincided with a period of rising interest rates.

One measure of the behaviour of chequeable deposits is shown in Figure 12–4—M1-A excluding currency holdings. This is not a perfect measure because it includes some nonchequeable deposits at chartered banks and excludes the chequeable deposits at near-banks. Nonetheless, the sensitivity of chequeable deposits to interest rates is obvious in the figure; in fact it is too obvious. Events in financial markets discussed below have exaggerated the responsiveness of this aggregate to interest rates. The role of interest rates has been well established statistically, however.[12]

We can summarise the previous discussion about the demand for currency and chequing deposits in two demand functions,

$$CU = CU(R,PY) \tag{12–10}$$

$$D = D(R_o,PY), \tag{12–11}$$

where CU is currency and D is chequing deposits. The first equation shows that the demand for currency is a function of the market interest rate R and

---

[11] See Stephen Goldfeld, 'The Demand for Money Revisited,' *Brookings Papers on Economic Activity*, Number 3, pp. 577–683, 1973.

[12] Evidence drawn from many countries, including Canada, is summarised in David E. W. Laidler, *The Demand for Money: Theory, Evidence and Problems*, 3rd edition, Harper & Row, 1985.

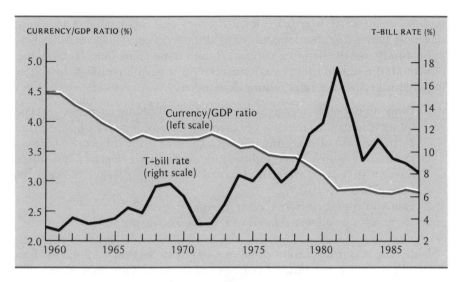

Figure 12–3.   CURRENCY DIVIDED BY GDP.
Holdings of currency relative to GDP have declined in recent decades. The upper line is the total amount of currency in circulation, divided by nominal GDP—a measure of nominal demand. The interest rate is also shown in the diagram. Sources: *Canadian Economic Observer*, Tables 1.1 and 10.1, and *Bank of Canada Review*, Table E1.

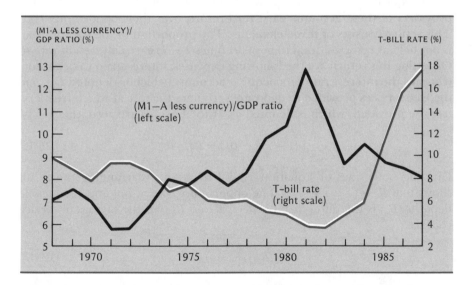

Figure 12–4.   M1-A LESS CURRENCY DIVIDED BY GDP.
The types of bank deposits included in M1-A declined as a proportion of GDP until changes in the nature of these deposits were made in the early 1980s. These changes (which are discussed on pages 338–339) coincided with the period of high interest rates shown in the figure. Sources: *Canadian Economic Observer*, Tables 1.1 and 10.1, and *Bank of Canada Review*, Table E1.

nominal income PY (the price level P times real income Y). The second equation shows that the demand for chequing deposits is a function of the opportunity cost of chequing deposits R_0 and nominal income. Total money demand is the sum of these two demands. Our discussion implies the following characteristics for total money demand:

1. Demand depends negatively on the costs of holding currency and chequing balances. In the case of currency, the cost is just the interest rate, R. In the case of chequing deposits, the cost is the difference between the market interest rate and the rate on chequing deposits, less the reduction in service charges obtained by having a larger balance. We have called this cost R_o.
2. Demand is positively related to the price level P.
3. Demand is positively related to real income or output Y.

Note that in our discussion of money supply in Section 12.2 (p. 315), we defined $c = CU/D$, the ratio of currency to deposits. Our discussion in this section shows that this ratio is not a simple constant. Rather it depends on movements in R and R_o.

How are R and R_o related? We can analyse this easily under the assumption that providing chequeable deposits is a competitive industry. This assumption, while not strictly correct, is becoming more accurate as the growth of near-banks and deregulation of the financial industry proceed.

If chequeable deposits are provided by a competitive industry, then the providers of these accounts earn zero return over their opportunity cost. This return consists of three elements. The proportion of the deposits that is not held as reserves (total deposits D times $1 - r$) earns interest at rate R. Offsetting this return are the following expenses: interest paid to depositors (D times the interest rate on chequing accounts, which is denoted R_c), and the free services provided to depositors (D times the rate at which free services are provided, which is denoted q). If total profits are zero, then

$$D(1 - r)R - DR_c - Dq = 0. \tag{12-12}$$

Dividing both sides of Equation 12–12 by D and rearranging the result shows that $R_c = (1 - r)R - q$. The opportunity cost of holding chequeable deposits (R_o) is the difference between R and R_c plus the savings in service charges.

$$R_o = R - (R_c + q) = rR. \tag{12-13}$$

Thus the opportunity cost of holding chequeable deposits depends on the interest rate. Changes in reserve ratios will change the relationship between the opportunity cost of chequeable deposits and the interest rate.

Velocity and Money Demand

Velocity is an old and controversial concept in monetary economics. The term is still used quite frequently when discussing the Bank of Canada's policy. The term is meant to convey the speed at which the money stock is turned over from one individual to another during a period of time such as a year. In practice velocity is usually calculated by dividing the money stock into nominal GDP. Using M1-A, this would be $MU = PY$ $V = \dfrac{PY}{M}$

$$\text{Velocity} = \frac{\text{Nominal GDP}}{\text{M1-A}}$$

If the value of this velocity ratio is 6, for example, then one might be tempted to say that the money stock has turned over six times in spending on a year's GDP. However, since total GDP is only a small fraction of the total number of transactions in the economy—all transactions in intermediate goods and all financial transactions are excluded—money really turns over much more frequently than six times in a year.

Velocity is best thought of in terms of the demand for money. When the demand for money as a function of nominal income shifts up, because of a fall in interest rates, for example, velocity shifts down. Conversely, when the demand for money as a function of nominal income shifts down, velocity moves up. The value of velocity is shown in the figure below for the 20-year period from 1968 to 1987. The growth of velocity increased dramatically until it collapsed in 1982.

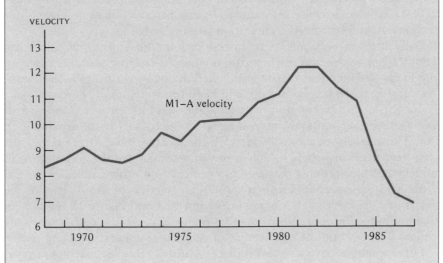

> The inverse relationship between velocity and money demand is most easily seen by comparing this figure with Figures 12–3 and 12–4, which show the ratios of currency to GDP and M1-A less currency to GDP, respectively. The sum of these two ratios is simply the ratio of M1-A to GDP, which is precisely the inverse of velocity. When the sum of the ratios declines—as it has through much of this period—velocity must increase. As an exercise, explain the movements in velocity in the figure above using what you know about changes in the demand for currency and chequing deposits during this period.

The Demand for Money

1. The demand for currency depends negatively on the interest rate and positively on income and the price level.

2. The demand for chequing deposits depends negatively on the difference between the market interest rate and the rate on chequing deposits, and positively on income and the price level.

INNOVATIONS IN FINANCIAL MARKETS

Many aspects of the behaviour of the monetary aggregates can only be understood by considering the recent changes in Canadian financial markets. These changes have been caused by the introduction of new computer technology and increased competition from near-banks.

Daily interest accounts were introduced in the late 1970s and early 1980s. Prior to this, interest was paid on interest-bearing accounts based on the lowest balance that the depositor had maintained during each month. As a result, there was no incentive to keep funds in an interest-bearing account for less than one month, as no additional interest would be earned. Daily interest accounts pay interest based on the balance in the account each day. These accounts, some of which are chequeable, have attracted deposits that were previously held in non–interest-bearing chequing accounts, or in nonchequeable accounts that paid interest on a monthly basis.

Daily interest accounts form a substantial fraction of M1-A. Part of the very rapid growth of M1-A noted in Section 12.1 and Figure 12–4 is simply due to this transfer of funds from other financial assets into daily interest accounts. It should not be mistaken for a very expansionary monetary policy.

Other changes have also taken place. Automated teller machines (ATMs) were introduced in the early 1980s. Their popularity has reduced the amount of inconvenience involved in transferring balances from one type of asset to another. In the mid-1970s banks began to offer their large commercial customers sophisticated strategies for managing their deposits. These allowed the firms to reduce the size of the balances that they maintained in chequeable deposits without reducing the volume of transactions they could undertake. These were extended to smaller commercial customers in the early 1980s.[13]

All of these innovations have changed the way in which money demand responds to changes in its other determinants, income and interest rates. This is termed **instability in money demand.** It can be thought of as changes in the numerical values of the parameters k and h in our money demand equation.

More changes are on the horizon. In 1988, for instance, tests of an electronic system that could replace paper cheques with instant electronic transfers of funds were under way in Canada.

12.5 The Bank of Canada's Policy Rule for the Monetary Base

We saw in Section 12.2 how the Bank of Canada can use open-market operations to change the monetary base and thereby change the money supply. The central question of monetary policy is how the Bank decides upon the level of the monetary base. Consider four alternative instructions for open-market operations that the governor of the Bank of Canada can give the bond traders at the Bank:

1. *Target the Level of* M. The bond traders are to keep the total amount of money (M) at a prescribed target level. If M goes above target, they are to sell bonds, which reduces the monetary base and so reduces M. If M goes below target, the traders are to buy bonds, raise the monetary base, and thus stimulate the level of M.

2. *Target the Interest Rate.* The bond traders are to keep an eye on the short-term interest rate and to keep it at a prescribed target level. If the rate goes over the target, they are to buy more bonds. This lowers the interest rate. If the rate goes below the target, they are to sell bonds, reduce the monetary base, and raise the rate back to the target.

3. *Target the Exchange Rate.* The exchange rate is to be kept at a target level. If the exchange rate begins to fall the foreign exchange traders are to buy Canadian dollars using foreign reserves. The reduction in foreign reserves will reduce the monetary base, thereby reducing the

[13] These innovations and their implications for monetary policy are discussed in C. Freedman, 'Financial Innovation in Canada: Causes and Consequences,' *American Economic Review,* Vol. 73 (May 1983).

Monetary Control without Reserve Requirements

The federal government has proposed a sweeping reduction in the regulations governing the financial industries.* Among the proposed changes is the elimination of reserve requirements on chartered banks. At present, chartered banks are at some disadvantage relative to near-banks because they are forced to hold a larger proportion of their deposits as non–interest-bearing reserves. Elimination of reserve requirements would end this disadvantage (so would extending reserve requirements to near-banks or paying interest on required reserves).

Eliminating reserve requirements would force the Bank of Canada to change the way it controls the money supply. The chartered banks would continue to hold some reserves, but they would be free to decide both the amount and the form of these reserves. As long as the Bank of Canada continued to supply currency as demanded, the Bank would no longer be able to control the amount of bank reserves.

The Bank has given an outline of the procedure that it plans to use. This procedure uses what are called **clearing balances.** Suppose that you write a cheque drawn on your account at Bank A to someone who banks at Bank B. The two banks settle this claim as follows. Once per day all of the cheques transferring balances from Bank A to Bank B are totalled, as are all of the cheques from Bank B to Bank A. Whichever bank owes the other more writes a single cheque for the difference to the other bank. The largest of the banks and near-banks do their cheque clearing by transferring to one another some of the balances that they maintain at the Bank of Canada. Even in the absence of reserve requirements many banks and near-banks would maintain these clearing balances at the Bank of Canada.†

The Bank of Canada plans to continue to control the size of these clearing balances. If the Bank reduces the amount of the balances, this will force some banks to borrow from other banks or the Bank of Canada, driving up the interest rate charged for lending clearing balances. The increase in this interest rate will affect other interest rates, and the change in these rates will affect the public's demand for those financial assets that make up the money stock.

This procedure seems rather indirect as it relies on the interest rate set in a specialised market to influence other interest rates (but we should note that the Bank has long described its approach to monetary control as acting on interest rates, and through them, on money de-

* New Directions for the Financial Sector, tabled in the House of Commons on December 18, 1986.

† This procedure is outlined in a statement by the governor of the Bank: John W. Crow, 'Some Responsibilities and Concerns of the Bank of Canada,' *Bank of Canada Review,* June 1988. See also 'Implementation of Monetary Policy in the Absence of Reserve Requirements,' Bank of Canada Discussion Paper No. 1, September 1987.

mand). Another potential problem is that the elimination of reserve requirements will reduce the sensitivity of the demand for chequing balances to the prevailing interest rate. This will come about because it will allow banks to reduce the proportion of their deposits held as non–interest-bearing reserves (r), and this in turn will reduce the sensitivity of the opportunity cost of holding chequing balances to the interest rate. This is shown by Equation 12–13.

However, the Bank of Canada is not concerned about a potential loss of monetary control. Perhaps the economists at the Bank take courage from the experience of other countries that make do without reserve requirements. For example, New Zealand eliminated reserve requirements in 1985 without any apparent loss of control over the money supply.[‡]

[‡] See Grant Spencer and David Carey, *Financial Policy Reform: The New Zealand Experience, 1984–1987*. Reserve Bank of New Zealand, 1988.

money supply, raising the interest rate, and attracting a capital inflow that will bid the exchange rate back up to target level.

4. *Target the Level of GDP.* The bond traders are to keep GDP at a prescribed target level. If GDP goes above target, they are to sell bonds, which will raise interest rates, contract the economy in general, and lower GDP. If GDP goes below target, they are to buy bonds and expand the economy.

We will look at each of these four policies in turn, to see what are the implications of the policy for the relations between the interest rate and the level of output.

MONEY SUPPLY (M) TARGET

The first policy for setting the monetary base is to adjust it as necessary to keep the money supply M at a prescribed level. What kind of adjustments of the monetary base are likely to be required? Recall that the relationship between M and the monetary base M_B can be written

$$M = mM_B, \tag{12–14}$$

where m is the money multiplier. The money multiplier depends on the ratio of reserves to deposits (r) and on the ratio of currency to demand deposits (c)—the **currency deposit ratio**. Recall that the exact formula for a narrow aggregate is $m = (1 + c)/(r + c)$. When the reserve ratio (r) is high, the base multiplier is low. When the currency deposit ratio (c) is high, the base multiplier is low. (For example, suppose that r is .04. Then when $c = .2$ the money multiplier is about 5.0, and when $c = .4$ the money multiplier is about 3.2.) The reserve ratio and the currency deposit ratio will depend on the interest rate and consumer preferences.

As a close approximation, the ratio of reserves to deposits is equal to the *required* reserve ratio and will therefore not change by much as long as reserve requirements are not changed. Suppose also that the currency deposit ratio is constant, independent of the interest rate. In that case, the relation between the monetary base and M is one of strict proportionality. The multiplier m is constant. To hold M at a prescribed level, all the Bank of Canada has to do is keep the base at the corresponding level. The money stock cannot shift when the base is held constant.

For three reasons, however, the money multiplier is not constant and is likely to be affected by interest rates.

First, recall that some reserves are held in excess of required reserves. These excess reserves decline when interest rates rise because reserves do not pay interest. Hence, r declines when interest rates rise. On this account, the money multiplier m increases when interest rates rise. Conversely, the money multiplier will decline when interest rates fall. Although this effect is probably small, it means that the Bank will have to decrease the base when interest rates rise in order to keep M on a fixed target.

Second, the currency deposit ratio will also depend on the interest rate. The demand for chequing balances is probably more sensitive to interest rates than is the demand for currency. High interest rates make the public economise on chequing balances relative to paper money. Thus, when interest rates rise the multiplier goes down. The Bank of Canada has to raise the base in order to keep M at its prescribed level.

Third, if the Bank of Canada is considering a broad monetary aggregate, then the base multiplier will also depend on the behaviour of deposits at near-banks, as discussed in Section 12.2. The public's choice of the ratio of their bank deposits to near-bank deposits, and the near-banks' choice of the proportion of their deposits to hold in reserve, may both be sensitive to the interest rate.

The LM curve for a money supply target is simply an upward-sloping line shown in Figure 12–5, the same line we derived in Chapter 5. We will want to compare the slope of this line with the other three policies: the interest rate target, the exchange rate target, and the monetary base target.

INTEREST RATE TARGET

Under the second policy the Bank of Canada is to keep the interest rate at a prescribed level. This is a very different policy. Under this policy, the base would change every day as necessary to keep interest rates at the target. If the demand schedule shifted upward because of a higher level of GDP, the supply of the monetary base would rise by enough to intersect the monetary base demand curve at the same interest rate. To analyse this case graphically it is convenient to use a horizontal line at the level of the interest rate target,

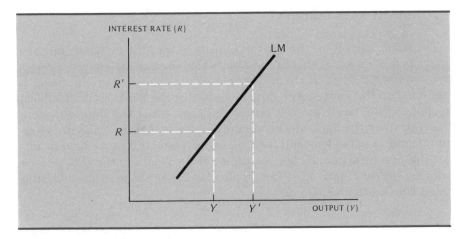

Figure 12–5.   LM CURVE WITH A MONEY SUPPLY (*M*) TARGET.
This LM curve is identical to the one derived in Chapter 5. The LM curve shows all the possible combinations of GDP and the interest rate when the price level is held constant. Because the Bank of Canada is holding the money supply constant, a higher level of GDP requires a higher interest rate. When GDP rises from Y to Y', the interest rate rises from R to R'.

instead of the LM curve. This line is labelled $\Delta R = 0$ in Figure 12–6. Much as in the fixed exchange rate case, the money supply will be chosen so that the LM curve always intersects the IS curve where the IS curve crosses the $\Delta R = 0$ line.

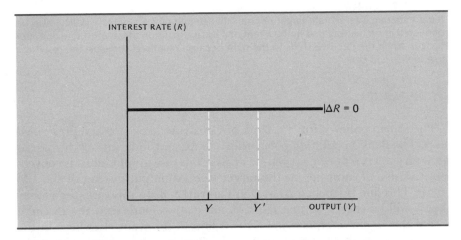

Figure 12–6.   GRAPHICAL REPRESENTATION OF AN INTEREST RATE TARGET.
If the Bank of Canada is using an interest rate target it is convenient to use a horizontal line at the height of the target instead of drawing the LM curve. This is labelled $\Delta R = 0$.

EXCHANGE RATE TARGET

The third policy is for the Bank of Canada to keep the exchange rate at a prescribed level. Recall that this will imply that the Canadian interest rate is equal to the U.S. rate. If the U.S. rate does not change, then this policy is equivalent to the interest rate target except that the Bank has no flexibility in choosing the target interest rate in this case. If the U.S. interest rate is changing, then the Bank must constantly adjust so that the Canadian interest rate moves in tandem with the U.S. interest rate. It is convenient to analyse this case by drawing a horizontal line at the height of the U.S. interest rate, as done in Figure 11–1 (see Figure 12–7). As we know (p. 292), this line is labelled the $BP = 0$ curve.

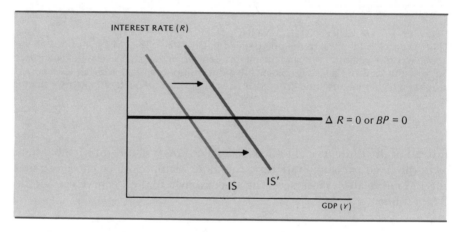

Figure 12–7.   FISCAL EXPANSION WITH AN INTEREST RATE OR EXCHANGE RATE TARGET.
Under either an interest rate target or an exchange rate target monetary policy must be conducted in such a way that in the event of a fiscal expansion the interest rate does not change. When the IS curve shifts to the right because of a fiscal stimulus, the result is a large increase in GDP.

GDP TARGET

The fourth policy is for the Bank of Canada to keep GDP at a prescribed level. The Bank's operating policy rule is to expand and contract the base as necessary to keep GDP on target. To analyse this case graphically it is convenient to use a vertical line at the target level of output instead of the LM curve. This line is labelled $\Delta Y = 0$ in Figure 12–8. In this case, the money supply will be chosen so that the LM curve always intersects the IS curve where the IS curve crosses the $\Delta Y = 0$ line. If an event elsewhere in the economy causes interest rates to rise, the Bank's operating rule would call for it to lower the base as needed to keep real GDP on target. The event would stimulate GDP if the Bank were pegging the money supply, but, in-

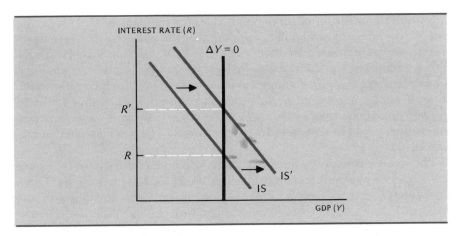

Figure 12–8.   FISCAL EXPANSION WITH A GDP TARGET.
When the Bank of Canada conducts monetary policy so as to keep GDP constant, it is convenient to use a vertical line at the GDP target instead of drawing the LM curve. A shift in the IS curve has no effect on GDP—it only raises the interest rate.

stead, the Bank is 'leaning against the wind' to keep GDP constant. Note that targeting GDP may be more difficult than targeting interest rates because GDP is observed with a lag.

12.6 How the Bank of Canada's Rule Determines the Effect of Fiscal Policy

Suppose that the Bank of Canada holds the money supply constant. Now consider a fiscal stimulus which increases aggregate demand and GDP rises. At a higher level of GDP, with no change in interest rates, consumption and investment will be higher. This increase will be partly offset by higher imports. But if GDP rises and interest rates remain the same, the money market will be out of balance. Higher interest rates are needed to offset the higher money demand that goes with higher GDP. Higher interest rates depress investment and possibly consumption. They also cause the exchange rate to appreciate and so depress net exports. Consequently, the rise in GDP is dampened. The IS-LM analysis sorts out all of these considerations and finds the point where both GDP and the interest rate have risen by just the right amount to restore expenditure balance and equality of demand and supply for the monetary base.

Diminished private spending in response to higher government spending is called **crowding out.** Under a money supply target the extent of crowding out depends on the interest rate sensitivity of the demand for money. If account-holders can benefit from higher interest rates by leaving funds in their chequing accounts rather than shifting to other investments, the LM curve will be steeper and there will be more crowding out.

Consider how the other three policy rules for the Bank of Canada can influence the effect of fiscal policy. Suppose that the Bank tries to keep the interest rate constant. Under this policy, the Bank eliminates the feedback effects of interest rates that normally limit the ramifications of fiscal policy. Investment, consumption, and net exports are not held back by a rise in the interest rate. GDP rises by the full amount of the rightward shift in the IS curve. A monetary policy that keeps interest rates constant when fiscal policy changes is said to **accommodate** the fiscal policy (as was illustrated in Figure 12–7).

The same is true of the fixed exchange rate policy (also shown by Figure 12–7). As we have just seen, a fiscal stimulus would tend to raise the Canadian interest rate causing an appreciation of the Canadian dollar. If the Bank of Canada wants to fix the exchange rate it must offset the effect of the fiscal stimulus on the interest rate by expanding the money supply.

At the other extreme, suppose the Bank adjusts the monetary base as necessary to keep GDP constant. In this case, the negative feedback effect through the interest rate is complete. Fiscal policy raises the interest rate without altering GDP. However, the composition of GDP may well be changed. If the fiscal stimulus takes the form of higher government purchases of goods and services, consumption, investment, and net exports must fall if GDP is to remain the same. The interest rate rises by enough to depress these categories of spending just enough to offset the increase in government purchases. Similarly, if the fiscal stimulus comes from higher transfers and lower taxes, higher interest rates depress investment and net exports by enough to offset the increase in consumption. Then the LM curve is a vertical line and fiscal policy does not affect GDP at all (as was shown in Figure 12–8).

12.7 Unavoidable Shocks to the IS Curve and LM Curve

One of the factors that enter into the choice of policy rule for the Bank of Canada is the likelihood of unanticipated and unavoidable shifts in the IS and LM curves. Suppose, for example, that the IS curve shifts around a lot because of erratic investment demand. The situation is illustrated in Figure 12–9. Then the best thing for the Bank to do is maintain a steep LM curve by using a money supply target. Any drop in investment thereby brings a drop in interest rates, which mitigates the decline in investment.

But suppose that the LM curve shifts repeatedly, perhaps because of changes in financial technology or changes in the public's desire to hold currency. Then the steep LM curve is not a good idea. An interest rate or exchange rate target would result in fewer of these financial shocks affecting aggregate demand. This is shown in Figure 12–10.[14]

---

[14] The idea that random shocks are important for deciding how steep the LM curve should be was first shown by William Poole, 'The Optimal Choice of Monetary Policy in a Simple Stochastic Macro Model,' *Quarterly Journal of Economics*, Vol. 84 (May 1970), pp. 197–216.

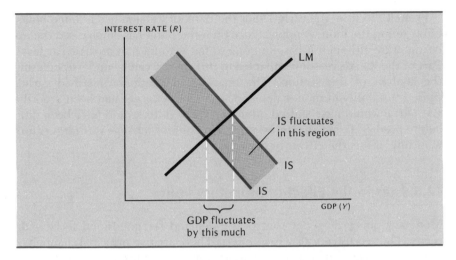

Figure 12-9. RANDOM SHIFTS IN THE IS CURVE.
The band around the IS curve illustrates the random shifts. A steep LM curve insulates real GDP from such shifts, indicating that a money supply target should be used.

What if the exchange rate is subject to exogenous shocks? The real exchange rate would change, causing the IS curve to shift. If changes in the exchange rate also have a strong immediate effect on prices then the LM curve would shift as well due to the change in real money supply brought about by the price change. If the Bank of Canada fixes the exchange rate it can eliminate these particular disturbances to the IS and LM curves. But it does so only by sacrificing its ability to respond to any other shocks that move the IS curve.

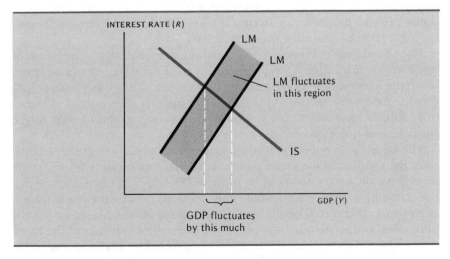

Figure 12-10.   RANDOM SHIFTS IN THE LM CURVE.
In this case, GDP fluctuations would be reduced by using an interest rate or exchange rate target instead of keeping a constant money supply.

From 1976 until the early 1980s the Bank of Canada had a stated policy of targeting the money supply. Since then the Bank has emphasised the exchange rate although it has not gone so far as to fix it at a particular level. Part of the Bank's reasoning that led to this change can be understood using the analysis of this section. The financial innovations described earlier caused instability in money demand. If a money target had been used the LM curve would have shifted often and these shifts would have been difficult to predict. Using an interest rate target or an exchange rate target automatically offsets the effects of these shifts.

12.8 Lags in the Effect of Monetary Policy

Monetary policy does not control the demand for goods and services directly. There is usually a lag in its effect. There are two principal channels of monetary policy and both act through interest rates: the response of investment and the response of net exports through the depreciation of the dollar.

In Chapter 9, we stressed the lags in the investment process. Businesses take months to get almost any investment plan into effect; those involving the construction of new plants or the ordering of special equipment can take years. Housing investment takes six months or a year to respond strongly to a change in the interest rate.

Less is known about the lags in the response of net exports to dollar depreciation. Exchange rates respond immediately to changes in the interest rate. But buyers in Canada and abroad do not switch their purchases immediately when Canadian goods become cheaper. Canadians who have learned that Japanese cars offer good value do not immediately reconsider Canadian-produced alternatives when the value of the dollar declines causing the dollar price of Japanese cars to rise. It takes time for foreigners to discover the advantage of Canadian products as well.

The peak effect of monetary expansion on GDP probably occurs between one and two years after the expansion. At first, a monetary expansion drives down the interest rate without much effect on GDP. The money market handles the monetary expansion through lower interest rates instead of higher GDP. After a year or so, the response of spending to the interest rate is stronger and GDP expands.

The lag in the economy's response to monetary expansion greatly complicates the conduct of monetary policy. As we have mentioned before, recessions generally hit the economy by surprise. The Bank of Canada learns that the economy is headed for trouble only a few months before the trouble is at its worst. It can step on the gas to try to head off the recession, but the peak effect of the stimulus will occur well after the worst part of the recession. In fact, if the recession is brief and is followed by a brisk recovery, the monetary stimulus may hit hardest when it is least needed; in the worst case, it can worsen the boom that follows the recession.

Because the main effect of monetary expansion occurs in the year after the expansion is launched, when formulating monetary policy the Bank of Canada must always think about the likely conditions in the economy a year in the future. Even if the economy is in bad shape this year, the Bank will not expand if it anticipates that the economy will recover on its own by next year. There is little the Bank can do to help the economy this year; any stimulus it adds now will only create problems next year.

The Bank never knows with any confidence what will happen in the future. Even if it does not know confidently that the economy will be in good shape on its own next year, the Bank will not take vigorous action this year. If it is 50 percent likely that the economy will be below potential next year and 50 percent likely that it will be above potential, the best action for the Bank is to do nothing. As a general matter, the more uncertain the Bank is about conditions next year, the more cautious it will be about policy actions this year.

Lags in Monetary Policy

1. Monetary policy operates through interest rates. Consequently, there is a lag before the policy influences GDP.

2. The evidence suggests that the peak effect of monetary policy on GDP occurs after a lag of between one and two years.

3. Today's monetary policy has to be formulated with the state of the economy a year from now in mind. Even if GDP is well below potential, it may not be desirable to launch a monetary expansion.

4. Uncertainty about the future state of the economy adds to the caution of monetary policy makers.

5. The net effect is to limit the monetary policy to much smaller adjustments than would be used if the effect of the policy occurred instantly.

12.9 Coordinated Fiscal and Monetary Policy

Fiscal expansion raises GDP and raises the interest rate. Monetary expansion raises GDP and lowers the interest rate. Therefore, mixes of fiscal and monetary policies can bring any desired combination of changes in GDP and the interest rate. For example, to raise GDP and keep the interest rate constant, an expansionary monetary and expansionary fiscal policy could be combined. To raise the interest rate and keep GDP constant, a combination of expansionary fiscal policy and contractionary monetary policy could be used.

A similar combination of policies would be necessary if the goals of the policy makers include international considerations such as the exchange rate or net exports. Suppose that policy makers want to keep both the exchange rate and GDP constant after an increase in the U.S. interest rate. Then they should choose a mix of fiscal and monetary policy that raises the Canadian interest rate without changing the level of GDP. Now suppose that an increase in GDP is sought but policy makers do not want the trade surplus to decline. As the increase in income would tend to reduce the trade surplus by increasing imports, the policy mix must also lower the interest rate. That way the Canadian dollar would depreciate, thereby offsetting the decline in net exports. This calls for simultaneous use of expansionary monetary and fiscal policies.

As Canadian fiscal and monetary policies are not set by the same people there is no assurance that coordination will occur. For example, in 1982 the Bank of Canada sharply reduced the growth of the real money supply in an effort to reduce inflation. At the same time the federal government's fiscal policy was expansionary.

Just as the IS-LM model predicts, this policy mix resulted in high interest rates. The federal deficit increased sharply. The monetary contraction added to the deficit by keeping GDP at low levels, limiting revenue and increasing transfer payments. The high level of interest rates also contributed to the deficit by raising the government's interest bill. The federal deficit rose from $7 billion in 1981 to $20 billion in 1982. (Fiscal policy and the federal deficit are discussed in more detail in the next chapter.)

This suggests that fiscal policy makers may have felt undermined by the decisions of those in charge of monetary policy, and vice versa. Indeed, the Bank of Canada subsequently encouraged the federal government to reduce the size of its budget deficit.

Review and Practice

MAJOR POINTS

1. A monetary system is an agreement on the way to quote prices and convey purchasing power.

2. The Bank of Canada issues currency and also reserves. Reserves are accounts at the Bank equivalent to currency. The sum of currency and reserves is the monetary base.

3. Through open-market operations, the Bank of Canada can set the monetary base to whatever level it chooses. To increase the base, the Bank purchases government bonds and issues new reserves to pay for the purchase. To decrease the base, the Bank sells government bonds.

4. The three major motives for holding money are as follows: the transactions demand; as a way to store wealth; and to pay the bank for the services it provides.

5. The effects of a fiscal stimulus depend on the Bank of Canada's policy rule. If the Bank targets the interest rate or exchange rate, fiscal stimulus raises GDP strongly.

If the Bank targets GDP, then fiscal stimulus raises interest rates but has little or no effect on GDP.

6. Monetary policy influences GDP with a lag. The immediate effect of monetary stimulus is to lower interest rates. After the lags in investment and foreign trade work themselves out, the stimulus raises GDP. Because of the lag and because of the Bank of Canada's uncertainty about the future, monetary policy needs to be used with caution.

7. Fiscal and monetary policy can be used in tandem to achieve any desired combination of GDP and the interest rate. Fiscal and monetary expansion together can raise GDP without changing the interest rate. Fiscal expansion and monetary contraction can raise the interest rate without changing GDP. Monetary expansion and fiscal contraction can lower the interest rate without changing GDP.

8. Monetary policy influences the exchange rate and net exports. Monetary expansion makes the dollar depreciate but has an ambiguous effect on the trade deficit.

KEY TERMS AND CONCEPTS

Means of payment	Monetary base	Compensating balances
Unit of account	Velocity	Open-market operation
Currency	Reserve requirements	Discount rate
Reserves	Transactions motive	Interest rate target
Chequing deposits	Precautionary motive	Exchange rate target
Money supply	Speculative motive	M target
Financial intermediaries	Store of wealth	GDP target
Near-banks		

QUESTIONS FOR DISCUSSION AND REVIEW

1. Why is the dollar the unit of account and the medium of exchange in Canada?

2. In what sense do chartered banks play a role as financial intermediaries? What other role do they play in determining the nation's money supply?

3. Why doesn't the Bank of Canada have separate control over both the quantities of reserves and currency?

4. What is the bank rate and how is it set? Is it correct to say that the bank rate sets the trend for other interest rates in the economy?

5. How does the Bank of Canada control the monetary base? What types of open-market operations increase the monetary base?

6. Why do banks require businesses to maintain compensating balances on deposits at the banks rather than simply charging them a service charge?

7. Does the demand for currency depend on the real rate of interest or on the nominal rate of interest?

8. What are the advantages and disadvantages of each of the following targets for monetary policy: the money supply, the interest rate, the exchange rate, and GDP?

9. What happens when monetary policy is contractionary and fiscal policy is expansionary?

PROBLEMS

Numerical

1. Suppose that money demand is given by the expression in Equation 12–9,

$$M = \sqrt{\frac{kW}{2R_o}}$$

where the opportunity cost of holding money is given by the expression in Equation 12–13,

$$R_o = rR$$

and the transaction cost k is equal to 2.

a. Assuming $r=.1$, what is the level of money demand at $W=2,500$ and $R=.08$? Suppose the money supply is set equal to this value. Find the interest rate at which money supply equals money demand for $W=1,000$ and $W=4,000$. Plot the points to scale on a graph.

b. Now let $r=.08$ and suppose that the money supply is set equal to the same level that you used in answering Part a. Find the level of money demand at $W=2,500$ and $R=.08$. Find the interest rate at which money supply equals money demand for the values of W given in Part a. Plot these points on the same graph.

c. Suppose the Bank of Canada's policy rule is to target M. Also suppose that household income W is the same as national income Y. For which value of r given above will the LM curve be steeper? Give a brief economic interpretation of your result.

d. Suppose that the federal government implements its proposal to eliminate reserve requirements. Suppose that this causes the banks to reduce the proportion of their deposits that are held in reserve. Would spending shocks be more or less destabilising to output after reserve requirements are eliminated?

2. In this problem we consider the relationship between monetary policy and the financing of the deficit.

a. Suppose that the reserve ratio, r, is equal to .1, and the currency ratio, c, is equal to .2. Assume that $G-T+F=\$200$ billion. By how much would the money supply, the monetary base, currency, and bank reserves have to change if the Bank of Canada were to finance the entire budget deficit?

b. Suppose now that the money supply is initially equal to $600 billion with output equal to potential. Suppose further that potential output is increasing by 2 percent per year, prices are expected to grow by 3 percent, and monetary velocity is expected to remain constant. If the Bank of Canada wishes to keep output at potential, what percentage of the deficit will it finance?

3. Suppose that the required reserve ratio is .12 for deposits and that there are no excess reserves. Suppose also that the total demand for currency is equal to .3 times deposits.

a. If total reserves are $40 billion, what is the level of the money supply?

b. By how much does the money supply change if the Bank of Canada increases the required reserve ratio to .20? Assume that total reserves are unchanged at $40 billion.

c. By how much does the money supply change if the Bank of Canada purchases $1 billion of government bonds in the open market? (Keep the required reserve ratio at .12.)

Analytical

1. Suppose that as a result of tax cuts, the amount of activity in the underground economy was significantly reduced.
   a. What effect would this have on the demand for currency?
   b. Explain why such a change would have an expansionary effect on the economy (holding the Bank of Canada's open-market operations fixed).
   c. Describe the Bank of Canada's response to such a change under each of the four policy rules discussed in Section 12.5.

2. Use Equation 12–9 to write an expression for real money demand as a function of real income and real transactions costs. Assuming that nominal income and nominal transactions costs increase proportionately with changes in the price level, describe how real money demand is affected by a change in prices. How is the nominal demand for money affected?

3. Consider the following cash management problem. An undergraduate student earns $400 a month which she uses to meet personal expenses. All expenses are paid for in cash. She maintains a savings account at a local bank which pays 1 percent per month (12 percent annually) in interest. At the beginning of each month she deposits her $400 paycheque in her savings account, and makes periodic cash withdrawals throughout the month. Cash withdrawals are made through an automatic teller at a service charge of 25 cents each.
   a. Calculate the student's average currency holdings and the number of withdrawals made each month.
   b. Suppose it's observed that the student always withdraws $40. There are several possible explanations. Perhaps she doesn't wish to risk losing larger amounts of cash. Protection against such loss is one of the benefits of a savings account. In addition, she may wish to avoid the temptation of spending more money than she can really afford. Call this the 'piggy bank' value of savings accounts. What must the value of such benefits be, expressed as a rate of return, in order for her withdrawals of $40 to be optimal?

4. Suppose that competition in the credit card industry drives down the cost of using credit cards.
   a. How is that likely to affect money demand? Illustrate the macroeconomic impact using an IS-LM diagram.
   b. If the Bank of Canada is aware of such a trend, but cannot be certain of its timing, what kind of policy rule should it use?

5. Suppose that banks began both to pay market rates of interest on all chequing accounts and to charge the full costs of providing such accounts. These costs would not be waived, regardless of one's average balance. Describe the possible effects of such a change on money demand.

6. The velocity of money, V, is defined by the expression

$$V = PY/M.$$

Another policy rule that could be used by the Bank of Canada can be described as follows. First, it is assumed that the velocity of money remains roughly constant from year to year. Next, the Bank forecasts this year's rate of inflation (which is viewed as being predetermined, and thus beyond their control). Finally, the Bank chooses its target rate of growth for real output. This results in a target rate of growth for the money stock.
   a. Suppose that inflation for the current year is forecasted to be 5 percent and that the Bank of Canada's target rate of growth for output is 2 percent. By how much should it increase the money stock this year?

b. Suppose now that money demand is given by the expression

$$M/P = kY - hR.$$

Derive an expression for the velocity of money, V. On what does V depend?

c. What kinds of changes in the economy could affect V? Consider both the cases where $h > 0$ and $h = 0$.

d. Explain why the policy rule described above is only useful when money demand is not very sensitive to interest rates.

7. Suppose that the federal government budget deficit is reduced through a cut in government purchases.

a. First assume that the Bank of Canada targets the *money supply* and does not change the target when the budget deficit is reduced. What happens to the exchange rate, net exports, and private saving? Use an IS-LM diagram and an aggregate demand curve with a price line to illustrate your answer. Be sure to distinguish between the short-run and the long-run effects, and describe in words how the economy adjusts over time as prices adjust.

b. Now assume that the Bank of Canada targets the *interest rate* and does not change the target when the budget deficit is reduced. Answer the questions in Part a for this alternative policy. Explain your answer using diagrams.

8. Both the interest rate target and the exchange rate target require the Bank of Canada to maintain a particular interest rate. Does this mean that they would have identical effects? Why or why not?

9. Monetary policy is one of the most hotly debated issues in macroeconomics. Yet, the policy implications of the IS-LM model would seem to be rather clear: Assuming that the Bank of Canada wishes to maintain output at potential, simply set the LM curve to intersect the IS curve at Y^*. Provide a brief explanation of why monetary policy isn't so simple a matter.

Appendix: Extending the Money Multiplier Analysis to a Broad Monetary Aggregate

In this appendix we show how the money multiplier analysis can take into account the existence of the near-banks. Define a broad monetary aggregate (M^+) as the sum of the currency held outside the chartered banks (CU) plus deposits at chartered banks (D^B) plus deposits at near-banks (D^N). It will be convenient to divide CU into the currency held by the public (CU^P) and the currency held by the near-banks as reserves against their deposits (CU^R). As before, the monetary base (M_B) is defined as the sum of CU and the chartered banks' reserve deposits at the Bank of Canada (RE). And as before $RE = rD^B$.

Let the ratio of the public's currency holdings to its holdings of bank and near-bank deposits be c. Then

$$CU^P = c(D^B + D^N).$$

Let the ratio of the public's near-bank deposits to its chartered bank deposits be d so that

$$D^N = dD^B.$$

Finally, suppose that the near-banks hold proportion r_N of their deposits as reserves in the form of currency. Then

$$CU^R = r_N D^N.$$

Thus

$$M^+ = CU^P + CU^R + D^B + D^N$$

$$= c(D^B + dD^B) + r_N dD^B + D^B + dD^B$$

$$= (1 + c)(1 + d)D^B + r_N dD^B,$$

while

$$M_B = CU^P + CU^R + RE$$

$$= c(D^B + dD^B) + r_N dD^B + rD^B$$

$$= c(1 + d)D^B + (r_N d + r)D^B.$$

Dividing M^+ by M_B we get

$$M^+ = \frac{(1 + c)(1 + d) + r_N d}{c(1 + d) + r_N d + r} M_B.$$

Thus when we consider a broad aggregate the money multiplier depends not only on c and r, but also on the public's choice of its ratio of near-bank deposits to chartered bank deposits (d) and the near-banks' choice of the proportion of their deposits to hold as reserves (r_N).

13

The Government's Budget Deficit and Aggregate Demand

WE are accustomed to referring to government budget balances as 'budget deficits' because federal government outlays have exceeded revenues in every year from 1975 to 1988. But government deficits are not inevitable. Prior to the mid-1970s the federal government often ran a budget surplus. And some of the provincial governments have enjoyed sizable budget surpluses even in recent years.

The federal deficit jumped from about 2 percent of GDP in 1981 to over 5 percent in 1982 and continued to increase to a peak of 6.5 percent of GDP in 1984 and 1985 before declining. The deficit remains large by peacetime standards. As a result the federal government had accumulated debts totalling 41 percent of GDP by 1987.

How does the budget deficit affect the economy? First, government purchases contribute directly to demand. Second, transfer payments such as Canada Pension Plan (CPP) cheques or unemployment insurance (UI) augment income. Third, personal and business income taxes reduce income. In the latter two cases demand is indirectly influenced because incomes change. The effect of the budget deficit is best analysed in terms of the components of the deficit: *purchases* plus *transfers* plus *interest on the national debt* less *taxes*. In this chapter we will examine in detail the effects of these components on the economy.

Traditionally in macroeconomics government purchases have been considered exogenous—not explained in the model. This was so, for example, in the basic model of Part I where government purchases G were taken as an exogenous variable. Empirically speaking, however, the government sector reacts to the state of the economy—partly because of conscious attempts to affect the economy. Transfers and taxes react to the state of the economy even more than purchases do.

One of the most significant recent developments in macroeconomics is the effort to describe the government's reaction to economic fluctuations and to build this behaviour into the model. The equation describing government behaviour is typically called a **reaction function.** Sometimes it is called a **policy rule** because, as we saw in Chapter 7, government actions are policy in one way or another, and if the behaviour is systematic it is like a rule. For example, generally, government taxes decline in recessions.

There are two ways to look at economic policy—from the **normative** perspective and from the **positive** perspective. Normative policy analysis asks what is the best policy and how one policy is better than another. For instance, normative analysis might study what policy can give the lowest rate of unemployment consistent with a prescribed rate of inflation. Positive analysis tries to describe policy actions without inquiring whether or not they are good for the country. In Chapter 7 we took the normative perspective and will do the same in Chapter 18. In this chapter, on the other hand, most of our discussion will be positive and descriptive.

13.1 Government Budgets

Because Canada has a federal system of government we need to distinguish between the different types of government: federal, provincial, and local. In 1987 federal government outlays accounted for 40 percent of the spending of all levels of government in Canada. Federal purchases of goods and services accounted for only 23 percent of the goods and services purchased by all Canadian governments combined.

THE FEDERAL GOVERNMENT BUDGET AND DEFICIT

The best place to start looking at the budget deficit's effect on the economy is with the federal **budget.** The federal government budget summarises all three of the types of effects on aggregate demand: purchases, transfers, and taxes. The overall budget totals do not distinguish between purchases and transfers. Rather, purchases of goods and services and transfers are lumped together as government **outlays.** The federal government's budget for 1987 is shown in Table 13–1.

Government outlays consist of purchases and transfers. Purchases involve the use of goods and services by the government, while transfers move funds to people outside the government. Less than one-quarter of federal

Table 13–1.   THE 1987 BUDGET OF THE FEDERAL GOVERNMENT
(billions of dollars during the calendar year)

RECEIPTS	99.1
Personal income taxes	53.9
Corporate income taxes	10.5
Indirect taxes	23.2
Investment income	8.8
Other	2.7
OUTLAYS	122.5
Purchases of goods and services	
National defence	9.6
Other goods and services	14.9
Transfers to persons	34.5
Transfers to other levels of government	22.7
Interest on the public debt	27.7
Subsidiaries	7.0
Other	6.1
DEFICIT	23.4

Figures are given on a national accounts basis. Source: Department of Finance, *Quarterly Economic Report,* Annual Reference Tables, 1988, Tables 51 and 52.

outlays take the form of purchases of goods and services. National defence accounts for about 40 percent of federal purchases. In 1987 total federal purchases of goods and services were about 4.5 percent of GDP.

Note that a substantial part of the government's expenditures is interest on the debt. As the debt has risen with high deficits in recent years, these interest payments have also risen. In 1987 interest payments on the debt represented about $2,111 for each person in the labour force on average. There is little that the government can do to change interest payments in a given year. The payments depend on past deficits and on the interest rate on past borrowing.

A major role of the federal government is to take in funds through taxes and pay them out as transfers. Most of the transfer takes the form of taxing families through the personal income tax, Canada and Quebec Pension, and unemployment insurance contributions and then paying out the proceeds as pensions, unemployment benefits, welfare, and family allowances.

The $23.4 billion deficit at the bottom of Table 13–1 is simply expenditures less tax receipts. The deficit in 1986 was about the same: $24.1 billion.

PROVINCIAL AND LOCAL GOVERNMENT BUDGETS

Canada's constitution gives the provinces responsibility for many of the functions of government, notably education and health care. Coupled with their broad taxing powers, this gives the provincial governments a large role in overall fiscal policy.

Table 13–2 shows the combined receipt and outlay figures for provincial and local governments in 1987. Over half of provincial and local outlays are purchases of goods and services that add directly to demand. Transfers are

Table 13–2.   THE 1987 COMBINED BUDGET OF PROVINCIAL AND LOCAL GOV-ERNMENTS (billions of dollars during the calendar year)

RECEIPTS	147.5
Personal income tax	41.1
Corporate income tax	4.5
Indirect taxes	47.3
Investment income	20.7
Transfers from federal government	22.7
Other	11.2
OUTLAYS	149.2
Purchases of goods and services	82.0
Transfers to persons	32.9
Interest on the public debt	17.5
Subsidies	5.5
Other	11.3
DEFICIT	1.7

Figures are given on a national accounts basis. Source: Department of Finance, *Quarterly Economic Report,* Annual Reference Tables, 1988, Tables 49–52.

about 20 percent of total outlays. The combined deficit of provincial and local governments was much smaller than the federal deficit. In fact, the provincial-local sector ran an overall budget surplus as recently as 1984.

Aggregating all of the non-federal governments into one obscures some important differences between them. In every year from 1975 to 1987 between six and all ten of the provinces have experienced budget deficits. In all but one of those years the Alberta government enjoyed budget surpluses because of the royalty payments it received from oil and gas producers. The Saskatchewan and British Columbia governments often ran surpluses during that period as well. Manitoba, Ontario, Nova Scotia, and Newfoundland ran deficits in every year of that period.

For most of the provinces, income tax receipts are set as a proportion of the federal income tax payments originating in that province. As a result, the behaviour of this revenue source over the business cycle is very similar for both the provincial and federal governments. The indirect taxes used by each level of government are different, however. For example, local governments are the only users of property taxes, provincial governments are the only recipient of retail sales taxes, and the federal government has the only claim to tariff revenues. As a result, the state of the economy may have somewhat different implications for the budget balances of each level of government.

13.2 Fluctuations in the Deficit: Purchases, Transfers, and Taxes

From the point of view of macroeconomic **fluctuations,** what matters most about the government budget deficit is not its average level, but the way the budget responds to conditions in the economy. How large is this response?

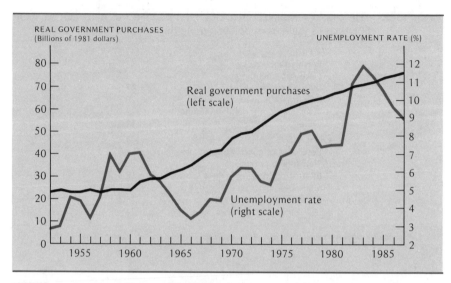

Figure 13–1. REAL GOVERNMENT PURCHASES AND UNEMPLOYMENT.
Purchases of goods and services have not responded in any systematic way to the state of
the economy, as measured by the unemployment rate. Sources: *Canadian Economic Observer*, Tables 1.3 and 2.1, and *Historical Statistics of Canada*, Series D233.

How do the fluctuations in the government deficit compare with the fluctuations in the economy as a whole? We will try to answer these questions separately for the three components of government spending.

First, purchases of goods and services do not seem to change much as real
activity in the private economy fluctuates. This is shown in Figure 13–1.
Every recession brings programs to raise spending and provide added government employment. In fact, however, spending programs have been
small and have taken some years to get into gear. Programs launched in the
depths of a recession frequently do not generate a significant contribution
to aggregate demand until some years later. By then, the economy might be
approaching boom conditions. This is another example of the lags in the effect of policy that we mentioned in Chapter 7.

On the other hand, government transfers usually do fluctuate in the right
direction, offsetting other movements in the economy. Government
transfers rise when unemployment rises, as can be seen clearly in Figure
13–2.

Government transfers rise in recessions and fall in booms largely through
the normal operation of benefit programs. No discretionary intervention on
the part of government officials is required. When unemployment rises and
incomes fall, a number of government programs automatically increase
their income transfers to families. For this reason they sometimes are called
automatic stabilisers.

The major programs that act as automatic stabilisers are unemployment
insurance and welfare. The unemployment insurance program pays bene-

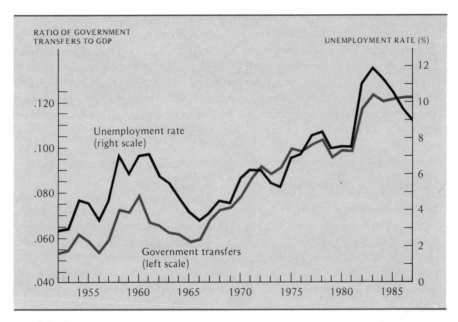

Figure 13–2.   GOVERNMENT TRANSFERS AND UNEMPLOYMENT.
Government transfer payments tend to rise in years of high unemployment and fall in years of low unemployment. The synchronisation has been achieved mainly through unemployment insurance and other programs that make the rise in transfers during recessions automatic. Sources: *Canadian Economic Observer*, Tables 1.7 and 2.1, and *Historical Statistics of Canada*, Series D233.

fits to workers who have lost their jobs. As a result, payments rise directly with unemployment. Welfare payments are available to people who are unable to support themselves, including people who have exhausted their unemployment insurance benefits. Lowered incomes and prolonged unemployment combine to raise welfare payments during recessions.

Taxes also rise and fall with the level of economic activity. During the last 20 years when real GDP fell or rose by 1 percent, real federal tax receipts fell or rose by about 1 percent. That is, the **elasticity** of year-to-year changes in real tax receipts with respect to changes in real GDP was about 1 (an elasticity is the percentage change in one variable induced by a 1 percent change in another variable).[1]

Each type of tax has a different elasticity with respect to GDP; the elasticity of total tax revenues with respect to GDP is the result of the mix of taxes used. The elasticity of real indirect taxes with respect to real GDP is close to 1. The elasticity of real corporate tax revenues with respect to real GDP is much greater than 1. Corporate taxes are based on corporate profits and

[1] The elasticity is the slope of the linear relationship between the percentage change in real federal tax receipts and the percentage change in real GDP. The slope was estimated by fitting a line through observations made during a 1969–87 sample period.

these profits are strongly procyclical; they increase a great deal during booms and fall sharply during recessions. For example, when real GDP fell 3.2 percent in 1982, real corporate profits fell by 34 percent. The elasticity of real personal tax revenues with respect to GDP is somewhat less than 1. One reason is that personal income tends to fluctuate less than GDP itself and this in turn is due in large part to the automatic stabilisers discussed above. The average of these responses, weighted by the extent to which governments rely on each form of tax, yields an elasticity of close to 1.

Indexing the Tax Brackets

It is important to realise how inflation can change tax rates in a progressive tax system. Canada's income tax system is called a **progressive system** because the more taxable income a person has, the greater the proportion of that income that is collected in income taxes. Consider two people whose tax is calculated according to the federal government's 1987 tax reform plan. The first person has taxable income of $27,500. He would pay 17 percent of that ($4,675) in federal income taxes. The second person has taxable income double that of the first, $55,000. She would pay 21.5 percent of her taxable income ($11,825) in federal taxes. On her first $27,500 in taxable income she is taxed at 17 percent but the next $27,500 falls into a higher tax bracket and is taxed at 26 percent (thus the average tax rate on her total income is 21.5 percent).

Now suppose that inflation of 10 percent took place but the tax brackets were not changed. Suppose that the real income of the first person had not changed. Solely due to inflation, his nominal income would have increased 10 percent, to $30,250. He would now pay more than 17 percent of his income in tax, however, because all of the nominal increase falls in the higher (26 percent) tax bracket.

One way to avoid this is to index the tax brackets. For example, the government could increase the lower limit of the 26 percent bracket to $30,500 due to the 10 percent inflation. As a result, no one would change tax brackets solely due to inflation. Tax indexing has occurred in Canada but it has varied over time. Under the 1987 tax reform proposal the tax brackets would be partially indexed. The lower limits of the brackets would be increased to the extent that inflation exceeds 3 percent (thus 10 percent inflation would raise the tax brackets by 7 percent).

In Chapter 4 we wrote tax receipts T as a constant proportion of income Y:

$$T = tY, \qquad (13-1)$$

where t is the constant tax rate. The discussion of the previous two paragraphs means that this is fairly accurate as a descriptive measure because the elasticity of real tax collections with respect to real GDP is close to 1. If the government changed its tax policies, for example, by relying much more heavily on corporate taxes, then the proportion of real GDP collected in taxes (the parameter t) would change over the course of the business cycle.

Much of the overall impact of the government's influence through taxes and transfers eventually shows up in personal disposable income. Recall that in Chapter 8 we looked at the relation between disposable income and GDP and found that the fluctuations in disposable income were much smaller (look back to Figure 8–3 for a review). Disposable income changes by only about 45 percent as much as total income. Consumers see only about 45 percent of the total loss in the economy's income when a recession hits.

Note that the effect of such countercyclical movements in taxes and transfers is to reduce the multiplier of the IS-LM model. When there is an increase in investment spending, for example, the increase in GDP leads to a smaller increase in disposable income and hence a smaller effect on consumption. The multiplier effect is smaller due to the automatic stabilisers.

13.3 The Effects of the Government Deficit

A great deal of controversy and concern surround government budget deficits. In Canada, attitudes towards the deficit vary across the political spectrum. Ironically, the Conservative Party has expressed concern over the size of the federal deficit while they have been in power (and hence at least partly responsible) while at the same time the opposition New Democratic Party was arguing that this concern was groundless.

The Canadian public is similarly split in their views. A survey taken in late 1982, when the federal deficit had recently taken a sharp increase, produced the following results. Sixty-seven percent of Canadians surveyed thought that reducing the deficit would help the economy. A companion survey of people who worked in the financial sector found a smaller number in favour of deficit reduction, 58 percent.

The U.S. federal budget deficit also receives a great deal of publicity in Canada. The dramatic fall of the Toronto Stock Exchange in October 1987 has been blamed on the U.S. budget deficit by some observers, although others dispute this.

Why is the government deficit so controversial and mysterious? Part of the reason is that the deficit is just a summary statistic that reflects the behaviour of many other variables. It is really just the tip of an iceberg. We emphasised that the budget deficit is simply the difference between government *expenditures* (purchases and transfers) and *receipts*. Moreover, from the government accounting identity discussed in Chapter 2, we know that deficits must be financed by issuing *bonds* or *money* to the public. The overall impact of the budget on the economy can thus be pieced together by looking at the effects of receipts, expenditures, bonds, and money.

In this section we address some of the questions raised about the deficit in the 1980s by examining the cyclical behaviour of the deficit, the implications of the simple fact that the government must borrow to finance its deficits the empirical relation between deficits and interest rates.

CYCLICAL VERSUS STRUCTURAL DEFICITS

The combined government budget deficit tends to increase during recessions. We know the reasons for this from the last section: Expenditures rise and receipts fall during recessions. The automatic stabilisers exacerbate the swing of the deficit during a recession.

Figure 13–3 shows the relationship between the deficit and the cyclical fluctuations in unemployment for the years 1952 to 1987. Increases in the unemployment rate, which signify that the economy is falling below potential output, are accompanied by increases in the deficit. This suggests that a deficit experienced during a recession (as, for instance, in 1982) could perhaps disappear without any change in government policy as the economy recovers and output returns towards potential.

To determine whether economic recovery alone would be sufficient to eliminate a deficit it is necessary to ask what the government budget balance

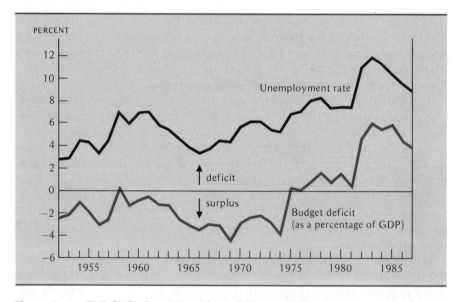

Figure 13–3. THE CYCLICAL BEHAVIOUR OF THE DEFICIT.
The chart shows the budget deficit, as a percentage of GDP, and the unemployment rate. The latter is a measure of the state of the economic cycle. Over the years 1952–87 the federal budget was in deficit when the economy was in a slump. The deficit is strongly cyclical. Sources: *Canadian Economic Observer* Tables 1.7 and 2.1, and *Historical Statistics of Canada,* Series D233.

would be if the economy were at full employment. This is termed the **full-employment deficit**.[2]

Calculations by Pierre Fortin of Laval University indicate that not all of the recent deficits can be attributed to the fact that output was below potential. Fortin estimates that under the tax and expenditure policies in place in 1984 the federal deficit would have been $13 billion even if output had been equal to potential. While this is substantially less than the actual $29.6 billion deficit experienced in 1984, it is still appreciable (about 3 percent of GDP). The fact that the budget would have been in deficit even at full employment indicates that the recent deficits have not been solely due to output levels below potential. Rather, the tax cuts and expenditure increases enacted in the early 1980s have also contributed to the explosion of the deficit.

In recent years the concept of the full-employment deficit has usually been discussed by distinguishing between the structural and cyclical parts of the deficit. The **structural deficit** is the same thing as the full-employment deficit, and the **cyclical deficit** is the difference between the actual deficit and the structural deficit.

How the Economy Destroys Budget Projections

A good way to get a feel for the influence of the economy on the government budget is to look at the difference between projected and actual budget totals. For example, the federal budget of November 1981 included projections of the outlays and receipts for the 1982–83 fiscal year to begin the following April. Outlays were expected to be $75.5 billion, receipts were expected to be $65 billion, and thus the expected deficit was $10.5 billion. But as is often the case, the actual budget turned out to be appreciably different from these projections. Outlays, at $78 billion, were greater than expected, receipts were less than expected at $58.6 billion, and the deficit thus turned out to be $19.6 billion. What happened?

The government had overestimated the strength of the economy in the coming year. The budget projections were based on the assumption that real output would grow by 2.2 percent when in fact it fell by 3.2 percent. Tax receipts were much less than expected simply because income was much less than expected. With less income people paid less taxes. The fall in corporate profits, and hence in corporate taxes, was particularly sharp and unexpected. Moreover, with a sagging economy the unemployment rate jumped to 11.0 percent in 1982, far higher

[2] The idea of the full-employment deficit was used by E. Cary Brown, 'Fiscal Policy in the Thirties: A Reappraisal,' *American Economic Review*, Vol. 46 (December 1956), pp. 857–879. He showed that the actual deficits observed in the early 1930s in the United States were large surpluses in the full-employment deficit.

than the expected rate of 7.8 percent.* As a result, transfer payments for unemployment and welfare were higher than expected. The fiscal 1982–83 tax shortfall is an excellent illustration of the impact that the economy has on the budget.

The strong impact of economic conditions on the budget is more than just a good illustration; it creates serious problems for budget planners. Because the deficit is the difference between two large numbers, relatively small errors in projecting outlays and receipts can cause very large errors in projecting the deficit. Note that in this example the expenditure forecast was off by 6 percent and the revenue forecast was off by 15 percent but the resulting deficit forecast was off by 135 percent.

* The budget projections are from the *Budget Papers*, November 12, 1981, the economic projections are from *The Current Economic Situation and Prospects for the Canadian Economy in the Short and Medium Term*, November 1981, and the actual budget figures are from the *Fiscal Plan*, February 15, 1984. All of these are Department of Finance publications.

THE DEFICIT AND THE EXPLOSION OF GOVERNMENT DEBT

When the government runs a deficit it must borrow from the public. The top panel of Figure 13–4 shows how budget deficits have led to an explosion of outstanding national debt in recent years, especially since 1975. Most of the debt consists of interest-bearing bonds, but part is non–interest-bearing money. As we saw in Chapter 12, the Bank of Canada **monetises** part of the government debt when it purchases it and issues currency and non–interest-bearing deposits. The Bank of Canada has monetised only a small amount of the debt. It monetises the debt primarily to provide sufficient money for the economy to work efficiently, rather than to raise revenues.

During World War II the government also ran a large deficit as is typical of most wars. Government expenditures were, of course, abnormally high in the war years; rather than raise taxes temporarily to pay for the war the government borrowed the money. This shifted some of the burden of the war to future generations who would have to pay the interest on the borrowings. After the war years the federal government often ran a surplus. The debt fell slightly during the surplus years, but was relatively unchanged compared to the increase during World War II.

Scaling the debt by nominal GDP gives a better perspective of the importance of the debt for the whole economy. At the end of World War II the government debt relative to GDP reached an all-time high of over 100 percent. Since World War II the public debt divided by GDP fell steadily until the mid-1970s, as shown in the bottom panel of Figure 13–4. Since then the stock of outstanding debt has again begun to grow relative to GDP as we have

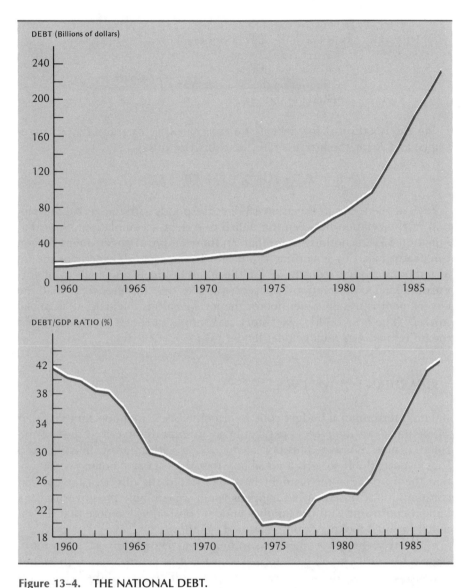

Figure 13–4. THE NATIONAL DEBT.
The national debt has had two big periods of rapid growth: during the war years in the 1940s and since the mid-1970s. In between the debt stayed fairly constant. It dropped as a ratio of GDP during this middle period. Sources: *Canadian Economic Observer,* Table 1.1, and *Bank of Canada Review,* Table G4.

had a series of large deficits. The ratio of the debt to GDP is still below the levels reached at the end of World War II, but the ratio is growing rapidly, and continued large deficits will raise the public debt to levels about which we know relatively little empirically.

We can express the relation between the deficit and the accumulation of debt formally as

Debt at the start of next year
   = Debt at the start of this year
   + Purchases this year
   + Transfers this year
   + Interest on the debt this year
   − Receipts this year.
$$\left.\begin{array}{c} \\ \\ \\ \\ \\ \end{array}\right\} \text{Deficit}$$

Using the notation D for debt, G for purchases, F for transfers, T for receipts, and R for the interest rate, we can write this as

$$D_{t+1} = D_t + G_t + F_t + RD_t - T_t. \tag{13-2}$$

Each of the terms in Equation 13–2 corresponds with the verbal description of the relation between the deficit and debt accumulation. Note that Equation 13–2 is nothing more than an **intertemporal government budget constraint** faced by government officials. It corresponds exactly to the intertemporal budget constraint for the households in our analysis of forward-looking consumption (Chapter 8). The only difference is that the government is usually a net debtor; hence we call its outstanding financial stock D. The household's asset stock was simply called A; we assumed that the household was usually a net lender.[3]

RICARDIAN EQUIVALENCE

The intertemporal budget constraint emphasises the important fact that when the government reduces taxes in an attempt to increase disposable income, it must borrow. This borrowing, along with interest, must be paid back eventually. If so, it is a possibility that the forward-looking consumption theory of Chapter 8 might have overstated the effect of tax cuts on consumption. Consider what happens when we combine the government's budget constraint with the family's budget constraint. Suppose that the rational forward-looking family reasoned as follows:

Ultimately, the government has to finance its expenditures. If it grants a tax cut this year, it will have to make up for it in future years with higher taxes to pay off the debt. We aren't any better off because of the tax cut; it is no more than a rearrangement of taxes, not truly a cut at all. We should not change our consumption. Moreover, all other families will see the situation the same way, so total consumption will not rise.

The possibility that tax cuts would be discounted against future tax increases was first pointed out by the British economist David Ricardo. Although he ultimately rejected the possibility, the proposition is still usually referred to as the **Ricardian equivalence.** The idea has been reviewed and

---

[3] Note that the government budget is balanced when the stock of government debt is not growing. The stock of government debt is usually stated in nominal terms. A reasonable alternative is to measure the stock in real terms. If there is inflation then the nominal budget is in deficit when the *real deficit* is balanced. The real deficit is simply the change in the real debt.

elaborated on by Robert Barro of Harvard University.[4] Ricardian equivalence says that the large budget deficits in the 1980s have had no effect on interest rates to the extent that they were due to tax cuts. According to the Ricardian equivalence proposition these tax cuts would not stimulate consumption because consumers would realise that future tax increases would be necessary to pay interest on the government debt. The experience of the 1980s may prove to be the crucial test of the Ricardian equivalence proposition.

One potentially important criticism of the Ricardian equivalence proposition is that people do not live forever. What if the government doesn't plan to repay the taxes until this generation is gone and the next generation has to pay the bills? The typical family still might not adjust its consumption if it cares about the next generation; it will want to make sure that the next generation does not have to restrict its consumption in order to pay off the government's tax liability. Barro has argued that the family should be viewed as a dynasty in which future generations are as important as the current generation. If so, tax cuts that are expected to result in future tax increases will not affect consumption even though individual generations do not live forever.

One implication of Ricardian equivalence is that the public debt does not 'burden future generations,' as is often argued. While it is true that future generations will have higher taxes, they will also receive larger bequests from their parents in order to be able to pay these taxes.

Even without Ricardian equivalence it is easy to overstate the burden on future generations. The bonds that are sold to finance a government deficit will pay interest to the bondholders in the future. The citizens who are alive at that time will have to remit the taxes to pay this interest. But these citizens will also be the bondholders at that time. Thus the national debt does not burden future generations as a group; they will receive in interest what they will pay in additional taxes.

There are two qualifications to this analysis, however. First, while it may be true for future citizens as a group, it need not be true for any individual citizen. A taxpayer who neither inherits nor purchases government bonds will receive no interest payments. Second, some of the public debt is held by non-Canadians. These people will receive interest payments without paying taxes. In 1986 and 1987 about 16 percent of the federal government's debt was held by foreigners. In each of the years between 1978 and 1985 the level was roughly 10 percent.

DEFICITS AND INTEREST RATES

The relation between the deficit and interest rates is one of the most important issues with respect to the government's role in aggregate demand.

[4] See Robert Barro, 'Are Government Bonds Net Wealth?' *Journal of Political Economy,* Vol. 82 (November–December 1974), pp. 1095–1117.

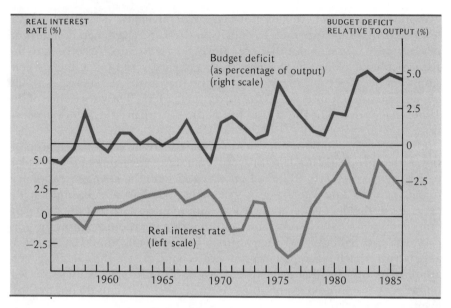

Figure 13–5.   BUDGET DEFICITS AND REAL INTEREST RATES IN THE UNITED STATES.
During much of the past 30 years U.S. interest rates have fallen during periods when the
U.S. federal government was running a deficit. However, this does not mean that deficits
cause lower interest rates. Falling interest rates and deficits are both largely the result of
recessions. The mid-1980s was one of the few periods where high budget deficits and
high interest rates occurred at the same time. Note: The real interest rate is the 3-month
Treasury bill less the average of the rate of change in the output deflator during the previous 3 years.

In Chapters 4 and 5 we showed that an increase in the government's budget
deficit, brought about by either an increase in expenditures or a cut in
taxes, would raise interest rates and expand output by shifting the IS curve
to the right. How does that theory fit the facts?

Sorting out the effect of deficits on interest rates can be difficult because
there are many factors that can influence interest rates, especially in an
economy like Canada's that is quite open to influences from abroad. One
way to try to simplify this problem is to look first at the U.S. economy. The
United States is less affected by foreign events, largely because of the sheer
size of the American economy, but it has experienced a pattern of budget
deficits that is quite similar to that of Canada.

Figure 13–5 shows the historical relation between a measure of the real
interest rate and the budget deficit in the United States. Two things are important from the chart.

First, over short-run periods and for much of the last 30 years, it appears
that the real interest rate falls when the deficit goes into the red. Deficits do
not appear to cause high real interest rates. Before you jump to any conclusions recall the previous discussion that pointed to the cyclical behaviour of
the deficit. Deficits occur when the economy is in a slump. Now, there are

many reasons for interest rates to be low during a slump; the demand for money is low and investment demand is low. It is thus likely that much of the relation between interest rates and the deficit during the last 30 years is due to other factors in the U.S. economy.

Second, there seems to be evidence of a positive relation between the budget deficit and interest rates during the 1982–86 period. Real interest rates were higher than normal rates during this period and the budget deficit reached a high-water mark as well.

This evidence tends to be contrary to Ricardian equivalence. U.S. interest rates have not skyrocketed as a result of the American budget deficits of the 1980s, but as Figure 13–5 shows, real interest rates do seem relatively high. Consumption expenditures also seem high given the level of disposable income. Recall that under Ricardian equivalence consumers would be saving more in order to cover their future tax liabilities rather than spending more. Savings would increase enough that the interest rate would not rise even though government borrowing was increased by the larger deficit.

Suppose then that Ricardian equivalence does not hold in the United States and that the U.S. budget deficit has raised U.S. interest rates. If the Bank of Canada is pursuing a policy of stabilising the exchange rate (perhaps to avoid positive price shocks) then the U.S. deficit will indirectly lead to an increase in Canadian interest rates. Under a fixed exchange rate, for example, Canadian monetary policy would ensure that the increase in the U.S. interest rate was matched in Canada, as discussed in Chapter 11. This is one reason the U.S. budget deficit receives a great deal of attention even in Canada.

Now suppose that Ricardian equivalence does not hold in Canada either. Would the Canadian budget deficit also raise Canadian interest rates? Once again it depends on what other policies are in place. Under a fixed exchange rate policy the deficit would not affect the interest rate, which would still be set to match the U.S. rate. If monetary policy does not respond to the exchange rate, then policies that lead to larger deficits will also affect the interest rate. For example, a tax cut or spending increase will shift the IS curve, increasing output and the interest rate, and increasing the budget deficit at the same time.

13.4 The Government and the IS Curve

Fiscal policy can shift the IS curve in two ways. First, government purchases of goods and services G enters spending directly. In Chapter 5 we looked at how changes in G shift the IS curve through the multiplier process. We noted in this chapter that over the last 30 years governments rarely offset the fluctuations in aggregate demand by altering their purchases of goods and services. One reason is that any increase in government purchases of goods and services G must be planned if it is to avoid being wasteful. Suppose that a recession in the United States reduces the demand for Canadian goods, causing a recession in Canada. Suppose also that the government wants to stimulate the economy by embarking on a series of public works projects to offset the loss of demand from the United States. The new construction projects will require that plans be drawn, tenders be put out for bidding, and approvals be obtained from other levels of government. By the time construction starts the recession may well be over. Historically government purchases do not appear to be an effective instrument to control aggregate demand but rather another shock or disturbance to aggregate demand. Recent experience with large deficits does not indicate that this situation is likely to change soon.

Second, policies on taxes and transfers can influence consumption. A tax cut increases income and stimulates consumption and so shifts the IS curve to the right. However, the magnitude of this shift is highly uncertain because of people's uncertainty about how permanent the tax cut will be. Moreover, there is a possibility that some people may increase their saving because they figure that taxes will rise in the future in order to pay the interest on the increased government debt.

Fiscal policy also influences the *slope* of the IS curve. We noted in this chapter that the automatic stabilisers operating through taxes and transfers reduce the multiplier. Because of the automatic stabilisers an increase in interest rates along the IS curve brings about a smaller decline in consumption and GDP. Therefore the IS curve is steeper as a result of the automatic stabilisers.

Review and Practice

MAJOR POINTS

1. Government purchases, transfers, and receipts are not exogenous. They respond to the state of the economy.

2. Expenditures rise and receipts are reduced by recessions. Real tax receipts fall by about the same percentage as real GDP during recessions.

3. The deficit fluctuates cyclically in time with the overall economy.

4. The structural or full-employment deficit has had these cyclical effects removed.

5. The government budget constraint relates the deficit to the public debt.

6. The debt has declined relative to GDP for most of the period since World War II. In recent years it has begun to increase again.

7. Higher government purchases of goods and services shift the IS curve to the right, though the federal government has not used this policy instrument to try to stabilise the economy very often in the past few decades.

8. Taxes influence both the position and the slope of the IS curve. A tax cut shifts the IS curve to the right, though the magnitude of the shift is uncertain. Automatic stabilisers make the IS curve steeper.

KEY TERMS AND CONCEPTS

Outlays

Purchases

Policy rule

Reaction function

Full-employment deficit

Indexing

Elasticity of tax revenues

Progressive taxes

Automatic stabilisers

Government budget constraint

Government debt

Ricardian equivalence

QUESTIONS FOR DISCUSSION AND REVIEW

1. Explain the differences between government purchases and government transfers. Which is larger for the federal government? For provincial and local governments? Which fluctuates more with the business cycle? In which direction?

2. What are the major automatic stabilisers? What is their significance for economic fluctuations?

3. Why is the budget typically in deficit during periods when the unemployment rate is high? What is the full-employment budget deficit? Does the full-employment deficit fluctuate with the state of the economy?

4. Why has the U.S. deficit usually been large when interest rates have been low? Does this mean that the deficit does not cause interest rates to rise as predicted by the IS-LM model?

5. Describe the behaviour of the government debt since World War II. Why has the debt declined as a fraction of GDP until recently?

6. Why do many Canadians pay attention to the level of the U.S. government deficit?

PROBLEMS

Numerical

1. Use the following example of a progressive tax schedule to compute what happens to average tax rates in the economy during a typical recession.

Income Bracket	Marginal Tax Rate
$0–$9,999	0
$10,000–$29,999	.2
$30,000–$49,999	.4
$50,000 and above	.6

To make it easy suppose that there are just three income groups of taxpayers. Just before the recession there are 200,000 taxpayers making $20,000, 700,000 making $40,000, and 100,000 making $60,000.

    a. Compute the average tax rate for the whole economy before and just after the recession if everybody's income drops by $10,000 during the recession. Has anyone moved to a different tax bracket?

    b. What happens to the average tax rate if everybody's income is reduced by $20,000?

    c. Suppose that the government introduces a 'flat tax' whereby everyone making equal to or more than $10,000 pays the same proportional tax of 25 percent. For this new tax system recalculate your answers to Parts a and b.

    d. Comment on the effect on stabilisation policy of a move from a progressive tax rate system to a flat tax rate system.

2. Suppose that federal tax receipts, transfers, and purchases are given by $T = .25YP$, $F = .15YP$, and $G = 400$, all in billions of *current* dollars. Suppose that at the start of 1990 the federal debt D was $800 billion, the interest rate R was 9.5 percent, real GDP was $3,500 billion, and the price level P was 1.08.

    a. Calculate the actual and full-employment budget deficit for 1990 in current dollars assuming that real potential output is $3,700 billion. Include interest payments in your calculation of the deficit using Equation 13–2.

    b. Now suppose that the following occurred:

	Real GDP Growth	Inflation	Interest Rate
1991	3.6	3.6	8.2
1992	2.8	3.9	8.9
1993	3.4	4.4	9.4
1994	3.6	4.8	8.4

Assuming that G increases at 5 percent per year calculate the deficit for 1991 through 1994. Start with the 1990 figures in Part a. Be sure to use Equation 13–2 to calculate the change in federal debt.

3. Assume that government outlays and taxes are initially zero, as is the stock of government debt. In Year 1 the government begins to spend $50 billion per year, in real terms, on environmental protection. Each year the government issues enough debt to finance this program, as well as to repay the interest on the previous stock of debt. The stock of government debt and the deficit, measured in current dollars, obey the equations

$$D_t = (D_{t-1} + G_{t-1})(1+R)$$
$$DEF_{t-1} = D_t - D_{t-1}$$

where G is measured in current dollars. The initial price level is 1.

    a. For an interest rate of 5 percent and an inflation rate of zero, calculate the real and nominal values of government debt and the deficit for each of the first five years.

    b. Now suppose prices rise at an annual rate of 5 percent. Assuming that the interest rate remains at 5 percent, repeat your calculations for Part a.

    c. Finally, assume an inflation rate of 5 percent and an interest rate of 10.25 percent. Again, repeat your calculations for Part a.

    d. Compare the path of real debt under Parts a, b, and c. Explain any differences.

    e. Comparing Parts a and c, you should find that the real debt stock is the same for Part c, but that the real deficit each year is higher. Why doesn't a higher deficit lead to a higher stock of debt?

    f. In which case was inflation anticipated by financial markets? Explain your answer.

4. Suppose that instead of G being exogenous it is given by the formula

$$G = 750 - .1(Y - Y^*)$$

where Y^* is potential GDP and is equal to $4,000 billion. Suppose that the other relationships in the economy are given by the example considered in Chapter 5:

$$C = 80 + .63Y$$
$$I = 750 - 2,000R$$
$$M = (.1625Y - 1,000R)P$$
$$X = 425 - .1Y - 500R$$

where the price level is predetermined at $P = 1$ and the money supply is 600.

  a. Derive an algebraic expression for the IS curve for this model. Plot it to scale. Compare it with the IS curve of Chapter 5 in which government purchases are exogenous. Which is steeper? Why?

  b. Derive the aggregate demand curve and plot it to scale. How does it compare with the aggregate demand curve when government spending is exogenous?

  c. Calculate the effect on GDP of an increase in the money supply of $10 billion. Is the effect larger or smaller than the case where government spending is exogenous? Explain in words what is going on.

  d. Is this equation an accurate description of government purchases in Canada? If not, what other components of the government budget act as automatic stabilisers? How is the impact of aggregate demand and price shocks affected by such stabilisers?

5. (Simple proof of the Ricardian equivalence.) Consider the intertemporal budget constraint for families that we introduced in Chapter 8 and the intertemporal budget constraint for the government that we introduced in this chapter. Suppose that taxes are cut by $1,000 in Year 1 and the government debt increases.

  a. If the interest rate is 5 percent, by how much will taxes have to increase next year if the government debt is to come back to normal by the end of next year?

  b. What is the effect of this decrease and subsequent increase in taxes on the intertemporal budget constraint for consumers? How would you expect this change to affect consumption?

Analytical

1. Suppose our model of the economy is the simple spending balance model of Chapter 4. The equations of the model are

$$Y = C+I+G$$
$$C = 100+.9Y_d$$
$$Y_d = Y+F$$

where $I=750$ and F stands for government transfer payments.

  a. You are told that government outlays equal 500, and there are no taxes. With this information can you calculate the point of spending balance?

  b. What is the maximum value of income for which there could be spending balance? What is the minimum value?

  c. Explain why government transfers and spending affect aggregate demand differently. Be specific.

2. Explain why imports act as automatic stabilisers. Compare the case where imports consist mainly of necessities to the case where they consist mainly of luxury goods.

3. Suppose it is 1993, and the newly elected federal government, in order to win, has promised (i) not to raise taxes, (ii) not to tamper with pensions, unemployment insurance, and other transfer programs, and (iii) not to cut government purchases. At 7 percent unemployment, output is very close to potential. There still, however, are the nagging two problems of the government budget deficit and the current account deficit.

  a. In the short run, how can the government reduce the budget deficit without breaking any of its campaign promises? Be specific about the policy. What effect will the policy have on output and interest rates? How will this policy reduce the budget deficit? Describe the effect of this policy on the current account deficit. Is it unambiguous?

b. Will this policy reduce the budget deficit in the long run? Again, be specific. What are its long-run effects on the current account deficit?

c. What will the effects of such a policy be, in the short run and in the long run, on the real value of government debt outstanding?

d. Recall the relationship between nominal interest rates and expected inflation discussed in Chapter 5. How might the expectations of such a policy have affected long-term nominal interest rates in the 1980s?

e. By comparing nominal interest rates with the actual rate of inflation, it has been suggested that real interest rates in the mid-1980s were at nearly an all-time high. How would the preceding analysis affect such a judgement?

4. Suppose that government spending is increased when the economy is below potential GDP. Why doesn't the decrease in government saving lead to a decline in total saving and to a drop in investment?

5. Sketch an IS-LM diagram. Compare two cases, one in which government spending is exogenous, the other where government spending declines when the economy rises above potential GDP and increases when the economy is below potential GDP. Which curve is steeper? For which curve is monetary policy most powerful?

6. Suppose that the federal government implemented an income tax increase in order to reduce the federal deficit. Specifically, suppose that it decided to increase the income tax take by $10 billion per year in 1989, 1990, and 1991. After 1991 the income tax would revert to its previous levels. What would be the effect of this tax increase on *consumption demand*? Use the forward-looking theory of consumption to explain what the impact of the tax increase would be.

7. Consider once again the simple spending balance model of Chapter 4. Suppose now that the model is

$$Y = C+I+G$$
$$C = 100+.9Y_d$$
$$Y_d = Y+F-T$$

where $I=750$ and G, T, and F are initially zero.

a. Calculate the initial point of spending balance.

b. Suppose the country goes to war for a year, requiring government expenditures of 100, and that taxes are temporarily raised to 100 in that same year. Calculate consumption and the point of spending balance in the war year and in all future years.

c. Now suppose that the government issues war bonds instead of raising taxes. The war bonds are 5 percent consoles. Consoles are bonds on which interest is paid forever and the principal is never repaid. Again, calculate consumption and the point of spending balance in the war year and in all future years.

d. What is the net effect of the government running a deficit in the war year instead of raising taxes? Is your result consistent with the idea of Ricardian equivalence? If not, how can you explain the difference?

PART III

The Micro
Foundations of
Aggregate
Supply and Price
Adjustment

14

Aggregate Supply and Economic Growth

AN ECONOMY in which prices and wages are perfectly flexible is always exactly in full employment because wages and prices can adjust instantaneously to offset the effect of disturbances. The full-employment economy is an abstraction, but it provides a useful framework that economists employ when they want to focus on the problems of long-term growth of potential output, rather than on short-run economic fluctuations. In the longer run, the Canadian economy behaves in the way described in the flexible-price economy.

The **aggregate supply** of productive factors—labour and capital—is the driving force determining total output in the full-employment economy. Monetary policy determines the price level and the inflation rate, but the money supply has no effect on total output. Fiscal policy determines the division of output among consumption, investment, net exports, and government purchases. Because fiscal policy influences investment, it affects the growth of physical capital and thereby the long-run growth of aggregate supply. We will also see that fiscal policy—in particular tax policy—can influence the growth of potential output by altering the supply of labour.

Macroeconomic models that assume flexible prices and wages bear the name **classical,** because it was this assumption that was used by the classical economists of the early twentieth century—for example, Alfred Marshall and A. C. Pigou of Cambridge University. In the 1930s, John Maynard Keynes began to emphasise the importance of wage and price rigidities. The classical models still play an important role in economic analysis. The term

neoclassical growth model is sometimes used to refer to the classical model because it was revived in the 1950s to study the problem of long-term growth.

14.1 The Microeconomics of the Labour and Capital Markets

We have already shown that a firm's production can be represented by a **production function** that governs how much output can be obtained from a specified amount of labour and capital. As we showed in Chapter 6, aggregate supply, or potential output, in the economy can be similarly described by an aggregate production function that relates total output to total labour and capital inputs:

$$Y = F(N,K), \tag{14–1}$$

where Y is output, N is employment, and K is the stock of capital. Because aggregate supply depends on labour and capital, the microeconomics of aggregate supply can be approached through the microeconomics of the capital and labour markets.

In Chapter 9 we discussed the microeconomics of the capital market: the demand and supply for capital. The *demand* for capital K depends negatively on the rental price of capital. The *supply* of capital depends on the amount of saving that has occurred in the past. As an accounting identity, saving equals investment, and the capital stock is the accumulated investment of the past. The stock of capital is a predetermined variable set by past investment and saving decisions. Time must pass for investment to occur and for the capital stock to change.

As for the microeconomics of the labour market, Figure 14–1 shows how production depends on labour for a given capital stock. The production function curves towards the horizontal axis. The **marginal product of labour** declines as the amount of employment increases. Recall that the marginal product of labour is the additional output that is produced by one additional unit of work. The marginal product of labour is the slope of the production function in Figure 14–1. Note how the production function gets less steep as more labour is employed.

THE DEMAND FOR LABOUR

If the labour market is competitive and firms take the market wage and the market price of their product as given, then they will choose the level of employment so that the marginal product of labour equals the real wage. The real wage is the dollar wage W divided by the price level P; that is, W/P. This demand for employment is implied by profit maximisation. If firms had employment below this level, the marginal product of labour would ex-

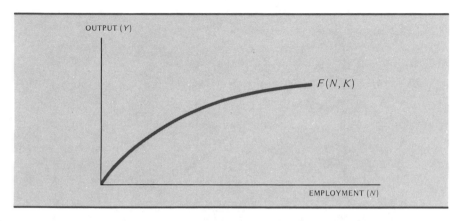

Figure 14–1.   THE PRODUCTION FUNCTION IN TERMS OF LABOUR INPUT.
With a given capital stock, the volume of output Y produced from various levels of employment N shows diminishing marginal product.

ceed the real wage and an opportunity for improved profit would exist. A firm could hire a worker for the wage W, produce more output in the amount given by the marginal product of labour, sell that output at price P, and make a profit on the deal. Firms will pursue this opportunity for profit until their additional hiring pushes the marginal product of labour down to the real wage. The point of maximum profit is shown in Figure 14–2.

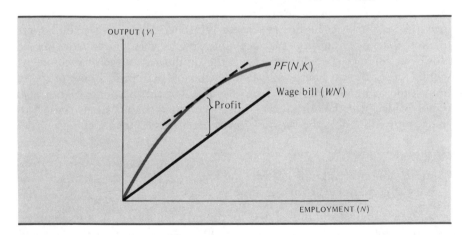

Figure 14–2.   PROFIT MAXIMISATION.
Profit is the difference between the value of output, P times $F(N,K)$, and the wage bill, W times N. It reaches a maximum when the slope of P times $F(N,K)$ equals the slope of W times N; that is, the value of the marginal product of labour equals the wage.

The demand function for labour is a negative function of the real wage because the marginal product of labour declines with increased labour input, as shown in Figure 14–3.

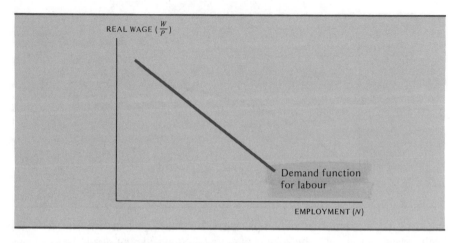

Figure 14–3.   THE DEMAND FUNCTION FOR LABOUR.
The demand function for labour is a downward-sloping relation between the real wage,
W/P, and the level of employment, *N*. For each real wage, it gives the level of employ-
ment that firms will choose by equating the marginal product of labour to the real wage.

THE SUPPLY OF LABOUR

The supply of labour is determined by the decisions of individual workers
about how much of their time to spend working. Some people have the alternative of spending time away from work. The real wage determines the
incentive to work. At higher real wages, the incentive to enter the labour
market is stronger and, on that account, people will want to work more.
However, for most people, wages are the dominant source of income. At
higher wages, they are better off. People who are better off choose to spend
more time at home and away from the job. On this account, higher real
wages bring lower labour supply. Microeconomic theory labels these two
contrasting influences the substitution effect and the income effect.

Microeconomic Estimates of Income and Substitution Effects in Labour Supply

Many labour economists have attempted to measure the size of the
income and substitution effects in labour supply by looking at individual behaviour. The earliest studies were based on samples of individuals for a single year. More recently researchers have used *panel* data
sets in which the hours of work and the wage rate of thousands of individuals are observed for a number of years. Panel data sets were discussed in Chapter 8 on consumption. Other recent studies are based
on negative income tax *experiments* in the 1960s and 1970s. In these
experiments, groups of individuals were given a cash grant and then

taxed at a higher rate on additional income. Other groups—the control groups—were not given a cash grant and faced the normal tax rates. By comparing the experimental groups with the control groups the size of the income effect and the substitution effect could be directly estimated.

The table below summarises the findings of several researchers who have used panel and experimental data on employment behaviour in the United States. In all cases total labour supply elasticity is small and sometimes negative, indicating a steep or even backward-sloping labour supply curve. Hence, there is much empirical support for the steep labour supply curve.

However, the estimates of the substitution and income effects have a wider variation. In some studies the substitution effects are quite large, but in others they are small, sometimes even negative. Unfortunately, this wide variation in estimates of substitution effects makes it difficult to calculate with much certainty the impact on labour supply of tax rate changes that hold income constant.

Researchers	Labour Supply Elasticity	=	Substitution Effect	+	Income Effect
Panel Data					
Orley Ashenfelter, James Heckman	−.15		.12		−.27
Farrel Bloch	.06		.12		−.06
Michael Boskin	−.29		.12		−.41
John Ham	−.16		−.05		−.11
Jerry Hausman, Paul Ruud	−.08		.55		−.63
Marvin Kosters	−.10		.04		−.14
Terrence Wales, A.D. Woodland	.14		.84		−.70
Experimental Data					
Jerry Hausman and David Wise	.10		.11		−.01
Terry Johnson and John Pencavel	.02		.19		−.17
Michael Keely and Phillip Robins	−.09		.05		−.14

Source: John Pencavel, 'Labor Supply of Men: A Survey,' in O. Ashenfelter (ed)., *Handbook of Labor Economics*, Amsterdam, North-Holland, 1987.

Substitution Effect. As something becomes more expensive, people substitute away from it. In the case of labour supply, as time at home becomes more expensive (as its opportunity cost, the real wage, rises) people substitute away from time at home and towards time in the labour market. To put it another way, the real wage provides an incentive for work, and people substitute toward work when the real wage rises.

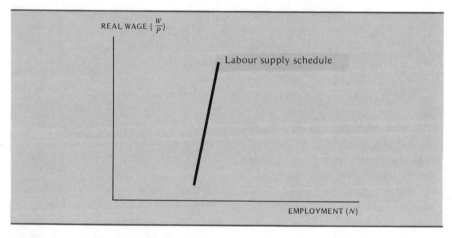

Figure 14-4. LABOUR SUPPLY SCHEDULE.
The labour supply schedule gives the amount of labour offered in the labour market for various levels of the real wage. At higher real wages, the incentive to work is greater, but people have more income, and this tends to offset the incentive. The evidence suggests that the labour supply schedule is almost vertical.

↑ income ↑ normal goods (leisure)

Income Effect. As income rises, people tend to consume more of most things. In this case, they consume more of their own time at home and offer less of their time in the labour market. Higher real wages make people better off and they work less on that account.

The labour supply schedule, illustrated in Figure 14–4, shows the net effect of these two offsetting influences. Research by a number of economists has agreed rather closely that the net effect of the two influences of the real wage on labour supply is roughly zero.[1] However, it is important to keep in mind that the agreement is that the net effect is zero, not that each of its components is zero. The substitution effect, prompting people to work more when the real wage rises, has been shown to be strong in some studies. In these studies the income effect happens to be equally strong in the opposite direction. If the substitution effect is large then an increase in work incentives without an increase in income could increase labour supply dramatically.

Classical **EMPLOYMENT WITH FLEXIBLE WAGES AND PRICES**

If both the wage W and price P can adjust, then the real wage W/P can also adjust. Employment in the labour market occurs at the intersection of the supply and demand schedules. This is shown in Figure 14–5. At the real

[1] The most recent econometric studies have used experimental data or panel data of the type we described in Chapter 8 in our analysis of consumption (see page 383 for a summary). A useful survey of available results is found in John Pencavel, 'Labor Supply of Men: A Survey,' in Orley Ashenfelter (ed.), *Handbook of Labor Economics,* Amsterdam, North-Holland, 1987.

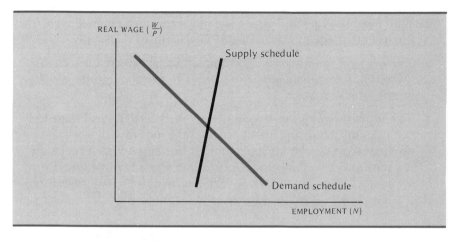

Figure 14–5.   LABOUR MARKET EQUILIBRIUM.
In the model with perfectly flexible wages and prices, the real wage fluctuates to equate
the supply and demand for labour. There is no unemployment.

wage W/P, the quantity of labour N chosen by firms equals the quantity
supplied by the public. The labour market is in a standard microeconomic
equilibrium. Unemployment cannot occur—if the real wage were too high
to provide jobs for everyone interested, the real wage would fall, stimulating labour demand by firms and discouraging labour supply by workers. It
would fall immediately to the point where supply and demand were equal
and unemployment disappeared.

An interesting and important feature of the model with flexible wages
and prices is that the level of output in any one year is determined solely by
the labour market. We showed above how the level of employment and the
real wage are determined at the intersection of the supply and demand
schedules. At any point in time the stock of capital K is predetermined by
past investment decisions. The level of output comes immediately from putting the level of employment N and the predetermined level of the capital
stock K into the production function $Y = F(N,K)$. The labour market is dominant in this model because it determines aggregate supply, or potential output. And with perfectly flexible wages and prices, output is always equal to
potential output.

Full Employment with Flexible Wages and Prices

1. The classical model assumes that wages and prices are completely
   flexible. It uses basic microeconomic principles to study the capital
   and labour markets and describe the equilibrium level of employment, capital, and output.

2. With flexible wages and prices, the real wage moves immediately to the level that equates the demand for labour to the supply.

3. The demand for labour is determined by employers. They choose the level of employment that equates the marginal product of labour to the real wage.

4. The supply of labour is determined by workers. The real wage has two roles in labour supply—it provides the incentive to work and it provides most families the bulk of their income. A higher real wage has substitution and income effects in the opposite directions. Consequently, labour supply is not very sensitive to the real wage.

14.2 The Natural Rate of Unemployment

When the labour market is in equilibrium, at full employment, not everyone who wants to work has a job. Unemployment is a feature of the economy even at full employment. In fact, there is unemployment even when the economy is in a boom. Thus the unemployment rate has not fallen below 2 percent in Canada since the end of World War II even though we have sometimes experienced substantial booms. Although excess unemployment is a sign of excess supply of labour, there is a certain level of unemployment, which we saw in Chapter 3, called the **natural rate of unemployment,** which exists even without excess supply.

Part of the unemployment present in equilibrium is *frictional*. Every month, millions of people move from one activity to another. In the spring, for example, high school and university students finish the school year and move into the labour market, hoping for either summer work or permanent work. Even more important, people are constantly changing jobs, either because they feel they can find better jobs or because their earlier jobs have ended. Frictional unemployment occurs because it takes time for people to find jobs. During the period when they are looking, they count as unemployed.

Another reason that substantial unemployment exists even in equilibrium is that not every labour market is in equilibrium at the same time. Even when equilibrium prevails, roughly speaking, in the economy as a whole, some markets will have excess supply and some will have excess demand. In the 1980s, employers had trouble finding software engineers at the same time that construction workers were out of work in large numbers. In 1988 employers in Toronto were advertising many job vacancies while employers in St. John's were not. The markets with excess supply contribute positive amounts of unemployment, but those with excess demand cannot have negative unemployment. The average unemployment rate must always be positive.

A third important reason for significant unemployment in equilibrium is the adverse experience suffered by certain groups in the labour market. Young people, members of some racial minorities, and the unskilled contribute disproportionately to the unemployment that is found when the economy as a whole is at full employment. These people spend long periods between jobs because of their difficulty in finding work; to the extent that they meet the survey's requirement for having made some type of job-seeking effort, they are counted as unemployed. They tend to find jobs that last only a few months, so they are thrown back into the market fairly quickly. Of all the weeks of unemployment suffered in the economy, a large number is contributed by a fairly small fraction of the labour force who tend to spend many weeks each year looking for work and relatively few weeks working.[2]

We have been discussing unemployment in equilibrium. When the economy is out of equilibrium, unemployment can be above or below its natural rate. When it is above, all the types of unemployment we listed become more severe.

MEASURING THE NATURAL RATE OF UNEMPLOYMENT

Estimating the natural rate of unemployment is of course extremely important for policy-making. In 1987, for example, the unemployment rate dropped to just below 8 percent. If the natural rate of unemployment is 9 percent, then policy makers should have become concerned that the economy was expanding at a dangerous pace. If the natural rate is 7 percent, then the economy could safely expand for a while longer.

Unfortunately, economists differ on how to measure the natural rate and on the numerical estimates they come up with. Some try to define the natural rate as the point of equilibrium where actual inflation equals expected inflation. That is, years when the rate of inflation turns out to be the same as the amount of expected inflation are years when the actual unemployment rate equals the natural rate. Such a measurement is dependent on a way of measuring expected inflation.

A more straightforward way to measure the natural rate is based on the idea that, over a sufficiently long span of years with about the same number of booms as slumps, the average unemployment rate should be equal to the natural rate. Sometimes the market is perturbed in one direction, sometimes in another. The average unemployment rate should be close to the natural rate.

The average unemployment rate for all workers from 1950 through 1987 was 6.2 percent. Based on the logic we just reviewed, this average can be considered an estimate of the natural rate of unemployment. But most

[2] The research on Canadian labour market dynamics is summarised in Morley Gunderson and W. Craig Riddell, *Labour Market Economics: Theory, Evidence and Policy in Canada*, 2nd edition, McGraw-Hill Ryerson, 1988.

economists would consider 6.2 percent an optimistic estimate of the natural rate in the 1980s.

One problem with this simple approach to measuring the natural rate is that the rate might be changing gradually over time. There are a number of reasons to expect such a change.

The composition of the Canadian labour force has changed substantially due to increases in the labour force participation rates of women and young people. Members of these groups tend to have higher turnover rates than men over the age of 25, the group that used to dominate the labour force. People with higher turnover rates are more often seeking to enter employment. During the period in which they are seeking a new job they are classified as unemployed.

In addition, the dispersion of disequilibrium across the economy apparently rose in the 1980s. This may have been due to shifts in activity between different sectors of the economy, or between different geographic regions.[3]

Finally, changes in the provisions of the unemployment insurance program have also affected the natural rate. The UI program was changed in the early 1970s to provide more income over a longer period of time to the unemployed. As a result, unemployed people spent longer looking for new jobs. This need not be interpreted as 'freeloading.' Even a conscientious job seeker will spend longer looking for a new job under these circumstances because he or she can afford to pass up the first job that comes along if it is not quite what the job seeker wants.

Average unemployment has been much higher since the early 1970s. The average unemployment rate rose from 4.8 percent for 1950–74 to 8.9 percent for 1975–87. This rise points in the direction of a higher natural rate but is not conclusive evidence. The later period saw three major events all pushing toward disequilibrium with unemployment above the natural rate. Two oil shocks raised unemployment. An abrupt shift in monetary policy that successfully lowered inflation also pushed unemployment to extraordinary heights in 1982; the unemployment rate reached a peak of 12.8 percent in October 1982. It is possible that almost the entire period from 1975 through 1987 was one of unemployment above the natural rate. In other words, the single decade included in the computation of the recent average unemployment rate may not be long enough to average out disequilibrium to zero. It may take another decade of experience, we hope without so many adverse shocks, to reveal the current natural rate.

The Natural Rate of Unemployment

1. The natural rate is the amount of unemployment present when the overall economy is in equilibrium.

---

[3] See Lucie Samson, 'A Study of the Impact of Sectoral Shifts on Aggregate Unemployment in Canada,' *Canadian Journal of Economics,* Vol. 18 (August 1985), and Janet Neelin, 'Sectoral Shifts and Canadian Unemployment,' *Review of Economics and Statistics,* Vol. 59 (November 1987).

2. The natural rate is positive because people are continually entering the labour market to find work or moving from one job to another. Another reason is that some sectors or regions may have excess supply even when the economy as a whole is at full employment. A third reason is that some disadvantaged groups spend a large fraction of each year out of work.

3. The average amount of unemployment since 1950 has been 6.2 percent, and there is an argument that this is a good measure of the natural rate. However, there are reasons to believe that the natural rate rose in the 1970s and was above 6.2 percent in the 1980s.

14.3 Long-Term Economic Growth

Compared to the fluctuations in actual output, potential output appears to grow rather steadily from year to year. The labour force increases, the capital stock usually rises, and productivity improves. We can study the process of growth with the production function. Because we are concerned about changes from one year to the next, we need to keep track of the dates of the variables involved. We do this with a subscript on the variable to indicate the year. Further, we need to set up the analysis so that the role of productivity improvement is made explicit.

We will define A_t as an index of *overall* productivity in year t. If A_t grows by 1 percent, it means that the economy can produce 1 percent more output from the same amount of labour and capital. A_t is a measure of **total factor productivity;** it incorporates the increased productivity of both labour and capital. Total productivity should be distinguished from labour productivity, which we discussed in Chapter 3. In terms of the production function, the productivity index fits into the analysis in the following way:

$$Y_t = A_t F(N_t, K_t). \tag{14-2}$$

The production function with the productivity index in front provides a way to determine the sources of growth of output. When output grows, it must be the result of some combination of growth in labour, in capital, and in productivity. In most years, all three forces are contributing.

There is a simple formula that growth specialists—economists such as Edward Denison of the Brookings Institution—use to assign credit for growth. The rate of growth of output equals the rate of growth of productivity plus the weighted rates of growth of labour and capital:

$$\Delta Y/Y = \Delta A/A + .7\Delta N/N + .3\Delta K/K. \tag{14-3}$$

The derivation of this formula is shown in Appendix A in this chapter. The growth formula shows how total growth relates to growth in the three de-

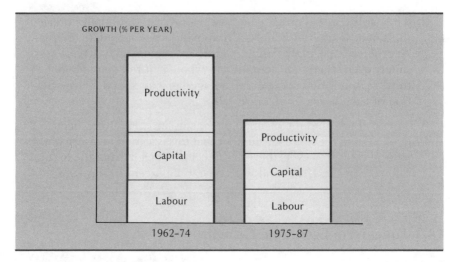

Figure 14–6. SOURCES OF GROWTH.
The height of each bar shows the actual annual growth rate of real GDP over 13-year intervals. Each bar is broken into blocks showing the contributions from labour growth, from capital growth, and from productivity growth. The contributions are calculated using Equation 14–3 in the text. Sources: *Canadian Economic Observer*, Table 1.3, and Statistics Canada, Nos. 13-211 and 15-204.

terminants. In words the formula says that the rate of growth of output is equal to the rate of growth of productivity plus .7 times the rate of growth of labour input plus .3 times the rate of growth of capital input. What is interesting about the formula is its lack of dependence on the details of the production function. All that matters from the production function is the weight .3 and its complement .7. These can be derived from data on the relative shares of capital and labour in national income. In Chapter 2 we saw that these income shares are roughly .3 and .7.

The formula can be used to study the change that took place in the mid-1970s. The right-hand bar of Figure 14–6 shows the sources of growth averaged over the years 1975–87. The left-hand bar pertains to an equal number of years preceding 1975. It is clear that growth has slowed considerably from the earlier period to the later. All of the sources of growth have made diminished contributions but the most striking decline has been the slowdown in productivity growth.

14.4 Policies to Stimulate Growth

The government can influence all three of the determinants of growth—productivity, capital formation, and labour input. Disappointing rates of growth since the mid-1970s have led to a number of suggested policies to stimulate growth.

POLICIES TO IMPROVE PRODUCTIVITY

Of the three factors, productivity growth has fallen most significantly, and the idea of stimulating productivity has been attractive to policy makers. But there have been few proposals for concrete action. Unfortunately, the process of improvement in productivity growth is not well understood by economists.

Perhaps the most important role that the government can play in improving productivity growth is in the area of education. In Canada all levels of government provide support for primary and secondary schools and universities. A highly skilled labour force is obviously a key ingredient to successful productivity growth.

Many observers point to Canada's low spending on research and development (R&D) relative to countries like the United States and Japan when discussing Canadian productivity. And indeed Canadian R&D spending as a percentage of GDP declined in the years leading up to the start of the productivity slowdown in the mid-1970s although it has recovered since then. The importance of this factor in the productivity slowdown remains an open question, however. In a small and open economy productivity gains can be made through research conducted in other countries that results in new equipment or processes that Canadian firms can use. And it may be difficult for an economy such as Canada's to capture a large share of the gains that would accrue from any increased R&D conducted within its borders.

The federal government has used grant programs and tax incentives to try to encourage R&D in Canada. These programs have increased Canadian R&D spending somewhat but their effect on Canadian productivity growth is uncertain.

POLICIES TO STIMULATE CAPITAL FORMATION

Canadian governments have also used grants and the tax system to encourage capital formation. A rising capital stock will add to economic growth; our growth formula in the previous section made this clear. Numerically, an extra percentage point of capital growth will add about .3 percentage point to growth in output. To get an added 1 percent of growth in output, the capital stock would have to grow 3.3 percent per year.

Consider a numerical illustration. At the end of 1987, the capital stock was about $600 billion 1980 dollars, excluding housing. The 3.3 percent growth in capital needed to add a point to growth of output would be

3.3 percent times $600 billion = $20 billion in added investment (1981 dollars).

Total fixed investment in 1987 was $57 billion 1981 dollars. Investment would have to rise by $20/57 = 35$ percent to add just 1 percentage point to growth in output. Of course, 1 percent more growth would take us a long way to restoring the previous growth path that Canada experienced in the mid-1960s, and would compound itself to an impressive increase in living standards in 20 years. Moreover, it is possible that the increase in new plants and machines would bring forth additional technical innovations which could spur productivity growth.

Under the right combination of economic conditions, a large increase in investment is possible. For example, real investment spending rose 50 percent from 1978 to 1981. This occurred mainly because firms expected that large energy-related projects would be profitable. The investment tax credit was also increased from 5 to 7 percent in 1978. However, the importance of the tax change should not be overemphasised. Nothing like the investment boom of 1978–81 followed the introduction of the original investment tax credit in 1975.

Although an increase in investment of 35 percent is feasible, it does not appear to be sustainable. Output growth can be raised by a percentage point for a few years, but then investment tends to decline to more normal levels. For example, investment spending declined 17 percent in the two years after 1981 despite the tax credit. This decline formed a substantial part of the recession that took place at that time.

As we discussed in Chapter 9, the federal tax reform plan of 1987 phased out the investment tax credit and, although the corporate tax rate was also reduced, the overall effect is negative for the growth of total investment. On this account the recent tax reform is bad for economic growth. On the other hand, the tax reform eliminated some of the dispersion of tax rates in different industries and this should make the allocation of capital more efficient, thereby stimulating economic growth for a period of time.

Growth through Capital Formation

1. Because the coefficient of capital growth in the growth formula is about .3, it takes about 3.3 percent of growth in capital to add 1 percent to output growth.

2. In 1987, it would have taken a 35 percent increase in the amount of investment to raise the growth of the capital stock by 3.3 percent.

3. Increases of this magnitude in investment have occurred in the past, but only under very favourable conditions. Even then, the high levels of investment were sustained only for a few years.

POLICIES TO INCREASE LABOUR SUPPLY

In the growth equation, employment growth has over twice the leverage of capital growth. Each percentage point of extra growth of employment

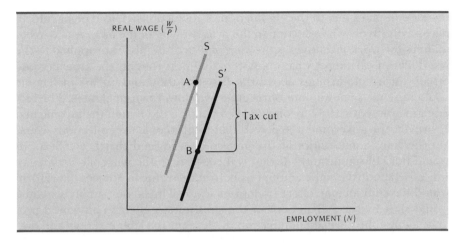

Figure 14–7.   SHIFT IN LABOUR SUPPLY FROM A TAX CUT.
A tax cut shifts the labour supply function downward in proportion to the cut. S is the labour supply schedule before the tax rate cut; A is an arbitrary point on it. S' is the supply schedule after the cut. B is a point on S' where the real wage after tax is the same as the real wage after tax on S. B is below A by the amount of the tax cut. The amount of labour supplied at B is the same as at A because the real wage received by workers is the same at B as at A. A downward shift in a schedule that is nearly vertical has almost no substantive effect.

adds .7 percent to output growth. To put it the other way around, it takes 1.4 percent of added employment growth to increase output growth by 1 percent per year. One of the main arguments put forward by tax reform advocates such as Arthur Laffer is that income tax cuts would increase work incentives.

The income tax depresses the incentive to work by reducing the wage that workers receive for their work. On this account, one might expect that a cut in income taxes would stimulate work by improving incentives. But a cut in income taxes also makes people better off, which depresses labour supply. The net effect of a simple tax cut could therefore be quite small. This is illustrated in Figure 14–7. If the labour supply curve is steep, as statistical evidence seems to suggest, the intersection of supply and demand occurs at almost the same level of employment. A prediction of large stimulus to employment and output from tax cuts would be contrary to the evidence.

Supply-side policies need not take the exclusive form of tax cuts. In fact, the federal government's need for revenue makes it impossible to improve work incentives dramatically by cutting taxes. Another type of supply-side policy is tax reform. A tax reform could be revenue-neutral—it could keep revenue the same although tax rates are cut. This could be done by eliminating deductions and lowering tax rates on earned income. Because revenue is the same, the typical taxpayer pays the same amount of tax and there is no income effect. The cut in taxes due to the lower tax rate is offset by the increase in taxes due to the elimination of deductions. This type of reform necessarily involves a reduction in the progressivity of the income tax. What matters for work incentives is the *marginal* tax rate, the rate applied to the last dollar of earnings. A flat tax system that puts roughly the same tax rate on all dollars of earnings above the first few thousand dollars of income could raise the same amount of revenue with lower marginal rates. The federal government's 1987 income tax reform plan did flatten the income tax. However, the government expected that total income tax collections would also decline. Some critics of the government argued that tax collections would not fall significantly. If that is the case then the personal income tax will raise about the same amount as before the reform. Hence, the reform would have no income effect to depress work. The labour supply schedule would shift by the full amount of the substitution effect. This would produce a one-time permanent effect on the level of the labour supply and output.

Growth through Increased Work Effort

1. The classical model provides a good way to analyse programs to stimulate growth through improved work incentives. However, the analysis applies only in the long run.

2. Because the labour supply schedule is nearly vertical, even a large tax cut has only a small effect on employment. The incentive effect of lower tax rates raises incentives to work, but the higher level of income depresses work.

3. If the tax change is a tax *reform*, which keeps tax receipts constant, rather than a tax *cut*, it improves incentives without changing average income. Then the incentive effects are not offset by income effects.

Classical Model

14.5 Fiscal, Monetary, and Exchange Rate Policy in a Full-Employment Economy

The aggregate demand side of the economy, as expressed in the IS-LM model, is relevant for an economy with perfectly flexible prices and wages, but the implications of the analysis are much different from a model with price rigidities. With price rigidities, aggregate demand—the consumption, investment, net export, and money demand relations—determines the level of output in the short run. With perfect price flexibility, output is determined purely by aggregate supply; aggregate demand determines the price level, the interest rate, the exchange rate, and the allocation of output between consumption, investment, government, and net exports.

We first touched on this result in Chapter 6, when we introduced gradual price adjustment. When prices adjust, actual GDP eventually moves towards potential GDP. After an increase in the money supply, the price level eventually increases by the same proportion. After an increase in government spending, the price level eventually rises by enough to completely crowd out investment. With perfectly flexible prices, all these adjustments take place *instantaneously*. The long-run results also apply in the short run. With perfectly flexible prices, output is always equal to its potential.

FISCAL POLICY IN THE CLASSICAL MODEL

An expansionary fiscal policy is one that stimulates spending. Because total spending always equals potential, an expansionary fiscal policy only drives up the interest rate; it has no effect on output. The only exception to this rule is a fiscal policy change that alters incentives in such a way as to change full-employment output. An example is the tax reform discussed in the previous section.

These effects are shown in Figure 14–8. Fiscal expansion moves the IS curve to the right. The price level rises, pushing the LM curve to the left and increasing the interest rate. We have already described how and to what extent the interest rate rises—by enough to depress total spending by the

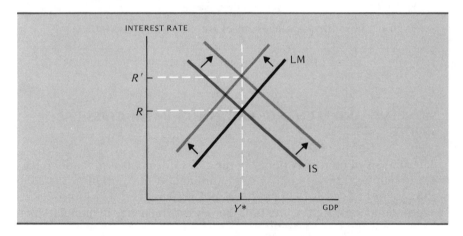

Figure 14–8. FISCAL EXPANSION IN THE CLASSICAL MODEL.
An expansionary move, such as an increase in government purchases, shifts the IS curve upward. But prices rise immediately, pushing up the LM curve. The interest rate rises so as to depress spending by the same amount that the fiscal stimulus raised it. Real output does not change. The intersection with the LM curve occurs at the higher interest rate (R') and at a higher price level. The price level rises because the higher interest rate depressed money demand; that is, the price level rises to offset the effect of the interest rate.

same amount that fiscal policy raised spending. This is what keeps output equal to potential. The amount of the increase in the price level depends on the *slope* of the LM curve.

Even though fiscal policy does not influence the level of real output on the demand side in the classical analysis, it has substantive economic effects on the interest rate, on the composition of output, and on the price level.

Because the classical model views the economy as always at full employment, fiscal policy would be unnecessary for stabilisation purposes. The motivation for a change in fiscal policy would always be to alter the composition of output, not to stabilise the total level of output.

Effects of Fiscal Policies with Flexible Prices

1. Increased government purchases of goods and services raise the interest rate and depress consumption, investment, and net exports. Private spending falls by exactly the amount that government purchases rise.

2. Income tax cuts raise consumption. The interest rate rises by enough to depress investment and net exports by the amount of the increase in consumption.

3. Investment incentives raise investment. The interest rate rises by enough to keep the sum of investment and net exports at its previous level.

4. Each of these three policies raises the price level as well.

MONETARY AND EXCHANGE RATE POLICY IN THE CLASSICAL MODEL

The analysis of monetary policy in the classical equilibrium model is particularly simple. Monetary policy cannot influence total output or the composition of output. Only the price level and exchange rate are affected by a change in monetary policy. The IS-LM analysis of a change in monetary policy is shown in Figure 14–9.

The monetary expansion has only two effects—to raise the price level and reduce the exchange rate. Nothing else in the economy changes. Because monetary policy does not influence output or employment, none of the agonising choices facing monetary policy makers in the real world exists in the classical model. Monetary policy can be given the simple task of keeping the price level at a certain prescribed level. As it does so, it will never interfere with the goal of full employment. Monetary policy is *neutral*.

Why does the exchange rate change during a monetary change in the

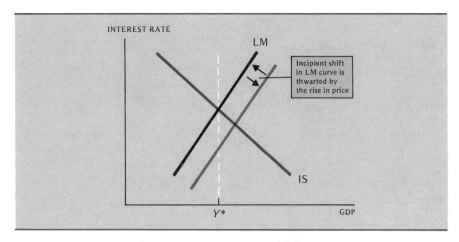

Figure 14–9. MONETARY EXPANSION IN THE CLASSICAL MODEL.
A monetary expansion shifts the LM curve to the right. But prices rise immediately and
push it back to the left. The net effect is zero. Not only is the total amount of output unaffected by the monetary expansion, but the composition of output among consumption,
investment, government, and net exports is unaffected by the move. The price level rises
in the same proportion as the increase in money.

classical model? In a classical world purchasing power parity would always
hold. That is, the U.S. dollar price of all tradeable goods would be equal
whether the goods were produced in Canada or the United States. If, for
example, Americans found that Canadian goods cost less to purchase than
U.S. goods, the resulting increase in demand for Canadian goods would
drive up the U.S. dollar price of Canadian goods immediately. Either the
Canadian dollar prices of Canadian goods would rise or the exchange rate
would rise, or both.

We will ignore non-tradeable goods for simplicity (the analysis with non-
tradeable goods is similar, but more complicated). We can write the fact that
the U.S. dollar price of all goods would be equal whether the goods were
produced in Canada or the United States in algebra as follows:

$$PE = P_u. \qquad (14\text{--}4)$$

We have already seen that an increase in the money supply would lead to a
proportional increase in the price level (P). Given a fixed value for the U.S.
price level (P_u), this implies that the exchange rate must depreciate so that
Equation 14–4 will hold.

We can use Equation 14–4 to analyse the implications of a fixed exchange
rate policy in a classical economy. Suppose that the IS curve is unchanging
and the foreign price level is fixed. We have shown that under these assumptions an increase in the money supply would increase the price level.
According to Equation 14–4, this would cause the exchange rate to depreciate. But this would violate the fixed exchange rate rule. Therefore, the
money supply cannot be changed under these conditions.

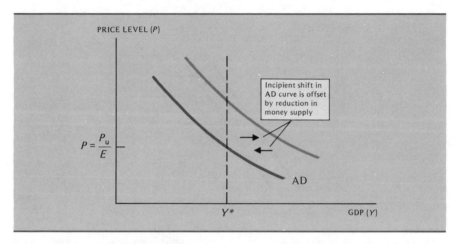

Figure 14–10. MONETARY REACTION TO A FISCAL EXPANSION IN A CLASSICAL MODEL UNDER A FIXED EXCHANGE RATE.
In the classical model the price level is given by the value that sets output equal to potential given the AD curve. A fiscal expansion would tend to shift the AD curve, raising the price level. In order to prevent the price increase, which would cause the exchange rate to fall, the money supply must be reduced so that the AD curve returns to its original position.

The money supply would be changed under a fixed exchange rate under two circumstances. First, suppose there was a fiscal expansion that would shift out the AD curve. This would increase the price level, as discussed above. But to fix the exchange rate when the foreign price level is unchanged the domestic price level must also be held constant. This would require a monetary contraction, as shown in Figure 14–10.

The other situation in which the money supply would change under a fixed exchange rate in a classical model is if the foreign price level changed. Suppose that the foreign price level increased. In that case the domestic price level must also increase so that Equation 14–4 will hold without a change in the exchange rate (E). To raise the price level the monetary authority would increase the money supply, shifting the AD curve up, as shown in Figure 14–11. Thus the potential problem of 'importing inflation' under a fixed exchange rate also occurs in the classical model. If we fix our exchange rate with the United States, we must expect to have roughly the same inflation experience as the United States in the long run.

Monetary and Exchange Rate Policy in a Classical Economy

1. A change in the money supply will affect the price level and the nominal exchange rate, but no other variables.

2. Under a flexible exchange rate a monetary expansion will cause an increase in the price level and a fall in the nominal exchange rate.

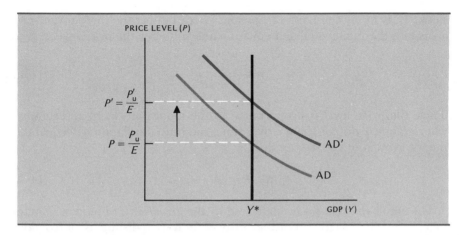

Figure 14–11.   EFFECT OF AN INCREASE IN FOREIGN PRICES ON A CLASSICAL ECONOMY WITH A FIXED EXCHANGE RATE.
To keep the exchange rate from changing when foreign prices rise the monetary authority must cause domestic prices to rise by increasing the money supply.

---

3. Under a fixed exchange rate the money supply can only be changed in response to a shift in the IS curve or a change in the foreign price level.

14.6 Long-Run Output Growth and Inflation

We have just seen that increases in money raise the price level with no effect on output or the interest rate in the classical model. Does it follow that continual increases in the money supply—say 5 percent per year, year after year—will continually increase the price level, year after year, without affecting output? In other words, does a higher rate of growth of the money supply merely lead to a higher inflation rate without affecting the growth of output? For the IS-LM model with perfectly flexible prices, the answer is clearly yes. A succession of years can be analysed simply by piecing together the results from each year.

Recall the algebraic form of the money demand function from Chapter 5:

$$\frac{M}{P} = kY - hR, \tag{14-5}$$

where k and h are constant coefficients. With flexible prices, the two variables on the right-hand side of the money demand function are determined outside the money market: The interest rate, R, is set by spending balance, and the level of real GDP, Y, is set by aggregate supply. Moreover, the money stock, M, is set by the Bank of Canada. We can insert the three given variables into the money demand equation and solve for the price level:

$$P = \frac{M}{kY - hR}. \tag{14-6}$$

Thus, the price level is proportional to the money stock. In an economy where R and Y do not change over time, the rate of inflation will equal the rate of growth of the money stock:

$$\Delta P/P = \Delta M/M. \tag{14-7}$$

The result that output is unaffected by the *growth rate* of money is sometimes referred to as the **superneutrality of money,** to distinguish it from the notion of neutrality that we discussed in Section 14.5. It is a property of the classical model, but, to the extent that the classical model represents the real world in the long run, it is a result that should apply in reality in the long run.

There are several reasons why superneutrality may not hold in the real world—even in the long run. First, the tax system might not be superneutral. For example, firms can deduct interest payments from their taxes. But nominal interest rates and therefore interest payments rise with inflation, giving firms a tax break. This lowers the rental price of capital.

Second, a higher rate of inflation makes it more attractive for people to hold real capital—factories, houses, trucks—compared to currency or non–interest–bearing deposits. This tends to increase the amount of real capital in the economy, and thereby increase aggregate supply. James Tobin of Yale University and Robert Mundell of Columbia University have emphasised this departure from superneutrality.

Third, in practice, high inflation rates are usually accompanied by *fluctuations* in inflation from year to year, and in fluctuations in relative prices. The relationship between the level and the variability of inflation is illustrated in Figure 14–12. These fluctuations in inflation make business planning difficult and could lead to inefficiencies in the production process. If so, then aggregate supply will be reduced. This negative effect of inflation on real output was emphasised by Milton Friedman in the address he gave when accepting the Nobel Prize in 1976.

A final reason that inflation might reduce real output is that it makes holding currency and reserves very costly. This creates inefficiencies in the monetary system and could reduce productive efficiency. Because currency and reserves do not pay interest, people will try to economise on them when inflation and interest rates rise. Economising on currency and reserves requires using time (trips to the bank) or resources (computers that automatically transfer funds from checking to savings accounts) that could be put to more productive or enjoyable use. In countries with extremely high inflation rates people spend much time just completing transactions. In extreme cases people begin to use foreign currencies—as in Israel in the inflation of

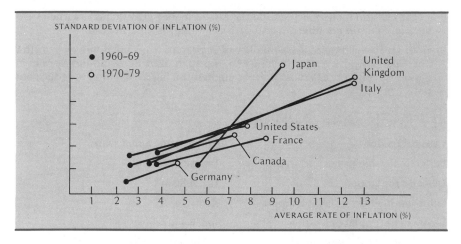

Figure 14–12. INFLATION AND FLUCTUATIONS IN INFLATION FOR SEVEN COUNTRIES.
The chart shows the year-to-year variability of inflation on the vertical axis and the average rate of inflation on the horizontal axis. As inflation increased in all seven countries the variability also increased. The standard deviation is a measure of variability with the property that about two-thirds of the observations are within a band of plus or minus one standard deviation.

the early 1980s. If they can't use alternative means of payment, then the monetary system may break down as in the hyperinflations in Eastern Europe in the 1920s.

Review and Practice

MAJOR POINTS

1. The classical model is one in which prices and wages are perfectly flexible. The economy is always operating at full employment in the classical model.

2. Even when the economy is operating at potential, there is some unemployment. This level of unemployment is called the natural rate.

3. The natural rate of unemployment has probably increased during the last 25 years.

4. Monetary policy only affects the price level and the nominal exchange rate in the classical model. Money is neutral. The levels of employment and real output are determined by aggregate supply.

5. At any one time, when the capital stock is predetermined, aggregate supply is determined in the labour market. Employment is given by the equality of labour demand and labour supply.

6. Over the longer run the capital stock grows as investment accumulates and this further increases aggregate supply.

7. During the last 25 years the decline in the rate of total factor productivity growth has been largely responsible for the decline in real output growth.

8. In the classical model, increases in the rate of money growth increase the rate of inflation, but do not affect output growth. Money is superneutral.

9. In the real world there are a number of reasons to expect that money growth is not superneutral, even in the long run. Taxation distortions and increases in inflation variability are two factors that might cause higher inflation to reduce output.

KEY TERMS AND CONCEPTS

Classical model

Perfectly flexible prices and wages

Demand for labour

Substitution effect in labour supply

Income effect in labour supply

Labour market equilibrium

Natural rate of unemployment

Sources of economic growth

Labour and capital share

Tax rate cut

Tax reform

Neutrality

Superneutrality

Inflation variability

Tax distortions from inflation

Total factor productivity

QUESTIONS FOR DISCUSSION AND REVIEW

1. Why is the demand for labour a negative function of the real wage?

2. Explain why microeconomic theory predicts that for labour supply the income effect is negative and the substitution effect is positive. What do empirical studies indicate about the sum of these two effects?

3. Explain why the classical model predicts that the level of real GDP in any one year is determined solely in the labour market. What would happen to the real wage, the price level, and the nominal wage if the money supply was increased?

4. Describe how economists measure the natural rate of unemployment. Did the natural rate of unemployment increase or decrease from the early 1960s through the early 1980s? Why?

5. Explain the difference between labour productivity and total factor productivity.

6. Does an increase in the rate of growth of labour add more or less to the growth rate of output than the same size increase in the rate of growth of capital? Explain why.

7. Describe three different policies that could be used to increase the growth rate of potential GDP. Identify whether the policy is aimed at productivity, capital formation, or labour supply.

8. Does fiscal policy completely crowd out private spending in the classical model? Explain.

9. Give three reasons why a change in the growth rate of money might affect potential GDP.

10. What determines the price level in a classical economy with a fixed exchange rate if world prices are fixed?

11. What determines the price level in a classical economy with a floating exchange rate?

PROBLEMS

Numerical

1. Consider the following two tax schedules (the same schedules used in Numerical Problem 1 of Chapter 13):

Income Bracket	Marginal Tax Rate	
	Progressive	Flat
$0–$9,999	0	0
$10,000–$29,999	.2	.25
$30,000–$49,999	.4	.25
$50,000 and above	.6	.25

   a. Calculate the taxes paid by someone earning $20,000, $30,000, and $40,000 under each schedule. For each salary level, indicate whether the income effect of changing to a flat tax will increase or decrease labour supply.

   b. Describe the effect that the flat tax will have on the marginal tax rate for each salary level in Part a. Again, indicate for each salary level whether the labour supply will increase or decrease due to the substitution effect.

   c. For each of these salary levels, indicate whether the supply of labour will increase, decrease, or whether it is ambiguous. Give the economic intuition behind your result in each case.

   d. Explain why tax payments from workers currently earning $30,000 will unambiguously increase under the flat tax. Is the same true for workers earning $20,000 and $40,000? Why or why not?

2. Assume that over a 10-year period the growth rate of capital is 4 percent, the growth of employment is 2 percent, and the growth rate of real output is 5 percent. Calculate the growth rate of total factor productivity. Suppose that a permanent cut in the budget deficit increases investment, and the growth rate of capital rises by 1 percent. How much does the growth rate of output increase? Suppose that a tax reduction increases the supply of labour by 1 percent in one year. What happens to the growth rate of real output?

3. Suppose that the production function takes the special form $Y = AN^{.7}K^{.3}$. By taking logarithms and first differences of this production function show that the growth formula is satisfied. (If you have had calculus, calculate the marginal products of labour and capital. Derive the labour demand function. Calculate the labour share and the capital share.)

4. Suppose that the equations in Numerical Problem 1 of Chapter 11 (p. 309) refer to a small classical open economy in which the price level P is perfectly flexible, Y is always equal to potential output, and $Y^* = \$4,000$ billion. Calculate what happens when government spending G increases by $10 billion. How do your results compare with the long-run results in Numerical Problem 2 of Chapter 11?

Analytical

1. In a model with perfectly flexible prices, explain why inflation depends only on current spending shocks and not on past spending shocks. Is the same true of the models of sticky prices developed in Part I? Compare the predictions of the model of flexible prices and the model of sticky prices with respect to the persistence of inflation. In which model does inflation tend to change slowly over time? In which model can inflation jump from low to high or positive to negative from one period to the next?

2. In the text it was suggested that the income tax reform plan of 1987 may have no income effect. If so, what effect would the reform have on the total amount of income taxes paid?

3. Consider a tax reform package that contains positive incentives for labour supply and negative incentives for investment. Assume that prices are perfectly flexible.
   a. Suppose that such reform is unanticipated. How do output, prices, and the interest rate in the first year of the tax reform compare with what they would have been without tax reform? Is investment unambiguously reduced?
   b. Suppose such legislation was announced a year in advance. Describe its impact on output, prices, the interest rate, and investment in the year of the announcement and in the implementation year.
   c. Suppose that $K^* = .5WY/R^K$ as in Chapter 9, where W is the real wage. Describe the factors that determine investment in the long run and how such reform affects these factors.

4. Suppose that there is a reduction in investment incentives in an economy with perfectly flexible prices.
   a. Show what happens to the aggregate demand curve.
   b. Show what happens to the IS and LM curves.
   c. Assume that neither consumption nor net exports varies with the interest rate. Does investment fall? Why or why not?
   d. Now assume that net exports vary negatively with the interest rate. What happens to investment?

5. Consider a model with perfectly flexible wages and prices. Suppose that the real wage W/P is fixed because labour contracts are perfectly tied to the price level. In other words, whenever the price level P rises by 1 percent the nominal wage W rises by 1 percent as well, so that the real wage W/P stays fixed. Labour contracts of this type are called 'indexed' contracts. Draw a labour supply-demand diagram in which the fixed real wage is greater than the point of interaction of the labour supply and labour demand curves.
   a. Indicate the amount of excess supply of labour on the diagram. Does this excess supply measure the total amount of unemployment in the economy?
   b. Explain what happens in this setup if the central bank increases the growth rate of money supply. What happens to the excess supply of labour? What happens to inflation?

6. Using an IS-LM diagram, illustrate how a change in the mix of monetary and fiscal policy can be used to lower the interest rate without affecting the price level. Why would policy makers be interested in changing the mix in this way?

7. Describe what happens in a small classical open economy with a fixed exchange rate when the price level abroad falls. Illustrate your answer with an IS-LM diagram.

8. In Section 5 of Chapter 12 we discussed different policy rules for the Bank of Canada. There we used a model with sticky prices. Here we want to consider the effect of such rules in an economy with flexible prices.
   a. Compare the effects of IS and LM shocks in an economy with sticky prices with the effects of such shocks in an economy with flexible prices, assuming that the Bank of Canada targets the money supply.
   b. Explain why an interest rate target is, in general, infeasible in an economy with flexible prices. Is the same thing true in the long run in an economy with sticky prices?
   c. Discuss the use of an output target in an economy with flexible prices.
   d. How would the monetary authorities implement a fixed exchange rate policy (exchange rate target) in a classical economy? How does this differ from the case where prices are sticky?

9. Here we examine another of the Bank of Canada's policy options in an economy with flexible prices: targeting the price level.
   a. Diagram what happens to the IS and LM curves in the event of an IS shock, assuming the Bank of Canada does nothing.
   b. Now suppose the Bank of Canada wants to reestablish the initial price level. Show how it should move the LM curve.
   c. Diagram the IS shock and the Bank's response on an aggregate demand graph.
   d. Does the Bank's policy of targeting the price level affect C, X, or I? If so, explain why. If not, can you relate this result to the neutrality of money in an economy with flexible prices?

10. Suppose that there is a sudden reduction in total factor productivity.
   a. Describe what happens to output, the marginal product of capital, the optimal capital stock, and investment demand in the year of the productivity shock.
   b. Is the shock inflationary, deflationary, or is it not possible to tell?

Appendix A: Deriving the Growth Formula

Suppose that A, N, and K grow by rates $\Delta A/A$, $\Delta N/N$, and $\Delta K/K$. We will derive a formula for the growth rate of output, $\Delta Y/Y$. First, we approximate the growth rate of output using the production function of Equation 14–2:

$$\Delta Y/Y = \Delta A/A + \Delta F(N, K)/F(N, K). \tag{14–8}$$

In other words, the growth rate of the *product* of A and $F(N,K)$ is the *sum* of the growth rates of A and $F(N,K)$.

Second, the part of the change in output that comes from changes in employment and capital can be further broken down using the marginal products of the two. Let M_N be the marginal product of labour and M_K be the marginal product of capital. Then

$$\Delta F(N,K)/F(N,K) = M_N \Delta N/Y + M_K \Delta K/Y. \tag{14–9}$$

In words this expression states that the proportional change in F can be divided up into two components that measure the contributions of the proportional changes in N and K. (If you have had calculus, this formula can be derived by taking the total derivative of F and dividing by Y.) Putting this into the formula for $\Delta Y/Y$ we get

$$\Delta Y/Y = \Delta A/A + M_N \Delta N/Y + M_K \Delta K/Y. \tag{14–10}$$

If firms are using labour and capital up to the points where their marginal products are equal to the real wage and real rental prices, then

$$M_N = W/P \text{ and } M_K = R^K/P. \tag{14–11}$$

Now the formula is

$$\Delta Y/Y = \Delta A/A + (W/P)\Delta N/Y + (R^K/P)\Delta K/Y. \tag{14–12}$$

We can rewrite this as

$$\Delta Y/Y = \Delta A/A + (WN/PY)\Delta N/N + (R^K K/PY)\Delta K. \tag{14–13}$$

WN/PY is the fraction of revenue, PY, paid out to labour in the form of compensation, WN. Similarly, $R^K K/PY$ is the fraction of revenue earned by capital. From the national income accounts, we find that these fractions are about .7 and .3. Thus,

$$\Delta Y/Y = \Delta A/A + .7\Delta N/N + .3\Delta K/K,$$

which is the growth formula (Equation 14–3).

Appendix B: The Algebra of Rational Expectations in the Classical IS-LM Model

The IS-LM model with perfectly flexible prices is a convenient framework for illustrating some of the techniques economists use for rational expectations analysis. It is convenient because the effects of changes in money are so simple—only the price level changes. In a more complete model the effects of changes in money on real output and the real interest rate have to be taken into account. Here we show algebraically how the classical model works when expectations are rational.

Where do expectations enter the IS-LM model with perfectly flexible prices? In the difference between the real and the nominal rates of interest. That is, in the **expected rate of inflation.** Suppose that the demand for money takes the form:

$$M_t = hY - k(R + P_{t+1} - P_t) + P_t, \tag{14–14}$$

where the symbols are defined as usual. The term $R + P_{t+1} - P_t$, that is, the real rate of interest plus the expected rate of inflation, is the nominal rate of interest. (Note that inflation is usually defined as the *percentage* change in the price rather than the actual change; this is an approximation that works fairly well for low to moderate inflation rates.) Equation 14–14 is a standard money demand relationship, in which we have emphasised how the nominal interest rate depends on the expected inflation rate. During year t, people do not know what the value of the price level will be in the following year, P_{t+1}; they must therefore form expectations of P_{t+1}. The rational expectations approach is to assume that people have a fairly good idea about how the economy works when they form these expectations of the future.

The classical model works in such a way that M_t affects the price level P_t, but not output Y or the interest rate R. To emphasise this, rearrange the symbols in Equation 14–14 to get

$$P_t = nP_{t+1} + M_t/(k + 1) - g, \tag{14–15}$$

where $g = (hY - kR)/(1+k)$ and $n = k/(1+k)$. The last term on the right of Equation 14–15—represented by the symbol g—depends only on the real interest rate and real output. It is therefore independent of monetary policy in the classical model; it can be treated as if it were a constant. For simplicity let's assume that this term is zero. That is, set $g = 0$. This simplifying assumption makes no difference for the points illustrated here. The remaining terms contain the money supply, the price level, and the expected price level next year. The entire relationship between money and prices in the classical model is thus contained in this formula.

Note that if we knew the expectation of next year's price level it would be straightforward to determine the effect of the money supply on this year's price. For example, if P_{t+1} equals 1, then an increase in M_t of 1 unit would increase P_t by $1/(1+k)$ units. However, next period's price is not known and people must forecast it using the information that they have about how the classical model works. This information is reflected in Equation 14–15. People who literally understand Equation

14–15 will try to forecast P_{t+1} using Equation 14–15. They could do this by looking forward using the same equation but applying it to the next year. That is,

$$P_{t+1} = nP_{t+2} + M_{t+1}/(k+1) \qquad (14\text{--}16)$$

where we have simply added 1 to each subscript to give the next year. Note that we have set $g = 0$. This equation could be used to forecast P_{t+1} except for the fact that it now depends on P_{t+2}, which is unknown. But this unknown could be handled by leading Equation 14–16 one more period; that is,

$$P_{t+2} = nP_{t+3} + M_{t+2}/(k+1). \qquad (14\text{--}17)$$

Clearly this same idea can be used again and again with forecasts of prices being pushed further and further into the future.

By successive substitution, the three previous equations can be combined to get

$$P_t = \underbrace{n^3 P_{t+3}}_{\substack{\text{future price} \\ \text{level}}} + [1/(1+k)] \, [\underbrace{M_t}_{\substack{\text{this year's} \\ \text{money}}} + \underbrace{nM_{t+1} + n^2 M_{t+2}}_{\substack{\text{money in two} \\ \text{future years}}}] \qquad (14\text{--}18)$$

which shows how this year's price depends on the expectations of the money supply in future years plus an expectation of the price level in the future. This process of successive substitution can be continued for an arbitrary number of periods, but eventually the coefficient that multiplies the future price level will get very small and can be ignored.[4] This coefficient is $n = k/(k+1)$ multiplied by itself many times. Since $k/(k+1)$ is less than 1, this coefficient will be small. Thus, eventually we will be left with an expression for the price level of the form

$$P_t = [1/(1+k)] \, [\underbrace{M_t}_{\substack{\text{this} \\ \text{year's} \\ \text{money}}} + \underbrace{nM_{t+1} + n^2 M_{t+2} + n^3 M_{t+3} + \ldots}_{\substack{\text{money in all} \\ \text{future years}}}]. \qquad (14\text{--}19)$$

Equation 14–19 is a relationship that shows how the price level depends on the money supply. It looks messy, but its message is quite simple. It says that the price level depends on the money supply this year, *and* on the anticipated money supply many years in the future. Of course the importance of future money supplies diminishes as we go further into the future. This dependence of the price level on anticipated future values of the money supply is a fundamental feature of rational expectations.

What does Equation 14–19 tell us about the effect of changes in money on the price level? Two cases need to be distinguished: a temporary and a permanent increase in money. Suppose that the money supply increases by one unit. If the increase in money is permanent, then Equation 14–19 tells us that the price level will increase by the same amount as the increase in money. This is because the coefficients on the M terms in Equation 14–19 sum to 1. On the other hand, if the in-

---

[4] There is a subtle issue here that macroeconomists have been hotly debating since rational expectations was introduced. The future price term can be ignored only if the price level is not exploding exponentially. But there is nothing in the model itself to rule out such a 'speculative bubble.' Some macroeconomists have attempted to test for the existence of such bubbles in price data. See Robert Flood and Peter Garber, 'Market Fundamentals versus Price-Level Bubbles: First Test,' *Journal of Political Economy,* Vol. 88 (October 1980), pp. 745–770. Others have focused on bubbles as potentially important parts of the workings of models. See Olivier Blanchard and Mark Watson, 'Bubbles, Rational Expectations, and Financial Markets,' NBER Working Paper No. 945, Cambridge, Mass., 1982.

crease in money is temporary, for 1 year only, then the price level only increases by $1/(1+k)$—the coefficient of M_t in Equation 14–19. This increase may be substantially less than 1. For example, if $k = 4$, then the temporary increase in money increases the price level by only 20 percent of the amount that it increases when the money change is permanent. The rational expectations of future behaviour of money growth can be quite important quantitatively.

What happens if the money supply is anticipated to increase temporarily 2 years from now? Then, according to Equation 14–19, the price level will increase by $[1/(1+k)] [k/(1+k)]^2$ today. The mere anticipation of a future money increase can have effects today.

While the classical model is a convenient framework for illustrating the algebra that lies behind rational expectations it also gives us a simple way to make some actual computations. Macroeconomists use these same algebraic techniques in more complete models with price and wage rigidities. Because output, prices, and real interest rates respond to changes in money in such models, the technical analysis is somewhat more involved.

15

New Classical Theory

THE WORLD appears to behave much differently from the predictions of the classical model with perfectly flexible wages and prices that we discussed in the previous chapter. GDP is not always equal to potential GDP. The evidence we examined in Chapter 1 indicates that actual GDP frequently departs from its normal level. The departures do not last forever; eventually actual GDP returns to its potential. In the longer run, the classical model of Chapter 14 does appear to be a good description of how the economy works. But the classical model has problems explaining the short-run economic fluctuations that constitute the study of macroeconomics. The model lacks features that explain why output departs from potential for prolonged periods.

There is another important feature of economic fluctuations that is missing from the classical model: the behaviour of prices. There is a general tendency for prices to gradually rise when GDP is above potential and to fall when GDP is below potential. The movement of prices sometimes lags behind real GDP, and sometimes outside price shocks like higher oil prices mask the correlation. In times of significant inflation, the price-GDP correlation can be detected only by looking at the inflation rate—not at the price level. If inflation is high, a decline in real GDP will bring about a decline in the inflation rate—the rate of change in the price level. No absolute decline in the price level will be observed. For example, during the decline in real GDP relative to potential GDP in the early 1980s, the price level—the GDP deflator—did not fall. However, the rate of inflation declined markedly. Before the Second World War, on the other hand, actual declines in the price level were sometimes observed.

This chapter and the next take up theories of the persistent departures of

GDP from potential and of the tendency for prices or inflation to rise in booms and fall in slumps. In this chapter we look at theories that maintain the flexible price-wage assumption of the classical model, but that differ from the classical model by incorporating *information problems* that may exist in the economy. These theories bear the name **new classical**, because they maintain the basic classical assumptions of flexible prices and wages. In the next chapter we look at theories based on price and wage rigidities—the explanation of macroeconomic fluctuations that underlies the basic model of this book.

15.1 Real Business-Cycle Theories

Before incorporating informational factors into the classical model, let's ask in what way the pure classical model does not appear to be capable of explaining economic fluctuations. In Chapter 14, we suggested that the classical model describes an economy that grows smoothly and never experiences recessions and booms. But the basic logic of the neoclassical model does not rule out short-run fluctuations in output. After all, potential GDP—or aggregate supply—could fluctuate. The prolonged deviations of unemployment from the natural rate might represent the optimal response of labour supply to such fluctuations in potential. Explanations of economic fluctuations that rely on fluctuations in aggregate supply are called **real business-cycle** theories, to distinguish them from other theories that emphasise monetary factors and shifts in aggregate demand. Finn Kydland of Carnegie-Mellon University and Edward Prescott of the University of Minnesota have argued that real business-cycle models provide a good explanation of economic fluctuations.[1] As we saw in Chapter 14, the level of employment in the classical model is determined in the labour market at the intersection of the supply and demand functions for labour (Figure 14–5). What might make the level of employment fall, as it does in every recession? There are only two answers: Either the *demand* schedule shifts downward or the *supply* schedule shifts downward.

SHIFTS IN LABOUR DEMAND

The demand schedule for labour shows the marginal product of labour for each level of employment. If the schedule shifts downward, it means that the marginal product of labour is lower at a given level of employment.

---

[1] See, for example, their paper: 'A Competitive Theory of Fluctuations and the Feasibility and Desirability of Stabilization Policy,' in Stanley Fischer (ed.), *Rational Expectations and Economic Policy,* University of Chicago Press for the National Bureau of Economic Research, 1980. Robert King and Charles Plosser have emphasised real theories in 'Money, Credit and Prices in a Real Business Cycle,' *American Economic Review,* Vol. 74 (June 1984), pp. 363–380.

That is, for the demand function to shift downward, the productivity of labour has to fall. It is hard to think of recurrent events that make all workers throughout the economy less productive for prolonged periods of time and then gradually become productive again. For example, one is hard put to identify a technological reason for a downward shift in productivity in 1981 and 1982 when Canadian output and employment fell in that recession. Models that emphasise aggregate demand would point to the behaviour of the Bank of Canada in fighting inflation. But some events do bring about shifts in productivity. For example, an increase in the price of oil will make firms use less oil and may therefore reduce the marginal productivity of labour. Most frequently, however, productivity shifts seem to influence only one sector—say the demand for Canadian auto workers drops because the Japanese have made sudden improvements in their cars. Or labour demand in oil-producing regions of Canada falls when the price of oil falls as in 1985–86. For events to influence all sectors, there must be some relationship between sectors. An example suggested by Edward Prescott is that business schools could start teaching a new productivity-increasing management technique that quickly becomes known throughout the economy.

Moreover, in order for a shift in labour demand to cause a noticeable change in employment in the classical model, it is necessary for the labour supply schedule to be reasonably sensitive to changes in the real wage. Recall that, as long as the labour supply schedule is not perfectly vertical, when labour demand shifts down employment falls. But employment wouldn't fall at all if the labour supply schedule were vertical, as in Figure 15–1. A good theory of recessions and booms within the neoclassical model has to show that labour supply is reasonably sensitive to the real wage. Some real business-cycle economists have suggested that labour supply is quite elastic in the short run, even though people will not raise or lower their volume of

Figure 15–1.   DECLINE IN LABOUR DEMAND WITH INELASTIC LABOUR SUPPLY.
The labour demand schedule shifts downward. Because the labour supply schedule is vertical—insensitive to changes in the real wage—employment does not fall.

work very much in the long run in response to permanent changes in real wages.

Another way to explain the large labour supply responses is to assume, realistically, that households must supply labour in an 'all-or-nothing' fashion (0 or 8 hours per day). Gary Hansen of the University of California, Santa Barbara, and Richard Rogerson of the University of Rochester have shown that such an assumption may help to explain high employment variability.[2]

SHIFTS IN LABOUR SUPPLY

The second way that the classical model could explain fluctuations is through shifts in labour supply. If some outside factor makes people want to work more hours, then the economy will move down and to the right along the labour demand schedule and employment will rise. One outside factor identified by the economists favouring this interpretation of the business cycle is the real interest rate. As we discussed in Chapter 8, when the real interest rate is high, people will seek to work more hours (at the same real wage) than they would at a lower real interest rate. A high real rate makes it attractive to work more now and consume later, because the saved earnings will be augmented by the high real rate. Thus the labour supply curve—drawn as a function of the real wage—shifts out.

Many macroeconomists are skeptical of both versions of the real business-cycle model of recessions and booms. They question whether shifts in labour demand are large and persistent enough to explain economic fluctuations and whether the labour supply schedule is sufficiently sensitive to the real wage. They also question whether the shift in labour supply associated with changing real interest rates is big enough to explain the large movements in employment that occur over the business cycle.[3]

15.2 Imperfect Information: The New Classical Theory

An important modern view of fluctuations sees them as the outcome of people not being fully informed about what is happening in the economy. These **information-based models** attempt to explain the departures of ac-

---

[2] See Gary Hansen, 'Indivisible Labor and the Business Cycle,' *Journal of Monetary Economics,* November 1985, pp. 309–328, and Richard Rogerson, 'Indivisible Labor, Lotteries, and the Business Cycle,' Unpublished paper, 1985. For a recent survey of microeconomic empirical work on intertemporal substitution in labour supply see Orley Ashenfelter, 'Macroeconomic Analysis and Microeconomic Analysis of Labor Supply,' *Carnegie-Rochester Series on Public Policy,* Vol. 21, pp. 117–156, 1985 (North Holland).

[3] See, for example, the comments of Martin Feldstein on Finn Kydland and Edward Prescott in Stanley Fischer (ed.), *Rational Expectations and Economic Policy,* University of Chicago Press for the National Bureau of Economic Research, 1980, pp. 187–189, or Lawrence H. Summers, 'Some Skeptical Observations on Real Business Cycle Theory,' *Federal Reserve Bank of Minneapolis Review,* Fall 1986, pp. 23–27.

tual GDP from potential GDP using the microeconomic theory of firm supply. Prices and wages are assumed to be flexible in these models. The positive relation between price and output is attributed to movements along firms' supply curves. The original research establishing the information-based model was done by Robert Lucas of the University of Chicago. The resulting positive relationship between prices and output is usually called the **Lucas supply curve.**[4]

The role of information is very important in these models. According to microeconomic theory, a firm produces up to the point where its *price equals marginal cost.* Marginal cost depends on the price of the firm's inputs to production. If the price of the firm's output rises *relative* to the price of other goods in the economy, including its inputs, then the firm will produce more. However, if all other prices rise by the same amount that the firm's output price rises, then there will be no incentive for the firm to produce more. In other words, the firm will produce more only if the price of its output rises relative to some other prices in the economy—in particular, its input prices. Yet when the *general* price level rises, as it does in booms, there is not necessarily any change in relative prices. Hence, the firm's output price will not rise relative to its input price. So how do we explain the boom that usually occurs when the general price level rises?

Something must be added to the model to generate the price-output relation that we know is an important characteristic of the departures of GDP from potential. The addition is an assumption about the information available to different firms. This information assumption is what provides a connection between general price movements and the supply decisions of firms. Lucas refers to the model as being 'rigged' by these information assumptions.[5]

THE FIRM'S INFORMATION ABOUT THE PRICE LEVEL

Firms are assumed to have difficulty getting information about prices in the economy other than their own output price. There are temporary information barriers through which firms cannot see what is going on in other markets. Put another way, firms specialise in monitoring conditions in their own market. They know very quickly when demand drops off, and prices begin to fall. On the other hand, they are relatively uninformed about developments in other markets and learn relatively slowly what is happening in these other markets.

Some algebra and graphs will help to explain how this works. We will use the subscript i to represent an individual firm. The representative firm's

[4] See Robert E. Lucas, Jr., 'Some International Evidence on Output Inflation Trade-offs,' *American Economic Review,* Vol. 63, pp. 326–334, 1973.

[5] See Robert E. Lucas, Jr., 'Tobin and Monetarism: A Review Article,' *Journal of Economic Literature,* Vol. 19, pp. 558–567, 1982.

supply curve is given by

$$Y_i = h(P_i - P) + Y_i^*,\qquad\qquad(15\text{--}1)$$

where Y_i is the firm's production, P_i is the firm's price, P is the aggregate price, and Y_i^* is the firm's potential or normal production. In words the equation says that the firm's output Y_i is greater than the normal Y_i^* by an amount equal to a constant h times the difference between the firm's price P_i and the general price level P. We enter the general price level into the supply curve as an indicator of the prices in all other markets. As we described above, the firm will supply more output only if its price rises relative to these other prices. The supply curve is upward sloping ($h > 0$) in terms of the difference between P_i and P, and is shown graphically in Figure 15–2.

Note that, if the price of the firm's product rises by the same amount as the overall price level, there will be no change in the firm's supply, according to the supply equation. The firm will see that, although it can receive more for its output, the prices of all other items in the economy have increased by the same amount. Hence, in relative terms there has been no change.

Suppose, however, that the firm did not know what was going on in other markets in the economy. The information about the rest of the economy could arrive late, or the managers of the firm might not have the time to monitor economic conditions throughout the economy. Suppose, further, that each firm is on an island, so to speak, where instantaneous communication among islands is not possible.[6] When information is restricted in this way, firms will not know the prices of other commodities in the economy, even if they are perfectly rational in their forecasts. Hence, they do not know the aggregate price level; they have to guess it. We therefore rewrite Equation 15–1 to reflect this fact:

$$Y_i = h(P_i - P^e) + Y_i^*.\qquad\qquad(15\text{--}2)$$

The superscript e on the P indicates the firm's *estimate* of the overall price level. We simply have replaced P by P^e in changing Equation 15–1 into Equation 15–2.

Now consider again the case where all prices in the economy rise by the same amount. Each firm will observe only the increase in price of its own product, and will have to make a guess about all the other prices as summarised in the index P. If the firm does not adjust its guess of P, then it will clearly produce more. The firm thinks that its own relative price has increased. If the other firms in the economy behave the same way, then they

---

[6] In describing one of the early information-based models, Edmund S. Phelps of Columbia University used the island analogy. The imaginary islands are sometimes called Phelpsian islands. See his edited volume *Microeconomic Foundations of Employment and Inflation*, W. W. Norton, New York, 1970, pp. 1–26.

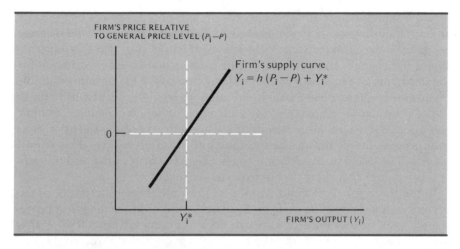

Figure 15-2. THE FIRM'S SUPPLY CURVE.
The firm's supply decision depends on its own price relative to the general level of prices in the economy. If P_i and P rise in the same proportion, then Y_i does not change.

could all produce more as a result of the general increase in prices. In this way, all the firms in the economy would mistake the general price rise for an increase in their own price. With all firms producing more than their potential Y_i^*, output in the economy as a whole will surely be above potential. Hence, we have an explanation of a departure of real GDP from potential GDP, based on the confusion within individual firms about what is going on elsewhere in the economy.

THE FIRM'S INFORMATION ABOUT THE PRICE LEVEL: A MORE SOPHISTICATED VIEW

In the explanation given above, firms do not change their expectations of the aggregate price level when they observe the prices of their own products. In an economic environment where there is a close relationship between economic activity in different industries, a firm would be naive not to guess that other firms in the economy were having the same type of experience. In other words, the observation that the price is high in one firm's market is an indication to that firm that prices are likely to be high in other markets. This would be especially true in a highly inflationary economy, where an increase in the price of one commodity is usually only an indication that inflation is continuing: The price of everything is going up, too.

Consider, first, an extreme case where economic conditions are such that relative prices of different products never change; that is, all the fluctuations in prices are due to general inflation where all prices move together. If relative prices never change, then firms would realise that any change in their own price simply represents an equal change in all prices. The firms would instantaneously adjust their expectations of other prices by the same amount that their own price increased. In Equation 15–2, P^e would increase by exactly the amount that P_i increased. Hence, the firm's production would not change. In this example, the information-based explanation for the departure of real GDP from potential disappears. Although this example is extreme, even in a less extreme situation we would expect firms to make use of information available in their own market when guessing economic conditions elsewhere. More specifically, when a firm observes the price of its own product it will adjust its expectation of prices elsewhere. This adjustment will be based on the relationship between the firm's price and the general price level that the firm has experienced over time.

In the three panels of Figure 15–3, we illustrate three different price experiences of a representative firm. Each of the points in the diagrams represents a year's experience of two variables: the general price level P that prevailed in the economy, and the firm's own price P_i that it received for its product. On the vertical axis of each diagram we indicate the general price level P. We measure P compared to the firm's forecast, before each year begins, of the general price level P. This forecast is done without any knowledge of (or is not conditional on) events in its own market. This could be next year's forecast of the overall price level from an econometric consulting firm. We represent this forecast by $\hat{P}$. On the horizontal axis of each of the diagrams is the firm's own price. It also is measured relative to the unconditional forecast of the general price level at the start of each year.

A point toward the top of each diagram indicates a year with a high general price level, compared with what was forecast at the start of the year. Points at the bottom represent a surprisingly low price. Looking in the other two directions, points to the right indicate years when the firm experienced a relatively high price for its product. Points to the left show low prices at the firm. Each of the diagrams has many such points, indicating many years of experience for the representative firm.

Two positively sloped lines appear in each of the diagrams. One line is a 45-degree line with a slope of 1. This line shows the points where the firm's price is equal to the overall price level; there is no relative price advantage to the firm for movements along this line. As we move up the line, both the firm's price and the general price move up in the same proportion, leaving

Figure 15–3. THREE ALTERNATIVE PRICE EXPERIENCES OF A FIRM. ▶
(1) In the top panel there is a large relative price variability and a small general price variability. The firm's best-guess line is fairly flat. Its slope b is near zero. The firm's own price is not very informative in helping the firm guess the general price level. (2) In the middle panel the general and the relative price variabilities are the same. There is a large general price variability compared with the top panel. The best-guess line is now steeper than in the top panel. Its slope b is about halfway between zero and 1. (3) In the bottom panel there is a small relative price variability compared with the top panel. The best-guess line is much steeper than in the top panel. Together the three panels show that the smaller the relative price variability and the larger the general price variability, the steeper the best-guess line.

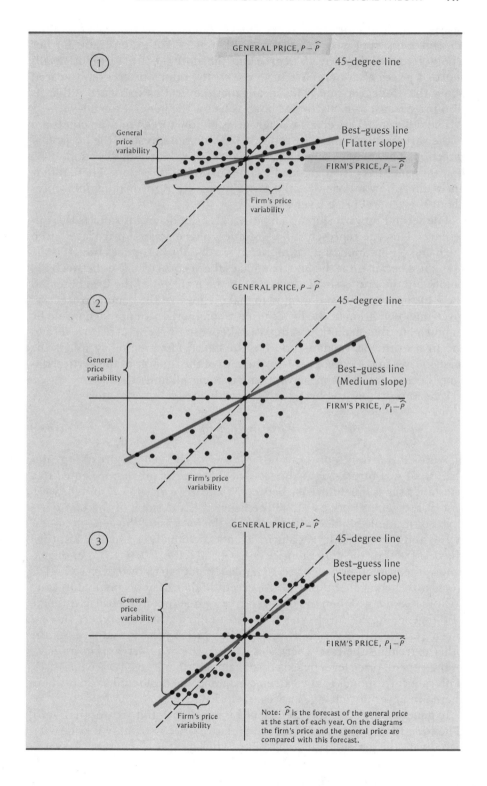

Note: $\widehat{P}$ is the forecast of the general price at the start of each year. On the diagrams the firm's price and the general price are compared with this forecast.

relative conditions for the firm unchanged. Points to the *right and left* of the 45-degree line represent relative price differences. For example, the farther a point is to the left of the 45-degree line, the more the firm's own price falls short of prices elsewhere. We have drawn the points to be evenly spaced about the 45-degree line. This means that the firm's experience is that its own price is just as likely to be above as below the general price level.

The difference between the diagrams is in how spread out the points are in the various directions. The top panel has a large spread in the horizontal direction. The middle panel has about equal spreads in both directions. The bottom panel has a small spread in the horizontal direction. These differences affect how informative the firm's own price is for making inferences about the general price level.

The second upward-sloping line in each of the diagrams reflects this difference. This line represents the best guess of the general price level given the firm's observation of its own price. We call it the **best-guess line**. It is the best guess because it is the line that makes the vertical distances between the points and the line as small as possible. If the manager of the firm observed these historical points and wanted to make a guess of the general price level given an observation of the firm's price, a commonsense approach would be to find a line that makes the differences between the general price level and the firm's price as small as possible. In statistical terminology this is the least-squares line, because actually the sum of the squares of the vertical distances between the points and the line is being minimised.

We can represent the best-guess line with an algebraic formula:

$$P^e = \hat{P} + b(P_i - \hat{P}). \tag{15-3}$$

In words this means that the firm's guess P^e of the general price is greater than what was forecast $\hat{P}$ at the start of the year by an amount equal to a constant b times the difference between the firm's own price P_i and the forecast of the general price $\hat{P}$. The coefficient b is the slope of the best-guess line. For example, if the coefficient b is .3, the forecast of the general price $\hat{P}$ is 1.0, and the firm observes a price P_i in its own market equal to 1.1, then the best guess of the general price is $1.0 + .3(1.1 - 1.0) = 1.03$. In the example, the firm observes a price 10 percent higher in its own market, and its guess is that the general price is 3 percent higher than originally forecast.

Note that if $b = 0$ then the firm's own price does not influence its estimate of the general price level. This is the least informative case, where there is much relative price variability and little general price variability. At the other extreme is the case where $b = 1$. Then the firm increases its estimate of the general price level by exactly the amount that its own price increases. This case corresponds to the extreme example we considered earlier, where there are never any changes in relative prices.

In general, however, the coefficient b is less than 1 and greater than zero. The size of b depends on whether the relative price variability is large compared with the general price variability. The larger the general price variability, the steeper the best-guess line and the more the firm changes its estimate of the general price level when it sees its own price increase. For example, in a typical high-inflation economy, the general price variability is high. Firms usually guess that their own price increase is a signal for another increase in inflation. The relation between price variability and the slope of the best-guess line is an important implication of the information-based theory, as we show below.

THE LUCAS SUPPLY CURVE

If we substitute the firm's best guess (Equation 15–3) into the firm's supply equation (15–1) we get

$$Y_i = h[P_i - \hat{P} - b(P_i - \hat{P})] + Y_i^* \qquad (15\text{–}4)$$

or,

$$Y_i = h(1 - b)(P_i - \hat{P}) + Y_i^*. \qquad (15\text{–}5)$$

Equation 15–5 shows how the representative firm produces more when its own price is greater than the unconditional forecast of the general price level. It has the same form as the firm's supply function except for the fact that the supply coefficient is related to the coefficient b. If b is near 1, then $h(1 - b)$ is near zero and the firm does not supply much additional output. At the other extreme, when b is near zero the supply coefficient is larger.

The aggregate supply curve for the entire economy is obtained by adding up all the representative firms' supply curves. Real GDP, which we continue to denote by Y, is the sum of all the individual firms' Y_i. The aggregate price level P is simply the sum of the individual firms' prices P_i divided by n, the number of firms.

If we use this notation, and add up Equation 15–5 for all the firms in the economy, we get

$$Y = nh(1 - b)(P - \hat{P}) + Y^*, \qquad (15\text{–}6)$$

which is the Lucas supply curve for the entire economy. We illustrate the Lucas supply curve in Figure 15–4, where the price level is the vertical axis and output is the horizontal axis. Note that the slope of the Lucas aggregate supply curve depends on b, the slope of the best-guess line. Because the slope b in turn depends on the importance of general versus relative price variability, we now can see that the aggregate supply curve itself depends on these variabilities. When the variability of the general price level is greater, the slope of the Lucas supply curve is steeper.

It will be useful to compare the Lucas supply curve with the price-adjustment curve we introduced in Part I. To do this, we rewrite the Lucas supply

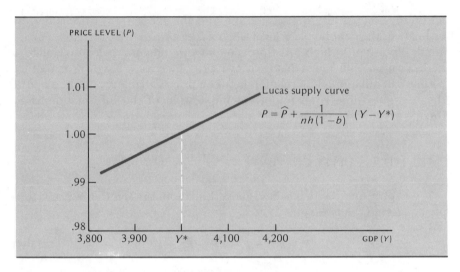

Figure 15–4. THE LUCAS SUPPLY CURVE.
When aggregate price variability is large compared with relative price variability, the slope of the aggregate supply curve is steep. Firms do not respond by much to changes in their own prices because they suspect that such changes represent changes in the general price level. ($\hat{P} = 1.0$ in this diagram.)

curve with the price level on the left-hand side:

$$P = \hat{P} + \frac{1}{nh(1 - b)} (Y - Y^*). \qquad (15\text{–}7)$$

The main difference between the Lucas supply curve (written in this way) and the price-adjustment curve is that, in the former, prices adjust without any lag. Prices must be viewed as perfectly flexible in the Lucas aggregate supply curve, rather than predetermined as in the price-adjustment curve. In terms of the algebra of the equation, one can see that there is no lag, because the current value of Y is on the right-hand side of Equation 15–7, rather than the lagged value of Y. By contrast, the price-adjustment equations in Chapter 6 had lagged Y on the right-hand side.

The Lucas Supply Curve

1. Because of imperfect information, firms cannot observe exactly what is going on in other markets. They make a best guess about what is going on by looking at their own market. In particular, if the prices of the goods they are selling are high, that is an imperfect signal that other prices are high.

2. Firms produce more when all prices rise more than the firms expected. Each firm in the economy sees a higher price but mistak-

enly thinks that it represents a relative price increase. Conversely, firms produce less when the price is unexpectedly low.

3. The positive relationship between GDP and unexpected price rises is called the Lucas supply curve.

15.3 Policy Implication of the Imperfect Information Model

In Figure 15–5 we combine the Lucas aggregate supply curve with the standard aggregate demand curve that we derived in Part I. To determine the impact of an increase in the money supply on real GDP and the price level, we want to shift the aggregate demand curve to the right. If the aggregate supply curve stays put, then the rightward movement of the aggregate demand curve will stimulate real GDP and raise prices.

Whether or not the aggregate supply curve stays put depends on whether people's expectations of the price level change. If these expectations adjust upward in response to the increase in the money supply, then the aggregate supply curve will shift up. As is shown in Figure 15–5, the expectations-induced shift in the aggregate supply curve will tend to reduce the impact of the increase in the money supply.

The case where expectations are rational is of particular interest because much of the policy effectiveness debates of the 1970s centered on it. Expectations are rational if people in the economy make the most of the informa-

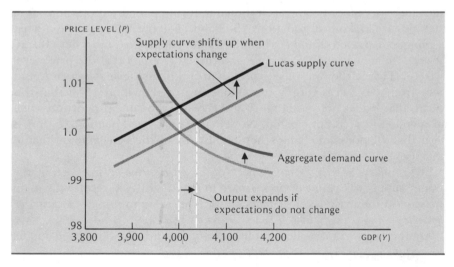

Figure 15–5.   AGGREGATE DEMAND AND THE LUCAS SUPPLY CURVE.
A rightward shift of the aggregate demand curve causes the aggregate supply curve to shift as well, because expectations change. Output stays the same and the price level rises.

tion that is available when making forecasts. To make the concept operational, economists have generally assumed that the information available to people includes a model of the economy—for example, the same model that we have been using—as well as complete knowledge of economic policy. No economist actually thinks that many people go through the formal process of solving a model. Rather, here, as in many other areas of economics, the model is a reasonable summary of a more informal thought process.

To derive the policy implications of the Lucas supply function with rational expectations, let us focus on a model with the aggregate demand curve:

$$Y = k_0 + k_1 (M/P). \tag{15-8}$$

The coefficients k_0 and k_1 are the intercept and slope of the aggregate demand schedule. For example, if k_0 equals 2,287 and k_1 equals 2.855, the aggregate demand curve is the same as the one in Chapter 5. (The coefficient k_0 incorporates government spending.) The rest of the model is given by the Lucas supply function, Equation 15–6, which we rewrite as

$$Y = c(P - \hat{P}) + Y^*, \tag{15-9}$$

with c equal to $nh(1 - b)$.

Now suppose that the economy is operating at potential GDP ($Y = Y^*$), and that the Bank of Canada increases the money supply. That is, M rises. Looking closely at Equation 15–8, we can see that the price level P, or output Y, must increase. Since people are rational in forming their expectations of P, they also are looking at Equations 15–8 and 15–9 trying to figure out what is going to happen to Y and P when the money supply goes up. They also anticipate the money supply increase and therefore *expect* that the price level will rise. That is, their rational expectation of the price level $\hat{P}$ increases. But note from the Lucas supply function shown in Equation 15–9 that this means that Y does not rise at all: P and $\hat{P}$ rise in the same proportion when an increase in M is anticipated. Now looking back at Equation 15–8 it is clear that if Y does not change then P must rise by the same amount that M increases.

In summary, with rational expectations, an *anticipated* increase in the money supply will result in no increase in real GDP. It will result only in an increase in the price level that matches the increase in money. *Anticipated monetary policy is ineffective: It has no effect on real GDP.*[7]

Another important policy implication of the information-based model

Can reduce π without affecting GDP ∴ no recession

[7] This implication of the Lucas supply function and rational expectations was first pointed out by Thomas Sargent and Neil Wallace in 'Rational Expectations, the Optimal Monetary Instrument, and the Optimal Money Supply Rule,' *Journal of Political Economy*, Vol. 83, pp. 241–254, 1975.

concerns the problem of disinflation. Recall that, in the model of Chapter 7, there was no painless way to bring down the rate of inflation. Some reduction of actual GDP below potential GDP was necessary if we were to get a reduction in the rate of inflation. The implications of the information-based model are quite different.

Suppose that we want to reduce the rate of inflation from 10 to 3 percent. Then if the Bank of Canada reduces the rate of money growth from 10 to 3 percent immediately—announcing that it will do so—the information-based model with rational expectations implies that the price level and the expected price level will immediately change their inflationary path from 10 to 3 percent. Prices can adjust instantaneously, and people know this. Since P and $\hat{P}$ never diverge, real GDP never departs from potential GDP. The disinflation is achieved without any recession! If true, this would be extremely important for policy makers in an inflationary situation. In order to reduce inflation instantaneously and painlessly, they would merely have to announce a sharp decline in the growth rate of money. People would immediately reduce their expectations of inflation, and actual inflation would be reduced by exactly the same amount.[8]

The policy ineffectiveness results are illustrated in Figure 15–5 above. When expectations are rational the supply curve shifts up by the same amount as the aggregate demand curve. Compare this with the case where expectations are sluggish or otherwise dependent on the past. Then the aggregate supply curve does not shift up as much. Hence, anticipated changes in money do affect output.

There are two crucial assumptions behind the policy ineffectiveness and instantaneous disinflation results: (1) Prices are perfectly flexible, and (2) expectations are rational. We showed in Figure 15–5 that monetary policy can be effective if people's expectations adjust slowly. Alternatively, if the money supply is increased unexpectedly, so that people do not anticipate the increase, then their expectations will not adjust and monetary policy will have an effect.

The "new classical" policy results derived from the information-based model should be distinguished from those of the "classical" model of Chapter 14. While both analyses assume that prices are perfectly flexible, the analysis using the Lucas supply function generates movements in real GDP that are consistent with departures of real GDP from potential. Recall that in the classical model there were no departures of real GDP from potential; monetary policy was always neutral. In the analysis presented in this section, anticipated increases in the money supply are neutral, but unanticipated or surprise increases are not.

[8] See Thomas J. Sargent, 'The Ends of Four Big Inflations,' in Robert E. Hall (ed.), *Inflation: Causes and Effects,* University of Chicago Press for the National Bureau of Economic Research, 1982, pp. 41–97.

New Classical Theory in Ottawa and Washington, D.C.

Some policy makers in both Canada and the United States appeared to have been influenced by the information-based model in the early 1980s. Gerald Bouey, the governor of the Bank of Canada, justified the Bank's restrictive policy by arguing that a stimulative policy would produce more inflation but no additional output:

When people have expectations . . . of high or rising inflation they tend to see in stimulative financial [i.e., monetary] policy evidence that their expectations . . . are warranted. The actions that they then take to protect themselves push up costs and prices . . . and reduce the benefits to employment and output that the financial stimulation was undertaken to achieve.*

In the United States, advisors to the Reagan administration argued that the rate of inflation could be brought down very quickly, with little or no recession, by announcing an immediate reduction in money growth. Their forecast was heavily influenced by the Claremont Economics Institute Econometric Model, which attempted to incorporate some of the rational expectations ideas; the Claremont modellers prepared such an optimistic inflation-output forecast for the administration.

While some of the ideas behind the Lucas supply curve and rational expectations were used in the political debates, such applications were not endorsed by Lucas or other developers of the theories. Lucas was quoted in *BusinessWeek* at the time (March 2, 1981), stating that applications of rational expectations ideas to such new or unfamiliar policies were likely to be inaccurate: 'For that purpose rational expectations doesn't have much to add.' Nevertheless, the policy debates and the actual decisions to have contractionary monetary policies were probably influenced by these theories—however inappropriately or inaccurately. Perhaps a better understanding on the part of policy makers, or at least by their advisors, of the actual meaning and empirical validity of the information-based models might have prevented this.

* Gerald Bouey, *Annual Report of the Governor to the Minister of Finance*, 1982, p. 61.

15.4 Does the Imperfect Information Theory Explain the Departures?

Perhaps the most remarkable thing about the Lucas aggregate supply function is that in principle it can explain the major patterns of economic fluctuations without the use of sticky prices. This is in sharp contrast to the model developed in Part I, where we rely on sticky prices to explain the fluctuations. This fact perhaps more than anything else underlies the early enthusiasm for imperfect information models. As we have just seen, without sticky prices, economic policy works quite differently from the models we have focussed on in this book. In fact, monetary policy can lose its effectiveness altogether when prices are not sticky.

Stating that a theory can explain the fluctuations *in principle* is much different from stating that it explains the actual fluctuations. In principle, the theory can explain the departures of real GDP from potential GDP as coming from price surprises, and it can explain the positive relation between output and prices from the basic theory of firm supply along with certain information barriers. To check whether the theory works *in practice*, however, we need to look at the magnitude and timing of the actual fluctuations, and compare these with the magnitude and timing of the price surprises. For this we can make use of the available empirical research.

There have been many empirical investigations designed to determine whether the theory does explain the facts of economic fluctuations. Some of these investigations compare price surprises—that is, the difference between P and $\hat{P}$—with the fluctuations in the economy. If positive price surprises usually occur when the economy goes into a boom, and if negative price surprises usually occur when the economy goes into a slump, then there would be good evidence for the theory. Note that even measuring price surprises is a difficult empirical undertaking, for it requires getting a measure for $\hat{P}$ to subtract from P. Most studies attempt to measure $\hat{P}$ by using statistical techniques to infer the public's forecasts. Others attempt to obtain direct measures of people's forecasts by using survey data. Because it is very difficult to get a good measure of $\hat{P}$, these empirical tests must be interpreted with some caution.

Nevertheless, based on research completed over the last 10 years, it does not appear that price surprises are of sufficient magnitude or are timed appropriately to explain the departures. Statistical studies have shown that there is a very weak relation between price surprises (that is, $P - \hat{P}$) and the departures of real GDP from potential GDP. Moreover, for recent years, the relation seems to go the wrong way! [9]

Some researchers have attempted to test the information-based theory by looking for a relationship between money surprises and the departures of real GDP from potential GDP. For most theories of aggregate demand, there is a close relationship between price surprises and money surprises. When the Bank of Canada increases the money supply, there usually is a surprise increase in prices. This was illustrated in the previous section on policy. Robert Barro of Harvard University has been the champion of this approach. Early research on the United States and Canada seemed to indicate that money surprises were important—even more important than actual or

[9] See Thomas Sargent, 'A Classical Macroeconometric Model of the United States,' *Journal of Political Economy*, Vol. 84, pp. 207–238, 1976, and Ray Fair, 'An Analysis of a Macroeconomic Model with Rational Expectations in the Stock and Bond Markets,' *Journal of Political Economy*, Vol. 67, pp. 539–552, 1979.

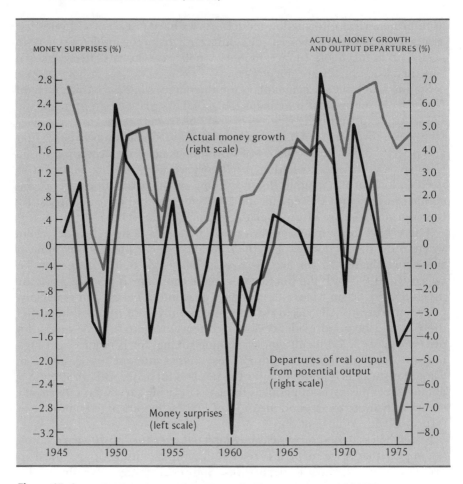

Figure 15–6. MONEY, UNANTICIPATED MONEY, AND REAL ACTIVITY.
Plotted are Barro's data on actual money, money surprises, and the departures of U.S. real output from potential output, $(Y - Y^*)/Y^*$.

forecasted money.[10] In Figure 15–6 we show some of the data used by Barro in his empirical work on the United States. As the figure shows, there clearly is a close relation between money surprises and the movements of the departures of actual GDP from potential GDP. However, except for the 1970s, there is also a fairly close relation between actual money and the departures, a result that supports the sticky-price models we have used in this book. Actual money does not fare very well in the 1970s, however. Apparently, the actual money supply is increasing more rapidly because of inflation, and this tends to blur the usual relation between actual money and the departures of actual GDP from potential GDP.

[10] See Robert J. Barro, 'Unanticipated Money, Output, and the Price Level in the United States,' *Journal of Political Economy*, Vol. 86, pp. 549–580, 1977, and Gillian Wogin, 'Unemployment and Monetary Policy under Rational Expectations: Some Canadian Evidence,' *Journal of Monetary Economics*, Vol. 6, pp. 59–68, 1980.

Figure 15–6 indicates that Barro's finding that money surprises are much more important than actual money might not stand up to attempts to deal with the longer-run movements in money in the 1970s. In fact, Barro's results have been brought into question by later researchers, and it now appears that actual money is also a factor in the departures of actual output from potential output in Canada and the United States.[11] This casts further doubt on the information-based model as an alternative to the sticky-price model.[12]

Finally, the information-based models—without some additional changes—are not capable of explaining the *persistence* of the departures of actual GDP from potential GDP. Recall that such persistence is an important feature of the fluctuations. The information-based models imply that real GDP always snaps right back to potential GDP. To explain the longer persistence, other things—like slow adjustment of employment to changes in demand—must be added to the model.

Two other problems with the theory should be mentioned. First, the informational restrictions placed on firms do not appear to be realistic in many situations. In particular, the assumption that firms know the price of the goods they are selling, but not the price of the goods they are buying, does not seem plausible for most firms. Second, the assumption of perfectly flexible prices does not appear to describe how most markets work. While it is true that some auction markets—such as the Toronto Stock Exchange—have rapid changes in prices, most markets have some rigidities in their prices. Many firms *set* their prices for a period of time. Rather than being price takers as in the information-based model, they are price setters. The price of labour—the wage rate—is particularly sticky. In labour markets the wage paid to workers is frequently set for a number of years.

If the new classical theory seems to have all these problems, what is the reason for spending so much time developing and studying it? The theory has had enormous impact on the way that all macroeconomists work. As James Tobin, the Keynesian macroeconomist from Yale University, has stated, 'The ideas of the [new classical macroeconomics] are too distinctive and powerful to be lost in the shuffle. They are bound to shape whatever orthodoxy emerges.'[13] Although rational expectations is an appropriate and useful assumption in models with sticky prices, the assumption was first introduced in new classical models. The use of rational expectations to analyse consumption, investment, and the exchange rate, as described in Part II, incorporates techniques developed in the new classical models. Moreover, the

[11] See Frederic Mishkin, 'Does Unanticipated Money Matter? An Econometric Investigation,' *Journal of Political Economy,* Vol. 91, pp. 22–51, 1982, and Mostafa Askari, 'A Nonnested Test of the New Classical Neutrality Proposition for Canada,' *Applied Economics,* Vol. 18, pp. 1349–1357, 1986..

[12] For a further discussion of the data presented in Figure 15–6 and more elaboration on this theoretical presentation of the information-based models, see John B. Taylor, 'Rational Expectations Models in Macroeconomics,' in K. Arrow and S. Honkapohja (eds.), *Frontiers of Economics,* Basil Blackwell, 1986.

[13] James Tobin, 'The Monetarist Counterrevolution Today—An Appraisal,' *Economic Journal,* Vol. 91, pp. 29–42, 1981.

new classical theory illustrates in a very simple and elegant way the difference between anticipated and unanticipated macroeconomic policy. In the information-based model, there is an enormous difference between anticipated and unanticipated policy. Anticipated policy has no effect on real GDP, whereas unanticipated policy has a powerful effect. There is also a difference between the effects of anticipated and unanticipated policy in models based on sticky prices—as we will show in Chapter 16—but the difference is not as pronounced, or as easy to illustrate.

Anticipated and Unanticipated Money: Policy and Tests

POLICY

1. The Lucas supply function with rational expectations implies that only unanticipated changes in the money supply affect real output. Anticipated changes in the money supply affect only the price level, leaving real output equal to potential. This is the 'policy ineffectiveness proposition.'

2. Two crucial assumptions underlie the policy ineffectiveness result: Prices and wages are perfectly flexible, and expectations are rational. If prices are sticky, anticipated changes in the money supply have an effect on real output, even if expectations are rational.

TESTS

1. The new classical theory, in which the Lucas supply function is central, is an improvement over the pure classical model because it can explain in principle the departures of output from potential, and the positive price-output correlation.

2. In careful statistical tests the theory does not seem to stand up to the facts, however. Anticipated money as well as unanticipated money affect output, and price surprises have a small effect on output.

Review and Practice

MAJOR POINTS

1. The pure classical model does not explain the departures of output from potential. It can explain the fluctuations in the economy only by hypothesising large and persistent fluctuations in potential output.

2. Real business-cycle theories are based on the pure classical model. In these theories fluctuations in potential output are due to changes in labour supply or labour demand. There is no role for monetary factors in economic fluctuations in these real models.

3. Another fact of the business cycle that is missed by the classical models is the positive correlation between prices and output.

4. The new classical theory was developed to explain the departures of real output from potential, while retaining the assumption that prices are flexible. In the new classical theory, output rises above potential because firms mistake general price increases for relative increases in their own prices. They are fooled into producing more than they would if they were perfectly informed. Imperfect information is crucial to the new classical models.

5. The relationship between prices and output in the new classical models is called the Lucas supply function. According to this function, GDP rises above potential when the price level is higher than was forecast at the start of the year. Conversely, GDP is below potential when the price level is lower than was forecast at the start of the year.

6. The slope of the Lucas supply curve depends on the variability of the general price level. The greater the variability of the price level, the steeper the Lucas supply curve, and the less firms increase their output when their own price rises above what was expected.

7. According to the Lucas supply function with rational expectations, only unanticipated changes in money affect output. An anticipated decrease in the money supply lowers the price level but does not reduce GDP. Unanticipated decreases in the money supply do decrease GDP, however.

8. Careful tests of the new classical theory indicate that it is not able to explain the actual fluctuations in the economy. Price surprises do not lead to large changes in output, and anticipated changes in money do seem to affect real output.

9. A crucial assumption behind the policy ineffectiveness result is that prices and wages are perfectly flexible.

KEY TERMS AND CONCEPTS

Price-output correlation

Real business-cycle theories

New classical theory

Imperfect information

Firm supply curve

Relative price

Local price

General price

Unconditional forecast of general price

Guess of general price given local price

Best-guess line

Price surprises

Relative and general price variability

Lucas supply curve

Slope of Lucas supply curve

Price-adjustment curve

Anticipated money

Unanticipated money

Policy ineffectiveness proposition

QUESTIONS FOR DISCUSSION AND REVIEW

1. What are the real theories of economic fluctuations? What do they assume about shifts in labour supply and labour demand? What do they assume about the slopes of labour supply and labour demand?

2. Why might the real interest rate increase labour supply?

3. What is the Lucas supply function? Why do the deviations of output from potential depend on price surprises?

4. Why does the Lucas supply curve require that firms are misinformed about what is happening in other markets?

5. Why is the Lucas supply curve steep if the variance of the general price level is high?

6. What is the policy ineffectiveness proposition? Explain what happens to the price level and output in the new classical model when the Bank of Canada increases the money supply and announces it in advance.

7. What two assumptions are crucial to the policy ineffectiveness proposition? If these two assumptions are dropped, explain what would happen when the money supply is increased.

8. Describe why prices and output are positively correlated during economic fluctuations according to the new classical theory. Compare this explanation to that using a slow price adjustment.

9. Describe how tests of the new classical theory have indicated that it cannot fully explain the facts of economic fluctuations.

PROBLEMS

Numerical

1. The labour supply schedule is $100 + 2W/P$. The labour demand schedule is $200 - 8W/P$. Find the levels of the real wage and employment in equilibrium. Now suppose that demand falls, so that the demand schedule is $190 - 8W/P$. By how much does the wage fall? By how much does employment fall? Explain why the wage falls by a larger percentage than does employment.

2. The aggregate demand schedule is $120 - 20P$. The Lucas supply curve governs the economy. There are 100 firms. Each one has the supply schedule $Y_i = 4(P_i - P^e) + 1$. Each one forms its forecast of the overall price level by using last year's price, P_{-1}, and its own price: $P^e = P_{-1} + .5 (P_i - P_{-1})$. Find the Lucas aggregate supply function by solving for P_i. Now assume that $P_{-1} = 1.00$. Find the levels of aggregate output and price at the intersection of the aggregate demand and Lucas aggregate supply curves. Suppose demand rises, so that the aggregate demand schedule is $131 - 20P$. Find output and price. Compute the price surprise and explain why output rises when the price surprise occurs.

3. Suppose that the Lucas supply curve is

$$Y = c(P - \hat{P}) + Y^*,$$

with $c = 20,000$ and $Y^* = 4,000$ (billions of dollars). For example, when the price level P is 1.01 and the expected price $\hat{P}$ is 1.0, output Y is 4,200, or 5 percent above potential output $Y^* = 4,000$. Suppose that the aggregate demand curve is

$$Y = 1,101 + 1.288\ G + 3.221(M/P).$$

a. Suppose that the economy has been at rest for some period with output at potential, and that no changes in policy are expected for the near future. The money supply M is 600 and government spending is 750. What is the price level? (Hint: If there are no surprises the actual and the expected price levels will be the same.)

b. Now suppose that the Bank of Canada announces that it will increase the money supply from 600 to 620. What are the new levels of output and price level?

c. Now suppose that the Bank of Canada announces that it will increase the money supply from 600 to 620 but actually increases it to 670. What are the new levels of output and price level?

4. Suppose that automatic stabilisers cause government purchases to rise when GDP is below potential and to fall when GDP is above potential. Algebraically we might represent this as

$$G = 750 - g(Y - Y^*),$$

where potential output Y^* is 4,000. The coefficient g measures the strength of the automatic stabiliser.

a. Substitute this expression for G in the aggregate demand function in Problem 3, and solve for output Y in terms of P (M is held fixed at 600). This is the aggregate demand curve incorporating the automatic stabiliser. Describe how the slope of the aggregate demand curve depends on the coefficient g.

b. For three different values of g (0, .01, and .1) describe the effect on output of an unanticipated increase in money like the one in Problem 3c. Assume that people know the value of g in each case. Do the effects on output depend on the value of the coefficient g? If so, then does it appear that even well-understood automatic stabilisers are effective in that they influence output? Explain your results intuitively. Why might automatic government spending stabilisers affect output while anticipated changes in money do not? (See B. T. McCallum and J. K. Whitaker, 'The Effectiveness of Fiscal Feedback Rules and Automatic Stabilizers under Rational Expectations,' *Journal of Monetary Economics*, Vol. 5, pp. 171–186, 1979, for a further discussion of this type of policy problem.)

Analytical

1. (Real business-cycle theory.) Consider an economy in which prices are flexible, but in which aggregate supply varies positively with the interest rate. Recall that this may be the case if labour supply shifts to the right with increases in the interest rate. Aggregate demand continues to be described by spending balance and money market equilibrium conditions. The economy is described by the following three equations:

$$Y = a_0 - a_1 R \qquad \text{(IS curve)}$$
$$M/P = kY - hR \qquad \text{(LM curve)}$$
$$Y = c_0 + c_1 R \qquad \text{(Aggregate supply)}$$

a. Describe how output, interest rates, and the price level are determined in this economy. Depict the situation graphically.

b. Describe the effects of an increase in the money supply on output, interest rates, the price level, consumption, investment, and net exports. Does monetary neutrality hold in this model?

c. Describe the effects of an increase in government spending on output, interest rates, the price level, consumption, investment, and net exports.

d. From Part c, is an increase in government spending necessarily inflationary, deflationary, or ambiguous? If it is ambiguous, on what does it depend?

2. If the Lucas supply function is written with output on the right and price surprises on the left, it looks like a Phillips curve. Explain what happens to this Phillips curve when relative price variability increases and when general price variability increases. Explain how your results can give rise to a test of the new classical theory.

3. Assume that agents know the true model of the economy, which is given by an aggregate demand curve and a Lucas supply curve. They may or may not, however, know the true value of the money supply.

a. On the same graph, draw two aggregate demand curves; one for $M=M_0$, and one for $M=M_1>M_0$.

b. On the same graph, draw a Lucas supply curve assuming agents believe that $M=M_0$. Explain how you know where to position this graph.

c. Assume now that M is actually equal to M_1. Depict the equilibrium price level, given the assumption of Part b.

d. Now assume that agents know that M equals M_1. Again, depict the equilibrium price level. For which equilibrium is the price level higher? Explain your result.

e. Compare the levels of Y, C, X, and I across the equilibrium of Parts c and d.

4. Suppose our model of the economy is given by an aggregate demand curve and a Lucas supply curve as in Equations 15–8 and 15–9. Assume further that agents have complete information about the model of the economy including the value of the money supply. Potential output is equal to 4,000. The aggregate demand curve goes through the point (4,000, 1.5).

a. Consider three possible Lucas supply curves going through the points (4,000, 1), (4,000, 1.5), and (4,000, 2). What is the value of $\hat{P}$ for each of these curves?

b. Which of the three curves in Part a is the rational expectations Lucas supply curve? In what sense would the other two curves not satisfy rational expectations?

5. In Chapters 6 and 7 we saw that output could deviate from potential in the short run, but that output would always return to potential in the long run after prices had time to adjust. In this chapter we also saw how output could deviate from potential. What defines the 'long run' in this model? That is, what must happen in order for output to return to potential? Is this likely to take a very long time?

6. On a graph (3 to 4 inches square) sketch an aggregate demand curve and a Lucas supply curve. Label their intersection point as Y^* and P^*. Now draw two aggregate demand curves, one each a quarter inch to either side of your initial curve. Label the intersection points with the Lucas supply curve Y_+, P_+ and Y_-, P_-. Finally, draw two more aggregate demand curves, three quarters of an inch or so to either side of the original curve, and label the intersection points with Y_{++}, P_{++} and Y_{--}, P_{--}.

a. What kinds of shocks can cause the aggregate demand curve to vary in the way shown on your graph? What is the relationship between the magnitude of those shocks and the variability in Y and P?

b. Suppose initially that shocks to the money supply cause the aggregate demand curve to vary within the narrow region. Assume that the Lucas supply curve shown in your graph is the appropriate curve given the magnitude of these shocks. In what sense is the curve 'appropriate'?

c. Now suppose that shocks to the money supply cause the aggregate demand curve to vary within the wider region. How will the Lucas supply curve appropriate to these shocks compare with your initial Lucas supply curve? Sketch the new curve. How do the swings in output and the price level compare with P_{--}, P_{++} and Y_{--}, Y_{++}?

d. Use these results to explain why output may not deviate much from potential in periods of either highly stable or highly variable prices, but that it may deviate considerably from potential in the transition period from stable to variable prices. Relate your analysis to the experience of the Canadian economy in the late 1960s.

16

The Theory of Wage and Price Rigidities

In this chapter we take a detailed look at the microeconomics of wage and price rigidities. Although the new classical models and the real business-cycle models with perfectly flexible prices are in principle able to explain economic fluctuations, many economists do not feel these models explain the actual empirical regularities very well. We considered the empirical evidence in the last chapter. The evidence suggests that models based on wage and price rigidities deserve consideration as the explanation of why real GDP departs from potential GDP for prolonged periods.

One of the most important concepts concerning wage and price rigidities is that they are temporary. The word 'sticky,' rather than 'fixed,' connotes the tendency for wage or price rigidities to give way under market pressures. Eventually prices and wages adjust and play their well-known role in allocating goods and employment in an efficient manner. As they do, the economy gradually returns to full employment. Once prices have fully adjusted, the levels of employment and production are given by the long-run classical conditions discussed in Chapter 14.

16.1 Wage Determination

The most comprehensive information about wage determination in Canada pertains to the formal contracts of workers who are members of large labour unions. We will consider this group of workers first, and then go on to discuss the non-union sector.

WAGE DETERMINATION IN THE LARGE UNION SECTOR

Of the 30 percent of Canadian workers who are unionised, about two-thirds are involved in collective-bargaining situations that are regularly tracked by a department at the federal government called Labour Canada. In total, this group consists of about 2.4 million workers. Although only 20 percent of the labour force, this group receives enormous attention in the media and in public policy discussions. The industries and unions that make up this group almost personify big business and big labour: It includes the steel, trucking, automobile, airlines, tobacco, aluminum, coal, and rubber industries as well as many government employees and health-care workers. Some economists, such as John Dunlop of Harvard and Lester Thurow of M.I.T., have argued that this group establishes wage patterns that other union and non-union workers imitate, although recent empirical studies on the subject indicate that the evidence is mixed.[1]

This group of unions is sometimes the focus of government policy. The wage controls imposed in the 1975–78 Anti-Inflation Program were applied to all of the unions included in the group monitored by Labour Canada, along with some other workers. The public sector wage restraint program of 1982–84 was aimed in large part at the government employees' unions included in this group.

Union contracts may last between one and three years. A union with a series of one-year contracts must negotiate a new contract each year. A union with a series of three-year contracts negotiates only once every three years, for example, 1979, 1982, 1985, and so on. Three-year contracts are more common in primary (mining, forestry, etc.) and manufacturing industries; one- and two-year contracts are more common for government employees. Because a large proportion of union members work in the public sector, where contracts tend to be relatively short, in recent years the average union worker has had a two-year contract. Figure 16–1 shows the number of workers whose unions signed new contracts in each year from 1978 to 1987.

The important fact that all workers do not sign contracts at the same time is evident in Figure 16–1. Contracts are unsynchronised. Wage negotiations are staggered over the contract cycle. At any one time, only a small fraction of the workers are signing contracts; the remaining workers either have recently signed their contracts or will sign their contracts in the future. The period in which one contract is in force overlaps the period in which other contracts are in force.

An example will be helpful to illustrate the characteristics of a typical long-term contract. The Western Canadian Regional Council of the International Woodworkers of America (IWA) signed a contract with the forest

---

[1] See Daniel J. B. Mitchell, *Union Wages and Inflation*, Brookings Institution, Washington, D.C., 1980, p. 171, or Richard B. Freeman and James L. Medoff, *What Do Unions Do?*, Basic Books, New York, 1984, Chapter 3.

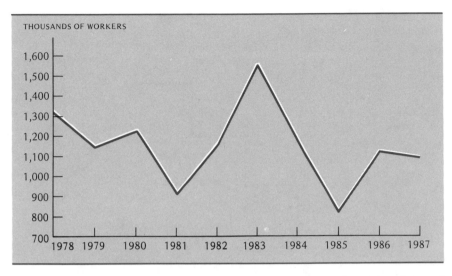

Figure 16–1. NUMBER OF UNION WORKERS IN MAJOR COLLECTIVE-BARGAINING SETTLEMENTS.
Each year only about one-half of the 2.4 million workers in major unions (500 or more workers) are involved in collective-bargaining negotiations. Source: *Canadian Economic Observer*, Table 2.13.

products industries in the coastal part of British Columbia in September 1988. The contract will run for three years. For the lowest-paid members of the union the contract stipulates the following increases; 85 cents per hour in the first year, 84 cents per hour in the second year, and 89 cents per hour in the third year. This pattern is illustrated in Figure 16–2.

Part of the wage increase in the agreement was deferred to the second and third years of the contract. These deferred increases indicate that management and labour had expectations of continued inflation. It would have been possible to **index** the contract to inflation. In an indexed contract wages automatically increase if there is inflation. But there were no indexing provisions in the IWA contract; these increases would—and did—occur regardless of economic conditions and indicate the extent of the nominal rigidity that such contracts impose on the economy. The IWA did have some indexing in their 1981–82 contract, when the rate of inflation was much higher than it was in 1988.

Some information on union wage settlements in Canada is given in Figure 16–3. The figure shows the average annual increase in the base wage over the life of the contract for all major agreements concluded in each year. The base wage is the lowest wage category in the contract (all major contracts specify different wage levels for workers with different skills or experience). The data exclude contracts that contain a cost-of-living allowance (COLA) clause because in those cases the actual wage increase depends on the future rate of inflation. In practice, workers with COLA clauses end up receiving roughly the same increases as workers without COLA clauses.

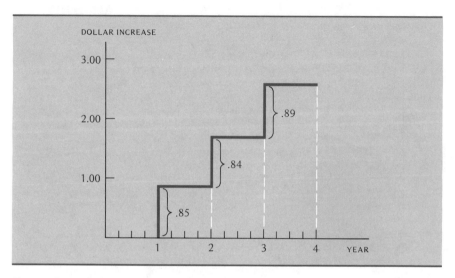

Figure 16–2. CURRENT AND DEFERRED WAGE INCREASES IN THE IWA CONTRACT.
A significant part of the wage increase was deferred to the second and third years. An inflation rate of about 5 percent was built into the contract; there was no indexing.

The effects of the severe recessions of 1975 and 1982 are quite apparent in the contract negotiations shown in Figure 16–3. For example, the unemployment rate increased dramatically from about 7 percent in mid-1981 to close to 13 percent by the end of 1982. During this period wage settlements

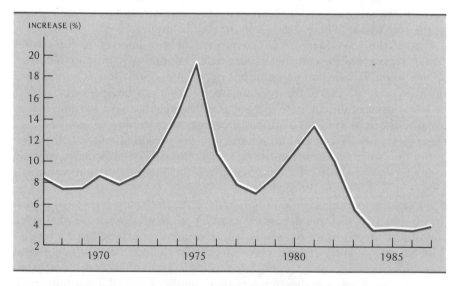

Figure 16–3. AVERAGE ANNUAL INCREASE IN BASE WAGE RATES IN MAJOR COLLECTIVE-BARGAINING AGREEMENTS WITHOUT COLA CLAUSES.
The rate of wage increases fell dramatically in the aftermaths of the recessions of 1975 and 1982. Source: *Bank of Canada Review*, Table H13.

dropped from over 10 percent to below 5 percent. Since 1982 wage settlements have remained under 5 percent. The huge step downward in wage increases, of course, underlies Canada's success with inflation since 1982.

In multi-year contracts it is common to find that wages rise in each year of the contract. That is, some of the wage increases are deferred until well into the life of the contract. There is often some front-end loading, however, in that the earlier years of the contract see larger increases. Table 16–1 shows the amount of front-end loading that occurred in a year of high inflation.

Table 16–1. AVERAGE INCREASE IN BASE WAGE RATES IN MAJOR AGREEMENTS WITHOUT COLA CLAUSES BY TIMING OF THE INCREASE: 1980 (percent)

	1st Year	2nd Year	3rd Year
1-year contracts	10.4		
2-year contracts	12.8	10.5	
3-year contracts	13.2	11.8	9.8

Source: Labour Canada, *Wage Developments*, 1980.

Thus far we have seen that most workers in large labour unions change their contracts about once every 2 years. What are the factors that determine the size of the wage adjustment when it does occur? Wage and salary decisions are made in collective-bargaining meetings for which both management and labour leaders spend extensive time preparing. While the outcome of any one bargaining situation cannot be predicted with much certainty, a number of factors clearly influence the outcome in particular directions.

The first and perhaps most important is the state of the labour market. If unemployment is high, then labour will be in a relatively weak bargaining position. Conversely, if unemployment is low, then workers will be able to bargain for larger wage increases. The threat of a strike is more credible in good times than in bad. Moreover, firms are likely to settle for larger wage increases in tight market conditions, because they will be better able to pass on their costs in the form of higher prices.

A second factor influencing wage bargaining is the wage paid to comparable workers in other industries. Because not all contract negotiations are synchronised, there are two components of this comparison wage: the wage settlements of workers who have recently signed contracts, and the expected wage settlements of workers who will be signing their contracts in the near future. Looking back at the wage settlements in recently signed contracts makes sense in a current negotiation because those settlements will be in force during part of the contract period under consideration. This backward-looking behaviour tends to give some built-in inertia to the wage determination process. If one union group gets a big increase, then the next group of workers in the wage determination cycle will also tend to get a big increase. Lester Thurow describes the process as follows: 'Suppose that this year the machinists' union is negotiating a new three year contract. Last year the auto workers negotiated a three year contract for a 10% rise per year. No leader of the machinists can settle for less than 10% and still remain in office. And in two years' time the auto leader will be similarly imprisoned by what the machinists negotiate today.'[2] But looking forward to future settlements also makes sense, because the current contract will be in force when these changes take place. In other words, wage determination generally combines elements of forward-looking and backward-looking behaviour.[3]

A third factor that will influence wage decisions is the expected rate of inflation. If inflation is expected to be high, then workers will ask for larger wage increases and management will be willing to pay them because their own prices are expected to rise. As with the effect of comparable wage increases, the effect of expected inflation will have both a backward-looking element and a forward-looking element.[4]

WAGE DETERMINATION IN THE NON-UNION SECTOR

It is very common for workers who are not in unions to receive wage and salary adjustments once each year. Although there is no formal contract involved it is unlikely that this wage decision will be changed before the next scheduled adjustment period. Hence, the nominal wage rigidity is very similar to that in the union contracts. One difference is that the entire wage adjustment usually occurs at one time rather than part being deferred as in the second and third years of the large union contracts. This is probably due to the shorter time between wage adjustments.

For example, our universities adjust our salaries once each year. We get a letter from the administration once per year giving our salaries for a 12-month period. This nominal wage rate is rarely changed before the next salary adjustment period the following year. This type of annual wage setting is common in many sectors of the economy.

In preparation for a wage adjustment, the management of non-union firms must obtain information very similar to that obtained by management of unionised firms preparing for a collective-bargaining meeting. In a large non-union firm there are usually specialists called wage and salary administrators who must make a wage decision. They obtain information about the current labour market situation. They conduct wage surveys or subscribe to a wage survey performed by an outside group. They also attempt to forecast the rate of inflation.

[2] Lester Thurow, 'Thurow's Third Way,' *The Economist,* January 23–29, 1982.

[3] The implication of staggered wage setting combined with rational expectations of future wage, price, and unemployment is discussed in more detail in John B. Taylor, 'Staggered Wage Setting in a Macro Model,' *American Economic Review,* Vol. 69 (May 1979), pp. 108–113.

[4] The impact of all three factors on wage setting in the Canadian unionised sector is estimated in W. Craig Riddell and Phillip M. Smith. 'Expected Inflation and Wage Changes in Canada, 1967–81,' *Canadian Journal of Economics,* Vol. 15 (August 1982), pp. 378–394.

Although the wage decision will usually be made under more competitive conditions than exist in a collective-bargaining situation, these factors—the state of the labour market and wage and price inflation—will influence the final outcome in similar directions. If unemployment is very low and is expected to remain low for the next year, then management will try to pay a relatively high wage compared to other firms employing similarly skilled workers. An attractive wage will prevent workers from quitting and help to lure workers from other firms if necessary for expansion. On the other hand, if unemployment is high, there will be less of a worry that workers will quit to look for jobs elsewhere. Moreover, if the year is expected to be bad for sales, an expansion of production requiring more workers would be unlikely.

If wages are expected to be relatively high at other firms—either because of recent wage decisions of these firms or because of expected wage increases at other firms—then the wage will necessarily be higher. Information about both recent wage decisions and intended wage decisions in the near future can be obtained from wage surveys.[5]

Although there is little direct evidence on when most non-union firms have their scheduled wage increases, it is unlikely that they all occur at the same time. Hence, there is a type of nonsynchronisation that we observe for the union sector. Figure 16–4 illustrates the simple situation where there

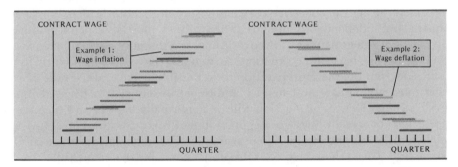

Figure 16–4. STAGGERED ANNUAL WAGE SETTING WITH FOUR WAGE-ADJUSTMENT PERIODS THROUGHOUT THE YEAR.
There are four groups of workers in each example. The contract wage of each worker group is denoted by a different colour shade from very dark to very light. Because wages are not all set at the same time (that is, they are not synchronised), the contract wage of one group overlaps that of all the other groups. This is shown in the diagram with the flat contract wage lines on top or below each other. In the left panel, there is a general inflation: Each group attempts to get ahead of the previous group. In the right panel, there is a general deflation: Each group tries to get below the previous group.

[5] Recently some formal theories have been developed to explain this relative wage setting. See Janet Yellen, 'Efficiency Wage Models of Unemployment,' *American Economic Review*, Vol. 74 (May 1984), pp. 200–205. Or see Lawrence F. Katz, 'Efficiency Wage Theories: A Partial Evaluation,' in S. Fischer (ed.), *Macroeconomics Annual*, Vol. 1, National Bureau of Economic Research, 1986, pp. 235–289. The term 'efficiency wage' theory is used for these explanations because paying a wage close to the going wage for similar work is usually supposed to increase efficiency by reducing turnover, or by making the workers feel better.

are four wage-adjustment periods through the year: January 1, April 1, July 1, and October 1. It is clear from this illustration that staggered wage setting gives rise to an overlapping of wage decisions.

WHY ARE WAGES SET FOR LONG PERIODS WITH FEW CONTINGENCIES?

We have just seen that unionised workers generally have their wages predetermined in 1- to 3-year contracts. Only a fraction of these contracts are contingent on the cost of living, and none, to our knowledge, is contingent on any other economic variable with the rare exception of profit-sharing provisions that are contingent on the firm's profitability. Furthermore, wage setting in non-union firms seems to operate in much the same way, though wages are reconsidered annually.

Adjustment Costs. The costs of adjusting wages and salaries may be high. Consider the situation where wage rates are determined in collective-bargaining negotiations between large corporations and labour unions. In preparation for these negotiations management spends months surveying wages in other industries, estimating changes in labour productivity, forecasting changes in the firm's own profits, and obtaining estimates of the general inflation during the upcoming contract period. To be adequately informed during the collective-bargaining sessions, labour leaders must be equally and independently prepared; hence, they must also spend months preparing for negotiations. Moreover, there is a threat of a strike in almost every collective-bargaining situation. An actual strike is obviously costly for both sides, but the mere preparation for a possible strike is also costly. The firm must accumulate and finance additional inventories to be used if a strike occurs. Hence, production will be abnormally high before negotiations, and abnormally low after negotiations as firms draw down inventories when a strike does not occur. These swings in production raise average costs to the firm. Given these high costs it is understandable that many collective-bargaining negotiations by private firms occur only once every 3 years.

Indexing. Why aren't the contracts that are negotiated contingent on events that may occur before the next renewal? We have noted that some of the contracts in recent years have included cost-of-living adjustments whereby the wage is indexed to the consumer price level. However, these clauses rarely involve 100 percent protection from cost-of-living changes, and most contracts do not have any such clauses. Moreover, cost-of-living clauses represent only one of many possible contingency clauses. For example, the contracts could be directly linked to the unemployment rate, GDP, or more local measures of the performance of the economy and the value of workers' time.

The primary reason that more contracts are not indexed to the cost of living is that such indexing can be harmful if prices are rising because of supply-side shocks. Suppose that the marginal productivity of labour is reduced because of a shift in the production function. Recalling the classical model of Chapter 14, we know that such a shift will eventually require a reduction of the real wage; that is, W/P must decline so that it is equal to the marginal productivity of labour. But a 100 percent indexed contract will prevent such a decline. The escalator clause will call for an increase in W in the same proportion as the increase in P. Hence, W/P remains constant and too high. It is understandable that many firms and workers are reluctant to institute an arrangement that rules out any adjustments in the real wage if prices should rise suddenly during the contract period. Of course, if the reason for the increase in prices is a general monetary-induced inflation, then there will be no need for a reduction in the real wage. Unfortunately there is usually no way to tell in advance whether the price rise is due to monetary effects or to shifts in the production process.

Why not index wages to unemployment, GDP, or other indexes that might indicate whether the shocks are to money or to productivity? Part of an answer is similar to the reason we gave for caution in indexing to the cost of living. For instance, some of the shifts in overall unemployment are not relevant for the productivity of a particular group of workers. When a special event, not a recession, makes unemployment zoom for auto workers, the unemployment rate may not reveal much about the jobs available to forestry workers.

A final reason that contracts do not have many indexing clauses is that they add complexity. There are good reasons to have a straightforward contract that the rank and file can easily understand and vote on. Similarly, contingency clauses appear to add uncertainty about the wage that the workers will actually get. Many workers would object to this added uncertainty, even though the economic theorist may argue that the uncertainty makes the worker better off.

Although we have focussed on labour union contracts, the same arguments pertain to the more informal wage-setting procedures used by firms employing non-union workers. A review of each worker's performance is costly, and obtaining survey information about wages paid elsewhere and forecasts of inflation requires time and expense. To make such an adjustment more than once a year is probably prohibitive for many firms. The arguments stated above against extensive contingency clauses also apply to this type of wage setting. Moreover, indexing would do little to improve the workings of annual wage-setting arrangements; waiting less than a year to make an adjustment after the fact is usually adequate.

WHY IS WAGE SETTING STAGGERED?

In a decentralised economy like that of Canada, firms and workers decide by themselves when their wages and salaries are adjusted. The fact that these decisions are not synchronised therefore seems natural; one would be surprised to see a coordinated wage (or price) adjustment without some centralised orchestration of such a move.

It is important to know whether the lack of synchronisation in Canada serves any microeconomic purpose. If it does not, then proposals for reforming the economic system to bring about more synchronisation would be innocuous for microeconomic welfare but could have some macroeconomic advantages.

Imagine what would happen if all wages and prices were set at the same time, and without a central planner to tell workers and firms what to do. A firm that thought that a relative wage increase was appropriate for its workers would have a difficult time knowing what other wages would be in order to achieve that relative increase. A wage survey would tell only about current wages in other firms, not the direction in which they were heading.

Staggered wage setting provides information to firms and workers about wages and prices elsewhere. Even though other wages will be adjusted before the current contract expires, there will be some period of time when the desired relative wage is in force. Nonsynchronised wage and price setting thus seems desirable in a decentralised economy.[6]

Moreover, staggered wage setting adds some stability to wages. Without staggering all wages and prices would be up for grabs each period; there would be no base for setting each wage. Tremendous variability would be introduced to the price system.

The situation is different in some other countries, especially in those where the government plays an active role in wage setting. For instance, a significant number of wage decisions are synchronised in Japan, where each spring there is a *shunto* or simultaneous wage adjustment for the large companies. However, the government is actively involved in the *shunto*. Prior to the *shunto*, extensive deliberations take place to determine the appropriate wage adjustment for that year. Here, the government is a prime player. Some economists feel that such a system would be desirable in Canada as well.

16.2 Price Determination

Basic microeconomic theory gives a detailed account of how the prices of individual items are determined in auction markets. In an auction market, the price fluctuates day by day or even minute by minute to keep demand and supply equal. Imagine an auction market for plywood, for example. The demand for plywood is based on the market price and on the price of substitutes for plywood—aluminum, plastic, etc. The supply of plywood depends positively on the price. Plywood producers make plywood up to the point where marginal cost equals the market price. Their supply schedule slopes

---

[6] See Gary Fethke and Andrew Policano, 'Will Wage Setters Ever Stagger Decisions,' *Quarterly Journal of Economics,* November 1986, for further discussion of the rationale for nonsynchronised wage setting.

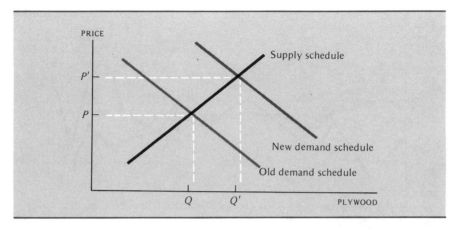

Figure 16–5. EFFECTS OF AN INCREASE IN DEMAND IN AN AUCTION MARKET
FOR PLYWOOD.
When the demand schedule for plywood shifts to the right, the price (*P*) and the quantity
(*Q*) rise. A higher price is needed to induce the production of the higher quantity, be-
cause marginal cost rises with output.

upward because marginal cost rises when output rises. When higher prices
of plywood substitutes shift the demand function to the right, both plywood
output and the plywood price rise, as shown in Figure 16–5.

One of the important conclusions of standard microeconomic analysis is
the following: *When the demand schedule shifts to the right, the price rises by
more than cost.* Firms earn extra profit, especially in the short run. The
profit arises because a higher price is needed to ration demand to the point
where it equals the added production that is feasible in the short run. In the
longer run, the price will fall to a point equal to long-run cost, as new firms
enter the market and existing firms raise their productive capacity by adding new factories.

Direct observation of many markets indicates that this prediction of standard micro theory of price fluctuations in response to demand fluctuations
does not hold. Demand can vary widely without appreciable movements in
the price. When prices change, it is usually because costs change, not because demand changes. For example, consider the U.S. steel market, which
is not an auction market. Figure 16–6 shows that demand seems to have little effect on price compared to cost.

The steel industry is not exceptional in having prices that are stable relative to costs in the face of wide fluctuations in demand. The same is true of
most manufactured goods and services. On the other hand, many raw materials, especially agricultural products, have prices that fluctuate a great deal
in response to changes in demand.

Consider the *ratio* of the average wage *W* to the price level *P*. Recall that
this ratio is just the real wage. If prices were determined just by costs for the
economy as a whole, then this ratio would be stable over business cycles. On
the other hand, if demand were important in pricing decisions, then the

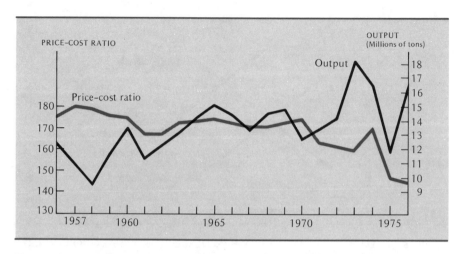

Figure 16–6. OUTPUT AND THE PRICE-COST RATIO IN THE U.S. STEEL INDUSTRY.
Steel is a cyclical industry and output has varied sharply, mainly due to shifts in the demand schedule for steel. The ratio of the price of steel to an index of costs of production
remained quite constant over the period. The price did not move up and down the marginal cost schedule of the steel industry. Source: Robert W. Crandall, *The U.S. Steel Industry in Recurrent Crisis: Policy Options in a Competitive World*, Washington, D.C., The
Brookings Institution, 1981, Appendix A.

ratio would fall when demand was strong as prices would be bid up relative
to wage costs. There is a general upward movement in the real wage due to
increase in labour productivity, but there is no noticeable extra upward
movement that might be related to a fall in demand. If anything, the real
wage fell during the most recent recessions.

One of the important implications of the stable relationship between
prices and costs is that a jump in costs very quickly results in a jump in
prices. We can express this algebraically as

$$\pi = \text{Wage cost contribution} + Z \tag{16–1}$$

where π is the rate of inflation (rate of growth of prices from one year to the
next) and Z is the change in an index of costs of production other than wage
costs.

The idea that prices respond quickly and fully to costs is called the
markup hypothesis. The markup is the gap between price and total cost of
production. The markup hypothesis says that the gap is close to constant.
Under the markup hypothesis, costs are the prime determinant of price and
changes in demand have little effect on price.

WHY DO FIRMS SET PRICES AS A FIXED MARKUP OVER COSTS?

According to the markup equation, prices are rigid, but in a somewhat
different way from wages. Like wages, prices respond relatively little to de-

mand. But, unlike wages, prices do seem to move quickly in response to changing costs. Some of the explanations for this behaviour are information limitations, long-term price contracts, customer relations, managerial rules of thumb, and oligopoly pricing.

Information Limitations. When the demand for a firm's product shifts, it is frequently unclear what the reason is. It could be a temporary change, in which case no change in price would be necessary. By waiting to see how persistent the change in demand is before changing the price, the firm obtains information about the nature of the shift. This strategy makes the firm's prices less sensitive to shifts in demand, and creates a lag in the adjustment of prices. Note that there is a certain similarity between these information limitations and those of the new classical models discussed in Chapter 15. Here, however, the prices are sticky rather than perfectly flexible.

There is also uncertainty about the effect of a change in a firm's costs. When there is an increase in the cost of fuel, for example, to run the firm's machines, it is not immediately clear to the firm what that change in cost will do to the economy in general. A reasonable strategy for the firm is to pass on the cost increase and see what happens to demand. If demand falls off then that is a sign that the cost increase is a genuine relative price increase, and the firm will eventually have to lower its price to maximise profits. In the case where the wages of the firm's workers increase, there is a similar tendency to pass on the costs, until it is clear that profits could be improved by doing otherwise.

Note that expectations of the future will affect these pricing strategies. If firms know that any increase in wages generally results in inflation, perhaps because the Bank of Canada accommodates the wage increases, then the tendency to pass on the wage increases in the form of higher prices will be even greater.

Contracts. Many firms have explicit contracts with the purchasers of their products. For example, steel companies make long-term agreements to supply steel to auto producers. In other cases, there is no formal contract, but there is a long-term understanding that continued purchasing will take place. The contracts provide that the purchaser can purchase however much it needs, at a price negotiated at the time the contract is signed. The contract lets the price rise in the future if costs rise, but does not make the price depend on the quantity sold by the producer to all of its customers.[7]

Customer Relations. A firm has an incentive to develop a reputation for charging a price related to cost. If it changes prices for other reasons, cus-

---

[7] The same type of nonsynchronised or staggered wage setting that we discussed in the previous section also occurs in price setting. That is, 'price contracts' are usually staggered. Olivier Blanchard of M.I.T. has studied the implications of staggered price setting in an input-output framework in his 'Price Asynchronization and Price Level Inertia,' in R. Dornbusch and M. H. Simonsen (eds.), *Inflation Debt and Indexation*, Cambridge, Mass., M.I.T. Press, 1983, pp. 3–24.

tomers will suspect they are being gouged. The customers will then have to spend resources verifying that the price increase is legitimate. It is in the mutual interest of the firm and the customer to develop a long-term relationship in which the customer does not have to worry about the firm making opportunistic price changes.

Managerial Rules of Thumb. Firms typically sell thousands of separate products. Setting prices is a critical management decision that cannot be delegated too far down in the company. Middle management usually does not have the discretion to set arbitrary prices for each product. Instead, top management formulates pricing rules that are handed down to middle managers. The typical pricing rule makes price depend on costs and not on the amount of the product being produced. To make the rule sensitive to the volume of production, top management must figure out the short-run marginal cost schedule for each product.

Oligopoly or Monopolistic Competition. In concentrated industries, firms may have an implicit agreement not to let prices drop to the competitive level. It is in their mutual interest to stabilise the price near the monopoly level. However, when the price is above long-run marginal cost, each firm has an incentive to cut the price a little and sell more output. A stable oligopoly needs a simple rule so that violations can be detected easily. The rule must allow firms to respond to costs, however. A simple agreement on a dollar price level could last only a year or so in an inflationary economy. The simplest viable rule in the longer run requires each firm to set a price based on costs, but prohibits price changes for any other reason.

The same type of pricing behaviour can exist in less concentrated industries where there is some short-run monopoly power for each firm because the products are slightly differentiated from other products. These industries are characterised by monopolistic competition. An example is the magazine business. *Time* and *Newsweek* are slightly different products, but a large price difference would shift sales from one magazine to the other. Stephen Cecchetti of New York University has studied the behaviour of American magazine prices and found striking evidence of sticky prices. He argues that this is consistent with a monopolistically competitive view of pricing.[8] He found that the average time between price changes in magazines was about *3 years* during the high inflation period of the 1970s when inflation averaged over 7 percent per year in the United States. Moreover, the average size of the price change—about 25 cents—was remarkably stable during the 1950s, 1960s, and 1970s. According to Cecchetti, 'It is very unlikely that the administrative costs of actually changing prices can explain this [infrequent price adjustment]. The obvious explanation is that each magazine fears that if it "moves" first to adjust its price for inflation, it will raise its relative price above that of the competition, losing sales.'

[8] Stephen G. Cechetti, 'The Frequency of Price Adjustment,' *Journal of Econometrics*, April 1986, pp. 255–274.

FACTUAL AND THEORETICAL RATIONALES
FOR WAGE AND PRICE RIGIDITIES: AN ASSESSMENT

Though the theoretical explanations we have discussed for long-term wage contracts, staggered wage setting, and markup pricing are plausible, they are not based on the standard auction model of microeconomic theory. For this reason, some macroeconomists remain unconvinced or skeptical of the theories.[9] Modifications of standard micro theory designed to explain wage and price rigidities have only begun in recent years, and it appears that no one single modification is enough to explain all the aspects of the rigidities. It is not an easy job to modify or improve basic micro theory, but the facts indicate that some such modifications or improvements are necessary. Attempts to build formal theoretical models of wage and price rigidities are one of the most important elements of current research in macroeconomics.

One such attempt—called *contract theory*—is examined in some detail in the appendix to this chapter. Optimal contract theory endeavours to generalise the standard microeconomic model of auction markets to allow for longer-term relationships between individuals lasting a year or more. The idea is to include in contracts contingencies for unpredictable events during the life of the contract, such as inflation, productivity changes, or higher profits. Labour union contracts between a union and a firm are an example, but optimal contract theory also addresses more implicit contracts such as the unwritten contracts between any worker and her employer. Thus far optimal contract theory has not been entirely successful in explaining wage rigidity and deviations of unemployment from the natural rate. One reason is that the optimal contracts are contingent on all possible events. Since we know that real-world contracts are not contingent on many variables, the challenge of optimal contract theory is to show why such contingency clauses are missing in the real world. One possibility is that some variables —like a firm's profit—are not perfectly observable by both parties to the contract; in particular the firm may have an incentive to claim to workers that profits are low.[10]

Even as such research is proceeding, we find the evidence in favour of long-term contracts, staggered wage and price setting, and markup pricing sufficiently convincing that we think it would be a serious mistake to ignore them in macroeconomics and rely instead on the classical model with perfectly flexible wages and prices. There seem to be good rationales for these

[9] See, for example, Robert E. Lucas, Jr., 'Methods and Problems in Business Cycle Research,' in Robert E. Lucas, Jr. (ed.), *Studies in Business Cycle Theory*, Cambridge, Mass., MIT Press, 1981, pp. 271–296, or Robert E. Lucas and Thomas J. Sargent, 'After Keynesian Economics,' in Robert E. Lucas and Thomas J. Sargent (eds.), *Rational Expectations and Economics Practice*, Minneapolis, University of Minnesota Press, 1981, pp. 295–319.

[10] Another approach to the microeconomic underpinnings of sticky wages and prices is the 'efficiency wage' model mentioned in Footnote 5 on page 439. Still another approach models firms in monopolistic competition where small costs of adjusting prices at the firm level can lead to large social welfare costs. See N. Gregory Mankiw, 'Small Menu Costs and Large Business Cycles: A Macroeconomic Model of Monopoly,' *Quarterly Journal of Economics*, May 1985, pp. 529–539.

aspects of wage and price rigidities—no one has proved that they are inconsistent with the basic idea of rational decision-making on the part of firms
and workers. They are certainly not inconsistent with rational expectations.
But we recognise that the details of the case are far from being worked out.

What Does a Union Labour Contract Look Like?

Sometimes the best method of economic research is to simply go out
and look carefully at how people do business. Consider, for example,
the labour agreement between the woodworkers' union and the forest
products industries discussed in the text. The entire agreement for
1988–91 is printed in a compact booklet, small enough for a worker to
carry in a shirt pocket or a lunch box. The contract is jam-packed with
108 pages of text describing worker-employer rights as well as wage
payments through 1991 for all types of workers from blacksmiths to

MASTER AGREEMENT
1988 - 1991

From Article II–Section 1:
'The management and the operation of, and the
direction and promotion of the working forces is
vested exclusively in the Management . . .'

From Article XX–Section 2:
'In the event of a reduction of the forces, the last
person hired shall be the first released . . . When
recalling forces after a period of layoff . . . an em-
ployee shall be recalled in order of his plant seniority . . .'

FOREST PRODUCTS INDUSTRIES
COAST REGION BRITISH COLUMBIA
Effective June 15, 1988

shake packers. The contract also specifies the extra payments for over-time—time-and-a-half or more beyond the 8-hour day and 40-hour week.

As with most labour contracts the firm is given a free hand in choosing employment as long as it pays according to the wage schedule. There is a layoff clause that ensures that the most senior workers are laid off last. The layoff clause guarantees that laid-off workers will be hired back in order of seniority and before new workers are hired.

The contract already tells us much about what happens when the demand for wood falls off. Suppose, for example, that Macmillan Bloedel—one of the operators who signed the agreement—starts getting fewer orders for lumber because of a decline in house construction. Clearly, the response of Macmillan Bloedel is not to lower the wage and thereby prevent a drop in profits. The wage is fixed by the contract that the company and the other operators signed. Instead, when demand drops Macmillan Bloedel will start producing less lumber and begin to lay off workers at its B. C. mills in order to reduce losses. The laid-off workers are then placed on a panel—as stipulated in the contract—from which they will be returned to employment on the basis of seniority when demand picks up. The behaviour of Macmillan Bloedel, as agreed to in this contract, is apparently just like what we assumed for the typical firm in this book.

Temporary Wage and Price Rigidities

WAGES

1. Union wage contracts in Canada last as long as 3 years. The contracts are not synchronised with one another. There is some indexing to inflation, but it is less than 100 percent and appears in well under half of the contracts.

2. Non-union workers typically have wage adjustments about once per year. These adjustments are staggered over time, much as the union contracts. Since the wage is rarely changed within the year, this wage-setting process creates rigidities much like formal contracts.

3. Wages are set for long periods because collective bargaining, threats of strikes, or simply careful reviews of worker performance make adjusting the wage costly. Wages are rarely indexed in Canada because supply shocks as well as demand shocks occur. With indexing, the real wage does not adjust enough after supply shocks. Moreover, extensive contingency clauses add complexity and apparent uncertainty to wage contracts.

PRICES

1. Prices are set according to a stable markup over costs. When demand falls, firms try to keep their profit margins constant, at least until they see if the change is permanent.

2. The real wage does not fluctuate much due to the business cycle. This stability is a reflection of the markup pricing strategies.

3. Firms use markup pricing because of information limitations, customer relations, simple rules of thumb, and oligopolistic strategy.

16.3 Policy Implications

Three important policy implications can be drawn from the theoretical and factual background of the previous section. The first concerns the problem of *disinflation;* that is, bringing the rate of inflation down from a level that is thought to be too high. The second concerns the *effectiveness of monetary policy when expectations are rational.* The third concerns the *long-run trade-off between inflation and unemployment.*

DISINFLATION AND THE REAL EFFECTS OF MONETARY POLICY

These issues are best understood by first considering an extreme case. In 1980 the average wage increase in union contracts was just over 11 percent. Suppose, for illustrative purposes, that *all* workers in Canada sign an 11 percent 3-year wage contract, but starting May 1991. All wages in the economy would be locked into 11 percent increases for 3 years. According to Equation 16–1, the markup pricing equation, prices would also be locked into 11 percent increases for 3 years. General inflation would be 11 percent. If real GDP was at potential and growing at 3 percent per year, then we know from our study of long-run growth in the classical model in Chapter 14 that the money stock would be increasing by 14 percent per year. With no shifts in the demand for money, real GDP growth plus inflation equals money growth.

With this economic situation in mind, imagine now that in June 1991 the governor of the Bank of Canada decides that this is too high, and decides to end inflation—to disinflate—by cutting money growth from 14 to 3 percent. The governor instructs the bond traders at the Bank to sell government securities at a sufficient rate to reduce reserve growth and hence money growth from 14 to 3 percent *immediately.*

The results of this hypothetical policy action should now be clear. With an 11 percent inflation built into the economy, the only possibility is that real GDP growth is reduced substantially, probably to a negative rate. (The amount of the reduction depends on the slope of the aggregate demand schedule.) The economy is thrown into a deep recession. As sales begin to fall, firms lay off workers and unemployment rises. Unless contracts are reopened, the recession will last 3 years—until the scheduled end of the labour contracts. Only then might we expect an end to the inflationary wage increases, a subsequent decline in inflation, and eventually an economic recovery as the 3 percent money growth permits 3 percent real GDP growth with zero inflation.

The fact that monetary policy can affect real output and employment, even if expectations are rational, is also demonstrated by this example. Everyone in the economy could be perfectly aware of the new policy action by the Bank of Canada. But as long as everyone is locked into contracts, the contractionary effect occurs. Note also that the Bank could have brought about a boom starting in June 1991 by increasing the rate of monetary expansion from 14 percent to some higher number. Policy that is anticipated in advance can have an effect with rational expectations, as long as knowledge of the policy change comes after the contracts are set.

In such a situation, a sharp decline in money growth is certainly costly. A far better approach would be for the Bank of Canada to *announce* its disinflation plans before the contracts are set. For example, in April 1991 the Bank could announce that it will reduce money growth from 14 to 3 percent in September 1994 when the labour contracts expire. This would give management and labour the chance to adjust their new contracts to incorporate the new anti-inflationary monetary policy; if the policy announcement were credible—this is a big if—then the recession could be entirely avoided. Disinflation without recession would be a reality.

Of course, we already know that the actual Canadian economy is not like the hypothetical economy in this extreme example. Contract signing is not synchronised in the major union sector and most non-union workers are employed under wage-setting arrangements in which the wage is set for 1 year. Hence, a sharp decline in money growth would begin to have some immediate effect on inflation as those workers signing new contracts see the rise in unemployment. Again, it would be better to announce the program in advance so that newly negotiated contracts could take account of the lower anticipated rate of inflation.

But the decline in inflation will be more gradual than the sharp 11 percent decline in money growth because only a small fraction of wages could be adjusted at first. A gradual decline in the rate of money growth would be better in that it would permit a gradual decline in inflation consistent with the configuration of contracts in the economy. An announced gradual reduction in money growth would be the least costly way to reduce inflation. Rather than an immediate reduction of 11 percent, recent studies suggest a reduction of about 1 percent in the first year, 2 percent in the second year, 6 percent in the third year, and 2 percent in the fourth year.[11] If such a policy could be announced in advance and be believed, it would minimise the

[11] See John B. Taylor, 'Union Wage Settlements during a Disinflation,' *American Economic Review,* Vol. 73 (December 1983), pp. 981–993.

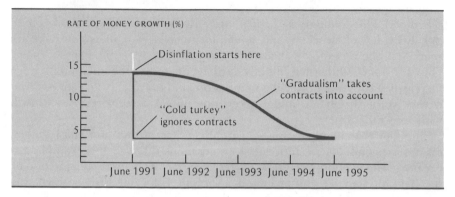

Figure 16–7. ALTERNATIVE DISINFLATION PATHS FOR THE MONEY SUPPLY.
The least costly policy is one that is gradual and announced. The largest deceleration
should occur near the third year because of the 3-year contracts that expire at that time.
Suppose that inflation has risen to 14 percent by mid-1991. The Bank of Canada wants to
reduce it. An immediate short reduction in money growth—'cold turkey'—would probably cause a big recession like that in the early 1980s.

harmful side effects of a monetary disinflation. The alternative paths for a
monetary disinflation are illustrated in Figure 16–7 for the hypothetical
1991–95 example.

The important role of contracts during a disinflation is recognised by
economists of differing persuasions. Arthur Okun, who was happy to be
identified as a Keynesian, emphasised contracts in much of his writings.[12] In
their best-selling book *Free to Choose,* Milton Friedman and Rose Friedman
argued:

> The most important device for mitigating the side effects is to slow inflation
> *gradually but steadily* by a policy announced in advance and adhered to so it be-
> comes credible. The reason for the gradualness and advance announcement is
> to give people time to readjust their arrangements—and to induce them to do
> so. Many people have entered into long-term contracts . . . on the basis of antici-
> pations about the likely rate of inflation. These long-term contracts make it dif-
> ficult to reduce inflation rapidly and mean that trying to do so will impose heavy
> costs on many people. Given time these contracts will be completed or renewed
> or renegotiated, and can then be adjusted to the new situation.[13]

What about reforming the wage-determination process in Canada so that
contracts are shorter and more synchronised? If all contracts were 1 year in
length and synchronised, then the above example indicates that it would be
possible to have a sharper reduction in inflation in a shorter period of time.
But it would still be important to announce the policy in advance and to
make it as credible as possible. The disadvantages of such a change would be

[12] A comprehensive discussion of Okun's view is found in *Prices and Quantities: A Macroeconomic Analysis,* Washington, D.C., Brookings Institution, 1980.
[13] Milton Friedman and Rose Friedman, *Free to Choose,* p. 273.

the increased negotiating costs and the likely increased volatility of relative wages and prices—as we discussed above.

Another reform that has been suggested by Milton Friedman and others would be to induce the private sector to use more wage indexing. This would in effect make wages more flexible because they could adjust before the contract expires. The problem with indexing—as we have already pointed out—is that it prevents real wage adjustments when these are needed because of changes in labour productivity.[14]

16.4 A Simple Model of Staggered Wage Setting

We have already seen that staggered wage-setting models predict that changes in the money supply will affect real output even if expectations are rational. But what happens in a sustained inflation with wages, prices, and the money supply increasing at a constant rate? What do the theoretical models of staggered wage setting and markup pricing indicate will happen to output and unemployment? Will there be a way for wage setting to adjust to such a situation so that the unemployment rate is equal to the natural rate for any sustained rate of inflation?

A simple stylised algebraic model of staggered wage setting and price determination will be useful in addressing this and other questions. The model brings together most of the facts about wage and price setting discussed in this chapter, and illustrates their macroeconomic implications in a simple way. Wage setting is nonsynchronised, prices are given by a markup over costs, and expectations are rational.

Suppose that all wage contracts last 2 years, that all the wage adjustment occurs at the beginning of each year, and that there is no indexing. Half the workers sign contracts at the start of even-numbered years and half at the start of odd-numbered years. This configuration of assumptions is shown in Figure 16–8, where X represents the contract wage and W the average wage. Since we need to distinguish between past and future variables, let the subscript '-1' represent the *previous* year and let the subscript '$+1$' represent the *next* year. Of course, events in the next year are not known; people must form expectations of them. The average is given by

$$W = \frac{1}{2}(X + X_{-1}). \tag{16-2}$$

In words, the wage W this year is the simple average of the contract wage signed last year, X_{-1}, which is still outstanding, and the contract wage signed

[14] Stanley Fischer, 'Wage Indexation and Macroeconomic Stability,' in Karl Brunner and Alan Meltzer (eds.), *Stabilization of the Domestic and International Economy,* Carnegie-Rochester Conference Series in Public Policy, New York, North-Holland, 1977, pp. 107–148, and Jo Anna Gray, 'Wage Indexation: A Macroeconomic Approach,' *Journal of Monetary Economics,* Vol. 2, pp. 221–36, 1976, have explored these effects of indexing on macroeconomic fluctuation.

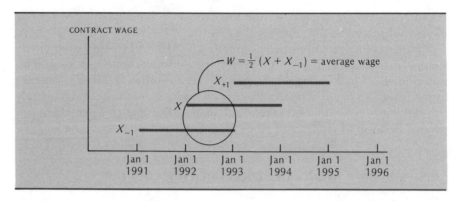

Figure 16–8. CONFIGURATION OF WAGE SETTING IN THE SIMPLE MODEL.
There are two groups of workers in the economy. One group has a wage adjustment
January 1 of the even years and the other group has a wage adjustment January 1 of the
odd years. The average wage W is shown to be equal to the average of this period's contract wage X and last period's contract wage X_{-1}. In the picture the average wage for 1992
is shown. It is the average of the contract wage set in 1991 and the contract wage set in
1992.

this year, X. For example, suppose that the contract wage is 10 in 1991 and
8 in 1992. Then the average wage is 9 in 1992 (the wage of 8 set in 1991 is
still outstanding in 1992).

An algebraic relationship that describes how the contract wage is set each
period might be given by

$$X = \frac{1}{2}(W + W_{+1}) - \frac{c}{2}[(U - U^*) + (U_{+1} - U^*)], \qquad (16\text{–}3)$$

<u>Effect of expected</u>   <u>Effect of current and future</u>
average wage   unemployment

where U is the unemployment rate and U^* is the natural rate of unemployment; c is a coefficient describing the response of wages to unemployment.

Equation 16–3 leads to an interesting observation. Rewrite Equation 16–
3 with W and W_{+1} replaced by the expressions in Equation 16–2. That is,

$$X = \frac{1}{2}\left[\frac{1}{2}(X + X_{-1}) + \frac{1}{2}(X_{+1} + X)\right] - \frac{c}{2}[(U - U^*) + (U_{+1} - U^*)]. \qquad (16\text{–}4)$$

W from Equation W_{+1} from Equation
15–2   15–2

Now gather together the X terms (without the subscripts) and put them on
the left-hand side of the equation. After some cancellation (you can work it
out in the margin), we get the simpler expression:

$$X = \frac{1}{2}(X_{-1} + X_{+1}) - c[(U - U^*) + (U_{+1} - U^*)]. \qquad (16\text{–}5)$$

Backward-looking   Forward-looking   Expected future unemployment
component   component   is also a factor

Equation 16–5 shows how wage determination has a backward-looking component X_{-1} and a forward-looking component X_{+1}. The backward-looking component—which we discussed in words above—is what makes inflation persistent from year to year. Workers base their wage decisions partly on what previous wage decisions were. The forward-looking component—also discussed previously in words—is what makes expectations of the future so important. Expectations of moderate wage settlements next year will tend to moderate wage settlements this year. For example, if wage settlements next year are expected to be 10 percent lower, then, according to Equation 16–5, actual settlements this year will be 5 percent lower. The coefficient of X_{+1} is $1/2$.

Equation 16–5 also shows how expected future unemployment conditions next year can affect wage settlements this year. If the unemployment rate is expected to rise next year by 2 percent, then wage settlements this year will be 2 times c percent lower. For example, if c equals .5 then wage settlements this year will be 1 percent lower. The expectation of a slump in the future with its accompanying increase in unemployment has a simple effect: It decreases wage inflation today.

Because of the markup relationship all these effects on wages will be passed through to prices. The policy implications are therefore clear. Expectations of a monetary policy that is noninflationary in the future and that will let unemployment rise if necessary in the future, should inflation rise, will have favourable effects on inflation today. These favourable effects on inflation can actually work with little or no adverse effects on unemployment. The expectation of a credible stance against inflation in the future should therefore have a favourable effect on the trade-off between inflation and unemployment.

Consider, finally, the operations of the model in a steady inflation. Say the contract wage X increases by the same amount each year. For example, let the amount of increase be 10. In a steady inflation the *change* in the contract wage this year, $X - X_{-1}$, and the change in the contract wage next year, $X_{+1} - X$, will be the same, namely 10. Equation 16–5 can then be written as

$$\underbrace{\frac{1}{2}(X - X_{-1})}_{5} = \underbrace{\frac{1}{2}(X_{+1} - X)}_{5} - \underbrace{c[(U - U^*) + (U_{+1} - U^*)]}_{0}. \qquad (16-6)$$

Notice that there is a $10/2 = 5$ on the left-hand side and a $10/2 = 5$ on the right-hand side. The two cancel out. The term involving unemployment must equal zero. This implies that $U = U^*$ and that $U_{+1} = U^*$. In other words, the unemployment rate is always equal to the natural rate. The same result holds, of course, for any steady change in prices, not just 10. Regardless of the rate of inflation, as long as it is steady and anticipated, there is no trade-off between inflation and unemployment in the long run.

The simple model consisting of Equations 16–1, 16–2, and 16–3 can be viewed as an alternative, more microeconomic-based, representation of the price-adjustment equation that we introduced in Chapter 6, Equation 6–6.

As such it can be combined with a model of aggregate demand that tells how the money supply and government spending shift demand when prices are predetermined. The 'gradualism' versus 'cold turkey' simulations described in Section 16.3 are based on such a model that combines staggered wage setting, markup pricing, and aggregate demand. Simulating such a model requires a large computer and sophisticated computer programs. Fortunately, most of the results can be conveyed in a more intuitive and less complex way by introducing some simple approximations to capture the essence of forward-looking and rational expectations behaviour. We turn to this in the next chapter.

Policy with Wage Contracts and Rational Expectations

1. Long-term contracts make it difficult for the economy to adjust immediately to changes in monetary policy. Even if expectations are rational, a deceleration of money growth will reduce output and employment, because workers and firms are locked into their contracts.

2. Since *new* contracts are negotiated with an eye to the future, they will be influenced by expectations of future policy actions. Old contracts will remain in place, unless extreme hardship develops.

3. In the long run, wage contracts adjust to expectations of higher rates of inflation. Regardless of the rate of inflation, as long as it is steady, the unemployment rate will return to the natural rate.

Review and Practice

MAJOR POINTS

1. Most detailed information about wage setting in Canada comes from the large labour union sector. About 30 percent of all workers in Canada belong to labour unions. The average union contract lasts 2 years.

2. Workers who are not in a large labour union typically have their wages adjusted about once each year. The size of the wage adjustment is influenced by expectations of inflation, expectations of the wages paid to other workers, and the level of unemployment.

3. Wage setting is staggered. Not all workers obtain wage adjustments at the same time. This staggering adds to the inertia of wage rigidities.

4. Prices are set as stable markup over costs, including labour costs. Prices are not as responsive to demand as they would be in an auction market.

5. Wage and price rigidities arising from overlapping contracts and other sources make the process of disinflation slow and painful.

6. A specific model of wage adjustment with overlapping contracts confirms that the same unemployment rate is consistent with any chronic rate of inflation.

KEY TERMS AND CONCEPTS

Three-year contracts

Two-year contracts

One-year wage adjustment

Large union sector

Staggered wage setting

Collective bargaining

Markup pricing

Adjustment costs

Oligopoly

Productivity shocks

Implicit contracts

Disinflation

Policy effectiveness with rational expectations

Income policies

Front-end loading

Indexing

Relative wage concerns

Long-run trade-off between inflation and unemployment

Contract theory

Monopolistic competition

Forward-looking component of wages

Backward-looking component of wages

Credibility

Gradualism

QUESTIONS FOR DISCUSSION AND REVIEW

1. Describe the typical long-term union wage contract in Canada. What is indexing? Are many contracts indexed? Why?

2. What is staggered wage setting? Why does it occur?

3. Describe the typical wage adjustment for workers who are not in unions. Are these wage-setting dates staggered? Why aren't wages adjusted more frequently?

4. What is markup pricing? Is it a good description of most firms' pricing strategies in Canada?

5. Explain how markup pricing might be the result of information limitations at firms about what is going on in the economy.

6. Is monetary policy effective when expectations are rational? Why? Do any wages adjust when expectations of future monetary policy change?

7. In disinflating, is it better to be gradual or to be quick in reducing money growth?

8. What are the forward-looking and the backward-looking components of wage determination? What is their significance?

9. Why is there no long-run trade-off between inflation and unemployment, even though there is a short-run trade-off?

10. What good does it do for the Bank of Canada to maintain its own credibility about its promise not to tolerate inflation in the future?

PROBLEMS

Numerical

1. A worker has a contract with an employer. The worker will work as many hours as the employer chooses and will be paid $10 for each hour. The marginal product of the worker is $25 - .125H$ dollars per hour when the worker is working H hours. The marginal value of the worker's time is $.5H - 50$ dollars per hour when he is working H hours. How many hours will the employer ask the worker to work? Is this the efficient level? What if the marginal product schedule is $30 - .125H$? How can you measure the inefficiency of this amount of work?

2. Using tight monetary policy, the Bank of Canada is able to bring about a deceleration of prices, so that inflation falls from 10 percent to zero. The time path of the price level is as follows:

Year	Price Level
1	1.000
2	1.100
3	1.188
4	1.259
5	1.310
6 and later	1.336

There are two groups of workers, those whose wages are set in odd years and those whose wages are set in even years. When the wage is set, it is equal to 10 times the price level in the preceding year, raised by the amount of inflation that occurred in that year relative to the year before; that is, $W = 10P_{-1}(1 + \pi_{-1})$. In the second year of the contract, the wage is increased in proportion to the inflation that occurred in the first year relative to the year before; that is, $W = W_{-1}(1 + \pi_{-1})$. Compute the wages paid to the two groups and the average wage across the two groups starting in Year 2. Compute the rate of wage inflation and the real wage. Comment on the problems that disinflation creates when there are lags in wage setting, using the numbers from this example.

3. A firm enjoys a monopoly; its average revenue schedule is $15 - .25Y$ and its marginal revenue schedule is $15 - .5Y$ (Y is its amount of output). Its marginal cost schedule is $(Z + W)(.3 + .01Y)$. Z and W are the price of materials and the wage rate, respectively. For $Z = 2$ and $W = 8$, find the price and amount of output that maximise the monopolist's profit. Now suppose that the intercept in marginal and average revenues rises from 15 to 21 because demand rises. Find the price and level of output. Compare these to the case of markup pricing, where $P = Z + W$, and P does not change when demand rises. Now go back to the original average revenue and marginal revenue schedules and compute price and output when Z rises to 3. Again, compare these to the case of markup pricing. Conclude by comparing the general nature of markup and monopoly pricing, using your calculations as examples.

Analytical

1. Suppose initially that the economy is in equilibrium with unemployment equal to the natural rate and inflation equal to 10 percent. The Bank of Canada would like to reduce inflation down to zero. Listed below are several different descriptions of the way in which wages and prices are set. For each of them, indicate a desirable strategy for disinflating, and explain in each case the short-run consequences of such a strategy.

   a. Wages and prices are perfectly flexible, as in the classical model of Chapter 14.

   b. Wages are governed by 3-year contracts, while firms use markup pricing. All wage contracts in the economy are renegotiated at the same time.

   c. Wages and prices are set as in Part b except that wage contracts are staggered. One-third are renegotiated each year.

   d. Wages are set annually. They are a function of the prior year's wage, the prior year's inflation rate, and the prior year's unemployment rate. Prices are set as a markup over cost.

2. Suppose that the government encouraged unions to moderate their wage increases in exchange for a promise of tax cuts if inflation should exceed wage increases. Explain why such a policy might be useful in an economy with staggered wage setting and markup pricing.

3. In what way does an economy in which prices are determined by the condition that marginal revenue equal marginal cost respond differently to an aggregate demand shock than an economy in which prices are set as a markup over cost? Does it matter how wages are set in the latter case? How does each type of economy respond to a price shock?

4. Suppose that wage contracts last for three years. Each year, one-third of the economy's wage contracts are renegotiated. Contract wages are set according to

$$X = \frac{1}{3}(W + W_{+1} + W_{+2}) - \frac{c}{3}\left[(U - U^*) + (U_{+1} - U^*) + (U_{+2} - U^*)\right].$$

   a. Provide an expression for the average wage rate, W.

   b. Derive an expression analogous to Equation 16–5. How far backward- and forward-looking is the wage-determination process? What determines the responsiveness of contract wages to *current* labour market conditions?

5. In this chapter we developed a model in which contract wages change in response to *current and expected future conditions* in the labour market. How does such a model provide the underpinnings for our price-adjustment equation of Chapter 6, where prices respond to output *with a lag*?

6. Evaluate the following statement: Synchronised wage contracts offer the best prospect for 'cold turkey' disinflation. But they also provide the Bank of Canada with the greatest temptation to cheat. Moreover, if the Bank loses credibility, disinflation with synchronised contracts can be very painful. Therefore, it is probably better that contracts are staggered.

7. 'If expectations are rational, monetary policy has no effect on output, and disinflation without recession is possible.' Is this statement true or false? Explain your answer, calling on both models with the Lucas supply function and models with wage contracts and sticky prices.

Appendix: Contract Theory: An Extension of Auction Market Theory

In this appendix we consider a very explicit and detailed theory that was developed by macroeconomists in the 1970s to explain wage rigidities in labour markets. The theory focusses on employment contracts between workers and firms—and for this reason it is called **contract theory.** Like the information-based new classical theory described in Chapter 15, it makes explicit use of the idea that both firms and consumers *optimise;* that is, they maximise profits or utility. Contract theory assumes that firms and workers enter into contracts that govern employment and wage payments for a number of years in advance. Because contracts predetermine the behaviour of firms and workers, they may cause rigidity in that they rule out quick adjustments in response to changing conditions.

Contract theory can be viewed as an attempt to extend economic theory systematically beyond *auction* markets so that it can deal with markets in which there are contracts. As we have seen, an **auction market** is one like the grain or stock markets where thousands of bidders are constantly buying and selling units of a homogeneous commodity. The labour market is completely different from an auction market. Each person's services are unique. Employers have to investigate each potential worker's qualifications carefully and a worker has to check out each potential employer. Once a good match is found and a worker has been trained for a job, both worker and employer have an incentive to preserve the match. Hence, employment relations need to be governed by some type of contract, even if it is not written down in a formal way.

Standard microeconomic theory treats the labour market as an auction market. Since we know that labour markets—and many other markets, for that matter—are not auction markets, contract theory is potentially an important area of economic research. Like the information-based theory, it has been the focus of much research over the last 15 years.[15]

THE AUCTION MARKET MODEL: A REVIEW

In Figure 16–9 we review the classical model using a supply and demand diagram for the labour market. The vertical axis is the real wage; the horizontal axis is employment. The intersection of the supply curve and the demand curve determines the real wage and the amount of employment.

Suppose that there is a disturbance that decreases the demand for labour. For example, suppose that labour becomes less productive because of a change in production technology. This shifts the labour demand curve to the left. The real wage immediately adjusts downward, as does employment.

Figure 16–9.   AN AUCTION MARKET FOR LABOUR.
A downward shift in the labour demand curve reduces the real wage and employment. The amount of employment at the intersection is efficient.

[15] The research began with papers by Costas Azariadis, 'Implicit Contracts and Underemployment Equilibria,' *Journal of Political Economy,* Vol. 83, pp. 1183–1202, 1975, and Martin N. Baily, 'Wages and Employment under Uncertain Demand,' *Review of Economic Studies,* Vol. 41, pp. 37–50, 1974.

The exact procedure through which the real wage instantaneously adjusts in the market is usually left unstated. In principle there must be some auctioneer calling out alternative real wages and obtaining information about demand and supply at those real wages. The fact that such auctioneers are not observed in labour markets is of course one of the reasons for developing an alternative to the auction market model.

An important property of the auction market model is that the amount of employment determined at the intersection of the demand and supply curves is **efficient.** That auction markets are efficient is a fundamental result of microeconomics. To understand the concept of efficiency, consider a furniture-manufacturing firm producing chairs and tables. The firm's managers hire carpenters (the workers) to make the chairs and tables. The number of hours that the carpenters actually work will depend on two things: (1) how valuable the carpenter's time is to the firm and (2) how valuable the carpenter's additional earnings are to the carpenter; less technically, (1) the firm's demand for labour and (2) the worker's supply of labour.

We first consider the firm. In deciding how many hours to employ the carpenters on a given day, the firm maximises profits by taking the real wage as given. (Think of the auctioneer calling out a real wage to the firm.) The basic result of the theory of the firm is that profit maximisation occurs at the level of employment where the *marginal productivity of an additional hour of work equals the real wage.* In terms of the example, the firm will be maximising its profits when the value of the chairs that a carpenter can make by working an additional hour equals the real cost of employing that carpenter for an additional hour. The reason for this result is fairly intuitive: If the marginal productivity of an additional hour of work were more than the real wage, then the firm could increase profits by having the carpenters work more hours. If the marginal productivity of an additional hour of work were less than the real wage, then the firm would want the carpenters to work fewer hours. The condition that the marginal product of labour equals the real wage is what generates the downward-sloping labour demand curve: As the real wage falls, the firm increases employment, thereby reducing the marginal productivity of additional employment.

Now consider the work decision of the carpenters. They will want to work up to the point where the increased utility through the higher income from an additional hour of work is equal to the decrease in utility from the loss in leisure time due to the additional hour of work. In other words, they want to balance the loss in leisure time from more work with the gain in income through more work. The point of balance will depend on the real wage, because the real wage translates hours of work into income. The higher the real wage, the more the worker will want to work. A higher real wage increases the gain from working relative to the loss.

These ideas can be stated more formally using a basic result from microeconomics: The carpenters will want to work up to the point where the *ratio of the marginal utility of an additional hour of leisure to the marginal utility of additional income is equal to the real wage.* If this condition is not satisfied, then the carpenters will be able to increase their utility by working a different number of hours. For example, if the real wage is greater than the marginal rate of substitution, then the carpenters will increase utility by working more hours.

At all points along the labour demand curve in Figure 16–9 the marginal product of labour equals the real wage. At all points along the labour supply curve, the marginal rate of substitution equals the real wage. Hence, at the intersection of these two curves—that is, at the point of equilibrium in the auction market—both marginal conditions are satisfied. With both conditions satisfied we know that the marginal rate of substitution is equal to the marginal productivity of labour. This is the fundamental condition of efficiency. The auction market—with the real wage determined by the auctioneer so that demand is equal to supply—generates this condition.

THE OPTIMAL CONTRACT MODEL

Now consider how this auction market model would be modified to deal with contracts. A basic property of a contract is that it specifies actions to be taken in the future. For example, it spells out a wage to be paid next year. Hence, in order to build a model of contracts, it is necessary to consider a situation where some events explicitly take place in the future. At the time that the contract is written these events are unknown.

The economic events are assumed to be the same as those that affected the auction model of the labour market in Figure 16–9. It is of interest to see how the response of the contract market to these shocks differs from that of the auction market. In particular, we assume that the disturbance that shocks the market is a shift in the labour demand schedule, and that this shock comes from a reduction in labour productivity. Unlike the auction market model, however, the labour contract must be written in advance of the time when the disturbance occurs. The contract is written this year and the shock occurs next year. (↓ labour prod.)

Neither the firms nor the workers know in advance what type of a disturbance will in fact occur. They are likely to have some idea of the probability of the disturbance to occur, however, and we will assume that everyone thinks that the chances are 50–50 that a negative shock will occur, and 50–50 that a positive shock will occur. It is as if a coin is tossed: heads, labour productivity shifts up; tails, labour productivity shifts down. In terms of the labour demand curve, the two possibilities are illustrated in Figure 16–10.

The contract is 1 year in duration, and applies only to the next year, when the uncertain disturbance will occur. Both workers and firms have a view of the world as illustrated in Figure 16–10 and agree that the probability of a good year (high productivity) is the same as that of a bad year (low productivity). That is, the objective probabilities correspond to the subjective probabilities of the workers and the firms; this is the *rational expectations* assumption. Under these circumstances it is op-

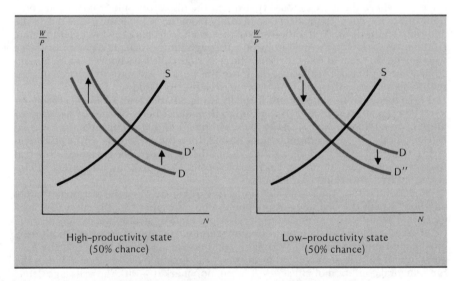

Figure 16–10. UNCERTAINTY ABOUT LABOUR DEMAND.
Which way the labour demand curve shifts in the next period is uncertain. Either it will shift up, as in the left panel, or it will shift down, as in the right panel. Both possibilities have an equal (50–50) chance of occurring.

timal for the contract to be written in the form of *contingency clauses* that stipulate what the level of employment and the wage rate will be in the case that the next period is a good year and in the case that it is a bad year. These contingencies will have the following form:

If productivity is *high*,
    employ workers for L_1 hours,
    pay real wage W_1/P_1.
If productivity is *low*,
    employ workers for L_2 hours,
    pay real wage W_2/P_2.

Note that the optimal contract entails a wage rate and number of hours that can be different in the two possible states of productivity. Presumably, the contract would specify that there be more hours worked in the case where productivity is high than in the case where productivity is low. (An example of a contingency clause is arrangements for indexing or cost-of-living adjustments as discussed in Section 16.1, in which the nominal wage changes automatically when the price level changes.)

What do the contingency clauses say about the levels of employment in the two states of productivity? The amount of work in each state must be efficient. That is, the marginal product of labour in the state must be equal to the marginal rate of substitution between income and leisure. Suppose the contract set a lower level of work where the marginal product of labour exceeded the marginal rate of substitution. Then another contract would be available that was better in that state for both the firm and the workers. It would set a higher level of employment; the extra profit to the firm from the additional output would be worth more than the time given up by the workers.

As a separate matter, the contract sets the real wage in each state. Think first about the average level of wages in the two states. The firm cannot make the terms of the contract too much in its own favour relative to the workers. If it did so the workers would go to another firm to sign a contract. The firm must take as given the opportunity that the workers have to sign such a contract with another firm, and thereby increase their expected utility. In the contract model, therefore, the firm takes as given the level of utility that the workers can obtain elsewhere. This proposition is a generalisation of the situation in the auction model where the firm takes the real wage as given, representing the opportunity that workers have if they go to another firm.

Now think about the levels of the wage in the two states. The workers' assessment of their utility in the next period will also involve an averaging of the two future possibilities. However, the uncertainty about the future productivity shock has a special additional effect on the preferences of workers. Optimal contract theory assumes that workers are *risk averse* when dealing with this uncertainty. If people are risk averse, they would prefer a certain outcome to an uncertain one with the same average value. Risk-averse workers would prefer a contract that gave them equal real incomes in the high-productivity case and in the low-productivity case. Paying the same income whether the workers are more or less productive reduces the risk to the worker.

While it is assumed that workers are risk averse, no similar assumption is made for firms. Firms are assumed to be *risk neutral,* which simply means that they are indifferent between a certain outcome and an uncertain outcome provided the two give the same amount of profit, on the average. The rationale for treating firms as risk neutral (while workers are risk averse) is that firms are owned by thousands of people, most of whom have investments in many other firms as well. Because of their diversification, they have less at stake with respect to this one firm. The workers, on the other hand, work only at this one firm. (The managers of the firms should be distinguished from the owners. Profits of the firm are paid out to the owners; except for profit-sharing arrangements, the managers are paid wages and salaries just like any other worker.)

Because of these considerations, the optimal contract has the striking property that the real wage may be *lower* in high-productivity states than in low-productivity states. Workers will achieve the same level of overall satisfaction in both states, but they will be working more hours in the high-productivity state.

By contrast, in the auction market, the real wage would be *higher* in the high-productivity state. The crucial difference is the following: In the contract theory, efficiency is achieved by the workings of the contract. *Essentially, there is a market in labour contracts, rather than in labour itself.* The wage that is set in the contract does not guide the allocation of labour—the firm does not decide each year how much labour to use in a given state by equating the marginal product of labour to the real wage. Instead, the contract stipulates the amount of work. The only function of the wage is to compensate the worker for accepting the contract. In contrast, the auction market is a market for labour services. Firms in the market equate their marginal product to the real wage they find in the market.

Labour contract theory was originally developed to explain the departures of actual employment from its efficient level. Contracts seemed to be a potential explanation of the price and wage rigidities that we know can lead to such departures. However, the simplest contract theory turned out to show the contrary: Contracts *per se* do not lead to inefficiencies. They may alter the short-run distribution of income, if some parties to the contract are more risk averse than others, as with the workers versus the firm.

There are other ingredients that can be added to the contract model in order to generate the observed inefficiencies. A key assumption underlying optimal contract theory was that the firm and workers both can observe the fluctuations in productivity. Workers would not agree to the contract if they could not verify the state of productivity. If management could fool workers into accepting a false statement about productivity, they might claim that productivity was high and the workers should work more hours. The additional work might cost the firm relatively little, because the firm might be committed to about the same amount of pay in high- as in low-productivity periods.

Contract theorists have examined this case; they call it 'asymmetric information.' Asymmetric information constrains the form of contracts so that they are 'incentive compatible.' That is, workers must be sure that the firm has no incentive to lie about productivity. The incentive compatibility constraints in effect limit the contingencies on which the contract can be based. It is not surprising that such limits can lead to inefficient contracts.[16]

---

[16] For more discussion of inefficient contracts see Guillermo Calvo and Edmund S. Phelps, 'Employment-Contingent Wage Contracts,' in Karl Brunner and Allan Meltzer (eds.), *Stabilization of the Domestic and International Economy*, Carnegie-Rochester Conference Series in Public Policy, 1977, pp. 160–168; Robert E. Hall, 'Employment Fluctuations and Wage Rigidities,' *Brookings Papers on Economic Activity*, Number 1, pp. 91–124, 1980; and Sanford Grossman and Oliver Hart, 'Implicit Contracts, Moral Hazard, and Unemployment,' *American Economic Review*, Vol. 71 (May 1981), pp. 301–307.

17

$\diamondsuit$ ━━━━━━━━━━━━━━━━━━━━━━━━━━━ $\diamondsuit$

Aggregate Dynamics and Price Adjustment

IN THIS chapter we develop a model of price adjustment that brings together the theories of price-wage rigidities and rational expectations. It thus responds to the important issues raised in the previous chapter, yet it is simple enough that we can incorporate it in our full model of the economy. In fact, the algebra and graphs that we use to analyse the price-adjustment model are very similar to those that we used to study the price-adjustment relationships in Chapter 6. Here, however, we examine *changes in the coefficients* of the model of price adjustment and of expected inflation that occur when macro policy or the economic environment changes. We also examine with more practical examples the *dynamic response of inflation and output to disturbances* that was presented in Chapter 7. Finally, we study *empirical tests of the model* using the actual macroeconomic data of Canada, the United States, and Germany during the 1970s and 1980s.

17.1 The Wage-Price Process as a Whole

In Chapter 6 we introduced the *Phillips curve* as our basic model of price adjustment: According to the Phillips curve, inflation rises when demand conditions are tight, when expectations of inflation rise, or when there are price shocks. Using algebra the Phillips curve can be written:

$$\pi = \underbrace{f\left(\frac{Y_{-1} - Y^*}{Y^*}\right)}_{\substack{\text{Market conditions} \\ \text{(slack or tight)}}} + \underbrace{\pi^e}_{\substack{\text{Expectations} \\ \text{of inflation}}} + \underbrace{Z.}_{\text{Price shocks}} \qquad (17\text{--}1)$$

$$\underbrace{\hspace{5cm}}_{\text{Determinants of wage inflation}}$$

[handwritten margin notes: deviation of real GDP from potential. real GDP > potential GDP. $\frac{Y_{-1} - Y^*}{Y^*} > 1$ π will not stop ↑]

The last term (Z), representing price shocks, was not made explicit in the discussion of Chapter 6; it represents the upward shift in the price-adjustment relationship that we discussed in Chapter 6 and again in Chapter 16.

One of the most important properties of Equation 17–1 is that there is no long-run trade-off between inflation and the level of GDP. A country with a high average inflation rate that is generally expected to continue will not have any higher output than a country with a low inflation rate that is generally expected to continue. This is easily seen from Equation 17–1: On average, the effect of supply shocks will be zero ($Z = 0$), and expected inflation π^e will equal actual inflation π in the long run regardless of the level of actual inflation. Hence, according to Equation 17–1, the market conditions term $(Y_{-1} - Y^*)/Y^*$ equals zero, or, equivalently, actual output equals potential output. As we saw in Chapter 6, the proposition that there is no long-run trade-off between output and inflation is sometimes called the *natural rate property* because the unemployment rate is equal to the natural rate regardless of the rate of inflation; it is also sometimes called the *accelerationist property* because attempts to keep output above normal result in accelerating prices.

Three specific aspects of the theory of wage and price rigidities of Chapter 16 provide a simple interpretation of Equation 17–1:

1. *Prices are set by Canadian producers as a markup over the costs of production,* including wage costs and the cost of materials, such as crude oil, iron ore, and timber. Because of markup pricing, if there are no changes in the price of crude materials then the rate of change in prices set by Canadian producers will equal the rate of change in wages. The first two terms on the right-hand side of Equation 17–1 reflect influences on the rate of change in wages—market conditions and expectations of inflation—as we will see in the next two paragraphs. The last term Z reflects changes in the prices of raw materials and imports. According to this interpretation, the primary reason for a shock to the prices set by Canadian producers is changes in the price of raw materials. A major example of this type of shock was the increase in the price of oil in 1973 and again in 1979 when a cartel of oil-producing countries increased the price of crude oil dramatically. A price shock Z can also come about due to a change in the price of imports. For example, if U.S. producers set the price of their exports to Canada

in U.S. dollars then a change in the Canada-U.S. exchange rate will change the Canadian dollar price of goods imported from the United States.

2. *Wages respond with a lag to unemployment.* When unemployment is high and the labour market is slack, currently negotiated wages fall, or rise by less than they would under favourable conditions. The average wage thus moves in the direction needed to bring the labour market into balance, but it moves only a fraction of the way each period because only a fraction of the wages are changed each period. As we have seen, there is a close relationship—Okun's law—between the unemployment rate and the departures of GDP from potential: When the unemployment rate is above normal, GDP is below normal, and vice versa. Using Okun's law, we can represent the pressure of labour market conditions on wage inflation by the output gap $(Y_{-1} - Y^*)/Y^*$. The subscript '-1' indicates that current wage change is related to market pressure in the previous period, reflecting the lags in wage adjustment.

3. *Wages respond to expected inflation.* When workers expect prices and other workers' wages to rise by 8 or 10 percent per year they will start off their negotiations asking for this much of an increase. One of the reasons that workers might expect inflation in the future is that other workers have recently signed 2-year or 3-year contracts with 8 to 10 percent increases in the second and third years. This is the reason for the expectations term π^e on the right-hand side of Equation 17–1. The price-adjustment equation says that the combined effect of a 1 percentage point increase in expected inflation is to raise wage inflation by 1 percentage point.

17.2 Changes in the Coefficients of the Price-Adjustment Model

The theory of wage and price rigidities underlying the price-adjustment relationship suggests that it would change if economic conditions or policy change. In particular, the sensitivity of inflation to recent market conditions (f) is likely to change when the economic environment changes. Here we consider two important examples of changes in the economic environment: an increase in the amount of indexing and a reduction in the size and length of business cycles.

THE EFFECT OF WAGE INDEXING

As we saw in Chapter 16, there is some indexing of union labour contracts (cost-of-living adjustment provisions) in Canada. Indexing is more prevalent in other countries—a good example is Italy. With indexing, each time the price level rises by 1 percent, wages rise by a fraction of a percent a, automatically. How would indexing affect the price-adjustment relationship? Indexing means that the wage will respond to the *current* rate of inflation as well as to the lagged rate of inflation. The effect of this is to speed up the overall response (*f*) of inflation to changes in unemployment. To see this, suppose there is an increase in output that initially increases wage inflation by 1 percent. Through markup pricing, this will quickly have an upward influence of 1 percent on prices. But, if wages are indexed, the upward adjustment of price inflation will mean a further upward adjustment of wage inflation of the amount *a*. This in turn will increase price inflation by *a*, through the markup process. Again indexing will raise wage inflation, now by an amount *a* times *a*, or a^2. And the process will continue for a third round, where inflation will increase by another multiple of *a* (a^3). The whole process is called a **wage-price spiral**. As long as indexing is less than 100 percent, the process will eventually settle down, but the end result has been to make wages adjust more to the increase in output than if there had not been any indexing. The total effect is

$$1 + a + a^2 + a^3 + \ldots = \frac{1}{1-a},$$

using the formula for the geometric series. Note that the total effect is much like the formula for the multiplier. For example, if *a* equals .5 then the effect of market conditions on inflation is doubled: $1/(1 - .5) = 2$. In general, *indexing makes nominal wages more responsive to market conditions,* as represented by a higher value for the coefficient *f* in Equation 17–1.

For the same reasons, indexing also increases the response of inflation to price shocks Z. When the cost of materials rises, firms increase their prices. But because of indexing, these price increases will raise wages. In turn, the increase in wages then increases prices again. The wage-price spiral thus multiplies the effect of a raw materials price on inflation. If there is no indexing, so that the wage does not respond at all to prices, other costs would go directly into prices with a coefficient of 1. But because wages rise when prices rise, there is a feedback effect—the wage-price spiral. The feedback effect more than doubles the impact of a price shock.

LENGTH AND SEVERITY OF BUSINESS CYCLES

In Chapter 16 we saw that long-term contracts are set in a forward-looking manner: Workers and firms look ahead to future labour market conditions, and to price and wage inflation. If workers expect a recession to be short then they will be more reluctant to accept lower wages than if they expect the recession to last for a number of years. In the price-adjustment equation, the market conditions term $(Y_{-1} - Y^*)/Y^*$ partially represents how recent excess supply or demand is indicative of future excess supply or demand. Usually business cycles last for a number of years, so, if output is below potential this year, that is an indication that output will probably be below normal for a few more years.

But suppose that departures of output from potential become less persistent; for example, suppose that the average length of business cycles is reduced from, say, 4 years to 2 years. Then if GDP is below potential today there is no implication that GDP will be below potential 2 years from now. The best guess is that GDP will be back to potential 2 years from now. As a result inflation will be less responsive to recessions. Algebraically, the coefficient f in Equation 17–1 will be smaller when recessions are expected to be less prolonged.

17.3 Models of the Expected Inflation Term

One of the most difficult issues in the price-adjustment equation is the measure of expected inflation, π^e. There are two important factors to consider:

1. *Forward-looking forecasts.* When wages are set, the fact that prices and other wages are expected to rise in the future influences the wage that emerges from whatever process the worker and the employer use to determine wages. For example, when a 3-year contract is negotiated, the built-in wage increases in the second and third years are larger if inflation is expected to continue during the contract. The amount of inflation that is forecast to occur in the future is therefore part of the expected inflation term. If workers and unions are informed about the economy, then these forward-looking forecasts will match rational expectations theory.

2. *Staggered contracts and backward-looking wage behaviour.* The influence of today's expectations on the expected inflation term is only part of the story, however. Because of wage contracts and staggered wage setting, the expectations term involves inertia that cannot be changed overnight. Workers and firms must take account of the wages that will be paid to other workers in the economy. Since wage setting is staggered over time, some wages must be set looking back at the previous wage decisions of other workers; once these wages are set they are not changed during the contract period unless economic conditions change drastically. Wage inflation has a momentum due to contracts and relative wage setting. The expectations term must take account of this momentum as well as of the pure expectational influence.[1]

There is no reason to choose between these explanations. Both are part of the simple algebraic model of staggered contracts with rational expectations discussed in Chapter 16.

---

[1] For more detail on this point and a contrast with other texts that emphasise only pure expectational effects, see John B. Taylor, 'Staggered Wage Setting in a Macro Model,' *American Economic Review,* Vol. 69 (May 1979), pp. 108–113.

CHANGES IN THE MODEL OF EXPECTED INFLATION

For macroeconomic policy the particular model of the expected inflation term is crucial. Any reasonable model of expectations will give the long-run result that there is no long-run trade-off between the levels of inflation and output. But much of macroeconomic policy is concerned about the short run, and here different models of expected inflation make quite a difference.

Any *model* of expected inflation must be consistent with the *actual behaviour* of inflation as observed over a number of years. If inflation typically tends to have momentum, then the public's model of expected inflation will also have momentum. But if inflation tends to be temporary, because of a policy to stabilise prices, for example, then people's view of expected inflation will incorporate the belief that a burst of inflation will probably not be followed by continuing inflation.

For the above reasons, any model of expected inflation is therefore itself endogenous to the type of economy or type of policy that is in operation. If policy changes, the model of expected inflation should change. Consider some examples:

1. *Changes in monetary policy.* When the Bank of Canada announces that it is switching to a new policy that puts more weight on controlling inflation, and the public believes it, the model of expected inflation will change.
2. *Introduction of specific policies for wage restraint.* The federal government has experimented with a variety of mandatory and voluntary programs for cutting wage inflation. Typically, these involve the announcement of a national wage norm and some method for punishing or exposing employers that exceed the norm. Economists have proposed alternative policies based on tax penalties for excessive wage increases. If the public believes that a policy of this type is working, the model of expected inflation will change.

If people are highly skeptical about promised changes in government programs, then they may well take the view that the only convincing evidence that expected inflation has changed is for actual inflation to change. If so, a simple backward-looking model of the expected inflation term is closer to the truth—at least for the period of time that it takes the government to convince people that it means business.

In what follows we will work through some of the implications of a particular example of a model of expected inflation and examine how the process might change.

A simple model says that this year's expected inflation depends on actual inflation last year and the year before:

$$\pi^e = .4\pi_{-1} + .2\pi_{-2}.$$ (17–2)

This equation is more complicated than the model of the expectations term that we considered in Chapter 6, but conceptually the same ideas are at work. In Chapter 6 we assumed that expected inflation depended only on the rate of inflation last year π_{-1}. In Equation 17–2, expected inflation also depends on inflation two years ago.

To illustrate the implications of this model of the expected inflation term, we will look at four examples of how prices adjust to different disturbances.

EXAMPLE 1: EFFECT OF A ONE-YEAR STIMULUS

The economy starts with zero expected inflation. Policy makers choose to push output above normal by 3 percentage points for one full year. From then on, output is kept at its normal level. Throughout the period, there is no contribution to inflation from materials prices or imports (Z is zero). What happens to the price level?

In order to answer this question, we need to know the numerical value of the coefficient, f, that governs the unemployment effect in Equation 17–1. A reasonable value, inferred from the last few decades of experience, is $f =$ .25. That is, if real GDP is 1 percent above potential in a particular year, inflation is .25 percentage point higher on that account.

In the first year, the output gap is above normal by 3 percent, which adds .75 percent to inflation in the second year through the first term in the price equation. Expected inflation is zero and there are no price shocks, so inflation π in Year 2 is .75. In the second year, output is back to normal, so there is no contribution from the first term. However, expected inflation is up because of the actual inflation the year before. Because last year has a coefficient of .4, expected inflation is .3. This is the only term affecting inflation, so inflation is .3 in Year 3. In the fourth year, again only expected inflation is contributing to actual inflation, so expected inflation is .4 times last year's inflation of .3 plus .2 times the .75 inflation of 2 years ago. The sum is .27. Thus, inflation in Year 4 is .27. In the fifth year, expected inflation is .4 times last year's rate of .27 plus .2 times the .3 inflation of the year before. That is, inflation in Year 5 is .17. This process continues year after year. If you keep computing in this way, you will get results that gradually approach zero. But the measurable effects of the one year of stimulus continue for quite a few years. The results are summarised in Table 17–1.

This example illustrates the *dynamic* nature of the trade-off between output and inflation in an economy where expected inflation responds to actual inflation, on the one hand, and then gets built into actual inflation, on the other hand. A 1-year period of lower unemployment brings a sustained increase in the inflation rate. The effect is dynamic because an effect in one year has an effect that lasts for many years.

The intuitive reason that a temporary period of higher output prompts a sustained increase in inflation is that higher output raises actual inflation. In

Table 17–1.   INFLATION EFFECTS OF A ONE-TIME STIMULUS TO OUTPUT

Year	Inflation (%)	Output Gap (%)
1	.00	3
2	.75	0
3	.30	0
4	.27	0
5	.17	0
.	.	.
.	.	.
.	.	.
∞	.00	0

the next year, expected inflation must be higher. Once expected inflation is up, it tends to remain up, because expected inflation feeds point for point into actual inflation. In our simple model, expected inflation gradually dies out if there is no further inflationary stimulus from lower unemployment or price shocks.

EXAMPLE 2: EFFECT OF A PRICE SHOCK

Price shocks can be caused by increases in the price of materials or the price of imports. The full story of the response of the economy to a price shock involves the aggregate demand side of the economy. But, even without the demand side, we can answer the question, what would happen to inflation if aggregate demand policy were manipulated in such a way that output remained at its normal level at the time of the price shock and during its aftermath?

Suppose that the rise in the price of materials or imports is 1 percent for 1 year and then is zero in future years. Also suppose that because of indexing, the contribution to the price-adjustment equation, Z, is 2.5 percent. Output is held at its normal level in every year. Expected inflation starts at zero. In the year of the shock, the price shock is the only contributor to inflation, so the immediate impact is to give 2.5 percentage points of inflation: Inflation π in Year 1 is 2.5. In Year 2, neither output nor the price shock of Year 1 is contributing to inflation, but expected inflation is up because of the actual inflation in the previous year. It gets a weight of .4, so expected inflation in the second year is 1.0, and that is the actual inflation rate as well: Inflation is 1.0 in Year 2. In the second year after the shock, expected inflation is .2 times actual inflation in Year 1 plus .4 times actual inflation in Year 2, or .9 percent: Inflation in Year 3 is .9. This process continues until inflation gradually reaches zero. The results are summarised in Table 17–2.

EXAMPLE 3: EFFECT OF A ONE-YEAR INFLATION

Another question we can answer using just the price equation has the opposite flavour of the two earlier ones: Suppose monetary policy is conducted

Table 17-2. EFFECT ON INFLATION OF A MATERIALS PRICE SHOCK WHEN OUT-
PUT IS HELD AT POTENTIAL

Year	Inflation (%)	Output Gap (%)
1	2.50	0
2	1.00	0
3	.90	0
4	.56	0
.	.	.
.	.	.
.	.	.
∞	.00	0

so that there is inflation in one year but no inflation in any later year. What happens to output in the inflationary year and in the subsequent years? In the first year, output will rise as the economy responds to the stimulus that brings on the inflation. But, in the second year, output must be below nor- $\overline{m} = \overline{u} + \frac{e}{f}$ mal. By assumption, inflation is to be zero, but expected inflation is positive because actual inflation was positive the year before. Hence there must be a negative contribution from output.

If inflation in the second year is to be 1 percent, and the contributions from price shocks and expected inflation are zero, it must be that output is 4 percentage points above normal in the first year. That is, inflation in Year 2 is 1 percent, which equals $.25[(Y_{-1} - Y^*)/Y^*]$ so that $(Y_{-1} - Y^*)/Y^*$ equals .04. Going into the third year, expected inflation is .4 times actual inflation in the second year, 1 percent, or .4 percent of expected inflation. We want actual inflation to be zero, so

$$.25[(Y_{-1} - Y^*)/Y^*] + .004 = 0.$$

Thus, the output gap is −1.6 percent. In the third year, the history of inflation is 1 percent 2 years ago and zero last year. Expected inflation is .2 percent. To make actual inflation zero, output must again exceed the fall below its normal level:

$$.25[(Y_{-1} - Y^*)/Y^*] + .002 = 0,$$

so that the output gap is −.8 percent. From this point on, expected inflation is zero. The unemployment rate drops back to its normal level in the fourth year and remains there. These calculations are summarised in Table 17-3.

Table 17-3. OUTPUT GAPS ASSOCIATED WITH A SINGLE YEAR OF INFLATION

Year	Inflation (%)	Output Gap (%)
1	0	4.0
2	1	−1.6
3	0	− .8
4	0	.0
>4	0	.0

The net effect of the policy of one point of inflation for 1 year is to push output 4 percent above normal in the year before. But in the two subsequent years, output has to be below normal by 1.6 and .8 percentage points. If you add up the total output gain from this policy you will see that it is positive: 4.0 minus 1.6 minus .8 equals 1.6. The economy achieves 1.6 percent more output. The inflation-output trade-off is sensitive to the way that expected inflation is related to actual inflation. The favourable trade-off in the example we just looked at arises because one point of actual inflation contributes less than one point of expected inflation. The one point of inflation in the first year generates .4 point of expected inflation in the second year and .2 point in the third year. If expected inflation is more sensitive to actual inflation, the trade-off would be less favourable. In particular, if one point of actual inflation ultimately contributed a whole point to expected inflation, the trade-off would be even—the total output loss associated with a rise and equal fall in inflation would be zero.

EXAMPLE 4: EFFECT OF EXTENDED HIGH OUTPUT

Finally, suppose that aggregate demand policy provides whatever stimulus is needed to keep output 3 percentage points above normal for every year starting with Year 1. What will happen to the rate of inflation?

We already know that an attempted policy of permanent stimulus will break down sooner or later, because expected inflation will respond to the policy and will move up to anticipate its effects. What happens in our simple model of expected inflation? It turns out that the simple model does not obey this accelerationist proposition. Even if the simple model worked fairly well in describing expected inflation over the last 30 years of Canadian experience, when inflation ebbed and flowed several times, it would clearly change under different conditions of extended periods of high inflation.

If we trace through the operation of the simple model under sustained stimulus, we get the following: The first year is exactly the same as the policy that kept output above normal just for the first year. Actual inflation is .75 percent in the second year. In the third year, expected inflation is .30 percent. In addition, because output is still 3 percentage points above normal, the first term of the price equation contributes another .75 percent. Actual inflation is 1.05 percent in Year 3. In the fourth year, expected inflation is $(.4)(1.05) + (.2)(.75) = .57$. Output remains 3 percentage points above normal and contributes its usual .75 percent. The sum is 1.32 percent: Inflation in Year 4 is 1.32. In the fifth year, expected inflation is .74 percent and actual inflation is 1.49. The process continues indefinitely, with actual inflation rising each year. Ultimately, inflation stabilises at 1.88 percent per year.

The behaviour we have just described is a complete violation of the natural rate–accelerationist proposition. The output gap is permanently 3 percentage points above normal, whereas the natural rate proposition says that output must be equal to potential, on the average. Inflation reaches a constant level of 1.88 percent per year, instead of rising to unlimited levels as predicted by the accelerationist proposition. The problem is that we are not allowing our simple model of expected inflation (Equation 17–2) to adjust to a fundamental change in the economic environment. If policy makers decide to introduce permanent inflation, then the simple model of expected inflation no longer makes sense.

To see the problem, note that, if inflation reaches the constant level of 1.88 percent, we can substitute 1.88 for π_{-1} and π_{-2} in Equation 17–2. Expected inflation is $\pi^e = 1.13$ percent per year. Expected inflation is chronically well below actual inflation. The government has tricked wage setters into thinking that inflation is less than it really is.

In the long run, people will not fall into this trap. They will revise expected inflation to the full level of actual inflation, and the natural rate–accelerationist proposition will hold. Our simple model of expected inflation will not work under sustained constant inflation. Instead, it is a model suited to a world where inflation is not sustained, but comes in occasional bursts that then subside.

It is likely that the model of expected inflation will change to something like

$$\pi^e = .5\pi_{-1} + .5\pi_{-2}.$$

This formula has the property that expected inflation becomes equal to actual inflation if the actual inflation is sustained for 2 years. If you go back over our calculations of the effect of a policy of keeping output 3 percent above normal permanently, you will find that the alternative model predicts that inflation will rise each year and become greater without limit. The amount of the increase is shown in Table 17–4. Eventually, the process settles down to a constant amount of increase in inflation of .5 percentage point each year.

The last example seems to show the accelerationist proposition at work. When policy makers hold output above normal year after year, inflation

Table 17–4.   INCREASE IN INFLATION WITH PERMANENT HIGH OUTPUT

Year	Inflation (%)	Output Gap (%)
1	.0	3
2	.750	3
3	1.125	3
4	1.688	3
5	2.156	3
6	2.672	3
.	.	.
.	.	.
.	.	.
∞	∞	3

Note: The expectations term is given by Equation 17-2 with a .5 coefficient on last year's inflation, and .5 on the previous year's inflation.

gets worse each year. If output is 3 percentage points above normal, inflation eventually worsens by .5 percentage point each year.

The alternative model of expected inflation is far from satisfactory, however. Although the *level* of expected inflation becomes equal to the level of
actual inflation, the rate of increase of expected inflation constantly lags behind the rate of increase of actual inflation. Even though the game policy
makers are playing must eventually become evident to everybody in the
economy, expected inflation constantly lags behind actual inflation. In reality, a policy that added .5 percentage point to inflation each year would
probably not keep output above normal indefinitely.

We could look at more complicated models of expected inflation that try
to keep up with the rate of change of inflation as well as its level, but the
main ideas should already be clear. There is a very general point at work
here: *No mechanical model of expected inflation is universally applicable.* If the
public has a particular way of arriving at expected inflation, the government
can design a policy that fools the public and makes actual inflation continually exceed expected inflation. But then the public will revise its method of
calculating expected inflation so that it will no longer be fooled.

If the government uses a policy that does not attempt to fool the public by
making actual inflation exceed expected inflation, then there can be a stable
way that the public arrives at expected inflation. In particular, if the government aims at a non-inflationary economy and acts to offset occasional bursts
of inflation from materials prices and elsewhere, then our simple model of
expected inflation is a reasonable description of the process. Inflation does
persist after it develops, but a point of past inflation does not contribute a
full point to expected inflation.

A policy that attempts to keep output above normal permanently will fail.
Eventually the public will catch on to the policy and revise expected inflation by a method that makes it keep up with actual inflation.

With any given method for determining expected inflation, the government can figure out an expansionary policy that keeps unemployment
below normal permanently. For example, with our simple model of expected inflation, a policy of continued inflation will keep unemployment
below normal. The model of expected inflation would not apply with such a
policy.

17.4 The Combined Operation of Price Adjustment and Aggregate Demand

We now integrate the price formulations, Equations 17–1 and 17–2, into a
model of aggregate demand, working in terms of a numerical example. A
simple form of the aggregate demand function is

$$Y = 2{,}067 + 3.221\frac{M}{P}. \tag{17–3}$$

Note that monetary policy is more powerful in this example than in the aggregate demand function in Chapter 5, which did not include the effect of interest on consumption goods such as automobiles. Fiscal policy determines the level of the constant, 2,067. Government spending is assumed to be fixed at $750 billion. The starting value for the money supply M is $600 billion. Potential output is assumed to be $4,000 billion.

Consider the case where the Bank of Canada targets M. Note that a higher price level means a lower level of aggregate demand. Recall the mechanism lying behind this conclusion:

1. If the price level rises more quickly than the money stock, the LM curve is farther to the left in the IS-LM diagram.
2. The intersection with the IS curve occurs at a lower level of real GDP and a higher interest rate.
3. Investment is lower because the interest rate is higher and because output is lower.
4. Net exports are lower because the interest rate is higher and the exchange rate is higher.
5. Consumption is lower because real income is lower and because interest rates are higher.

The second major element of the complete model is the price-adjustment equation, Equation 17–1. The third is the model of expected inflation.

The Four Relationships of the Numerical Example

Aggregate demand	$Y = 2,067 + 3.221(M/P)$
Price adjustment	$\pi = .25[(Y_{-1} - Y^*)/Y^*] + \pi^e + Z$
Expected inflation	$\pi^e = .4\pi_{-1} + .2\pi_{-2}$
Price level	$P = (1 + \pi_{-1})P_{-1}$

To analyse the three equations we can proceed graphically, as we did in Chapter 6, or algebraically. The graphical approach would use an aggregate demand diagram with price adjustment (see Figure 6–9). Each year we would treat the price level as predetermined and determine output at the intersection of aggregate demand and the flat price line; then calculate the price level for the next year using the price-adjustment diagram.

Here we proceed algebraically using the numerical example, but the analysis is equivalent: Take the price level as predetermined each year, and use the aggregate demand curve to determine output. Then use the model of the expectations term and the price-adjustment equation to determine the price level for the next year. At the new price level determine output in the next year and so on. We use this approach to look at the following four different examples: (1) recovery from a demand-deficient recession, (2) recovery from stagflation, (3) a boom, and (4) an oil price shock. In the first two examples we start the economy off from a position below full employment without asking how the economy got there. In the second two examples we start the economy at full employment and then push it away from full employment with a shock.

EXAMPLE 1: RECOVERY FROM A DEMAND-DEFICIENT RECESSION

Suppose the economy starts out at a position below full employment. Suppose, as well, that expected inflation at the outset is zero. How does the economy get back to equilibrium with full employment and stable prices?

In the first year, output is determined by the aggregate demand function given the initial price level and the money stock. This level of output is below potential. Consequently, the first term of the price-adjustment equation pushes the price level downward. Price shocks and expected inflation contribute nothing at this point. Inflation is negative. The price level falls slightly.

In the second year, the process continues. Output is still below potential, so the $(Y_{-1} - Y^*)/Y^*$ term in the price-adjustment equation pushes the price level down some more. But actual deflation in the previous year makes expected inflation negative in the second year. The result is a larger decline in the price level in the second year than in the first year.

In the third year, there is even more deflation, because the negative contribution from expected inflation is even larger. In the fourth year, deflation is about the same as in the third year. Expected inflation is making a somewhat larger negative contribution. But output has been improving steadily. As the price level falls, output rises, according to the aggregate demand function. Consequently, the negative contribution from the $(Y_{-1} - Y^*)/Y^*$ term is not as large as it was in earlier years.

In the fifth year, the price level falls some more, but not by as much as in the fourth year. The rate of inflation rises, in the sense that the rate of deflation is no longer as high. However, prices are still falling, and output rises some more.

Skipping to the ninth year, the price level has fallen far enough to restore full employment. However, the rate of inflation is still negative, because expected inflation is negative. The price level continues to fall and the economy enters a period that is slightly above full employment.

Some years later, the price level is again at equilibrium and output is at its potential level. But now expected inflation is very slightly positive. The economy overshoots a little and enters a period of less than full employment. By this time, the economy is so close to equilibrium that the rest of the process of cycling to equilibrium is almost invisible.

We now introduce a convenient diagram (Figure 17–1) to look at the

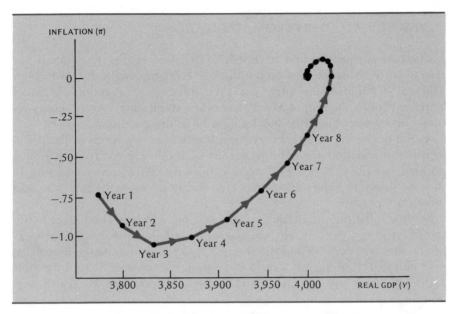

Figure 17–1.   ECONOMIC RECOVERY (EXAMPLE 1).
In the first year, real GDP is far below potential. In the next year inflation falls. In the year after that, inflation becomes even more negative because expected inflation becomes negative. Throughout the first nine years, the price level is falling, so aggregate demand rises and output approaches potential. Because of the momentum of deflation, the price level continues to fall after Year 7 and the economy enters a period with GDP above potential. The economy makes a spiral approach to equilibrium, where output equals potential and inflation is zero.

movements of output and inflation. This diagram shows that the rate of inflation is the vertical axis and the level of output is the horizontal axis.

The basic mechanism of a recovery is simple. From a point of deficient aggregate demand, the economy gets back to full employment by moving to a lower price level. As the price level falls, the LM curve shifts to the right, the interest rate falls, investment and export demand rise, and output rises.

The complete model describes this process. The most critical feature of the model is the response of the price level to output. In our portrayal of the complete model, a 1-year period in which output is 1 percent below potential lowers the price level by .25 percent below what it would have been if output had been at potential. It takes 9 years to restore full employment from a starting point below potential, with zero initial expected inflation and no price shocks throughout the recovery.

If the price level is significantly more sensitive to output, then the recovery would take place much faster. For example, if the coefficient in the price-adjustment equation is 1.00 point instead of .25 point of deflation per point of departure from potential, it takes only a little over 3 years to get back to full employment from a starting point below full employment.

EXAMPLE 2: RECOVERY FROM STAGFLATION

The case we just studied started with deficient aggregate demand but zero expected inflation. An even unluckier economy might start with both deficient demand and positive expected inflation—the condition Nobel laureate Paul Samuelson of M.I.T. has called **stagflation.**[2] An economy recently hit by a serious price shock might be in this condition.

At the beginning of a recovery from stagflation, two terms in the price-adjustment equation are fighting against each other. Expected inflation is positive, but the $(Y_{-1} - Y^*)/Y^*$ term is negative. Either one could win. In the case shown in Figure 17–2, expected inflation wins in the first year, and inflation is positive.

Because inflation won in the first year, the price level is a bit higher in the second year and the level of real GDP actually falls some more. Then expected inflation declines and the $(Y_{-1} - Y^*)/Y^*$ term dominates. The price level falls slightly going into Year 3 and output rises a bit. In Years 4 through 9, the price level falls some more and the recovery proceeds. By Year 9, out-

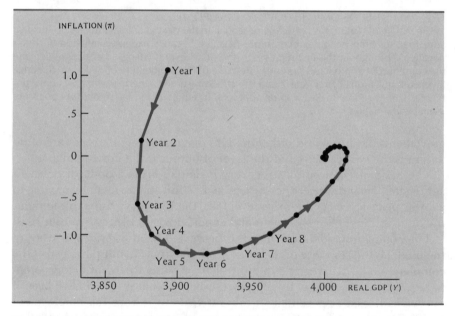

Figure 17–2. RECOVERY FROM STAGFLATION (EXAMPLE 2).
In the first year, inflation remains positive because of expected inflation. In the second year, real GDP is even lower because the price level has risen. From then on, the recovery is similar to the one in Figure 17–1, which started from zero expected inflation. The economy approaches equilibrium in a spiral.

[2] Paul Samuelson, 'Worldwide Stagflation,' in Hiroaki Nagatani and Kate Crowley (eds.), *The Collected Scientific Papers of Paul Samuelson*, Vol. 4, Cambridge, Mass., M.I.T. Press, 1975, pp. 801–807.

put is back up to potential but, because expected inflation is negative in that year, the economy overshoots a little. Output remains slightly above potential for a number of years.

If you compare Figures 17–1 and 17–2, you will see that the main effect of starting from a point of positive expected inflation is to delay the recovery for about 2 years. During these two years, the economy of Figure 17–2 is working off expected inflation and suffering from little growth of real output, while the economy of Figure 17–1 is getting started on its recovery. Again, falling prices are the key to recovery. In the two years when expected inflation is working against falling prices, the stagflation economy of Figure 17–2 cannot expand.

EXAMPLE 3: A BOOM

What happens in the short, medium, and long runs when an outward shift in aggregate demand sets off a boom? At first, higher aggregate demand raises output, in the way described by the IS-LM model. But higher output means inflation. After inflation gets started, expected inflation begins to catch up with it. As the price level rises, aggregate demand falls. Eventually, the economy gets back to equilibrium, with output equal to potential and inflation at zero. In the new equilibrium, the only effect of the increase in aggregate demand is to raise the price level. The path of the economy in response to an increase in aggregate demand is shown in the inflation-output diagram of Figure 17–3.

The path starts at equilibrium in Year 1. There is no inflation and output is at potential. In Year 2, the outward shift in aggregate demand raises output sharply. Because the price level does not respond immediately, output increases by the full amount of the shift in aggregate demand. For the next nine years, a series of increases in the price level depresses aggregate demand. At first, through Year 4, inflation gets worse each year, as expected inflation catches up with actual inflation. From then on, inflation gradually dissipates because output is less and less above potential. In Year 8, output is back to its potential level. However, expected inflation is still positive. Further price increases depress aggregate demand below potential, and the economy enters a very slight recession. The spiral approaches equilibrium rapidly thereafter.

EXAMPLE 4: AN OIL PRICE SHOCK

We can trace out the reaction of the complete model to a one-time increase in materials prices, Z, such as the oil price increases of the 1970s. Suppose Z is 2.5 percent in Year 2 and returns to zero for the indefinite future. The path of inflation and output is shown in Figure 17–4.

In Year 2, inflation jumps up to 2.5 percent from the contribution of oil

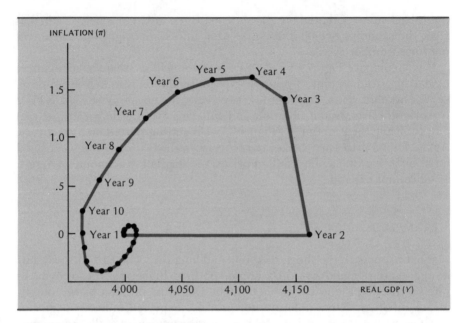

Figure 17–3.   A BOOM (EXAMPLE 3).
The economy starts in equilibrium in Year 1, with output equal to potential and zero inflation. In Year 2 the aggregate demand curve shifts outward. Real GDP shifts upward immediately. Inflation starts in Year 3. As the price level rises, aggregate demand falls and
output begins to recede toward equilibrium. In 8 years, output is back to equilibrium but
the economy overshoots because expected inflation is positive at that point. The approach to equilibrium is again a spiral.

prices to total costs and from the feedback through wages. The higher price
level depresses output; the economy is in a state of stagflation. The recovery
from stagflation proceeds as in Figure 17–2. At first, expected inflation
dominates the deflation that is associated with output that is below potential. The price level rises some more and output falls even further below potential. As expected inflation subsides and deflation from low output dominates, aggregate demand begins to recover. The recovery overshoots a little
and the economy experiences a little boom on the way to equilibrium.

17.5 Inflation-Output Loops in Canada, the United States, and Germany

How well does this model work as an explanation of the record of inflation
and output fluctuations in modern economies? Before proceeding with policy analysis in the next chapter it is important to check whether the theory is
consistent with experience.

The four inflation-output diagrams of the previous section (Figures 17–1,
17–2, 17–3, and 17–4) provide a fascinating and reasonably accurate way
for us to confront the theory with the facts. In all the cases we considered—
(1) recovery from a demand-deficient recession, (2) recovery from stagfla-

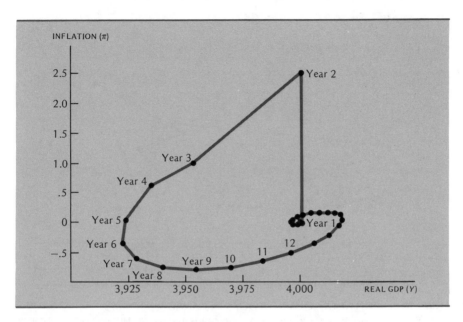

Figure 17–4. AN OIL PRICE SHOCK (EXAMPLE 4).
The economy starts at equilibrium in Year 1. In Year 2, inflation jumps up to 2.5 percent because of the 1 percent increase in total costs from the higher oil price. In Year 3, the level of output is much lower because the price level is higher. In Years 4, 5, and 6, the price level is even higher and output even lower because of expected inflation. Starting in Year 7, a recovery takes place because the price level begins to fall. Around Year 12, output is back to potential. The economy overshoots slightly on its way back to equilibrium.

tion, (3) a boom, and (4) an oil price shock—the model economy was displaced from its long-run potential. In each case the return path to potential displays a striking characteristic that is clear in the diagrams: The path is a **counterclockwise loop** because the economy tends to spiral back to potential in a counterclockwise fashion.

Do inflation and output actually behave this way? Since real-world economies are constantly being shocked by many events, it is difficult to separate out isolated episodes like the special shocks in the model economy. Nevertheless, inflation and output fluctuations do display such counterclockwise loops. They are not so smooth and circular as in the model economy, but they are there nonetheless.

In Figure 17–5 we show inflation and output pairs in Canada for each of the years from 1971 through 1987. Even at a quick glance two big loops are evident: one from 1971 through 1976, and another from 1976 through 1987. The first loop involves the boom of 1971–72, the oil price shock of 1974, and the recession of 1975. The second loop occurred under very similar circumstances: a boom in 1977–78 followed by another oil shock in 1979—this time related to the revolution in Iran, a major oil producer—and a subsequent large recession in the early 1980s. In both cases expected

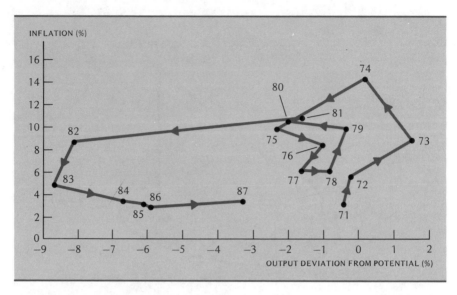

Figure 17–5.   INFLATION-OUTPUT LOOPS IN CANADA, 1971–87.
During the 1971–87 period there were two big loops in Canada. The second loop started
from a higher rate of expected inflation. Source: *Canadian Economic Observer,* Tables 1.3
and 1.13.

inflation first rose and then fell. Note that the second loop started at a
higher rate of expected inflation.

This type of output and inflation fluctuation is not unique to Canada. Figure 17–6 shows the data for a similar period in the United States. Again
there are two loops. The similarity between the two figures is not coinciden-
tal. Canadian output would tend to move in the same direction as U.S. output if only because the United States is such an important market for
Canadian goods. In addition, the two economies are often subject to similar
external shocks, such as the oil price increases of the 1970s. And Canadian
policies are often similar to those in the United States. This is especially true
when the Bank of Canada is attempting to stabilise the value of the Canada-
U.S. exchange rate, because in that case the Bank must try to make Canadian interest rates behave much like U.S. interest rates.

Other industrialised countries also experience counterclockwise loops in
output and inflation. Figure 17–7 shows that Germany has also experienced
two such loops in recent years. The size and shape of these loops differ from
those in Canada and the United States because the German economy un-
derwent different shocks and carried out different policies. But the basic
message is the same.

Overall, the model is consistent with the dynamic movements of inflation
and output. While these graphical tests focussing on loops may appear
overly simplistic, they are confirmed by more accurate statistical regression
techniques and we believe they capture the essence of the theory and the
facts.

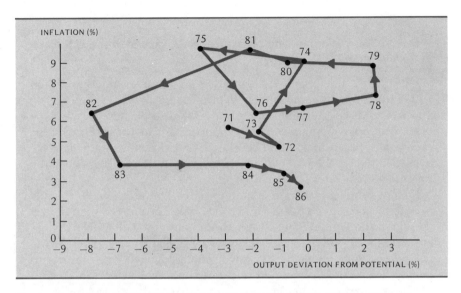

Figure 17-6. INFLATION-OUTPUT LOOPS IN THE UNITED STATES, 1971–86.
Note the similarity between this figure and Figure 17–5. Source: *Economic Report of the President,* 1985, Tables B–2 and B–3.

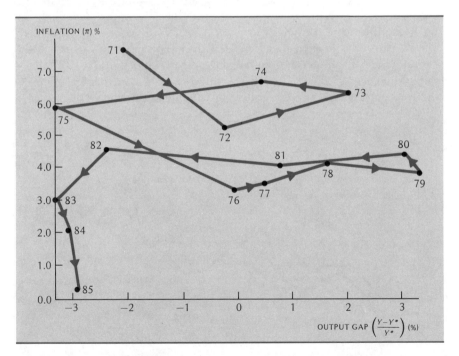

Figure 17-7. INFLATION-OUTPUT LOOPS IN GERMANY, 1971–85.
In Germany there were two loops during the 1971–85 period, and they appear flatter than those for Canada and the United States. Source: *International Financial Statistics,* International Monetary Fund, various issues.

Why Has the Canadian Unemployment Rate Exceeded the U.S. Rate in Recent Years?

Until 1982 the unemployment rates in Canada and the United States were usually quite similar. Not only did the rates tend to rise and fall at about the same time, they tended to be close to the same level. Unemployment rose in both countries during the recessions that each experienced in 1982. The rise in Canadian unemployment far exceeded that in the United States, however, and the difference in the unemployment rates has persisted since.

One possible explanation is quite simple. The recession in Canada may have been much deeper and much more prolonged than the recession in the United States. John McCallum of McGill University has argued that the fall in Canadian aggregate demand can explain the initial relative increase in the Canadian unemployment rate, but not its persistence. Orley Ashenfelter and David Card of Princeton University have tested a number of possible explanations—changes in the demographic and industrial composition of employment, changes in labour market regulations and the extent of unionisation, and changes in relative real wages between the two countries—but find all of these wanting.

Ross Milbourne, Douglas Purvis, and W. David Scoones of Queen's University have argued that a particular change in the Canadian unemployment insurance system may have been important. In 1977 the UI system was changed so that the number of weeks that an unemployed person is allowed to collect UI benefits automatically increases

UNEMPLOYMENT RATE (%)

Sources: Canadian Economic Observer, Table 2.1, and *Economic Report of the President*, 1988, Table B-32.

when the national unemployment rate rises. As a result, the sharp rise in unemployment in 1982 itself made the UI system more generous, contributing to the subsequent measured unemployment rate by encouraging people to stay in the labour force or to prolong their job searches.

It remains to be seen how much of the change in Canada's unemployment rate can be explained by this alteration of the UI system. It may be that no single factor can explain all of the change. David Gower of Statistics Canada has pointed out that the relative increase in the Canadian unemployment rate has resulted from a combination of relatively slower employment growth in Canada and relatively faster labour force growth.*

* See John McCallum, 'Unemployment in Canada and the United States,' *Canadian Journal of Economics,* Vol. 20, pp. 802–822, 1987; Orley Ashenfelter and David Card, 'Why Have Unemployment Rates in Canada and the United States Diverged?' *Economica,* Vol. 53, pp. S171–S195, 1986; Ross Milbourne, Douglas Purvis, and W. David Scoones, 'Unemployment Insurance, Unemployment Dynamics and the Natural Rate(s),' paper presented to the Canadian Macroeconomics Study Group, Montreal, 1988; and David Gower, 'The Labour Market in the 80s: Canada and the United States,' *Canadian Economic Observer,* August 1988.

Why Are Output Fluctuations in Japan So Small?

During most of the last 15 years fluctuations in real output have been much smaller in Japan than in many other countries, including Canada. As shown in the figure below, Japan did experience a recession when world oil prices rose sharply in late 1973. Other than that, however, actual real output in Japan behaves much like the smoothly changing potential output of Canada. For example, both the boom of 1981 and the bust of 1982 that are visible in the Canadian series are missing from the Japanese data.

What might explain this difference? The theory of aggregate demand and price adjustment described in this chapter offers one possible explanation. If prices and wages adjust very quickly to demand—that is, if the coefficient f in the price-adjustment equation is large—then relatively small fluctuations in output will be capable of stabilising inflation. For example, if the response (f) of prices and wages is high, then the effect of a price shock like that in Example 4 and Figure 17–4 would result in only a small drop in output. Similarly, a boom resulting from a monetary expansion like that in Example 3 and Figure 17–3 would be relatively small.

In Japan, wages and prices do seem to be more sensitive to demand conditions than in Canada. One reason is that a significant fraction of wage payments comes in the form of bonuses that can be easily adjusted. Another reason for the greater sensitivity of wages is that most wage changes are synchronised in the spring quarter in the *shunto* as described on page 442 in Chapter 16.

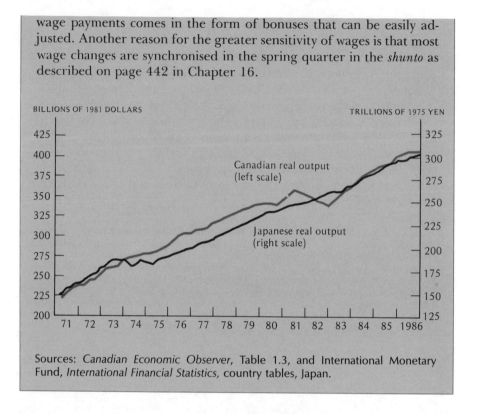

Sources: *Canadian Economic Observer*, Table 1.3, and International Monetary Fund, *International Financial Statistics*, country tables, Japan.

Review and Practice

MAJOR POINTS

1. A model of price adjustment must incorporate the response of wages to excess demand and to expected inflation.

2. Expected inflation has forward-looking features and backward-looking features. Expectations and contracts are both part of the micro underpinnings of the expected inflation term.

3. A simple model of price adjustment can be derived by combining wage adjustment with markup pricing behaviour. The model of price adjustment is the same as in the model of Chapter 6 except that the coefficients of the model can change.

4. No simple mechanical formula is satisfactory as a model of expected inflation. Any such model would be inconsistent with actual inflation behaviour if policy or the economic environment changed.

5. The accelerationist or natural rate hypothesis holds that, in the long run, unemployment will equal the natural rate regardless of how high inflation is, as long as it is steady.

6. A model that combines aggregate demand with price adjustment implies that inflation and output will fluctuate or spiral as the economy returns to potential after a shock.

7. During the 1970s and 1980s Canada and other countries went through economic fluctuations that displayed such spirals of counterclockwise loops.

KEY TERMS AND CONCEPTS

Expected inflation

Accelerationist hypothesis

Indexing

Expectations of future labour
   market conditions

Stagflation

Inflation-output loops

Markup pricing

Consistent model of expected inflation

Oil shock to price setting

Wage-price spiral

QUESTIONS FOR DISCUSSION AND REVIEW

1. What are the three elements included in the price-adjustment equation?

2. How is expected inflation related to forward-looking behaviour? To staggered wage setting?

3. Why might the total effect of an increase in materials prices be greater than the effect portrayed in the markup equation?

4. How can you determine potential output from the price-adjustment equation?

5. Why does a one-year stimulus cause inflation to remain higher for many years?

6. Trace out the effects over time of a price shock, assuming that output is held constant.

7. What happens if policy tries to hold output above the natural rate for an extended period?

8. What are the three relationships that make up the unified model that shows how the economy moves over time?

9. Explain why the economy approaches equilibrium in a spiral in the inflation–real GDP diagram.

PROBLEMS

Numerical
1. Example 1 of Section 17.3 looked at the inflation effects of a one-time stimulus to output. In this problem we show how such effects vary with different models of inflationary expectations. Consider the following alternatives to Equation 17–2:
(i) $\pi^e = \pi_{-1}$; (ii) $\pi^e = .9\pi_{-1}$; (iii) $\pi^e = .5\pi_{-1} + .5\pi_{-2}$; (iv) $\pi^e = .33\pi_{-1} + .33\pi_{-2} + .33\pi_{-3}$.
   a. For each of these expressions find the inflation effects of a one-time 3 percent stimulus to output. Calculate the inflation rate for Years 1 through 10.
   b. Estimate the long-run rate of inflation in each case.
   c. Based on your calculations and the calculations shown in Table 17–1, explain how inflation varies with (i) the sum of the coefficients in the expression for π^e, and (ii) the weight given to recent inflation compared to more distant inflation in the expression for π^e.
   d. Do any of the expressions for inflationary expectations given above lead to sys-

tematic errors in forecasting inflation? If so, which ones? If not, explain the relationship between expected and actual inflation when fiscal and monetary policy are used to keep output at potential. Is one expression for expected inflation more likely to prevail than another?

2. In this problem we consider the behaviour of the economy following a demand-deficient recession. We look at how the recovery is influenced by the model used for inflationary expectations. Suppose the economy starts off with output at potential ($Y=Y^*=4,000$), $\pi=0$, and $P=1$. Aggregate demand is given by Equation 17–3; price adjustment is given by Equation 17–1 with $f=.25$. In Year 1 the money supply is reduced from 600 to 570, creating a recession.
   a. Calculate the path of inflation, the price level, and output for Years 1 through 6 assuming (i) $\pi^e=.4\pi_{-1}+.2\pi_{-2}$, and (ii) $\pi^e=\pi_{-1}$. In performing your calculations compute P as $(1+\pi_{-1})P_{-1}$.
   b. For which model of expectations does the return to potential output take longer? For which model will there be more overshooting?
   c. We assumed here that the value taken by f in the price-adjustment equation was the same for both models in inflationary expectations. Explain why in reality the value of f might differ from one model to the other. (Hint: In Chapter 16 we discussed the relationship between f and the length of the business cycle.)

3. In this problem we look at how the recovery from an oil price shock is affected by the model used for inflationary expectations. Let the model of the economy and its initial conditions be the same as in Problem 2. Note that the money supply will remain at 600. In Year 1 let $Z=.025$.
   a. Calculate the path of inflation, the price level, and output in Years 1 through 6 under each of the models for π^e given in Part a of Problem 2.
   b. In each case, how long does it take inflation to first return to zero? Analyse the factors that cause inflation to fall in each case.
   c. In which case is the fall in output greater? How do you explain this result?

4. Reconsider the oil price shock of Problem 3, only now suppose that the aim of policy makers is to keep inflation equal to zero in every year possible. This is achieved by manipulating the money stock.
   a. Assuming that the oil price shock was unexpected, can anything be done about the rate of inflation in Year 1? Why or why not?
   b. Suppose π^e is always equal to zero. Find the values of M chosen by policy makers each year during and following the oil shock.
   c. Now assume that π^e is given alternately by π_{-1} and $.5\pi_{-1}+.5\pi_{-2}$. Repeat the calculations from Part b for each case.
   d. Is $\pi^e=0$ reasonable given the goals of policy? Use this example to explain the importance of policy makers maintaining their credibility.

Analytical

1. Explain why the inflation-output loops in Section 17.4 are vertical at the point where inflation equals zero. Would the same be true if the money supply was increasing each year?

2. In this problem we consider the policy actions underlying Example 1 of Section 17.3.
   a. Assuming that the natural rate of unemployment is 7 percent, what is the unemployment rate in Year 1 and Year 2 onward?
   b. Diagram the actions taken by policy makers in Year 1 and in Year 2 onward on an aggregate demand graph.
   c. Again, diagram the actions of policy makers each year on an IS-LM graph assuming that (i) all policy actions consist of fiscal policy, and (ii) all policy actions

consist of monetary policy. Explain why your diagram in Part b does not depend on the nature of the policy action taken.

3. Describe the behaviour of investment and interest rates during the boom described in Example 3 of Section 17.4 assuming that the boom was created by an exogenous increase in investment. How do interest rates and investment behave during and following an oil price shock?

4. What is the correlation between output and interest rates implied by the inflation-output loops of Section 17.4? What assumption is made about monetary policy in constructing these loops? Are the predictions of the model consistent with the data presented in Chapter 1?

5. Suppose that agents use all available information to make unbiased, but not error-free, forecasts of inflation. In that case, we can say that

$$\pi = \pi^e + e$$

where e is a forecast error whose average value is zero.
   a. What does this relationship between π and π^e imply about the average value of the output gap? (Hint: Use the price-adjustment equation.)
   b. Suppose now that π^e was formed such that π^e always differed from π by a constant, $\bar{e}$. Using the price-adjustment equation, show that the accelerationist hypothesis doesn't hold.

PART IV

Macroeconomic Policy Evaluation

18

Designing and
Maintaining a Good
Macro Policy

As WE have seen, modern macroeconomic theory incorporates new ideas about rational expectations and price adjustment into traditional Keynesian and monetarist frameworks. What are the policy implications of this theory? This chapter begins with a review of the principal features. After examining the problem of matching policy instruments to targets and the problem of uncertainty in implementing policy, we go on to apply these principles to macroeconomic policy problems in Canada. Then we consider how macroeconomic policies can be coordinated among countries.

18.1 General Principles of Macro Policy Analysis

Much of our discussion of the recent developments in macroeconomics—rational expectations, policy rules, time inconsistency, theories of wage rigidities, the nature of economic fluctuations—has been technical. It is important not to lose sight of the central ideas by focussing too much on the technical details. The central ideas are summarised in the following five propositions.[1]

[1] This discussion is related to that in John B. Taylor, 'An Appeal for Rationality in the Policy Activism Debate,' in R. W. Hafer (ed.), *The Monetary and Fiscal Policy Debate: Lessons from Two Decades*, Roman and Allanheld, Totowa, N.J., Allanheld, 1986.

1. *When making decisions, people think about the future, and their expecta-tions of the future can be modelled by assuming that they have a sense of eco-nomic fluctuations and use their information to make unbiased (but not error-free) forecasts.*

The notion that people make the most of the information available to them when forecasting the future was originally proposed by John Muth in 1960 for use in microeconomic applications, such as the demand and supply for agricultural commodities.[2] Farmers need to predict future prices in order to know how much to grow. Muth suggested that we model a farmer's expectations by simply assuming that the supply and demand model was known to the farmer.

Whatever its value in agricultural economics, the idea seems reasonable for macroeconomic applications. Many features of economic fluctuations are recurrent from one business cycle to another; there are established sta-tistical regularities. We have documented many of these regularities. Since business cycles have been observed for hundreds of years, it makes sense to assume that people have become familiar with them. Of course, in the face of new, unprecedented events, people will make significant errors in trying to look forward.

2. *Macroeconomic policy can be usefully described and evaluated as a policy rule, rather than by treating the instruments as exogenous and looking only at one-time changes in these instruments.*

Because people are forward-looking, their expectations of future policy actions affect their current behaviour and the state of the economy. Hence, in order to evaluate the effect of policy on the economy we need to specify not only current policy changes but also future policy changes. In other words, we need to specify a contingency plan that describes how policy will react to future events. Such a contingency is nothing more than a rule for policy. The contingency plan could be as specific as a constant growth rate rule for the money supply, but more generally it establishes a range of reac-tions depending on the state of the economy.

The rational expectations approach almost forces a macroeconomic ana-lyst to think about policy as a rule or a strategy. Once you are working with a rational expectations model you soon realise that you have little choice but to specify policy as a rule. We will see in our policy evaluation study in the latter part of this chapter that it is natural and convenient to specify policy as a rule.

Note that the focus on rules does not mean that the effect of one-shot changes in policy should never be calculated; such a calculation can be a useful exercise to help understand the workings of the model. We did this extensively in the previous chapter to see if our model was consistent with the facts.

---

[2] John Muth, 'Rational Expectations and the Theory of Price Movements,' *Econometrica*, Vol. 29, pp. 315–335, 1960.

In a famous critique of traditional policy evaluation, Robert Lucas of the University of Chicago argued in the early 1970s that traditional macro models, like the model of Chapters 4–6, could give incorrect answers to policy evaluation questions if expectations were forward-looking and there was a change in the policy rule.[3] Since these traditional models were based on adaptive backward-looking expectations, their parameters would change when the policy rule changed. This was the negative part of the critique, and it has clearly made policy analysts wary of using the traditional models. But there was also a positive side. The critique provided a general framework for modifying the traditional models; by stipulating policy as a rule it is possible to calculate by how much the parameters of the traditional models would change. An example of this was discussed in Chapter 17, where we showed how the sensitivity of inflation to recessions would diminish if business cycles became less prolonged, due, perhaps, to a change in policy. Similarly, the model of the expected inflation term in the price-adjustment equation (Equation 17–1) would change if monetary policy changed.

Some macroeconomists, such as Christopher Sims of the University of Minnesota, have argued that the focus on policy rules is irrelevant.[4] Sims argues that we rarely get big changes in rules anyway, so we might as well use conventional models for policy. Indeed there is a utopian flavour to the 'policy rules' approach. The search is for big policy reforms that would improve economic welfare over a long period of time. The reforms would probably require changes in the policy-making institutions, or the creation of new institutions. Such reforms are by their very nature rare. But they do occur. The creation of the Bank of Canada, the departure from the gold standard, and the shift to floating exchange rates are all examples. These reforms seem to have had substantial effects on the economy. A careful analysis of the effects of future policy reforms therefore seems quite relevant.

3. *In order for a particular policy rule to work well, it is necessary to establish a commitment to that rule.*

We briefly discussed the problem of time inconsistency in Chapter 7. The possibility that policy makers will find it tempting to change their plans in the future—be time inconsistent—is a reason for maintaining a commitment to a stated rule. The problem of time inconsistency was first pointed out in macroeconomics by Finn Kydland of Carnegie-Mellon University and Edward Prescott of the University of Minnesota, and independently by Guillermo Calvo of the University of Pennsylvania.[5]

---

[3] Robert E. Lucas, 'Econometric Policy Evaluation: A Critique,' in Carnegie-Rochester Conference Series, *The Phillips Curve*, 1976, pp. 19–46.

[4] Christopher Sims, 'Policy Analysis with Econometric Models,' *Brookings Papers on Economic Activity*, Vol. 1, pp. 107–164, 1982.

[5] Finn Kydland and Edward Prescott, 'Rules Rather than Discretion: The Inconsistency of Optimal Plans,' *Journal of Political Economy*, Vol. 85, pp. 473–491, 1977, and Guillermo Calvo, 'On the Time Inconsistency of Optimal Policy in a Monetary Economy,' *Econometrica*, Vol. 46,

In attempting to find optimal policies for economies where people are forward-looking, these researchers found that once policy makers began an optimal policy there was incentive in future periods for the policy makers to change the plan—to be inconsistent. Policy makers could make things better by being inconsistent. This was true even if the policy makers had the interests of the public in mind. One example close at hand is that of a teacher giving an examination. It is tempting to call off an examination after the students have studied and learned the material in a course in anticipation of the exam. Then the students do not have to sweat through the exam, and the teacher does not have to grade the exam papers. The government's patent laws provide a similar problem of inconsistency. Patent laws confer a temporary monopoly as a reward for inventions. Hence, they spur inventiveness. But the monopoly is undesirable: It would be tempting to remove patents when an invention is completed, so that the new product would be produced and marketed competitively. Another example from the government sphere is the construction of dams for flood plains. The government tells people not to build houses on a dangerous flood plain, because there will be no dams for flood control built. But when people move in anyway, the government will find it desirable to build the flood control project in order to protect them.

However, by being inconsistent the policy makers are likely to lose credibility; people would begin to assume that the policy makers will change the rules and this would lead to a new policy-making equilibrium that was generally inferior to the original policy plan of the policy makers. If the students began to expect that the exam would be called off, they probably would not study for it. The implication is that, to prevent this inferior outcome, it is better to maintain a firm commitment to a policy rule.

Returning to the patent example, a policy maker who had the discretion to award patents each year would indeed be tempted not to do so. By holding back the patent, the economic inefficiencies of a monopoly are avoided. Fortunately, reneging on patent promises does not occur in practice because it is so clear that future inventive activity would suffer. Instead, we have patent laws that limit such discretion. The time inconsistency research suggests that discretion should be limited for similar reasons in macroeconomic policy.

It is important to distinguish between **activist policy rules** and **discretionary policy.** Activist policy rules involve *feedback* from the state of the economy to the policy instruments, but the feedback is part of the rule. Sometimes the term **passive policy rule** is used to refer to special rules without feedback, like the fixed growth rate rule for the money supply. An example of an activist policy rule is the following: If the unemployment rate rises by a certain amount next year, then the money supply will increase by a

pp. 1411–1428, 1979. Also see Stanley Fischer, 'Dynamic Inconsistency, Cooperation, and the Benevolent Dissembling Government,' *Journal of Economic Dynamics and Control*, Vol. 2, pp. 93–107, 1980.

certain stated amount. Discretionary policy is formulated on a case-by-case and year-by-year basis with no attempt to commit to or even talk about future policy decisions in advance. Those in favour of discretionary policy disagree with the whole concept of a rule of the game approach, whether the rule is a feedback rule or a constant setting for the policy instruments. Activist and constant growth rate policy rules have much more in common with each other than do activist policy rules and discretionary policy. Both types of policy rules involve commitments and lead to the type of policy analysis suggested by the rational expectations approach.

4. *The economy is basically stable; after a shock the economy will eventually return to its normal trend paths of output and employment. However, because of rigidities in the structure of the economy, this return could be slow.*

The macro models we have looked at are *dynamic* systems continually disturbed by *shocks*. After each shock the economy has a tendency to return to the normal or natural growing level of output and employment, although there may be overshooting or a temporary cumulative movement away from normal. A smooth return is never observed in practice, however, because new shocks are always hitting the system. Since the economy is viewed as always being buffeted around the shocks, the equilibrium is really a random or stochastic equilibrium. The combination of the shocks and the dynamics of the model is capable of mimicking the actual behaviour of business cycles surprisingly well, as we saw in the previous chapter. The properties of the random equilibrium are much like the actual behaviour of business cycles.

The shocks can be due to many factors, but usually have been money shocks, demand shocks, or price shocks. The dynamics are due to many possible rigidities in the economy, but price-wage rigidities and slow adjustment of capital (including inventories) have been the most important empirically.

Because of these rigidities the impact of a shock to the economy takes time to sort itself out. Suppose, for example, that there is a shift in money demand with people wanting to hold more money at any level of income and interest rates. Eventually the price level will fall so that the real supply of money is effectively increased. But if there are wage and price rigidities this adjustment will take time: First the increase in money demand will cause an increase in interest rates; the higher level of interest rates will in turn depress demand for durables and have repercussions throughout the economy; depressed demand conditions will then begin to put downward pressure on prices; and the fall in prices then will begin to raise the real supply of money—this process will continue until the economy is back to its natural level of output and employment. The whole process could take more than a year.

Combined with these structural rigidities is the supposition that expectations are not restrained by similar rigidities. A shock can change expectations of inflation, exchange rates, and other variables overnight even though there are rigidities that cause the economy to take additional time to adjust fully to the shock. The expectations take account of the structural rigidities since these are part of the model. The combination of rigidities in the economy with perfectly flexible expectations is an essential feature of most rational expectations models.

There has been a tendency to get expectations assumptions mixed up with assumptions about how markets work. Hence, the comment that expectations might be rational in flexible auction markets but not in sticky wage labour markets is frequently heard. But there is no reason why expectations are not rational in both areas. Labour union staffs may spend more time predicting future wage and price inflation than the staffs of brokerage firms.

As we saw in Chapter 16, there has been much technical research on the effect of price and wage rigidities in rational expectations models. The important general feature of this research is that prices and wages have a forward-looking feature, whether they are sticky or not. When workers and firms set wages and prices they look ahead to the period during which the prices or wages will be in effect—to demand conditions, to the wages of other workers, and so on. This means that expectations of future policy actions will affect wage and price decisions, a property that is quite unlike models of wage and price rigidities with purely backward-looking expectations. The view that the economy will eventually return to normal—however slowly—after a shock is also inconsistent with the view that the economy stagnates permanently below potential.

5. *The objective of macroeconomic policy is to reduce the size (or the duration) of the fluctuations in output, employment, and inflation from normal levels after shocks hit the economy. The objective is to be achieved over a long period of time, which will in general include a larger number of business-cycle experiences. Future business-cycle fluctuations are not viewed as less important than the current one.*

By responding to economic shocks in a systematic fashion, economic policy can offset their impact or influence the speed at which the economy returns to normal. It thus can change the size of the fluctuations. How this should be done is a main area of disagreement among proponents of different policy rules.

From a technical viewpoint the disagreement can be addressed by inserting alternative policy rules into a rational expectations model and calculating how each rule affects the variance of output, employment, and inflation in the moving equilibrium that describes the business-cycle fluctuations. We want to choose a policy that provides the best economic performance. One simple criterion is the minimisation of the size of the fluctuations in output and inflation. Since in many models with price and wage rigidities there will be a trade-off between the reduction of output and inflation variability, it will usually be necessary to stipulate a welfare or loss function that reflects certain value judgements. Frequently one policy will so dominate another that the particular welfare weights do not matter much, however. This approach to policy will be featured later in this chapter.

The average rate of inflation can obviously be influenced by monetary policy, and it is important to choose a target rate that maximises economic welfare. The objective of macroeconomic policy, however, is to keep the inflation rate close to this target rate—that is, to minimise fluctuations around the target, regardless of what the actual value of the target is. Alternatively, if a zero inflation target is appropriate, the objective of policy is to keep the price level near some target; the specific target value itself is much less important.

18.2 Instruments and Targets

Generally stated, the macro policy problem is one of choosing policy rules that describe how the *instruments* of policy should respond to economic conditions in order to improve the performance of the *target* variables. The instruments of macro policy are things like the monetary base or tax rates—or, more generally, monetary policy and fiscal policy. The targets of policy are the endogenous economic variables that we care about: inflation, unemployment, capital formation, and economic growth. Sometimes it is useful to distinguish between *intermediate* targets and *final* targets. For example, for the Bank of Canada, the exchange rate may be an intermediate target while its instrument to control that target is the interest rate. The final targets for the Bank are real output and inflation.

To describe our objectives for the target variables it is necessary to define a **social welfare function** that summarises the costs of having the target variables deviate from their desired levels. Such a social welfare function should reflect the tastes of individuals in society. If people do not like inflation, then deviations of inflation from zero should register as a loss of welfare in the social welfare function. In practice, it is very difficult to determine what the social welfare function actually is. Since people are different, we cannot just choose policy to improve the welfare of some representative individual.

Once a social welfare function has been specified, we can view the macro policy problem much like any other economic problem: We want to choose policy rules for the instruments to maximise the social welfare function. Analogously, in a consumption problem the consumer chooses a contingency plan for consumption—a decision rule—to maximise utility.

In most macro problems we are faced with the typical economic problem of scarcity. Whenever there is scarcity in economics we are faced with a *trade-off* between competing goals. In fact, scarcity is the most fundamental problem in economics. An important principle of optimal macro policy is that whenever there is a scarcity of instruments—that is, the number of instruments is less than the number of target variables—there is a trade-off between the different target variables. Jan Tinbergen, the Dutch economist who won the Nobel Prize for his work on macro modelling and on techniques for macro policy evaluation, established this important principle relating the number of instruments to the number of targets.[6] As long as the number of instruments is less than the number of targets, society is faced with a cruel choice between meeting one goal or another. The choice between inflation and unemployment is the best example of this type of cruel choice in macroeconomics, and we will consider it in detail later in this chapter.

It is very important to note that equality between the number of instruments and the number of targets is not sufficient for avoiding a cruel choice. In many cases the different instruments are not independent enough in their effects on the target variables. Again, the best example of this is the inflation-unemployment trade-off. A simple counting of instruments and targets could lead to the following type of incorrect reasoning: 'We have two instruments, monetary policy and fiscal policy, and we have two target variables, inflation and unemployment. Thus there is no cruel trade-off. We can use monetary policy to control inflation and fiscal policy to control unemployment.' This reasoning is wrong because it assumes that monetary and fiscal policies affect inflation and output in different and independent ways. In fact, we already know from our macro model that monetary and fiscal policies affect output and inflation in the same way—by shifting the aggregate demand curve. Unless one instrument can directly affect inflation without going through aggregate demand, we are left with a trade-off. For example, if monetary policy had a separate effect on expected inflation, or if tax policy could affect price setting, then there would be a separate channel.

18.3 Uncertainty and Timing Considerations

In practice, the target-instrument approach described above is too simple. It ignores the inherent uncertainty that exists in our understanding of the economy. If there is uncertainty about the effect of an instrument of policy on the economy, then we must be careful not to exploit that relationship too much. Very active use of an uncertain instrument can be risky. This is one of the central reasons for using less active policies in practice.

When there are many instruments and uncertainty, the theory of economic policy tells us to use a mix of the instruments in a way that minimises the risk. William Brainard of Yale University showed how the choice of instruments under uncertainty is much like the problem of choosing an optimal portfolio of common stocks.[7] Just as an individual should attempt to diversify a portfolio of stocks—'don't put all of your eggs in one basket'—policy makers should diversify their instruments, in order to reduce risk.

Another reason that macroeconomic policy-making is difficult is that its benefits do not occur at the same time as its costs. An expansionary monetary or fiscal policy, for example, involves balancing the short-term benefits

---

[6] Jan Tinbergen, *On the Theory of Economic Policy,* Amsterdam, North-Holland, 1952.
[7] William Brainard, 'Uncertainty and the Effectiveness of Policy,' *American Economic Review, Papers and Proceedings,* Vol. 57, pp. 411–425, 1967.

of a stimulative move against the long-term costs of inflation the move will bring. Conversely, the costs of a contractionary policy occur in the short run and the benefits occur later and are perhaps drawn out over many years. We will start with a look at the benefits and costs. Then we will set up a framework within which policy makers can make an intelligent choice between expansion and contraction.

18.4 The Benefits of Full Employment and Price Stability

Macro policy makers should try to achieve the best combination of employment and inflation. Chapter 17 showed the difficulties that policy makers face in dealing with unemployment and inflation. No policy can give the ideal of low unemployment and zero inflation, year after year. A policy that concentrates on low unemployment will permit a good deal of price instability; one that keeps prices on target will bring serious recessions and booms. Policy makers face a trade-off between unemployment stability and price stability.

Economic analysis deals with trade-offs of many types. For example, consider a consumer who cannot afford an expensive car and an expensive home—to buy a better car, the consumer will have to settle for a more modest home, and vice versa. Micro theory describes the consumer's preferences in terms of indifference curves. The consumer chooses the combination of car and house on the best indifference curve within the consumer's budget. The combination is at a point of tangency of an indifference curve and the line showing all the different combinations of car and house the consumer can afford.

We can look at the nation's choice between employment and price stability in the same way. Preferences give a set of indifference curves. The behaviour of the economy, as described by the model of Chapter 17, gives the set of different combinations of employment and price stability that can be achieved. We call the curve showing those combinations the **policy frontier.** The optimal policy is at the point of tangency of an indifference curve and the policy frontier.

The starting point for the analysis is to choose the two axes for the indifference curves and for the policy frontier. One axis has something to do with price stability and the other something to do with unemployment. For inflation, it seems clear that the desirable level is near zero. Large departures above zero have been a big problem in recent decades. Departures below zero were the problem in the depression of the 1930s and in some earlier contractions. There is no good reason to think that the cost of a positive error is any different from the cost of a negative error. In addition, it seems reasonable to suppose that *the marginal cost of an inflation or deflation error rises with the magnitude of the error.* A simple measure of the loss with these properties is the **squared error.**

This suggests that a good general summary of the inflation side of the performance of the economy is the average of the squared deviation of the inflation rate from its target, near zero. We will call this the **inflation loss.** If everything else is held the same, the ideal macro policy will keep the inflation loss at zero. In real life, the inflation rate cannot be kept exactly at zero, and the average inflation loss will be positive.

For the output-employment-unemployment side of the economy, the situation is a little different. For a number of reasons, the *natural* unemployment rate is probably not the *optimal* unemployment rate. Because of taxes and unemployment compensation that make the social cost of unemployment exceed the private cost, and because of monopoly power, it is likely that social welfare rises whenever unemployment drops below the natural rate. But, in the last chapter, we stressed that macro policy cannot influence the average rate of unemployment. It can only influence the fluctuations of unemployment around the natural rate. Consequently, macro policy makers should do what they can do: limit the fluctuations of unemployment about the natural rate. Based on this logic, we define the **unemployment loss** as the average squared departure of unemployment from the natural rate.

Social preferences about inflation and unemployment can be displayed in a family of indifference curves as shown in Figure 18–1. Note that the indifference curves bend in the opposite direction from the usual ones for the theory of the consumer. Consumer theory deals with things people like. Inflation and unemployment losses are things the public does not like, so the indifference curves have the opposite curvature. At the upper left end of each curve, the public is willing to trade quite a bit of added unemployment loss to reduce their inflation loss a little from its high level. At the lower end, they will accept only a small added amount of unemployment loss to reduce

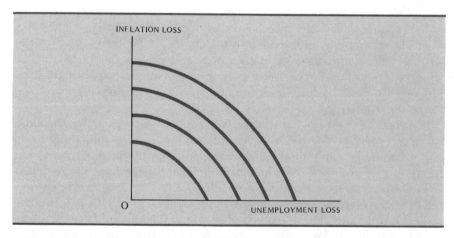

Figure 18–1. SOCIAL PREFERENCES ABOUT INFLATION AND UNEMPLOYMENT.
Each indifference curve shows the locus of combinations of average inflation loss and average unemployment loss that the public finds equally acceptable. The curve that is farthest from the origin is the worst one. The public prefers curves that are closer to the origin.

their inflation loss quite a bit. Curves closer to the o
ferred because they involve lower amounts of both u
flation loss.

WHY IS INFLATION UNDESIRABLE?

Public opinion polls have made it abundantly clear tnat mmm.
ular in Canada. Stringent anti-inflation policies in the early 1980s seem to
have been politically acceptable, even though they brought on a pair of recessions. Whenever inflation rises above 10 percent per year, public opinion
polls show that inflation is the number one economic problem, even when
unemployment is high.

Though some specific economic costs of inflation have been identified, it
is hard to quantify and assess them. The areas of economic costs include the
following:

1. *'Shoe-Leather Costs' of Holding Money.* When inflation is high, currency
   and non–interest-bearing chequing accounts are undesirable because
   they are constantly declining in purchasing power. People will make
   extra trips to the bank to avoid holding much money. These trips involve genuine economic costs, and these costs would be avoided with
   stable prices. One response to inflation has been the development of
   chequing accounts that pay interest closer to market interest rates.
   This change in banking has reduced the cost of inflation because people do not have to spend so much time and effort transferring money
   between accounts.
2. *Tax Distortions.* Originally, the Canadian tax system was written entirely in current dollars. In 1973 the brackets for the personal income
   tax were indexed, as we discussed in Chapter 13, but the brackets have
   not been raised enough to fully account for inflation since 1982. As a
   result, bracket creep due to inflation has not been eliminated. Many
   other parts of the tax system are not indexed, the presumption being
   that the purchasing power of the dollar is stable from one year to the
   next. For example, businesses take depreciation deductions that are
   based on the original dollar cost of plant and equipment investments.
   When inflation rages, the actual value of these deductions is much less
   than it should be, thanks to the declining purchasing power of the dollar. The tax law could be changed so that the deductions automatically
   rise at the same rate as the cost of living.
3. *Unfair Gains and Losses.* When inflation hits, some people gain and
   some lose. Retired people whose pensions are fixed in dollar terms lose
   (government pension payments are indexed to inflation, however).
   Homeowners gain because they can pay off their mortgages in less
   valuable dollars. In total, losses equal gains. In each transaction set in
   dollars, there is somebody paying who wins under inflation, and some-

body losing exactly the same amount. The social loss occurs because inflation makes long-term transactions more unreliable. There seems to be no clear tendency for inflation to favour the rich over the poor or the poor over the rich. Gains and losses from inflation are more or less randomly distributed in this respect.

4. *Nonadapting Economic Institutions.* Certain standard economic practices have not adapted readily to inflation, and the public has suffered as a result. The most important is private retirement arrangements. The typical private pension plan pays its retirees a certain number of dollars per month when they retire. The number of dollars is based on their earnings in the last few years of work. In this respect, the pension keeps up with inflation. But once retirement starts, the amount of the pension is fixed in dollars. A pension that starts out at a generous level may dwindle to inadequacy as a result of inflation. One way retirement plans could adapt would be to build in an allowance for, say, 5 percent inflation. Payments would rise by 5 percent every year. They would start at a lower level than they do now, but keep up better with inflation.

Many of these costs are avoidable by apparently simple means. Shoe-leather costs have been cut as banks now pay closer to market interest rates on chequing accounts. Changing the tax system to avoid distortions from inflation is not too difficult, and would be even easier if some other highly desirable tax reforms were instituted. Gains and losses could be avoided completely by linking payments and receipts to government price indexes, as many businesses do today in their transactions with other businesses. Better pension plans with cost-of-living indexation have been designed and put forward by a number of economists.

The public's negative view of inflation seems to come from sources other than these identifiable economic costs. One is the notion that the dollar is supposed to be a unit of purchasing power just as the yard is a unit of length. If the government decreased the length of the yard randomly by 5 or 10 percent each year, the public would be upset in a way that would also be out of proportion to the technical costs a changing unit of length would impose on us. It is a sign that the government is doing its job when its units of weights, measures, or purchasing power are reliable. Inflation is historically associated with the breakdown of government.

Perhaps another reason some people may be upset about inflation is that they do not take the same broad view as an economist, who sees inflation as a general rise in all prices and dollar incomes. Recall that, in a general inflation, wages and prices increase by the same amount. If wages increase less rapidly than prices, then something else in addition to inflation—like a drop in productivity—is affecting the economy. Someone who does not think about the economy in that way will not associate an increase in income with the increase in prices that goes with it. Such a person may imagine that the increase in income would have occurred even without the inflation. In that case, the inflation appears to diminish the purchasing power of the income, and so to be a loss. To put it another way, some people may not realise that both their incomes and the prices they pay will not rise as fast under an anti-inflation policy.

Costs of Inflation

1. There are some specific economic costs of inflation, but they are hard to quantify. These include:
   - Shoe-leather costs of conserving money holdings.
   - Distortions because much of the tax system is not indexed.
   - Capricious losses suffered by holders of dollar claims, though off-set by surprise gains enjoyed by those paying fixed dollar debts.
   - Problems caused by the failure of retirement plans and other in-stitutions to adapt to declining purchasing power.

2. People see inflation as a breakdown of the basic government re-sponsibility to provide a stable unit of purchasing power.

3. Some people may not understand the relation between their own incomes and rising prices. To them, higher prices represent dimin-ished real income.

COSTS OF OUTPUT LOSS AND UNEMPLOYMENT

There is less mystery about the output and unemployment losses, espe-cially on the downside. As we noted in Chapter 13, when real GDP falls by a billion dollars, people see about half a billion dollars immediately in the form of reduced disposable income. Reduced corporate retained earnings account for part of the reduction. The remainder, hundreds of millions of dollars, takes the form of reduced tax revenue for federal, provincial, and local governments. The public suffers from this reduction as well, either in the form of cuts in government services or in the form of higher taxes later.

In addition to the obvious economic costs of lost output, there are other serious costs of a period of low output and high unemployment. Young workers are particularly likely to become unemployed. Many of them are working in low-wage jobs where part of the benefit is the training they are receiving. When they stop work, the loss includes not just what they were producing, which is included in GDP, but also the value of the training, which is not included in GDP. The experience of unemployment itself may have social costs beyond reduced GDP. Unemployed people may be more likely to turn to crime or to become physically or mentally ill.

While each recession is different, it would not be surprising to see real GDP fall below potential by around 5 percent for two years in a recession. Total lost output would be about 10 percent of GDP, or about $55 billion at

1987 levels. There are about 9 million households in Canada, so the loss would be over $6,000 per household. Some recessions are deeper or more prolonged and involve even larger losses.

Of course, there are some benefits of lower employment and output that need to be evaluated. When people are not working as many hours on their jobs, they have more time for other pursuits. When jobs are hard to get, for example, more people go to school and fewer people quit school for work. The added education is a valuable use of time that offsets the lost GDP to a small extent. People with more time on their hands often do work on their own houses, another valuable use of time. But the offset to the lost GDP from alternative uses of work effort is probably a small fraction of the lost GDP. Because tax rates are high, the private value of time in the Canadian economy is much less than the social value. Further, as we mentioned in Chapter 14, labour supply functions are not very elastic with respect to wages. Consequently, the marginal value of a worker's time falls quickly if the worker is forced to work short hours.

Economists have thought less about the costs of episodes when GDP is above potential. The microeconomic argument supporting the idea that the costs are important is the following: The extra work effort needed to push GDP above potential is worth more than is the extra GDP. Instead of working as many hours as they do during a boom and consuming and investing the extra output, the public would be better off with less output and more time to spend with their children, on their houses, and in recreation. Again, because of high taxes, the private value of time is well below the social value of work, so there is at least a range where a boom is socially beneficial even though it is privately costly to workers to be working longer hours.

In terms of unemployment, there is little disagreement that the marginal social costs of unemployment are higher at higher rates of unemployment. Remember that it is not the overall level of the marginal social cost that matters, but the extent to which the marginal social cost of unemployment is higher in recessions than in booms. The value of the extra time at home that becomes available with higher unemployment is much lower for people who are already partly idle because of a recession than it is for people who are busy because of a boom. Consequently, keeping the variability of unemployment low is an important social goal.

Costs of Output Fluctuations and Unemployment

1. The marginal social cost of unemployment is higher when unemployment is high.

2. Because labour supply is inelastic, the marginal value of time in other uses falls if employment falls, and rises if employment rises above normal.

3. Because of these considerations, the economy is better off with stable output at its full-employment level, as against fluctuating output and employment.

18.5 The Policy Frontier between Inflation Loss and Unemployment Loss

In Chapter 7 we saw that, when aggregate demand shifts for some reason not related to macro policy, the shift can be offset through a policy that moves aggregate demand back to its original position. Then output and inflation will be back at their original levels as well. There is no need for aggregate demand shifts to cause either inflation losses or output-unemployment losses. Both can be avoided by a simple reversal of an aggregate demand shift.

In general, the best way to set up policy is to establish fixed rules for dealing with the foreseeable contingencies. One good fixed rule is to offset completely each aggregate demand disturbance. Another is to decide in advance how to deal with a shock that affects the price level. The choice of such a rule is a more complicated issue.

The price-adjustment equation from Chapter 17 is

$$\pi = f \frac{Y_{-1} - Y^*}{Y^*} + \pi_{-1} + Z. \tag{18-1}$$

Here we use the assumption that the expectations term is simply the lagged value of inflation, $\pi^e = \pi_{-1}$. But recall that alternative models of the expectations term may be more appropriate depending on the type of policy that is used. The last term in Equation 18–1, Z, represents price shocks, like increases in the price of oil. $\longrightarrow \mathcal{D} \uparrow \pi \ (\uparrow output)$

In Figure 18–2 we show how policy might handle a price shock. The diagram shows the price-adjustment equation (18–1). Output is the horizontal axis and inflation is the vertical axis. Policy can try to offset the price shock by lowering output, or policy can keep output at potential and ignore the increase in inflation. Keeping output at potential is a policy that is *fully accommodative to inflation*. The more policy lowers output below potential, the *less accommodative to inflation* is the policy. Because of Okun's law, the policy that lowers output below potential raises unemployment above the natural rate. When output stays at potential, unemployment stays at the natural rate. Policy cannot keep both unemployment and prices stable.

We can characterise the policy alternatives in terms of a coefficient of response, g. If g is zero, the policy response keeps output at potential (and unemployment at the natural rate) and permits every shift of the price-adjustment schedule to translate into the same amount of inflation.

Figure 18–2. ALTERNATIVE RESPONSES TO A POSITIVE PRICE SHOCK.
The economy starts in equilibrium with output at potential and inflation at zero. A positive price shock occurs, shifting the price-adjustment schedule upward. Policy can keep inflation at zero, which will require a decrease in output, as at point A. Or, it can tolerate an increase in inflation together with a smaller decrease in output, as at point B. A third alternative is to keep output at potential and let the shock raise inflation, as at point C.

With g equal to zero, there is no attempt to control inflation. Point C in Figure 18–2 is the one chosen for $g = 0$. If g is greater than zero, the policy response always lowers output and raises unemployment, in order to stabilise inflation. The larger g is, the larger the reduction in output when an inflation shock occurs. In Figure 18–2, point A represents a very large value of g and point B represents an intermediate value. The coefficient g measures how accommodative policy is to inflation. For $g = 0$, policy is fully accommodative to inflation. Larger values of g represent less accommodative policies.

   In mathematical form, the coefficient of response g is part of the policy response function. Thus:

$$\frac{Y - Y*}{Y*} = -g\pi. \tag{18–2}$$

In words, the output gap is reduced below zero if inflation rises above zero.

   We can use the price-adjustment equation to find out how much inflation will be reduced by different choices of the response coefficient g. If we substitute the policy rule, Equation 18–2, into the price-adjustment equation, we get

$$\pi = (1 - fg)\pi_{-1} + Z. \tag{18–3}$$

When g is large, past inflation affects future inflation less, and the effects of a single price shock are more quickly withdrawn from inflation. Define k as

$1 - fg$. The coefficient k measures how long and how much a price shock affects inflation. If g is zero (a fully accommodative policy), so that $k = (1 - fg) = 1$, then the price shock permanently raises the inflation rate by Z; in this situation the effects of the price shock are never withdrawn from inflation. If inflation was zero before the price shock, it will be permanently above zero after the price shock. If, at the other extreme, $k = 0$, then the effect of the price shock disappears after only one year. If k is in the intermediate range, between 0 and 1, then the effect of the price shock *gradually* disappears: Inflation is k times the price shock in the year after the shock, k^2 times the price shock in the second year, k^3 in the third year, and so on, eventually back to zero inflation. For example, if k is .8, and inflation is initially raised from zero to 10 percent because of the price shock, then inflation is 8 percent in the next year, 6.4 percent in the third year, 5.1 percent in the fourth year, 4.1 percent in the fifth year, and so on, eventually getting to zero inflation.

A policy that aggressively counters price shocks (with g large and k near zero) will incur large fluctuations in output and unemployment. This is clear from Equation 18–2. For example, suppose that the sensitivity of inflation f to output is .2. Then, to achieve a value of k equal to .8 we set g equal to 1. With these coefficients, now suppose that a positive shock initially raises inflation by 10 percent. With $g = 1$, then, according to the policy rule in Equation 18–2, this will reduce output below potential by 10 percent in the period right after the shock. Eventually output will come back to potential as inflation declines. When g is large, the drop in output is large and, because of Okun's law, the rise in unemployment is large. On the other side, a negative shock that lowers inflation by 10 percent will require output to rise by 10 percentage points above potential if g is 1. According to Okun's law, unemployment falls in this case. A policy that rolls completely with price shocks (g equal to zero) will have a completely stable level of output and unemployment.

The implications of the choice of the coefficient k for inflation and unemployment losses are shown in Figure 18–3. Because the inflation loss and unemployment loss are related to the squared deviations from normal, the two curves sag as k is raised from zero.

There is another way we can depict the same trade-off. In Figure 18–4, we draw a curve representing the policy frontier in a diagram where average unemployment loss is the horizontal axis and average inflation loss is the vertical axis.[8]

---

[8] The idea of constructing policy frontiers in terms of the squared deviations of output and inflation and choosing alternative policy rules to get to the best point on such a frontier was described in John B. Taylor, 'Estimation and Control of a Macroeconomic Model with Rational Expectations,' *Econometrica*, Vol. 47 (September 1979), pp. 1267–1286; the model used in that paper corresponds closely with that discussed in the text.

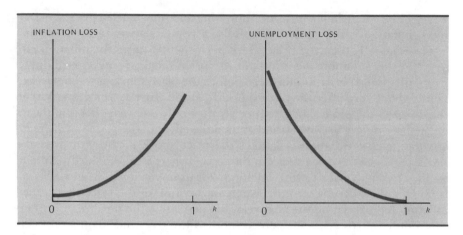

**Figure 18-3. AVERAGE INFLATION AND UNEMPLOYMENT LOSSES FOR ALTERNA-
TIVE POLICIES.**
For $k = 0$, policy changes unemployment enough to make price shocks disappear from
inflation after only one year. The average inflation loss is small, but the unemployment
loss is substantial. At $k = 1$, policy keeps unemployment at the natural rate and lets the
price shock influence actual inflation fully. Unemployment loss is at a minimum but inflation loss is high.

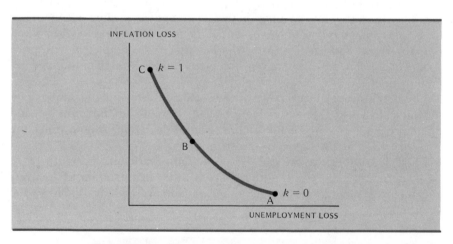

**Figure 18-4. THE POLICY FRONTIER FOR UNEMPLOYMENT AND INFLATION
LOSSES.**
Every point on the frontier can be achieved by a policy that lets unemployment respond
to inflation. At the upper left is the point of minimal unemployment loss and maximal inflation loss, corresponding to $k = 1$. At the lower right is the point of low inflation loss and
high unemployment loss, corresponding to the other extreme, $k = 0$. The points marked
A, B, and C are the same as in Figure 18-2.

The Inflation-Unemployment Policy Frontier

1. The optimal policy for dealing with a shift in aggregate demand is to reverse the shift through a compensating change in aggregate demand policy. In that case, the shift does not cause either an inflation loss or an unemployment loss.

2. A general policy for dealing with price-adjustment shocks is to let the actual amount of inflation be a fraction, k, of the amount of the shock. The rest of the shock is cancelled through aggregate demand policy.

3. An aggressive anti-inflation policy has a low k close to zero.

4. There is a policy frontier defined by different values of k from zero to 1. The frontier shows the available combinations of average inflation loss and average unemployment loss. The frontier curves towards the origin.

18.6 The Optimal Policy for Dealing with Price Shocks

The policy frontier of Figure 18–4 shows the alternative combinations of inflation and unemployment loss that are available from different policies. The best policy will achieve a compromise between the two types of losses. Remember that the best policy is the one closest to the origin, that is, the one that achieves low values of both unemployment and inflation losses. Uncompromising policies are unattractive for two reasons.

1. A policy of strict price stability ($k = 0$, the point at the lower right-hand end of the policy frontier) involves a large amount of unemployment loss. It takes large movements of unemployment to keep inflation exactly at zero in the face of oil price shocks and other shifts in the price-adjustment process.

2. A policy of strict unemployment stability ($k = 1$, the point at the upper left-hand end of the policy frontier) involves a large amount of inflation loss. When an inflationary shock occurs, the policy does nothing to offset the shock. Not only does inflation jump upward in the year of the shock, but inflation is higher in future years as well, because the shock raises expected inflation.

The uncompromising policies are unsuitable because, in both cases, the trade-off set by the policy frontier strongly favours making at least a small compromise. From strict inflation stability, a small move towards the middle of the frontier gives a large payoff in reduced unemployment loss with only a small sacrifice of inflation loss. From strict unemployment stability, a small

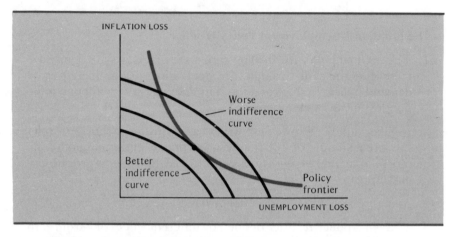

Figure 18–5.   THE OPTIMAL POLICY FOR RESPONDING TO PRICE SHOCKS.
The coloured line shows the policy frontier. At the upper left are policies that stabilise unemployment at the cost of higher average inflation loss. At the lower right are policies that stabilise inflation at the cost of higher average unemployment loss. The optimal policy is in the middle, where the frontier is tangent to the indifference curve that is closest to the origin of all the indifference curves that touch the policy frontier.

move to the middle gives a large payoff in reduced inflation loss with only a small sacrifice of unemployment loss.

To find the optimal compromise, we superimpose the policy frontier of Figure 18–4 on the family of social indifference curves from Figure 18–1. The best point on the frontier is the one tangent to the indifference curve closest to the origin, as shown in Figure 18–5.

In Chapter 17 we looked at the macro performance of Canada, the United States, and Germany for the 1970s and 1980s in terms of output-inflation loops (Figures 17–5, 17–6, and 17–7). In these diagrams inflation is the vertical axis and output is the horizontal axis. Flat loops represented large output fluctuations and small inflation fluctuations, performance corresponding to values of k near zero. The steep (standing-up) loops represented the reverse—large inflation fluctuations and small unemployment fluctuations, performance corresponding to values of k near 1. Therefore, according to this empirical evidence, Germany, with its flat loops during this period, followed a less accommodative policy than Canada or the United States: Output fluctuations were relatively large and inflation fluctuations were relatively small.

THE MESSAGE FOR POLICY MAKERS

It is not an easy matter to conduct macro policy in an optimal way. Our analysis has reached two conclusions about the appropriate response to shocks in the economy:

1. If the shock affects only aggregate demand, then a compensating change in aggregate demand policy (monetary or fiscal) will eliminate both the inflation loss and the unemployment loss.
2. If the shock affects the price-adjustment schedule, then the best policy divides its effects between inflation and unemployment according to the rule that the actual amount of inflation declines by a fraction k each year.

In general, to develop policy from our model, the policy maker needs to be able to separate shocks into their aggregate demand and price-adjustment components and then figure out the magnitude of the response needed to offset fully the aggregate demand shock and to offset partially the price-adjustment shock. Clearly some technical analysis is necessary to do this.

NOMINAL GDP TARGETING: A REASONABLE WAY TO EXPRESS POLICY?

There is another less technical way to express the optimal policy that may be useful to policy makers who also need to discuss economic policy with nonspecialists. The alternative begins with the observation that the optimal policy tends to stabilise nominal GDP. Suppose in some year a positive aggregate demand shock raises real GDP without much effect on prices. It shows up as above-normal growth of nominal GDP. A rule that calls for steady GDP would automatically offset aggregate demand shocks, just as our optimal policy recommends.

When a positive price-adjustment shock strikes, the optimal policy is to let part of the shock raise prices and part of the shock reduce output and raise unemployment. Keeping nominal GDP on a prescribed growth track does exactly that. Nominal GDP is the product of the price level and real GDP. If the price level jumps, real GDP must fall to keep nominal GDP growth at a prescribed rate. Keeping nominal GDP growth at a prescribed rate is a compromise policy of the type we just derived as optimal.

The degree of compromise in a policy that stabilises nominal GDP seems to favour unemployment stability over price stability. The value of the coefficient of response g for a nominal GDP policy is 1. As we showed above, when $g = 1$, the value of k is .8 for the numerical example of price adjustment used here. Eighty percent of a price-adjustment shock is tolerated as a continued increase in inflation the year after it occurs. Twenty percent is extinguished by permitting output to fall. Thereafter, 20 percent of inflation is offset each year, by keeping output below normal.

Suppose the initial inflation impact from a shock is 10 percent. Under the fixed nominal GDP policy, real GDP falls by 10 percent, and inflation in the following year is reduced to 8 percent. From Okun's law, this means that unemployment rises by about 5 percent in the first year.

If the public is so opposed to inflation that the optimal value of k is well below .8, then nominal GDP targeting is inappropriate—it gives excessive inflation losses that will not be made up, in the public's view, by the lower unemployment losses it will bring. Or, if the public cares less about inflation, nominal GDP targeting will bring excessive unemployment losses that will not be made up by its favourable influence on inflation losses. In either case it would be possible to change the policy goal and let nominal GDP respond to the price shock. If $k = .8$ is too large, then nominal GDP should be reduced when price shocks occur. If $k = .8$ is too small, then nominal GDP could be allowed to grow a bit when a price shock occurs. But the simplicity of a fixed nominal GDP may outweigh the benefits of modifying the path of nominal GDP in this way.[9]

If nominal GDP targeting were used explicitly in practice, the process might work in the following way: Each year the Bank of Canada (perhaps in cooperation with the federal government) would announce a target rate of growth of nominal GDP for the next two or three years. Then each month, as new information became available about the growth of nominal GDP, the Bank and the government could adjust monetary and fiscal policy to eliminate errors. If growth was above target, for example, the Bank would contract the monetary base. The Bank would sell government securities, which would reduce the monetary base and raise interest rates. If growth was below target, the Bank would expand the monetary base by raising the base and lowering interest rates.

Nominal GDP targeting should not be viewed as an alternative to the optimal policies described above. Rather, it is an easy and convenient way to talk about policy procedures and goals. For example, if there is a policy mistake that brings about a very high unemployment rate, then the optimal policy is to bring the economy back to normal quickly. There is no reason to hold output Y below potential Y^* if inflation is low. Holding nominal GDP growth to a fixed level might not allow for the economy to catch up and bring Y back to Y^*. But even in this case the policy makers should announce their intentions for nominal GDP.

EXCHANGE RATE TARGETING: HEADING OFF PRICE SHOCKS?

Our discussion of price shocks has assumed that such shocks are unavoidable and unpredictable. This assumption is appropriate for shocks such as changes in materials prices. But what about shocks that come about due to changes in Canada's exchange rates with other countries?

---

[9] See Robert E. Hall, 'Macroeconomic Policy under Structural Change,' in *Industrial Change and Public Policy*, Federal Reserve Bank of Kansas City, 1983, pp. 85–111, and James Tobin, 'Commentary,' in *Industrial Change and Public Policy*, Federal Reserve Bank of Kansas City, 1983, pp. 113–122. A review of the alternative proposals is found in John B. Taylor, 'What Would Nominal GNP Targeting Do to the Business Cycle?' *Carnegie-Rochester Conference Series on Public Policy*, Vol. 22 (1985), pp. 61–84.

As we saw in Chapter 11, some economists argue that a policy of targeting the exchange rate can prevent price shocks. As we will see here, this argument has had some influence on the Bank of Canada's behaviour. Under what conditions would a policy of fixing the exchange rate be preferable to a policy that responds to price shocks according to some chosen value of k?

First, exchange rate changes must be a very significant cause of price shocks in the economy. By fixing the exchange rate the Bank of Canada would give up its ability to respond to other types of price shocks and to aggregate demand shocks. This would clearly not be worthwhile if exchange rate changes had only a small effect on the economy. As we discussed in Chapter 10, it is not clear how important exchange rate changes have been in generating price shocks.

Second, the preferences of the policy makers in the country whose exchange rate we choose to match must be similar to our own. If, for example, Canadians prefer price stability and Americans do not, then we would not want to fix our exchange rate with the United States. Stimulative U.S. monetary policies that lower the U.S. interest rate while causing inflation would have to be matched in Canada, leading to inflation in Canada as well.

Evaluating Monetary Policy in 1981–83

In 1981 the Bank of Canada decided to place more emphasis on stabilising the Canada-U.S. exchange rate. There were three reasons for this change. First, the Bank became relatively more concerned with price stability and less with output stability. Second, like the central banks of many other countries, the Bank of Canada was concerned that any depreciation of the Canadian dollar relative to the U.S. dollar would cause significant price shocks. The Bank believed that such shocks would add to the already high rate of inflation in Canada. Third, changes in Canadian financial markets had made it difficult for the Bank to determine what levels of the monetary aggregates would bring about the desired level of output.

At roughly the same time, the monetary authorities in the United States also decided to embark on a program to reduce inflation. This was implemented by a very restrictive monetary policy that raised U.S. interest rates and brought about a recession in the United States. The resulting fall in U.S. demand for Canadian exports had a contractionary effect on the Canadian economy. Instead of offsetting this aggregate demand shock with a stimulative monetary policy, the Bank of Canada also embarked on a restrictive policy.

At least part of the motivation for this policy was to reduce the extent of the depreciation of the Canadian dollar relative to the U.S. dollar. The Bank's intervention in the foreign exchange market had the effect of raising the Canadian interest rate, as described in Chapters 11 and 12.

The combination of a negative aggregate demand shock and restrictive monetary policy sent the Canadian economy into the deepest recession of the postwar period. This recession subsequently brought about a dramatic fall in the rate of inflation in Canada.

Was this policy optimal? The answer that you would give to this question depends in part on your own preferences with regard to price and output stability. The dramatic fall in the rate of inflation was accomplished at the expense of a large drop in output and the highest unemployment rates experienced in Canada since the Great Depression of the 1930s. If you care much more about output stability than price stability, then the Bank's policy was clearly not optimal from your point of view.

Suppose, however, that your preferences were similar to the Bank's. Was the emphasis on exchange rate stability misplaced even then? Peter Howitt of the University of Western Ontario has argued that the Bank erred in concentrating so much on the exchange rate with the U.S. dollar. At the same time that the Canadian dollar was falling relative to the U.S. dollar, the value of the Canadian dollar was rising relative to the currencies of our other trading partners. Although the lion's share of Canada's imports come from the United States, a significant amount originates in other countries, notably Japan and Western Europe. As we saw in Chapter 1, to determine the overall impact of the foreign exchange market on Canada's import prices it is necessary to form a weighted average of the exchange rates between Canada and each of our trading partners.

The Bank of Canada calculates one such weighted average; it is called the **G-10 rate.** The figure below shows that even though the Canada-U.S. exchange rate fell sharply during most of 1981 through 1983, the G-10 weighted average exchange rate did not show the same trend. Although the G-10 rate did fluctuate, it was roughly constant

Sources: Canadian Economic Observer, Table 10.1, and International Monetary Fund, *International Financial Statistics*, country tables, Canada.

over much of this time period. The difference in the two exchange rates occurred because our exchange rates with countries other than the United States rose.

Another weighted average exchange rate is calculated by the International Monetary Fund (IMF). The economists at the IMF believe that the United States should be given less weight than it has been given in the G-10 index. According to the IMF's calculation, Canada's weighted average exchange rate actually rose during most of the 1981–83 period, as also shown in the figure above. Even given that the Bank was in a very anti-inflation frame of mind, there is no indication that it wanted the foreign value of the Canadian dollar to increase. Thus if the IMF calculation is correct the Bank's policy was too restrictive even by its own standards.*

* See Peter Howitt, *Monetary Policy in Transition: A Study of Bank of Canada Policy, 1982–85*, C. D. Howe Institute/Prentice-Hall, 1986.

18.7 International Policy Coordination

To this point we have assumed that Canadian policy makers must address Canada's macroeconomic problems taking the policies of other countries as given. Perhaps, however, every country could benefit if they coordinated their policy decisions. If so, then policy makers would do better to approach the policy-setting problem differently. We will consider the possible gains to cooperation under flexible exchange rates first, and then turn to the fixed exchange rate case.

POLICY COORDINATION UNDER FLEXIBLE EXCHANGE RATES

One of the most important properties of a floating exchange rate system is that it permits different countries to have different inflation rates. But floating exchange rates do not completely insulate one economy from the effects of macroeconomic policies in other countries. In principle, therefore, international coordination of macro policies might be useful. The optimal macro policy that we discussed for Canada might be different if the effects of Canadian policy on other countries were taken into account and if the effects of other countries' policies on Canada were taken into account.

Macro policy-making in the world economy can be thought of as a game. Each country is a player in the game. The objective of policy makers in each country might be the same as those we discussed earlier in this chapter. Each country has a social welfare function that includes output stability and price stability. Policy makers choose their instruments to minimise a combination of each type of loss (see Figure 18–1). But if there is an interaction among countries, then the choice of a policy rule in one country will affect the social welfare function in the other country. Country 1 might improve its macroeconomic performance by worsening Country 2's macroeconomic performance. But if Country 1 does so, Country 2 might retaliate, or at least watch out for itself, with harmful side effects for Country 1. This would be a **noncooperative policy choice. A cooperative policy choice,** on the other hand, is one in which each country agrees to use a policy rule that doesn't have an adverse effect on the other country, in exchange for getting the same treatment from the other country. Some international coordination or discussion about policies, like that at Bretton Woods after World War II which we discussed in Chapter 11, would probably be necessary for this cooperative outcome.

In recent years there has been an annual international summit meeting among the leaders of seven large industrial countries that interact with each other: Canada, France, Germany, Italy, Japan, the United Kingdom, and the United States. One of the stated purposes of these summit meetings is to discuss macro policy. The amount of actual international coordination that goes on varies from meeting to meeting. Under the administration of U.S. president Jimmy Carter, there was much effort by the United States to get other countries to expand. In the first term of Ronald Reagan's presidency, when contractionary policies were enacted in the United States to reduce inflation, these types of coordination efforts were abandoned. However, during President Reagan's second term there was more discussion about coordination.

Are the gains from coordination large? How different would optimal policies look if countries cooperated, rather than acting independently? For example, should countries be less or more accommodative to inflation than calculations like those earlier in the chapter indicated?[10] Or perhaps countries should use their monetary policies to reduce the size of the fluctuations in the exchange rate as well as of the inflation rate and the unemployment rate.[11]

We saw in Chapter 10 that changes in the U.S. money supply have effects on the Canada-U.S. exchange rate. A monetary contraction in the United States lowers the exchange rate and a monetary expansion in the United States raises the exchange rate. The same is true for the exchange rates between other countries and the United States. Consider the case of U.S. dollar appreciation associated with tight U.S. monetary policy or a loose U.S. fiscal policy. Obviously, an appreciation of the U.S. dollar is a depreciation

[10] Macroeconomic research on this question is just beginning. See Koichi Hamada, 'Macroeconomic Strategy and Coordination under Flexible Exchange Rates,' in Rudiger Dornbusch and Jacob A. Frenkel (eds.), *International Economic Policy: Theory and Evidence,* Baltimore, Johns Hopkins, 1979, pp. 292–324; Gilles Oudiz and Jeffrey Sachs, 'Macroeconomic Policy Coordination among the Industrialized Countries,' *Brookings Papers on Economic Activity,* Number 1, pp. 1–64, 1984; and John B. Taylor, 'International Coordination in the Design of Macroeconomic Policy Rules,' *European Economic Review,* Vol. 26, 1985.

[11] See Ronald I. McKinnon, *An International Standard for Monetary Stabilization,* Washington, D.C., The Institute for International Economics (distributed by M.I.T. Press), 1984.

of other currencies. A depreciation in the rest of the world has two effects that must be considered by policy makers.

First, the depreciation increases aggregate demand in the rest of the world. The depreciation is like an aggregate demand shock that increases net exports in the rest of the world—the aggregate demand curves shift to the right. According to our optimal policy analysis, the appropriate response of policy makers in the rest of the world is to offset this shift by effecting tighter fiscal or monetary policy. Policies should be coordinated to get this result, but since the effect of the U.S. policy can be offset by the appropriate choice of policies abroad, there is no loss in world welfare on this account.

The second effect cannot be offset so easily, however. *The depreciation of the foreign currencies will raise the price of imported products in the rest of the world.* For example, Japan Airlines will have to pay 2.5 billion more yen for a U.S. $50 million Boeing 747 jet made in Seattle if the yen depreciates from 150 yen per U.S. dollar to 200 yen per U.S. dollar. The second effect of the U.S. monetary policy is thus to create a price shock in the rest of the world.

As we already know, a price shock presents a cruel choice to policy makers: Inflation must rise, unemployment must rise, or both must rise. The magnitude of the inflation or unemployment depends on how much accommodation is built into policy in the rest of the world. Some loss, however, is inevitable. This effect of the U.S. policy, therefore, does result in a loss in welfare in the rest of the world and opens the possibility of cooperation. A cooperative policy would be one in which both the United States and other countries are more accommodative to inflation than they otherwise would be. This would make U.S. monetary policy less contractionary in the face of a price shock in the United States and would therefore have smaller harmful effects on the rest of the world. In return, other countries, including Canada, would agree to be more accommodative to inflation in their countries. Although it is clear that optimal cooperative policies should be more accommodative than noncooperative policies, the difference could be small. Since our historical experience with flexible exchange rates is still fairly short, there is unfortunately little empirical evidence about the size of the difference between the policies.

POLICY COORDINATION UNDER FIXED EXCHANGE RATES

We now know that if Canada pursues a fixed exchange rate policy the Bank of Canada must give up the opportunity for monetary policy to respond to destabilising shocks originating at home or abroad. This will be worthwhile only if exchange rate shocks are very important relative to all other shocks. Further, a fixed exchange rate policy will result in Canada experiencing roughly the same level of inflation as the country with which we fix our exchange rate (presumably the United States). Perhaps these two disadvantages of a fixed exchange rate—lack of flexibility and 'importing inflation'—can be reduced if a number of countries cooperate in fixing their exchange rates.

For example, under a policy coordination agreement all countries might pledge to avoid policy shocks that would affect other countries. For example, countries might promise to avoid sharp changes in government spending that would affect their demand for imports. Or all countries might pledge to pursue price stability so that no country is forced to import inflation.

Would the gains from this sort of policy coordination be enough to offset the disadvantages of a fixed exchange rate policy? Clearly most countries do not think so. If they did, then we would see a return to a Bretton Woods type of system. A partial exception to this is the European Monetary System described in Chapter 11.

The Annual Economic Summits

Each year the leaders of seven large Western countries get together to discuss economic policy. This is the highest-level forum that is regularly available for international policy coordination. The leaders have occasionally used the summits to reach or ratify a program of economic policy coordination, but these agreements have not been frequent or far-reaching.

One reason that the summits have had only a modest effect is that the countries often disagree about the appropriate policy. In 1978 and again in 1985 the United States asked the other countries to agree to stimulative policies in order to reduce the U.S. trade deficit and stimulate the world economy in general. Canada was in broad agreement with these proposals, but Germany and Japan in particular resisted these requests, fearing that this would lead to excessive inflation in their countries. During the 1981 summit the U.S. monetary policy that had led to very high interest rates was criticised by Canada, Germany, France, and Italy. At that time these four countries felt that U.S. policy was overemphasising the fight against inflation. The United States, supported by the United Kingdom, declined to change its policy, however.

Canadian leaders have occasionally committed Canada to particular policies at these summits, but only when the promised policy was already what the leader had had in mind. For example, in 1978 Canada agreed to foster growth, but the target of 5 percent agreed to at the summit had already been Canadian government policy. At the 1979 summit Canada and the United States were asked to raise oil prices in their countries as a conservation measure. Then–Prime Minister Joe Clark agreed to do this, but once again the decision had been made before the summit. The subsequent defeat of the Clark government in a general election largely because of this policy did nothing to encourage Canadian politicians to make commitments to coordinate policies with other countries.

As prime minister, Pierre Trudeau twice announced new policies shortly after returning from a summit. In 1978 he announced an austerity plan, and in 1982 he announced the '6 and 5' anti-inflation program. However, neither of these fulfilled commitments to policy coordination made at the summit.

Although the annual summits were originally intended to focus on economic policy, their scope has since expanded to include issues such as terrorism, nuclear proliferation, and relations with developing countries. Much (but not all) of the economic policy issues have been devolved to meetings of the finance ministers of the countries. Canada and Italy are not always included in these meetings. For example, the Plaza agreement on exchange rates described in Chapter 11 involved only France, Japan, the United States, the United Kingdom, and West Germany (the G5). Some of the subsequent finance minister meetings have included all seven of the summit countries.

International Policy Coordination

1. A policy coordination agreement under a flexible exchange rate system would see all countries becoming somewhat more accommodative to price shocks than they are in the absence of such an agreement. However, the change in policies and the benefit from coordination might be quite small.

2. A policy coordination agreement under a fixed exchange rate system could involve pledges to reduce shocks that affect other countries and to pursue price stability. Such coordination does not appear to be enough to make fixed exchange rates attractive to most countries.

18.8 Changing the Policy Frontier

In Section 18.6 we described a policy for responding to price shocks. This policy involved choosing a point on the policy frontier for unemployment and inflation losses. The policy is optimal in the sense that it tells policy makers how to make the best of a bad situation. But the policy does not make the situation good. We should spend at least as much effort thinking about how to move the policy frontier toward the origin as we spend thinking about choosing the best point on the frontier. If the frontier were closer to the origin, both inflation loss and unemployment loss would be lower.

STREAMLINE THE LABOUR MARKET

The policy frontier lies far from the origin because wages do not respond quickly and vigorously to the situation in the labour market. When an inflation shock strikes, policy has to raise unemployment to get inflation back down. When wages are less responsive, a larger rise in unemployment is necessary. If wages could be made to adjust rapidly to surpluses and shortages of labour, then the average unemployment loss needed to keep inflation loss at a given level would be lower. The policy frontier would be closer to the origin.

Because the reasons for sluggish adjustment of wages are not well understood, it is not obvious what types of new policies would speed up the process. Some proposals include:

1. *Better Job Matching.* In the highly decentralised Canadian labour market, employers have trouble getting in touch with potential workers. There may be a large number of qualified people ready to work at a particular job at a low wage. If the employer cannot let them know about the job, it may be necessary to hire a nearby worker at a higher wage. Some kind of electronic job listing might make it possible to draw from a larger number of potential workers. Or, if there were better information available about the number of qualified job seekers, firms would be in a better position to tailor wage offers to the state of the market. The federal government has tried to perform this service for many years, but has found it increasingly difficult to do so. The government's Canada Employment Centres were involved in about one-sixth of new hires in 1956; 20 years later this had fallen to one-tenth. Firms are reluctant to use these services, even though they are not charged for them, because the Centres are not able to screen applicants well enough before sending them to potential employers or to find enough well-qualified workers.

2. *Eliminate Government Price Fixing.* Various levels of government affect price setting in the economy by providing goods and services directly (for instance, public transportation), requiring regulatory approval for price changes (for instance, telephone rates), or instituting controls on the supply of products (for instance, marketing boards for agricultural products). Over 15 percent of consumer expenditures excluding housing and energy are for goods and services whose prices are regulated by government in one way or another. A study by Maurice Levi and Albert Dexter of the University of British Columbia found that these prices were less responsive to economic conditions than unregulated prices.[12]

3. *Reform Unemployment Compensation.* Unemployment compensation serves a vital purpose but some reforms would improve the inflation-

[12] Maurice Levi and Albert Dexter, 'Regulated Prices and Their Consequences,' *Canadian Public Policy,* Vol. 9, pp. 24–31, 1983.

unemployment trade-off. In 1982 the federal government established the Royal Commission on the Economic Union and Development Prospects for Canada. In their report, the MacDonald Commission (as it is commonly known) recommended that the treatment of both firms and workers should be changed. At present the contributions that each firm must make to the UI fund do not depend on how often the firm lays off its workers. This subsidises firms and industries with unstable employment patterns at the expense of those with stable patterns. Charging firms on the basis of their layoff experience would correct this. While many workers use UI compensation as a temporary means of support while searching for new jobs some workers use the system as a way to work for only a fraction of the year. As of 1988 a person could work only 10 weeks and then receive up to 40 weeks of UI benefits at 60 percent of the wage they had earned, depending on the region they lived in and the national unemployment rate. This encourages regular lengthy spells of unemployment and discourages workers from moving to regions with better employment prospects. Among its other recommendations the MacDonald Commission suggested raising the number of weeks of work needed to qualify for UI benefits and linking the length of the benefit period to the length of the previous employment period.

4. *Legislate the Share Economy.* Martin Weitzman of M.I.T. has proposed a structural reform of the labour market that he calls 'the share economy,' which has received a good deal of popular attention.[13] Under Weitzman's plan, the government would provide tax incentives to businesses to induce them to pay workers under a share system in place of existing wage systems. In a share system, part or all of a worker's earnings would be set as a share of the firm's revenue, rather than as a fixed hourly wage. The share system has two virtues, according to Weitzman. First, it automatically makes earnings respond to the state of the economy. Unemployment rises less during a recession in a share economy than in a wage economy. However, as we discussed in Chapter 16, an optimal labour contract should not link the wage to the success of the firm, but to the economy as a whole. Second, when compensation is set as a share of revenue, the firm faces no cost to add another worker. Weitzman foresees an economy where employers pursue the few remaining unemployed workers relentlessly, because their marginal products are above their costs of employment. But the workers already employed suffer wage loss every time the firm adds a new worker. Whether the economy would run more efficiently, taking all the effects of the share economy into consideration, is an open question.

[13] Martin L. Weitzman, *The Share Economy*, Cambridge, Mass., Harvard University Press, 1984. The *New York Times* called Weitzman's plan 'the best idea since Keynes' in a March 28, 1985, editorial.

IMPROVE INDEXATION

In Chapter 17 we saw that when wages are linked directly to prices through cost-of-living indexation the impact of outside price shocks is amplified—a price shock goes immediately into wages, then into costs, and finally into prices again, all within the same year. Although indexation prevents workers from being left behind by general inflation, it is harmful to the economy when wages rise in response to oil or other outside price shocks.

The ideal method of cost-of-living escalation would omit price increases that arise from imports and other materials costs. Though economists have suggested price indexes that would perform better than the CPI for wage indexation, nobody has started to use them for actual wage setting. It is not easy to persuade a skeptical employer or labour union that a new price index is superior to the tried-and-true consumer price index. Proposals to make much smaller changes in the indexes used for wage indexation have encountered stiff resistance. There are no grounds for optimism that wage setters will voluntarily adopt new indexation methods. Nor is it clear that the government can or should try to force changes in this area.

AVOID GOVERNMENT PRICE SHOCKS

Sometimes the government itself creates a shock in the price-adjustment process. An important example occurred in Britain in 1979. The government cut income taxes and substituted a value-added tax to raise the same revenue. Because the value-added tax is imposed on firms, it adds to costs just as does an increase in the price of a material input. The VAT is much like a sales tax. In terms of the price-adjustment model of Chapter 17, the value-added tax adds an inflationary impetus Z in the year that it goes into effect.

In Britain, the value-added tax shock and the oil price shock occurred simultaneously. The British economy suffered from more inflation and a larger reduction in output than did other economies, which suffered only from the oil price shock. If self-inflicted government price shocks can be kept to a minimum, the policy frontier will be closer to the origin.

Avoiding government price shocks need not prevent tax reform or other useful changes in the government's influence on the economy. For example, a value-added tax can be changed in a simple way that does not change its favourable properties as a tax—it could be instituted so that the cost falls on workers rather than on businesses. Then the switch to the tax will not create a price shock. Changes in all types of economic policies need to be designed with the harmful effects of macro price shocks in mind.

CONTROLS AND INCENTIVES

The reason the policy frontier is so far from the origin is that the government influences inflation only indirectly through its control of demand. If the government could simply dictate the price level, then there would be no need for either inflation losses or unemployment losses. Moreover, there need not be shortages or excess supplies in such an economy. The government could set the price level and the position of the aggregate demand schedule so as to have them intersect exactly at full employment.

Only once has the Canadian government tried to set prices and wages directly in peacetime. The Trudeau government formed the Anti-Inflation Board (AIB) in late 1975. The AIB was empowered to review major wage settlements and order reductions if these exceeded guidelines set by the government. The AIB also had some power to review prices and penalise firms whose price increases were deemed to be excessive. The AIB program was ended in 1978.

The AIB exerted a (probably modest) restraining influence on the rate of wage increases during 1975–78.[14] But this slower growth of wages was only achieved at some cost. The AIB spawned a large and cumbersome bureaucracy whose interference in private agreements about wages was widely resented. In addition, the uneven impact of the AIB on wages and prices probably reduced economic efficiency by distorting the way prices allocated resources throughout the economy.

For these reasons the wage and price control program was not politically popular (indeed, the Trudeau government had been reelected in 1974 on a platform that opposed the wage and price control proposal of the opposition). Thus the next time that the federal government instituted an anti-inflation program it contented itself with setting an example of restraint and urging the private sector to follow. Specifically, in the federal budget of June 1982 pay increases for government employees were limited to 6 percent in the first year and 5 percent in the next. Federal regulatory agencies were asked to limit increases in prices that they controlled or approved to 6 and 5 percent as well. No controls were placed on the private sector, however.

Economists looking for a permanent policy to shift the inflation-unemployment policy frontier toward the origin have proposed systems based on incentives rather than controls. **Tax-based incomes policies** would reward businesses and workers who followed government guidelines for price and wage increases. Businesses would lose tax deductions for cost increases beyond the guideline rates and would pay extra taxes on revenue attributable to excess price increases. In the aftermath of a price shock, policy could get inflation back down by setting a low guideline for wage and price increases. The disincentive cost to taxpayers would be less than the cost of the unemployment that would result from achieving the same degree of disinflation through higher unemployment.

Since we do not have any practical experience with incentives, it is hard to know how well they would work. Any incentive program would have to be designed with great care, as shown by an example drawn from the United

[14] For a review of the research on this topic see W. Craig Riddell and Phillip M. Smith, 'Expected Inflation and Wage Changes in Canada, 1967–81,' *Canadian Journal of Economics*, Vol. 15, pp. 377–394, 1982.

States. In 1978, President Jimmy Carter submitted an incentive plan to the U.S. Congress. In addition to specific incentives for individual price and wage setters, it offered workers a general assurance that the program could not hurt them. Labour had been concerned that they might be required to moderate their wage growth while businesses did nothing to cut price inflation. Carter's program included 'real wage insurance.' In the event that prices did rise more than wages, workers would have received income tax cuts large enough to make up their loss in real wages.

Only a few months after the real wage insurance proposal was made, real wages fell by several percentage points, thanks to an event that had nothing to do with the anti-inflation program. World oil prices almost tripled. That event was never contemplated in designing real wage insurance. Had real wage insurance gone into effect in 1978, huge tax cuts would have occurred quite accidentally in 1979 and 1980, when the U.S. federal budget was already in deficit. Fortunately, real wage insurance died in Congress and this accident never took place.

TRADE POLICY

International agreements largely limit Canada's ability to raise barriers to trade. As a result, protectionist measures that could raise domestic prices and thus cause a positive price shock are seldom observed. One exception was the restriction on the import of Japanese cars that was imposed in the early 1980s (this did not violate international agreements because the Japanese government agreed to do this 'voluntarily'). The result was some upward pressure on the prices of imported and domestic cars.

A reduction in tariffs or trade barriers could provide a negative price shock. The Canadian government is reluctant to lower trade barriers unilaterally even when this is desirable because our existing trade barriers can be used as a bargaining chip when asking other countries to reduce their restrictions on Canadian products. As a result, reducing trade barriers can only rarely be used as an anti-inflation tool.

Improving the Policy Frontier

1. Policies for streamlining the labour market could push the inflation-unemployment frontier toward the origin. The same amount of inflation loss would be achieved with less unemployment loss if inflation responded more vigorously to unemployment.

2. Public job placement has not been very successful. Reduced government price and wage fixing might be a small help. Reform in unemployment compensation would also improve the frontier.

3. Controls on prices and wages are another option, but in practice they have been difficult to administer and have not had a lasting impact on inflation.

4. The government should be careful not to create unnecessary price shocks.

Review and Practice

MAJOR POINTS

1. The general policy implication of recent research in macro is that policy should be formulated as a rule or contingency plan.

2. Macroeconomic policy can be logically formulated and evaluated using the target and instrument framework. A social welfare function could be used to represent goals for the target variables.

3. Much as in most areas of economics, trade-offs are widespread in macroeconomics. As long as the number of instruments is scarce we will face a tough trade-off between the goals of the target variables.

4. Uncertainty in the models leads to less active use of the policy instruments.

5. High inflation is bad because it causes people to hold too little money. It is also difficult to adjust the tax system to be neutral to inflation. Inflation also sometimes brings higher uncertainty, which can interfere with efficient resource allocation. Deflation is undesirable for similar reasons.

6. Variations in unemployment are undesirable because the social costs of periods of high unemployment outweigh the benefits of periods of low unemployment.

7. Indifference curves between inflation loss and unemployment loss curve away from the origin. Higher indifference curves represent poorer macroeconomic performance.

8. Policy rules describe how accommodative the monetary policy makers are to inflation. More accommodative policy results in better output performance, but worse inflation performance.

9. In principle, countries may want to pursue somewhat different policies if they agree to coordinate their macroeconomic policies than if they always act independently.

10. The only type of policy move that could improve both inflation and unemployment performance would be an inward shift of the policy frontier, but unfortunately the prospects seem limited for this type of policy.

KEY TERMS AND CONCEPTS

Lucas critique	Commitment to a policy
Social welfare function	Final targets
Time inconsistency	Intermediate targets
Model uncertainty	Scarcity of instruments

Policy trade-offs   Unemployment loss

Activist policy   Social indifference curve

Policy coordination   Policy frontier

Discretionary policy   Policy rule

Shoe-leather cost of inflation   Accommodation of inflation shock

Marginal social cost of unemployment   Nominal GDP target

Inflation loss

QUESTIONS FOR DISCUSSION AND REVIEW

1. If the purpose of the final exam is to motivate students to study, why will the instructor not cancel the final at the last minute, after all studying has occurred, in order to save everybody's time and effort?

2. What is the basic argument against discretionary policy?

3. If the effect of a policy instrument is uncertain, will policy makers be more or less aggressive in the use of the instrument than they would be under certainty?

4. Give some of the reasons that both inflation and deflation are undesirable.

5. Explain why both high and variable unemployment are undesirable. Why does the policy frontier deal just with the variability and not with the level of unemployment?

6. Explain the consequences for unemployment and inflation if policy makers fully accommodate a price shock. Repeat for zero accommodation and for 50 percent accommodation.

7. Describe the axes of the policy frontier diagram and how to find points on the frontier.

8. How should policy makers choose the best point on the frontier?

9. How much accommodation of price shocks occurs if nominal GDP targets are followed?

10. List some of the proposals that have been made to shift the policy frontier inward.

11. Trace out the effects of a restrictive quota on auto imports.

PROBLEMS

Numerical

1. Calculate the value of k that corresponds to the policy of keeping nominal GDP at a given level in the year that a price shock occurs. Assume that f equals 1. Assume that the economy starts in equilibrium, with $Y = Y^*$, $\pi = 0$, and $P = 1$. Then an inflationary shock of 10 percent, $Z = .1$, occurs. Compute the change in the price level, using Equation 18–1. Compute the change in output from Equation 18–2. Show that the percentage change in real GDP plus the percentage change in the price level equals zero, the percentage change in nominal GDP.

2. An economy has an aggregate demand schedule $Y = 2,067 + 3.221(M/P)$. It starts at potential $(Y = Y^* = 4,000)$ with a money stock of 600. Then it is hit by an inflation shock of $Z = .1$. Policy uses a value of k of .9. Assume that $f = .25$. Com-

pute the change in the money stock necessary to achieve the policy. Also compute the change in P and Y. Repeat the calculations for $k = .1$. Explain the differences.

3. The purpose of this exercise is to illustrate the trade-off between inflation and unemployment. However, we focus on the output gap rather than on unemployment because the two are closely related due to Okun's law. Suppose that the policy rule

$$(Y - Y^*)/Y^* = -g\pi \qquad \text{(Policy Rule)}$$

is substituted into the price-adjustment equation to get

$$\pi = (1 - .2g)\pi_{-1} + Z. \qquad \text{(Inflation)}$$

   a. Starting from $Y = Y^*$ and from $\pi = 0$ (zero percent inflation), use the second equation to calculate the effect on inflation for Years 1 through 10 of a price shock $Z = .1$ (a 10 percent shock to the price level). Set $g = .5$.
   b. Using the values of inflation that you calculated in Part a, calculate the value of the GDP gap, $(Y - Y^*)/Y^*$, for all 10 years using the policy rule.
   c. Plot the values of inflation and the output gap for all 10 years on two time series diagrams (put the variable on the vertical axis and the year on the horizontal axis).
   d. Plot the values of output and inflation on a diagram with inflation on the vertical axis and output on the horizontal axis (like Figure 17–5 of Chapter 17).
   e. Calculate the average squared loss for inflation. That is, square each value of inflation (π^2) for all 10 years, sum up the squares, and divide by 10. Calculate the average squared loss for the output gap in the same way. Now repeat the calculations in Parts a through d and the inflation loss and output loss for $g = .1$ and $g = .9$. You should now have three pairs of inflation loss and output loss, one for each of the three values of the policy rule (g). Plot the three pairs on a diagram with average inflation loss on the vertical axis and average output loss (output gap) on the horizontal axis. Comment on the position of the three points. Is a trade-off between inflation loss and output loss evident? Compare your diagram with that of Figure 18–4. (Note that the output gap loss and the unemployment loss will occupy similar relative positions because of Okun's law.)

4. The purpose of this exercise is to illustrate that a 'stochastic' dynamic model with shocks can lead to business-cycle fluctuations. Suppose that the income identity is

$$Y = C + I + G,$$

where $G = 750$. Consumption is equal to

$$C = 80 + .63Y_{-1},$$

and investment is a random variable given by

$$I = 650 + (7 - \text{Number from a roll of a pair of dice}) \text{ times } 93.$$

   a. Roll a pair of dice twenty times, and record the number for each roll. Use the investment function to calculate investment for each roll. This gives 20 years of stochastic investment. Investment in Year 1 is the first roll and investment in Year 20 is the last roll. Plot the values of investment on a time series chart with investment on the vertical axis and the year on the horizontal axis. The values should look random, with investment fluctuating around 650.
   b. Now use the values of investment for the 20 years to calculate income Y. Substitute the consumption function into the income identity. Start with Y_{-1} equal

to 4,000 and with investment equal to the value that you calculated for Year 1. Then calculate the second year's income by substituting in income for the first year for Y_{-1} and investment in the second year. Do the same thing for the third year and so on through Year 20.

c. Plot the resulting values of income Y for the 20 years with the year on the horizontal axis. The average value should be near 4,000 but you should see some prolonged fluctuations around this average value that look like business cycles. Compare the prolonged nature of the fluctuations of Y with the random but less prolonged fluctuations of investment I. Calculate the average time between peaks for each series. Unless your dice are loaded, the average time between peaks for income will be longer than that for investment. Try to explain why.

5. Suppose that price-adjustment and inflationary expectations are given by Equations 17–1 and 17–2 respectively. Policy is given by Equation 18–2 with $g=0$. Initially there is an oil price shock of 2.5 percent ($Z=.025$).

a. Calculate inflation and expected inflation for Years 1 through 4. Are expectations rational?

b. Is the monetary authority using a constant money stock target, a constant nominal GDP target, or neither? Explain your answer.

Analytical

1. Derive the policy rule schedule for the case where the Bank of Canada maintains nominal GDP at a given target level.

2. In Chapter 12 we showed how monetary policy affects the economy with a lag. What are the implications of these lags for our suggestions about optimal policy in this chapter? What do lags in the effect of money imply for nominal GDP targeting?

3. Compare monetary aggregate targeting by the Bank of Canada (as described in Chapter 12) with targeting nominal GDP. Prepare a brief argument in favour of each type of targeting, listing advantages and disadvantages.

4. Using the IS-LM method, show what the Bank of Canada must do to the money supply to reduce output by a certain percentage when there is a price shock. Could the same actions be undertaken by fiscal policy? Why might a mix of monetary and fiscal policies be used to reduce output after a price shock?

5. Suppose that in response to a large and unexpected oil price shock the Bank of Canada acts to keep output at potential. Inflationary expectations are given by the expression $\pi^e=.9\pi_{-1}$. Prices are sticky and price adjustment is given by an equation like 17–1. The changes in the money stock, prices, and output for the first 4 years are:

Year	%ΔM	%ΔP	%ΔY
1	10	10	0
2	9	9	0
3	8.1	8.1	0
4	7.3	7.3	0

a. How large was the oil price shock?

b. An economist writing for a popular magazine comments: 'The Bank of Canada is up to its old tricks again, fueling inflation with money stock growth.' The economist goes on to note that every time the Bank increases the money supply by X percent it leads to an increase in prices of X percent, just as predicted by the classical model. Is this economist right; that is, has inflation over the last 4 years been caused by increases in the money stock?

c. The economist ends his column with an admonition to the Bank of Canada to stick to a constant money stock rule. This, he asserts, will give us noninflationary full employment. If the Bank had held the money stock constant over the last 4 years, would output have remained constant? Diagram the path the economy would have followed using an output-inflation loop.

6. Suppose that as a result of the Bank of Canada's policy rule, inflation is given by Equation 18–3, where the parameter k lies between 0 and 1. Sketch the output-inflation loop for the case of an oil price shock. Is there overshooting as in the output-inflation loops of Chapter 17? Why or why not?

7. The Canadian economist Ronald McKinnon of Stanford University is one of the most ardent and eloquent supporters of fixed exchange rates. In his monograph *An International Standard for Monetary Stabilization* (Institute for International Economics, 1984) he argues as follows:

> Assigning responsibility to the central bank for stabilizing the national money's purchasing power [i.e., targeting the exchange rate] may seem excessively narrow to many readers concerned with unemployment, national output growth, or fluctuations in interest rates. Yet, a strong case can be made that [such] a monetary policy. . .will, incidentally, be quite successful at output and employment stabilization. For an open economy, eliminating sharp fluctuations in the 'real' exchange rate due to monetary imbalances would also tend to reduce frictional unemployment. . . Most important, the stipulation that the government prevent surprise inflations or deflations in the general price level is very strong in a countercyclical sense. . . On the other hand, asking the monetary authority to target nonmonetary or 'real' variables [such as unemployment and real income] is not feasible.

Write a short essay evaluating McKinnon's argument (if you want to be scrupulously fair you should read the small book from which the quotation is drawn). Is it possible that fixing the exchange rate could foster both price and output stability: If it is indeed possible, do you think that a different policy could do an even better job? Justify your answer using the analysis developed in this book.

8. Suppose that policy makers in Canada decided that it would not be a good idea to fix Canada's exchange rate unilaterally. Now suppose that at one of the annual summits it is suggested that all of the countries maintain fixed exchange rates. Is it possible that Canada would welcome a multilateral return to fixed rates even though declining to go to a fixed rate unilaterally? If so, what sort of multilateral agreement must take place? If not, why not?

9. Explain why aggregate demand shocks need not lead to a policy conflict between countries while a price shock might (Hint: Take account of the effect of the exchange rate on prices.)

10. Explain why a depreciation of the exchange rate could have an inflationary impact in one country and a deflationary impact in other countries.

Index